The Economic Development of Northeast Asia
Volume IV

Wherever possible, the articles in these volumes have been reproduced as originally published using facsimile reproduction, inclusive of footnotes and pagination to facilitate ease of reference.

For a list of all Edward Elgar published titles visit our site on the World Wide Web at
http://www.e-elgar.co.uk

The Economic Development of Northeast Asia
Volume IV

Edited by

Heather Smith

Fellow
Australian National University, Australia

An Elgar Reference Collection
Cheltenham, UK • Northampton, MA, USA

338.95
E192
VOC. 4

Published by
Edward Elgar Publishing Limited
Glensanda House
Montpellier Parade
Cheltenham
Glos GL50 1UA
UK

Edward Elgar Publishing, Inc.
136 West Street, Suite 202
Northampton
Massachusetts 01060
USA

A catalogue record for this book is available from the British Library.

Library of Congress Cataloguing in Publication Data

The economic development of Northeast Asia / edited by Heather Smith.
      p. cm. — (Elgar mini series) (Elgar reference collection)
   Includes bibliographical references and indexes.
   1. East Asia—Economic policy. 2. Monetary policy—East Asia. 3. Fiscal policy—East Asia. 4. East Asia—Foreign economic relations. 5. East Asia—Economic integration. 6. East Asia—Economic conditions. 7. Industrial policy—East Asia. I. Smith, Heather, 1965– II. Series. III. Series: Elgar reference collection

HC460.5 .E3635 2002
338.95—dc21   2002022245

ISBN   1 85898 867 5 (4 volume set)

Printed and bound in Great Britain by MPG Books Ltd, Bodmin, Cornwall

Contents

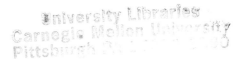

Acknowledgements

The editor and publishers wish to thank the authors and the following publishers who have kindly given permission for the use of copyright material.

Blackwell Publishers Ltd for articles: Keijiro Otsuka and Yujiro Hayami (1985), 'Goals and Consequences of Rice Policy in Japan, 1965–80', *American Journal of Agricultural Economics*, **67** (3), August, 529–38; Stephen D. Prowse (1992), 'The Structure of Corporate Ownership in Japan', *Journal of Finance*, **XLVII** (3), July, 1121–40; Heather Smith (1995), 'Industry Policy in East Asia', *Asian-Pacific Economic Literature*, **9** (1), May, 17–39; Heather Smith (1997), 'Taiwan's Industrial Policy in the 1980s: An Appraisal', *Asian Economic Journal*, **11** (1), March, 1–33.

Frank Cass & Co. Ltd for article: John C.H. Fei and Gustav Ranis (1974), 'A Model of Growth and Employment in the Open Dualistic Economy: The Cases of Korea and Taiwan', *Journal of Development Studies*, **11** (1), October, 32–63.

Economic Record for article: Peter Drysdale (1995), 'The Question of Access to the Japanese Market?', *Economic Record*, **71** (214), September, 271–83.

Harvard Business School Press and The President and Fellows of Harvard College for excerpt: Linsu Kim (1997), 'Government as a Learning Facilitator', in *Imitation to Innovation: The Dynamics of Korea's Technological Learning*, Chapter 2, 21–58, notes.

Institute of Developing Economies for article: Makoto Abe and Momoko Kawakami (1997), 'A Distributive Comparison of Enterprise Size in Korea and Taiwan', *Developing Economies*, **XXXV** (4), December, 382–400.

John F. Kennedy School of Government, Harvard University for excerpt: Joseph J. Stern, Ji-hong Kim, Dwight H. Perkins and Jung-ho Yoo (1995), 'Overview of Results', in *Industrialization and the State: The Korean Heavy and Chemical Industry Drive*, Chapter 4, 63–106, references.

Korea Development Institute for excerpt: Seong Min Yoo and Sung Soon Lee (1997), 'Evolution of Industrial Organization and Policy Response in Korea: 1945–1995', in Dong-Se Cha, Kwang Suk Kim and Dwight H. Perkins (eds), *The Korean Economy 1945–1995: Performance and Vision for the 21st Century*, Chapter 10, 426–67.

Oxford University Press for articles and excerpt: Ha-Joon Chang (1993), 'The Political Economy of Industrial Policy in Korea', *Cambridge Journal of Economics*, **17**, 131–57; Yoon Je Cho (1996), 'Government Intervention, Rent Distribution, and Economic Development in Korea', in Masahiko Aoki, Hyung-Ki Kim and Masahiro Okuno-Fujiwara (eds), *The Role of Government in East Asian Economic Development: Comparative Institutional Analysis*, Chapter 7, 208–32; Denis Fred Simon (1996), 'Charting Taiwan's Technological Future: The Impact of Globalization and Regionalization', *China Quarterly*, **148**, December, 1196–223.

Gustav Ranis for excerpt: Howard Pack (1992), 'New Perspectives on Industrial Growth in Taiwan', in Gustav Ranis (ed.), *Taiwan: From Developing to Mature Economy*, Chapter 3, 73–120.

Routledge for excerpt: Otto C.C. Lin (1998), 'Science and Technology Policy and Its Influence on Economic Development in Taiwan', in Henry S. Rowen (ed.), *Behind East Asian Growth: The Political and Social Foundations of Prosperity*, Chapter 9, 185–206.

M.E. Sharpe, Inc. for article: Paul Sheard (1991), 'The Economics of Japanese Corporate Organization and the "Structural Impediments" Debate: A Critical Review', *Japanese Economic Studies*, **19** (4), Summer, 30–78.

Stanford University Press and The Board of Trustees of the Leland Junior University for excerpt: Daniel I. Okimoto (1989), 'Industrial Policy Instruments for High Technology', in *Between MITI and the Market: Japanese Industrial Policy for High Technology*, Chapter Two, 55–111, notes.

Tokyo Club Foundation for Global Studies, Japan and the Institute of Southeast Asian Studies, Singapore for excerpt: Edward K.Y. Chen and Kui-wai Li (1997), 'Industrial Policy in a Laissez-Faire Economy: The Case of Hong Kong', in Seiichi Masuyama, Donna Vandenbrink and Chia Siow Yue (eds), *Industrial Policies in East Asia*, Chapter 4, 91–120.

University of Chicago Press for articles: Sophia Wu Huang (1993), 'Structural Change in Taiwan's Agricultural Economy', *Economic Development and Cultural Change*, **42** (1), October, 43–65; Yoong-Deok Jeon and Young-Yong Kim (2000), 'Land Reform, Income Redistribution, and Agricultural Production in Korea', *Economic Development and Cultural Change*, **48** (2), January, 253–68.

Every effort has been made to trace all the copyright holders but if any have been inadvertently overlooked the publishers will be pleased to make the necessary arrangement at the first opportunity.

In addition the publishers wish to thank the Marshall Library of Economics, Cambridge University, the London School of Economics and Political Science and the Library of Indiana University at Bloomington, USA for their assistance in obtaining these articles.

Part I
Structural Change and Development

[1]

A Model of Growth and Employment in the Open Dualistic Economy :

The Cases of Korea and Taiwan

By John C. H. Fei and Gustav Ranis*

*In this paper, the pressing problem of unemployment in the con-
temporary developing world is studied from an historical perspective of transition growth, i.e. the process representing the
termination of economic colonialism and the initiation of modern
growth. This problem is investigated for a particular type of LDC,
namely, the open dualistic labour surplus economy. The post-war
(1950–70) experience of Taiwan and Korea were analyzed from
this viewpoint—emphasizing the fine differences as well as the
family resemblance among these countries. As ex-Japanese colonies,
both these countries shared a relatively strong agricultural infrastructure and the open dualistic and labour surplus characteristic
at the beginning of the transition in the 1950s. However, as we
show, Taiwan had an initially more favourable set of institutional
and economic conditions in agriculture.*

In the post-war decade, we indicate that both countries experienced
two sub-phases of transition: an import substitution sub-phase followed by
an export substitution sub-phase. In the former, entrepreneurial experience was accumulated along with a further strengthening of the rural
infrastructure, e.g. by land reform. In the latter, both countries rapidly
developed labour intensive manufacturing exports to the world market.
It was this latter development that contributed substantially to the solution
of the unemployment problem and permitted the labour surplus condition
to be gradually terminated. This major 'turning point', as well as other
turning points related to the historical role of the agricultural sector, are
deduced theoretically in the paper as well as verified empirically.

The overall experience of the '50s and '60s seems to indicate a worsening
of the unemployment or underemployment problem in the developing
world, even where per capita income growth has been quite satisfactory.
When this experience is then projected forward, given the knowledge that

*Economic Growth Center, Yale University. The authors wish to acknowledge the
substantial contributions of Professor Sung Hwan Jo of Sogang University, Korea and
Professor Chi-Mu Huang of National University, Taiwan to this paper, especially its
empirical portions. Portions of this research were financed by funds provided by the
Agency for International Development under contract CSD/2492. However, the views
expressed in this paper do not necessarily reflect those of AID.

even the most successful population control programmes cannot affect labour force size for some 15 years to come, the gloom thickens. Something has to be done for employment—even if it means sacrificing the GNP growth rate.

The purpose of this paper is to demonstrate, with the help of a theoretical framework applicable to at least one type of LDC, that the necessity of contemplating a trade-off between employment and GNP may, in fact, be illusory and based on a misinterpretation of the historical record. The model presented 'opens up' the traditional closed dualistic model of development [*Lewis, 1954*], based on the notion that the full potential complementarity between growth and employment is best demonstrated when the focus of analysis is broadened from the process of domestic 'labour' reallocation within the closed dualistic setting, to include the possibility of labour reallocation through trade. While we believe that the solution of the employment problem in the context of growth, as demonstrated by the model, applies to all but the very large (and therefore domestically-oriented) labour surplus LDCs, our empirical test is concentrated on Korea and Taiwan.

In historical perspective, the post–war performance of most LDCs is a transition between a long epoch of colonialism and a long epoch of modern growth.[1] Korea and Taiwan share the colonial heritage of a heavy dependence on traditional land–based production and exports, moving gradually to a non-traditional labour-based output mix as they successfully solve their employment problem, mainly through trade.

We shall accept the 'initial' period of transition as 1952–4 for Taiwan and 1953–7 for Korea,[2] with the 'terminal' period as 1968–70, in both cases. In Section I we present a comparative static model, with statistical evidence, to examine the initial and terminal structural characteristics of the two countries under observation. Section II identifies several important turning-points during the transition process. In Section III we present our conclusions and the implications of our analysis for employment and output policy in labour-surplus LDCs.

I. COMPARATIVE STATIC ANALYSIS

The basic purpose of our comparative static analysis is to identify the structural change within the economy between the initial and terminal years. In the open dualistic labour surplus economy this structure can be described by a set of indices such as shown in Table 1, including production, consumption, saving, investment, trade, labour allocation, each of which has its place in the context of the model we intend to develop in the course of this section.

Since countries of this particular type are overwhelmingly agricultural, at least at the initial point, we begin our analysis with relations focussing on agricultural productivity, the allocation of labour between sectors, and trade in agricultural goods. The labour surplus condition is eliminated by the reallocation of unemployed or inefficiently employed (underemployed) workers from the subsistence to the commercialized sectors, where they

TABLE 1

COMPARATIVE STATIC ANALYSIS*

(1)	(2) Taiwan 1952–54 a	Initial Period (3) Korea 1955–57 b	(4) Parity b/a	(5) Taiwan 1967–69 c	Terminal Period (6) Korea 1968–70 d	(7) Parity d/c
1. v agricultural labour productivity	$273·4	$198·5	·73	$668·0	$386·8	·57
2. θ labour allocation ratio	42·3%	32·0%	·76	58·0%	49·5%	·84
3. $E\Delta$ 'per capita' agricultural net exports	$ 19·4	$—8·3	—	$ 9·3	—38·9	—
4. $C\Delta_a$ 'per capita' consumption of agricultural goods	$138·5	$142·4	1·04	$263·2	$223·14	·77
4a. GDP/X 'per capita' GDP	$131·2	$83·4	·64	$276·8	$150·5	·54
5. w_a agricultural real wage	303·8	195·4	·64	472·5	$317·3	·67
6. w_i industrial real wage	$313·9	$219·0	·69	$529·2	$367·8	·69
7. — internal terms of trade P_a/P_i	95·5%	96·1%	1·0	96·5%	119·7%	1·24
8. $C\Delta_i$ 'per capita' consumption of industrial goods	$221·0	$139·5	·63	$416·1	$240·0	·57
9. $K^* = K/W$ industrial capital-labour ratio	$2543·0	$4508·0	1·77	$2372·0	$3051·0	1·28
10. $q = Y/W$ industrial labour productivity	$659·6	$541·3	·82	$1442·9	$906·2	·62
11. $Y\Delta = Y/P$ 'per capita' industrial output	$279·1	$169·9	·61	$837·5	$453·0	1·84
12. $E\Delta_i$ 'per capita' industrial exports	$ 16·0	$6·8	·43	$223·5	$110·0	·49

Continued overleaf

#	Symbol	Description						
13.	E/GDP	export ratio	11·2%	4·1%	·37	27·6%	25·4%	·92
14.	E△	'per capita' exports	$43·8	$11·0	·25	$251·9	$123·0	·48
15.	Ei/E	industrial share of exports	37·2%	61·6%	1·65	88·5%	89·8%	1·01
16.	Ea/Q	agricultural export ratio	12·2%	3·1%	·25	3·3%	6·9%	2·09
17.	Mc/Cd	import substitution potential index	8·5%	6·5%	·76	10·2%	6·5%	·63
18.	Mc/M	industrial consumer goods share of imports	23·0%	13·3%	·57	15·9%	7·5%	·47
19.	Ma(Ma+Q)	agricultural import fraction	5·1%	8·1%	1·58	6·4%	21·3%	3·32
20.	(Sa+Si)/GDP	domestic saving rate	10·0%	−4·1%		34·4%	18·5%	
21.	I/GDP	investment rate	17·2%	15·4%		33·0%	35·4%	
22.	Sa/I	agricultural saving contribution	18·5%	15·2%		23·5%	2·1%	
23.	Si/I	industrial saving contribution	40·0%	−43·5%		80·7%	49·5%	
24.	Sf/I	foreign saving contribution	41·0%	128·3%		−4·4%	48·2%	
25.	X	population	8·438 mil.	22·263 mil.		13·313 mil.	32·056 mil.	
26.	P	labour force	2·828 mil.	6·924 mil.		4·926 mil.	9·886 mil.	

Cumulative Contribution to Investment During Transition

	Taiwan	Korea
agricultural saving ΣSa/ΣI	25·9%	8·6%
industrial saving ΣSi/ΣI	68·6%	29·7%
foreign saving ΣSf/ΣI	5·7%	61·6%

*See Appendix for data sources.

U.S. $ figures for Korea are in 1965 constant prices, and those for Taiwan, in 1964 constant prices.

36   EMPLOYMENT, INCOME DISTRIBUTION AND DEVELOPMENT

are efficiently or competitively employed.[3] In the early phase of the transition growth, 'this' is the heart of the employment problem.

Suppose the economy's total initial labour force (P) is divided into an agricultural labour force (L) and a non-agricultural labour force (W), i.e. $P = W + L$. Let us denote $\theta = W/P$ as the fraction of the total labour force in the non-agricultural sector (i.e. $1 - \theta = L/P$ is the fraction in the agricultural sector). Suppose the total output of agricultural goods is Q and the average productivity of agricultural labour is $v = Q/L$. Then the demand and supply of agricultural goods is

$$Lv = Q = C_a + E_a \qquad (1)$$
(supply) (demand)

where the demand for agricultural goods is either for domestic consumption (C_a) or for export (E_a)—as is typical in the colonial pattern. Dividing throughout by total population (and letting $x^\triangle = x/P$, i.e. per capita x), we have

$$(1-\theta)v = Q^\triangle = C_a^\triangle + E_a^\triangle \quad \text{or} \qquad (2a)$$
$$v = (E_a^\triangle + C_a^\triangle) / (1-\theta) \qquad (2b)$$

From (2b) we can see that a higher agricultural productivity (v) can lead to a combination of a higher consumption standard of agricultural goods ($C_a^\triangle$), a higher per capita export level ($E_a^\triangle$), and a higher fraction of the labour force already allocated to industry (θ).

Let us assume that land and labour are the only important traditional factors of production in agriculture.[4] If the supply of land is approximately fixed, the total productivity of labour, say for Taiwan, in the initial year. may be represented by the Q_T-curve in Figure 1a (i.e. the agricultural labour force L_T is measured on the horizontal axis to the left). If the total population is represented by a point 'P' in Figure 1a, the industrial labour force is PL_T, while the agricultural labour force is OL_T, leading to an initial agricultural labour productivity v_T represented by the slope of the straight line Oa_T in Figure 1a. In Figure 1b (below 1a) with the same fixed initial population P, the per capita output for the economy as a whole is represented by the $Q_T^\triangle$ curve (i.e. $Q_T^\triangle = Q_T/P$). The initial supply of agricultural output per head for Taiwan is then equal to $L_T b_T$ as indicated in Figure 1b. For the case of Korea, in a similar way, the initial agricultural output (Q_K-curve in Figure 2a), output per head ($Q_K^\triangle$ curve in Figure 2b) and labour allocation point (L_K) are shown.

What we have just portrayed is a realistic comparative picture of the agricultural condition of the two countries at the initial point. Taiwan inherited a more favourable agricultural infrastructure, reflected in a higher initial productivity of agricultural workers (slope of Oa_T in Figure 1a > slope of Oa_K in Figure 2a).[5] As indicated in Table 1, row 1, Korea's initial agricultural labour productivity was only 70 per cent of that of Taiwan. However, possibly due to their common colonial experience, the agricultural consumption standard (C_a^A) in both countries is seen to be

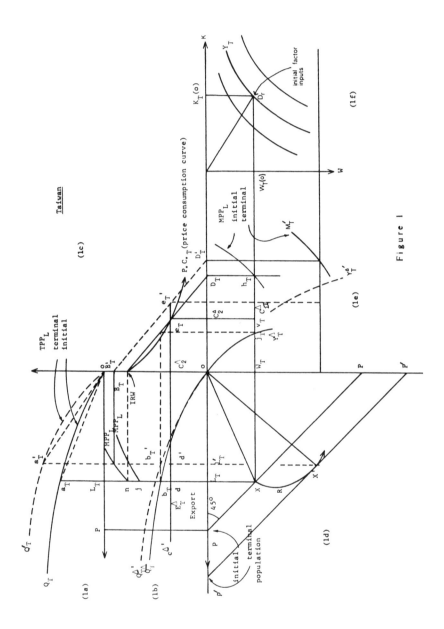

Figure 1

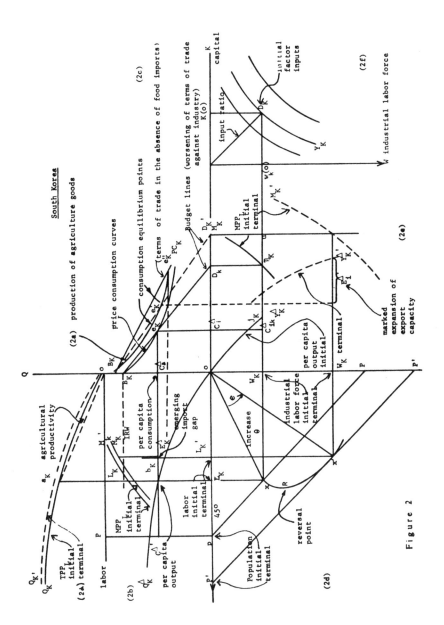

Figure 2

approximately the same (Table 1, row 4). Moreover, Table 1, row 2, indicates that initially Taiwan had already allocated 42 per cent of her labour force to non-agriculture, in sharp contrast to Korea with only 32 per cent. Thus, using equation (2b), the higher productivity in Taiwan led to *both* a higher fraction of labour in the non-agricultural sector (θ) *and* a higher level of agricultural exports on a per capita basis.

Even more startling is the contrast summarized in row 3. While Korea was initially already a net importer of agricultural goods, Taiwan exported a hefty $19 per capita and thus provided capacity to import capital goods and raw materials for the growing non-agricultural sectors.[6] This means that, from the very beginning, the agricultural sector in Taiwan played a much more positive role in fuelling the expansion of the industrial activities than Korea, in which the relative backward agricultural sector constituted a burden for industrialization. In the case of Korea, the agricultural sector was 'pulled along' by a dynamic non-agricultural sector rather than an important 'push' for industrialization, as in the case of Taiwan.

Since the individual worker consumes two kinds of commodities (agricultural goods, measured on the vertical axis of Figure 1c, and non-agricultural goods, measured on the horizontal axis), the agricultural real wage level for a typical Taiwanese worker may be represented by the budget line $B_T D_T$ (in Figure 1c). In other words, OB_T, (OD_T) is the level of the real wage in terms of agricultural (non-agricultural) goods, while the slope of the budget line represents the initial terms of trade. In a similar fashion, the budget line for Korea may be shown as $B_K D_K$ in Figure 2c. $B_K D_K$ is meant to lie below $B_T D_T$ since Korea's initial real wage in terms of agricultural goods, OB_K, is lower than Taiwan's, OB_T (see row 5), as well as in terms of industrial goods (row 6). Since the wage parity in terms of both conditions are approximately the same ('·64' and '·69', column 4) the internal terms of trade are approximately the same for the two countries (row 7). This means that, in the context of an open economy, the possibility of the import of agricultural goods in Korea compensated for her relatively backward condition in agriculture and that, initially the internal terms of trade in both countries are governed by a common international terms of trade in the Japanese market.[7]

In the context of a labour surplus dualistic economy, the real wage in terms of agricultural goods (e.g. OB_T in Figure 1c for Taiwan) may be thought of as the institutional real wage (IRW) which is determined by the institutional forces prevailing in the agricultural sector. In such an economy the IRW is likely to be above agricultural labour's marginal product (MPP_L), signifying the existence of surplus labour in the economy.[8] During the transition process, the IRW, moreover, is likely to increase only moderately, certainly less than the MPP_L, as long as IRW > MPP_L. However, once the labour surplus is exhausted and labour becomes scarce, IRW = MPP_L, and we can expect the wage to follow the MPP_L thereafter.

In Figure 1c, given the fixed IRW at level OB_T, the price-consumption curve PC_T, for Taiwan, is shown.[9] Where this curve intersects the typical worker's budget line ($B_T D_T$), *i.e.* at point e_T, locates the initial consumption equilibrium point for Taiwan (OC_2^a units of agricultural goods and OC_1^a of non-agricultural goods). Similarly, for Korea, the price-consumption curve PC_K may be drawn in Figure 2c. As we have noted earlier, virtually the same $OC_{\dot{a}}^a$ is seen to prevail in both Korea and Taiwan initially. Thus, in the case of Taiwan, we can show (see row 3) the existence of a substantial agricultural export surplus per head ($E_T^a = b_T d$ in Figure 1b), while in the case of Korea, there exists a need to import agricultural goods at the outset.[10] Since Korea's budget line ($B_K D_K$ in Figure 2c) is lower than Taiwan's ($B_T D_T$ in Figure 1c) the fact that the two countries consume about the same amount of agricultural goods per capita, implies, moreover, that Korea's farmers initially consume substantially less non-agricultural goods on a per capita basis. This is confirmed by the data in row 8, columns 2 and 3.

Let us turn next to the production of and demand for non-agricultural (or, in shorthand, industrial) output. With respect to industrial output, there are two factors which differentiate the industrial from the agricultural sectors: first, the primary factors of production are now labour (W) and capital (K); and second, the industrial sector is assumed to be commercialized in that the real wage (in terms of industrial goods) may now be equated with the marginal productivity of labour. In Figures 1f and 2f, with labour (W) and capital (K) being measured on the vertical and horizontal axes, respectively, the production contour map, for Taiwan and Korea, for the initial period, is represented by the solid production contour maps indexed by Y_T and Y_K. Given the initial capital stock, e.g. ($K_T(o)$) for Taiwan, the MPP_L-curve is represented by the solid M_T-curve in Figure 1e, 'below' 1f. To show the consistent equilibrium position for the case of Taiwan, let the 45-degree line PP be drawn in Figure 1d with the aid of which the initial industrial labour force P_T^L (in Figure 1b) can be projected as OW_T on the vertical axis (downward). Since the initial non-agricultural real wage in Taiwan is OD_T,[11] the MPP_L-curve (i.e. the M_T-curve) passes through the point h_T in Figure 1e, indicating that OW_T units of labour are demanded at the real industrial wage OD_T. Similarly, for Korea, with capital stock $K_K(o)$ in Figure 2f, the MPP_L-curve is represented by the M_K-curve in Figure 2e, with an employment equilibrium point at h_K —indicating that OW_K units of workers are demanded at the industrial real wage OD_K.

A possible important initial difference in the state of industrial technology in Korea and Taiwan should be noted. From the theoretical standpoint, if the initial production functions of the two countries were exactly the same, then the higher level of the industrial real wage in Taiwan would imply that Taiwan also has (1) a higher industrial capital-labour ratio ($K^* = K/W$) and (2) a higher average productivity of industrial labour ($q = \dfrac{Y}{W}$). However, the empirical evidence (rows 9 and 10) indicates otherwise. Korea has an initially higher industrial capital-labour ratio than Taiwan—in spite of the lower Korean real wage level—and nevertheless sports a lower level of labour productivity—than Taiwan.[12] The cause of this difference may be traced once again to the Japanese colonial heritage; while the Japanese lavished relatively more attention on agricultural infrastructure in Taiwan, they pushed industrialization more heavily in Korea, which probably led to a more capital intensive, less innovative industrial structure.[13]

With respect to the demand and supply of industrial goods a formula symmetrical to (2a) is

$$\theta\, q = Y^\triangle = C^\triangle + E_i^\triangle \qquad (3)$$
$$\text{(supply)} \quad \text{(demand)}$$

where $Y^\triangle$ ($= Y/P$) is the per capita output of industrial goods and q is industrial labour productivity. From row 11, we see that the initial $Y^\triangle$ is much higher in Taiwan than in Korea (the parity is ·61) in spite of a much smaller gap in q (row 10 with a parity of ·82), simply because a larger proportion of the population has already been allocated to the non-agricultural sector (see row 2). On the demand side, a much larger fraction of Korea's non-agricultural output is exported at the outset—i.e. the percentage E_i/E is 50 per cent larger in Korea than in Taiwan (see row 15)—even though the actual magnitudes are small in both cases (see row 12).

Let us turn next to the overall magnitude and structure of international trade in the initial years in both countries. As far as the volume of total trade is concerned, given the already established fact that per capita GDP (row 4a) was higher in Taiwan initially, we would expect foreign trade to be quantitatively more important in Taiwan. Two indicators—exports as a fraction of GDP (row 13) and exports per capita (row 14)—are shown to corroborate this fact.

The contrast in the structure of the two countries' trade is even more dramatic than the difference in external orientation. While the initial export pattern of Taiwan was dominated by agricultural goods, Korea's modest exports were dominated by non-agricultural commodities (row 15). In fact, Taiwan inititally exported nearly 12 per cent of her agriculural output while Korea exported only 3 per cent of hers (row 16).

On the import side, during the initial years of transition growth total imports (M) consisted of imported industrial consumer goods (M_i) and producers' goods (M_p), i.e. capital goods and/or raw materials destined as productive inputs into the industrial sector ($M = M_i + M_p$). This breakdown will be seen to be significant for any analysis of the phenomenon of *import substitution (I-S) growth* which often characterizes the initial phase of transition.

By I-S growth we shall mean a sub-phase dominated by the development of the indigenous consumer goods industry with tradiional consumer goods imports (M_i) gradually being replaced. In order to build up these import substituting industries the LDC, however, usually needs to import more raw materials and capital goods M_p. Bearing this in mind, rows 17 and 18 attempt to describe the initial potential for I-S growth. Row 17, for example, shows that, while Taiwan initially imported 8.5

per cent of her total requirements for industrial consumer goods, the corresponding figure for Korea was 6·5 per cent. In the case of Taiwan, moreover, the imported industrial consumer goods accounted for 23·0 per cent of her total imports while the corresponding figure for Korea was only 13·3 per cent (row 18). Thus, both from the viewpoint of the domestic market and from the viewpoint of the allocation of foreign exchange, the importation of industrial consumer goods was more important in Taiwan than in Korea in the initial period under observation—allowing more scope for I-S growth.

The above description of the structure of trade reveals a contrasting pattern during the early phase of transition growth in the two countries under examination. In the case of Taiwan, there is in evidence a pattern of triangularism, i.e. the agricultural sector produces an exportable surplus which, in turn, provides the import capacity used for two types of industrial imports, consumer goods and producers' goods. The same agricultural exports, moreover, generate the incomes and demand for the larger volume of industrial consumer goods now produced at home. In this manner, agriculture fuels I-S growth as M_p imports permit the continued building up of the domestic import substituting capacity that gradually replaces M_i imports.

In the case of Korea, on the other hand, the growth dynamics represent more of a bilateral interaction between industry and the foreign sector as agriculture remains relatively stagnant. The industrial sector in consequence has to be depended upon to produce an exportable surplus which, together with the provision of capital from abroad, is used to import the capital goods and raw materials needed by the import substitution process. Moreover, as we shall see below, and especially during the later subphase of transition, the industrial sector, instead of being supported by agricultural exports, is saddled with the responsibility of diverting a part of the import capacity it generates for the purchase of food abroad.

The case of Taiwan is described in Figure 1e in which the $Y_T^\triangle$ curve is shown. The initial value of per capita output is seen to be $W_T j_T$, while the initial value of the per capita demand for consumer goods $C_i^\triangle$ is $W_T C i_T^\triangle$ ($=OG^\triangle$).[14] Thus, there exists a shortage of $j_T C i_T^\triangle$ units of industrial goods which must be imported. Since, from Figure 1b, the initial per capita agricultural export is seen to be $E_T^\triangle$ ($=b_T d$), at the initial terms of trade, the import capacity generated by these agricultural exports is $C_i^\triangle v_T$ (Figure 1e). The other portion of industrial goods required (i.e. $v_T j_T$ units on a per capita basis) is financed by foreign capital.

In the case of Korea, in Figure 2, the inital $Y^\triangle$-curve is labelled $Y_K^\triangle$ leading to an initial per capita output of $W_K j_K$ units. This output is actually higher than domestic demand $W_K C i_K^\triangle$, signifying that Korea's industrial sector is already producing an exportable surplus, to finance its own import needs. The agricultural sector, on the other hand, is not involved in the financing process; in fact, to the extent that there is a food deficit, it is already drawing on the import capacity provided by industrial exports and foreign capital inflow.

The above presents a fairly accurate picture of the comparative structural conditions of the two countries under observation at the initial point in time. The purpose of comparative structural analysis is to contrast these initial characteristics with those obtaining in the terminal periods. The forces that brought on the marked structural change observable in columns 5–7 of Table 1 include (1) capital accumulation, (2) population growth, and (3) technology change in both the agricultural and non-agricultural sectors.

Let us first concentrate on capital accumulation. The saving fund available to these entrepreneurs, in both the public and private sectors, was composed of three sources: foreign capital (S_f), the reinvestment of industrial profits (S_i), and agricultural saving (S_a), i.e. [15]

$$I = S_a + S_i + S_f \qquad (4)$$

Turning once again to Table 1, we have indicated the relative contribution to the total investment fund of the three sources of saving, both for the initial and terminal period—in rows 22–24. In the same table, moreover, we have presented the cumulative contribution of each between the initial and terminal period. In terms of these cumulative figures, the dramatic differences between Taiwan and Korea during the transition period is demonstrated by the fact that foreign capital financed $61 \cdot 6$ per cent of total investment in Korea and only $5 \cdot 7$ per cent in Taiwan. Agricultural saving contributed about three times as much to a higher investment rate in Taiwan than in Korea. This lack of domestic saving capacity, especially in agriculture, to finance her own investment needs and the heavy continued reliance on foreign capital, remains the most serious problem facing Korea's development.

Other evidence of marked structural change can be analyzed in terms of a comparison of (1) the role of agriculture; (2) the behaviour of wages and consumption; (3) the progress of industrial technology and the structure of international trade. While there continues to exist a marked family similarity between these two countries, differences in observed structural change are also instructive for the understanding of the employment problem.

The Role of the Agricultural Sector

To begin with the non-agricultural sector in both countries has grown rapidly enough to absorb the unemployed and underemployed in agriculture in spite of substantial population increase. Thus the centre of gravity of both economies, in terms of the allocation of labour between the two sectors, has shifted markedly. Returning to Figures 1d and 2d, the growth of population may be represented by the parallel and outward shift of the population lines PP to P'P'. At the same time the allocation points have shifted from L_T (L_K for Korea) to L_T^1 (L_K^1 for Korea), representing an increase in θ for both countries, as indicated. Rows 25 and 26 of Table 1 yield an average annual rate of growth between the initial and terminal period of $2 \cdot 9$ per cent in population and $3 \cdot 7$ per cent in the labour force for Taiwan, and $2 \cdot 5$ per cent and $2 \cdot 7$ per cent, respectively, for Korea. In spite of this, as we can see from row 2, Taiwan registered an increase in θ from 42 to 58 per cent and Korea from 32 to 49 per cent. This demonstrates the rapidity of the growth and industrial sector labour absorption process in both countries.

Associated with this marked structural change in terms of labour reallocation, is a markedly different role played by the agricultural sector. In the case of Taiwan, the initially more favourable agricultural infra-structure, and the encouraging policies led to dramatic advances in technology and agricultural labour productivity. This is depicted by the upward shift of the total output curve from Q_T to Q_T^1 (in Figure 1a) and of the per capita output curve from $Q_T^\triangle$ to $Q_T^{\triangle 1}$ (in Figure 1b). Coupled with the labour reallocation effect, agricultural labour productivity has thus advanced from the slope of Oa_T in Figure 1a to the slope of Oa_T'.[16] The exportable per capita agricultural surplus in the terminal period is now $d'b_T'$, in Figure 1b, compared with db_T earlier.

From row 1 we see that agricultural labour productivity in Taiwan advanced by more than 244 per cent. As a result, in spite of substantial gains in the per capita consumption of agricultural goods (row 4) agricultural exports, even on a net per capita basis, could be sustained at a high level (row 3). All this in the face of the fact (row 2) that the agricultural labour force is now a much smaller fraction of the total labour force than in the initial period, and, in fact, declined absolutely after a point.

In the case of Korea, the initially relatively unfavourable agricultural infra-structure, reinforced by the relative government neglect over time thereafter, has led to a situation of comparative agricultural stagnation. Agricultural productivity here also registered some gains. But, as seen from row 1, the gains were more modest leading to a further substantial decline in the relative position of the two agricultural sectors (see row 1, columns 4 and 7). Consequently, the increase in Korea's agricultural consumption standard is modest (row 4—note especially the decline in the parity ratio) from domestic sources; instead, increasing volumes of food imports have been required (see row 3).

To obtain a clear picture of the contrast we can look at the net import or export figure for food only over the relevant period. While Taiwan has been continuously exporting food during the entire transition period, Korea's food deficit problem has been steadily worsening, with more than $300,000 annually being spent on net food imports in recent years. The contrast is best summarized in Figure 3, showing food imports as a percentage of total food consumption in Korea and food exports as a percentage of total food consumption in Taiwan.

Thus, in the case of Taiwan, rapid growth, industrialization and labour reallocation were financed in considerable part by gains in agricultural productivity. In the case of Korea, on the other hand, rapid industrialization, growth and labour reallocation were financed in large part by the inflow of foreign capital. In the case of Korea the agricultural sector was 'pulled along' by a dynamic non-agricultural sector rather than providing an important 'push' for industrialization, as in the case of Taiwan. This contrast was also demonstrated vividly by our earlier analysis of the comparative cumulative sources of finance during the transition.

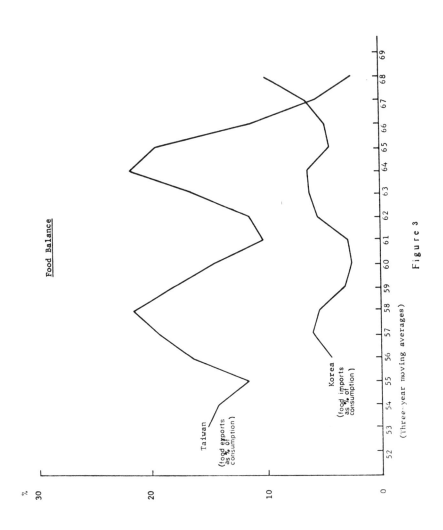

Food Balance

Taiwan
(food exports
as % of
consumption)

Korea
(food imports
as % of
consumption)

(Three-year moving averages)

Figure 3

Real Wage and Welfare

From the viewpoint of welfare, the impact of economic development may be examined in terms of an economy's (1) consumption level, (2) saving capacity and/or (3) the distribution of income between labour and property-owning classes. All these dimensions are in turn closely related to the behaviour of the real wage through time. An increase in the level of the real wage can be described by an upward shift in the budget line of a typical worker in Figure 1c. In the case of both Korea and Taiwan two facts may be noted. First, the real wage did go up between the initial and terminal years (see rows 5 and 6).[17] This is due to an upward revision of the IRW in agriculture as productivity change occurs[18] and means that, for example, for Taiwan, the budget line has shifted, from $B_T D_T$ to $B_T^1 D_T^1$ in Figure 1c. Secondly, the terms of trade have remained about constant in Korea, but worsened slightly against the industrial sector in Taiwan (see row 7). As far as the consumption standard is concerned, both the consumption per head of agricultural goods (row 8) and of industrial goods (row 9) rises with the increase in real wage. Accordingly, the consumption equilibrium point moves from e_T to e_T^1 and e_K to e_K^1 in both cases. Large food imports made this possible without a deterioration of the industrial sector's terms of trade in Korea.

As far as income distribution is concerned, labour's distributive share in any sector is $\emptyset = (Lxw)/z$ where 'z' is the total output of that sector. Consequently the rate of increase of $\emptyset$ is

$$\eta_\emptyset = \eta_w - \eta_{z/L} \tag{5}$$

which is the difference between the rate of increase of the real wage (η_w) and the rate of increase of labour productivity in that sector. Thus, for each sector, the distribution of income moves against labour when the increase in the real wage lags behind productivity gains during the un-limited supply of labour phase.[19]

As the company moves through its transition, changes in income distribution and in the participation of medium and small scale entrepreneurs under a more market-oriented policy setting, enhance the economy's saving capacity. Row 2, Table 1, indicates that Taiwan's gross domestic saving rate had, in fact, increased spectacularly during the transition period. The same is true of Korea where negative saving rates initially gave way to a very satisfactory saving performance at the $18 \cdot 5$ per cent level at the end of the period. From rows 22, 23, and 24 we may, moreover, gather that these gains in domestic saving capacity were largely based on the increasing contribution over time of the non-agricultural sector which, especially in Taiwan, replaced foreign capital as the main source of developmental finance.

The relative failure of Korea's agricultural sector also resulted in a less dramatic increase in her domestic saving capacity as we have already noted (row 20). In fact, rows 22–24 permit us to see precisely how the agricultural sector's contribution to the economy's total investment fund declined dramatically during the transition period. Consequently, even in the terminal period, foreign capital still had to be relied on for close to 50 per cent of Korea's total investment fund. Thus, while the saving

GROWTH AND EMPLOYMENT IN KOREA AND TAIWAN   47

capacity of the industrial sector increased dramatically, the gap left by the failure of agriculture's contribution had to be filled largely by foreign capital.

Industrial Sector and International Trade

Turning, finally, to a brief examination of the non-agricultural sector in the same comparative static setting, we should, first of all, note that it is the performance of this sector that has marked off the path of both Korea and Taiwan from that of other contemporary open dualistic economies, Recalling equation (3), we see that the dramatic increase in θ (proportion of the population already efficiently allocated or employed) and in q (non-agricultural labour productivity) has led to a large increase in the per capita output of industrial goods $Y^\triangle$. Although there has been some increase in the domestic use of that industrial output, the most conspicuous result of this development has been in the spurt of industrial exports.

Referring to row 11, the availability of industrial output per head $(Y^\triangle)$ sustained an annual rate of increase of 8·0 per cent in Taiwan and 7·5 per cent in Korea during the transition period. This high rate of increase followed from both the increase in θ (row 2) and the increase in q (row 10). The spectacular change in the extent of external orientation of both countries' rapidly growing non-agricultural sectors is summarized in row 12. In Taiwan (Korea), industrial exports per head grew at the remarkable rate of 19·3 per cent (24·0 per cent) annually, yielding a 14-fold (16-fold) increase during the transition period.[20]

This dramatic increase in the external orientation of the industrial sector brought with it a corresponding change in the structure of foreign trade. First of all, in terms of the overall involvement in trade, as measured by the export ratio (row 13), while Korea participated much less in trade at the outset, the export ratio rose substantially in both countries so that, by the terminal year, more than 25 per cent of GDP was exported in both cases. Furthermore, as seen from row 15, in the case of Taiwan, the initial dominance of the agricultural sector in exports was completely reversed so that in the terminal year almost 90 per cent of exports are seen to be non-agricultural. In the case of Korea which had a relatively much more industrial orientation (including exports) to start with, exports are now also almost exclusively industrial in origin. The fact that agricultural exports lagged along with agricultural output is further confirmed in row 16, i.e. the fraction of agricultural goods exported remains small in Korea and substantial in Taiwan.

II. LANDMARKS IN THE TRANSITION PROCESS

We have thus tried to compare and contrast the economic structure of the two countries under observation during both the initial and terminal periods of the transition process to obtain two flashlight exposures. But it is inadequate in the sense that we are still lacking a picture of the process of continuous change over more than a decade which, of course, brought about the structural changes observed. In this section we will attempt to describe the highlights of this process, in terms of the turning points by

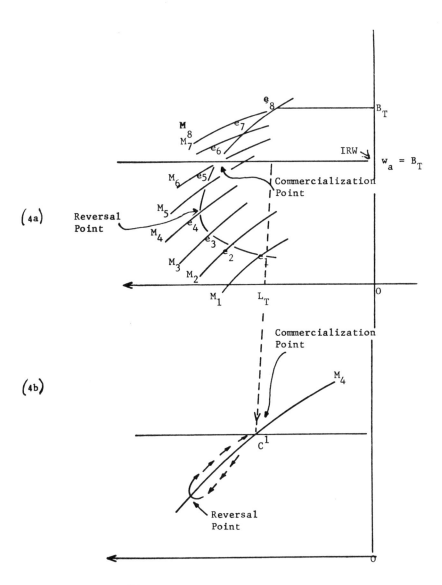

Figure 4

GROWTH AND EMPLOYMENT IN KOREA AND TAIWAN   49

which the sub-phases of the transition process can be marked off.[21] In what follows we shall explore the economic significance of four turning points:

Turning Points	Taiwan	Korea
(a) Commercialization point	65–66	66–67
(b) Reversal point	64–65	66–67
(c) Export substitution point	60	64
(d) Switching point	75 (?)	80 (?)

For a closed labour surplus dualistic economy, the *commercialization point* indicates the termination of the labour surplus condition.[22] From this point on, real wage in the agricultural sector is equated with the marginal productivity of labour (i.e. determined by 'commercial principle' rather than 'institutional forces') which signifies that labour now becomes a scarce factor (from the economic standpoint) and tends to increase rapidly. This concept can be applied to an open dualistic economy.

In the case of Taiwan the causes of the arrival of the commercialization point must be found in a combination of the 'push' effects of continuous technology change in agriculture combined with the 'pull' of industrial demand for labour in a balanced fashion. In Figure 4, which 'blows up' Figure 1b, we indicate the changing marginal product of labour curves M_i as technological change takes place in agriculture. Thus the movement from M_1 (i.e. the MPP_L curve of 1b) to M_8 (the MPP_L' curve of 1b) is replicated in Figure 4. The dynamic process of labour reallocation may then be depicted by a sequence of points e_i which, consistent with a continuously rising θ, or a relative decline in the size of the agricultural population, show, first, an absolute increase in agricultural population (e_1 to e_4), followed by an absolute decrease (from e_4 onward).[23] The commercialization point is reached at e_6.[23] Thus the commercialization point arrives earlier, the faster the upward shift of the MPP_L curve, the slower the rate of population growth, the slower the upward creep of the institutional real wage and the faster the demand for labour increases in the industrial sector.[24]

The above thesis is supported by the actual long-term behaviour of the real wage in the two countries under observation. As shown in Figure 5, the real wage in both countries shows only a minor upward creep until very recently (i.e. after 1965). It thus appears that the commercialization point may have been reached in both Korea and Taiwan[25] towards the end of the '60s—with agricultural 'push' forces contributing much more in Taiwan, and industrial 'pull', fuelled by foreign capital, much more in Korea.[26] If so, we can also expect a further acceleration of real wage increases to characterize their development in the '70s.

The increase of real wages has a profound impact on income distribution, on saving capacity and on the economy's consumption pattern. As income distribution within each sector now shifts in favour of labour, any decline in the propensity to save will be accompanied by a more sustained expansion of the domestic market for consumer goods. In other words, the commercialization point heralds an end to the relative natural austerity typical of the 'unlimited supply of labour' condition. After the commercial-

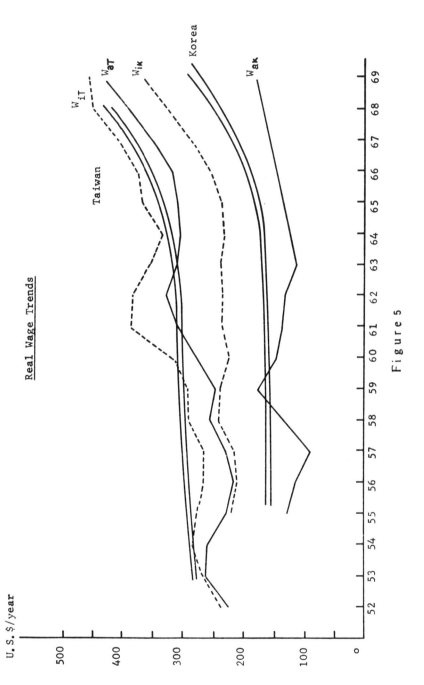

Real Wage Trends

U.S. $/year

Figure 5

ization point, *ceteris paribus*, we can expect the saving rate and the GDP growth rates to level off. Furthermore, in an open dualistic labour surplus economy the commercialization point is also likely to usher in changes in the structure of international trade. The external orientation of the industrial sector, which was previously based on the continuation of maturing entrepreneurs taking advantage of cheap labour,[27] now gives way gradually, to the incorporation of skills and capital goods as the basis for exports. Simultaneously we can expect a shift in the orientation of the industrial sector in the direction of satisfying the growing domestic market for industrial consumer goods, including more durable consumer goods.

The second turning point is the *reversal point* signifying an absolute decline in the agricultural population or labour force. It can be shown that when the rate of increase of the industrial labour force (η_w) is sustained long enough at a level higher than the growth rate of the total labour force ($\eta_w > \eta_p$), not only does θ ($=W/P$) increase continuously, as we have already observed, but a reversal point is reached after some time, when an absolute increase of the agricultural labour force gives way to an absolute decline. In Figure 1d, associated with an increase of the total population or labour force from OP to OP′, the initial labour allocation point X changes to X′ in the terminal years, representing an increase of θ (slope of OX′ > slope of OX) as well as an absolute decline of the agricultural labour force. The movement of the labour allocation point through time is depicted by the locus XRX′ in Figure 1d, where R is the reversal point. The same reversal point R can be observed in Figure 4. In the case of the two specific countries under observation here, our data indicate that the reversal point was reached in Taiwan a couple of years before commercialization, while in Korea both seem to have arrived more or less simultaneously, i.e. near the end of the '60s.[28]

When the supply of land is, for all practical purposes, fixed, the arrival of a reversal point signifies that the law of diminishing returns is beginning to work in a reverse direction, as both marginal and average productivities of labour begin to increase even when technology is stagnant. For Taiwan, this implies that the pressure is beginning to appear for the adoption of labour-saving technology (e.g. mechanization) in agriculture—as there is now an absolute shortage of manpower under the old technology. For Korea, this means that it is *possible* to solve the problem of agricultural stagnation by a strategy of 'pulling' this sector up by rapid industrial development. Whether or not this strategy will be successful remains to be seen.[29]

The third turning point is the *export substitution point*. During the long period of growth under colonialism, prior to transition growth, the economy was clearly a land based economy fuelled by primary product exports. During the import substitution sub-phase, which characterizes the initial period of transition growth, the system continued to rely on land based exports, to build up its import substitution industries. The meaning of 'export substitution' is that labour intensive manufacture export (e.g. textile) replaces (i.e. 'substitutes for') the traditional exports (e.g. rice and

52   EMPLOYMENT, INCOME DISTRIBUTION AND DEVELOPMENT

sugar in Taiwan and the traditional exports in Korea) as the dominant export items of the economy.

Turning to time series in our effort to identify sub-phases in the transition we see that the potential for primary (i.e. consumer goods) import substitution (measured by the share of total industrial consumer goods which is imported, M_c/C_d is initially higher in Taiwan than Korea (see the M_c/C_d curves in Figure 6). Moreover, this potential is being steadily explored (and thus reduced) until around 1960 in Taiwan and 1964 in Korea after which point these curves turn up. Similarly, if we trace the share of consumer goods imports to total imports (M_c/M curves in Figure 6) we see the same turning points 1960 and 1964, respectively, occurring in the two countries. What lies behind these statistical results was the import substitution strategy adopted by the government (high tariff protection for domestic import substituting industries, overvalued domestic currency in the world market by the official exchange rate, artificially low domestic interest rates, etc.) to encourage the use of foreign exchange receipts (earnings by traditional exports) to build up import substitution industries.

When the domestic markets for industrial consumer goods is supplied almost exclusively by the new import substituting industries, the import substitution phase comes to an end (i.e. exhausted). In the case of a relatively small labour surplus economy, the natural development is the emergence of the export substitution phase—i.e. selling labour intensive manufacturing exports in the world market. This transition was facilitated by a change in government policy to promote exports (e.g. realistic foreign exchange rate or even undervaluation of domestic currency) based on labour efficiency (e.g. adoption of realistic interest rate through interest reform to eliminate the artificial 'capital cheapening' condition under the import substitution phase). The results are seen in Figure 7 which shows a marked shift in the composition of exports—with industrial exports as a fraction of total, shooting up in Taiwan after 1960 and a few years later in the case of Korea.[30] The change in export structure is nothing less than spectacular.

For a small labour surplus economy with a colonial heritage of primary product export, the emergence of the export substitution phase, replacing the import substitution phase is a highly significant phenomenon.[31] In respect to the unemployment problem, the import substitution phase was not a period conducive to full employment leading to the, by now popular, slogan of a 'necessary' conflict between 'employment and growth'. In reality, there is no such conflict when the export substitution phase arrives. For the embodiment of labour service in export to the world market is conducive to both rapid growth and full employment—as the country has, for the first time, found a way to make full use of her abundant labour supply. As this process continues it leads to both the 'commercialization point' and the 'switching point' signifying the termination of the labour surplus condition in the economy as a whole as well as in the agriculture sector in particular. For this reason, the export substitution point precedes the other turning point in both countries just mentioned.[32]

GROWTH AND EMPLOYMENT IN KOREA AND TAIWAN   53

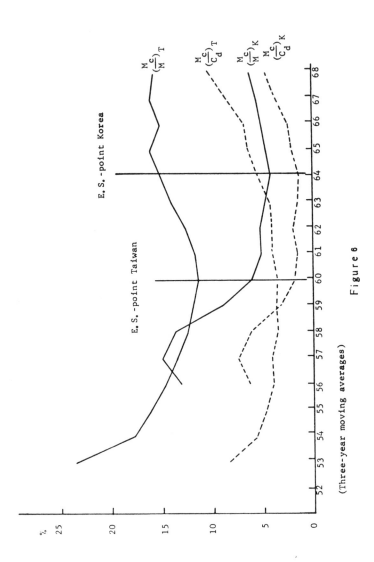

Import Substitution and Export Substitution

Figure 6

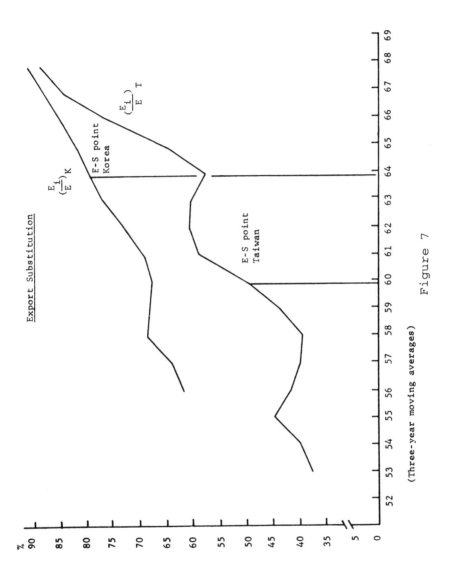

Figure 7

Another turning point in the transition of the open dualistic economy is the *switching point*. It is based on the notion that countries which are basically natural resources poor will at some point in their history have to become net importers of agricultural goods. This is as true of Korea and Taiwan as of historical Japan which became a net importer of agricultural goods from her colonies around the turn of the century.[33] Taiwan's agricultural sector, in spite of its superior performance, through the application of land reform, non-traditional inputs, etc., is, as we have already observed, reaching its natural limits—witness the determination of her industrial sector's terms of trade and the declining level of per capita agricultural exports (rows 3 and 7).[34] Korea, on the other hand, as we have also noted, became a net importer of agricultural goods virtually from the beginning of the transition period; her agriculture sector, we feel, has not fulfilled its historical mission.

The phenomenon of land-based exports at the beginning of the transition must be viewed as a temporary phenomenon in long run historical perspective. A 'switch' from an agricultural exporting to importing position is bound to occur at some stage in the development process in the future. But *when* it occurs and on the basis of *what* kind of agricultural performance remains an all important issue. It matters greatly for Korea whether or not existing reserves of agricultural productivity have been harnessed *en route* to the successful solution of the LDC employment problem. The alternatives may well be failure of the total effort—true for many contemporary LDCs of the type under discussion—or an unacceptably heavy reliance on foreign capital, as in the case of Korea.

III. CONCLUSION AND IMPLICATIONS FOR POLICIES

In the transition process of a labour surplus open dualistic economy, the solution of the unemployment problem may be identified with the arrival of the commercialization point which signifies the termination of the labour surplus condition inherited from the colonial epoch. After commercialization, we can expect to observe a sustained increase in real wage; the 'unemployment problem' will then be of a different type.

The increase in real wage is expected to be accompanied by some reduction in the savings rate, a relative decline in the importance of trade and a shift toward a more skill and capital intensive technology and output mix—an increased concern with the provision of an adequate supply of high talented manpower. These are the major development issues confronted by Taiwan (and to a lesser extent Korea) at the present time and for the near future.

On the road to commercialization, the most important landmark is the export substitution point based on labour intensive export. There will no longer be a sharp conflict between growth and employment objectives—as was the case under import substitution growth. The arrival of the export substitution point 'facilitates' the arrival of the commercial point that terminates the labour surplus condition.

The whole array of government policy measures (e.g. high protective tariffs, exchange controls, low interest rates, overvalued currencies, price

56   EMPLOYMENT, INCOME DISTRIBUTION AND DEVELOPMENT

inflation) adopted to facilitate the import substitution process—via the exclusion of foreign competition and the augmentation of the profits of the domestic industrialists—are, of course, subject to changes. Both Taiwan and Korea, did, in fact, effect major changes in their policy environment around 1960 and 1963, respectively, to facilitate transitions to export substitution. Stabilization plus dismantling of the various existing direct control measures, on trade, interest rate and foreign exchange rates, thereby created a more market orientated economy most conducive to access for large numbers of domestic entrepreneurs seeking efficient utilization of the economy's relatively abundant resources via embodiment in labour-intensive industrial exports. The experience of Taiwan and Korea teaches us that unemployment problems can be solved through growth in 'this' way.

At some point during its life cycle, the open dualistic labour surplus economy is, moreover, likely to move from the successful exploitation of its agricultural potential to its 'natural' long term position as an importer of agricultural goods. The arrival of such a switching point signifies that the country will ultimately have to accelerate its industrial exports to acquire the needed food and raw materials—a phenomenon which may occur before commercialization point, as in historical Japan, or after commercialization point, as in Taiwan, or Korea in the future.

Finally, given the rates of population growth, a reversal point indicating an absolute decline in the size of the agricultural labour force is likely to occur before the switching point. Thus the policy focus may shift to labour saving techniques in agriculture in order to prolong labour using techniques in industry, while the economy gets ready for the skill and capital intensive phase. At the present time, this is precisely the central policy issue in Taiwan. In the case of Korea, however, due to its neglect of agriculture in the past, the country is still faced with the problem of first building up its rural infrastructure and utilizing the still unexploited slack in agricultural productivity—a process likely to release additional supplies of labour without the need to resort to extensive mechanization.

In Taiwan, the agricultural sector has already fulfilled its historical mission during the early phase of transition. In the case of Korea the story is quite different as it cannot be denied that Korea's agricultural sector has been relatively stagnant.[35] Consequently, throughout the import substitution sub-phase, while industrial entrepreneurial maturation took place, much of the potential domestic fuel for further growth was never generated. Consequently, after the export substitution point had been reached, a tremendous burden fell upon the industrial sector, fuelled largely by foreign capital, to continue to 'pull' the agricultural sector along with it, including the continuous 'pulling out' of agricultural workers.

The rather heavier burden which Korea's non-agricultural sector has consequently had to carry has, in turn, led to certain distortions in that sector. For example, industrial exports have undoubtedly been pushed, at least in some areas, beyond the point of efficiency, and that a good deal of 'premature' backward linkage type of import substitution has conse-

GROWTH AND EMPLOYMENT IN KOREA AND TAIWAN   57

quently taken place[36] (especially since 1968, with the help of a large assortment of special subsidies and other incentives). The simple reason is that, with agriculture's push not forthcoming,[37] industrial exports have had to 'run' ever faster, with the consequence that some fairly technology and capital intensive sub-sectors have been expanded, ahead of what the, admittedly changing, endowment picture would call for. Moreover, Korea was consequently forced to admit an unusually heavy flow of foreign aid, more recently private investment, to keep the process going.

As far as the future is concerned, it is, of course, 'mathematically' conceivable that the present trends continue during the decade ahead—until the non-agricultural sector and the non-agricultural labour force become so predominant that the Korean economy begins to operate something like the city-states of Hong Kong and Singapore, i.e. importing virtually all needed agricultural goods and depending entirely on her industrial exporting sector. Such a strategy is, however, not likely to be successful as a practical choice. Korea's agricultural sector and population remain too large relative to the total economy to permit the hinterland to be 'dragged along' into modernity in this fashion. It is difficult to conceive of trade able to expand fast enough in a competitive fashion; it is equally difficult to conceive of foreign capital as continuing to flow in at the rates required. The increasing import intensity of industrial exports, the heavy foreign debt structure, the growing food gap are all symptoms of difficulties ahead. Whether or not the commercialization point has already been reached, Korea will clearly have to reconsider its policy of agricultural neglect by pursuing a more balanced growth strategy in the years ahead.

APPENDIX 1

In Figure 8bcde, we reproduce the initial equilibrium position of Taiwan described in Figure 1bcde. In Figure 3b, out of a total labour force OP, the agricultural labour force is OL_T producing a per capita output of L_Tb_T. Total agricultural output is represented by the area OPab. With respect to the allocation of this output, we see that, since the real wage in terms of agricultural goods is OB_T, labour's share is OB_TcL_T ($= B_1 + B_2 + B_3$).[38] Let us assume that wage earners do not save; then the consumption by farmers of food is B_1 (at the consumption standard for agricultural goods Oe), while the income exchanged by farmers for industrial consumer goods is $B_2 + B_3$. To see the magnitude of the landlord or rent share, let the auxiliary straight line dc be drawn; then from point 'e' let a straight line parallel to cd be constructed, thus obtaining point 'f'. The area B_4 ($= dhgf$) then equals $B_2 + B_3$ by construction.[39] Since the wage share is $B_1 + B_4$ ($= B_1 + B_2 + B_3$), the remaining total output or rent share is $B_2 + B_5 + B_6$. Under the assumption that all rental incomes are saved, this constitutes agricultural saving (S_a).

The total output of agriculture is thus allocated in the following way: B_1 is consumed by agricultural workers; $B_2 + B_5$ is exported (hB_T being per capita exports); the remaining output $B_4 + B_6$ is destined for consumption by workers in the industrial sector. The latter two types of shipments summarize the contribution that agriculture makes to non-agricultural development, first in providing import capacity ($B_2 + B_5$) and second in providing food for industrial workers ($B_4 + B_6$).

Let us turn now to the industrial sector (in Figure 8e), where the equilibrium is established at point h_T, i.e. where the M_T-curve intersects the real wage level in terms of industrial goods, OD_T. With a given labour force (OW_T), the total industrial output is then divided into the wage share ($A_1 + A_2 + A_3$) and the profit share (A_4), the latter constituting industrial saving (S_i). Out of the total wage share, A_1 is consumed by industrial workers, while $A_2 + A_3$ is exchanged for agricultural goods for purposes of consumption. At the given terms of trade (slope of B_TD_T) the exchange value of $A_2 +$

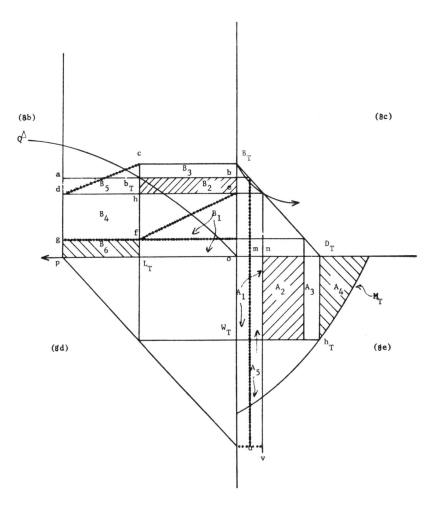

Figure 8

A_3 is $B_4 + B_6$. Notice that A_2 comprises industrial consumer goods exchanged for B_4 units of agricultural goods delivered by the farmers; A_3, on the other hand, represents investment goods exchanged for the landlord's agricultural saving B_6. Notice also that total agricultural export proceeds ($B_2 + B_3$) which accrue to the owners of the agricultural surplus, enable the system to import A_5 ($=$ mnuv) units of investment goods. [40] Thus the total domestic investment fund is $A_3 + A_4 + A_5$ and financed in the following way:

$$\text{(A1)} \quad \underset{(A_3 + A_4 + A_5)}{I} \quad = \quad \underset{(A_5 + A_3)}{S_a} \quad + \quad \underset{(A_4)}{S_i}$$

Since, in addition, there exist also inflows of foreign capital (S_f), the finance equation may be slightly modified to obtain (4). [41]

What we have just presented is pertinent to the case of Taiwan and would have to be modified in a by now predictable fashion to capture realistically the case of Korea. As we indicated in the context of our discussion of Figures 1 and 2, the essential differences are (1) the agricultural contribution to the saving fund here is much lower because of the low level of agricultural productivity; (2) whatever contribution the agricultural sector does make to industrial finance is through the 'domestic route', i.e. inter-sectoral finance; (3) foreign capital plays a much larger role in the financing of domestic capital formation.

APPENDIX 2

Data Sources: (Korea)

(a) *National Income Statistical Yearbook* 1968, 1969 (The Bank of Korea)

(b) *Korea Statistical Yearbook* (1960–69) (Economic Planning Board, Republic of Korea).

(c) *Annual Economic Review* 1955–1959 (The Bank of Korea)

(d) *Economic Statistical Yearbook* 1960–71 (The Bank of Korea).

(e) *Inter-Industry Relations Tables* 1960, 1963, 1966, 1968 (The Bank of Korea).

(f) *Price Statistical Summary* 1961, 1964, 1966, 1968 (The Bank of Korea).

(g) *Yearbook of Agriculture and Forestry* 1964, 1968, 1969 (Ministry of Agriculture and Forestry, Republic of Korea).

(h) *Foreign Trade of Korea* 1964–69 (Ministry of Finance, Republic of Korea).

(i) *Monthly Economic Review* (The Korea Development Bank).

(j) *Agricultural Cooperative Monthly Survey* (National Agricultural Cooperative Federation, Korea).

(k) *Estimates of Korean Capital and Inventory Coefficients in 1968* (by Kee Chun Han, Yonsei University).

(l) *Analysis of Household Spending-Saving Behaviour in Korea*, 1970 (by Sung-Hwan Jo, Sogang University).

Data Sources: (Taiwan)

(a) *National Income of the Republic of China*, 1951-1970 (Directorate-General of Budgets, Accounts and Statistics, Executive Yuan).

(b) *Industry of Free China* (CIECD), 1970

(c) *Commodity-Price Statistics Monthly, Taiwan District*, 1971 (Directorate-General of Budgets, Accounts and Statistics, Executive Yuan).

(d) *Monthly Statistics of the Republic of China* (Directorate-General of Budgets, Accounts and Statistics, Executive Yuan).

(e) *Input-Output Table* (CIECD), 1961, 1964, 1966.

(f) *Taiwan Agricultural Year Book*, 1962-1970 (Department of Agriculture and Forestry, Provincial Government of Taiwan).

(g) *Taiwan Economic Statistics* (CIECD).

(h) *Taiwan Statistical Data Book* (CIECD), 1970.

(i) 'Household Registration' of Provincial Department of Civil Affairs.

(j) *Taiwan Area Report on the Year-End Household Check and Population Registration Statistics* (of Provincial Department of Civil Affairs).

(k) *Export and Import Foreign Exchange Settlements Statistics*, 1970 (Foreign Exchange Department, the Central Bank of Taiwan.)

60   EMPLOYMENT, INCOME DISTRIBUTION AND DEVELOPMENT

(l) *The Republic of China, Taiwan Industrial Production Statistics Monthly* (Ministry of Economic Affairs).

(m) *Quarterly Report on the Labour Force Survey in Taiwan*, 1963-69, (Labour Force Survey and Research Institute).

(n) *Taiwan Agricultural Price Monthly* (Department of Agriculture and Forestry, Provincial Government of Taiwan).

(o) *Monthly Statistics on Price Received and Price Paid by Farmer in Taiwan* (Bureau of Accounting and Statistics Provincial Government of Taiwan, Republic of China).

(p) *The Republic of China, Report on Industrial and Commercial Surveys*, 1954, 1962, 1966 (Ministry of Economic Affairs).

(q) *Taiwan Food Statistics Book*, 1970 (Taiwan Provincial Food Bureau)

NOTES
1. S. Kuznets [*1966*]; see also Fei and Ranis [*1969*]. This process, linked to the achievement of political independence, began earlier in Latin America.

2. These dates, coming a few years after the move from the Chinese Mainland, in the first instance, and after the Korean War, in the second, are commonly accepted as appropriate base years.

3. We recognize the incompleteness of the mapping between agriculture and subsistence, on the one hand, and non-agriculture and commercialized, on the other 'Agriculture' is viewed as a proxy for sectors in which wages or income exceed the marginal product and are institutionally determined, and 'non-agriculture' as a proxy for sectors where there is an approximation to a competitive solution. The statistical problem remains and has not been solved in the context of this paper. It would require a careful disaggregation of the services sector, as well as of agriculture and even industry, into their commercialized and non-commercialized components.

4. If desirable, capital can be combined with land.

5. The reasons for this are complicated, but related to the greater attention paid by the Japanese to irrigation and organizational infrastructure in colonial Taiwan where a cash crop, sugar, was to be promoted, along with the staples.

6. In a predominantly agricultural economy, we would expect the relationship in relative agricultural productivities between the two countries to also be reflected in their relative per capita GDP levels. This is borne out by the parity calculations in Table 1, row 4a, column 4.

7. Thus, in column 7 of the statistical table, the internal terms of trade reflect the common international terms of trade.

8. This is shown by the distance nj in Figure 1b.

9. The absolute fixity of the IRW is, of course, only an approximation to reality The model could easily be amended to incorporate a more realistic upward 'creep' in the IRW level. The price-consumption curve (PC_T) is derived by taking the typical worker's income at OB_T and determining his consumption of agricultural and non-agricultural goods at different terms of trade, i.e. it is the locus of tangencies between the worker's indifference map and a 'swivelling' budget line anchored at point B_T.

10. Given Korea's lower level of agricultural productivity (v) approximately the same level of per capita consumption of agricultural goods (C_a^Δ) and plus more people still in agriculture, if follows that E_a^Δ must be smaller here (see equation 2b). This is not shown clearly in Figure 2b because the net export is negligible.

11. In the absence of a wage gap between the agricultural worker's real wage in terms of industrial goods and the industrial worker's real wage in terms of industrial goods. The existence, realistically, of a wage gap can be easily accommodated.

12. Suppose the production functions of the two countries were the same. Given the higher input ratio (at D_K, Figure 2f) for Korea than for Taiwan (at D_T, Figure 1f), the equilibrium point for Korea (h_K, Figure 2e) would have implied a higher level of both the marginal and average productivities of labour. For example, the Korean MPP_K-curve would have passed through a higher point such as 'u' in Figure 2e. Compared with such a point, the actual point 'h_K' indicates the presence of 'labour saving innovations' in Korea as compared with Taiwan.

13. Our understanding of the precise causes of such differences in colonial heritage

GROWTH AND EMPLOYMENT IN KOREA AND TAIWAN   **61**

a phenomenon which must be traced to profit maximization under colonialism, given differential resource endowments in the two colonies—is clearly incomplete at this point. [see, however, *Samuel Ho 1971*].

14. The domestic demand for industrial goods which includes not only consumption but also industrial demands is actually higher than this (i.e. a certain multiple of $W_T C \stackrel{\triangle}{i}$) We have, however, for simplicity's sake, assumed that $W_T C \stackrel{\triangle}{i}$ represents the total per capita demand for industrial goods.

15. The forces that determine these contributions to the total saving fund may be traced to the distribution of income as well as to the rules governing intersectoral exchange in the context of our analytical framework. The theory of determination of savings in an open dualistic economy will be explained in Appendix 1.

16. While technological progress (i.e. the upward shift of the Q-curve) increases average labour productivity, the labour allocation effect itself will also increase labour productivity if the agricultural labour force declines absolutely. We shall examine this issue briefly below.

17. While agricultural productivity in Taiwan, for example, increases by 130 per cent during the period, agricultural real wages increased only 50 per cent (rows 1 and 5). The existence of labour surplus is indicated in Figure 1b, by point 'n' (corresponding to the IRW) lying above point 'j' (indicating MPP_L) in the initial year. This signifies the existence of disguised unemployment during much of the transition. In the case of Korea, agricultural real wages lag much less behind productivity gain. This signifies the more rapid 'pulling out' of agricultural labour with the help of foreign capital inflow and the earlier termination of disguised unemployment. We will return to both these points in the next section.

18. And/or, once the more realistic possibility of a wage gap (between agricultural and industrial workers) is admitted, due to a change in the size of that gap.

19. Nevertheless, for the economy as a whole, the distribution of income may well improve for labour, as a consequence of the existence of a wage gap between the two sectors and the shift of the economy's centre of gravity from one to the other. The full analysis of income distribution in the two-sector world under discussion is a complicated one and really beyond the scope of this paper.

20. In recent years, total industrial exports have been rising at close to 35 per cent annually in both countries.

21. In this paper we are not concerned with the formulation of a truly deterministic dynamic theory. Our analysis, it is hoped, can provide some guidelines as to how such a theory should be formulated and tested by time series.

22. For a fuller discussion of commercialization point, see Fei and Ranis [*1964*].

23. Before 'e_6' there exists disguised unemployment in agriculture as the MPP_L is below the institutional wage w_a; after 'e_6' the labour surplus condition terminates as the wage now follows the MPP_L, signifying the fact that the reservoir of the unemployed has been 'mopped up' and wages are henceforth determined according to neo-classical rules. If, more realistically, the IRW itself rises, from B_T to B_T^1 the commercialization point does not occur until productivity level M_8 (leading to point e_8) has been reached.

In the absence of technology change in agriculture, only a major absolute decline in the agricultural population could permit the commercialization point to be reached, i.e. by moving along a constant MPP_L curve.

24. This is traced, in turn, to the rate of capital accumulation and the degree of labour using bias in the industrial sector.

25. This, in fact, has definitely been occurring in Taiwan. The question of whether or not the commercialization point and a condition of labour shortage has really been reached in Korea or whether the recent rise in real wages may be due to a short run deterioration of the industrial sector's terms of trade (as agricultural stagnation continues and P.L. 480 imports are becoming more expensive) is still not entirely clear and the subject of continuing investigation by the authors. One thing is clear, however, i.e. that, if the commercialization point has, in fact, already been reached in Korea it is more by moving upward along given M curves, while in Taiwan there was more of an upward shift in the M curve itself. On this general subject, see also Roger Sedjo (*1971*).

26. A similar pattern of the behaviour of real wages can be observed for historical Japan whose earlier experience as an open labour surplus economy is relevant here.

Here also the pattern of real wage increases shows a modest upward creep in the nineteenth century followed by a substantial acceleration after World War One [see *Fei and Ranis, 1971*].

27. See the discussion of the 'Export Substitution Point'.

28. In historical Japan the reversal point occurred during the last decade of the nineteenth century, thus preceding the commercialization point by at least several decades. It is also quite possible for the reversal point to occur after the commercialization point. A systematic investigation of the sequential order of all the turning points is the purpose of a more formal dynamically determistic theory yet to be developed.

29. The crucial factors are (1) the population growth rate (2) the relative size of the labour force in the agricultural sector, (3) the population size relative to the demand for the products of this country in the world market. Hong Kong can solve her 'agricultural problem' by this strategy because all these factors are favourable. There is a serious doubt in our mind that this strategy can be successful in Korea.

30. It should be noted that Korea's E_i/E ratio is substantially higher from the very beginning, as a consequence of the economy's relatively weak agricultural base from the outset. Export substitution here means, in part, a shift from traditional non-agricultural exports (e.g. mining) to non-traditional non-agricultural exports (e.g. labour intensive textiles and electronics). The small differences in determining the E-S point from the import and export sides (in Figures 6 and 7) should not surprise us. 'Nature does not make jumps' and we are really talking about turning ranges rather than turning points. The change in trend and in the structure of the two economies is clearly established. In the case of Korea, there is more of an over lapping between the end of I-S and the beginning of E-S growth.

31. Many theoretical issues and interpretations can be raised, but not elaborated, in this paper. The phenomenon may be approached from the viewpoint of international trade and comparative advantage which emphasized the inefficiency of import substitution (see, for example, Little, Scitovsky and Scott [*1970*] which would view the emergence of export substitution phase essentially as correcting the mistakes of the import substitution strategy). On the other hand, from the growth theoretical point of view the import substitution phase may be viewed as an essential pre-requisite of the export substitution phase (see Paauw and Fei [*1973*] for a full exposition of this view; also see Ranis [*1972*] for an international comparison).

32. Again, these issues can only be explored with further study by dynamic models.

33. Before that point was reached, however, i.e. during the three decades following the Meiji Restoration in 1868, she had been very successful in generating substantial agricultural productivity increases. [see, for example, *Johnston, 1952; Ranis 1959; Ohkawa and Rosovsky, 1960*].

34. A full exploration of the relation between the 'international terms of trade' and the 'internal terms of trade' between agriculture and non-agriculture goods requires an understanding of whether 'free trade' prevailed in these countries and whether they are small countries. We feel that initially, 'free trade' prevailed in these two countries so that the internal terms of trade reflected the common international terms of trade. However, in the process of development in the last 20 years, internal terms of trade gradually diverged from the international terms of trade—a theoretical observation which needs to be investigated further.

35. While there admittedly exist important differences in the soil, climate and other elements of the natural endowment as between Korea and Taiwan—and no one is suggesting that every country has equal reserves of agricultural productivity ready for activation—there is ample evidence that much of the relative failure of Korea's agriculture to date is man-made. We know, for example, that the Japanese left a relatively inferior agricultural infrastructure in Korea, not only in terms of irrigation facilities, but also, and probably more important, in terms of organizational infrastructure. It is our distinct impression—though admittedly, it is risky to be categorical on this point—that much more could have been done to repair this differential. To cite one example, Korea's rural organization (the NACF) represents an attempt to do too many things in agriculture, including the provision of information, of inputs, as well as the power to tax. It is but a pale reflection of Taiwan's Farmers' Associations, hooked up with the JCRR structure, which farmers could view more as their own instrument. Moreover, agri-

cultural price policies in Korea are directed much more towards income redistribution objectives *after* production decisions have already been made rather than providing *ex ante* incentives for increased productivity, as in Taiwan. There seems, in short, to be a substantial consensus among agricultural economists and agronomists that while the 'Green Revolution' potential of Korea may be below that of Taiwan, the actual performance of Korea's farmers also remains substantially below that potential.

36. Research on this issue is currently under way. For the current use of a variety of special incentives ranging from tariff and tax reductions, to linkage systems, import wastage allowances, deposit rate preferences, differential interest, electricity and freight rates, see Kim Kwang Suk [*1971*].

37. Worse, with industry having to help pay for net agricultural imports.

38. $B_1 = oL_The$; $B_2 = hebb_T$; $B_3 = bb_TcB_T$. B_1, $B_2 \ldots B_6$ are rectangular areas.

39. $hf/he = ch/dh$. This means $hfxdh = chxhe$.

40. In Figure 8e total domestic output of the industrial sector is $A_1 + A_2 + A_3 + A_4$, with an output capacity for consumer goods of $A_1 + A_2$. For Taiwan, in fact, the domestic consumer goods production capacity is less than the domestic demand $(A_1 + A_2)$ or the capacity for investment goods production is greater than $A_3 + A_4$. In that situation, a part of imports takes the form of industrial consumer goods.

41. When foreign capital inflows are admitted, the magnitudes of 'investment', 'supply of industrial goods', 'industrial imports' are all augmented by the value of 'S_f'.

REFERENCES

Fei, J. C. H. and G. Ranis, 1964, *Development of the Labour Surplus Economy: Theory and Policy*, Homewood, Ill.: Richard D. Irwin.

Fei, J. C. H. and G. Ranis, 1969, 'Economic Development in Historical Perspective', *American Economic Review*, May.

Fei ,J. C. H. and G. Ranis, 1971. 'On the Empirical Relevancy of the Fei-Ranis Model of Economic Development: A Reply', *American Economic Review*, September.

Ho, S., 1971, *The Development Policy of the Japanese Colonial Government in Taiwan, 1895–1945*, in G. Ranis (ed.), *Government and Economic Development*, New Haven: Yale University Press.

Johnston, B. F., 1952, 'Agricultural Productivity and Economic Development of Japan', *Journal of Political Economy*, 7: 2.

Kim, Kwang Suk, 1971. *Export Promotion and Industrial Incentive Policy in Korea*.

Kuznets, S., 1966, *Modern Economic Growth: Rate Structure and Spread*, New Haven: Yale University Press.

Lewis, W. A., 1954, *Development with Unlimited Supplies of Labour*, Manchester School of Economics and Social Studies.

Little, I., T. Scitovsky and M. Scott, 1970, *Industry and Trade in Some Developing Countries—A Comparative Study*, London: Oxford University Press.

Ohkawa, K. and H. Rosovsky, 1960, 'The Role of Agriculture in Modern Japanese Economic Development', *Economic Development and Cultural Change*, 9: 1, Part 2, October.

Paauw and Fei, 1975, *Development of the Open Dualistic Economy*, New Haven: Yale University Press.

Ranis, G., 1959, 'Financing Economic Development', *Economic History Review*, March.

Ranis, G., 1972, *Relative Prices in Planning for Economic Development*, in D. J. Daly (ed.), *International Comparisons of Prices and Output*, NBER, Columbia University Press.

Sedjo, R., 1971, 'The Turning Point in Korea', paper presented to the ILCORK Conference, Seoul, Korea, August 22–27.

[2]

New Perspectives on Industrial Growth in Taiwan

Howard Pack

1. Introduction

In the general euphoria that has accompanied the extraordinary growth of the four East Asian export oriented countries, there has been only limited exploration of the sources of the growth of supply. The sustained growth in aggregate demand at 10 percent per year is less difficult to comprehend insofar as even a small increase in the share of worldwide exports generates very large increases in demand relative to the small domestic economy of a country like Taiwan. The possibilities offered by rapid growth in exports reduce the policy skills and consensus that would otherwise be required to pursue a fiscal-monetary mix that aims for such high growth in demand based largely on domestic components. On the other hand, the protracted growth in supply over a quarter-century that allows a country to achieve near-developed-country status requires careful attention.

Given a rapid growth in supply and per capita income, many structural changes that accompany such a development are set into motion: income elasticities partly determine that households will demand a changing set of goods; factor prices will be altered as employment growth leads to tighter labor markets; perhaps the size distribution of firms and their location will change. In the case of an open economy such as Taiwan, some of these effects will be attenuated as export earnings permit a looser connection between the growing sectoral demands for consumer and producer goods and local production of them.

In a well known and provocative analysis, Alexander Gerschenkron argued that latecomers to the development process, including presumably Taiwan of the 1950s, would be able to achieve rapid growth as they could take advantage of the benefits of "relative backwardness." Changing terminology, this hypothesis could be rephrased as implying that best practice technology in the developed countries (DCs) exhibited very high total factor

productivity (TFP) while the actual technology employed in the LDCs generated lower TFP. Hence, obtaining command of both the hardware and
"software" of advanced technology would enable the LDCs to generate
rapid growth in TFP as they eliminated the gap between actual and best
practice technologies. In effect, their capital accumulation and additions to
the labor force would have a magnified growth impact. One implication of
this view, not spelled out by Gerschenkron, was that once the gap was closed, it would be increasingly difficult to maintain rapid growth, an issue that
Taiwan is likely to confront in the coming decade.

For most LDCs the opportunities offered by the highly productive technologies of the DCs have not been a source of rapid growth. For the
industrial sector, with which this chapter is concerned, most LDCs encouraged excessively capital-intensive technology adoption. Even where modern
technologies were efficiently absorbed,[1] they benefitted a small group of
workers and plant owners. In contrast, in Taiwan there were limited factor
price distortions (Little 1979; Ranis 1979; Fields 1985) and both the industry mix and technologies chosen within an industry were consonant with the
country's factor endowments. The gains from closing the best practice gap
were widely diffused, with many sectors, firms, and their employees benefiting. This undoubtedly helped the *aggregate* productivity performance in
Taiwan whereas in most LDCs a handful of firms have experienced higher
productivity over time which did not have a significant quantitative overall
impact. This difference may go some way towards explaining the fact that
Taiwan has experienced positive total factor productivity growth in the
industrial sector whereas most LDCs have not (Pack 1988). Moreover, the
diffusion of better practice partly explains the failure of significant income
inequality to emerge during three decades of rapid growth (Fei, Ranis and
Kuo 1979).

Kuznets (1979), using the Gerschenkronian framework in an analysis of
Taiwan, noted that "the useful knowledge must be accessible -- through
trade, capital flows, direct investment, and the like . . ." (p. 129). He then
pointed out that such accessibility is far from sufficient -- both the institutional and policy framework conducive to fruitful deployment of these
technologies must be set into place. Moreover, there will inevitably be
severe costs imposed on some groups as a result of the rapid transformation of the economy implied by widespread adoption of newer technologies.
Without considerable political skills being exercised by the government, the
possible "losers" may oppose many of the potentially beneficial changes (p.
130). Analysis of the political and social requirements of successful development have now become the staple of the (non-Marxist) political economy
approach to development (Deyo 1988).

In analyzing Taiwan's industrial development, I pursue several themes.
First, what were the sources of the growth of supply? Can one identify the

New Perspectives on Industrial Growth in Taiwan   75

economic role of exports themselves as a contributor to the growth of total factor productivity; more broadly, did they somehow help strengthen the institutional and political framework that were conducive to growth? Within this framework more traditional concerns about the industrial sector will appear, such as the changing sectoral structure of production, the role of small scale enterprises, and so on. As will be clear, I do not think that exports were the sole source of the spectacular performance of Taiwan. Nevertheless, one is ignoring the obvious if no attempt is made to speculate on the impact of exports on the ability of Taiwan to close the best practice-actual practice gap and to facilitate the transformation of the economy. More precisely, one difference between Taiwan and some other countries that have saved almost as much and have had rapid labor force growth is that Taiwan has experienced a fairly high rate of growth of TFP, and part of this long-term TFP growth may be attributable to its export orientation.[2]

For expository purposes, much of the following assumes that the growth phenomena to be explained are those of the manufacturing sector. Insofar as manufacturing and its export growth were the primary determinants of Taiwan's aggregate growth, the exposition does not distinguish between the two. At points where this convenient didactic framework misses key phenomena, they will be explicitly discussed. The role of the service sector is considered separately. To understand past Taiwanese experience and the probable evolution of its growth in the future, a better understanding of the determinants of productivity growth is critical. In recent years the OECD countries have all undergone a considerable slowing in their overall growth rates. Much of this reflects lower rates of growth of total factor productivity since 1973 (Baily and Blair 1988). While the source of this slowdown has not been determined, and there is no inevitable contagion that will spread to Taiwan, setting out the issues in the context of TFP growth may allow policy-makers to consider the future in a broader context.

Under this wide umbrella that focuses on productivity growth, other aspects of Taiwanese growth that have been cited as critical can be placed within a more rigorous and comprehensive framework. For example, a few scholars, most notably Robert Wade (1990), have recently argued that Taiwan, far from being a *laissez-faire* economy, has seen considerable government intervention ranging from ownership of public enterprises to an extraordinarily sophisticated use of import-limiting measures, special credit facilities, and so on. It is maintained by these analysts, who have provided careful documentation supporting their views, that Taiwan, like Japan and Korea, followed a wide-ranging industrial policy that was an important component of its considerable success. These views contrast strongly with those scholars (Little 1979) who aver that the major sources of Taiwan's achievement were: (a) allowing exporting firms to obtain inputs at world

prices; (b) low-cost labor, at least during the initial phases of industrialization; (c) high real rates of interest; and (d) a roughly balanced government
budget. Interestingly, a re-examination of evidence presented by analysts
who helped establish the conventional explanation partly supports the revisionist view. For example, Scott (1979), who largely agrees with Little,
presents a number of tables showing the quite high nominal tariff rates and
the importance of quantitative restrictions well into the 1970s, more than
ten years after the initiation of the rapid growth rate of Taiwanese exports.
While exporters may have faced international prices for both inputs and
outputs, many producers were nevertheless protected and initiated production on the basis of protection in the domestic market, a phenomenon well
documented by Wade.

The canonical analysis of development economists that Taiwan, like
Korea, simply got the prices right may need some subtle modification.
Nevertheless, the case that *selective* intervention was a critical component
of the Taiwanese policy mix must demonstrate that intervention increased
productivity growth rates.[3] Simply altering the sectoral structure will not
confer beneficial effects unless productivity growth is increased. Industrial
policy as used by Wade and others is a term employed to describe
attempts to influence the structure of production through interventions that
are not neutral across sectors: selective (among industries) credit policy,
non-uniform protection whether in the form of tariffs or quantitative
restrictions, research subsidies for specific products, and so on. Most
analyses of efforts at industrialization of the LDCs during the last quarter-
century have, of course, described industrial policy, though the term has
emerged largely in recent discussion of manufacturing competitiveness
among OECD countries.

One characteristic of Taiwan often noted is the greater importance of
small-scale enterprises (SSEs) in manufacturing than in other developing
countries. Static advantages may accrue in terms of employment generation if such firms choose socially appropriate lower capital-labor ratios in
producing a given product than do larger firms (Ho 1980; Ranis 1979).[4]
While correct factor choices may generate a greater output for a given
commitment of capital and labor,[5] it is not easy to establish a link between
the size distribution of firms and productivity growth rates. One possibility
is that the greater flexibility of such enterprises allows them to adjust to
changing markets more quickly than do their larger compatriots. The relation between total factor productivity growth and firm size will thus be
considered.

The plan of this paper is as follows. Section 2 considers the determinants of intermediate-term growth in output. Section 3 briefly reviews
Taiwan's export experience and suggests a new view of the overall strategy
informing its policy. Section 4 considers the potential sources of techno-

logical change associated with exports. Section 5 investigates the probable impact of industrial policy on Taiwan's growth rate. Section 6 considers the evolving industrial structure and the size distribution of firms. Section 7 analyzes the evolution of the service sectors. Views about the future of Taiwanese growth are contained in Section 8.

2. Intermediate Term Growth Accounting

The Sources of Growth

A surprising omission in the literature analyzing development in outward oriented economies has been the failure to explain why export orientation will allow sustained growth in supply over a period as long as twenty to thirty years. Although the literature commending export orientation is quite good at delineating the short- and medium-term *level* effects to be derived from a switch to export promotion, it fails to set out the longer term growth *rate* augmenting effects. While a move from inefficient import substitution to neutrality in profitability between import substitutes and exports can generate once-and-for-all gains in allocative efficiency, perhaps spread over a number of years, such gains were presumably exhausted in Taiwan by 1970 or 1975, depending on one's preferred dating schema.[6] Not only were there intersectoral allocative benefits as the economy exploited its comparative advantage in particular sectors during the first decades of rapid export growth, but some gains in technical efficiency were obtained from greater capacity utilization and more product specialization. Moreover, new plants could be built on a large scale. But most of these benefits would presumably have been reaped by the early 1970s.[7] Yet Taiwan's TFP continued to grow with great rapidity after 1976.

The sources of growth equation for Taiwan has been calculated for several subperiods for 1951-1987 (Table 3.1). This equation is

$$Q^* = A^* + bK^* + (1-b)L^* \tag{1}$$

where asterisks denote rates of growth, Q is constant price value added in manufacturing, K is the constant price fixed stock of capital, L is the number of workers in the manufacturing sector, and A is the unexplained growth of output. A^* is 5.3 percent per annum for 1961-1987 or about 40 percent of total growth (Table 3.1).[8] The figures for such a long period are unlikely to be affected by transitory phenomena such as changing rates of capacity utilization. The explanation of A^* implied by the trade and development literature suggests that it is due to learning effects and scale effects, greater utilization of capacity, growing education, and so on. But these lump together mechanisms that can work only in the long run (educa-

TABLE 3.1   Growth Rates of Input, Output and Total Factor Productivity
in Manufacturing

Years	Value added	Labor	Capital	A	A/VA
1952-1961	12.1	2.7	8.7	6.8	.56
1961-1976	14.9	7.8	11.7	5.4	.36
1976-1987	10.7	5.1	6.6	5.0	.47
1961-1987	13.1	6.7	9.5	5.3	.40

Note: TFP is calculated using actual factor shares from national accounts
for the subperiod.

Source: 1952-1961, Columns 1-3, Kuo (1983); columns 4 and 5 calculated
by author using factor shares from *Statistical Yearbook of the Republic of
China*, 1989, Table 45.   1961-1987, value added and capital stock from
*Yearbook of Earnings and Productivity Statistics, Taiwan Area, Republic of
China, 1988*, Table 92; labor from *Taiwan Statistical Yearbook, 1989*, Table
2-9a; factor shares from *Statistical Yearbook of the Republic of China*, 1989,
Table 45.

tion) with those that exert a short- and medium-term effect (greater capacity utilization).

For the developed countries, a ratio of A^*/Q^* of .40 or .50 has been calculated for both the total economy and manufacturing.   For most LDCs,
this ratio has been zero or negative (Pack 1988).   The latter has been
attributed to import substitution policies though the usual calculation of the
impact of ISI is one of static income loss rather than reduced A^*.   Nevertheless, the standard for a successfully functioning economy has typically
been the performance of the OECD countries over varying periods until
1973 in which TFP growth has been a major source of output growth.
Normatively, output growth that is not attributable to that of primary inputs
is critical insofar as growing labor and capital inputs have a welfare cost in
terms of foregone leisure and current consumption.   Taiwan has certainly
done much better than other LDCs, roughly as well as the OECD norm
(Baily and Blair 1988).

Table 3.1   also presents the growth rates for each of the variables contained in Equation 1.   Growth in value added has been very high in the
three periods shown, 1952-1961, 1961-1976 and 1976-1987.   Between the
first and second periods, the rate of absorption of factors into the manufacturing sector increased enormously yet TFP growth declined only

slightly, an extremely impressive performance. The contribution of the residual to output growth declined from 56 percent of output growth in the 1952-1961 period, to 36 percent in 1961-1976. Nevertheless, it was the latter period that saw the transformation of Taiwan into a major exporter, a process begun roughly in the middle of the first period. This surprising result implies that even during its intensive import substitution phase the allocative inefficiency of ISI may have been offset by rapidly growing technical efficiency. If this tentative finding is correct, the factors that allowed the sector to perform well in contrast to other ISI regimes constitutes a fascinating area for additional research.

Taiwan's achievement in productivity is particularly impressive insofar as the A^*/Q^* figure in the OECD countries has been achieved with considerably lower growth rates of the primary inputs, typically capital growth rates of less than 4 percent and labor growth rates less than 2 percent. To me it appears that a signal achievement of the Taiwanese manufacturing sector has been to maintain positive TFP growth while absorbing enormous increases to its initial factor endowments. At the growth rates shown in Table 3.1, the capital stock doubles roughly every five years, the labor force every fourteen years. To deploy productively this many additional resources in so short a period is quite remarkable and a major characteristic of the economy to be explained. Thus, the productivity raising mechanisms to be discussed have to be viewed in a context of their ability to avoid diminishing returns to the rapid addition of factors to small existing stocks. An important question then is whether exports themselves helped to forestall the likely onset of diminishing returns. It will also be argued in Section 7 that the size structure of manufacturing may have been an important contributor to this performance.

The Import of New Technology

After 1965, it seems likely that some part of productivity growth was accounted for by the importation of new equipment which embodied productivity-increasing characteristics, the effect both Gerschenkron and Kuznets thought would be decisive.[9] One path of escape from relative backwardness is to be achieved by importing newer technology though, as I have shown elsewhere, realization of the promised productivity benefits is not automatic (Pack 1987).[10] Knowledge, particularly of production engineering, must also be obtained, a question to which I return below. To attach some magnitudes to the role of imported technical change, it is useful to expand upon the simple growth accounting formula contained in (1).

Nelson (1964) derived the following expression for the rate of growth of output in the presence of embodiment:

$$Q^* = A^* + (1-b)\lambda_k - (1-b)\lambda_k\Delta\bar{a} + (1-b)K^* + (1-b)L^* \qquad (2)$$

where $\Delta\bar{a} = 1 - (K^* + \delta)a_{t-1}$ is the rate of change of the average age of equipment, λ_k is the rate at which the productivity of equipment of new vintages increases, $\bar{a}$ is the average age of equipment, δ is the rate of depreciation, and b is the elasticity of output with respect to capital.

During most of the period under consideration Taiwan has imported a major fraction of its new machinery, though to be sure some was produced domestically. Moreover, a considerable percentage of investment in manufacturing has consisted of factory buildings for which it seems unlikely that embodied productivity growth is an important characteristic.[11] Assume that construction and locally produced equipment account for one half of total manufacturing investment. Then, λ_k should equal half of the rate of embodiment calculated for imported equipment. Recent estimates of Hulten (1989) suggest that the rate of improvement of equipment in the U.S. is about 5 percent per annum. Using one half of this figure plus the other appropriate numbers for equations (1) and (2), I calculate that of the TFP growth rate of 5.3 percent for 1961-1987, about 1.5 percentage points, or 29 percent, could plausibly be attributed to embodiment of more productive technologies in new equipment, leaving 3.8 points to be accounted for by other sources of productivity growth. This calculation suggests that the benefit from importing equipment containing new technology was a very important source of industrial growth in Taiwan, but it was only part of the story. Other sources of productivity growth must be analyzed.

It would be particularly useful to calculate the share of output growth accounted for by the changing quality of the labor force. As discussed below in Section 5, it is likely, given the aggregate changes in education levels, that it has had a major impact on the growth process. Unfortunately, as of now it is impossible to obtain employment in manufacturing by education and wages, thus precluding the standard calculation.

Clearly, all growth accounting should be taken as providing rough orders of magnitude and indications of where to search for explanations of growth rather than as precise measures (Nelson 1973, 1981). Nevertheless, several observations follow for the calculations for 1961-1987. First, the share of output growth accounted for by the residual was larger than in other LDCs, comparable to the now advanced countries at similar stages of development. The growth of total factor productivity was an important driving force behind Taiwanese industrial success. Second, the performance was in an important sense even better than a simple calculation of TFP growth rates suggests. In particular, the DCs in which TFP growth has accounted for a similar percentage of total output growth, had much slower growth rates for primary factors and much slower changes in industrial structure (examined below).[12] The ability to even maintain initial levels of TFP, let alone increase them in the face of the absorption of such massive amounts of factors, was an extremely impressive achievement implying considerable organizational ability at both the micro and national levels.

The continued rapid growth in TFP is intriguing, and absent any detailed microeconomic studies of the sources of this growth, several strands are worth pursuing. I consider in turn the possible role of exports in stimulating productivity growth, then, more conventionally, scale economies and learning by doing.

The Impact of Productivity on Export Growth Productivity

If exports are to explain long term *growth* rather than *level* effects, a link must exist between exports and productivity growth. Section 4 explores this question and attempts to set out the probable channels through which exports may affect productivity growth quite apart from those short- and intermediate-term benefits most often cited. Recent advances in the understanding of technological development are incorporated within the framework of growth accounting to explain the maintenance of output growth rates which are extraordinarily high by international standards. It is obviously a possibility that the causality works in another direction, namely, that productivity growth, originating in the local economy, reduces costs and generates exports if profitability of sales to the domestic and foreign markets are roughly kept at parity. However, as is often noted by analysts of the super-exporters, the sequence in which industries became exporters roughly conforms to their labor intensity, exports being based initially on low real wages rather than productivity growth.[13] Although it is possible that the initial export boom began as a result of initial productivity growth in the labor-intensive sectors based on accumulating production experience, this hypothesis is not testable with the data that are available. It is also not evident that the sectors which succeeded in increasing exports would have benefitted more from productivity growth than other sectors. For Taiwan, the Heckscher-Ohlin model works well in the early stages of development.[14]

3. The Export Experience of Taiwan

The Acquisition of Technology

The standard and probably most important explanation of Taiwan's spectacular growth in exports is that the foreign trade regime made exporting profitable (Lee and Liang 1982; Little 1979; Ranis 1979; Scott 1979). Early exports consisted mainly of labor intensive products (Ranis 1979; Scott 1979) such as clothing, textiles, athletic equipment, canned pineapple, and so on.

The technology underlying these products was mastered by three mechanisms: (a) experience during the Japanese colonial period; (b) knowledge brought to Taiwan from the mainland by industrialists fleeing the revolution; and (c) knowledge initially obtained from non-proprietary and inexpensively available sources on the world market, more recently from direct foreign investors, joint ventures, and licensing agreements.   Ho (1978, Chapter 5) describes the growth of manufacturing, primarily food processing, until 1930 and then in a broader spectrum of industries during the 1930s. Although he does not discuss the extent of transfer of technical knowledge such as production engineering to the Taiwanese during this period, it is plausible to assume that many important production skills were learned by the indigenous residents. It seems unlikely that the rapid and broad growth of the 1930s could have been achieved simply by Japanese managers without some knowledge being appropriated by local employees. The fact that by 1951, despite the withdrawal of the Japanese and the devastation of World War II, industrial output had reached 1937 levels (Ranis 1979, p. 209) implies that considerable managerial and technological knowledge must have been absorbed during the colonial period, undoubtedly supplemented by the industrialists leaving the Mainland in the late 1940s.[15]

It seems probable that the huge number of small-scale enterprises (SSEs) characteristic of the 1950s and 1960s was made possible partly by skills acquired before 1949 both on the Mainland and under the Japanese. Unfortunately, the evidence collected on the small-scale sector (summarized by Ho 1980) does not report the background of small entrepreneurs. Although it may be conjectured that the initial conditions for industrial development were probably more favorable, just as they were in agriculture (Thorbecke 1979), than in many other LDCs, initial conditions are not automatically transmuted into good performance. Policy is important.

With respect to obtaining knowledge from external sources, as late as 1978, Taiwanese royalty payments were only US$52 million per year and remained below US$100 million through 1983 (Liang and Liang 1988). However, such formal methods of knowledge acquisition were undoubtedly dwarfed by the ability to absorb non-proprietary knowledge in the relatively uncomplicated sectors that formed the basis of the early industrialization drive. One benefit, often overlooked, of sectoral growth and technology choice that is consistent with relative factor prices is the greater availability of non-proprietary knowledge in simpler sectors and technology. It is not an accident that the most vocal criticism of the high cost of technology transfer (royalties or licensing fees) emanates from those countries following import substitution policies that lead to an early emphasis on capital- and technology-intensive production in which much of the knowledge is proprietary. As will be noted below, as Taiwan enters new technology-intensive areas, access to technology may become a major issue.

Given the relative ease of acquiring and mastering the relevant technology, the combination of low wages and a foreign exchange regime neutral between production for the domestic and foreign markets is probably a sufficient explanation of the early rapid growth in labor-intensive exports.[16]

In new products, the explanation for success is that substantial investment, made possible by the growing domestic saving rate and to a much lesser extent by foreign investment (Ranis and Schive 1985), was allocated according to comparative advantage. New investments were directed to sectors along the ladder of comparative advantage as measured by the domestic resource cost.[17] Additions to the labor force were similarly allocated as were those workers reallocated from agriculture and the informal urban sector to the industrial sector. An alternate interpretation is put forth by those who argue that some industries were established earlier than would have been "natural" according to the DRC ladder (Wade 1990).

The Structure of Incentives

I will return to an evaluation of these conflicting views in Section 5. The important issue here is that, whatever the investment allocation mechanism, much of the investment in new sectors resulted in exports, leading to a rapid change in the commodity composition of exports. Such exports may have been encouraged by a variety of government promotional measures, but the new sectors were not allowed simply to produce for the protected domestic market as in the import-substituting countries. Thus, old and new sectors grew because of relatively neutral incentive policies, new ones also benefiting from some promotional measures.

The growth in exports in turn was the primary source of growth in aggregate demand between 1956 and 1971 and was decisive in altering the structure of production as shown by the decomposition of deMelo (1985) presented in Table 3.2. This decomposition, following a method developed by Chenery and a variety of collaborators, divides the deviation of manufac-

TABLE 3.2 Decomposition of Sources of Growth of Taiwan's Gross Output

Deviation of manufacturing output from proportional growth	28.2
Percentage source of output deviation	
Domestic demand	2.5
Exports	71.3
Import substitution	10.6
Changes in input-output coefficients	15.6

Source: Calculated from deMelo (1985), Table 9.2.

turing's growth of gross output from that of the economy-wide average into four components, namely, the expansion of domestic demand, export expansion, import substitution, and a category attributable to changes in the input-output coefficients. Table 3.2 shows that roughly 71 percent of the disproportionate expansion in manufacturing gross output was attributable to the non-proportional growth of exports, the only remaining large source being the deepening of the input-output structure. While this calculation has not been updated, it is clear from successive input-output tables that exports have played a very large role as a source of demand for manufacturing in the ensuing period.[18]

Two aspects of the trade regime have been cited in Taiwan and other countries as important in generating allocative efficiency, namely, the low dispersion of rates of effective protection across production sectors and the neutrality of incentives as between exports and domestic sales. However, in the case of Taiwan these studies have largely been carried out for the early years of the industrialization process. For example, the analysis of Lee and Liang (1982) stops with 1970. Anecdotal evidence collected by Wade (1990) and often cited in journalistic accounts suggest that in some selected sectors effective rates of protection have continued to be very high up to the present time. The absence of systematic evidence precludes analyzing the possible anomaly of rapid and efficient growth in sectors that have continued to be protected,[19] though as noted in Section 2, the value of A^*/Q^* during the import-substituting 1950s was quite high.

Perhaps more important than the intersectoral variation in protection across manufacturing sectors is the fact that, with the exception of the post-oil-price-increase years of 1974 and 1975, Taiwan has exported more goods and services than it has imported in every year since 1971 (Table 3.3). The

TABLE 3.3   Export Surplus as a Percentage of Gross Domestic Product (current prices)

Year	Average of yearly figures
1952-1956	−6.2
1957-1961	−6.9
1962-1966	−1.7
1967-1971	0.6
1972-1976	0.5
1977-1981	2.7
1982-1986	12.1
1987-1988	14.4

Source: Taiwan Statistical Data Book 1989, Table 3.8b.

implied undervaluation of the currency must have contributed significantly to the continuing export surge across a broad spectrum of sectors.

The Role of Undervaluation

Undervaluation and the continuing surplus on goods and services account is often viewed as simply a misguided mercantilist policy. There is much merit to this view, known since Adam Smith. But it is possible to view it in a different light if exports are viewed as providing benefits, both economic and political. The economic externalities are discussed in detail in Section 5 and may provide some (limited) economic justification for the policy that was pursued. Politically, the accumulation of large foreign currency reserves and their potential use as a source of foreign aid and as an easy-to-assess measure of the government's intention of maintaining an environment conducive to business that would attract direct foreign investment would surely not go unnoticed in the world.

The increasing number of countries opening formal and informal relations with Taiwan is surely related to its economic strength, partly perceived as its GNP per capita, but partly reflecting its accumulated hard currency reserves and the potential for either Taiwan-based DFI or aid. As a means of preventing increasing political isolation given the sheer numbers and international strength of Mainland China, it would be difficult to design a better instrument of policy.

Exports and Aggregate Demand

Finally, the role of export growth in the maintenance of rapid growth in demand is often overlooked. Sustaining rapid growth in demand and incomes would have been extremely difficult without the contribution of exports. While it is theoretically possible to employ a monetary-fiscal policy that would sustain 10 percent per annum growth in GNP, it is likely that such a program, if dependent on domestic sales, would have been more susceptible to cycles that would have led investors to be more cautious and undermined the ability to maintain the requisite growth in domestic investment. I have argued elsewhere (Pack 1988) that the export orientation of the super-exporters allowed them to avoid the declining internal terms of trade that would have ensued had they accumulated factors as rapidly as they did but had to sell them to the more slowly growing domestic non-manufacturing sector. This would have led to declining profitability of investment and a slowing in its rate of growth. It is for this reason that the early closed economy, two-sector models of development such as Lewis and Fei-Ranis pay attention to the conditions for balanced growth, particularly the maintenance of a constant terms of trade between sectors. For the large, much less open economies which these models envisioned, internal balanced growth remains an important issue. For smaller, more open economies like Taiwan, exports reduce, to some extent, the overlapping issues of macroeconomic balance and micro-sectoral adjustment. As shown in Table 3.2, domestic demand was not an important source of non-proportional growth in manufacturing. However, the emphasis on non-proportional growth should not obscure the fact that as of 1986 the share of domestic absorption of manufactured gross output was 70 percent, exports being 30. The absolute size of domestic demand matters as well.[20]

4. Exports and Productivity Growth

Exports contribute to growing demand and to the reaping of the once-and-for-all gains from reallocation of resources from inefficient to efficient sectors. The major gains from greater utilization of capacity and scale economies are realized early in the process. Why then does the supply in Taiwan continue to grow at such rapid rates -- is there some characteristic of exports themselves that helps to increase TFP growth? It will be seen in Section 6 that I attribute part of the success of Taiwan's industrial growth to the structure of industry and other characteristics of the economy that are conducive to development. Nevertheless, consistency requires an attempt to answer the question of whether exports have a supply augment-ing effect that contributes more to growth than would a comparable increase in domestic sales.

Reduction in Opposition to Structural Change

The changing structure of production resulting from the growth of manu-factured exports, along with fast aggregate overall growth, was the source of an important benefit which might be described as an externality, namely, the reduction in opposition to a range of policies that were critical for Taiwan's continuing development. Mancur Olson (1982) has argued that a distinctive difference between high-growth countries (The Gang of Four, Japan and Germany) and other more slowly expanding countries is the ab-sence of growth-obstructing interest groups. For Taiwan, this view would assert that land reform and the great upheavals accompanying the reloca-tion of the Kuomintang government from the mainland in 1949 permitted the implementation of growth fostering policies without the need to over-come domestic resistance from groups that lost either relative income or power.[21]

As is usual in broad-brush views, there is some truth, but it is easy to neglect the possibility that, once growth begins, sectoral interests begin to emerge and may oppose growth-enhancing policies. In recent years the

Japanese government has had to design "exit" policies for no longer profitable industries, presumably because of the potential of these "sunset" sectors for disrupting the policies necessary to a continuing shift to more competitive sectors. The alleged "consensual" nature of Japan may be an endogenous outcome of specific policies rather than the result of socialization from the cradle.

In Taiwan, relatively low protection levels limited the rents accruing to factors employed in industrial sectors, hence limited their losses from policies that reduced rents (Lee and Liang 1982). Given the lower rewards from rent seeking, the resources devoted to such activities were presumably smaller. Equally important, the continuing extraordinary expansion of exports undoubtedly lessened the opposition to growth enhancing policies, as those engaged in relatively declining sectors such as food, beverages, and tobacco, non-metallic minerals, and chemical products (Table 3.4) under-

TABLE 3.4   Sectoral Structure of Employment and Value Added (percentage shares)

Sector	Share of value added current prices		Share of employment	
	1966	1986	1966	1986
Food, beverage, tobacco	.29	.11	.23	.06
Textiles	.12	.08	.17	.11
Cloth, leather, fur	.03	.08	.03	.08
Wood products	.04	.03	.06	.05
Paper, printing, publishing	.05	.04	.05	.04
Chemical, petroleum	.20	.15	.12	.05
Plastics	.00	.07	.00	.11
Rubber	.01	.01	.02	.02
Non-metallic minerals	.07	.03	.08	.04
Basic metals	.03	.06	.03	.03
Fabricated metals	.02	.05	.04	.08
Machinery	.03	.03	.05	.04
Electrical equipment & machinery	.05	.13	.06	.10
Transportation equipment	.04	.06	.04	.05
Precision instruments	{.02	.01	{.04	.01
Miscellaneous		.06		.06

Source: Value added, *National Income in Taiwan Area, the Republic of China*, 1989, Table 1. Employment, 1986, *The Report on 1986 Industrial and Commercial Census*, Table 3.8; 1966, Ho (1978, Table 10.9), based upon the 1966 industrial and commercial census.

stood that the rapid expansion in others would allow their absorption in newly profitable sectors. Not only does fast growth allow the sleeping dogs of class warfare to lie dormant, but it also reduces the anticipation of danger from the inevitable changes accompanying growing urbanization and industrialization.[22] This virtuous circle of growth-adjustment-growth may shed light on the inability of inward oriented countries to engage in the reforms necessary for more rapid growth. Fear of prolonged structural unemployment in these nations is not mitigated by the rapid growth in exporting sectors.

The shifting structure of production (Table 3.4), made possible by export growth, permitted a movement by factors from industrial sectors with low or declining marginal value productivity to those with higher or growing marginal value products. This was especially important in the early stages of growth, until the disguised and overt unemployment were eliminated. Although such a transformation would have occurred in any event, the time taken for it was probably compressed as the result of the large impact of exports on the production structure as shown in Table 3.2.[23] This change in structure must also have improved productivity growth in the intermediate term after 1975 given the continuing rapid change in the sectoral structure of employment and output, now in response to evolving profitability of various sectors and a rapidly changing constellation of products.

Knowledge Transfers from Foreign Purchasers

Research in Korea, as far as I know not replicated in Taiwan, suggests one mechanism through which productivity growth was probably enhanced in Taiwan as well. A study by Westphal, Rhee, and Pursell (1981) found that a considerable amount of the knowledge of production engineering possessed by Korean firms came from purchasers of Korean exports. Scott (1979, p. 367) reports some evidence of similar mechanisms in Taiwan. The continuing transfer of manufacturing "know-how," particularly in production engineering, to Taiwanese firms by importers desiring still lower cost, higher quality products must also have been an important feature of Taiwanese experience. A continuing flow of technical knowledge improves firms' total factor productivity and will have a larger impact insofar as firms are under competitive pressure to reduce costs and possess sufficient technical ability to effectively absorb this knowledge. Recent work by Lall (1987) demonstrates that Indian firms that were technically competent often did not translate new knowledge into cost reductions because of the absence of a competitive atmosphere.

Still another probable source of growth in TFP made possible by exports was knowledge obtained from purchasers of exports about both process and product *innovations* as opposed to better command of *existing* production engineering. The literature on diffusion of innovation suggests that process innovations are more appropriable and less easy to learn from the general knowledge pool. Nevertheless, it is likely that major importers of Taiwanese products were, in their own interest, quite willing to provide proprietary knowledge of processing improvements in order to obtain either lower prices or better quality from Taiwanese manufacturers, and hence increase their own competitiveness.

Product-specific knowledge conveyed by importers presumably allowed greater value added per unit of primary inputs as the price for final products would, on the average, be greater as Taiwan was enabled to shift among products, away from those whose price was declining (relatively) towards new products still in the early part of the product cycle.[24]   A growth impact may also have been obtained insofar as advice about quality control increased value added per unit of combined inputs each year.

In all of these knowledge-transferring activities, growth rate-augmenting effects as compared to a once-and-for-all increase would have required continuing transfers. If, for example, the impact of advice from importers was merely to indicate quality requirements and to show how these could be met on a one-shot basis, there would have been a level effect but no growth rate impact from export orientation. In the context of a major exporter whose products were an important component of the ability of many importers to maintain profit margins, an ongoing transfer seems a more plausible specification, and the same would be true for other modes of knowledge transfer. There is no Taiwan-specific evidence on these issues and they constitute a fruitful area for further research.

Knowledge Transfers from Returning Nationals

In Korea, it has been documented that a large part of growing technical competence was obtained from returning nationals who had received American education and remained to work in the U.S. only temporarily (Westphal, Rhee, Pursell 1981). Korea, and presumably Taiwan, have experienced a much smaller brain drain than other developing countries as a result of rapidly rising income levels which enabled employers to offer salaries which, if not equal to those in the U.S., were close enough to induce a return home. Anecdotal journalistic evidence depicting this phenomenon is accumulating, many returning nationals having received education in the U.S. and then worked for an American firm.[25] Liu (1987, Tables 24 and 25) shows that more than 20 percent of executives in large Taiwanese firms had studied abroad, largely in Japan and the United States. One can speculate that the return of foreign-trained Taiwanese nationals helped provide part of the technical change that improved productivity and helped to avoid the slowdown inherent in an economy as diminishing returns set in to capital accumulation.

In contrast to Taiwan, nationals may fail to return to import-substituting countries insofar as the skills they have lead to employment in sectors in which exports rather than domestic sales are the natural outlet, yet these exports are discouraged by the international trade regime. Thus, the environment that is conducive to exports, if not the latter themselves, may induce the inflow of technology embodied in individuals; while not an externality, such an inflow may prove as important as more formally acquired technological knowledge.

The Purchase of Knowledge and the Location of MNCs

The hard currency earnings permitted by exports also enabled firms to purchase consulting services and engage in licensing agreements which required payment of royalties in hard currencies. This type of knowledge transfer must have been an important component in allowing some firms, particularly in newer sectors in which knowledge acquired under the Japanese or from mainland businesses did not suffice, to establish themselves and move towards world best practice. Although as noted earlier, royalty payments were relatively small until the late 1970s, even inexpensive technology licensing agreements can provide critically important knowledge for improving productivity and quality.

Unlike Japan and Korea, Taiwan's industrial development was characterized by a more substantial presence of MNCs whose willingness to locate was at least partly dependent on the stability implied by a growth commitment[26] which may also have been signaled by a growing level of exports. Insofar as the presence of MNCs enabled local firms to obtain knowledge, from emulation, from the movement of workers, and from the general atmosphere effects, they must have contributed to a continuing learning process.[27] Moreover, the small size of manufacturing firms in Taiwan probably enabled local employees of MNCs to leave and begin their own firms fairly easily.[28]

Ranis and Schive (1985) have shown that MNC activities accounted for less than 10 percent of manufacturing value added and employment through the late-70s. Nevertheless, the cumulative spillover effects can be quite substantial if even a small percentage of employees each year leave the firms and either go to existing locally owned ones or begin their own. Scott (1979, p. 339) cites anecdotal evidence that this occurred. Evidence from labor force surveys indicates quite substantial labor market turnover though separate data on MNCs, joint ventures, and local firms are not available. As can be seen in Table 3.5, the separation rates in manufacturing exceed 3 percent per year, few of these reflecting retirement or a move

TABLE 3.5   Separation Rates per 100 Employees

Industry	1978	1982	1986	1988
All manufacturing	3.43	3.77	3.55	3.69
Electric and electronic equipment	3.09	4.75	4.72	5.07

Source: Yearbook of Earnings and Productivity Statistics, Taiwan Area, Republic of China, 1988, Directorate-General of Budget, Accounting and Statistics, Executive Yuan, Republic of China, Tables 102, 103.

to unemployed status. While some of the same workers leave firms each year, the aggregate rates suggest that substantial knowledge must be transmitted from firm to firm as workers move. To the extent that MNCs bring in knowledge that is closer to the best practice frontier, some fraction must be diffused by employee mobility.   Moreover, the separation rates are greater in newer higher technology sectors which Ranis and Schive find are often entered by non-Chinese owned MNCs.

Ranis and Schive (1985) provide a detailed account of the benefits conferred upon other firms of the interaction with the Singer Sewing Machine Company. The linkages described and the productivity gains obtained by other firms as a result constitute a good example of rarely documented real external economies. In the case of Singer, the external benefits arose at least partly as the firm attempted to satisfy local content requirements imposed by the government.[29]

In summary, the undervaluation that encourages exports confers an externality as the expansion of exports reduces the political opposition to rapid structural change and allows a more rapid transfer of resources, especially labor, to more (socially) profitable industries. More generally, exports generate knowledge transfers from potential purchasers, indirectly encourage the return of nationals residing abroad and their knowledge, provide the means to purchase knowledge that expands productivity still more, and may encourage the location of MNCs, the latter generating knowledge spillovers.

The above (non-exhaustive) list of the possible growth *rate* augmenting effects of exports runs the risk of attributing many features of a successful economy to exports excluding the purely domestic activities that contribute to a higher growth rate of TFP. Thus, the location of MNCs and the contribution at the margin of knowledge obtained from returning expatriates and consultants, would surely have been lower had there not been a high and growing level of education.[30] Similarly, fewer MNCs and Taiwanese trained abroad would have located there had there not been a reasonable level of social overhead ranging from communication to transportation services. Contrary to the provocative hypothesis of Hirschman that the absence of social overhead capital may serve as a catalyst to the breaking of bottlenecks, it seems more likely that the provision of communications, transport, and power ahead of demand was, as Ranis (1979) maintains, an important contributor to the successful initial industrialization effort.

In this sense, export growth may have been an important contributor, given the existence of a range of other conditions: it was, as Kravis would put it, a handmaiden to growth rather than the sole locomotive. Countries trying to emulate Taiwan by duplicating the trade regime but ignoring the many other policies, from education to the provision of social overhead capital, are likely to be disappointed. On the other hand, those providing critical nontradeable services but ignoring the benefits conferred by exports are unlikely to succeed in the same dramatic way. While the past quarter-century of export-propelled growth and its analysis have yielded many important lessons about the importance of trade regime, success in Taiwan was built on two foundations, the non-traded one having been subordinated in most analytic efforts to derive growth prescriptions from the East Asian experience.

5. The Role of Industrial Policy

As noted earlier, a number of scholars contend that Taiwan's success has been at least partly attributable to an intensive effort by the government to direct the sectoral evolution of the economy. To evaluate these views, it is necessary to briefly review the arguments most often made to support the potential beneficial effects of government intervention.

The Case for Industrial Policy

Consider the general case for government intervention in the manufacturing sector or industrial policy. Such activity can be welfare improving in the presence of real external economies or capital market imperfections. The latter can arise because of high failure rates by borrowers and the consequent need of financial institutions to charge high interest rates to insure acceptable rates of return. The externality is the loss in real income as some projects with high expected private and social rates of return are not financed. The imperfection here is the high cost of screening or asymmetric information between borrowers and lenders. Arguments about learning by doing and static scale economies, often invoked to justify intervention, are also encompassed under the capital market failure argument insofar as perfectly informed lenders would find it worthwhile to lend to projects whose present discounted value is positive. They do not lend because of risk aversion, an inability to lend the requisite minimum amount given the size of project required, or myopia.

The second valid argument for intervention stems from the possibility of real external economies conferred by a new firm or industry. In an open economy, such externalities must consist of allowing goods to be produced at less than the imported c.i.f. price.

In Taiwan there is reason to be skeptical of the quantitative importance of the impact of government intervention in the capital market. The view that government lending made a decisive difference in the sectoral *pattern* of investment is not very plausible in an economy in which domestic saving was at a high level (Table 3.6), rapidly growing, and the capital market closed for much of the period, making investment abroad difficult. Such conditions must have led to a growing and intense effort by private investors to identify high quality local projects. While the impact of asymmetric information would continue to be felt, the growing ratio of investment to GNP implies that an increasing number of projects with positive present discounted value at market rates would be financed. While it is possible that the sectoral structure of investment was affected, the overwhelming fact is the rapid growth of the capital stock for the entire manufacturing sector as was shown in Table 3.1.

As is well known, the first-best intervention in the case of either market failure is to direct policy to correct the specific failure. A second-best policy would subsidize industries during their learning period, provided that the Mill-Bastable criterion is satisfied. It is difficult to evaluate retrospectively whether these normative criteria were met by the policies that

TABLE 3.6   Gross Saving Rate

Year	Average of yearly figures
1952-1956	14.2
1957-1961	16.2
1962-1966	19.5
1967-1971	24.7
1972-1976	31.4
1977-1981	32.8
1982-1986	32.9
1987-1988	36.7

Source: Taiwan Statistical Data Book 1989, Council for Economic Planning and Development, Republic of China, Taipei, China, 1989, Table 3-11.

56 *The Economic Development of Northeast Asia IV*

94 *Howard Pack*

were followed, though in principle it could be done. It is not much less challenging to determine whether the various interventions[31] had a major quantitative impact as it is hard to construct a counterfactual scenario of growth without intervention. Nevertheless, it is possible to obtain some sense of the importance of industrial policy.

The Impact of Taiwan's Industrial Policy

Wade and others have vigorously argued that a critical component of Taiwan's success has been an industrial policy that: (1) established public enterprises when private initiative was not forthcoming or the capital market was reluctant or unable to fund very large projects; (2) extensively employed import restrictions; and (3) occasionally financed private enterprise. Although his evidence is anecdotal, I find Wade's case that wide intervention was employed to be persuasive. Such government direction raises two critical questions in terms of the preceding discussion: (a) did it matter -- was the sectoral structure of production affected with respect to the time at which various sectors were initiated or did its depth (the extent of forward and backward linkages) differ compared to what would have transpired in the absence of industrial policy; (b) was this intervention welfare enhancing? In both dimensions, Wade's view is affirmative -- government direction had decisive effects upon the structure of production and it improved welfare.

Before examining the impact of policy on structure and growth, it is worth noting that the role of government enterprises has declined continuously, their economy-wide value added share decreasing from 12.9 percent of domestic value added in 1951 to 11.6 in 1965 and 10.5 in 1988.[32] There was a corresponding decline in the current price economy-wide share of investment of these enterprises from 29 to 21 to 19 percent in these years.[33] Even more important is the decline in the share of constant price value added of government manufacturing enterprises, the figures for selected years being shown in Table 3.7. These shifts presumably reflected the increasing skill levels and capital available in the private sector. The decrease in the importance of government enterprises' share of value added from the early years occurred in the period of rapidly rising exports and changes in the structure of production toward more technologically complex activities. While it is possible that some important sub-sector activities were undertaken by such entities, it seems unlikely that they were critical to the growth of the entire sector. On the other hand, public enterprises may have been an important training ground for entrepreneurs: Liu (1987, Chapter 5) reports that, among executives in large companies, 30 percent of Mainland-born executives and 10 percent of Taiwan-born executives had earlier been employed in public enterprises.

TABLE 3.7   Share of Public Enterprise in Value Added in Manufacturing

1952	56.2	1975	14.2
1957	48.7	1980	14.5
1964	38.9	1984	14.2
1970	20.6	1988	11.1

Note: Share of 1981 constant price value added through 1980, share of 1986 constant price value added share afterwards.

Source: Taiwan Statistical Data Book, 1989, Council for Economic Planning and Development, Table 5-4.

Effects of Intervention on the Structure of Production.   Are the views that contend that government intervention had important effects correct? First, the evolution of Taiwan's industrial structure can be compared with that of other developing countries. In particular, Taiwan's industrial structure can be compared to that of other countries of similar income undergoing a growth in income per capita employing the normal patterns calculated by Chenery and Syrquin (1986). . A second, complementary method is to determine whether the industrial structure of Taiwan deepened more than other countries of similar income (and size), one goal of government direction being an increase in backward and forward linkages. There are well known problems with each method, for example, the intersectoral pattern of evolution of value added across nations includes the impact in all countries of changing levels of effective rates of protection as determined by government policy; hence in no sense can normal patterns be considered normative. Nor do linkages convey any information about social optimality unless direct measures of efficiency of the linked sectors are available. Nevertheless, to obtain a proximate insight into the impact of government intervention in the absence of a detailed computable general equilibrium model for Taiwan, such international comparisons provide a useful benchmark, keeping in mind their limitations.

The evolution of the sectoral structure of Taiwan has been compared to that of other developing countries in studies by Chenery and Syrquin (1986) and Kubo *et al.* (1986). Although their analysis ends in 1971, this is presumably the period in which the greatest quantitative impact of government policy would have been experienced as government enterprise was more important, savings rates were not as high, and the role of import restrictions loomed larger in the recently liberalized economy. Nevertheless, the evolution of the sectoral structure of manufacturing, at least at the two digit level, looks similar to that in the other countries contained in the study. Sectors promoted by the government, such as metals and chemicals, did not grow more rapidly than would have been expected from a typical country achieving Taiwan's level of income in successive years, although it could be conjectured that a comparable study over the succeeding fifteen years would demonstrate a growth in electronics that exceeded that attained in other countries.

Similarly, calculations that I have carried out (Table 3.8) show that while backward and forward linkages in Taiwan exceed those in other countries in an international sample, in most cases the differences are not statistically significant.[34]   While it is possible that at a more detailed sectoral breakdown significant differences from international patterns would appear, it is not plausible to assert that for the entire manufacturing sector, government intervention had a decisive effect on economic structure.

It is possible, of course, that the other countries in the study were all pursuing policies to encourage a similar evolution. Hence, Taiwan's policy may have altered the "natural" pattern of its development but not have shown up in such comparisons. Other explanations can be offered given the limitations of cross-national comparisons. But I suspect that the broad conclusions would stand up to a more finely honed empirical analysis, namely, that at the two-digit level Taiwan's sectoral evolution appears similar to that of other countries.

Was industrial policy, in the sense of intentionally altering the sectoral composition of output, then largely irrelevant to Taiwan's development? To answer this question it is necessary to examine the major individual products whose growth has been large and to determine the importance of

TABLE 3.8   Linkages in Taiwan and Other Countries

Sectors	Taiwan		Other	
	Forward	Backward	Forward	Backward
Food, beverage, tobacco	.36	.71	.26	.71
Textiles, clothing, leather	.52	.74	.36	.63
Wood, paper, printing, etc.	.53	.71	.57	.61
Rubber product, chemical	.78	.66	.64	.65
Non-metallic minerals	.77	.63	.81	.50
Metals and machinery	.63	.71	.46	.62

Note: Calculation for Taiwan is for 1984. Date of calculation for other countries varies.

Source: Taiwan, calculated from input-output table for 1984 reported in *Statistical Yearbook of the Republic of China*, 1988. Other countries from Syrquin (1989).

industrial policy, on the margin, in their development. However, a disaggregated breakdown of industrial production by value added, by units of production, and by major exports, shows any number of products exhibiting rapid growth in one or more of these dimensions. Many of them, particularly in electronics, would have been natural candidates for investment as Taiwan moved up the capital- and technology-intensive hierarchy. To separate "natural" sources of growth from those induced by government is probably impossible. Government encouragement may have led to a somewhat earlier initiation of production in some products or to slightly lower initial (private) costs, but hardly to the establishment of productive capacity in sectors that would not have been begun at all absent such efforts.

Table 3.4 presented evidence on the sectoral evolution of employment and value added, the point there being that considerable structural change did occur, my conjecture being that rapid aggregate growth and the promise of new opportunities reduced the political or social opposition to such changes on the part of those adversely affected. The implicit model of those who believe that industrial policy has had an important effect is that changes in the deployment of resources were not based on conventional comparative advantage but that the government created comparative advantage in new sectors. In the case of Taiwan, this implies that sectoral growth occurred in capital- or technology-intensive sectors rather than the more labor-intensive sectors which would have been "natural" for Taiwan given its initial resource endowment which was, of course, rapidly changing. While a rigorous test of this hypothesis is very difficult to construct, a simpler one is available.

Table 3.9 presents data on the ratio of value added and employment in 1986 relative to that in 1971 for each sector along with various characteristics of the sector, indexed to the sector-wide average for manufacturing. The characteristics include the ratio of fixed capital (at historic acquisition cost) to labor in 1986,[35] the average wage in 1986, and the ratio of value added to total employment in the sector.

Several results of analyzing these data are noteworthy. First, multiple regression analysis whose results are not shown does not find significant correlation between sector expansion, measured as either share of value added or employment, and the various sectoral characteristics. Second, the sectors that exhibited a large expansion in employment (or value added) -- clothing and footwear, plastics, electrical equipment, and metal products -- are all characterized by *below* average wages and value added per worker. Below average wages even at the end of the period in rapidly expanding sectors tends to confirm the standard view of the determinants of sectoral evolution. Lower than average value added per worker suggests no rents are being earned either by owners of capital or those who possess unusual skills. While it is possible that some of the development, for example, in

TABLE 3.9   The Evolution of Sectors and Their Characteristics

Sector	N_{86}/N_{71}	VA_{86}/VA_{71}	$\overline{W}$	VA/N	K/L
Food, beverages	.48	.38	1.07	1.91	1.64
Textiles	.56	.67	1.07	.76	1.05
Apparel	1.14	2.67	.90	1.00	.31
Wood products	.69	.75	.85	.63	.58
Paper and paper products	.95	.80	.99	.98	1.16
Chemical products	1.16	1.10	1.39	1.83	2.13
Petroleum products	.69	.63	1.43	7.95	7.85
Plastics	10.00	.98	.62	.52	.68
Rubber	.92	1.00	1.05	.60	
Non-metallic minerals	.74	.43	.93	.76	1.46
Basic metals	1.16	2.00	1.28	2.07	3.99
Metal products	1.80	2.50	.86	.66	.65
Machinery	.84	1.00	.97	.70	.77
Electrical equipment	1.59	2.60	.87	.77	.75
Transportation equip.	1.59	1.50	1.13	1.30	1.23
Precision, misc.	1.63	1.40	.89	.98	.43

Definitions: N, employment; VA, value added; $\overline{W}$, average wage; K/L, fixed capital at historical cost/persons employed.

Source: Value added, employment, same as Table 3.4. Value added per employed person, wage per employed person, fixed capital stock per employed person, *The Report on 1986 Industrial and Commercial Census Taiwan-Fukien Area*, Table 19.

electronics would not have come about without specific efforts by the government to establish research institutes and industrial estates,[36] the main burden of the evidence is that even in the period of economic growth which saw the introduction of new technology-based products, the sectoral pattern of expansion is not consistent with assigning a major role to industrial policy. Indeed, the picture that emerges from Table 3.9 is very neoclassical. The cross-sector dispersion of wages is very small compared to other LDCs, comparable to that in the OECD countries, and is consistent with the hypothesis that labor markets are very competitive, it being likely that skill differentials account for the intersector variation that exists. While it is not possible to obtain rates of return on equity across sectors, it seems unlikely that these would vary greatly given the enormous pool of saving, seeking, at least initially, local reinvestment.

Effects on Growth. Given the difficulty of demonstrating any quantitatively unusual behavior in the growth of Taiwan's industrial structure as well as the complexity of demonstrating at the individual product level the contribution of industrial policy versus the natural evolution of industry, what may be concluded about the impact of industrial intervention by the government on growth rates? The major benefit of industrial policy would be to increase the rate of long-term productivity growth. But the view of Wade and others is that industrial policy induced individual sectors to emerge much earlier than they would have absent such a policy. It is not an argument about rates of productivity growth as much as about the timing of the changing industrial structure. Their view is implicitly that new sectors exhibit a higher level of total factor productivity, in which case initiation of production in new sectors does yield a greater level of total factor productivity for a given commitment of resources. As in the case of static international trade models, there is a level effect but no rate of growth impact. To obtain a conclusion that rates of TFP growth are increased, the introduction of new sectors with higher levels of TFP must occur on a continuous basis or the sectors introduced must themselves exhibit higher rates of TFP growth than older sectors.[37] However, no evidence has been adduced that such is the case.

Chen and Tang (1990) have calculated rates of TFP growth for two digit sectors for the period 1968-1982 (see Table 3.10). There is no systematic relation between the type or age of the sector and TFP growth rates. Thus, chemicals had a negative TFP growth rate for the period while that for textiles, an older sector, is quite high. While TFP growth in machinery is high, it is exceeded by that for leather and furs. TFP growth in electronic and electrical equipment is not much higher than that in apparel.

TABLE 3.10 Growth Rates of Total Factor Productivity by Sector, 1968-1982

Food processing	-.0015	Petroleum & coal	-.0063
Beverages & tobacco	.0088	Rubber	.0207
Textiles	.0346	Clay, stone, glass	.0099
Apparel	.0202	Basic metals	.0004
Leather & fur	.0413	Fabricated metals	.0142
Lumber & furniture	-.0076	Machinery	.0363
Paper & paper products	-.0001	Electronics & elec.	.0212
Chemicals	-.0067	Transportation equip.	.0226

Source: Chen and Tang (1990).

Contrary to the results of Chen and Tang obtained for two-digit branches, assume that for the period since 1982 each new sector has a higher value of A^* than the average earlier one. If this were the case, the need for government intervention to induce the establishment of the sector is not obvious, though one can postulate the existence of capital market failures or excessive risk aversion by private investors. While it is possible that the government's attention to a sector accelerated its introduction, to have an impact on measured TFP growth rates requires not an occasional success but a continuing stream of them. The existing evidence shown in Table 3.10 does not support this view.

Industrial Policy and the Sources of Growth

An alternative view of the contribution of industrial policy is possible, namely, that it increased the elasticity of substitution, slowing the decline in the marginal product of capital. The view behind such a formulation is that the government is more far-sighted than the private sector, anticipates changes in aggregate relative factor availability and relative factor prices, and initiates discussions and focuses attention on new industries (perhaps new technologies) before the private sector would have done so. The move to more capital-intensive sectors is faster and more efficient.

To ascertain whether such intervention could have increased the growth rate, an expanded form of the intermediate term growth equation, (1), the Nelson-Kmenta approximation, is useful.

$$Q^* = A^* + bK^* + (1-b)L^* + \frac{1}{2}b(1-b)[(\sigma-1)/\sigma][K^* - L^*]^2. \qquad (3)$$

This equation assumes that the underlying production function is a constant elasticity of substitution one, σ being the elasticity of substitution. The first three terms provide the conventional Cobb-Douglas explanation of output growth contained in (1) while the last term introduces a correction if σ, the elasticity of substitution, differs significantly from unity. When capital grows much more rapidly than natural units of labor, labor supply may constrain output growth rates as the sector encounters diminishing marginal rates of return to its fastest growing factor. Nevertheless, the greater the ease with which capital can be substituted for labor, the less is any such restrictive effect. A higher σ slows the onset of diminishing returns. Given the rapid increase in capital-labor ratios in Taiwan shown in Table 3.1, this explanation could be of considerable importance. Because of a high degree of collinearity, (3) cannot be estimated. But consider some hypothetical values. If the elasticity of substitution had in fact been 1.2, the unexplained residual for 1961-1987, A^*, declines from 5.25 to 5.09. For the period of the most rapid growth in the capital-labor ratio, 1961-

1976, the residual decreases from 5.39 to 5.09, hardly a significant fall. While some types of selective intervention were undoubtedly followed, it is very difficult to discern their impact either in terms of higher rates of growth of TFP in newer sectors or by positing that the government was more prescient in anticipating changes in the overall endowment of the manufacturing sector.

Such calculations do not preclude the possibility that industrial policy had a major effect on the growth path. It could be argued that the counterfactual scenario would have been an elasticity of substitution of 0.5 and that selective government intervention raised it to unity. The differences in realized growth rates would then have been much larger and industrial policy assumes a quantitatively significant role in the growth process. My own sense of the evidence is that if any one factor allowed the rapid changes in sectoral structure that permitted the staving off of the diminishing returns attributable to the growing capital-labor ratio, it is likely to have been the dramatic rise in education levels discussed below. At this point in our state of knowledge, it would be premature to isolate one aspect of the development process, whether learning derived from exports, selective industrial policy, or education. All had a role and these were surely mutually reinforcing. Without considerably more extensive and precise quantitative micro evidence, assigning priority to one aspect or another of the development process is impossible. With a particular choice of explanatory model and judiciously chosen parameters, any of these can be shown to be decisive.

Foreign Exchange and Education in the Intermediate Run

Within the intermediate-term framework and continuing to utilize equation (3), two other issues are relevant: the role of the availability of foreign exchange and the role of education.

To switch to more capital intensive industries (and technologies within existing sectors) as factor endowments changed often required the importation of new equipment and obtaining technical foreign production knowhow. As indicated in Section 4, some of this knowledge was probably transferred by importers and returning nationals. But some was also derived from technology licensing agreements and from imported new equipment. Given the imperative to alter the structure of the economy in response to the increasing capital-labor endowment, the availability of foreign exchange undoubtedly allowed a less difficult transition. Some countries have increased their saving rate but have been able to earn insufficient foreign exchange to allow such a transition, particularly the import of more modern capital equipment and intermediate inputs. Thus, export orientation and the foreign exchange it provides has a benefit of allowing the *de facto* production function along which the economy produces to avoid the onset of diminishing returns to its saving and investment effort. Again, the payoff to this capacity depends on the value that would have prevailed had the economy been dependent solely on its own capital goods sector, but the qualitative point is clear.

While those advocating the importance of industrial policy in facilitating a changing industrial structure focus on the government, an alternative complementary approach to the ability of Taiwan's industrial sector to evolve with continuing growth in TFP is the quality of its labor force. The growth of education levels in Taiwan has been striking (Table 3.11).

The growth in the capital-labor ratio shown in Table 3.1 along with the maintenance of very low unemployment rates required changes in the labor-intensive technology employed in existing sectors to a more capital-intensive one in response to changing relative factor prices. While the initial choice of appropriate labor-intensive technologies and sectors in response to undistorted price signals was important in achieving both output and employment growth (and an excellent income distribution) in the early decades of rapid growth, the ability to adjust to a rapidly growing capital-labor ratio, growing real wages, and changing international product markets, required considerable flexibility. The shift to new industries characterized by more capital- and technology-intensive processes and the adoption of new technologies such as shuttle-less looms within textiles, was facilitated by the simultaneous growth in the level of education.

Development as rapid as Taiwan's necessitates many types of technological development. Inevitably, much of the relevant technology is imported and successful absorption requires a large group of educated workers.

TABLE 3.11   Education Levels (percentage distribution)

Education level	*1964*	*1987*
Illiterate	22.9	5.1
Self-educated	4.3	2.1
Primary school	55.0	32.6
Junior high	8.0	19.8
Senior high	3.0	7.3
Vocational	3.8	19.2
Junior college	⎰ 3.0	7.6
College & graduate school	⎱	6.2

Source: Statistical Yearbook of the Republic of China, 1989, p. 60.

Moreover, insofar as the product mix is changing quickly, the investigation of new products, market niches, and new export financing arrangements were required, all of these being skill-intensive activities. While industrial policy may somewhat accelerate the inter-industry and intra-industry shifts in technology, a key enabling factor is the high level of education which facilitates the efficient introduction of the requisite technologies. Without the corresponding growth in education, the economy would have been forced, despite its rapid capital accumulation, to remain with more traditional sectors and technologies, yielding a lower return on new investment than was in fact realized. Rather, the growing level of education altered the constellation of production possibilities. In terms of equation (3), with lower levels of education, the elasticity of substitution of the production function along which the manufacturing sector operated would have been lower than that which was realized. If education had been lower, the elasticity of substitution would itself have been lower, and the growth impact of the high national saving rate would have been considerably decreased insofar as capital would have encountered rapidly diminishing marginal returns. Unfortunately, as noted earlier, the data required to estimate the impact of the growing education levels of workers employed in the manufacturing sector are not yet available. If employment by education in the manufacturing sector even roughly resembles the overall trends shown in Table 3.11, the effect might be substantial.

Just as higher education is critical for permitting a shift in structure, so is new investment. Existing capital is not truly malleable. Sewing machines cannot, until replacement, become lathes. To take advantage of changing relative efficiency of a sector requires investment. Similarly, shifts of labor among sectors in accordance with changing social marginal product of labor requires investment.[38] Education and investment are thus complementary in permitting a shifting industrial structure, a characteristic feature of Taiwan's development. Assuming that these changes have been socially profitable, both were important.

6. Small-Scale Enterprises

Most analyses of the industrial development of Taiwan have noted the importance of small-scale enterprises (SSE) (Ho 1980; Levy 1988; Ranis 1979; Scitovsky 1985). Rather than repeat the comprehensive discussion in these studies, the following attempts to link the role of SSEs to total factor productivity growth discussed in Section 2.

Many inquiries into the sources of TFP growth assert the importance of scale economies.[39] This view is also maintained in the disaggregated two digit studies of TFP growth for 1968-1982 by Chen and Tang (1990) reported above. In particular, they find that the TFP growth rate across sectors is correlated with the rate of growth of output. For this explanation to carry a behavioral economic underpinning, the typical firm in each sector would have had to undergo an expansion in size to benefit from an increasing size of plant. While some growth in the average size of plant has occurred, available data suggest that the reaping of scale economies is not likely to have been a major source of productivity growth. Thus, Table 3.12 reports the average number of employees per establishment reported in the 1986 Census of Manufacturing. By international standards the typical size of firm in each sector is remarkably small. Although the measurement of

TABLE 3.12   The Size Structure of Taiwanese Manufacturing

Sector	Average number of persons engaged	Number of firms 1966-1970	1986
Food processing	17	1,129	217
Beverages, tobacco	160	13	9
Textiles	37	428	1,039
Clothing	44	112	417
Leather, fur	63	156	618
Wood products	15	505	760
Paper, printing, publishing	12	478	1,093
Chemical materials	67	70	73
Chemical products	25	265	113
Petroleum, chemicals	465	2	1
Plastic products	29	388	1,603
Rubber products	28	88	283
Non-metallic minerals	27	270	402
Basic metals	27	189	213
Fabricated metals	9	722	3,728
Machinery	11	504	1,091
Electrical equipment	61	274	1,010
Transportation equipment	30	209	445
Precision equipment	29	53	169
Miscellaneous	26	261	765

Source: Number of firms, *The Report on 1986 Industrial and Commercial Census Taiwan-Fukien Area*, General Report, Table 28; average firm size, ibid., Table 19.

firm size by employment can understate the ability to realize scale economies if each plant is very capital-intensive, it is extremely unlikely that firms at this level of employment are obtaining them.[40]

Table 3.12 also reports the growth in the number of firms operating between the period 1966-1970 and 1986. The absolute growth in the number of firms is extraordinary, especially in fast growing sectors such as plastics and electronics. While the expansion of firms is considerably less than that of the growth of output (the "elasticity" of the number of firms with respect to constant price value added being typically below 10 percent) it is nevertheless an important component in the explanation of the growth of TFP. In particular, small firms are likely to have: (1) exhibited great flexibility in movement among product lines; (2) managed employees more intensively to obtain high and growing productivity from a given set of factors; and (3) allowed the benefits of considerable subcontracting and the realization of economies of scope. While the average size of existing firms did increase given the slower growth of the number of firms compared to value added, the small average size and the limited size of even the largest one-fifth of firms relative to international competitors, suggests that scale economies were unlikely to have been a major source of growing total factor productivity.

The small average size of firms may have contributed to the growth of TFP. Levy (1988) documents the ability of relatively small Taiwanese firms to adjust to changing product markets in goods as diverse as athletic shoes, computer keyboards, and personal computers. Such firms have been able to move towards products which have just been developed or towards existing ones whose relative price has increased. For the same level of total factor productivity in purely physical terms, the ability to avoid declining prices clearly adds to the TFP of a sector as real value added will be greater. An important permissive factor that allows a rapid change in industrial structure is the large supply of trading firms which search for new product niches appropriate for Taiwan's smaller producers. The effect of this complex structure is to enable firms to begin production with small amounts of capital for both production facilities and for "the acquisition of specialized market information." While this is similar to the superior choice of technique emphasis of earlier discussions of Taiwanese industrial organization, it highlights two additional features: the ease of entry for new innovative participants and the ability to avoid large investment in informational requirements which is arguably more constraining, especially in the Taiwan context, than obtaining financing.

In addition, Levy maintains that Taiwanese firms have benefitted considerably from the ability to avoid complex organizational decisions about how to vertically organize large numbers of workers and departments. Setting adequate wage incentive systems when large numbers of employees are involved is one of the most difficult of management tasks and is best left to a later stage of development, as is organization of many "job-shops" within a large firm. The ability to maintain a small firm structure surely contributed to productivity growth over the first three decades of industrialization though some concerns about its implication for the future are surfacing (see section 8). The Taiwanese structure enabled firms to engage in considerable subcontracting, thus allowing supplier firms to realize economies of scope in the utilization of specialized capital and labor.[41]

What features contributed to the remarkable elasticity of entrepreneurs and the establishment of trading networks? Levy emphasizes the extremely high level of education of the population, contrasting it favorably with Korea, in which the supply of trading firms was quite low. I would argue that other factors were also at work, but they would take us beyond the scope of this paper. The critical point is that a plausible argument can be made that, given the enormously rapid increase in the capital stock and the labor force shown in Section 2, it seems unlikely that a more centralized form of economic organization would have been able to absorb such re-sources without much lower marginal returns. As noted in Section 2, although computed TFP growth rates were very impressive, it is even more remarkable in contrast to countries that have achieved similar ratios of A^*/Q^* only with much lower rates of factor accumulation. The smaller firm structure permitted more detailed supervision and the avoidance of principal-agent problems, flexibility in product niches, subcontracting and the exploitation of economies of scope, and the tapping of the ability of many innovative skillful entrepreneurs who would have been consigned to employee status in a larger industrial structure.

While the importance of competitive market pressure as a source of pro-ductivity growth is surely important, the size structure seems to me to have played an equally important role. Moreover, Chen and Tang (1990) do not find any evidence that intersectoral growth rates in exports, one measure of competitive pressure, are significantly correlated with TFP growth rates. It is likely that all the pieces contributing to Taiwan's performance were in fact interconnected. Even if it becomes possible to document the productivity-promoting effects of the discipline imposed by exporting, it is very likely that the size structure was an important complementary condi-tion for such rapid industrial development, in particular, the high rates of TFP growth.

All of this is of more than just historical interest. A key question that often arises in the context of Taiwan's probable future performance is whether the emphasis on small-scale structure is likely to hurt it, an issue discussed in Section 8.

7. Services

In looking at cross-country patterns, Clark, Kuznets, Chenery, and others have noted that as per capita income grows, the share of the service sector in both employment and value added grows. This evolution reflects high income elasticities of demand for some household services (education, health, entertainment), growing demand for business services such as insurance and banking, and to some extent the fact that some services initially performed within other productive sectors, for example, accounting, become specialized and appear under the service rubric. Insofar as high income elasticities exist, and the services demanded are not tradeable, the share of services within Taiwan is likely to increase over time. During the 1980s the main growth in the share of services in GDP occurred in the business services such as finance, insurance, real estate, and banking (Table 3.13). Commerce (wholesale and retail trade, restaurants, and hotels) and transport (transport, storage, and communications) remained a roughly constant share of current price GDP. Nevertheless, despite its relative constancy, commerce required a significantly increased share of employment. This implies that the commerce sector had, on the margin, lower labor productivity compared with the rest of the economy.

For the first two service sectors, the share of value added is roughly similar to that of employment. Although marginal labor product may differ from average, it is likely that, in both sectors, marginal labor product is not far from the economy-wide average. In contrast, the average labor product

TABLE 3.13   The Share of the Service Sector in Value Added and Employment

Sector	VA_{1980}	VA_{1988}	N_{1980}	N_{1988}
Wholesale, retail, restaurants, hotels	.13	.14	.114	.154
Transport, storage, communications	.06	.06	.050	.045
Finance, insurance, real estate, business insurance	.13	.16	.020	.026

Source: Value added, National Income in Taiwan Area of the Republic of China, 1989, Table 1. Employment, Statistical Yearbook of the Republic of China, 1989, Table 9.

in business services (0.16/0.026) is about five times the economy-wide average, a level reflecting its higher capital-labor ratio rather than a higher level of total factor productivity. The greater capital-labor ratio reflects not fixed capital but working capital, presumably financial assets.[42]

To see the implications of the growth of the service sector, or some of its components, consider a simple transformation of equation (1), namely,

$$N^* = \left\{Q^* - A^* - bK^*\right\}/(1-b) \tag{4}$$

Assume that Q^* is set exogenously.[43] Then the absorption of labor in a given sector depends on the rate of growth of total factor productivity and the rate of growth of the capital stock in the sector. To obtain some insight on the evolution of Taiwan's service sector, consider the rates of growth of Q and N shown in Table 3.14 for the period 1980-1988.

For the two largest sectors, the growth rate of *labor* productivity shown in the last column is considerably less than that of *total factor productivity* for all manufacturing shown in Table 3.1, though for different periods. Moreover, the growth in labor productivity in these sectors reflects both the effect of capital deepening and growth in TFP. Assume that in Taiwan, as in other countries, A^* will be low or close to zero, in any case much lower than in manufacturing. Equation (4) implies that there will be a higher rate of growth of employment in services than in manufacturing. Moreover, one reason for the relatively high average product of labor in business services is the very high ratio of total assets per worker compared to other sectors. Thus, if the service sector grows, particularly its business service component as is widely forecast, it will require disproportionate shares of both labor and capital, reflecting both low values of A^* and high capital-labor ratios in the business service subsector. Given that the economy-wide value of total factor productivity growth rate is a weighted sector average, it seems likely that the changing structure will reduce the overall Taiwanese growth rate unless (1) the growth rate of TFP in manufacturing can be further increased or (2) TFP growth in services can be accelerated.

TABLE 3.14   Rates of Growth of Constant Price Value Added and Employment, 1980-1988

Sector	Value added	Employment	V^*-N^*
Commerce	9.6	6.6	3.0
Transport	9.1	1.4	7.7
Business	10.3	6.7	2.6

Source: Calculated from data underlying Table 3.13.

Greater productivity growth in the service sector is, however, likely to be difficult to achieve. TFP growth in this sector largely (but not completely) arises from entering service areas with high prices rather than improvement in physical productivity. Yet rents in this sector can be earned only from unusual knowledge including organizational ability, the devising of new financial services or software, and so on. While Taiwan may have the ability to obtain rents in some areas such as software development, it is likely to be difficult to generate such rents in most of these areas in competition with the huge financial service institutions that exist in the U.S., Japan, and a few of the European countries. As in manufacturing, the best promise (see below) is entry into niche markets.

8. Summary and Conclusions

It is perhaps inevitable, given Taiwan's remarkably successful growth, that some analysts will seek an Achilles heel in the process that may bring down a house of cards. Certainly, such a development would delight members of the "inward-orientation is best" chorus. Every time a transition point or a slowing of growth occurs, for example after the oil shocks, new variations on the "we told you so" theme are developed. Such well-wishers, having failed to see their dreams fulfilled in Japan, eagerly await the stagnation of Korea and Taiwan.

Even within Korea and Taiwan, analysts often maintain that the other country has chosen a better path. To evaluate the accuracy of such perceptions, a brief summary of the past decades and a broad view of likely evolution of the next two decades is necessary.

Both Korea and Taiwan entered world export markets by taking advantage of the relatively low wages of a fairly well educated labor force. In both countries, the quality of the labor force was continuously upgraded via high expenditures on education. The technology in the industries that formed the initial base of their export drives was relatively simple and was derived by obtaining non-proprietary information from machinery manufacturers and readily available trade literature, from returning nationals, from purchasers of exports, and so on. From the viewpoint of international trade theory, both countries were in a Hecksher-Ohlin world for much of the 1965-1980 period.

With the inevitable rise of unit labor costs, and the appearance of still lower wage countries seeking to export, Taiwan increased its share of more capital- and technology-intensive sectors in the 1980s, though many labor intensive activities continue to be of major importance. The latter have become more "technology"-intensive; for example, in athletic shoes the design component generates considerable product differentiation and they are no longer simple standardized goods. Both Korea and Taiwan entered the low end of the product spectrum of newer consumer goods such as microwave ovens, compact disc players, and color televisions. Often the technology was licensed from the Japanese. The overwhelming issue facing firms in Taiwan in the decade of the 1990s is their ability to identify new products that will enable them to maintain an inevitably slower but respectable rate of export growth. Services will play an increasing role but only a small fraction of them are likely to be characterized by high income per worker.

The critical export market will continue to be the U.S. While the European market offers potential for growth, the effort to integrate the East European countries into the planned 1992 unification will probably result in substantial investment to establish production in the Eastern European countries of many of the consumer products, from clothing to electronics, now produced in the Far East.

Given this tentative scenario, what are the prospects for the East Asian super-exporters and what conclusions may be reached about the appropriateness of their past evolution for addressing the next generation of problems? In particular, some analysts have argued that Korea's reliance on the chaebol confers an advantage that the smaller average size firms in Taiwan cannot match. Others have asserted that Taiwan's smaller firms are likely to be more nimble in responding to rapidly changing conditions.

There are two issues related to firm size. First, it is increasingly clear that the larger Korean firms provide an obvious target for extracting larger wage-increases. Korea's unit labor costs are thus likely to rise more rapidly than those in Taiwan. Second, a new generation of products will require new technical knowledge, usually based on proprietary information. In both Korea and Taiwan, the era of low-cost acquisition of non-proprietary knowledge is coming to a close. While both countries have done brilliantly in many sectors at moving towards best world practice, the move into new product areas will be vigorously contested by OECD firms.

It is not clear *a priori* whether entry into new product markets will be better served by large or small firms. Insofar as there is a fixed cost component in licensing fees as well as largely fixed costs of absorbing the technology, firms that can allocate these over larger production runs will derive an advantage. Moreover, large firms with many products in their portfolio will have a lower firm-wide risk than smaller one or two product firms. However, the former may encounter reluctance to share new technology by the developers of the technology insofar as they present a threat in third markets given their size. In contrast, the smaller Taiwanese firms may encounter more willingness to license given the lesser threat they pose.

Other supposed differences between small and large firms are equally ambiguous. Thus, the many studies designed to investigate the Schumpeterian hypothesis about differential innovative success in large and small firms have been largely inconclusive. Moreover, there are no studies of which I am aware that investigate productivity growth by firm size. Hence, despite the fashionable trend asserting the probable superior performance of Korea given its industrial organization, the argument is far from compelling.

Taiwanese firms will undoubtedly face an increasingly difficult world in the 1990s. New product areas will have to be identified, their characteristics and production technology understood, and become the basis for another set of exports. This path is likely to be much more difficult than that of the past quarter-century. Moreover, the very success of the East Asian model has led to exporting becoming the goal of many countries, not least in some of the Latin American NICs whose debt service problems have led to new government policies that make exporting a more profitable activity compared to domestic sales.[45]

Although it is hard to document, it is fairly clear that product cycles are becoming increasingly short for many of the products in which Taiwanese firms are interested. When compact disk players were introduced in 1983, their price was about US$1,200 and they were largely produced by Japan and Holland. By 1990, retail prices for typical mass market players have declined to about US$200, with *ex factory* prices being less than half of this. Such rapid learning leaves very small profit margins in many newer consumer products after a very short period of production. Indeed, it seems likely that firms that were not producing CD players between 1983 and 1986 missed the bulk of profits. Yet, the technology in comparable new industries may become more difficult to acquire in the early period of production as developers try to recoup increasingly large research expenses. For example, in high density television, once a standard is adopted in the U.S., the bulk of profits are likely to accrue to the developers in the first few years of sales.

In view of this, the evolving comparative advantage of Taiwanese firms is likely to be in market niches that are being abandoned in the developed countries rather than in the newest consumer or producer products. In such markets, the relative smallness and the ability to act quickly of Taiwanese firms may confer an important advantage. With respect to new products, there is likely to be a temptation to try to compete in some of the advanced areas, such as the development of new chips. While this might be done as part of a technology sharing consortium, going it alone is likely to be exceptionally expensive. To take one example, IBM and Siemens have recently announced plans to undertake joint research on the production of 64 megabyte chips. Their combined annual sales are US$130 billion, yet neither is willing to undertake the new technology by itself.

The IBM-Siemens example is also instructive in another dimension. It is occasionally argued that a country must participate in the development of a current technology in order to keep its options open for the next generation. Yet the new x-ray lithography method being explored for the production of the 64 megabyte chip is totally different from that employed for the 256K and one megabyte chip. The losses incurred by latecomers to the latter market, particularly by Korean firms, cannot be viewed as an investment for the next stage. Their knowledge simply doesn't confer any advantage.

It seems unlikely that the growth rate of supply in Taiwanese manufacturing and services can be maintained at its rate of the past quarter-century. The likely shift to services will slow the rate of growth of capital given its higher capital-output ratio. The rapid growth rate of TFP in manufacturing is likely to slow because of the decline in rents accruing to the manufacturing sector. Moreover, part of TFP growth in manufacturing was attributable to the import of equipment embodying new technology, and some was ascribed to disembodied knowledge obtained from abroad. Given the relative modernity of its industrial equipment, the potential gains from importing new equipment are perforce more limited. Taiwan is in the enviable position of being relatively advanced. Hence, obtaining new equipment in existing industries is not likely to be a major source of productivity growth. While benefiting from new product research abroad will be possible, it will become increasingly expensive. Similarly, process research which is typically more easily appropriated by developers will become more expensive.

Joint ventures or technology agreements in which Taiwanese firms deploy their considerable production engineering skills combined with (still) relatively low-cost labor to produce products designed abroad is one possible direction. It avoids the pitfalls of entering product markets which experience rapid change as a result of intensive research, development, and design expenditures by major firms in the OECD countries. The great difficulties being encountered by Korea's huge Hyundai automobile manufacturing operation is instructive. After extraordinarily successful penetration of the U.S. market with a low-priced car, its sales have fallen precipitously as a result of the inability to introduce design changes. Although the possibility of increasing the size of the machinery sector is currently being discussed in Taiwan, the design issue suggests caution.[46]

A large literature attests to the slowdown in the rate of growth of total factor productivity in the OECD countries, including Japan, since 1973. Taiwan has averted this decrease through a variety of mechanisms discussed in this paper that allowed it to maintain high rates of TFP growth. But many of these are unlikely to be as important in the future as Taiwanese firms are already close to the best practice frontier in existing industries. In sum, the opportunities to increase productivity by inexpensive acquisition of external knowledge will inevitably decline. While a prospective decline in TFP growth rates could be offset by faster capital accumulation, it is not clear that the requisite decrease in consumption levels would be welfare enhancing at Taiwan's current levels of per capita income. As in Japan, increased levels of social satisfaction may militate in favor of a gradual shift towards the production of non-tradeable goods.

Taiwan in the 1990s thus faces difficult problems of competing in an increasingly complex world economy. Its problems now closely resemble those of the OECD countries in terms of where to fit into the evolving world economy. While there are dilemmas ahead, 140 governments surely wish they faced the future with the extraordinary achievements of Taiwan behind them.

Notes

1. In the sense that they exhibited similar TFP in their new locale as in the original one.

2. Pack (1988) reviews the available evidence on TFP growth for LDCs. For most LDCs for varying periods, TFP growth has been negligible.

3. An alternative is to examine the rates of return on investment in those sectors fostered by government policy, an empirically difficult path.

4. One obvious source of different factor choices is differential interest rates which result in differing user cost of capital and wages that differ by firm size.

5. Output will be larger, for a given capital stock, if the socially appropriate capital-labor ratio is chosen rather than if a higher capital-labor ratio is chosen.

6. Intersectoral variation in effective protection rates were already low by 1968 (Hsing 1970), corroborated by Lee and Liang (1982) for 1972. Different authors have varying views of the impact of reforms leading to rapid export growth. See, for example, Galenson (1979) and Kuo and Fei (1985).

7. There may be increases in technical efficiency if expansion in capacity is achieved with larger plant size relative to that which would have been built if sales were largely oriented to the domestic market. These gains will be particularly large if the initial structure is primarily small-scale and there is a substantial shift in typical plant size to one taking advantage of scale economies. As discussed in Section 7, the size of firms expanded over the period but the industrial structure does not imply that large gains from scale economies were obtained. Moreover, with respect to industrial sectors, Taiwan did not experience a large concentration of new production in those industries in which static scale economies are important, such as basic metals and chemicals.

8. The factor shares were obtained from *Statistical Yearbook of the Republic of China*, various years. Kuo also estimates the rate of technical change by estimating a Cobb-Douglas production function rather than weighting input growth rates by factor shares, assumed to reflect the elasticity of output with respect to each share. She finds lower values for A^* in the 1961-1980 period but a parallel decline from the earlier period.

9. In long term growth models capital embodiment does not affect the steady-state rate of growth, at least with a Cobb-Douglas production function (Phelps 1962). However, the intermediate-term growth rate will be affected by rates of embodiment.

10. Kuznets (1979, p. 97) explicitly drew attention to the fact that investment in equipment would be a major determinant of Taiwanese productivity growth though he did not distinguish between domestic and imported capital.

11. The breakdown of investment among equipment and structures is available for aggregate investment but not for investment by one digit sectors. See *National Income in Taiwan Area of the Republic of China*, 1989, Directorate-General of Budget, Accounting and Statistics, Executive Yuan, Republic of China, Table 15.

12. See, for example, Kuznets (1966).

13. See Ho (1978) and Kuo (1983) for evidence on the labor intensiveness of exports.

14. On the sources of success of the initial export drive see Fei and Kuo (1985), Ranis (1979), and Scott (1979).

15. Liu (1987, Chapter 5) presents data culled from biographical information of executives about the sectors in which they are engaged, though evidence on their earlier experience is not available.

16. Scott (1979, pp. 351-57) provides substantial evidence for this view for the period through 1975. He also examines (pp. 357-364) the cost structure of a number of major exporting sectors and shows the decisive role of low wages and the availability of intermediate inputs at international prices.

17. This is the thrust of Ranis' (1979) argument that the industrial sector succeeded because factor endowments were allowed to "speak."

18. Current price input-output tables are presented in various issues of *The Statistical Yearbook of the Republic of China*, an annual published by the Directorate-General of Budget, Accounting and Statistics.

19. The anomaly would disappear if an additional instrument of government policy such as explicit export targeting (as in Korea) were used systematically (Pack and Westphal 1986). However, I have found no evidence of such additional instruments in the existing literature though Wade (1990) reports some policies that might have such effects.

20. Little (1979) notes the income of domestic purchasers is affected to a considerable degree by income received from exporting, hence the

accounting partition between exports and domestic demand as a source of changing structure is somewhat arbitrary.

21. Little (1979) notes that the Mainland government, once established on Taiwan, owed no allegiance to *Taiwanese* landlords.

22. The undercutting of social and political opposition to industrialization may be the best defense of the "big push" argument of Rosenstein-Rodan and others. Whereas they were concerned with the ability to escape a low-level equilibrium trap, whether as a result of the growth of supply not conforming to existing income elasticities of demand or Malthusian concerns, three decades of additional observation suggest that overcoming the opposition of recipients of rents and those bearing the costs of transition from the current regime is more important.

23. Also see deMelo (1985) and Kuo (1983).

24. Levy (1988) provides evidence that Taiwanese export traders were also very important in this process. See also Section 6 below.

25. See, for example, the *Wall Street Journal*, June 1, 1990.

26. For an exhaustive study of the role of MNCs in Taiwan through the late 1970s and their motives for locating in Taiwan see Ranis and Schive (1985). Cohen (1975) provides case study material on MNCs in Taiwan and other Asian countries.

27. For a model of the potential beneficial impact of MNCs on local knowledge see Findlay (1974).

28. Scitovsky (1985) suggests that the small size structure of firms encouraged workers to begin their own firms and made it easier to accumulate enough capital through informal channels to finance the establishment of the firms. He also links this phenomenon to the rapid growth in the household saving rate.

29. Westphal and I (1986) have pointed out in the case of Korea that many of the policies pursued by the East Asian NICs are very similar to those pursued by the import substituting countries, in this case local content requirements. The difference in their success may be due to the more appropriate economic environment, for example, local suppliers in Taiwan being able to obtain specialized inputs without applying for licenses.

30. The role of education is discussed below.

31. For a very detailed list with large numbers of examples culled from government documents, newspapers, and periodicals see Wade (1990).

32. *National Income in Taiwan Area of the Republic of China, 1989*, Directorate-General of Budget, Accounting and Statistics, Executive Yuan, Republic of China, Table 3.

33. *Ibid.*, Table 14.

34. Significance tests have been carried out employing the standard deviations reported by Syrquin (1989). It is possible, of course, that the other countries in the study were all pursuing policies to encourage a simi-

lar evolution. Hence, Taiwan's policy may have altered the "natural" pattern of its development but not have shown up in such comparisons. Other explanations can be offered given the limitations of cross-national comparisons. But I suspect that the broad conclusions would stand up to a more finely honed empirical analysis, namely, that at the two-digit level Taiwan's sectoral evolution appears similar to that of other countries.

35. The value of all assets, rather than fixed assets per worker, could also be used, but the correlation is .99. The use of capital-labor ratios at historical cost is likely to be a fairly good indicator of true capital-labor ratios insofar as much of the equipment in each sector has been installed relatively recently and there is no reason to believe that machinery price inflation has differed significantly across various purchasing sectors. Nevertheless, in the absence of constant price estimates of capital stock, the comparisons in the text should be viewed as subject to some measure of error.

36. Some of these institutions are briefly described by Li (1988).

37. In an interesting paper analyzing the potential impact of industrial policy, Justman and Teubal argue that new sectors will exhibit higher *levels* of TFP.

38. Nelson (1964) emphasizes this important reallocative role of investment.

39. There is some inconsistency in the methodology employed. If indeed there are scale economies, observed factor shares do not necessarily equal elasticities of output with respect to each factor, hence the method for obtaining weighted factor growth is dubious.

40. For comparative international data and discussion see Berry (1990) and Lee (1990).

41. For examples of the costs in machinery production of the inability to engage in subcontracting and the consequent need to establish "captive" internal production facilities that are inadequately employed see Pack (1981).

42. *The Report on 1986 Industrial and Commercial Census, General Report*, Table 19 reports that net assets per person engaged in business services is roughly 34 fold that in all manufacturing.

43. In fact, Q is endogenous, depending on both income and price elasticities of demand.

44. I am not a partisan of the new export pessimism for all LDCs as a group. However, many of the specific industrial product markets, particularly the ones in which Taiwan has excelled, are attractive to many of the NICs and may become the arena for fierce competition.

45. See Pack (1981) for a discussion about the prospects of NICs, including Taiwan, in the machinery sector.

References

Baily, Martin Neal, and Margaret M. Blair. 1988. "Productivity and American Management," in Martin Neal Baily *et al.*, *American Living Standards, Challenges and Threats*. Washington, D.C.: The Brookings Institution.

Behrman, Jere. 1990. "Thoughts on Human Resource Led Development Possibilities." Processed, University of Pennsylvania.

Berry, R. A. 1990. "Intra-industry Firm Heterogeneity in the Analysis of Trade and Development Allowing for Small and Medium Enterprises," in G. Helleiner, ed., *Trade Policies, Industrialization and Development: New Perspectives*. London: Oxford University Press.

Chen, Tain-Jy, and De-Piao Tang. 1990. "Export Performance and Productivity Growth: The Case of Taiwan." *Economic Development and Cultural Change* 38: 577-86.

Chenery, Hollis B., and Moshe Syrquin. 1986. "Typical Patterns of Transformation," in H. Chenery, S. Robinson, M. Syrquin, *Industrialization and Growth: A Comparative Study*. New York: Oxford University Press.

Cohen, Benjamin I. 1975. *Multinational Firms and Asian Exports*. New Haven: Yale University Press.

deMelo, Jaime. 1985. "Sources of Growth and Structural Change in the Republic of Korea and Taiwan: Some Comparisons," in V. Corbo, A. O. Krueger, and F. Ossa, eds., *Export-Oriented Development Strategies*. Boulder, CO: Westview Press.

Deyo, Frederic C. 1988. *The Political Economy of the New Asian Industrialism*. Ithaca: Cornell University Press.

Fei, John C. H., Gustav Ranis, and Shirley W. Kuo. 1979. *Growth With Equity: The Taiwan Case*. New York: Oxford University Press.

Fields, Gary. 1985. "Industrialization and Employment in Hong Kong, Korea, Singapore, and Taiwan," in Walter Galenson, ed., *Foreign Trade and Investment*. Madison: University of Wisconsin Press.

Hsing, Mo-Huan, John H. Power, and Gerardo P. Sicat. 1970. *Taiwan and the Philippines, Industrialization and Trade Policies*. London: Oxford University Press.

Ho, Samuel P. S. 1978. *Economic Development of Taiwan, 1860-1970*. New Haven: Yale University Press.

_____. 1980. "Small-Scale Enterprises in Korea and Taiwan." World Bank Staff Working Paper No. 384, The World Bank, Washington D.C.

Hulten, Charles, Jr. 1989. "The Embodiment Hypothesis Revisited." Processed, University of Maryland.

Justman, M., and Morris Teubal. 1990. "The Structuralist Perspective to Economic Growth and Development: Conceptual Foundations and Policy Implications," in R. Evenson and G. Ranis, eds., *Science and Technology in Developing Countries*. Boulder, CO: Westview Press.

Kubo, Yuji, Jaime deMelo, Sherman Robinson, and Moshe Syrquin. 1986. "Interdependence and Industrial Structure," in H. Chenery, S. Robinson, M. Syrquin, *Industrialization and Growth: A Comparative Study*. New York: Oxford University Press.

Kuo, Shirley W. Y. 1983. *The Taiwan Economy in Transition*. Boulder, CO: Westview Press.

Kuo, Shirley W. Y. and John C. H. Fei. 1985. "Causes and Roles of Export Expansion in the Republic of China," in Walter Galenson, ed., *Foreign Trade and Investment*. Madison: University of Wisconsin Press.

Kuznets, Paul. 1988. "An East Asian Model of Economic Development," Japan, Taiwan, and South Korea." *Economic Development and Cultural Change* 36: S11-S44.

Kuznets, Simon. 1966. *Modern Economic Growth*. New Haven: Yale University Press.

————. 1979. "Growth and Structural Shifts," in W. Galenson, ed., *Economic Growth and Structural Change in Taiwan*. Ithaca: Cornell University Press.

Lall, Sanjaya. 1987. *Learning to Industrialize*. London: Macmillan.

Lee, Norman. 1990. "Market Structure and Trade in Developing Countries," in G. Helleiner, ed., *Trade Policies, Industrialization and Development: New Perspectives*. London: Oxford University Press.

Lee, T. H. and Kuo-Shu Liang. 1982. "Taiwan," in B. Balassa and associates, *Development Strategies in Semi-industrial Countries*. Baltimore: Johns Hopkins.

Levy, Brian. 1988. "Korea and Taiwan as International Competitors." *The Columbia Journal of World Business*, Summer.

Li, K. T. 1988. *The Evolution of Policy Behind Taiwan's Development Success*. New Haven: Yale University Press.

Liang, Kuo-shu, and Ching-ing Hou Liang. 1988. "Development Policy Formation and Future Policy Priorities in the Republic of China." *Economic Development and Cultural Change* 36: S67-S102.

Little, I. M. D. 1979. "An Economic Reconnaissance," in W. Galenson, ed., *Economic Growth and Structural Change in Taiwan*. Ithaca: Cornell University Press.

Liu, Alan P. L. 1987. *Phoenix and the Lame Lion modernization in Taiwan and Mainland China 1950-80*. Stanford, CA: Hoover Institution Press.

National Income in Taiwan Area, the Republic of China. 1989. Taipei: Directorate-General of Budget, Accounting and Statistics, Executive Yuan.

Nelson, Richard R. 1964. "Aggregate Production Functions." *American Economic Review* 54: 575-606.

_____. 1973. "Recent Exercises in Growth Accounting: New Understanding or Dead End." *American Economic Review* 73: 462-468.

_____. 1981. "Research on Productivity Growth and Productivity Differences." *Journal of Economic Literature* 19: 1029-64.

Olson, Mancur. 1982. *The Rise and Decline of Nations.* New Haven: Yale University Press.

Pack, Howard. 1981. "Fostering the Capital-Goods Sector in LDCs." *World Development.* Pp. 227-250.

_____. 1987. *Productivity, Technology, and Industrial Development.* New York: Oxford University Press.

_____. 1988. "Industrialization and Trade," in Hollis B. Chenery and T. N. Srinivasan, eds., *Handbook of Development Economics.* Amsterdam: North-Holland.

Pack, Howard, and Larry E. Westphal. 1986. "Industrial Strategy and Technological Change: theory vs reality." *Journal of Development Economics* 22: 87-128.

Phelps, E. S. 1962. "The New View of Investment: A Neoclassical Analysis." *Quarterly Journal of Economics* 76: 548-567.

Ranis, Gustav. 1979. "Industrial Development," in W. Galenson, ed., *Economic Growth and Structural Change in Taiwan.* Ithaca: Cornell University Press.

Ranis, Gustav, and Chi Schive. 1985. "Direct Foreign Investment in Taiwan's Development," in Walter Galenson, ed., *Foreign Trade and Investment.* Madison: University of Wisconsin Press.

The Report on 1986 Industrial and Commercial Census of Taiwan. 1986. Taipei: Committee on Industrial and Commercial Census of Taiwan, Executive Yuan.

Scitovsky, Tibor. 1985. "Economic Development in Taiwan and South Korea." *Food Research Institute Studies* 19: 215-64.

Scott, Maurice. 1979. "Foreign Trade," in W. Galenson, ed., *Economic Growth and Structural Change in Taiwan.* Ithaca: Cornell University Press.

Statistical Yearbook of the Republic of China. 1989. Taipei: Directorate-General of Budget, Accounting and Statistics, Executive Yuan.

Syrquin, Moshe. 1989. "On Linkages." Discussion Paper 8925, Department of Economics and Business Administration, Bar Ilan University, Ramat Gan, Israel.

Taiwan Statistical Data Book. 1989. Taipei: Council for International Economic Cooperation and Development.

Thorbecke, Eric. 1979. "Agricultural Development," in W. Galenson, ed., *Economic Growth and Structural Change in Taiwan.* Ithaca: Cornell University Press.

Tsiang, S. C., and Rong-I Wu. 1985. "Foreign Trade and Investment as Boosters for Take Off: The Experiences of the Four Asian Newly Industrializing Countries," in Walter Galenson, ed., *Foreign Trade and Investment*. Madison: University of Wisconsin Press.

Wade, Robert. 1990. *Governing the Market: Economic Theory and Taiwan's Industrial Policies*. Princeton, NJ: Princeton University Press.

Wall Street Journal, June 1, 1990, "Taiwan, Long Noted for Cheap Imitations, Becomes an Innovator."

Westphal, Larry E., Yung Rhee, and Garry Pursell. 1981. "Korean Industrial Competence: Where it Came From." World Bank Staff Working Paper 469, Washington D.C.

Yearbook of Earnings and Productivity Statistics, Taiwan Area, Republic of China. 1988. Taipei: Directorate-General of Budget, Accounting and Statistics, Executive Yuan.

A
Agricultural Policy

[3]

Structural Change in Taiwan's Agricultural Economy*

Sophia Wu Huang
U.S. Department of Agriculture

I. Introduction

Taiwan's near double-digit rate of economic growth since the 1960s dramatically transformed a relatively impoverished agrarian society into a relatively affluent industrial and export-led economy. However, the agricultural sector, once the backbone of the economy, has rapidly lost ground. Gone is the buoyant period before the 1970s when agriculture was the main foreign exchange earner and contributed greatly to Taiwan's economic development. Agriculture has slowly declined and increasingly depends for its survival on government protection as the 1990s get under way.

While Taiwan has become a showcase of economic development, the changing perceptions of its role in the international economy also have made its agricultural trade policy a focal point of trade friction. Like Japan and South Korea, Taiwan is a rich market that has attracted the attention of world agribusiness. It has been accused of unfair trade practices and has been under increasing pressure to open up its agricultural market. This pressure was intensified in the mid-1980s when the trade surplus with the United States, the largest market for Taiwan's exports, grew rapidly. The trade surplus with the United States averaged $12.4 billion during 1985–89, although it decreased to $9.1 billion in 1990.

As Taiwan's agricultural sector comes under heavy internal and external pressure, the issues of structural adjustment have become increasingly important and will occupy government policy decision making for years to come. How will Taiwan's agriculture of small family farms survive? What are the barriers to future structural adjustments? What is the direction of Taiwan's future agricultural policy? To throw some light on these questions, a major part of this article will recapitulate the course of Taiwan's structural change in agriculture since 1960. Because the government has always played an important role in Taiwan's economic development, a discussion of the evolution of agricultural policy and programs is also included.

II. Structural Changes in Agriculture

The center of gravity of Taiwan's economy has shifted rapidly away from agriculture during the fast economic development of the past decades. Agriculture's contribution to the net domestic product (NDP) decreased from 30% in 1960–64 to 6% in 1985–89, and agricultural trade changed from a yearly average surplus of $54 million (in nominal value) to a deficit of $1.6 billion over the same period. Over this period, agricultural production, consumption, trade, farm operations, and income have changed dramatically.

The materials discussed in this section are based mainly on data compiled in tables 1 and 2, in which average figures for each 5-year subperiod are presented. Table 1 shows the structural changes of Taiwan's agricultural production, consumption, and trade, while table 2 shows the changes in agricultural farm size, employment, and income. Agriculture will be restricted to the conventional definition of crops and livestock, excluding forestry and fishery unless otherwise specified, partly because of the relative importance of crops and livestock in the economy and partly because the primary focus is on the peasant economy to which the majority of crop and livestock farmers belong.

Increased High-Value Products in Production and Consumption
Taiwan's agriculture showed impressive growth during the 1950s and 1960s, with an average annual growth rate of gross agricultural production reaching more than 6% in the 1950s and about 5% in the 1960s (including forestry and fishery sectors).[1] Even in the 1970s, when agriculture began to encounter structural change problems, its gross production still had a near 5% growth rate, in part because of rapid growth in the livestock industry. In the 1980s, however, the growth rate was clearly much slower than before—only about 2%. The growth rate among different sectors also varied. Growth in livestock was much faster than for crops, while fruits and vegetables had the highest growth rate in the crop sector. As a result, the composition of agricultural production shifted considerably during the past decades.

In addition to backyard livestock raising, Taiwan's agricultural production used to depend primarily on a few crops. Rice, sweet potatoes, and sugarcane were traditionally the predominant crops. The value share of these crops in total crop and livestock products, however, has dropped steadily. The share of rice decreased from 40.2% in 1960–64 to about 17.3% in 1985–89, while the share of sugarcane decreased from 6.6% to 3.9%, and sweet potatoes from 7.7% to 0.6%.

Rice is still the dominant crop in Taiwan, but its relative impor-

TABLE 1

TAIWAN'S AGRICULTURAL PRODUCTION, CONSUMPTION, AND TRADE

	1960–64	1965–69	1970–74	1975–79	1980–84	1985–89
Agricultural produc-tion (%):*						
Share in NDP	29.7	23.6	15.1	12.5	8.7	6.3
Production index (86 = 100)	41.1	53.8	66.4	80.6	92.4	105.5
Production growth rate	4.5	4.8	4.2	5.0	1.7	2.4
Percentage of crop-livestock value:						
Crops	74.5	73.6	67.5	64.1	62.6	59.7
Rice	40.2	35.2	30.7	29.1	24.4	17.3
Sugar	6.6	4.8	4.5	5.7	4.0	3.9
Sweet potatoes	7.7	7.7	5.7	2.9	1.6	.6
Fruits and vegeta-bles	8.2	14.7	17.0	18.0	24.4	28.0
Others	11.8	11.2	9.6	8.4	8.2	9.9
Livestock and products	25.5	26.4	32.5	35.9	37.4	40.3
Hogs	17.7	17.2	20.7	20.5	20.3	24.9
Chickens and eggs	3.2	4.7	5.9	9.6	11.4	11.1
Others	4.6	4.5	5.9	5.8	5.7	4.3
Per capita consumption (kg):						
Rice	134.2	138.1	133.3	120.6	92.8	75.9
Sweet potatoes	53.8	38.9	15.5	7.1	2.7	1.1
Meats	16.8	23.8	27.0	34.1	46.0	57.4
Eggs	1.8	3.0	4.4	6.6	9.3	11.3
Fish	25.7	29.0	35.0	36.1	35.6	43.0
Milk	6.3	6.0	12.4	20.2	27.1	34.8
Vegetables	58.3	60.9	91.8	118.6	121.3	123.1
Fruits	20.4	34.5	49.1	59.1	73.1	94.7
Agricultural exports (1,000 tons):						
Rice	88.5	110.6	21.8	159.4	280.4	125.1
Sugar and products	712.9	758.6	509.1	455.1	275.2	85.6
Hogs and pork	3.1	2.3	16.3	18.4	30.2	102.9
Processed fruits and vegetables	95.8	211.6	363.5	505.8	517.4	391.0
Agricultural imports (1,000 tons):						
Corn	4.5	200.8	968.5	2,003.0	2,876.3	3,721.1
Soybeans	142.8	306.8	601.7	869.0	1,192.2	1,814.7
Cotton	53.6	82.4	148.6	201.8	256.6	382.4
Hides and leather	3.4	7.2	16.3	41.0	114.1	190.1
Wheat	298.2	420.3	632.7	613.2	675.7	834.6
Beef	0	0	.8	1.2	1.9	3.4
Dairy products	4.2	9.5	24.6	53.5	66.0	87.6
Fruits and nuts	2.1	6.7	10.2	22.2	227.4	162.0
Vegetables	9.6	24.0	37.0	50.6	71.2	261.0
Agricultural trade balance (millions of dollars at current value):*						
Exports	165.6	268.2	540.0	1,246.2	1,937.6	3,162.8
Imports	111.2	203.8	712.6	1,855.4	3,416.2	4,730.8
Balance	54.4	64.4	−172.6	−609.2	−1,478.6	−1,568.0
Share of agricultural exports (%)*	61.9	41.7	17.6	12.9	8.2	6.5

SOURCES.—*Taiwan Statistical Data Book* (Taipei: Council for Economic Planning and Development, 1990); *Taiwan Food Balance Sheet* (Taipei: Council of Agriculture, 1960–89); *Basic Agricultural Statistics* (Taipei: Council of Agriculture, 1990); *Taiwan Agricultural Yearbook* (Taichung: Taiwan Provincial Department of Agriculture and Forestry, 1960–90).

* Including agriculture, forestry, and fishery.

TABLE 2

TAIWAN'S AGRICULTURAL FARM SIZE, EMPLOYMENT, AND INCOME

	1960–64	1965–69	1970–74	1975–79	1980–84	1985–89
Farm size:						
Cultivated land (1,000 ha)	873	901	904	919	897	890
Planted area (1,000 ha)	1,623	1,687	1,615	1,575	1,359	1,237
Farm households (thousands)	811	867	904	906	838	754
Average farm size (ha)*	1.08	1.04	1.00	1.01	1.07	1.18
Under 1 ha (%)	66.5	66.7	71.5	71.3	72.6	72.6
1–3 ha (%)	30.3	29.7	25.3	26.1	24 9	24.8
Over 3 ha (%)	3.3	3.6	3.2	2.6	2.5	2.6
Multiple crop index (%)†	186	187	178	172	151	139
Agricultural employment:						
Percentage of total employment	50.9	42.8	33.3	26.5	18.7	15.3
Agricultural employment (thousands)	1,806	1,731	1,660	1,570	1,284	1,203
15–29 years old (%)	N.A.	39.6	31.1	26.7	20.6	15.9
30–59 years old (%)	N.A.	57.3	66.0	67.2	68.9	71.6
60 years old and over (%)	N.A.	3.1	2.9	6.1	10.4	12.4
Composition of crop farms:*						
Farm households (thousands)	776	N.A.	879	N.A.	872	772
Full-time farms (%)	49.3	N.A.	31.2	N.A.	9.0	11.4
Part-time farms (%)	50.7	N.A.	68.8	N.A.	91.0	88.6
Class I part-time (%)	30.9	N.A.	42.0	N.A.	36.0	19.8
Class II part-time (%)	19.8	N.A.	26.8	N.A.	55.0	68.8
Composition of incomes:‡						
Farmer income (1,000 NT$)	N.A.	32.1	52.5	115.7	232.1	309.7
Net agricultural income (%)	N.A.	59.3	46.6	38.5	33.8	37.2
Nonagricultural income (%)	N.A.	40.7	53.4	61.5	66.2	62.8
Farm-urban laborers' incomes:§						
Per capita	N.A.	79	78	81	83	87
Per household	N.A.	101	91	89	84	79

SOURCE.—*Basic Agricultural Statistics* (Taipei: Council of Agriculture, 1990).
* Data refer to the beginning year of each period.
† The ratio of planted area to cultivated area.
‡ Data for 1965–69 are the average of 1966 and 1968.
§ The ratio of farm to urban laborers' income.

Sophia Wu Huang   47

tance has diminished substantially. While increased production costs led to the uncompetitiveness of Taiwan's rice in the world market, fast economic growth ended the role of rice as a "wage good" in the domestic market. Even with the almost uninterrupted increase of postwar rice production up to 1968, the decreased importance of rice production was obvious. The riceland diversion program initiated in 1984, which cut rice production by more than one-fourth during 1984–90, further accelerated the decline.

Drastic changes also occurred in the sugar industry, which was the world's third-largest producer in 1934–35, next to India and Cuba. Sugar exports were once vitally important to the economy. Because of volatile international prices and high production costs, the volume of Taiwan's sugar exports have headed downward since the 1970s. Taiwan has been phasing out its sugar operations particularly since the 1980s when its export-oriented sugar policy was gradually changed to focus mainly on the domestic market. As a result, the importance of sugar production diminished quickly.

The changes in sweet potatoes, once the most important feedstuff for hog raising and, next to rice, an important staple especially for the poor, were as dramatic as those for rice and sugar. The commercialization of the hog industry since the 1970s has resulted in replacing sweet potatoes with imported coarse grains in modern livestock rations. In addition, as a result of fast economic growth since the mid-1960s, people have changed their diets from sweet potatoes to other high-value foods. As a result, planted acreage of sweet potatoes has dropped from about 14%–15% of Taiwan's total crop area before the 1970s to only 1% in 1990.

On the other hand, the production of hogs and chickens, under the government's guidance and with the help of imported coarse grains and soybeans, has been transformed from traditional backyard sideline farm operations into large business enterprises. The hog industry has grown rapidly ever since the government in 1967 modified its trade regulations by reclassifying imports of coarse grains and soybeans from the "controlled" to the "permitted" category. Pork became the leading agricultural export in the late 1980s, and hog production value surpassed rice as the most valuable agricultural product in 1985–89. The value share of hog production in total crop and livestock products increased from 17.7% in 1960–64 to 24.9% in 1985–89. Similarly, the share of chickens and eggs grew from 3.2% to 11.1% during the same period. Taiwan's poultry production, however, has not yet achieved international competitiveness. The production share of fruits and vegetables has also grown rapidly to supply the increasing domestic and sometimes foreign demand; the value share of fruits and vegetables increased from 8.2% in 1960–64 to 28% in 1985–89.

The changes in agricultural production, together with the relaxation of import controls, are closely related to the changing patterns
of food consumption. Because of increasing income, people can afford
to consume more high-value products, such as meats, and a wider
variety of foods than ever before. Among the significant changes, per
capita consumption of rice, the main staple for the majority of people
in Taiwan, increased in the 1960s but decreased steadily since then
from about 138 kilograms in 1965–69 to only 76 kilograms in 1985–89.
Per capita consumption of sweet potatoes decreased drastically from
54 kilograms in 1960–64 to 1 kilogram in 1985–89. Per capita consumption of meats increased from 17 kilograms in 1960–64 to 57 kilograms
in 1985–89, fishery products from 26 to 43 kilograms, fruits from 20 to
95 kilograms, and vegetables from 58 to 123 kilograms over the same
period (all in retail weight).

Agricultural Trade Deficits Widened
Taiwan began its economic development as an agricultural exporter.
Agricultural exports, once the main source of foreign exchange earnings, contributed much in financing the required capital goods imports
for economic development. Taiwan's agricultural exports, however,
are increasingly overwhelmed by the exports from the rest of the economy. The role of agricultural exports diminished drastically from accounting for 61.9% of the value of Taiwan's total exports in 1960–64
(it was about 90% in the 1950s) to only 6.5% in 1985–89. In particular,
rising production costs have caused many of the formerly prominent
agricultural exports to lose ground in the international markets. More
recently, a near 50% appreciation in Taiwan's dollar against the U.S.
dollar between 1985 and 1989 has put substantial pressure on some of
Taiwan's export-oriented farm products.[2]
    In the 1950s, Taiwan exported rice, mainly to Japan, in exchange
for fertilizers. Rice exports, however, have decreased substantially
since the early 1960s because of Japan's self-sufficiency in rice production. Rice exports increased after 1977 in order to dispose of surpluses
through heavy government subsidies but were finally restrained by the
5-year U.S.-Taiwan rice agreement in 1984. Rice exports have been
small since then because of uncompetitive prices and concern over the
reaction from the U.S. rice industry, even though the agreement was
not renewed after its expiration in December 1988.
    More than rice, sugar was an export-oriented commodity and the
main foreign exchange earner. About 86% of sugar production during
the two decades of the 1950s and 1960s was for export; sugar exports
still accounted for more than half of Taiwan's total export earnings
until 1958.[3] Sugar's export share, however, dropped to a single digit
by the mid-1960s and has declined almost continuously since then be-

cause of decreased sugar exports and the fast growth of Taiwan's overall trade.

While the traditional exports of sugar and rice declined, new agricultural exports—processed fruits and vegetables, especially canned products—emerged.[4] Beginning with canned pineapple and followed by canned products of mushrooms, asparagus, and tomatoes, Taiwan's export-oriented processed fruits and vegetables increased through the 1950s to the 1970s until they became a world leader. They reached a peak of 517,400 tons in 1980–84 and then declined substantially. As production costs increased and the currency appreciated, competition from canners in developing countries emerged—notably China's canned tomatoes and mushrooms and Thailand's canned pineapple. Taiwan's processed fruit and vegetable industry lost its comparative advantage and was no longer a major world supplier by the end of the 1980s.

Since the mid-1980s, the scope of exportable agricultural products from Taiwan has shrunk substantially. Pork exports, mainly to Japan, are the latest star. Led by the Taiwan Sugar Corporation, the government-owned monopoly producer of centrifugal sugar that diversified into other businesses, such as hog raising, Taiwan's pork successfully made inroads into Japan.[5] Compared with Japan's other foreign pork suppliers—Denmark, Canada, and the United States—Taiwan's geographic and cultural proximity to Japan has been advantageous. In addition to low transportation costs, Taiwan can provide chilled pork to Japan and is able to make all cut specifications available, with the quality and flavor that suits Japanese tastes. Exports started in the late 1950s, but Taiwan has become one of Japan's leading foreign pork suppliers since the mid-1970s. The long-run prospects for Taiwan's pork exports, however, are not good because serious water pollution problems caused by hogs' waste may require a cut in production.

While the role of agricultural exports is fading, there has been an upward trend in imports of agricultural products. Because of limited resources and climate constraints, Taiwan has to depend almost totally on imports of inputs for its modern livestock, flour-milling, and export-oriented textile and leather goods industries. Fast growth in these industries has spurred the rapid growth of agricultural imports. In 1985–89, the yearly average of imported wheat was 835,000 tons, while corn and soybeans reached 3.7 and 1.8 million tons, respectively, and imported cotton and hides and leather reached 382,400 and 190,100 tons, respectively.

Although importing mostly bulk commodities, increasing income and relaxed trade barriers since the 1980s also have stimulated imports of fruits, nuts, and vegetables as well as dairy products and beef to satisfy Taiwan's increasingly diversified taste. In fact, Taiwan has reversed its agricultural trade balance from surplus to deficit since 1970 and has become an important agricultural importer, ranking as the sixth most important U.S. overseas farm market in 1990, valued at $1.7 billion (excluding fishery and forestry products).

Farms Remained Small but Land Use Became Less Intensive
Table 2 shows the changes in agricultural farm size, employment, and income. With a dense population and only a quarter of the island's 13,900 square miles being arable, Taiwan's agriculture has limited areas for cultivation, which have remained relatively stable for the past several decades. Partly because of the government's farmland policy, Taiwan's farming is characterized by small-scale family operations with an average farm size of about 1 hectare. In addition, the distribution of the land is increasingly concentrated in small-size farms. Farm households under 1 hectare increased from 66.5% in 1960 to 75.2% in 1990, while farms above 3 hectares decreased from 3.3% to 2.5%.

The government's extensive land reform has fundamentally altered Taiwan's postwar farmland system. As noted in Ho, armed with political flexibility as an "outsider" with no tie to the local establishments, while urgently fighting for political survival caused by the defeat on the mainland, the Nationalist government was able, and had the determination, to put into practice in Taiwan its old political rhetoric—the equilization of land ownership.[6] Beginning with a compulsory rent-reduction program in 1949, followed by the sale of public lands in 1951, the reform was completed with the land-to-tiller program in 1953.

In addition to other far-reaching and positive impacts on both agricultural growth and income distribution in rural Taiwan, the direct and immediate effect of the land reform on land distribution was obvious. Tenant farm households as a share of total farm households dropped from 39% in 1949 to 21% in 1953 and to about 4% in 1989; that of owner-cultivator households grew from 36% to 55% over the same period and reached close to 86% in 1989.[7] In other words, within a short period, the government dramatically converted Taiwan's postwar farmland system from one based mainly on tenants into one relying on a large number of very small farms of owner-cultivators.

While land was distributed equally after the reform program, the land tenure system has become a major institutional impediment for enlarging farm size. Partly because of the association of a free land market with landlordism, high land prices, concentration of ownership of land, and other undesirable consequences, the government has more or less faithfully executed the rigid laws and regulations of the land reform. Thus, in addition to a custom of equal inheritance rights among children, some land reform regulations that imposed limitations on the size of landholdings, on reclaiming leased land, and on freely selling farmland have seriously hampered the enlargement of farm size.[8]

Because land that could be economically farmed was already under cultivation, and because labor was still in abundant supply, multiple cropping systems were encouraged and widely practiced by farmers in Taiwan, where subtropical climates and good irrigation render year-round farming possible. Although multiple cropping had been around for centuries, it was practiced heavily in the 1950s and 1960s before turning downward. During that period, with heavy agricultural investment and technical innovations assisting in the development of intensive agriculture, Taiwan was able to increase crop area substantially, which in part contributed to its impressive postwar agricultural growth.

The expansion of manufacturing and service sectors, causing out-migration of young farmers, however, changed the costs and benefits of multiple cropping.[9] The agricultural labor force in total employment steadily decreased from 50.9% in 1960–64 to only 15.3% in 1985–89, while the absolute number of agriculturally employed declined almost steadily since the late 1960s. In fact, the 1970s were widely agreed on as a turning point that marked the beginning of a new phase in Taiwan's agricultural development—one without an abundance of labor.

In addition, because the out-migrants were relatively young, farm labor was aging. Farmers older than 60 years were 3% of the agriculturally employed in 1965–69, but 12% in 1985–89. Instead of a labor surplus as in the earlier years, labor shortages led to surging wages, and labor costs became the fastest growth component among all agricultural inputs.[10] As increases in real labor costs eroded the benefits of practicing multiple cropping, the multiple cropping index, defined as the ratio of planted area to cultivated area, after reaching a peak of 187% in 1965–69, decreased steadily to 139% in 1985–89.

Part-Time Farmers and Nonfarm Income as the Norms
The most prominent change in farm households during Taiwan's rapid economic growth is the substantial rise in the participation of part-time farmers. Part-time farm households as a percentage of total crop farm households surged from 50.7% in 1960 to 91% in 1980 but declined slightly to 87.0% in 1990. As a result, nonfarm income became the main source of farm household income.

Taiwan's part-time farming has been particularly encouraged by the decentralized character of the rapid industrialization that was stimulated by the government's export-oriented policies. Unlike the experiences of some other countries, such as South Korea, which concentrated their industrialization in a few centers and a few big companies, Taiwan's experience, aided by its compact size, good infrastructure, and the government's policy of focusing on labor-intensive light industries, was characterized by relatively dispersed small- and medium-size businesses that allowed industry to tap much rural labor without physical migration. As a result, Taiwan's farm management was rapidly converted to one relying preponderantly on part-time employment.

In addition to the opportunity of off-farm employment, the mechanization of many farm operations and the desire of farmers to maintain landholdings as an asset have also contributed to the popularity of part-time farming. In particular, the government's protection of the rice sector and the proliferation of rice nursery centers and machine centers, which have standardized paddy field rice production, have given rice farmers a stable return without much managerial effort and thus greatly encouraged part-time farming.[11]

Taiwan (like Japan and South Korea) classifies part-time farm households into class I if their farm income comprises more than 50% of total household income and the remainder into class II or sideline households. The proportion of class II part-time farm households increased substantially from 19.8% in 1960 to 69.8% in 1990. Full-time farm households, however, decreased from 49.3% to 13.0% over the same period. Moreover, Taiwan's full-time farmers also evolved into two extreme types: (1) aged farmers who retain their status as full-time farmers but whose income is mainly transfer income from relatives or other sources, and (2) those new-breed, young full-time farmers who depend for most of their income on farming. According to an estimate, the former group accounts for more than 30% of the full-time farmers, while the latter group accounts for about 20%.[12]

The various farm types, namely, full-time, class I, and class II part-time farms, possess different characteristics. According to the 1985 agricultural census, among the three types of farms the average class II part-time farmer operated the smallest amount of cultivated land per farm, had the highest rate of ownership of farmland, and relied proportionately more on rice planting but with the lowest yield.[13] In addition, household members of this farm type possessed the following characteristics: the lowest percentage of working-age (15 or older) members who were 65 or older, the lowest percentge of unschooled working-age members, and the highest percentage of females as major workers. On the other hand, the full-time farm households possessed characteristics opposite those of the class II part-time farms (table 3).

Because of the prevalence of part-time farming, Taiwan's farm families have depended for more than one-half of their income on nonfarm sources since the 1970s. Average off-farm income increased from 40.7% in 1965–69 to 66.2% in the early 1980s and then decreased slightly to 62.8% in 1985–89. In addition, although for class II households farming is a sideline activity, their income per farm household was the highest, while income of full-time farm households was the

Sophia Wu Huang   53

TABLE 3

Profile of Farm Households, 1985

Items	Full-time	Class I	Class II
Number of farms	89,313	154,759	535,825
Cultivated land per farm (ha)	1.14	1.28	0.61
Land ownership (%)	82.60	82.32	87.51
Percentage of rice farms	57.77	64.81	64.82
Rice yield (kg/ha)	4,894	4,786	4,742
Age over 65 (%)	17.54	8.39	8.21
Education:			
Unschooled (%)	29.13	21.19	20.19
High school and above			
(%)	18.29	24.02	25.42
Sex of major workers:			
Male (%)	83.21	81.71	76.03
Female (%)	16.79	18.29	23.97

Source.—*The Report on 1985 Agricultural and Fishery Census, Taiwan-Fukien District* (Tapei: Directorate-General of Budget, Accounting and Statistics, 1987).

lowest.[14] The result was not surprising because, as mentioned earlier, the work force in class II farm households was younger and more educated than in other types of farm households.

Farm household income, on either a per capita or a per household basis, however, was lower than for any nonfarm household group. For example, in 1985–89, per capita farm income was about 87% of that of urban laborers, and it was only 79% on a per household basis. These income gaps between farm and nonfarm households perhaps can be explained by two of the most important characteristics of a household, namely, education and age.

Household heads in farm families tend to have less education than those of nonfarm households. The 1985 survey of income and expenditures shows that, of household heads 35–40 years of age, 11% of the household heads of farm families had high school or higher education, while this was true for 38% of nonfarm households. Similarly, only 4% of the farm household heads 45–50 years of age had high school and beyond while 24% of the nonfarm household heads had at least a high school education. As to age factor, the 1985 agricultural census data indicate that the proportion of farm households' working members older than 65 in 1985 was 11%, but only 7% among all Taiwanese households.[15]

The income gap between farmers and urban laborers narrowed in particular after the 1980s on a per capita basis, but grew on a per household basis probably because of changes in family structure. While household population decreased in farm and nonfarm households alike, since 1983 the number of members in urban laborers' households has been larger than that in farm households.[16]

III. Evolution of Agricultural Policies

It is well known that rich countries tend to assist agriculture while poor countries tax it; Taiwan has not been an exception in its course of economic development. Taiwan's postwar agricultural policy and programs were initially focused on increasing food production while transferring resources from the agricultural sector to assist in general economic development. After Taiwan's agricultural development reached a turning point in the late 1960s when agricultural growth began to show signs of stagnation, Taiwan reoriented its policy and began to subsidize farmers in the early 1970s.

Agriculture as the Base for Economic Development

The development of Taiwan's economy was to a significant extent based on savings transferred from agriculture. On the one hand, after the war a series of agricultural programs, including the extensive land reform measures, undertaken by the government in 1949–53 laid the groundwork for further growth of the economy. Once the economy was stabilized, with the assistance of U.S. economic aid, the government immediately turned its attention to development.[17] Beginning in 1953, Taiwan's economic development was encouraged through a series of economic plans. Between 1953 and 1968, in which four 4-year economic plans were carried out consecutively, agriculture as the premier sector of the economy supplied funds and raw materials to a budding industrial sector, and rural areas became a major market for industrial products. During this period, increased land productivity through labor-intensive farming was particularly emphasized because of abundant rural labor.

On the other hand, the bitter experiences of food shortages and the hyperinflation of the 1940s that contributed to the loss of the Chinese mainland provided an important setting that deeply influenced Taiwan's postwar agricultural policy. Against this historical background, Taiwan's agricultural policy gave the highest priority to price stability and food production for basic foodstuffs, especially rice. In addition, the shortage of foreign exchange and the rapid increase in population, caused by the large population influx from the Chinese mainland[18] and the high rate (more than 3%) of natural increase in population, forced the government to adopt an agricultural policy that served the multiple objectives of government revenue, self-sufficiency, foreign exchange, and price stabilization.

Since rice is traditionally the staple food in Taiwan and was regarded as a wage good, a sufficient rice supply was necessary for economic stability and as a hedge against inflation. Rice and sugar were also important for earning foreign exchange needed in the initial stages of postwar economic rehabilitation and development. Thus, in addition to a government-owned sugar industry, the government fo-

Sophia Wu Huang 55

cused on controlling every aspect of rice marketing from production through trade.

While increasing rice production and controlling rice marketing were the main targets, the rice policy distorted the rice market and kept domestic rice prices low but stable.[19] In addition, there was systematic regulation of rice exports to generate foreign exchange. To serve these purposes, the government used the paid-in-kind land tax, compulsory procurement programs, and the rice-for-fertilizer barter program to control a sizable share of the rice marketed. Furthermore, the government's purchase prices under the programs were typically only 70%–80% of the prevailing free markert prices, while the exchange ratio of rice for fertilizer was consistently unfavorable to rice farmers.[20]

According to Samuel Ho, during the 1950s and 1960s, the average annual government procurement was 650,000 tons of paddy, which accounted for about one-half of off-farm rice. Approximately 50%–60% of the rice collected was rationed to the armed forces and distributed to military dependents and civilian government employees. The remaining rice was either sold on the free market to stabilize rice prices or exported, a trade that the government monopolized.[21]

Despite agricultural policy being unfavorable to farmers in the early stages of Taiwan's economic development, significant increases in agricultural output and productivity were achieved because of public investments in research, extension, irrigation, and other rural infrastructure. Gains in agricultural productivity made possible the transfer of large amounts of capital and labor from agriculture to other sectors. According to T. H. Lee, the net real capital outflow from the agricultural sector in the form of rents, interest payments, taxes, and others was positive throughout this period.[22] The rice compulsory purchase scheme and rice-for-fertilizer barter program were implicit taxes that, according to the estimate by Kuo, exceeded the total income tax of the whole economy almost every year before 1963.[23]

Policy Reorientation from Taxing to Subsidizing Farmers
As Taiwan's agricultural development reached a turning point in the late 1960s when the supply of rural labor for the first time began to shrink, the focus of agricultural development was broadened. The agricultural program of the fifth economic plan (1969–72), which called for the improvement of labor productivity instead of land productivity with the increase of farmers' income as its principal objective, signified the end of an era of so-called Development of Agriculture to Foster Industry. Later, the government announced the so-called Accelerated Rural Development Program in 1972 to begin a new chapter of agricultural policy. Since then, in addition to increased production in agriculture, policy was reoriented from taxing to subsidizing farmers.

In fact, the undercurrent of protectionism gathered substantial strength after a series of international events in the early 1970s. The worldwide grain shortage in 1972–73, which coincided with Taiwan's lowest rice production in 10 years, and the oil crisis that followed the Middle East War in October 1973, provided a strong backdrop for shifting agricultural policy. Moreover, Japan, Taiwan's much advanced neighbor and in some respects its model, was in the process of increasing its protection for rice; self-sufficiency has been the national policy for both countries.

To provide incentives for rice farmers, programs detrimental to rice farmers, notably the rice-for-fertilizer barter system, were abolished in 1973. The government also established a rice stabilization fund in 1974 to guarantee producer prices for rice; the official procurement prices were raised too and then kept above free-market levels. As a consequence of increasing incentives to rice producers, a large rice surplus developed after the mid-1970s. Official purchase prices for rice were frozen during 1975–78 and have remained almost unchanged since 1982. Also, the government was forced to give up the original practice of unlimited rice purchases in 1976 because of insufficient storage space and funds, while rice exports were no longer price competitive. As of 1990, the government purchased about half of the total rice production, and farmers had to sell their remaining rice in the free market at prices lower than the guaranteed prices.

Taiwan's rice prices, however, were much higher than required for self-sufficiency, and this resulted in a persistent surplus. Rice exports—once a major alternative for surplus disposal—were effectively restricted by the signing of the 5-year (1984–88) U.S.-Taiwan rice agreement, which limited the volume and destination of Taiwan's rice exports. In turn, the government decided to start a costly 6-year (1984–89) riceland diversion program to encourage farmers to divert their riceland to other crops, particularly to soybeans and coarse grains for which Taiwan has low self-sufficiency. Because the production of these feed-related crops is not cost competitive, the government has to subsidize farmers by paying a higher purchase price than the imported price for sale to feed millers. Despite the costs, the government renewed the diversion program for another 6 years (1990–95) after the end of the first diversion program.

In fact, Taiwan subsidizes its rice sector through the riceland diversion program to serve another government objective—increase of farm income—in addition to the pursuit of self-sufficiency. Taiwan's other agricultural protection measures include trade barriers on many agricultural imports and high purchase prices for many domestically produced farm products such as wheat, sugar, milk, grapes, and tobacco. In addition, the government also provides measures to subsidize the improvement of production and marketing systems.

Sophia Wu Huang 57

Agricultural Protection

While Taiwan's government has made much effort to intervene in agriculture, the dominant form of agricultural protection has come from the restrictive border measures that have long existed, in part because of a severe shortage of foreign exchange in the early years. Taiwan used to suffer chronic balance-of-payments deficits to such an extent that during 1951–61, when U.S. aid (it was terminated in 1965) was in full swing, it paid for more than 30% of Taiwan's total imports.[24] Nowadays, instead of pursuing the original goal of conserving scarce foreign exchange, Taiwan's trade barriers have increasingly become a protectionist scheme.

Although trade liberalization is a relatively new concept in Taiwan's agricultural policy, tariff barriers and import controls on agricultural products have been relaxed over the years. Taiwan started to reduce tariffs and relaxed import controls on wheat, feed grains, and soybeans in the mid-1960s. These bulk commodities, however, were subject to government control mechanisms on price, quota, and group purchase requirements, and to a special levy on the imported bulk commodities until these were finally abolished in 1988, with the exception of wheat.

A big step toward relaxing trade barriers came in the 1978–79 bilateral agreement between Taiwan and the United States; provisions were comparable to those applicable to developing countries set forth in nontariff agreements concluded in the Tokyo round of multilateral trade negotiations, even though Taiwan was not a contracting party to the General Agreement on Tariffs and Trade (GATT). Taiwan agreed, in exchange for U.S. concessions on industrial products, to lower tariffs on a number of products stage by stage and gave concessions on some nontariff measures.

Since then, scheduled reductions in tariffs and nontariff barriers have taken place. For example, the tariff rates for wheat decreased from 13% before the agreement to 6.5% as of 1992, for corn from 6% to 1%, for soybeans from 5% to 1%, for raw cotton from 16% to no tariff, for ducks from 75% to 35%, and for pork from 75% to 15%. The import controls on U.S. apples, pears, and whole ducks were removed in 1979, 1986, and 1990, respectively. The uplift factor on tariffs, under which tariffs on imported products were levied against 120% of the landed or cost and freight value, began to be phased out in 1980 and was totally eliminated in 1986.

Agricultural trade liberalization, however, has encountered some setbacks since 1987 because of rapid political liberalization, which in part was caused by the lifting of the 38-year martial law. Taiwan's farmers, long obedient and staunch supporters of the government, have begun to take more rebellious action against the government's trade liberalization policy. In response, the government excluded most agricultural products from Taiwan's otherwise broad tariff cuts and temporarily banned imports of turkey meat in 1988 and beef in 1989. Bureaucratic inertia and what are usually referred to in GATT talks as "non-trade" concerns such as food security, the environment, and the cultural and social heritage also countered trade liberalization efforts. Thus, despite years of relaxing trade barriers, tariffs on many agricultural imports remain high, and other import barriers, such as bans, import licensing restrictions, and unique sanitation or purity standards, persist.

To understand the level of Taiwan's agricultural protection, the producer subsidy equivalents (PSEs), defined as the ratio of policy transfers including the value of direct and indirect government supports to the value of production, were calculated for 11 major commodities covering 1982–89. Among the price distortion measures for these commodities, Taiwan uses import controls on rice, chicken meat, fresh milk, and sugar, while paying high guaranteed prices on domestic production of rice, wheat, corn, sorghum, soybeans, sugar, tobacco leaves, and milk. For 1982–89, Taiwan's policy interventions are mainly linked to strict border measures, which account for about 90% of policy transfers to producers. These results, along with those for other countries and the European Community, have been compiled annually by the U.S. Department of Agriculture (USDA), Economic Research Service, since 1986, and they have been published in detailed country specifications since 1988.[25]

Although it is difficult to have a precise comparison of PSEs across countries, for example, because different commodities across countries are included, conclusions can still be drawn about the relative degree of government protection. The international comparison from the USDA study shows that although Taiwan's agricultural protection might be high by the standard of developing countries, it was low in comparison with those of most developed countries. Table 4 shows that among seven countries—Taiwan, Japan, South Korea, Australia, New Zealand, Canada, and the United States—and the European Community, Taiwan had a lower rate of agricultural protection than other countries except for New Zealand and Australia. In particular, the yearly average of Taiwan's PSEs for 1982–89 was 23%; it was much lower than those of Japan and South Korea, which were 74% and 70%, respectively.[26]

Prospects for Changes in Agricultural Policies
After intense economic development in past decades, Taiwan's agriculture faces unprecedented challenges as the last decade of the twentieth century gets under way. The very success of its industrialization

Sophia Wu Huang   59

TABLE 4

AVERAGE PRODUCER SUBSIDY EQUIVALENTS (%) FOR SELECTED COUNTRIES

	1982	1983	1984	1985	1986	1987	1988	1989	Average
Taiwan	16	19	21	24	24	25	28	29	23
Japan	66	71	71	72	79	80	79	72	74
South Korea	63	65	64	64	67	70	77	88	70
European Community	28	26	27	36	48	51	39	N.A.	36
Australia	12	9	9	9	11	7	7	6	9
New Zealand	33	25	18	22	10	6	4	3	15
Canada	23	25	30	39	42	41	32	30	33
United States	17	26	22	24	34	32	24	18	25

SOURCE.—Estimates are provided by Economic Research Service, U.S. Department of Agriculture. Data for Taiwan, Japan, South Korea, Australia, New Zealand, and Canada are published in *Pacific Rim Agriculture and Trade Report,* no. RS-91-4 (Washington D.C.: U.S. Department of Agriculture, Economic Research Service, 1991).

has resulted in rising production costs and a shrinking and aging supply of farm labor in the agricultural sector. Labor-intensive farming has become uneconomical, yet substantial mechanization of Taiwan's current small farms is often impractical. Furthermore, increasing import competition and other problems of Taiwan's overall economy— pollution, strong currency, labor shortages, and dwindling water resources—have become major policy concerns.

As to the traditionally important crops, rice and sugarcane, the government has modified its previous "more is better" policy by adopting the riceland diversion program and phasing out sugar operations. Thus far, much of the government's efforts to keep agriculture viable are centered on rice farmers. The protective rice policy, however, in addition to causing costly budgetary expenditures to dispose of surplus rice, has in fact benefited mostly sideline part-time farms. This is ironic given the government's stated policy of promoting the full-time enterpreneurial type of so-called nucleus farmers. According to one estimate, part-time sideline farm households were responsible for 69.3% of total earnings in rice production in 1987.[27]

Taiwan's once world-renowned canned food exports have almost ended, ever since various export corporations for pineapple, mushrooms, and asparagus ceased operation in 1988 and 1989. The prospects for finding new exports as successful as these products appear to be slim. Even the potential of pork and chicken is rather limited, although they are the fastest-growth products in agriculture with a value share accounting for more than one-third of total value of crop and livestock production. Chicken production is uncompetitive internationally; its prosperity is in part due to the protection derived from a ban on chicken imports. Although hog production is efficient, pollution from hog's waste in the densely populated island has reached a serious level.

Policymakers have been well aware of the need to enlarge the size of farm operations ever since the labor surplus gave way to scarcity in the late 1960s and mechanization became the only way to overcome the labor constraint. The second phase of the farmland reform program was launched in 1983 with the intention of establishing a new land-tenure system that allows the enlargement of farm operations without affecting land ownership.[28] The program includes joint decision making in specific operations, joint management, contract farming, and the promotion of specialized production areas. Also, during the past de-cades, the government has initiated and partly subsidized a farmland consolidation program for about 365,000 hectares—more than 40% of Taiwan's total cultivated land area.[29] However, factors such as the traditional attachment to land, the fragmented nature of rural landhold-ings, and the lack of an open land market caused by the government's adherence to rigid land regulations have continued to restrain the en-largement of farm size.

Perhaps the most ambitious and comprehensive part of Taiwan's farm programs so far is the Integrated Agricultural Adjustment Plan (IAAP), which is a complementary plan for agriculture within the new 6-year (from July 1991 to June 1997) National Development Plan (NDP). While the NDP is aimed at catapulting the island into the ranks of a fully developed nation economically, socially, and culturally, the IAAP is intended to usher Taiwan across the threshold from a pro-tected, traditional agriculture to a liberalized, modern agriculture in a developed society.[30]

The IAAP charts a new course for Taiwan's agricultural develop-ment in the 1990s. For the first time, agricultural production is to convert from an export orientation to minimum self-sufficiency over the next 6 years. Government resources will focus on products that are deemed competitive, using criteria such as marketing and techno-logical potentials, returns to labor input, environmental costs, food security, farm numbers, and location of production. In particular, the term "quality agriculture," which was introduced in the mid-1980s, is now being actively paraded before the island's farmers. While ac-knowledging that trade liberalization on agricultural products is inevi-table, the IAAP will provide production and marketing assistance to those farmers whose product sales have been adversely affected by imported goods.

Apparently, the IAAP plan is intended to balance the interests of a declining agricultural industry and rural population with the trade liberalization demands of international trading partners and local con-sumer groups. Although many detailed measures are still being de-bated, the message is unmistakable. In the face of Taiwan's transfor-

Sophia Wu Huang 61

mation to an industrial and service-based economy, the direction of Taiwan's farm policy has been changed from a production-driven to a market-oriented and environmentally sensitive one. In particular, the IAAP plan establishes a new role for agriculture: it is being broadened to include environmental and landscape management and agrotourism.

IV. Concluding Remarks

Although the contraction of agriculture's share of gross domestic product in the course of economic development is universal, Taiwan's dramatic experience provides an extreme version of the structural changes in a rapidly industrializing and resource-poor economy. The traditional agricultural products such as rice, sugarcane, and sweet potatoes are giving way to higher-valued products such as pork, chicken, and horticultural products. Instead of playing its traditional role of contributing foreign exchange earnings, the agricultural sector depends heavily on imports to keep the livestock, flour-milling, and export-oriented industries of textile and leather goods in operation. Despite land always being the most limited production factor in Taiwan's agriculture, the intensity of land use is declining. There is a substantial rise in the role of part-time farmers, and the portion of nonfarm receipts in total farm income is increasing. Most of all, Taiwan's agriculture is facing surging production costs, shrinking numbers of and aging farm workers, lack of an efficient farming scale, and concern for pollution, as well as increased demands from trading partners for trade liberalization.

The structural changes in agriculture would have been even more dramatic had it not been for the shifting of agricultural policy from taxing to subsidizing farmers after the early 1970s, while many of the restrictive border measures on agricultural imports remain. Although Taiwan has gradually relaxed agricultural trade barriers in the past years, there has been heavy pressure demanding further trade liberalization from major trading partners. Because of the recent political reforms, farmers' discontent on agricultural trade policy has received considerable political attention and has complicated the liberalization process. The farm sectors' political leverage in Taiwan, however, appears insufficient to stave off further market liberalization because, unlike Japan, Taiwan has not yet developed complicated legal, institutional, and ideological frameworks designed for agricultural protection policies. Therefore, the question of agricultural trade liberalization is not whether it will proceed but, rather, how quickly and to what degree. In fact, the government has announced intentions to relax barriers against agricultural products for which Taiwan has no comparative advantage while continuing to seek protection for some politically sensitive farm products such as rice.

Faced with a dwindling sector and increasing pressure for trade liberalization, Taiwan's agriculture is in need of reform. The recently implemented 6-year farm programs starting July 1991 would help to ease the transition of the agricultural sector to a smaller but more efficient market-oriented and environmentally sensitive farming operation. Besides, Taiwan's application for membership in the GATT in 1990 and its willingness to join the organization as a developed economy represent a milestone in Taiwan's agricultural policy. If Taiwan is successful in joining GATT, which formed a working party to review Taiwan's membership application in late 1992, its agricultural markets will open further in order to conform to the GATT rules on agricultural trade. The prospects of trade liberalization depend in part on domestic structural adjustments, while the pressure for trade liberalization will certainly intensify the need for restructuring agriculture.

Notes

    * I would like to thank D. Gale Johnson for helpful comments and suggestions, and John Dyck and Carol Goodloe of the Economic Research Service, U.S. Department of Agriculture, for reviewing the earlier manuscript. The views expressed in this article are mine and do not necessarily represent those of the Economic Research Service or the U.S. Department of Agriculture.

    1. *Taiwan Agricultural Yearbook* (Taichung: Taiwan Provincial Department of Agriculture and Forestry, 1950–91).

    2. While the Taiwan dollar was essentially stable at 40 to 1 against the U.S. dollar between 1960 and 1985, the near 50% appreciation of Taiwan's dollar between late 1985 and 1989 was second only to that of the Japanese yen. The effects of the exchange rate on Taiwan's agricultural exports varied among different commodities partly because of their different competitors. For example, the Taiwan dollar's appreciation constituted a big disadvantage for Taiwan's exports of canned products because the biggest competitors for Taiwan's canned products were Thailand and China. In addition to their lower production costs, the exchange rate with respect to the U.S. dollar was quite stable for both countries between 1985 and 1989. China's exchange rate depreciated slightly, while Thailand's appreciated marginally during 1985–89.

    3. *Taiwan Sugar Statistics* (Taipei: Taiwan Sugar Corporation, 1950–90); and *The Trade of China* (Taipei: Inspectorate General of Customs, Republic of China, 1950–91).

    4. The emergence of processed fruits and vegetable exports was mainly due to the government of Taiwan's initiative in providing guidance from production through marketing. Because of the termination of U.S. aid in 1965, the government urgently needed to find new sources of earning foreign exchange. These labor-intensive products provided a way for the government to use its abundant labor force while earning foreign exchange.

    5. The Taiwan Sugar Corporation (TSC) is Taiwan's largest single pork producer. Although it is 98% government owned, it is supposed to run on a business base with no direct government funding. The TSC has a number of different farm operations, some of which appear to turn a profit, while others do not. In Taiwan's hog industry, TSC has been the cornerstone of research and innovation for the private-sector firms in terms of breeding, slaughtering, and marketing. The TSC, however, does not have monopoly privileges in domestic or export markets and faces active private-sector competition in both.

    6. Samuel P. S. Ho also provided an analysis of the effect of land reform

Sophia Wu Huang   63

on equity in his *Economic Development of Taiwan, 1860–1970* (New Haven, Conn.: Yale University Press, 1978), pp. 159–74.

7. *Taiwan Agricultural Yearbook,* various issues.

8. Yu-kang Mao, "Current Land Problems and Policies of Taiwan, the Republic of China," *Industry of Free China* (June 1987), pp. 11–13; and Teng-hui Lee and Yueh-eh Chen, "Agricultural Growth in Taiwan, 1911–1972," in *Agricultural Growth in Japan, Taiwan, Korea, and Philippines,* ed. Y. Hayami, V. W. Ruttan, and H. M. Southworth (Honolulu: University Press of Hawaii, 1979), p. 88. For details of all the relevant laws and regulations see Hui-sun Tang, *Land Reform in Free China* (Taipei: Chinese-American Joint Commission on Rural Reconstruction, 1954); and Cheng Chen, *Land Reform in Taiwan* (Taipei: China Publishing, 1961).

9. By assuming that in the absence of net migration the agricultural labor population would have grown at the same rate as the total labor population, T. H. Lee estimated net migration of the agricultural labor force. On the basis of this method, Y. K. Mao and Chi Schive estimated the net migration sequence during 1952–88. They showed that the permanent migration rate out of the agricultural population was about 2.4% during 1960–69, about 6.7% in 1970–79, and about 4.2% in 1980–88. In addition, much of the flow from agricultural to nonagricultural activity was of young people. According to a study, laborers under the age of 24 comprised 66.3% of total labor absorption in manufacturing between 1966 and 1972. For details see Yu-kang Mao and Chi Schive, "Agricultural and Industrial Development of the Republic of China" (paper presented at the conference Agriculture on the Road to Industrialization, cosponsored by the Council of Agriculture, Republic of China, and International Food Policy Research Institute, Washington, D.C., September 1990); T. H. Lee, "Wage Differential, Labor Mobility and Employment in Taiwan's Agriculture," in *Proceedings of the Sino-American Conference on Manpower in Taiwan* (Taipei: Academia Sinica, 1972).

10. Tso-Kwei Peng, "Price, Income, and Farm Policy in Taiwan" (manuscript for the symposium Chinese Rural Development: Strategies and Experience, organized by the China Committee of the American Agricultural Economics Association, Baton Rouge, La., July 1989). According to his estimate, the annual growth rate of input prices during 1951–87 was as follows: farm wages, 11.8%; farm machinery, 5.0%; fertilizer, 4.9%; and feed, 5.3%.

11. A rice nursery center (RNC) raises seedlings, chemically treats the seeds to be free from pest and disease, and supplies the seedlings to farmers in its service area for machine transplanting. The seedlings are raised in a box about 60 by 30 centimeters. Each hectare of paddy land needs 200–240 boxes of seedlings. The RNCs in Taiwan are all privately owned, but their establishment requires approval by and registration at the county government office. Each RNC is designed to provide healthy seedlings for 100–200 hectares. The RNCs work closely with the farmers' association, irrigation association, and agricultural offices of the local government. In fact, an RNC becomes multifunctional, its services similar to those of a small extension office. It helps government extension workers organize farmers into joint operation teams and provides the teams with information on the availability of farm machinery and innovations in cultivation practices. In addition to supplying seedlings, the RNCs are also responsible for regulating and coordinating the supply of and demand for farm machinery including power tillers, transplanters, sprayers, combines, and driers for farmers in each RNC service area. For details, see Shao-er Ong, *Development of the Small Farm Economy in Taiwan* (Taipei: Council of Agriculture, 1987), pp. 24–25.

12. Data provided by Y. C. Wang, Senior Specialist, Economics and Planning Department, Council of Agriculture, Executive Yuan, Taiwan.

13. *The Report on 1985 Agricultural and Fishery Census, Taiwan-Fukien District, Republic of China* (Taipei: Directorate-General of Budget, Accounting, and Statistics, Executive Yuan, 1987).

14. Data provided by Y. C. Wang, Senior Specialist, Economics and Planning Department, Council of Agriculture, Executive Yuan, Taiwan.

15. *1985 Report on the Survey of Family Income and Expenditure, Taiwan Province, Republic of China* (Taichung: Taiwan Provincial Department of Budget, Accounting, and Statistics, 1986); and *Taiwan Statistical Data Book, 1990* (Taipei: Council for Economic Planning and Development, 1990).

16. By dividing the time-series data on income per household by the series of income per capita, one can obtain the population of an average household over time.

17. After the war, agricultural planning and development tasks were undertaken by the Chinese-American Joint Commission on Rural Reconstruction (JCRR), a bilateral agency initially set up on the mainland in 1948 before the move to Taiwan. The unique character of the JCRR was its dual role—it served as the agency comparable to the department of agriculture of the Taiwanese government and later as the agricultural division of the U.S. Aid Mission as well. During its whole lifetime from 1951 to 1965, total U.S. aid obligations amounted to $1.465 billion. For details see, e.g., E. Thorbecke, "Agricultural Development," in *Economic Growth and Structural Change in Taiwan: The Postwar Experience of the Republic of China*, ed. Walter Galenson (Ithaca, N.Y.: Cornell University Press, 1979), pp. 171–72 and 182–84.

18. Immediately after the government moved its headquarters to Taiwan, Taiwan experienced, in addition to hyperinflation, a large population influx from the Chinese mainland. Population was estimated at about 6 million in 1949 before the sudden influx of nearly 2 million civilian refugees and soldiers. See, e.g., S. C. Tsiang, W. L. Chen, and A. Hsieh. "Progress in Trade Liberalization, Taiwan, Republic of China," *Industry of Free China* (June 1985), p. 1.

19. Statistics provided by the Provincial Food Bureau reveal that between 1955 and 1969 the rice price index was consistently 22%–36% lower than the general price index. For details see H. Y. Chen, W. F. Hsu, and Y. K. Mao, "Rice Policies of Taiwan," *Food Research Institute Studies* 14, no. 4 (1975): 415–16.

20. For details, see ibid., pp. 403–17; and Ho (n. 6 above), pp. 175–85.

21. Ho, p. 182.

22. On the basis of the data calculated by T. H. Lee, E. Thorbecke concluded that the net capital outflow from agriculture fluctuated between 20% and 30% of Taiwan's agricultural production before World War II, amounted to 22% in 1950–55, and around 15% between 1956 and 1969. Although Lee's data have been discontinued since then, Thorbecke believed that "it is most likely that the net outflow in the mid-1970s must be disappearing." T. H. Lee, *Strategies for Transferring Agricultural Surplus under Different Agricultural Situations in Taiwan* (Taipei: Chinese-American Joint Commission on Rural Reconstruction, 1971); and Thorbecke, pp. 189, 203.

23. Wanyong Kuo, "Effects of Land Reform, Agricultural Pricing Policy and Economic Growth on Multiple Crop Diversification," *Philippine Economic Journal* 14, nos. 1/2 (1975), p. 161, table 10.

24. Kuo-shu Liang and Ching-ing Hou Liang, "Development Policy Formation and Future Policy Priorities in the Republic of China," *Economic Development and Cultural Change* 36, no. 3, suppl. (1988): S68.

25. While the revised and updated version is forthcoming, the most recently available publication is A. J. Webb, M. Lopez, and R. Penn, eds., *Estimates of Producer and Consumer Equivalents, Government Intervention*

Sophia Wu Huang   65

in Agriculture, 1982–87, ERS Statistical Bulletin no. 803 (Washington, D.C.: U.S. Department of Agriculture, 1990).

26. In related research, Shun-Yi Shei and Kym Anderson measured agricultural protection for Taiwan from 1955 to 1982 by using nominal rates of agricultural protection (NRAPs), defined as the percentage by which domestic price exceeds the border price. Their results showed that Taiwan's NRAPs, which moved upward from minus to positive, particularly after 1970, grew at a slower rate and were lower than those in Japan and South Korea. Shei and Anderson, "Taiwanese Agricultural Protection in Historical and Comparative Perspective," Pacific Economic Papers, no. 104 (Australia-Japan Research Centre, Australian National University, Canberra, 1983).

27. Data provided by Y. C. Wang, Senior Specialist, Economics and Planning Department, Council of Agriculture, Executive Yuan, Taiwan.

28. Mao (n. 8 above).

29. Data provided by Economics and Planning Department, Council of Agriculture, Executive Yuan, Taiwan.

30. "Agricultural Situation Report—1991," unpublished attaché report no. TW1016 (U.S. Department of Agriculture, Foreign Agricultural Service, Washington, D.C., 1991).

[4]

Goals and Consequences of Rice Policy in Japan, 1965–80

Keijiro Otsuka and Yujiro Hayami

The change in welfare of producers and consumers, government cost, and the deadweight loss arising from the various forms of government interventions into the rice market in order to protect domestic producers in Japan are estimated in a partial equilibrium framework. Results of the quantitative analysis indicate that the motivation of the government was to minimize budget costs in achieving the target level of producer price support, while consumer welfare had an insignificant weight in the government's objective function. It is also found that acreage control is a "second best" policy to reduce social inefficiency produced from other forms of market distortions.

Key words: acreage control, import restriction, revealed motivation of government, rice price support, social cost.

Japan's rice policy in the past two decades represents a major departure from having production take place according to international comparative advantage. Domestic rice production has been protected by import restriction (virtual prohibition) since the mid-1960s. The domestic rice price has been raised further above the equilibrium of domestic demand and supply (autarky) by means of government purchases at a support price. As a result, the domestic producer price of rice in Japan has been two to four times higher than the international price since the late 1960s. The high level of price support has created a large excess supply, despite subsidies for the diversion of paddyfield areas to non-rice crops. The government has been forced to dispose of the accumulated surplus via concessional exports or for feed and industrial uses at a price much lower than the purchase price.

This paper attempts to estimate the social costs involved in those protectionist policies in Japan since the mid-1960s. The analysis focuses on the decomposition of the effects of various policy measures, especially import restrictions, acreage diversion, producer price

supports, and deficiency payments. The "second-best" implication of the supply control policy to reduce the social cost resulting from the high level of producer price support is emphasized. The implied objective function of government in policy choice is identified from the results of the quantitative analysis.

Model of Rice Policy

The effects of government policies on the rice market may be illustrated in figure 1. Curves S and C on the left-hand panel represent, respectively, total supply and producers' home consumption demand schedules. The difference between S and C is the market supply, which is shown by curve M on the right-hand panel. The market demand schedule of consumers is shown by curve D. Curve $(1 - \psi)S$ represents a leftward shift of total supply by $\psi\%$ due to the introduction of the acreage control program, and curve M' shows the corresponding shift in market supply.

Assuming a perfectly elastic supply of rice from the world to the Japanese market (a small-country assumption), a market demand equilibrium would be established at point k and a market supply equilibrium at point i. This would occur in the absence of government intervention into the market, at which market supply, demand and import are M'_p, M'_c and $(M'_c - M'_p)$, respectively, whereas total production and farm consumption are Q'_p

Keijiro Otsuka and Yujiro Hayami are an associate professor and a professor of economics, respectively, at Tokyo Metropolitan University.

The authors wish to thank Kym Anderson and the anonymous referees for helpful comments on earlier drafts of the paper.

Review was coordinated by Bruce Gardner, associate editor.

530 *August 1985*   *Amer. J. Agr. Econ.*

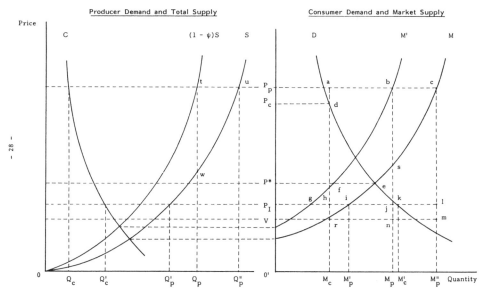

Figure 1. Effects of government policy

and Q'_c, respectively, for a given international price (P_I). When imports are prohibited, the market equilibrium would move to point e.

The Japanese government purchased rice from producers at P_p, which was higher than the equilibrium price under autarky (P^*), and even higher than the government sale price to consumers (P_c).[1] As a result, excess supply was created by the amount $(M''_p - M_c)$. In fact, during the 1960s, since the enactment of the Agricultural Basic Law in 1961, the purchase price increased at a very rapid rate and exceeded the sale price by a wide margin (table 1, columns 1 and 2).[2] The high support price stimulated domestic production to expand in excess of consumption, resulting in the accumulation of surplus rice in government storage (columns 3 and 4). The government deficit from the rice-control program

multiplied and exceeded 300 billion yen at the end of the 1960s, which accounted for almost 40% of the central government budget for agriculture or nearly 5% of the total national budget (column 5).

The rapidly increasing rice surplus and the rice-control program deficit finally arrested further increases in rice prices in 1968. The government purchase price was frozen for 1968–70. Meanwhile, an acreage control program was launched, wherein incentive payments were made to the paddyfields retired from production or diverted for non-rice crops (column 6).[3] In terms of figure 1, this program shifted the total supply curve to the left by $\psi\%$ with the effect of a reduction in the total supply by $(Q''_p - Q_p)$ or $(M''_p - M_p)$.[4]

---

[1] In the derivation of the market supply curve, we assumed that producer's decision concerning the consumption of rice was made with respect to the producer price, P_p, and not the consumer price, P_c, despite the fact that the former was higher than the latter. It must be noted that in our analysis we abstract from marketing and processing costs and define both prices in brown rice terms. Even if the consumer price was lower than the producer price, the retail price which includes the retail and other cost margins was not lower than the "effective" price that producers paid for the home consumption of their rice produce. In fact, producers very seldom purchased rice from retailers.

[2] For the review of evolution of the rice policy, see Hayami and Hayami and associates (pp. 72–80); for the political decision process in rice price determination, see Hemmi.

[3] The acreage control program was essentially voluntary, as is evidenced by the fact that the area actually diverted tended to exceed the area planned to be diverted by the Ministry of Agriculture, Forestry, and Fishery.

[4] According to the estimate by Otsuka (1984b), the elasticity of total supply, with respect to the planted acreage, is not significantly different from unity, even though the land removed under the acreage control program tended to be inferior to the land that remained in production. For simplicity, we assume that the total supply curve shifts to the left by the ratio of diverted paddy area. We do not deny, however, the possibility that the supply curve under acreage diversion program is identical to that under no diversion program for the smaller volume of output and has an upward kink at the certain level of output. However, the adoption of such assumption makes the calculation of welfare effects intractable. Thus, we are compelled to use the assumption of a proportional supply shift à la Floyd.

Table 1.   Major Statistics of the Rice Policy

	Rice Prices[a]		Annual Excess Supply[b] (3)	Government Stock of Old Rice as of 1 Nov. (4)	Deficits in Rice Control[c] (5)	Ratio of Diverted Paddy Area (6)	Surplus Rice Disposed (7)
	Government Purchase (1)	Government Sale (2)					
	-- (1,000 yen/ton) --		---- (1,000 ton) ----		(billion yen)	(%)	(1,000 ton)
1961	74	72	−216	500	50		
62	81	81	−979	100	53		
63	88	80	−400	17	89		
64	100	80	−335	14	123		
65	109	93	205	52	134		
1966	119	101	242	205	223		
67	130	117	1,970	645	242		
68	138	126	2,198	2,976	268		35
69	138	125	2,038	5,530	348	0.2	432
70	138	124	741	7,202	474	10.6	1,096
1971	142	123	−972	5,891	446	17.1	2,507
72	149	131	42	3,074	445	17.8	1,866
73	172	130	71	1,477	636	17.7	1,183
74	227	171	259	615	719	9.9	268
75	260	203	1,198	1,142	799	8.3	
1976	276	224	−47	2,641	815	6.7	
77	287	246	1,612	3,675	841	6.7	
78	288	246	1,225	5,722	987	13.9	
79	288	257	740	6,517	1,020	14.8	1,130
80	294	266	176	6,693	929	18.3	1,020

Sources: Japan, Ministry of Agriculture, Forestry, and Fishery, *Statistical Yearbook of Food Control* for prices, deficits, and stock of old rice; *Statistical Yearbook of Ministry of Agriculture, Forestry, and Fishery* for the agricultural budget; unpublished data of the Food Agency for annual excess supply and surplus rice disposed; and *Pocket Statistics of Ministry of Agriculture, Forestry, and Fishery* for diverted paddy area.
[a] In terms of brown rice.
[b] Actual production minus food consumption.
[c] The rice control deficits in the Food Control Special Account plus subsidy payments to paddy areas retired and diverted to non-rice production.

The excess supply of rice induced by the high price support forced the government to dispose of the accumulated old rice stock for uses other than domestic food (column 7). The sale prices of old rice for exports and/or industrial use in the surplus rice disposal program were nearly one-half of the government's normal sale price for domestic consumption. The price for feed use was one-sixth of this normal domestic consumption price. Japan, however, was forced to limit rice exports because of strong objections from commercial rice-exporting countries. The demand for feed use was elastic but only at a very low price comparable to feed grain prices. The government limited the sale of old rice for industrial use in order to keep its price higher than the sale price for feed use. On average, the salvage value of the surplus rice (V) was significantly lower than the international price (P_I). The average salvage value of surplus rice tends to decline sharply when the quantity of

surplus rice for disposal increases as a larger proportion of the disposal must be redirected toward feed use.

Those programs were successful in eliminating the excess supply of rice, in both flow and stock terms, by 1974–75. The successful reduction of surplus rice stock coincided with the world food crisis of 1973–74. Sharp increases in world food prices, coupled with the U.S. soybean embargo, resulted in increased domestic political pressures for self-sufficiency in food production. The farm block took advantage of this by having the government raise purchase prices and relax acreage controls. Consequently, the experience of the 1960s was repeated—increased excess supply, accumulation of surplus stocks, thereby multiplying the government budget deficit. This forced a price freeze, and hence the strengthening of acreage control in the late 1970s was inevitable.

The welfare implications of these govern-

532   *August 1985*   *Amer. J. Agr. Econ.*

ment interventions in the rice market are formulated as follows. Since producers consume a part of the rice produced, an increase in the producer price of rice raises producer surplus and reduces their consumer surplus. In order to evaluate the producers' net welfare position, we define the net producer surplus as the difference between the producer surplus and a portion of the consumer surplus accruing to producers.[5] An increase in the net producer surplus (ΔPS) due to the government rice policy (compared to the free trade situation) is given by

(1) $\Delta PS = area\ P^*eiP_I + area\ P_pceP^*,$
$$for\ Z = 0$$

$= area\ P^*eiP_I + area\ P_pceP^*$
$$- area\ tuO + Z \cdot \Delta L,$$
$$for\ Z > 0$$

$$= \int_{P_I}^{P^\circ} M(P)dP + \int_{P^\circ}^{P_p} M(P)dP$$

$$- \int_0^{P_p} \psi S(P)dP + Z \cdot \Delta L$$

where $M(P)$ and $S(P)$ denote the market supply and the total supply functions, respectively; and ΔL and Z are the area of paddyfields diverted from rice production and the government subsidy per hectare of diverted area, respectively. The first term in equation (1) represents the increment of net producer surplus due to the prohibition of imports. The second term represents the producers' gain due to the price support above the equilibrium price under autarky. The third term, in the case when the acreage control program is introduced ($Z > 0$), is the producer surplus foregone due to the reduced supply. The last term is the total amount of subsidy payments for the diverted paddyfield area. The last two terms are zero when the acreage control program is not introduced.

A corresponding change in the consumer surplus (ΔCS) is defined as

(2) $\Delta CS = - area\ P^*ekP_I - area\ P_cdeP^*$

$$= - \int_{P_I}^{P^*} D(P)dP - \int_{P^*}^{P_c} D(P)dP$$

[5] The share of rice consumed by the farm sector amounted to as large as 25% in Japan. As was cogently recognized by Hayami and Herdt; and Tolley, Thomas, and Wong, the welfare analysis of policy intervention into the rice market in the Asian context—in which a large number of small producers consume a large portion of their produce—must take account of the price effect on the consumer surplus of producers.

where $D(P)$ denotes the market demand function. In both equations (1) and (2), the first term represents the effect of trade protection and the other terms represent the effect of domestic price support programs, including the acreage control.

The government (or taxpayers') cost of the rice policy programs is denoted as

(3) $G = area\ P_padP_c + area\ acmr,$
$$for\ Z = 0$$

$= area\ P_padP_c + area\ abnr$
$$+ Z \cdot \Delta L, \qquad for\ Z > 0$$

$= (P_p - P_c)M_c + (P_p - V)[M''_p$
$$- \psi Q''_p - M_c] + Z \cdot \Delta L$$

where $M''_p - \psi(Z)Q''_p = M_p$ when $Z > 0$. In the above equation the first term is the marketing loss from the rice sale for current food consumption at a negative marketing margin, the second term is the loss associated with the future sale of excess supply at a salvage price, and the third term is the subsidy payment for acreage control.

The deadweight or net social loss (DL) can be calculated by

(4) $DL = \Delta PS + \Delta CS - G$

$= area\ cli + area\ dkh$
$$+ area\ hlmr, \qquad for\ Z = 0$$

$= area\ sji + area\ dkh$
$$+ area\ hjnr + area\ twO,$$
$$for\ Z > 0.$$

Various components of DL in equation (4) can be evaluated by referring to figure 1. Let us first examine the case when $Z = 0$ and, hence, $\psi(Z) = 0$. Area cli disappears when P_p is equal to P_I, so that the producer price support can be identified as the cause of this element of social loss. Similarly, it is easy to establish that area dkh is caused by inefficient consumer pricing. Area $hlmr$ is the cost which arises from the need to dispose of excess rice supply at a salvage value lower than the international price. With the introduction of acreage control, the cost of surplus rice disposal declines from area $hlmr$ to area $hjnr$ at the expense of the additional production inefficiency measured by area twO.

The introduction of the acreage control program reduces the social cost that resulted from the price support (area $cmns$). In addition, the diminished supply may further reduce the social cost associated with the disposition of surplus rice to less than area $hjnr$ in that a decrease in the amount of excess supply reduces the disposition of surplus rice at relatively unlucrative outlets and thereby raises the salvage value. On the other hand, the subsidy payment for acreage control results in an inefficient production associated with the artificially increased cost of land input (measured by *area twO*). Therefore, if *area cmns* plus the possible gain arising from an increase in *V* is larger than *area twO*, the acreage control program increases social economic welfare—given other forms of market distortion such as the price support, as implied by the theory of second best (Lipsey and Lancaster; and Davis and Whinston).

Data and Estimation Procedures

In order to measure the social costs involved in the rice policy programs, as specified in the previous section, market equilibrium prices and quantities both under autarky (P^*, M^*) and under free trade (M'_p, M'_c) must be estimated from the empirically observable data of prices and quantities under government market interventions.

When the acreage control program was enforced, we observed M_p rather than M''_p (see fig. 1). Considering that the amount of subsidy was determined so as to maintain the total income of rice producers (including incomes from non-rice production), it is reasonable to assume that the amount of producers' home consumption did not change due to the acreage control program. This implies that the amount of market supply was reduced exactly by the amount of rice production curtailed. Thus, the following relation holds:

$$(5) \qquad M''_p = M_p + (Q''_p - Q_p)$$
$$= M_p + \left(\frac{\psi}{1 - \psi}\right) Q_p$$

where $Q_p = Q''(1 - \psi)$. The rate of supply shift due to the acreage control (ψ) is assumed to be the ratio of paddy area retired from production or diverted for non-rice crops, to total paddy field area.

The price elasticity of market supply (ϵ) is estimated from the underlying total supply and farm demand functions. It is assumed that the total supply and farm demand functions can be approximated by constant elasticity functions. Then, following Tolley, Thomas, and Wong, ϵ is obtained by differentiating total supply and farm demand functions with respect to producer price as:

$$(6) \quad \epsilon = \alpha\left(\frac{Q}{M}\right) + \beta\left(\frac{C}{M}\right) - \gamma\left(\frac{PQ}{Y}\right)\left(\frac{C}{M}\right)$$

where α and $(-\beta)$ are the price elasticities of total supply of and farm household demand for rice, respectively; γ is the income elasticity of farm household demand; Q is the total supply; M is the market supply; C is the household demand; P is the producer price; and Y is the farm household income.

Since rice imports have been nil since the mid-1960s, an estimate of the import price to Japan is required. The CIF price of imported rice equivalent to domestic rice is estimated by adding 15% freight and other expenses to the FOB price of Texas long grain, the highest quality rice among internationally traded rice products.

Another variable that needs to be estimated is the average salvage value of surplus rice disposed for nonfood use (V). The estimation is based on the following formula:

$$(7) \quad V_t = \frac{1}{E_t} \left\{ \sum_{s=1}^{N} (1 + r)^{-s}[p_{t+s}q_{t+s} - c_{t+s}] \right\}$$

where E is quantity of surplus rice produced in year t; r, real discount rate of 7% based on Kama; s, the lapse of years, up to N, for which the surplus rice was produced and disposed; p, average sale price of surplus rice; q, quantity of surplus rice sold ($\Sigma_s q = E$); and c is storage cost.

In order to analyze the hypothetical situation of no acreage control, the salvage value of surplus rice in the absence of acreage control must be estimated. Since the salvage value decreases when the quantity of surplus rice to be disposed increases, there is a close negative correlation between the salvage value of surplus rice produced in a year and the stock of old rice for the next year as follows:

$$(8) \qquad \hat{V}_t = 144 - 0.18 \, s_{t+1},$$
$$(7.73)$$
$$r^2 = 0.821$$

where $\hat{V}_t$ is the average salvage value of surplus rice (yen per kilogram) deflated by the consumer price index, 1975 = 100; s_{t+1} is the government stock of old rice (1,000 tons) in year ($t + 1$); and the figure in parentheses is the Student-*t* ratio. The hypothetical salvage value, in the absence of acreage control, was

534 *August 1985* *Amer. J. Agr. Econ.*

estimated from equation (8) by adding to the empirically observed s_{t+1} value the reduction of rice output due to the acreage control program, which was calculated as $\left(\dfrac{\psi Q_p}{1 - \psi}\right)$.

Once the hypothetical prices and quantities are estimated, it becomes straightforward to calculate the effects of rice policy programs on social economic welfare by carrying out integration. The basic data used for estimation are as follows.

Data of observable rice prices (P_p, P_c) and quantities (Q_p, Q_c, M_p, M_c) and of variables needed to estimate the average salvage cost (V) in equation (7) are obtained from MAFF publications. The producer price (P_p) is the average price of brown rice sold by farmers. The consumer price (P_c) is the average price of milled rice paid by consumers, which is converted into brown rice terms. Since the actual rice output fluctuates with weather changes, the "normal output" as estimated by Chino is used for Q_p.[6] The quantity of actual consumption is used for Q_c and M_c. The estimate of CIF import price converted from U.S. export price

[6] The normal output is estimated by using weather dummy variables in the estimated supply function.

is shown in table 2 in comparison with the domestic prices.

For the elasticities of total supply, producers' home consumption and market demand, we employed 0.18 for α, 0.10 for β, −0.10 for γ, and −0.12 for the price elasticity of market demand based on Otsuka (1984b). These are in close agreement with the estimates obtained by Bale and Greenshields, Bale and Lutz, Chino, and Yuize. The estimates of ϵ range from 0.37 in 1965 to 0.25 in 1980.[7]

Results of Simulation of Alternative Policies

The last three columns of table 2 show the postulated levels of rice imports and the corresponding levels of rice self-sufficiency in Japan in the absence of import restriction. They indicate that Japan should have been a major rice importer since the mid-1960s, barring the world food crisis years, when international rice prices rose sharply. In the late

[7] The estimated elasticities pertain to the short-run effects. To the extent that the long-run elasticities are larger than the short-run elasticities, our estimates involve overestimation bias in the case of welfare gain of producers and underestimation bias in the case of welfare loss of consumers.

Table 2. **Comparison of Domestic and Import Prices and Estimates of Import Quantity and Self-Sufficiency Ratio of Rice**

| | Prices | | | Estimate of Import Quantity | Self-Sufficiency Ratio | |
	Producer[a] P_p	Consumer[b] P_c	Import[c] P_I		Actual	Estimate
	--------- (yen/kg) ---------			(Million ton)	------ (%) ------	
1965	108	100	68	1.38	96	90
66	118	107	70	0.84	102	94
67	129	108	72	0.64	116	95
68	136	120	70	0.41	118	97
69	137	125	71	0.07	117	99
1970	137	129	83	−0.51	106	104
71	141	134	82	−0.49	92	104
72	148	142	103	−1.15	100	109
73	170	155	138	−1.15	101	109
74	224	171	181	−0.33	102	103
1975	258	216	147	0.65	110	95
76	278	252	110	2.01	100	84
77	292	272	134	1.04	114	92
78	300	287	99	1.59	111	87
79	302	289	102	1.51	107	88
1980	308	297	122	1.06	89	91

Source: MAFF, *Statistical Yearbook of Food Control* and FAO, *Production Yearbook*.
[a] Average sale price of producers.
[b] Average price of milled rice paid by consumers converted into brown rice terms.
[c] Unit FOB export value of milled Texas long grain multiplied by .906 to convert to a brown rice term plus an allowance for freight and other necessary costs assumed to be 15% of unit FOB value.

1970s the import quantity would have risen to 1 to 2 million tons, so that the self-sufficiency ratio would have declined under the small-country assumption from actual 110% to 90% or less if the rice imports liberalized.

Producer Surplus

Estimated increases in the net producer surplus due to rice policy programs are shown in table 3. ΔPST represents producers' welfare gain from the trade protection and ΔPSD represents their gain from additional price support above the market equilibrium under autarky by means of government price support and acreage control. ΔPST fluctuates significantly mainly because of variations in world rice prices, while ΔPSD shows a steadily increasing trend, though the rates of increase decelerated in the years when the surplus rice stock became very large. Altogether, the total gain of producers (ΔPS) from both trade protection and domestic support measures has increased sharply during the past decade and a half; from the mid-1960s to the late 1970s it increased by more than four times in nominal terms and almost doubled in

real terms if we use the consumer price index as a deflator; in the late 1970s the producers' gain became as large as about 20% of agricultural gross domestic product (GDP) and about 40% of total rice output value in farmgate prices.

Consumer Surplus

Estimated decreases in the consumer surplus due to rice policy programs are also shown in table 3. ΔCST represents the consumers' welfare loss due to trade protection and ΔCSD represents their loss due to additional domestic price support measures. On the whole, movements in those components of consumers' loss and their total parallel those of producers' gain and implied that the government intervention into the rice market was designed primarily for income transfer from consumers to producers.

Government Cost

The cost of rice policy programs shouldered by the government (or taxpayers) is estimated

Table 3.   Decomposed Estimates of Changes in Net Producer and Consumer Surpluses, Current Prices (Billion Yen)

	Increase in Net Producer Surplus[a]			Decrease in Consumer Surplus[b]		
	Trade Protection ΔPST	Domestic Price Support ΔPSD	Total ΔPS	Trade Protection $-\Delta CST$	Domestic Price Support $-\Delta CSD$	Total $-\Delta CS$
1965	236	80	316	258	11	269
66	141	254	395	146	152	298
67	123	372	495	128	171	299
68	71	541	612	72	347	419
69	15	615	657	15	435	450
1970	-99	578	479	-94	478	384
71	-100	603	503	-98	552	454
72	-280	655	375	-263	612	349
73	-384	580	196	-359	519	160
74	-422	722	300	-523	433	-90
1975	290	637	927	297	355	652
76	829	579	1,408	920	423	1,343
77	455	915	1,370	477	788	1,265
78	589	1.172	1,761	638	1,107	1,745
79	572	1,199	1,771	617	1,111	1,728
1980	442	1,181	1,623	468	1,153	1,621

[a] Based on equation (1):

$$\Delta PST = area\ P^* ei P_t$$
$$\Delta PSD = area\ P_\mu ce P^* - area\ twO + Z \cdot \Delta L.$$

[b] Based on equation (2):

$$-\Delta CST = area\ P^* ek P_t$$
$$-\Delta CSD = area\ P_c de P^*.$$

536   *August 1985*   *Amer. J. Agr. Econ.*

Table 4.   Decomposed Estimates of Government Costs, Current Prices (Billion Yen)

	Current Marketig Deficit GM	Cost of Surplus Rice Disposal GS	Acreage Control Subsidy GA	Total G = GM + GS + GA
1965	65	11		76
66	88	55		143
67	171	108		279
68	134	204		338
69	99	251	2	352
1970	72	76	114	262
71	60	14	184	258
72	57	8	203	268
73	139	−26	203	316
74	490	39	128	657
1975	380	156	106	642
76	234	297	79	610
77	178	455	96	729
78	115	281	305	701
79	116	235	365	716
1980	98	112	455	567

Note: Based on equation (3):

$$GM = area\ P_p ad P_c$$
$$GS = area\ acmr\ \text{for } Z = 0$$
$$= area\ abnr\ \text{for } Z > 0$$
$$GA = Z \cdot \Delta L.$$

in table 4. The government cost (G) consists of the loss from the Food Agency's deficit from current rice-marketing operations (GM), the loss from the disposal of surplus rice at a very low salvage value (GS), and the subsidy payments for acreage control (GA). Movements in these components may appear very different but, in fact, they are closely related. In the 1960s, GM increased first because the producer price was raised relative to the consumer price; the consumer price was soon raised in order to reduce GM but it had the effect of increasing the excess supply of rice and, hence, increasing the cost of surplus rice disposal (GS); when GS became unbearably large, the government introduced the acreage control program (1969), which reduced GS at the expense of GA. The same process was repeated after 1973, when the successful elimination of surplus rice stock coincided with the world food crisis and slackened the government effort to restrain farmers' demand for price hikes. From the data in table 4 it is clear that G and GA are inversely correlated for 1969–72 and 1977–80 periods when the acreage control was intensified. The negative correlation indicates that the acreage control given the high level of price support has had the effect of reducing the total government cost.

Deadweight Loss

The estimates of deadweight or net social loss due to rice policy programs are shown in table 5. The deadweight loss (DL) can be decomposed into welfare losses due to (a) producer and consumer prices raised above international prices (DLP), (b) disposal of surplus rice at salvage values below international prices (DLS), and (c) production inefficiency caused by the acreage control (DLA). Movements in those components in relation to the total deadweight loss were similar to those of the government cost. In both the 1960s and the 1970s, after the world food crisis, the price support was raised first, and this tended to increase DLP. The cumulating surplus stock worked as a brake on further price increases and, at the same time, increased the volume of surplus rice disposal, which reduced DLP and increased DLS. Sharp increases in the social cost of surplus rice disposal paralleled the increases in the government cost which forced the government to introduce the acreage control program. As a result, DLS was reduced at the expense of DLA. The negative correlation between DL and DLA for the periods when the acreage control was intensified suggests, given the high level of price support, that the acreage control program raised social welfare.

Table 5. Decomposed Estimates of Dead-weight Loss, Current Prices (Billion Yen)

	Price Distortion DLP	Surplus Rice Disposal DLS	Production Inefficiency Due to Acreage Control DLA	Total DL
1965	31	-2		29
66	40	7		47
67	48	36		83
68	60	84		144
69	65	105	3	173
1970	13	33	121	167
71	38	4	165	208
72	60	3	179	242
73	96	-14	198	280
74	50	25	192	267
1975	104	63	200	366
76	281	88	175	544
77	239	188	197	624
78	274	77	332	683
79	273	54	345	672
1980	247	33	383	663

Note: Based on equation (4):

$$DLP = area\ cli + area\ dkh,\ \text{for}\ Z = 0$$
$$= area\ sji + area\ dkh,\ \text{for}\ Z > 0$$
$$DLS = area\ hlmr,\ \text{for}\ Z = 0$$
$$= area\ hjnr,\ \text{for}\ Z > 0$$
$$DLA = area\ twO.$$

"Second-Best" Effect of Acreage Control

In order to test the hypothesis that acreage control was a "second-best" policy to reduce the social cost produced by high price support, the changes in social economic welfare from the actual situation to the hypothetical situation of no acreage control program are estimated in table 6. The results of the hypothetical analysis show that, if the acreage control were not introduced, the producer surplus would have increased.[8] However, the increases in producers' gain would have been substantially smaller than the additional government costs for surplus rice disposal, so that the deadweight loss would have increased.[9]

---

[8] This does not imply that producers were adversely affected by the acreage control policy. The acreage control policy was essentially voluntary, so that producers entered the program to the extent they gained from subsidy payments cum non-rice production activities.

[9] The deadweight loss might have been even larger to the extent that the acquisition of tax revenue for the subsidy payments entails the additional market distortion (Harberger 1978). Also note that the "efficiency" of welfare redistribution through the acreage diversion program is critically related to the supply and demand elasticities. For this point, see Gardner.

Table 6. Estimates of Changes in the Social Cost of Rice Policy Programs if the Acreage Control Were Not Introduced (Billion Yen)

	Change in Producer Surplus[a] $\Delta(\Delta PS)$	Change in Government Cost[b] ΔG	Change in Deadweight Loss $\Delta DL = \Delta G - \Delta(\Delta PS)$
1970	66	256	190
71	95	300	205
72	87	263	177
73	137	267	129
74	112	194	82
1975	144	230	86
76	117	157	40
77	125	245	119
78	203	729	526
79	189	811	622
1980	243	1,024	781

[a] Estimated by subtracting the estimates of ΔPS based on equation (1) under the actual situation from the estimates under the counterfactual situation of no acreage control.
[b] Estimated by subtracting the estimates of G based on equation (3) under the actual situation from the counterfactual situation of no acreage control.

These results are consistent with the hypothesis that the introduction of acreage control was a "second-best" policy to reduce social inefficiency or divergence from the Pareto optimum produced from other forms of market distortion.[10]

Conclusion

The results of our analysis suggest a hypothesis that the government's goal was to minimize the government's cost in achieving the politically determined level of price support for domestic rice producers and that the consumers' welfare had an insignificant weight in the government's objective function in policy choice. The government tried to transfer the cost of price support to the consumers in the form of high consumer prices. However, the transfer was limited, not because of the organized political protests of consumers but due to market forces that jeopardized the goal

---

[10] Since the acreage control program diverted some land to other crops such as wheat, soybeans, and barley, for which production was socially excessive due to price support policies for these crops, it entailed additional social welfare losses. Otsuka (1984a) estimated such welfare losses, using the estimation formula for welfare loss in a general equilibrium framework developed by Harberger (1971). The results show that the additional welfare losses accounted for only about 10% of the social loss incurred in the rice market, so that the second-best implication of the acreage control policy remains unchanged.

538 *August 1985* *Amer. J. Agr. Econ.*

of minimizing the government cost. The high support prices encouraged production and discouraged consumption, resulting in an excess supply of rice that had to be disposed of at prices lower than international prices. In order to prevent the government cost from rising, it became necessary to introduce the acreage control program. It appears that the sequence of such policy choices based on the motivation of government cost minimization was largely consistent with the "second-best" solution in terms of social economic welfare (given the desired level of domestic price support). In terms of the social welfare maximization model of price policy decision by Sarris and Freebairn, the Japanese government's behavior is consistent with the case in which the social welfare weight (as conceived by the government) of producer surplus is higher than that of government budget cost but the weight of consumer surplus is almost zero.

[Received March 1984; final revision received September 1984.]

References

Bale, M. D., and B. L. Greenshields. "Japanese Agricultural Distortions and Their Welfare Value." *Amer. J. Agr. Econ.* 60(1978):59–64.

Bale, M. D., and Ernst Lutz. "Price Distortions in Agriculture and Their Effects: An International Comparison." *Amer. J. Agr. Econ.* 63(1981):8–22.

Chino, Tetsuro. "Shijokainyu no Koseisonshitsu: Niju Beika to Seisan Chosei Seisaku" (Welfare Cost of Market Intervention: Rice Price and Acreage Control Policies in Japan). M.A. thesis, Tokyo Metropolitan University, March 1981.

Davis, O. S., and A. B. Whinston. "Welfare Economics and the Theory of Second Best." *Rev. Econ. Stud.* 32(1965):1–14.

Floyd, John E. "The Effects of Farm Price Supports on the Returns to Land and Labor in Agriculture." *J. Polit. Econ.* 73(1965):148–58.

Gardner, Bruce. "Efficient Redistribution through Commodity Markets." *Amer. J. Agr. Econ.* 65(1983): 225–34.

Harberger, A. C. "On the Use of Distributional Weights in Social Cost-Benefit Analysis." *J. Polit. Econ.* 86(1978):S87–S120.

———. "Three Basic Postulates for Applied Welfare Economics." *J. Econ. Lit.* 9(1971):785–97.

Hayami, Yujiro. "Rice Policy in Japan's Economic Development." *Amer. J. Agr. Econ.* 54(1972):19–31.

Hayami, Yujiro, in association with M. Akino, M. Shintani, and S. Yamada. *A Century of Agricultural Growth in Japan.* Tokyo: University of Tokyo Press and University of Minnesota Press, 1975.

Hayami, Yujiro, and Robert W. Herdt. "Market Price Effects of Technological Change on Income Distribution in Subsistence Agriculture." *Amer. J. Agr. Econ.* 59(1977):245–56.

Hemmi, Kenzo. "Agriculture and Politics in Japan." *U.S.-Japanese Agricultural Trade Relations,* ed. E. N. Castle and Kenzo Hemmi. Baltimore MD and London: Johns Hopkins University Press, 1982.

Japan. Ministry of Agriculture, Forestry, and Fishery (MAFF). *Pocket Statistics of Ministry of Agriculture, Forestry, and Fishery.* Tokyo, various issues.

———. *Statistical Yearbook of Food Control.* Tokyo, various issues.

———. *Statistical Yearbook of Ministry of Agriculture, Forestry, and Fishery.* Tokyo, various issues.

———. *Tensaku no Genjo to Kongo no Hoko* (Present Situation of Paddy Diversion Program and Future Policy Plan). Tokyo: Sozo Shobo, 1979.

Kama, Kunio. "The Determinants of Interest Rates in Japan, 1967–78." *Keizai Kenkyu* (Economic Review) 32(1981):21–33.

Lipsey, R. G., and Kelvin Lancaster. "The General Theory of Second Best." *Rev. Econ. Stud.* 24(1956/57):11–32.

Otsuka, Keijiro. "Beika Seisaku to Seisan Chosei Seisaku: Keizai Kosei no Henka to Seisan Chosei no Igi" (Rice Price and Acreage Control Policies: Their Welfare Effects and Significance of Acreage Control). *Kome no Keizai Bunseki* (Economic Analysis of Rice Economy), ed. S. Sakiura. Tokyo: Taimeido, 1984a.

Otsuka, Keijiro. "Kome no Juyokyoku Kansu no Suitei" (Estimation of Supply and Demand Functions of Rice). *J. Faculty of Econ. at Tokyo Metropolitan University,* no. 55, 1984b.

Sarris, A. H., and John Freebairn. "Endogenous Price Policies and International Wheat Prices." *Amer. J. Agr. Econ.* 65(1983):214–24.

Tolley, G. S., Vinod Thomas, and M. C. Wong. *Agricultural Price Policies and the Developing Countries.* Washington DC: World Bank, 1982.

Yuize, Yasuhiko. "Beikoku no Jukyu Model" (Economic Model of Rice, Wheat, and Barley under Government Management). *Nogyo Sogo Kenkyu* (Quart. J. Agr. Econ.) 32(1978):1–76.

[5]

Land Reform, Income Redistribution, and Agricultural Production in Korea*

Yoong-Deok Jeon
Taegu University, Korea

Young-Yong Kim
Chonnam National University, Korea

I. Introduction

The purpose of this study is to investigate the effects of agricultural land reform on the Korean economy. In addition to the land ownership transfer and the socioeconomic causes of the land reform, its effects on income redistribution and rice production will be addressed. This study emphasizes economic forces in terms of transaction costs as the cause of land reform, while most of the previous studies, by M. A. Taslim, for example, attributed its cause only to political factors.[1]

Most of the previous studies on land reform in Korea also have put emphasis only on the transfer of land ownership established by the Agricultural Land Reform Amendment Act (ALRAA) of 1950. In fact, the ratio of owner-cultivated land to total arable land reached about 96% in 1951 as a result of the ALRAA.[2] Unlike earlier work, however, we will investigate not only the sale of vested land by the U.S. military administration but also the transactions of land in the market pre-ALRAA.[3] The vested and redistributed land amounted to approximately 40% of the total land to be reformed, whereas the land sold by landlords in the market represents about 50% of the total, which is considered to be indirectly affected by the ALRAA. Also, there are noticeable effects of land reform on income redistribution and agricultural production. Therefore, we examined the entire process of the reform in order to identify its effects on the Korean economy.

Results of the analysis are summarized as follows. First, we claim that land reform evolved to reduce transaction costs. High transaction costs between landlords and tenants prevented the smooth functioning of the tenancy system. As a large majority, tenants gained political power at the cost of landlords. Thus, ALRAA, a new and formal institutional arrangement, was established. Second, land reform redistributed income from landlords to other economic agents, including tenants, government, and the general public. This income redistribution is comparable to the predictions of the median voter theorem.[4] Finally, the abolition of the tenancy system increased agricultural production and positively affected economic growth.

The remainder of the article is organized as follows. In Section II we briefly explore the history of land reform and investigate the transfer of land ownership. Section III examines the political and economic causes of the land reform. In Section IV we discuss the effect of land reform on income redistribution, and its effect on rice production is analyzed in Section V. Finally, some closing remarks are offered in Section VI.

II. The History of Agricultural Land Reform

Agricultural land reform has been an important social and economic issue in Korea since the end of the Chosun Dynasty. A small number of the ruling class possessed most of the agricultural land, and high rental rates seriously deteriorated the economic life of tenants who comprised most of the population.

An article of agricultural land reform was listed in the Constitution of the Republic of Korea in 1948. Based on the Constitution, the ALRAA was drafted and actually became effective on March 10, 1950.[5] The ALRAA contains three main features: first, any individual can own agricultural land but only if he or she cultivates or manages it for himself or herself; second, one can own three *jungbo* of land at maximum;[6] and third, tenancy arrangements and land-renting activities are legally prohibited.

The land reform proceeded as follows. After surveying landlord-tenant relationships in June 1949, the government purchased the land from landlords with land securities under the provision of the ALRAA. Land securities specified the compensation period (5 years) as well as the price of land as a percentage of annual crop yields from the land. However, actual compensation was made by cash, and the compensation period was prolonged to more than 10 years for some of the land under reform. Generally, land reform was completed by the beginning of the 1960s, and 97.3% of the compensation for landlords was completed by the end of 1961.[7] Altogether, it took well over 10 years to complete the land reform process. In addition, the government sold the land to tenants who made payments with rice and, in fact, acted as an arbitrageur between landlords and tenants.

Previous studies maintain that the impact of the ALRAA on land reform is negligible at best, since the amount of land sold by landlords on the free market was larger than that of the land redistributed.[8] How-

Yoong-Deok Jeon and Young-Yong Kim   255

TABLE 1

OWNERSHIP CHANGE IN AGRICULTURAL LAND AS A RESULT OF REFORM

Classification of Land	1,000 Jungbo (%)
Redistributed land through ALRAA by the Korean government	302 (21.0)
Vested land owned by the Japanese and sold to individuals by the U.S. military government	273 (18.9)
Land freely sold by landlords in the market before ALRAA	714 (49.2)
Land excepted by ALRAA*	74 (5.1)
Hidden land, not reformed	85 (5.9)
Total land targeted for reform in 1945†	1,447 (100)

SOURCE.—Korea Agricultural Economic Research Institute (KAERI), *Nongchikae-hyoksa Yonku* (A study on the history of agricultural land reform) (Seoul: KAERI, 1989), pp. 1030–31.

    * 90% of the excepted land was for the management of private cemeteries.

    † Total land is not exactly equal to the sum of each item due to round-off error.

ever, such a claim does not take into account the indirect effect of the ALRAA. Although agricultural land ownership had to be transferred from landlords to tenants as provided by the ALRAA in 1950, it is evident that land reform actually started in 1945, when a majority of the sharecropping land was transacted in the market while the legislation for land reform was still in process. S. H. Chang shows that about 60% of the total land sold in rural areas from 1945 to 1950 was transacted from 1948 to 1949.[9] The sale of sharecropping land to tenants before the enactment of the ALRAA provided a good environment for success because it eliminated to a significant degree the resistance of landlords against agricultural reform.[10]

A survey on the transfer of land ownership is presented in table 1. It shows that the vested and redistributed land amounted to 40%, while the market-transacted land reached 50% of the total land to be reformed. Table 2 shows the number of farmer households by tenure status. The number of owner-cultivating households increased drastically to 1,812,000 in 1950 from 349,000 in 1949, whereas the number of tenant farmer households decreased to almost zero in 1950. Since 1950, the number of tenant households gradually increased although the tenancy is illegal.[11]

III. Causes of Land Reform

There were two major forces that brought about agricultural land reform in Korea: economic and political. Prohibitively high transaction costs between landlords and tenants, and the strong political motives of land reform prevented the smooth functioning of the share tenancy system. There was a movement toward denying rental payments in the 1930s. Strikes against the tenancy system were frequent as well as destructive. While such disorder occurred in the agricultural sector, Korea in general

TABLE 2

NUMBER OF FARMER HOUSEHOLDS BY TENURE STATUS
(Unit = 1,000)

Year	Owner Cultivation	Tenancy	Mixed	Total
1937	550	1,581	738	2,869
1938	552	1,583	729	2,864
1939	540	1,583	719	2,842
1940	551	1,617	711	2,879
1941	548	1,647	723	2,918
1942	530	1,642	729	2,901
1943	536	1,481	984	3,001
1945	285	1,010	716	2,011
1946	337	990	810	2,137
1947	401	914	834	2,149
1949	349	1,133	992	2,474
1950	1,812	0	158	1,970
1959	1,808	43	406	2,257
1960	1,729	160	460	2,349
1965	1,742	176	589	2,507
1970	1,625	237	581	2,443

SOURCES.—Korea Agricultural Economic Research Institute (KAERI), *Nongopsashipnyonsa* (The forty year history of agriculture) (Seoul: KAERI, 1989), p. 106; The Chosun Bank, *Chosun Kyongje Yongam* (Annual economic review of Korea) (Seoul: The Chosun Bank, 1948), pp. iii–25.

was well controlled by the police and military forces of Japan during the colonial period, from 1919 to August 1945. Immediately after the colonial period, however, almost no social order was maintained. Later, the social order of rural areas was preserved only by local committees, consisting of tenants and small landowners. With the beginning of the U.S. military administration, a movement of denying rental payments as well as strikes demanding redistribution of the land previously owned by the Japanese became frequent and violent in regions that were dominated by committees and agricultural cooperatives. The target of the strikes was soon extended to include land owned by Korean landlords.

As Douglass C. North pointed out, an essential part of the functioning of institutions is the costliness of ascertaining violations and the severity of punishment.[12] Such institutional costs varied significantly between pre- and post-1945. Although political motives of land reform had been strong ever since the 1930s, land sales in the market did not occur to a significant degree before 1945. Law enforcement costs were relatively low before August 1945, as a result of the Japanese presence in Korea. However, costs of negotiation and law enforcement rose due to the weak or protenant government that prevailed in local areas from August 1945 to the beginning of the U.S. military administration. The government was so weak that landlords had no means of ascertaining and punishing violations of tenancy contracts, particularly in rural areas. For example, a landlord could collect as a share rent 1,500 *suk* of rice during the colonial period, 100 *suk* right after August 1945, and 400–500 *suk* after 1946 for the same acreage of sharecropping land.[13] This means that the share rent after 1945 was determined by tenants' discretion, not by a contract or negotiation. The decrease in share rent that the landlords could collect reflects increased transaction costs.

In addition, the landlords' political power became severely limited because of their pro-Japanese activities during the colonial period. At times even the personal security of landlords was in severe danger immediately after the colonial period. Transaction costs and law enforcement costs, in particular, rose so high by 1945 that landlords lost the incentives to keep their land. This phenomenon suggests that economic forces combined with political factors should explain the voluntary sale of land by landlords before the ALRAA became effective. In short, an inability of the government to secure socioeconomic order, combined with the political motives of land redistribution, were the reasons primarily responsible for the increase in transaction costs, which eventually broke down the tenancy system.

The ALRAA was made primarily for the purpose of income redistribution toward tenants at the cost of landlords. Tenants represented the largest portion of the population in the 1940s and 1950s. They were monolithic and strongly against sharecropping tenancy since the 1930s. As a large majority, they gained strong political power under the U.S. military administration. Furthermore, South Koreans with different ideologies, such as capitalism and socialism, were in severe confrontation, which resulted in social disorder after the colonial period. Approximately 77% out of 8,453 respondents in sample surveys that were conducted by the U.S. military administration in August 1946 responded ''yes'' in support of socialism and communism.[14] Also in 1946 the government of North Korea took landlords' land without compensation and distributed it to the people at no charge. Under such circumstances, the U.S. military administration wanted the South buffered from socialism and communism. Thus, it set the rental rate for tenancy at one third of annual crop yields, which was much lower than that before 1945. It also sold part of the vested land to individuals, which led landlords and tenants to expect that land reform would certainly materialize in the near future. In general, the agricultural policy of the U.S. military administration was in favor of tenants and against landlords.[15]

In 1948, when the new democratic government was established, the main socioeconomic issue was still land reform. Under democracy, the threat of communism and the redistribution of land in North Korea reinforced the political power of tenants, while the political power of landlords became increasingly limited, even though the Han-Min party, the ruling party of the South, represented the landlords. Without land reform the government would not have been able to prevent most tenants from shifting to communism. Finally, the government of South Korea made the ALRAA effective. Both the agricultural policies of the U.S. military administration and the ALRAA were an endogenously determined governmental policy consistent with the intuition of the median voter theorem.

In sum, the increase in transaction costs combined with strong political motives of tenants for land reform led the landlords to sell their land voluntarily, and eventually these factors broke down the tenancy system.

IV. The Impact of Land Reform on Income Redistribution

The land reform also redistributed income among those involved, as the median voter theorem generally predicts. In this section, we examine this issue of income redistribution.

Demand for and supply of agricultural land increased simultaneously after August 15, 1945. The population of South Korea increased substantially because of the immigration of North Koreans and from foreign countries such as China. The population size increased to roughly 20.2 million in 1949 from approximately 16.9 million in 1945. This demographic change increased demand for land. However, landlords only sold 714,000 *jungbo* in the market, approximately 37% of the total arable land.

Had that amount of land not been sold in the market during such a short period, the price of the redistributed land would have been much higher. Redistributed land was priced by the National Assembly at 1.5 times its annual crop yields, slightly lower than the market price. The survey on the market price of land demonstrates that its median value was 1.5 to two times its annual crop yields, and its weighted average was approximately 1.52 times its annual yields. However, the price was much lower than its market price during the colonial period, approximately five times the annual crop yields from the land. This significant shift in land price seems to reflect the fact that the increase in the supply of land was greater than the increase in the demand for land.

Although the explicit value of the redistributed land does not seem to be much different from the market price, we get a quite different result if we calculate the present value, 1.5 times the annual yields. Landlords who sold their land in the market were usually paid in cash at the time of sale. Tenants who purchased redistributed land from the government had to pay 30% of the annual crop yields within 1 year and then the same amount annually for the subsequent 4 years. The present value of all such payments amounts to 0.795 times annual crop yields if the market interest rate is applied as the discount factor and to 1.123 times the annual yields if the discount rate of a bill is applied.[16] Subsequently, the government prolonged the payment period to 8 years. Approximately

Yoong-Deok Jeon and Young-Yong Kim   259

70% of the total payment (cumulated) were made by 1954, 95% by 1960, and 100% by 1970. If we incorporate this extension of the payment period into calculating the present value, then the present value becomes much smaller than what we obtained from our previous calculations.

Redistribution was also accomplished when the government acted as an arbitrageur between landlords and tenants. It purchased land from landlords with cash and sold the land to tenants who made payments with rice and cash.[17] The payments in terms of rice amounted to 78% of the total, while the cash payments amounted to 20% of the total. The government applied the regulated price not only to the cash compensation to the landlords but also to the cash payments by the tenants. The point is that in the 1950s the regulated price of rice was much lower than the market price. Thus, the difference between the two prices was redistributed among the tenants, the government, and the general public. Table 3 provides the market price and the regulated price of rice, 1950–70. The regulated price converged to the market price that prevailed at the end of the 1960s.

To be specific about the income transfer from landlords to tenants and the government, we used the government's 1950–70 Special Accounts for the Agricultural Land Reform Project, shown in table 4. Column A shows total receipts from tenants that equal the sum of columns B, C, and D. Approximately 78% of total receipts was in terms of rice, 20% cash, and 1.4% land securities. When cash and land securities were used for payment, the government applied the regulated price of rice. Therefore, the difference between the market price and the regulated price of rice was transferred from landlords to tenants. Column E shows the amount of compensations made by the government to landlords. It was made in cash not rice. One-fifth of the total compensation was to be made the first year followed by the same amount each year for the subsequent 4 years. However, compensation was actually stretched out over a longer period than 5 years, since tenants were unable to make their payments due to a bad harvest and the Korean War. The government's compensations to landlords amounted to only 26.3% of total receipts by the government because the regulated price of rice was much lower than the market price.

Column F indicates the sum of administrative costs of land reform and agricultural investment for remodeling of arable land. In principle, both costs should have been paid by the tenants, since they were prime beneficiaries of land reform. However, they were actually paid by the landlords. This, too, illustrates the redistribution of income from landlords to tenants.

Subtracting columns E and F from column A, we obtain column G. In particular, subtracting columns C and D from column G results in the transfer of income to the government. It amounts to approximately 38% of total receipts. The general public benefited from land reform in that

Economic Development and Cultural Change

TABLE 3

THE MARKET AND THE REGULATED PRICE OF RICE: 1950–1970
(Unit = *Won* per *Suk*, %)

Year	Market Price (A)	Regulated Price (B)	B/A (× 100)
1950	29.1	14.8	50.8
1951	115.7	58.8	50.8
1952	419.4	180.6	43.6
1953	436.5	297.9	68.2
1954	354.9	475.5	134.0
1955	851.1	629.0	73.9
1956	1,336.7	953.1	71.3
1957	1,537.3	953.1	62.0
1958	1,255.7	953.1	75.9
1959	1,106.1	953.1	86.2
1960	1,283.3	953.1	74.3
1961	1,463.2	1,394.9	95.3
1962	1,594.5	1,489.3	93.4
1963	2,526.5	1,850.0	73.2
1964	3,130.0	2,377.3	76.0
1965	2,998.0	2,701.0	90.1
1966	3,122.0	2,889.7	92.6
1967	3,432.0	3,220.1	94.2
1968	3,868.7	3,779.6	97.7
1969	4,636.3	4,634.3	99.9
1970	5,217.2	5,686.9	109.0

SOURCES.—S. H. Chang, "Nongchikaehyok Kwachonge Kwan-han Shilchungjok Yonku" (An empirical examination of the process of land reform), in *Haebangchunhusaui Inshik* (The perspective of the history about the time of liberalization), M. K. Kang et al. (Seoul: Hankilsa, 1985), 2:350 and table 28. Some errors are corrected. Ministry of Agriculture, Forest, and Fishery (MAFF), *Hankukyangchongsa* (Rice policy history) (Seoul: MAFF, 1978), pp. 264, 308, 309.

NOTE.—1 *suk* = 180.4 liters (4.9629 bushels). The old currency unit is converted into *won*. The series of market prices after 1966 may seem to be somewhat underestimated. The regulated price is the price at which the government purchased the rice.

without it they would have had to pay much more. In sum, land reform mainly redistributed income from landlords to tenants, but the government and the general public benefited from it as well.

V. The Impact of Land Reform on Agricultural Production

Until recently, the theoretical modeling of sharecropping tenancy has followed two basic approaches. The first approach, called Marshallian productive inefficiency, assumes a prohibitively high cost of monitoring the tenants' activities and predicts lower input intensities on rented land than on owned land.[18] A fraction of marginal product is taxed away by the landowner under sharecropping, whereas owner-cultivators are presumed to receive the entire marginal product (Marshallian effect). Hence sharecropping results in an inefficient allocation of resources. In con-

TABLE 4

TOTAL RECEIPTS AND COMPENSATION (Unit = 1,000 *Suk*)

Total Receipts = Total Compensation (A)	Receipts in Rice (B)	Receipts in Cash (C)	Receipts in Land Security (D)	Compensation to Landlords (E)	Administration and Agricultural Investment (F)	Remainder (G)
11,578 (100)	9,022 (77.9)	2,291 (19.8)	165 (1.4)	3,048 (26.3)	1,680 (14.5)	6,850 (59.2)

SOURCE.—Korea Agricultural Economic Research Institute (KAERI), *Nongchikaehyoksa Yonku* (A study on the history of agricultural land reform) (Seoul: KAERI, 1989).

NOTE.—Total receipts = B + C + D (= A). E is annual compensation divided by the market price of rice. F is the sum of administrative costs and agricultural investment divided by the market price of rice. A is not exactly equal to the sum of B, C, and D, since the original data set has some errors. Numbers in parentheses are percentages.

trast, the "new school" or "monitoring approach," established by Steven Cheung and based on the Coasian framework, argues that landlords can monitor the tenants' activities effectively and inexpensively.[19] According to this approach, landlords can stipulate the intensity of inputs, and they have a sufficiently effective and inexpensive way of monitoring to ensure that the stipulation is fulfilled. Thus productive efficiency is achieved. In addition, sharecropping is used as an arrangement to share risks between the two parties, landlords and tenants, and to provide effort incentives to tenants. In testing the two theories, Radwan Shaban, among others, supports the productive inefficiency approach.[20]

The question arises then as to why sharecropping is more widespread. It is argued that if sharecropping is an inefficient contractual arrangement, landlords and tenants can make a fixed-rent contract, or landlords can sell their land to tenants. However, the fixed-rent contract is not frequently observed because landlords need to share risks with their tenants. Also, the tenants' limited wealth might cause them to default on fixed-rent obligations in times of a bad harvest. In addition, empirical findings suggest that land markets are thin. D. Mookherjee suggests that there would never be a mutually beneficial scope for land sales from landlords to tenants because of the tenants' inability to finance the land purchase. He indicates that this may arise from endogenous credit market imperfections in the presence of distortions such as moral hazard. He also suggests that the coercive transfer of land ownership from landlords to tenants will result in an increase in agricultural productivity and in welfare improvement, though it is not Pareto improvement. Therefore, landlords will presumably be losers while tenants will be winners.[21] As described in Section IV, income was actually redistributed from landlords to tenants in the case of Korea.

In a study on Korea, I. H. Yoo, for example, argues that the effect of land reform on agricultural production is insignificant, but this has not been tested systematically.[22] Note that tenancy arrangements in Korea were not based on fixed rent but on sharecropping. Therefore, our empirical test of the effect of the tenancy rate on agricultural production pertains to contractual arrangements, not to tenancy per se. Since land reform was mainly related to land for rice production, an investigation of its effect on rice production would provide some useful evidence.

To investigate the effect of land reform on agricultural production, we specify the rice production function as follows:

$$Q = Ae^{\lambda t}L^{b_1}N^{b_2}K^{b_3}e^{\epsilon}, \tag{1}$$

where Q represents rice output, A constant, λ productivity growth rate, t time trend, L labor, N cultivating land, K capital, e exponent, and ϵ error term. In addition, three dummies are included in the regression to cap-

Yoong-Deok Jeon and Young-Yong Kim   263

ture, respectively, the effect of weather condition (*WD*), the effect of a decrease in cultivating land due to the political separation of the Korean peninsula and the Korean War (*SEPD*), and the effect of an abrupt decrease in the tenancy rate for 1943–44 (*DU*). We also added the tenancy rate variable (*RSC*) in the equation to determine whether a decrease in tenancy rate increases rice production. Thus, the regression equation is of the following form:

$$\ln Q = \ln A = \lambda t + b_1 \ln L + b_2 \ln N + b_3 \ln K$$
$$+ b_4 WD + b_5 SEPD + b_6 DU + b_7 RSC + \epsilon. \quad (2)$$

The data used are annual observations recorded during 1937–44 and 1955–74.[23] The observations for 1945–54 are not included because consistent time series data are not available, since Korea's independence from Japanese rule and the Korean War occurred during this period. Thus, the sample contains 28 observations. The data in the Appendix were obtained from a 1978 publication by the Ministry of Agriculture, Forest, and Fishery.[24]

Average annual growth rates of the variables used are shown in table 5 for the three subperiods. After the land reform, rice production and inputs of labor and arable land increased, whereas capital input decreased at a lower rate. With the first 5-year economic development plan, started in 1962, rice production and inputs of arable land and capital increased, while the labor force devoted to the rice production decreased due to migration from rural to urban areas.

The definition of variables and the expected signs of the estimated coefficients are presented in table 6. Variables *Q*, *L*, and *N* are measured, respectively, using the quantity of rice produced, number of people employed for rice production, and the land designated for rice production in terms of hectare. The variable *K* is the sum of costs of working capital and depreciation indexed to the constant price of 1965. The time trend runs from 1 to 38, excluding from 9 to 18. The weather dummy variable,

TABLE 5

AVERAGE ANNUAL GROWTH RATES IN AGRICULTURE
(Unit = %)

Subperiod	Rice Production	Labor	Land	Capital
1937–44	−7.32	−.23	−2.99	−3.60
1955–61	2.62	6.10	.59	−1.14
1962–74	3.24	−3.82	.53	5.85

SOURCE.—Ministry of Agriculture, Forest, and Fishery (MAFF), *Hankukyangchongsa* (Rice policy history) (Seoul: MAFF, 1978).

264   *Economic Development and Cultural Change*

TABLE 6

DEFINITION OF THE VARIABLES AND THEIR EXPECTED SIGNS

Variable	Definition	Expected Sign
LnQ	Logarithm of annul rice production	. . .
T	Time: from 1 to 38 (excluding 9–18)	Positive
LnL	Logarithm of annual labor input for rice production	Positive
LnN	Logarithm of annual cultivating land for rice production	Positive
LnK	Logarithm of the sum of working capital and depreciation costs	Positive
WD	Weather dummy with one for bad and zero otherwise	Negative
SEPD	Dummy for the drastic decrease in arable land due to the political separation of Korea: one for the years after 1955 and zero otherwise	Uncertain
DU	Dummy capturing an abrupt change in tenancy rate: one for the years 1943–44 and zero otherwise	Negative
RSC	Tenancy rate	Uncertain

WD, is included with the value of one assigned to bad weather and zero otherwise. The second dummy variable, *SEPD,* is added to capture the effect of a decrease in arable land that resulted from the political separation of the Korean peninsula and from the Korean War. It is conjectured that the separation of the peninsula and the Korean War changed the structure of rice production. The value of one is given to the years after 1955 and zero otherwise. The final dummy variable, *DU,* reflects the effect of a sharp decrease in the ratio of sharecropping land in 1943 and 1944. Although we do not know exactly what happened in those years, *DU* is included in the equation to control for such a change, giving it the value of one for 1943–44 and zero otherwise. Finally, the data series for the tenancy rate, *RSC,* is incomplete, and since it is the key variable in this study, the missing observations were generated by interpolation.[25]

     The problem with the single equation estimation of the production function by ordinary least squares (OLS) is that the estimates are inconsistent because of the endogeneity of the input variables (*L, N,* and *K*). If agricultural firms try to maximize current money output, the level of use of inputs will depend not only on the price of output and inputs but also on the error term, ϵ. However, if we assume that the firms attempt to maximize anticipated money output, the solution for the inputs will not contain the error term. If this argument is assumed, then the single equation estimates obtain consistency.[26]

     The regression results are reported in table 7. The coefficient on *RSC* is estimated to be negative and is significantly different from zero at the 5% level. This suggests that the abolition of tenancy due to land reform favorably influenced rice production. Therefore, the hypothesis is incorrect that land reform failed to increase agricultural production.

Yoong-Deok Jeon and Young-Yong Kim   265

TABLE 7

PARAMETER ESTIMATE OF RICE PRODUCTION
FUNCTION (OLS) DEPENDENT VARIABLE: LnQ

Constant	2.75 (1.84)
T	.02 (3.45)**
LmL	.09 (.99)
LnN	1.21 (6.23)**
LnK	−.03 (−.24)
WD	−.14 (−5.59)**
SEPD	−1.88 (−2.51)*
DU	−.36 (−3.68)**
RSC	−3.57 (−2.68)*
Adjusted R^2	.93

NOTE.—*t*-values are given in parentheses.
* Statistically significant at the 5% level.
** Statistically significant at the 1% level.

Rather, the result supports the proposition that agricultural land reform raised agricultural production by enhancing economic incentives. This is similar to Justin Lin's finding that market-oriented institutional reforms contributed to China's agricultural output growth in 1978–84, although his context is different from ours.[27]

The estimated coefficient on time trend is significantly positive to imply that agricultural productivity increased over time. The coefficient on land is estimated positive, as expected, and significant at the 1% level. While the estimated coefficient on labor is positive, it is insignificant. This result may reflect the fact that workers were inefficiently used. The coefficient on capital has a wrong sign, but it is insignificant. Although farming capital increased after the colonial period, its effect on rice production is not significant. A further investigation of labor and capital is necessary, which is beyond the scope of this study.

The estimated coefficient on *WD* has the expected sign and is significant, which suggests that rice production in Korea critically depended on weather conditions. The dummy variable, *SEPD,* is significantly negative, implying that the political separation of the Korean peninsula and the Korean War produced a harmful effect on the rice production of South Korea.[28] Finally, the estimated coefficient on *DU* is of the expected sign and different from zero at the 1% significance level. In sum, the regression results show that a decrease in tenancy rate increased rice production, which may be interpreted as supporting the Marshallian productive inefficiency theory.

VI. Concluding Remarks

The effect of agricultural land reform on the Korean economy was tremendous. While most of the previous studies have focused on the changes in land ownership, they ignored the economic cause of land re-

266   *Economic Development and Cultural Change*

form and its effects on income redistribution and rice production. This
article addresses those issues as well as the political and economic
causes of land reform.

We emphasize that high transaction costs between landlords and
tenants eventually broke down the tenancy system. Also, land reform redistributed income mainly from landlords to tenants and, on a smaller
scale, to the government and the general public. This is consistent with
the intuition of the median voter theorem. In addition, the abolition of
the tenancy system increased agricultural production, which supports the
notion of the Marshallian productive inefficiency theory of sharecropping. It also made a contribution to stabilizing the political environment,
thus positively affecting future economic growth.

Appendix

TABLE A1

DATA APPENDIX

Year	Rice Output (1,000 *Suk*)	Labor (1,000 Men Equivalent)	Land (1,000 Hectare)	Capital (Million *Won*)	Tenancy Rate
1937	26,796	1,782	1,626	22,392	.579
1938	24,139	1,806	1,647	23,085	.580
1939	14,356	1,684	1,225	20,827	.584
1940	22,527	1,874	1,629	21,920	.586
1941	24,886	1,842	1,633	22,140	.585
1942	15,688	1,687	1,203	20,821	.588
1943	18,719	1,814	1,505	19,530	.546
1944	16,052	1,753	1,319	17,402	.524
1955	20,549	1,629	1,080	25,125	.052
1956	16,928	1,719	1,088	26,240	.055
1957	20,846	1,831	1,096	26,684	.058
1958	21,951	1,928	1,099	24,161	.061
1959	21,872	2,154	1,104	22,465	.065
1960	21,157	2,234	1,112	21,862	.068
1961	24,046	2,349	1,119	23,469	.064
1962	20,937	2,095	1,130	26,847	.060
1963	26,098	2,239	1,146	35,661	.056
1964	27,462	2,315	1,186	37,056	.052
1965	24,313	2,335	1,218	39,317	.070
1966	27,217	2,341	1,221	39,171	.075
1967	25,022	2,328	1,225	40,353	.081
1968	22,190	2,168	1,224	37,974	.086
1969	28,406	2,096	1,218	40,772	.092
1970	27,357	2,010	1,219	42,252	.097
1971	27,762	2,031	1,201	43,276	.089
1972	27,481	1,934	1,192	43,001	.081
1973	29,248	1,916	1,183	48,224	.073
1974	30,868	1,324	1,204	54,188	.077

SOURCE.—Ministry of Agriculture, Forest, and Fishery (MAFF), *Hankukyangchongsa*
(Rice policy history) (Seoul: MAFF, 1978).

Yoong-Deok Jeon and Young-Yong Kim   267

Notes

* An earlier version of this article was presented at the annual conference of the Southern Economic Association, 1996. Financial support from the Korea Center for Free Enterprise is gratefully acknowledged. We also thank Chip Filer, Seungjun Lee, and an anonymous referee for their helpful comments and suggestions.

1. See M. A. Taslim, "Redistributive Land and Tenancy Reform in Bangladesh Agriculture," *Journal of Developing Areas* 27 (April 1993): 341–75.

2. In the prereform period, a 50:50 division of output in sharecropping contracts was prevalent.

3. The U.S. Army occupied South Korea from October 1945 to August 1948, and during that period it acted as the government in Korea. From August to October 1945, there was no formal government, which resulted in social disorder.

4. On the median voter theorem, see Duncan Black, "On the Rationale of Group Decision-Making," *Journal of Political Economy* 56 (February 1948): 23–34, and *The Theory of Committees and Elections* (Cambridge: Cambridge University Press, 1958).

5. The Agricultural Land Reform Act was passed in June 1949, but it became ineffective, since President Rhee did not sign the act into law.

6. *Jungbo* is a measurement unit of area, and one *jungbo* is approximately equal to 0.992 hectare.

7. Korea Agricultural Economic Research Institute (KAERI), *Nongchikaehyoksa Yonku* (A study on the history of agricultural land reform) (Seoul: KAERI, 1989).

8. Landlords were classified into two groups, depending on the amount of land they owned. The first group owned more than 5 *jungbo* and earned income only from crop-share tenancy, while the second group owned less than 5 *jungbo*, and their income came from crop-share tenancy and self-cultivating. The ALRAA affected the two groups differently. Those in the first group sold most of their land to tenants before the ALRAA became effective, whereas those in the second group did not sell, expecting that their land would not be reverted. However, all the land over three *jungbo* owned by the two groups was reverted. Thus, the ALRAA had a greater effect on the second group.

9. See S. H. Chang, "Nongchikaehyok Kwachonge Kwanhan Shilchungjok Yonku" (An empirical examination of the process of land reform), in *Haebangchunhusaui Inshik* (The perspective of the history about the time of liberalization), M. K. Kang et al. (Seoul: Hankilsa, 1985), esp. 2:317.

10. As mentioned in n. 8, there were two groups of landlords. Sixty percent of the first group sold their land to tenants before ALRAA, whereas most of the second group, owning small amounts of land, did not sell their land to tenants, expecting that theirs would not be reverted. However, theirs was also reverted. We were not able to determine why the second group did not resist the reform.

11. Some tenant farmer households could not pay for the purchase of land at the time of ALRAA. They borrowed money to make the payment for the redistributed land but soon sold it to self-cultivating households, and subsequently they either became tenants again or migrated to urban areas.

12. Douglass C. North, *Institutions, Institutional Change, and Economic Performance* (New York: Cambridge University Press, 1990).

13. One *suk* is approximately equal to 180.4 liters (4.9629 bushels).

14. Y. B. Park, *Hankuksa 100 Changmyon* (One hundred scenes of Korean history) (Seoul: Karaum, 1993).

15. Y. I. Chung, "Mikunchongui Nongopchongchaek" (Agricultural policy of the U.S. military administration), *Mikunchongshidaeui Kyongchechong-*

chaek (Economic policy of the U.S. military administration) (Seoul: Korea Research Institute of Spirit and Culture, 1992).

16. The market interest rate was about 48% per annum in the mid-1950s. The official discount rate of a bill was 14.24% per annum before April 5, 1951; after that, 17.52% to October 9, 1951, 17.25% to June 2, 1953, and 17.52% to March 31, 1962. For computational convenience, 17% was applied as the discount rate of the bill.

17. As mentioned in Sec. II, the government purchased the land from landlords with land securities. However, actual compensation was made in cash.

18. D. Gale Johnson did not seem to accept the productive inefficiency argument, although his theoretical model lends support to the argument. See his "Resource Allocation under Share Contracts," *Journal of Political Economy* 58 (April 1950): 111–23.

19. See Steven N. S. Cheung, "Private Property Rights and Sharecropping," *Journal of Political Economy* 76 (November–December 1968): 1107–22; R. H. Coase, "The Problem of Social Costs," *Journal of Law and Economics* 3 (October 1960): 1–44.

20. Radwan A. Shaban, "Testing between Competing Models of Sharecropping," *Journal of Political Economy* 95 (October 1987): 893–920.

21. Mookherjee developed a model of the complete contract. He argued that a transfer of land ownership from a landlord to an owner cultivator enhances the bargaining power of the latter, which results in a higher level of effort incentives. See D. Mookherjee, "Informational Rents and Property Rights in Land," in *Property Rights, Incentives, and Welfare*, ed. J. Roemer (New York: Macmillan, 1997).

22. See I. H. Yoo, *Hankuknongchichedoui Yonku* (A study on farm land system in Korea) (Seoul: Baekmundang, 1975).

23. The observations for 1961–74 were included because the number of observations for 1937–44 and 1955–60 were not sufficient for a meaningful statistical inference.

24. Ministry of Agriculture, Forest, and Fishery (MAFF), *Hankukyangchongsa* (Rice policy history) (Seoul: MAFF, 1978).

25. As the referee recommended, it would be desirable to include the variables of crop prices and wage rates in the regression to separate out the effect of the reform. However, those variables were excluded because of the lack of consistent time series data for the period investigated.

26. This argument was first made by Hoch. See Irving Hoch, "Estimation of Production Function Parameters Combining Time-Series and Cross-Section Data," *Econometrica* 30 (January 1962): 34–53.

27. In assessing the contribution to China's agricultural growth of market-oriented institutional reform along with the adjustments in state procurement prices, Lin found that both factors are mainly responsible for the output growth during the period 1978–84. See, for details, Justin Yifu Lin, "Rural Reforms and Agricultural Growth in China," *American Economic Review* 82 (March 1992): 34–51.

28. We conducted the Chow test to further investigate the effect of the separation of the peninsula and the Korean War on rice production. The whole sample is grouped into the two subsamples, 1937–44 and 1955–74. The null hypothesis of there being no structural break is rejected at the 1% level. The F-statistic is calculated to be 4.94, whereas the critical value is 4.28 with (7, 14) degrees of freedom. In the test, we exclude the dummy variable (DU), capturing the effect of an abrupt change in tenancy rate, since the second subsample contains zeros only.

B
Industry Policy

[6]

Industry Policy in East Asia

Smith*

This survey examines the role of industry policy in the industrialisation of East Asian economies since the early 1980s. The first section outlines the 'neoclassical' model and the interventionist literature that has arisen to challenge it. It distinguishes three strands in this literature: the 'structuralist' and the 'strategic' trade models and the 'fair trade' argument. The following sections evaluate the empirical evidence for Northeast and Southeast Asian economies, discuss the analytical and empirical validity of the interventionist literature and in conclusion draw attention to the diminished relevance of industry policy, given the rapid market-driven integration taking place in the Asian–Pacific region.

The source of East Asia's industrial success lies in the eye of the beholder. Typically, the historical interpretation of the East Asian industrial experience differs depending on the chosen paradigm. Some contend that the 'East Asian evidence falsifies the idea that a high degree of state intervention in the economy is incompatible with successful capitalist development' (Berger 1987:156). Others view the East Asian experience as an exception; they admit the important influence of government in this experience, but argue that the same results could not be achieved in countries which are 'soft states' characterised by weaker political institutions, low administrative capacity and a high risk of 'government failure'.

It is difficult to draw definite conclusions about the overall effect of the role of government intervention in East Asian development. As Garnaut (1990:10) says, 'it depends on the nature of the intervention and of the society and the polity within which it operates'. East Asian regimes were undeniably interventionist. What remains controversial is

the contribution of industry policy interventions to this success. In the context of East Asian industrialisation, this is at the centre of a lively debate.

Industry policy can be thought of as having two main elements: functional interventions and selective interventions (Lall 1994:65). Functional interventions are those that remedy market failure without favouring any one activity over another. Selective interventions are designed to favour individual activities or groups of activities in order to correct suboptimal resource allocation, in a static or a dynamic sense. The definition adopted in this survey is the latter ('picking winners') which refers to policy measures to change the inter-industry allocation of resources. The instruments of selective industry policy to be found in the literature include trade policy (especially protection from imports and/or promotion of exports); financial sector policies (affecting the demand and supply of industrial credit); tax benefits and investment incentives; direct government investment and ownership; highly selective foreign investment regimes;

* Northeast Asia Program, The Australian National University.
  Thanks are due to Ross Garnaut, Stuart Harris, Hal Hill and Peter Warr for helpful comments and discussions, and to the ANU's Northeast Asia Program for financial support.

measures to encourage industrial agglomeration; and labour market regulation.

There is now an influential literature which asserts that East Asian—especially Northeast Asian—industrial success owes much to governments selectively intervening to overcome alleged market failure. Since the early 1980s, two distinct political-economy thrusts behind 'industry policy' have emerged to challenge what is known as the neoclassical (market forces) interpretation of East Asian industrialisation. The first, the 'structuralist' opposition to market-oriented policies, argues that the state in East Asia anticipated shifts in comparative advantage and intervened aggressively to develop new export industries. The second, the 'strategic trade' view, aims to show how a country that promotes industries characterised by particular external economies can help shift its pattern of comparative advantage and can accelerate growth. East Asian governments are said to have been accomplished practitioners of such policies. The two versions of industry policy overlap in that both identify high technology industries as those which are 'strategic', enjoying beneficial externalities and having high export potential.

A by-product of the strategic trade view has been emergence of the protectionist 'fair trade' opposition to free-trade policies, centred on the belief that the United States (and other developed countries) cannot hold their own vis-à-vis the East Asian countries if they rely on the 'level playing field'. In the main, this literature focuses on Japan and the Northeast Asian newly industrialising economies (NIEs). But as Hill (1995:forthcoming) notes, 'there is an intellectual spillover already evident to the next tier of high growth Southeast Asian economies. There is a presumption both in policy circles and in some of the literature that the path to industrial success lies in following the Northeast Asian recipe'. More recently, the 'fair trade' argument has been extended to

include issues such as labour rights and the environment and has been applied to China and Southeast Asia.

Some aspects of the literature have been covered in this journal by Islam (1992) on the political economy of Asian–Pacific development and by Adams and Davis (1994) on the role of government policy in East Asian economic development. Comprehensive surveys of industry policy in the Asian–Pacific region have been undertaken in recent years by Ariff and Hill (1985); Findlay and Garnaut (1986); Hughes (1988, 1993); Arndt (1987); Chowdhury and Islam (1993); and the World Bank (1993).

The industrial experience of Hong Kong and Singapore will not be discussed here. There is almost unanimous agreement concerning the non-interventionist role of the Hong Kong government, while the Singapore industrialisation experience will be discussed in a future issue of *APEL* by Dr Goh Keng Swee.

The debate on the East Asia 'miracle'

The neoclassical model

The beginnings of this debate can be traced to the literature on the relative merits of import-substituting industrialisation and export-oriented industrialisation of the late 1960s and early 1970s. The body of empirical research on trade and industrialisation undertaken in the 1970s,[1] along with improvements in the theoretical analysis in the 1960s,[2] undermined the 1950s arguments for protection and import substitution strategies by documenting 'the failures and disasters of regulatory, interventionist states' (Bardhan 1990:3). Many of these studies related to the economic success stories of the export-oriented East Asian economies and suggested that their development accelerated as they liberalised their foreign trade regimes and

1 See for example Little, Scitovsky and Scott (1970); Balassa (1971, 1982, 1983); Krueger (1978); Bhagwati (1978); World Bank (1983, 1987).
2 These included the distinction between domestic and foreign trade distortions (Bhagwati and Ramaswami 1963; Johnson 1965); the concept of effective protection (Balassa 1965; Corden 1966); and the concept of domestic resource cost (Krueger 1966).

adopted an outward-looking strategy of export promotion.

The outstanding performance of East Asia cannot be attributed to favourable external conditions

The original East Asian 'miracle' was Japan, followed by Korea and Taiwan which shared some similar conditions. With little in the way of natural resources, all three began rapid capital accumulation in their first decade of development. Korea in particular followed the Japanese model by competing directly in large industries such as steel, shipbuilding, and automobiles. Taiwan relied more on a range of smaller firms in most sectors, while Hong Kong and Singapore were initially entrepôt exporters. Export development was helped by the expanding US market of the 1960s and 1970s.

However, the outstanding performance of East Asia cannot be attributed to favourable external conditions. Other regions faced similar external conditions but did not do nearly so well. The East Asians committed themselves, almost from the outset, to become players on the global scene. Indonesia, Malaysia and Thailand were resource rich, but they did not really take off until manufactured exports were developed. These second-generation NIEs laid the foundation for their growth with stable macroeconomic policies and political stability which, together with low labour costs, appealed to foreign investors, increasingly from East Asia—Japan in the first instance, but later also from Korea and Taiwan. Japanese foreign investment, followed by that of the NIEs, provided the transfer of technology that the first generation NIEs had to secure by other means (World Bank 1993).

The neoclassical approach to the role of industry policy in East Asia has been to argue that, while relying on assistance at various stages, these economies ensured that their trade regimes were more neutral as between import substitution and export activities than those of most economies. This facilitated specialisation on the basis of comparative advantage. In other words, local prices of traded goods, on average, departed much less from world prices than in other developing regions, even though there were substantial variations for some individual items and for some countries. Neoclassical writers stressed that the successful economies were by and large those that had 'got their prices right' and had not greatly inhibited market signals driving resource allocation. To cite the World Bank (1987:71) definition, 'they had maintained a competitive exchange rate and implemented policies that do not in aggregate discriminate between broad groups of industrial activity'. The most important prices to get right were those 'governing incentives for export, relative to production for the home market'. 'Open foreign exchange policies and regimes were also important for getting the foreign trade prices right' (Garnaut 1990:14–15).

On this view, government industry policy interventions are not the *sine qua non*. Rather, good economic management is thought to account for superior economic performance. Specifically, 'the soundness of underlying policies—fiscal, monetary, financial, trade, labour and infrastructure—determined the speed, sustainability and equity of growth' (Hughes 1993:5). Macroeconomic stability and high rates of saving and investment, combined with judicious investment in human capital and infrastructure, are emphasised as the cornerstones on which East Asia's export success was built (World Bank 1993).

In highlighting the disadvantages of interventionist industry policy the neoclassical school did not argue that the state has no role to play in the process of economic development. Mainstream neoclassical economists stressed that 'dynamic' effects, such as learning-by-doing and externalities arising from R&D, provided the strongest, if not the only valid, reason for promoting industrialisation in the sense of allocating resources between industries on a discriminatory basis (Corden 1974). Functional measures, such as across the board R&D incentives, provision of training facilities and incentives to develop a broad-based venture capital market, were advocated rather than industry and firm-specific interventions (Baldwin 1969).

If government cannot deliberately create industrial 'winners', how do such winners emerge? Mainstream neoclassical economics treated the theory of changing comparative advantage as the central element in the analysis of industrial development. The comparative advantage case for free trade simply stated that a country would attain a higher level of welfare if it permitted trade at international prices, producing those commodities that are comparatively cheaper at home and exchanging them for those that would be relatively more expensive to produce (Krueger 1990:69). Trade generates gains by allowing specialisation between countries.

The neoclassical interpretation suggests that a great deal of empirical evidence can be found in support of the view that East Asian countries followed their comparative advantage based on factor endowment.[3] In East Asia, the shift from traditional labour-intensive industries to new industries characterised by more capital and technology-intensive processes and the adoption of new technologies was facilitated by the simultaneous growth in the stock of human capital (Pack 1992:102). Successful economic growth itself changed comparative advantage through accumulation of capital and through changes in relative technological efficiency across industries.

A country pursuing its comparative advantage also derives dynamic benefits in terms of learning-by-doing, technology acquisition and productivity growth (see Krueger 1993:27–8). An export-oriented trade regime tends to encourage the expansion of industries with a comparative advantage by concentrating resources in a country's most productive industries.

Competition induces greater attention to costs, and greater effort to cost reduction, than a sheltered domestic environment. Export growth assists the process of 'catching up' technologically by allowing imports of goods embodying new technology and by increasing overseas contacts and thus access to new ideas on production and management. There was thus 'a "virtuous trade cycle" linking trade expansion to technological improvement and back to trade expansion again' (Garnaut 1989:43).

The structuralist model

Since the early 1980s, an alternative explanation has emerged which has attributed the economic success of the Northeast Asian economies to selective intervention by the state. The neoclassical explanation has been challenged, in the words of Islam (1992:70), by a 'statist counter-revolution'. The dynamism of the Northeast Asian economies has been re-interpreted as flowing from 'the logic of the development state' (Onis 1991).

According to Henderson and Appelbaum (1992:14), the neoclassical orthodoxy has been successfully challenged in a steady stream of publications. Beginning with Chalmers Johnson's (1982) account of the role of MITI in Japan's post-war industrialisation, this literature includes Amsden's contributions on South Korea (1989) and Taiwan (1985); Gold (1986) and Wade (1990a) on Taiwan; Luedde-Neurath (1988) and Chang (1993) on Korea; and contributions by Cumings (1984), Chalmers Johnson (1987), Wade (1988), White (1988), and Biggs and Levy (1991) on the various aspects of the political economy of industry policy. Drawing on these studies, Henderson and Appelbaum (1992:14) claim 'that at least as far as Northeast Asia is concerned, it is now simply impossible to argue that free markets have

> **Export-oriented trade concentrates resources in a country's most productive industries**

---

3 A common theme in the industry policy literature is that the theory of comparative advantage has lost its relevance in the sense that it no longer captures the determinants of exporting success in the modern international economy, so-called 'competitive advantage'. For a discussion of the concepts of competitive advantage and comparative advantage, see Warr 1994.

been the primary determinants of economic growth'.

Various terms—'revisionist', 'statist', 'new political economy', 'development state'—have been applied to this literature. In originating the expression 'corporate state' or 'development state', Chalmers Johnson (1982) attributed Japan's post-war industrial growth to the 'special nature' of the government's approach to policy making, which in turn was thought to result from Japan's historical experience. In particular, the interventionist role of the Ministry of International Trade and Industry (MITI) in influencing corporate decision-making and other commercial outcomes was given much of the credit for Japan's strong industrial performance.

A large crop has since grown to explain the success of the Japanese economy. At one end of the spectrum stands a group of political scientists, business executives and government officials who see Japan as embodying a state-guided capitalist system in which MITI and industry policy have played a central role. Strategic industries have been backed by MITI with the collaboration of the private sector. Government leadership has been the key to Japan's economic success, with business a willing follower. An extreme version of this approach is encapsulated in the phrase 'Japan Inc.', though most scholars agree this concept is too simplistic and naive for what is a much more complex, variegated, multi-dimensional set of relationships between politicians, central government and business (Patrick 1986:17). But several authors have put Japan's industrial and trade policies at the heart of explanations of Japan's economic success (Chalmers Johnson 1982; Shinohara 1982; Tyson 1992; Zysman 1983; and Prestowitz 1988). The implication is that if Japanese firms were forced to compete on a 'level playing field', they would lose their advantage.

At the opposite end of the spectrum stand a group of mainstream economists who see the basic source of Japan's economic growth as being in a vigorous private sector which, taking advantage of the market mechanism, has energetically engaged in productive business investment and commercially oriented research and development, while also employing a supportive system of labour-management relations. Entrepreneurs were and are the engine of growth, but government is given credit for having pursued macro-economic and industrial policies beneficial to private sector growth (Trezise 1976, 1983; Patrick and Rosovsky 1976; Lincoln 1984; Abegglen and Stalk 1985; and Patrick 1986).

One of the more prominent structuralists, Robert Wade (1990a:26) has argued that Chalmers Johnson's 'development state' theory of East Asian industrial success 'is not much of a theory'. It is not clear what the developmental state is contrasted with. It also says little about the nature of policies and their impact on industrial performance. Instead, Wade encapsulates the central tenets of the structuralist literature in his 'governed market model'.

Wade argues that in Taiwan, as well as in Northeast Asia generally, governments have guided or governed market processes of resource allocation so as to produce production and investment outcomes different from those that would have occurred in a free market. Government intervention of a 'leadership' kind is considered to have focused on industries which are capital intensive, or which use technology that must be imported from a small number of potential suppliers (Wade 1990a:303). The state is thought to have anticipated shifts in comparative advantage and intervened aggressively to develop national champions for international markets (Wade 1984:65). Leadership is thus applied to a shifting band of industries (Wade 1990b:249). Sectoral interventionist policies are considered to have been important in supporting export expansion in the late 1960s, industrial deepening in the 1970s, and technological upgrading in the 1980s (see for example Simon 1992:119; Amsden 1992:46, 1991:284–5; Wade 1990a:11). In turn, sector-specific interventions are supported by a certain kind of organisation of the state and the private sector. In particular, the corporatist and authoritarian political arrangements of East Asia are said to have provided the basis for market guidance.

While acknowledging that the theoretical basis for a selective industrial strategy is less well developed than that which supports a non-interventionist approach, Wade argues that this merely reflects the neoclassical emphasis on trade rather than technological change as the central process of industrialisation (Wade 1988:152–3). When technological change is made the centrepiece, an economic rationale for selective promotion follows from two propositions. The first is that national comparative advantage is not simply the result of given endowments of resources, but also results from government promotion. The second is that some sectors have major 'externalities', in the sense that far more people are affected by a decision about production and price than the buyer and seller (Wade 1988:153). According to Wade, '[s]ome of their [East Asian] industry policies make sense as an attempt to lower entry barriers and thereby allow quick capture of economies of scale and learning-by-doing, and some make sense as an attempt to capture externalities (or spill-over effects) within national boundaries' (Wade 1990b:262). Moreover 'unassisted entrepreneurs may not have either the foresight or access to capital to follow long-term potential. Their decisions may lock the country into specialisation in industries with inferior prospects (an issue beyond the scope of comparative advantage theory)' (Wade 1990a:354–5).

This view suggests that the nature of the debate on industry policy has now shifted from a concern with old-fashioned protection of domestic markets (import substitution) to one aiming at export markets through strategic intervention in key industries—a view which is often summarised in the phrase 'strategic trade policy'. It is now argued that the risk of government failure inherent in activist industry policy can be minimised through appropriate institutional arrangements and that the East Asian experience supports such a contention (Islam 1992:70).

Amsden (1989) has proposed another variant of the structuralist view, drawn from

Industry policy has now shifted from protection to strategic intervention in key industries

the Korean experience. She argues that through the allocation of subsidies the Korean government has acted not only as a banker, but also as an entrepreneur, using the subsidy to decide what, when and how much to produce (Amsden 1989:143–4). Moreover, it has deliberately distorted the price structure by way of subsidies, protection, price controls, and restrictions on finance and investment. The end result has been an industrial structure different from that which the market would have produced.

The most controversial contention is that the state intervened to foster development through the creation of differential prices for loans—the implication being that a repressed financial system facilitates rapid economic growth (Amsden 1989, 1991; Wade 1988, 1990a). Credit, it is argued, was allocated by the government to selected firms at negative real interest rates in order to stimulate specific industries. In addition, importers and exporters faced different prices for foreign currency. By intervening to establish multiple prices in the same market, the state cannot be said to have got relative prices 'right'. Rather, it has set relative prices deliberately 'wrong' in order to create profitable investment opportunities (Amsden 1989:13–4). What distinguishes the experience of East Asia is that the state exercised discipline over subsidy recipients. In exchange for subsidies, the state imposed performance standards on private firms (Amsden 1989:14).

Incentive regimes

There are features of the industrial experience of East Asia that some structuralists agree fit the neoclassical accounts better than the structuralist explanation (Wade 1990a:71–2). Generally, it is agreed that the real exchange rate has been kept relatively stable and undistorted, and that East Asian economies have been outward-oriented in the sense that the inequality between incentives for producers to sell abroad or on the domestic market has not been significant (exports have not been discriminated against). However, structuralists claim that neoclassical research, particularly in the case of Taiwan and Korea, has understated both the level and dispersion of assistance to sectors (Wade 1990a; Alam 1989; Amsden 1989; and Luedde-Neurath 1988).[4] Because the empirical research used to support the neoclassical explanation has methodological weaknesses, caution is required in accepting the conclusion that protection in the domestic market has generally been quite low by international standards (Biggs and Levy 1988:22; Alam 1989:31–4; Wade 1990a:116). In particular, the dispersion of incentives is said to imply intersectoral differences and that this dispersion results from intended differences between industries rather than from accidental causes. Others argue, and supply evidence, that price distortions do not in fact correlate closely with inward or outward-oriented trade regimes or with measures of national economic performance (Bradford 1984). This questions the proposition that market liberalisation could have been the driving force behind the success of East Asia.

Authoritarian states

All proponents of the structuralist view emphasise the virtues of a strong state in being able to formulate and implement policies broadly in line with the national interest, as contributing to East Asian growth. The original proponent, Chalmers Johnson (1982), argued in the case of Japan—and this was later extended to Korea and Taiwan—that state intervention in East Asian capitalist countries relied on organisational and institutional links between politically insulated state development agencies and major private-sector firms (Chalmers Johnson 1987). The efficacy of intervention was amplified by fostering powerful, state-linked, private-sector conglomerates, banks and trading organisations that tended to dominate strategic economic sectors (Deyo 1987:19, 136–64). According to Amsden (1989), Korea has an outstanding growth record because the

institutions on which its late industrialisation has been based have been managed differently, and have functioned more effectively than elsewhere. In Taiwan, the bureaucracy is thought to operate as a 'filtering mechanism', focusing the attention of policy makers (and the private sector) on sectors, products and processes crucial to future industrial growth (Wade 1990a).

Haggard (1990:128), along with several others has qualified this argument. With the reform process during the 1980s phase of industrial restructuring the political context has changed. With political liberalisation, interest groups and opposition parties have mobilised around economic policy, and governments have become more responsive to public demands, including those from previously excluded groups, especially labour. For example, as a result of both the costs of financial repression and international pressures, financial market policies in both Taiwan and Korea in the 1980s began to converge around a liberalisation strategy (Haggard and Lee 1993:17).

The strategic trade model

While the structuralist literature was gaining prominence, some economists were developing a new theoretical rationale for active intervention by government to pursue a 'strategic trade policy'. Krugman (1984, 1987c) sought to encapsulate empirically what Givens (1982) referred to as the Japanese 'narrow moving band'. The government, it was said, targets a series of new industries in succession, leaving subsidies in place just long enough for long-run competitiveness to be assured. In this way, industries are 'sliced off' one after another. Baldwin and Krugman (1988) suggest that this policy may have been adopted by Japan as a means of overcoming the 'early start' advantage of the United States semiconductor industry and enabling Japan's industry to become a significant exporter of the 16K random

---

4   Reference is made in particular to Balassa (1982). See Smith (1994a:30) for a discussion of how Wade has a tendency to exaggerate these 'methodological weaknesses'.

access memory chip. Other East Asian economies are said to have pursued similar policies to establish export industries. Reference is often made to Yamamura (1986) on Japanese televisions, and Amsden (1989:85–8) on Korean and Wade (1990a, 1990b) on Taiwanese exports. It may be questioned whether a convincing causal relationship has been established between trade policy and establishment of the industry, or a measure of the the the welfare effect of such policies.

From the mid-1980s, much of the more informal academic discussion of strategic trade theory increasingly emphasised externalities as a reason for protecting or promoting strategic sectors. Krugman (1992:436) and other, predominantly US, academics raised the possibility that a country could advance its standard of living at the expense of other countries by systematically promoting industries subject to external economies of a particular kind. They cited the importance to modern industrial competition of economies of scale, of learning-by-doing, and of externalities stemming from research and development. These 'dynamic effects' associated with the development of 'strategic' high-technology industries were said to enhance productivity. Support for industries possessing these characteristics therefore was crucial if a country was to stay at the technological frontier (Tyson 1990).

Much of this research emerged from the United States at a time of increasing American fears of an East Asian challenge in trade and technology. A number of authors argued that the Japanese government's targeting of industries on the basis of their technological potential was the foundation of Japan's dramatic competitive success in world markets (Dosi, Tyson, Zysman 1989:3–34). Other East Asian governments were also said to have pursued such policies (Tyson 1990:4). In a survey of the literature and its relevance to the Asian–Pacific region Richardson suggests that:

> American and European perceptions are that selected Asian technological protectionism

The view that Japan's success is due to unfair trade practices is strongly held in the USA

and trade-policy activism have actually succeeded …[they] have come to believe that Japan, Korea, and probably Singapore and Taiwan as well, have been the most accomplished practitioners of new-view trade policies. Out of that perception comes the desire to establish new ground rules, to 'even the playing field'. (Richardson 1991:34)

But proponents of the more recent theoretical literature are not dogmatic on the issue of intervention to capture technological externalities. In arguing that the presence of externalities in high technology industries may provide a legitimate case for intervention, some new trade theorists have stressed that the circumstances giving rise to such externalities are likely to be very limited. Krugman (1987a; 1989) has discussed how a special national advantage from an externality-generating sector is likely to arise only if the sector generates broad spillovers to the rest of the economy which are country-specific. Even if technological or linkage externalities are national in scope, the benefits of the externality may still end up being shared internationally. The limited circumstances in which externalities may in fact give rise to a legitimate case for intervention suggests that the case for intervention to ensure their capture has been somewhat overstated.

Lawrence and Schultze (1990:46) pointed out that the case for protection of high technology industries based on external economies was misleading.

> An important part of the output of high technology industries is intermediate products, whose availability at reasonable prices is important to the pace of productivity and innovation in other high technology-using industries. Rather than promote productivity-raising spillovers, policies that restrict the availability and raise the price of high technology parts and components, as the new protectionism often does, may actually suppress them.

Empirical research does show significant patterns of spillovers or externalities arising from R&D and innovations that range from moderate to important (Richardson 1990). But these are not always associated with high technology industries. Moreover, most of the empirical research on government subsidies justified on these grounds concludes that subsidies are counterproductive.[5] Even if spill-overs and linkages are detectable, they would appear to be more accurately detected by information gathered efficiently by private sector agents (Richardson 1991:30–1). Moreover, an increasing trend among countries to share the burden of R&D costs or gain access to foreign markets via joint ventures and strategic alliances is complicating any definition of national economic interest, weakening the role of government in industry policy.[6]

The 'fair trade' argument

Another strand in the policy debate of the early 1980s was the view that the economic structure of some countries (especially Japan) was rendering the principle of free trade unachievable in practice. This argument justified government intervention by the need to counteract 'unfair' practices of other countries, as evidenced either by excessive penetration of domestic markets or by foreign 'discrimination' against imports. The view that Japan's success is due to unfair trade practices is strongly held, particularly in the United States at both official and popular levels.

Bhagwati and Patrick (1990) note that the emergence of the fair trade view in the United States can be traced to the surge of import protectionism with the rise of the dollar during the Reagan Administration. But according to Bhagwati (1988:65), the 'diminished giant syndrome' has also helped. The persistent belief that the East Asian countries are 'not playing by the rules' and that 'level playing fields' must be established to compete with

them, owes much to this syndrome. Since the mid-1970s market penetration by Japan and the developing East Asian economies has intensified competition, particularly in labour-intensive sectors. These developments, combined with increased popular awareness of strategic trade literature, have lent critical ideological support to the export lobbies seeking larger shares in foreign markets. Politicians also welcome a justification for aggressively opening foreign markets (Bhagwati and Patrick 1990:14).

The evidence: country cases

Japan

Among specialists on Japanese political economy there is no clear consensus regarding the effectiveness of Japan's industry policy:

> The results of MITI's policies in targeting specific industries have been mixed in practice. One can credit the combination of MITI policy, market forces, and the mixture of Japanese business leadership and follow-the-leader business behaviour for having created a generally high competitive environment in Japan. And there have been industries targeted successfully. However, industry policy has not been successful in a number of industries, with consequent high costs to consumers, savers or taxpayers. (Patrick 1986:21)[7]

MITI's record in 'picking winners' is by no means unblemished. As Arndt (1989:41–2) points out:

> MITI initially opposed the establishment of the steel industry (and, it is said, of Sony). It sought unsuccessfully to prevent the emergence of new motor car manufacturers and only thus failed to kill at birth one of Japan's success stories, Honda...MITI, like others,

---

5 See Smith (1994a:94) for a survey of this literature.
6 After several years of theoretical and empirical investigation, Krugman (1993) concludes that while an important contribution to the literature, the strategic trade argument is probably of minor real importance. The theoretical foundation of strategic trade policies are sound, but rather narrow. Small changes in assumptions lead to large changes in conclusions. These models have been applied to industries with a few large, dominant firms operating on global markets. It is largely of relevance to industrialised rather than the developing countries.
7 A recent study by Sazanami, Urata and Kawai (1995) estimates the cost of Japan's trade barriers to Japanese consumers at around 15 trillion yen ($US110 billion at 1989 exchange rates) or 3.8% of GDP.

failed to foresee the rise in energy prices that rendered these industries even less competitive. MITI encouraged a huge expansion of shipbuilding that was widely, and as it turned out, correctly expected to run into world-wide excess capacity. Among industries which MITI at various times saw as potential winners but had to abandon in the face of foreign competition were the production of construction equipment, chain saws, marine engines and plate heat-exchanges. The chemical industry that MITI pushed vigorously has remained fragmented and plagued by high costs.

There are a number of important industries, such as automobiles, consumer electronics and most consumer goods, which did not receive government support but succeeded on their own (Patrick 1986:18). 'MITI has long targeted the commercial aircraft industry with no commercial success. It could not prevent what it saw as excessive domestic entrants into vehicle production for the domestic market, and later was unable to effect mergers among competing smaller producers' (Patrick 1986:26). Bergsten and Noland (1993:68–9) in a survey of the relevant literature conclude that direct subsidies have played little role in fostering changes in Japan's industrial composition. On balance they have probably been welfare-reducing by shifting resources from high to low productivity uses.

Imai (1986) evaluated the effectiveness of Japanese industry policy over a wide range of high technology industries. Along with Okimoto (1986) he concluded that MITI has been most successful in the information industry and concurred with Saxonhouse (1986) that it has not been successful in biotechnology. Imai also found that industry policies have not done well in computer software, new materials, chemicals and new energy sources.

One problem that makes evaluation difficult is that Japan's industry policies were generally designed to allocate resources in conformity with already existing domestic and

> **'The USA dominated military electronics and Japan dominated consumer electronics'**

foreign market pressures (Lawrence 1993:5). MITI chose to target industries with high income demand elasticities and rapid productivity growth. But as Komiya (1988:6–7) points out, these are precisely the sectors that would be expected to grow rapidly in the absence of such policies. Aron (1986:234) argues that industries labelled as infant (such as computers and semiconductors) were infants also in every country of the world:

> Both Japan and the United States encouraged these industries, but under different auspices: the Department of Defense in the United States and MITI in Japan. This gave a military bias to United States efforts and a consumer bias to Japanese efforts. Ultimately the United States dominated military electronics and Japan dominated consumer electronics.

Since the late 1970s, two major trends have been discernible in the evolution of Japanese industry policy. Industry policy has become less important in overall government economic policy, and MITI is losing its historic role as the predominant initiator, agent, and implementor of industry policy (Patrick 1991:14). MITI has placed great emphasis on other aspects of industry policy—assisting in the structural adjustment process of major uncompetitive, declining 'sunset' industries such as those hit by high energy costs (aluminium, petrochemicals), low world demand (shipbuilding), or high labour costs (textiles, simple assembly operations). Japanese industrial policy during the 1980s has been most effective in dealing with industries in trouble and needing structural adjustment (Patrick 1986:29; Arndt 1987). On the whole these policies have been market-conforming, rather than market-obstructing, helping resources to get out of, rather than stay in, declining industries.

Korea

During the 1980s Korean industry policy underwent a fundamental reorientation (Young 1986, Smith 1994b). Its shift to technology-intensive industries was designed around functional policies supportive of industrial upgrading. This contrasted with the industry-specific interventions during the previous major shift in industrial structure in the 1970s when the government used trade and financial policies to direct resources to the heavy and chemical industry sector. The highly politicised heavy industry drive left a legacy of distorted credit markets, heavily indebted firms and a high concentration of industrial power (Nam 1991, 1992). In contrast, the industry policy strategy of the 1980s was based on the premise that direct intervention was no longer feasible or desirable in light of the economy's changing industrial structure and greater reliance on private sector decision-making.

What is conspicuously missing from the structuralist literature is a discussion of the most intractable problem in industry policy-making in Korea since the late 1970s, namely how to deal with financially distressed firms and the large volume of non-performing debts that has accumulated in the banking system.[8] Industries such as shipping and foreign construction which had been selected and fostered by the government as 'strategic' industries in the 1970s faced financial difficulties in the early 1980s. Overall, opinion differs as to whether the heavy and chemical industry policy should be judged a failure or a success. Some argue that Taiwan out-performed Korea without undertaking the costly heavy and chemical industry drive and that the rapid increase in these exports could equally have resulted from several other factors which gave Korean exports a competitive stimulus (Yoo 1990); others like Amsden (1989) and Chang (1993) judge it a success, and the World Bank (1993) a qualified success in that Korea paid a high price.

I have suggested that the structuralist and strategic trade models would appear to have limited relevance in explaining the role of the Korean government in technological upgrading in the 1980s (Smith 1994b). This upgrading has largely been driven by the private sector's push into high technology

industries through R&D investment. Rather than directing resources to industries considered 'strategic', the government's industrial initiatives have instead focused on the restructuring of declining industries and measures to promote a greater role for small-scale enterprises. This tendency for the Korean government, like Japan's, to become less *dirigiste* in response to changing economic circumstances has received little attention in the structuralist literature.

Moreover, despite occasional early backsliding, Korean progress on trade liberalisation, particularly since the mid-1980s, has been both consistent and significant. The government has considerably reduced border protection, wound back its use of direct production subsidies and no longer employs extensive export subsidies. Korea will have reduced its (unweighted) average tariffs from around 32 per cent in 1982 to 8 per cent by 1995, and the coverage of quantitative restrictions to less than 5 per cent of items. Ongoing financial liberalisation is improving the access of small and medium firms to finance. While several significant formal barriers still remain, industry promotion policies, particularly with respect to the high technology sector, are being tailored to avoid trade friction.

Taiwan

In the early 1980s Taiwan embarked on a development program designed to shift its economy away from reliance on labour-intensive industries towards the development of technology-intensive products and industries. External pressure, particularly from the United States, was influential in bringing about trade reforms in the early 1980s. But trade liberalisation was also taking place in response to domestic pressures. The pace of trade liberalisation accelerated after 1985. Non-tariff barriers were considerably reduced and average tariff rates wound back from 31 per cent to 9 per cent between 1985 and 1990 (Smith 1994c).

While continuing to pursue ongoing trade liberalisation, the Taiwan government in 1982

8   See Maxwell Fry in this issue, p.46

ASIAN–PACIFIC ECONOMIC LITERATURE

also adopted a sectoral policy of identifying and promoting 'strategic' industries as a means of furthering industrial development and restructuring industry. Preferential fiscal measures (tax exemptions, tax credits, accelerated depreciation) and financial incentives (long-term, low interest loans) were made available to high technology sectors, with the following criteria for selection of strategic industries: high technology intensity, market potential, high value-added and large linkage effects between industries.

However, empirical investigation into this policy has revealed that the beneficiaries of industry policy interventions in this period were not strategic industries. The incentive structure to industry was aimed more at sustaining losers than picking winners (Smith 1994a). Relative to other sectors, those industries regarded as 'strategic' (high technology) industries, such as the electronics, machinery and information sectors, exhibited low rates of effective assistance and subsidy. The major recipients of subsidies were in fact those with a declining comparative advantage such as textiles, and industries in which Taiwan did not have an established export specialisation or comparative advantage. Indeed, the incentive structure discriminated against high technology industries, in favour of industries with low skill and technology-intensity and with low international competitiveness.

Southeast Asia

In a recent book, MacIntyre (1994:2) notes that the absence of careful cross-regional comparisons has contributed to the emergence of a popular—but untested—perception that the economic transformations under way in Southeast Asia are largely replicating what might be thought of as a Northeast Asian model. This vacuum is now beginning to be filled by a number of contributions which, while noting the diversity of individual country experience, show that Southeast Asian countries

(with the exception of the Philippines) are industrialising within a policy and polity quite different from that of Northeast Asia.[9] Interventionist industry policies appear to have played a less substantial role in the transition to export-led growth than in the Northeast Asian NIEs—the bureaucracies are less competent and the governments less insulated from political pressures.

Indonesia

Indonesia, like Malaysia and Thailand, was initally import-substitution oriented. In the 1970s growth was high, but based on the oil boom. Industrial development was state-led and inefficient. Manufacturing began to grow rapidly following the major liberalisation in the 1980s, led by exports and private investment. Hill (1995), as one of the first to test the Northeast Asian interventionist literature against the Indonesian experience, concludes that there is little evidence that Indonesia's rapid industrial growth can be attributed to the kind of selective industry policy advanced by the structuralists.

From 1973 to 1985 the government sought to accelerate industrialisation through a combination of import substitution policies, regulation of investment and state ownership (Hill 1988). The participation of the state in the manufacturing sector was justified on strategic grounds (cement, fertilisers and steel), technology (aircraft) and increasing value added (oil refining, LNG, petrochemicals, pulp and paper) (Pangestu 1993:272). But the productivity and long-run financial performance of most of the state enterprises have been poor, and it is difficult to discern any compensating features in their record. Moreover, their concentration in sectors that faced limited domestic or import competition, meant that their output was often priced well above world prices, putting a burden on other segments of the economy (Bhattacharya and Pangestu 1993). 'The much-vaunted "high-tech" projects of Minister Habibie, for example, have yet to earn a profit, despite over a decade of

---

9   Apart form the empirical literature surveyed here, this literature includes MacIntyre (1994); Islam (1992); and Haggard, Lee and Maxwell (1993).

operation and a range of implicit subsidies' (McKendrick 1992, Hill 1995: forthcoming).

Fane and Phillips (1991) and Warr (1992b) find that while the distorting effects of Indonesia's trade policies declined markedly during this period, the most highly protected industries, unsurprisingly but damagingly, continue to be those in which its comparative advantage is least. After 20 years of heavy intervention, the automotive industry is intensely regulated with tariffs in the range of 175–275 per cent in 1993. It remains an infant industry, with no evidence that production has approached minimum average cost levels. Other unsuccessful examples include plywood and the state-owned steel industry which until 1988 received very high protection.

Similarly, most authors writing on the political economy of Indonesia concur that one does not find in Indonesia, the 'strong state' so widely credited with steering the Northeast Asian NIEs through rapid economic transformation. Bureaucratic agencies have lacked the institutional capacity to monitor the use of government subsidies by industry (MacIntyre 1994; Biggs and Levy 1991; Bhattacharya and Linn 1988; Hill 1995). Certainly, there is no sign of the state attempting to 'discipline' corporate recipients of preferential credit along the lines Amsden has described in Korea (MacIntyre 1993:150). Hill (1995:forthcoming) suggests that the Indonesian government has been a 'hard state' in macroeconomic management. But in its micro interventions, it displays all the hallmarks of a 'soft state'—prone to corruption and vulnerable to capture.

Malaysia

Bowie (1994) suggests that Malaysia, like Indonesia, has never closely resembled the developmental state model often associated with Korea and Taiwan. In the early 1980s, frustration at the pace of economic development

> *Malaysia, like Indonesia, has never closely resembled the developmental state model*

prompted a state-led attempt at industrial upgrading. The 'Look East' policy adopted in 1981 (Awanohara 1987) was an explicit attempt to emulate the heavy industrialisation efforts of Japan and Korea. The government created a holding company, the Heavy Industries Corporation of Malaysia, to 'plan, identify, initiate, invest [in], implement and manage projects in the field of heavy industries' (Malaysia 1985:10) by creating a nucleus of industries, including basic metals, machinery and equipment, automobiles, building materials, pulp and paper, and petrochemicals (Bowie 1991:111–52). Several of these state-owned enterprises have been poor performers (Salleh and Meyanathan 1993). The record of HICOM's best-known project, Proton, the national car manufacturer (a joint venture with Mitsubishi) has been a decidedly chequered one (Jayasankaran 1993). Until recently Proton has recorded large losses, operating well below the minimum efficient scale for car plants.[10] Unlike Korea's HCI push, which was aimed at achieving international competitiveness, HICOM industries, although monitored by the government, were under no such compulsion. Faced with mounting deficits, the government changed policy and began a major program of privatisation (Salleh and Meyanathan 1993:19).

The period 1986–90 was a period of adjustment and liberalisation, prompted by a sharp recession in 1985, which highlighted the costs of the drive toward industrial upgrading and the large external debt it had generated. Investment incentives were introduced in an attempt to increase foreign direct investment (FDI) and stimulate private enterprise, state enterprises were privatised, and state expenditure now concentrates on infrastructure provision (Lim 1992; Hill 1993). These policies have been successful: Malaysia has recorded rapid growth since 1986 and is a favoured location for FDI among the Asian NIEs. The

---

10 Currently Proton commands nearly 74 per cent of Malaysia's car market, largely because the preferential treatment accorded Proton has made its competitors prohibitively expensive. The cost to consumers has been high, with a tripling of car prices in Malaysia over the past decade (*Far Eastern Economic Review* 1994).

ASIAN–PACIFIC ECONOMIC LITERATURE

flexibility of Malaysia's government has been a crucial factor—it has been willing to pronounce certain policies and their implementation as outright failures (Salleh and Meyanathan 1993).

Since protection builds up and entrenches vested interests...

Thailand

Thailand has had consistent and fairly rapid growth since 1955, with government emphasis on private sector development, outward orientation, and macroeconomic stability. In the 1960s and 1970s, the government made various efforts to protect and promote domestic industry by interventionist policies but, compared with Korea, they were not highly co-ordinated. Balance of payments problems and concerns about the pattern of industrialisation prompted a shift in the early 1980s to export development and import liberalisation. Protection for manufacturing was reduced by the mid-1980s (although it was much higher and more variable than in Korea and Malaysia), and again quite sharply in the early 1990s.

The main instruments of industry policy have been the trade regime and the Board of Investment (BOI), which have combined to favour large industry (Christensen et al. 1993). In the 1960s and 1970s, they supported capital-intensive, import-substituting activities, discriminating against agriculture and labour-intensive manufactures, sectors in which Thailand enjoys a comparative advantage. In the 1980s, they shifted in favour of exporters, but were still biased towards large-scale producers. However, Christensen et al. (1993) emphasise that the importance of the BOI in this export drive should not be exaggerated. For example, the BOI began to favour electronics in the early 1980s, yet the industry did not make much progress. It was not until the mid-1980s, with the large devaluation in the real exchange rate, that electronics really took off. There are other sectors that the BOI did little to promote until they were already very successful: canned tuna, canned fruit and jewellery are examples.

Warr (1995:220–2) argues that while, in the mid-1970s, 'export promotion' was stressed over 'import substitution' in the plan documents, this change of language was more a matter of intellectual fashion than policy commitment. Protection of inefficient manufacturing sectors actually increased during this period, as it did through the remainder of the 1970s. While export promotion policies were introduced, supposedly to promote manufactured exports. Warr finds little empirical evidence that industry policy interventions were being designed to promote manufacturing exports. It was industries whose export performance worsened, not successful exporters, that received increasing support. There is evidence that import-substituting policies did not succeed in 'picking winners' either. Wiboonchutikula's (1987) study found that total factor productivity (TFP) growth has been low in import-competing sectors and relatively high in export industries.

Following reforms in the mid-1980s, the level of state involvement in the Thai economy has been modest, although policy continues to discriminate against small producers. State-owned enterprises in Thailand have been relatively few, tariff and non-tariff barriers have not been particularly high by developing country standards (with the exception of automobiles), there has been relatively little state intervention in credit allocation for industrial purposes, and foreign investment has generally been welcome (Warr 1993; Doner and Unger 1993; Findlay and Garnaut 1986).

Philippines

Hutchcroft (1993:18) argues that the Philippine state is more often 'plundered than plunderer', with public policy almost wholly captured by interests of a narrow elite. Despite its rich endowment with human capital and access to foreign aid and credit, the Philippines stands out as a country that has yet to achieve sustained export competitiveness. There is fairly general agreement in the literature that domestic structures, in particular deeply entrenched class divisions and weak political institutions, have prevented the government from adopting export-promotion policies. The Philippines has long had an extensive system of preferential credit, but the allocation of credit has done little to promote goals of economic development. Although the government has repeatedly published lists of economic activities to be targeted by selective credit, these lists commonly have become so all encompassing as to lose their ability to achieve specific development goals. Because of the state's vulnerability to particularistic interests, it is incapable of playing a more coherent role in guiding economic development.

Trade reform, aborted during severe balance of payments difficulties in 1983, resumed in 1986. As a result of the cumulative actions of ongoing liberalisation efforts undertaken in the early 1980s, the Philippine economy is now more open and transparent in its trade regime than it has been in the last three decades. The average nominal tariff was reduced to about 24 per cent in 1992, and the dispersion narrowed from 0 to 100 per cent to 10 to 50 per cent with a few exceptions (Soesastro 1994a:13).

The structuralist interpretation: summing up

The bulk of the structuralist literature on East Asia presents evidence of various forms of government assistance to specific industries and then argues that they were provided in anticipation of comparative advantage. It is doubtful whether the structuralist writers have satisfactorily established the effectiveness of such policies. Islam (1992:77–8) suggests that the developmental state is a historically specific phenomenon, more relevant in some periods than in others. Several authors have pointed out that the dense organisational network which, according to the structuralist

> *...governments tend to protect industries with low comparative advantage*

model, exists between policy makers and the private sector is of a subtle and informal nature and hence not readily observable. Structuralists tend to treat the policy-making process in a too-mechanical fashion, with the private sector responding passively to bureaucratic initiative and guidance (Chowdhury and Islam 1993:54).

Hughes (1993:11–13), in her critique of the structuralist case, argues that Wade (1990a) and Amsden (1989) have neglected the distortions created by the unreformed components of policy and the extent to which interventions were necessary to offset these distortions. They pay too little attention to the costs imposed by rent-seeking corporations and public officials. Reformers were not politically strong enough in either Taiwan and Korea to abolish protection or to induce a competitive financial system because of the build-up of vested interests in protection and regulation during the 1960s and 1970s. Both countries therefore attempted to reach 'neutral' policies by offsets to protection in agriculture and for exports and by credit rationing. The fiscal and macroeconomic costs created by distorting policies reduced the availability of funds for social and environmental concerns. 'Financial "repression" distorted investment among, and within, sectors. Elaborate rural poverty alleviation programs were introduced to offset the effect of biases against agriculture which by the early 1980s had become agricultural protection policies, damaging the Korean and Taiwan economies' (Hughes 1993:11). The structuralist literature cannot accommodate the conspicuously high levels of inefficient agricultural protection with which Asia was saddled (Anderson and Hayami 1986). It does not explain why the agricultural sector, although lacking economic clout, constituted such an important political constituency (Islam 1992:78).

A more general criticism of structuralist writers is that they have failed to come to grips with the neoclassical theory of government failure. Since the early 1970s, many studies have analysed in quantitative terms the relationship between the level of protection afforded different industries and the political and economic characteristics of sectors or groups that appear to influence the level of protection.[11] Since protection builds up and entrenches vested interests, governments tend to protect industries with low and decreasing comparative advantage. It has little to do with the promotion of industries which are expected to become internationally competitive in the future.

A general criticism of the industry policy literature is that its advocates have not convincingly demonstrated its effectiveness. As Haggard (1990:14) has pointed out, 'the effect of industry policy was… never measured against the more substantial influence of consistent and credible macroeconomic policies, the provision of public goods and incentives to private risk taking'.

Chowdhury and Islam (1993), however, note that the structuralist literature has made a contribution in drawing attention to some of the less balanced neoclassical interpretations of East Asian economic success. Brander (1987:36) while concluding that much of the industry policy literature is logically flawed, points out that professional economists are inclined to discount the popular industry policy work simply because it does not meet the standards of precision and logical rigour that are normal in economic research. This is unfortunate because this literature does contain substantive ideas that should be addressed carefully.

Where from here?

Earlier interventionist policies are probably not replicable today, given a less receptive trading environment for export subsidies, more open capital markets, and freer labour markets. Several developing East Asian countries still have fairly high tariff rates—for example, around 20 per cent in Indonesia and

the Philippines and 30 to 40 per cent in Thailand, while effective rates of protection, particularly in manufacturing remain in the 30 to 60 per cent range (Soesastro 1994a:1) (see table 1).

There are also informal, quantitative restrictions to trade and investment in the developing and industrial economies of East Asia. However, as Soesastro (1994b) notes, governments are now committed to continuing the process of opening their markets in the interests of achieving increased efficiency. This process of progressive opening among Northeast and Southeast Asian economies, has been described as a game of 'prisoners delight'—each country's success in internationally oriented economic growth depends on its own trade liberalisation (Drysdale and Garnaut 1993a; 1993b).

Some have suggested a role for APEC in speeding up this process by, for example, preparing sectoral liberalisation agreements to be negotiated globally through the WTO. Sectors where significant gains could be expected from early liberalisation would include: steel and steel products, processed minerals (such as aluminium), grains, textile, clothing and fibres, and aviation. Recent analysis suggests there are potential gains to Asian–Pacific economies through such joint initiatives (see for example Garnaut and Ma 1992). Results in a specific sector such as steel could act as a model for future co-operation efforts in specific areas of regional trade and industry policy (Drysdale 1993).

As the economies of the region become more intertwined, government policies encouraging particular sectors are increasingly irrelevant. The economic interdependencies being created by the burgeoning economies of Hong Kong, Taiwan and parts of China are the most obvious examples. Other examples of open economic associations are the 'growth triangles' around Singapore, the increased interaction between China and Korea and the

---

11 The quantitative approach to analysis of industry-government interaction has been most frequently applied to the area of tariff policy-making in developed countries. See Baldwin (1984) for a survey of the relevant literature for industrial countries. In the case of the Asian-Pacific region, see Findlay and Garnaut (1986) for ASEAN and Australia, Miller (1987) for Japan, and Smith (1994a) for Taiwan.

SMITH — *INDUSTRY POLICY IN EAST ASIA*

Table 1
Select industry policies of Asian–Pacific countries

	Tariffs and other import taxes		Non-tariff barriers	
	Nominal rate of assistance	*Effective rate of assistance (manufacturing)*[a]	*Import licensing*	*Quantitative restrictions (QRs)*
Japan	On industrial products 2%. 12% average on agricultural products, will be reduced and bound in WTO			Commitment to tariffication of quota/bans on agricultural goods, and reduction in tariffs by 2000
Korea	7.9% (1994). 6.2% (manufacturing). 30%+ on meat, most fruits, dairy products	23% (1990) all industry, 6% manufacturing	Required for all goods, 99% of which are automatic	3-year import liberalisation program (1992–94) phased out restrictions on 133 (mostly agricultural) items are scheduled to be either liberalised or brought into conformity with WTO provisions by 1997.
Taiwan	6.5% (1994) industrial products, falling to 4% on industrial goods, and 15% on farm goods on entry to WTO. 20–50% on some fruits and vegetables	57% (1989)	Number of items gradually being reduced. Will replace with simplified negative list	De facto bans or onerous quarantine restrictions for some meats and vegetables. Most full-sized cars on the prohibited list, though other car imports from USA, Europe are permitted. Ban on car imports from Japan is being eased.
Singapore	Average tariff rate 0.5% (excluding petroleum) 96% of imports enter duty-free. Following Uruguay Round 99% of tariff lines bound at zero rate		Virtually none. Rice importers required to keep buffer stock	QRs or bans on amusement machines, chewing gum, and certain toys, plants, animals
Indonesia	Applied tariff rates from from 5% to 30%. 83% of items tariffs <30–35%. Import surcharges for about 200 tariff categories mostly in the 5–25% range. Following Uruguay Round will bind 94% of tariff lines at highest rate of 40%	52% (1992) 44% (1987)	269 tariff categories to be removed over 10-year period. Imports subject to NTB 3.4% (1994) of tariff lines but protect 30% manufacturing and 35% agriculture	QRs on several agricultural products, including milk and rice
Malaysia	<10% average (1990). Following Uruguay Round tariffs on 80% of import value will be bound at 9.5%	17% (1990)	For about 3.3% of all tariff lines	Manufactured imports prohibited in 'pioneer' (new) industries
Thailand	17% (1994). 16.8% trade-weighted (1991). 9.3% ratio of tariff collected to total imports. 60% on most agricultural products. Following Uruguay Round tariffs on 64% of import value will be bound at the rate of 32%	51% (1988)	Restrictive licensing on 47 product categories, or 4% of 4-digit HS lines (1994)	Certain chemicals, selected food products: converting QRs to tariffs as part of Uruguay Round agreement
Philippines	24% (1992). 4 tiers in tariff structure: 3%, 10%, 20%, 30%. By end 1995, 50% for about 200 'strategic' products	32% (1992)	More than 100 items regulated through non-automatic licensing	QR 3% of all tariff lines. QR/bans on about 150 items

Note: Under the ASEAN Free Trade Area (AFTA), ASEAN countries have committed to reduce tariffs on manufactured products to a common effective preferential tariff rate of <5% by 2003 (covering 95% of trade). An accelerated or fast track program reduces tariffs on 15 product groups to 5% by 1998.

[a] Effective rate of protection (ERP), measures are not strictly comparable because of differences in methodology.

Sources: Edwards (1990); Fane and Phillips (1991); Hong (1992); GATT (1993); Kwak (1994); Naya and Iboshi (1994); Smith (1994); Soesastro (1994a); World Bank (1994).

'production networks' being created all around the Asian–Pacific region by investment from Northeast Asia (Elek 1994:6). Arguments for domestic industry policies are being weakened by the rapid growth of FDI. The World Bank (1994:41) has pointed out that 'to attract multinational companies and state-of-the-art technology, governments must offer an economic environment as free as possible from import barriers, regulations, taxes, and other interventions'. Some of the most spectacular recent stories of East Asian

development, in Malaysia and Thailand, for instance, have been led by export-oriented FDI from Japan and the NIEs. China is using FDI for development of competitive industries in textiles and electronics. Foreign investment promotion will continue to be helped by liberal trade regimes, and is in turn creating economic and political pressures for further trade liberalisation. This virtuous circle, not sector-specific industry policy, is the key to the future development of sophisticated manufactures in East Asia.

References

Abegglen, James and Stalk, G. 1985. *Kaisha: The Japanese Corporation*, Basic Books, New York.

Adams, Gerard F. and Davis, IngerMarie. 1994. 'The role of policy in economic development: the East Asian and the Latin American experience', *Asian–Pacific Economic Literature*, 8(1):8–26.

Alam, M. Shahid. 1989. *Governments and Markets in Economic Development Strategies: lessons from Korea, Taiwan, and Japan*, Praeger, New York.

Amsden, Alice. 1985. 'The state and Taiwan's economic development', in Evans, Peter; Rueschemeyer, Dietrich and Skocpol, Theda (eds), *Bringing the State Back In*, Cambridge University Press, Cambridge and New York.

— 1989. *Asia's Next Giant: South Korea and late industrialisation*, Oxford University Press, New York.

— 1991. 'Diffusion of development: the late industrialising model and Greater Asia', *American Economic Review Papers and Proceedings*, 81(2):282–6.

— 1992. 'Taiwan in international perspective', in Wung, N. T. (ed.), *Taiwan's Enterprises in Global Perspective*, M.E. Sharpe, Armonk, NY, USA.

Anderson, K.; Hayami, Y.; et al. 1986. *The Political Economy of Agricultural Protection: East Asia in perspective*, Allen and Unwin, London and Sydney.

Ariff, Mohamed and Hill, Hal. 1985. *Export-Oriented Industrialisation: the ASEAN experience*, Allen and Unwin, Sydney.

Arndt, H.W. 1987. 'Industrial Policy in East Asia, 1950–1985', in *Industry and Development*, UNIDO, Vienna. Reprinted 1989, National Centre for Development Studies, No. 2, Australian National University, Canberra.

Aron, Paul H. 1986. 'Comment' on Thomas A. Pugel: 'Industry policy in Japan: implications for technological catch-up and leadership', in Pugel, Thomas A. (ed.), *Fragile Interdependence: economic issues in US–Japanese trade and investment*, D.C. Heath, Massachusetts/Toronto.

Awanohara, Susumu. 1987. 'Look East: the Japan model', *Asian–Pacific Economic Literature*, 1(1):75–89.

Balassa, Bela. 1965. 'Tariff protection in industrial countries: an evaluation', *Journal of Political Economy*, 73(6):573–94.

— 1971. *The Structure of Protection in Developing Countries*, John Hopkins University Press, Baltimore.

— (ed.). 1982. *Development Strategies in Semi-industrial Economies*, John Hopkins University Press, Baltimore.

— 1983. 'Outward versus inward orientation once again', *The World Economy*, 6(2):215–18.

Baldwin, Richard and Krugman, Paul R. 1988. 'Market access and international competition: a simulation study of 16K random access memories', in Feenstra, R. (ed.), *Empirical Methods for International Trade*, MIT Press, Cambridge, Mass.

Baldwin, Robert E. 1969. 'The case against infant-industry tariff protection', *Journal of Political Economy*, 77:295–305.

— 1984. 'Trade policy in developed economies', in Jones, R. W. and Kenen, P. B. (eds), *Handbook of International Economics*, vol. 1, North-Holland, Amsterdam.

Bardhan, P. 1990. 'Symposium on the state and economic development', *Journal of Economic Perspectives*, 4(3):3–8.

Berger, Peter L. 1987. *The Capitalist Revolution*, Wildwood House, England.

Bergsten, Fred C., and Noland, Marcus. 1993. *Reconcilable Differences?*, Institute for International Economics, Washington, DC.

Bhagwati, Jagdish N. 1978. *Foreign Trade Regimes and Economic Development: anatomy and consequences of exchange control regimes*, Ballinger, Cambridge, MA, USA.

— 1988. *Protectionism*, MIT Press, Cambridge, MA, USA.

Bhagwati, Jagdish and Ramaswami, V.K. 1963. 'Domestic distortions, tariffs and the theory of optimum subsidy', *Journal of Political Economy*, 7(1):44–50.

Bhagwati, J. and Patrick, H. T. (eds). 1990. *Aggressive Unilateralism*, University of Michigan Press, Ann Arbor.

Bhattacharya, Amarendra and Linn, Johannes F. 1988. 'Trade and Industrial Policies in the Developing Countries of East Asia', World Bank Discussion Paper No. 27, World Bank, Washington, DC.

Bhattacharya, Amarendra and Pangestu, Mari. 1993. *Indonesia: development transformation and public policy*, Lessons of East Asia series. World Bank, Washington, DC.

Biggs, Tyler and Levy, Brian. 1988. 'Strategic interventions and the political economy of industrial policy in developing countries', paper presented for Harvard Institute for International Development Conference on Development Reforms, Morocco.

— 1991. 'Strategic intervention and the political economy of industrial policy in developing countries', in Perkins, Dwight and Roemer, Michael (eds), *Reforming Economic Systems in Developing Countries*, Cambridge, MA, USA.

Bowie, Alasdair. 1991. *Crossing the Industrial Divide: state, society, and the politics of economic transformation in Malaysia*, Columbia University Press, New York.

— 1994. 'The dynamics of business-government relations in industrialising Malaysia' in MacIntyre, Andrew (ed.), *Business and Government in Industrialising Asia*, Cornell University Press, Ithaca, NY, USA.

Bradford, C. 1984. 'The NICs: confronting US "autonomy"', in Fienberg, R. and Kallab, V. (eds), *Adjustment Crisis in the Third World*, Transactions Books, New Brunswick.

Brander, James A. 1987. 'Shaping comparative advantage: trade policy, industrial policy, and economic performance', in Lipsey, Richard G. and Dobson, Wendy (eds), *Shaping Comparative Advantage*, Policy Study No. 2, C.D. Howe Institute, Prentice-Hall, Ontario.

Chang, H-J. 1993. 'The political economy of industrial policy in Korea', *Cambridge Journal of Economics*, 17:131–57.

Chowdhury, Anis and Islam, Iyanatul. 1993. *The Newly Industrialising Economies of East Asia*, Routledge, London and New York.

Christensen, Scott; Dollar, David; Siamwalla, Ammar and Vichyanond, Pakorn. 1993. *Thailand: the institutional and political underpinnings of growth*, The Lessons of East Asia series, World Bank, Washington, DC.

Corden, W. M. 1966. 'The structure of a tariff system and the effective protective rates', *Journal of Political Economy*, 74(3):221–37.

— 1974. *Trade Policy and Economic Welfare*, Clarendon Press, Oxford.

Cumings, B. 1984. 'The origins and development of the Northeast Asian political economy: industrial sector, product cycles, and political consequences', *International Organisation*, 38(1):1–40; Reprinted in Deyo, Frederic C. (ed.), 1987, *The Political Economy of New Asian Industrialism*, Cornell University Press, Ithaca, NY, and London.

Deyo, Frederic C. (ed.). 1987. *The Political Economy of New Asian Industrialism*, Cornell University Press, Ithaca, NY, and London.

Doner, Richard and Unger, Daniel. 1993. 'The politics of finance in Thai economic development', in Haggard, Stephan; Lee, Chung E. and Maxfield, Sylvia (eds), *The Politics of Finance in Developing Countries*, Cornell University Press, Ithaca, NY, and London.

Dosi, Giovanni; Tyson, Laura D'Andrea and Zysman, John. 1989, 'Trade, technologies, and development: a framework for discussing Japan', in Johnson, Chalmers; Tyson, Laura D'Andrea and Zysman, John (eds), *Politics and Productivity: how Japan's development strategy works*, Ballinger, Cambridge, MA, USA.

Drysdale, Peter. 1993. *The Proposal for an East Asian Steel Community*, paper presented at the Fourth Global Contribution Seminar on the Asia–Pacific's Further Development and Ongoing Global Economic Growth, Tokyo.

Drysdale, Peter and Garnaut, Ross. 1993a. 'The Pacific: an application of a general theory of economic integration', in Bergsten, C. F. and Noland, M. (eds), *Pacific Dynamism and the International Economic System*, Institute for International Economics, Washington, DC.

— 1993b. 'East Asia in the international system: APEC and the challenge of discriminatory trade', paper presented at 'Sustaining the Development Process', a Festschift seminar held in honour of Helen Hughes, Australian National University, Canberra. To be published in Garnaut, Ross, Grilli, Enzo, and Riedel, James, 1995, *Sustaining Export-Oriented Development: ideas from East Asia*, Cambridge University Press, Cambridge.

Elek, Andrew. 1994. 'An open economic association in the Asia Pacific: a conceptual framework for Asia Pacific Economic Cooperation', paper presented to 'Australian, Indonesia and Japanese Approaches Towards APEC', Australian National University.

Fane, G. and Phillips, C. 1991. 'Effective protection in Indonesia in 1987', *Bulletin of Indonesian Economic Studies*, 27(1):105–25.

Far Eastern Economic Review. 1994. 'Retuning needed', October 13:64.

Findlay, Christopher and Garnaut, Ross (eds). 1986. *The Political Economy of Manufacturing Protection: experience of ASEAN and Australia*, Allen and Unwin, Sydney.

Garnaut, Ross. 1989. *Australia and the Northeast Asian Ascendancy*, Australian Government Publishing Service, Canberra.

— 1990. 'The Market and the State in Economic Development: some questions from East Asia and Australia'. The 1990 Shann Memorial Lecture. University of Western Australia. Reprinted in Siddique, M. A. B. (ed.), 1993, *A Decade of Shann Memorial Lectures and the Australian Economy 1981–90*, Academic Press International, Western Australia.

Garnaut. Ross and Ma, Guonan. 1992. *Grain in China*, Australian Government Publishing Service, Canberra.

GATT (General Agreement on Tariffs and Trade). 1993. *International Trade and the Trading System*. Report by the Director-General 1992–93. Geneva.

Givens, N. L. 1982. 'The U.S. can no longer afford free trade', *Business Week*, 15, November 22:11.

Gold, Thomas. 1986. *State and Society in the Taiwan Miracle*, M.E. Sharpe, Armonk, NY, USA.

Haggard, Stephan. 1990. *Pathways from the Periphery*, Cornell University Press, Ithaca, NY, and London.

Haggard, Stephan and Lee, Chung E. 1993. 'The political dimension of finance in economic development', in Haggard, Stephan; Lee, Chung E. and Maxfield, Sylvia (eds), *The Politics of Finance in Developing Countries*, Cornell University Press, Ithaca, NY, and London.

Haggard, Stephan; Lee, Chung E. and Maxfield, Sylvia (eds). 1993. *The Politics of Finance in Developing Countries*, Cornell University Press, Ithaca, NY, and London.

Helpman, Elhanan and Krugman, Paul R. 1985. *Market Structure and Foreign Trade: increasing returns, imperfect competition, and the international economy*, MIT Press, Cambridge, MA, USA.

Henderson, J. W. and Appelbaum, Richard P. (eds). 1992. *States and Development in the Pacific Rim*, Sage Publications, CA, USA.

Hill, Hal. 1988. *Foreign Investment and Industrialisation in Indonesia*, Oxford University Press, Singapore.

— 1993. 'Southeast Asian Economic Development: an analytical survey', Economic Division Working Papers 93/4, Research School of Pacific Studies, Australian National University, Canberra.

— 1995. (forthcoming) 'Indonesia's Industrial Policy and Performance: Orthodoxy Vindicated', Economic Division Working Papers No. 1, Research School of Pacific and Asian Studies, Australian National University, Canberra.

Hong, S. D. 1992. *The Structural Change in Nominal and Effective Protection Rates 1975–1990*, Korea Development Institute, Seoul (in Korean).

Hughes, Helen (ed.). 1988. *Achieving Industrialisation in East Asia*, Cambridge University Press, Cambridge.

— 1993. 'Is there an East Asian model?', Economics Division Working Papers No. 4, Research School of Pacific Studies, Australian National University, Canberra.

Hutchcroft, Paul D. 1993. 'Selective squander: the politics of preferential credit allocation in the Philippines', in Haggard, Stephan; Lee, Chung E. and Maxfield, Sylvia (eds), *The Politics of Finance in Developing Countries*, Cornell University Press, Ithaca, NY, and London.

Imai, Ken-ichi. 1986. 'Japan's industrial policy for high technology industry', in Patrick, Hugh (ed.), *Japan's High Technology Industries*, University of Washington Press, Seattle and London.

Islam, Iyanatul. 1992. 'Political economy and economic development', *Asian–Pacific Economic Literature*, 6(2):69–101.

Jayasankaran, S. 1993. 'Made-in-Malaysia: the Proton project', in Komo K. S. (ed.), *Industrialising Malaysia*, Routledge, London.

Johnson, Harry G. 1965. 'The costs of protection and self-sufficiency', *Quarterly Journal of Economics*, 79(3):356–72.

Johnson, Chalmers. 1982. *MITI and the Japanese Miracle: the growth of industrial policy, 1925–1975*, Stanford University Press, Stanford, California.

— 1987. 'Political institutions and economic performance: the government-business relationship in Japan, South Korea, and Taiwan', in Deyo, Frederic C. (ed.), *The Political Economy of*

New Asian Industrialism, Cornell University Press, Ithaca, NY, and London.

Komiya, Ryutaro. 1988. 'Introduction', in Komiya, Ryutaro; Okuno, Masahiro; and Suzumura, Kotaro (eds), *Industrial Policy of Japan*, Academic Press, Tokyo.

Krueger, Anne O. 1966. 'Some economic costs of exchange control: the Turkish case', *Journal of Political Economy*, 74:466–80.

— 1978. *Foreign Trade Regimes and Economic Development: liberalization attempts and consequences*, vol. 10, National Bureau for Economic Research, Ballinger Press, New York.

— 1990. 'Free trade is the best policy', in Lawrence, Robert Z. and Schultze, Charles L., *An American Trade Strategy: options for the 1990s*, The Brookings Institution, Washington, DC.

— 1993. 'The role of trade and growth and development: theory and lessons from experience', paper presented at 'Sustaining the Developing Process', a Festschrift seminar for Helen Hughes at the Australian National University, Canberra.

Krugman, Paul R. 1984. 'Import protection as export promotion: international competition in the presence of oligopoly and economies of scale', in Kierzkowski, H. (ed.), *Monopolistic Competition and International Trade*, Oxford University Press, Oxford.

— (ed.). 1986. *Strategic Trade Policy and the New International Economics*, MIT Press, Cambridge, MA, USA.

— 1987a. 'Strategic sectors and international competition', in Stern, Robert M. (ed.), *US Trade Policies in a Changing World Economy*, MIT Press, Cambridge, MA, USA.

— 1987b. 'Targeted industrial policies: theory and evidence', in Salvatore, D. (ed.), *The New Protectionist Threat to World Welfare*, MIT Press, Cambridge, MA, USA.

— 1987c. 'The narrow moving band, the dutch disease, and the competitive consequences of Mrs Thatcher', *Journal of Development Economics*, 27:41–55.

— 1989. 'New trade theory and the less developed countries', in Calvo, Guillermo; Findlay, Ronald; Kouri, Pentii and de Macedo, Jorge Braga (eds), *Debt, Stabilisation and Development*, Basil Blackwell, Oxford and New York.

— 1992. 'Does new trade theory require a new trade policy?', *The World Economy*, 15(4):423–41.

— 1993. 'Free trade: a loss of (theoretical) nerve?', *American Economic Review*, 83(2):362–66.

Kwak, H. 1994. 'Changing trade policy and its impact on TFP in the Republic of Korea', *The Developing Economies*, 32(4):398–421.

Lall, Sanjaya. 1994. 'Industry policy: the role of government in promoting industrial and technological development', *UNCTAD Review 1994*, UNCTAD, Geneva.

Lawrence, Robert. 1993. 'Japan's different trade regime: an analysis with particular reference to Keiretsu', *Journal of Economic Perspectives*, 7(3):3–19.

Lawrence, R. and Schultze, C. L., (eds) 1990. *An American Trade Strategy: options for the 1990s*, The Brookings Institution, Washington, DC.

Lim, David 1992. 'The dynamics of economic policy-making: a study of Malaysian trade policies and performance', in MacIntyre, Andrew and Jayasuriya, Kanishka (eds), *The Dynamics of Economic Policy Reform in South-east Asia and the South-west Pacific*, Oxford University Press, Singapore.

Lincoln, Edward J. 1984. *Japan's Industrial Policies*, Japan Economic Institute of America, Washington, DC.

Little, I.; Scitovsky, T.; and Scott, M. 1970. *Industry and Trade in Some Developing Countries*, Oxford University Press, London.

Luedde-Neurath, Richard. 1988. 'State intervention and export-oriented development in South Korea', in White, G. (ed.), *Developmental States in East Asia*, Macmillan, London.

MacIntyre, Andrew. 1993. 'The politics of finance in Indonesia: command, confusion, and competition', in Haggard, Stephan; Lee, Chung E. and Maxfield, Sylvia (eds), *The Politics of Finance in Developing Countries*, Cornell University Press, Ithaca, NY, and London.

— (ed.). 1994. 'Business, government and development: Northeast and Southeast Asia comparisons', in MacIntyre, Andrew (ed.), *Business and Government in Industrializing Asia*, Cornell University Press, Ithaca, NY, USA.

Malaysia, Government Printer. 1985. *Heavy Industries Corporation of Malaysia (HICOM), Annual Report 1984*, Kuala Lumpur.

McKendrick, David. 1992. 'Obstacles to "catch-up": the case of the Indonesian aircraft industry', *Bulletin of Indonesian Economic Studies*, 28(1):39–66.

Miller, B. 1987. The political economy of Japan's tariff policy: a quantitative analysis, unpublished PhD dissertation, Australian National University, Canberra.

Nam, Sang-Woo. 1991. 'The Korean economy at crossroads: recent policy efforts and new challenges', Korea Development Institute Working Paper 9124, Korea Development Institute, Seoul.

— 1992. 'Korea's financial reform since the early

1980s', Korea Development Institute Working Paper 9207, Korea Development Institute, Seoul.

Naya, Seiji Finch and Iboshi, Pearl Imada. 1994. 'A new agenda: setting up the "building blocks" of free trade', Asia–Pacific Issues No. 17. East–West Center, Honolulu.

Okimoto, Daniel I. 1986. 'Regime characteristics of Japanese industrial policy', in Patrick, Hugh (ed.), *Japan's High Technology Industries*, University of Washington Press, Seattle, USA, and London.

Onis, Z. 1991. 'The logic of the developmental state', *Comparative Politics*, 24(1):109–26.

Pack, H. 1992. 'New perspectives on industrial growth in Taiwan', in Ranis, Gustav (ed.), *Taiwan: from developing to mature economy*, Westview Press, Boulder.

Pack, H. and Westphal, L. 1986. 'Industrial strategy and technological change: theory versus reality', *Journal of Development Economics*, 22:8–128.

Pangestu, Mari. 1993. 'The role of the state and economic development in Indonesia', *The Indonesian Quarterly*, 30(3):253–83.

Patrick, Hugh (ed.). 1986. *Japan's High Technology Industries*, University of Washington Press, Seattle and London.

— (ed.). 1991. *Pacific Basin Industries in Distress*, Columbia University Press, New York.

Patrick, Hugh and Rosovsky, Henry (eds). 1976. *Asia's New Giant: how the Japanese economy works*, The Brookings Institution, Washington, DC.

Porter, Michael E. 1990. *The Competitive Advantage of Nations*, Free Press, New York.

Prestowitz, Clyde. 1988. *Trading Places: how we allowed Japan to take the lead*, Basic Books, New York.

Richardson, J. David. 1990. 'The political economy of strategic trade policy', *International Organisation*, 44(1):107–35.

— 1991. '"New" trade theory and policy a decade old: assessment in a Pacific context', paper presented at the First Australian Fullbright Symposium, 'Managing International Economic Relations in the Pacific in the 1990s', Australian National University, Canberra.

Salleh, Ismail and Meyanathan, Saha Dhevan. 1993. *Malaysia: growth, equity and structural transformation*, The Lessons of East Asia series, World Bank, Washington, DC.

Saxonhouse, Gary R. 1986. 'Industry policy and factor markets: biotechnology in Japan and the United States', in Patrick, Hugh (ed.), *Japan's High Technology Industries*, University of Washington Press, Seattle and London.

Sazanami, S.; Urata, S. and Kawai, H. 1995. *Measuring the Costs of Protection in Japan*, Institute for International Economics, Washington, DC.

Shinohara, Miyohei. 1982. *Industrial Growth, Trade, and Dynamic Patterns in the Japanese Economy*. Tokyo University Press, Tokyo.

Simon, Denis Fred. 1992. 'Taiwan's strategy for creating competitive advantage: the role of the state in managing foreign technology', in Wang, N. T. (ed.), *Taiwan's Enterprises in Global Perspective*, M.E. Sharpe, Armonk, NY, USA.

Smith, Heather. 1994a. The role of government in the industrialisation of Taiwan and Korea in the 1980s, unpublished PhD dissertation, Australian National University, Canberra.

— 1994b. 'Korea's industry policy during the 1980s', *Pacific Economic Papers*, no. 229, March.

— 1994c. 'Taiwan's industry policy during the 1980s and its relevance to the theory of strategic trade', *Pacific Economic Papers*, no. 233, July.

Soesastro, Hadi. 1994a. 'Trade reforms in the ASEAN economies', paper presented at the China and East Asia Trade Policy Conference, Australian National University, Canberra.

— 1994b. 'Indonesian approaches to APEC', paper presented at 'Australian, Indonesian and Japanese Approaches Towards APEC', Australian National University, Canberra.

Trezise, Philip H., with the collaboration of Yukio Suzuki. 1976. 'Politics, government, and economic growth in Japan', in Patrick, Hugh and Rosovsky, Henry (eds), *Asia's New Giant: how the Japanese economy works*, The Brookings Institution, Washington, DC.

Trezise, Philip H. 1983. 'Industrial policy is not the major reason for Japan's success', *The Brookings Review*, Spring, pp.13–18.

Tyson, Laura D'Andrea. 1990. 'Managed trade: making the best of the second best', in Lawrence, Robert Z. and Schultze, Charles L. (eds), *An American Trade Strategy: options for the 1990s*, The Brookings Institution, Washington, DC.

— 1992. *Who's Bashing Whom?*, Institute for International Economics, Washington, DC.

Wade, Robert. 1984. 'Dirigisme Taiwan-style', *Institute of Development Studies Bulletin*, 15(2):65–70.

— 1988. 'The role of government in overcoming market failure: Taiwan, Republic of Korea and Japan', in Hughes, Helen (ed.), *Achieving Industrialisation in East Asia*, Cambridge University Press, Cambridge.

— 1990a. *Governing the Market: economic theory and the role of government in East Asian industrialization*, Princeton University Press, Princeton, USA.

— 1990b. 'Industrial policy in East Asia: does it lead or follow the market?', in Gereffi, G. and Wyman, D. (eds), *Manufacturing Miracles: paths of industrialisation in Latin America and East Asia*, Princeton University Press, Princeton, NJ, USA.

Warr, P. 1992a. 'Comparative advantage and competitive advantage', Economic Development Institute Working Paper, World Bank, Washington, DC.

— 1992b. 'Comparative advantage and protection in Indonesia', *Bulletin of Indonesian Economic Studies*, 28(4):41–70.

— 1993. 'Thailand's Economic Miracle', Information Paper No. 1, *National Thai Studies*, Australian National University, Canberra.

— 1994. 'Comparative and competitive advantage', *Asian–Pacific Economic Literature*, 8(2):1–14.

— 1995. 'Myths about dragons', *Agenda*, 1(2):215–28.

White, G. (ed.). 1988. *Development States in East Asia*, Macmillan, London.

Wiboonchutikula, Paitoon. 1987. 'Total factor productivity growth of manufacturing industries in Thailand', in Thai Development Research Institute (TDRI), *Productivity Changes and International Competitiveness of Thai Industries*, TDRI, Bangkok.

World Bank. 1983. *World Development Report 1983*. Oxford University Press, New York.

— 1987. *World Development Report 1987*. Oxford University Press, New York.

— 1993. *The East Asian Miracle, Economic Growth and Public Policy*, Oxford University Press, New York.

— 1994. 'East Asian leadership in liberalisation, a discussion paper on building on the Uruguay Round', World Bank, Washington, DC.

Yamamura, Kozo. 1986. 'Caveat emptor: the industrial policy of Japan', in Krugman, Paul (ed.), *Strategic Trade Policy and the New International Economics*, MIT Press, Cambridge, MA, USA.

Yoo, Jung-ho. 1990. *The Industrial Policy of the 1970s and the Evolution of the Manufacturing Sector in Korea*, Korea Development Institute Working Paper No. 9017. Korea Development Institute, Seoul.

Young, Soogil. 1986. Impediments to Trade Liberalisation, unpublished manuscript. Korea Development Institute, Seoul.

Zysman, John. 1983. *Governments, Markets, and Growth: financial systems and the politics of industrial change*, Cornell University Press, Ithaca, NY, USA.

[7]

THE ECONOMIC RECORD, VOL. 71, NO. 214, SEPTEMBER 1995, 271–283

The Question of Access to the Japanese Market*

PETER DRYSDALE

Australia–Japan Research Centre,
Research School of Pacific and Asian Studies,
Australian National University,
Canberra, ACT 2600

It is now widely accepted that Japan has relatively low official barriers to merchandise, particularly manufactured goods, trade relative to other industrial countries. Yet, Japan's current account and trade surpluses have encouraged the view that there must be special 'hidden barriers' to accessing the Japanese market, and a literature has developed on the premise that Japanese business organizations (keiretsu) limit foreign penetration of markets of manufactured goods. This paper surveys the main elements of this literature and questions some of the assumptions upon which recent American policy in this area seems to have been developed.

The question of access to the Japanese market has again become a central issue in the high politics of the relationship between the world's two largest economies. The settlement of the impasse over automobile and automobile parts trade (Hashimoto and Kantor, 28 June 1995) within the context of the Framework Agreement talks between the United States and Japan, has not resolved the issue—rather it underlines the continuing importance in American thinking of new trade policy strategies towards Japan and, perhaps, more broadly the whole of East Asia.

Of course, Japan still has an agricultural sector which is among the most highly protected in the world, and Japanese agricultural protection for those commodities, like rice, the import of which is subject to quantitative restriction, rose rapidly over the past two decades of yen appreciation at a time when, otherwise, Japanese commercial policy was pointed towards trade liberalization.[1]

Restrictions on a whole range of service trades are also pervasive, from construction and civil aviation to legal services. These restrictions are a prime target of the stalled reform package introduced by former Prime Minister Hosokawa in 1993.[2]

Ostensibly, Japan has the cleanest import system for manufactured goods among virtually all OECD countries: on average tariffs are lower and official non-tariff barriers have almost no effect on trade at all. Moreover, Japan, like Australia, is not a participant in the Multi Fibres

---

[1] In this respect, Japan is, of course, only a front runner among the industrial country pack and even in agriculture, the liberalization of the beef market in Japan after 1988 represents among the most significant agricultural trade liberalizations by any industrial country in recent times. At last, there is also a narrow opening in the rice market under the Japanese government's Uruguay Round commitments.

[2] Yet, in this sector too, the barriers are on the way down and, insofar as it is possible to devise objective measures of services trades affected by the regulatory system, Japan is not so far behind the United States in the openness of its services markets to foreign competition (see table following).

---

*I am grateful to John Kunkel for assembling all the bibliographical material on which this paper is based and for other assistance in its preparation. I am also grateful to Paul Sheard, Ross Garnaut, Ben Smith, Luke Gower, Tony Warren, Gordon de Brouwer, and Bill Norton for comments on a draft. I alone, of course, am responsible for the final form of the argument.

Arrangement (MFA) so that its market for the most important labour-intensive exports from developing economies is more open than that of all other large industrial countries. Thus far, Japan has largely resisted the temptation of seeking 'voluntary export restraint' on this sensitive area of manufactured goods trade.

Paradoxically, it is in manufactured goods trade—the heartland of Japan's industrial competitiveness—that the question of access to the Japanese market now looms largest.

There may be few official barriers to trade in manufactured goods, but the import share in Japanese markets is low in comparison with other

TABLE 1

Measures of the Frequency of Application of Restrictions on Services Trade for APEC Countries[a]

	All Commitments	Market Access	National Treatment	Mode 1[b]	Mode 2	Mode 3	Mode 4
Australia	49.6	49.5	49.7	46.5	43.0	40.4	68.6
Brunei	95.0	95.7	94.3	94.9	93.2	95.9	96.2
Canada	61.2	62.1	60.2	58.6	53.0	58.1	75.0
Chile	90.2	90.3	90.1	91.1	92.5	85.3	91.8
China	88.2	88.5	87.9	96.8	78.7	90.6	86.7
Hong Kong	88.1	83.4	92.8	97.7	85.1	71.9	97.6
Indonesia	91.6	91.0	92.2	91.2	89.8	92.7	92.8
Japan	46.5	44.0	48.9	38.8	31.3	47.5	68.4
Korea, Rep	70.7	75.1	66.2	70.7	67.4	65.0	79.5
Malaysia	78.8	80.4	77.2	74.9	74.0	80.3	86.1
Mexico	71.9	74.1	69.7	73.0	62.3	70.8	81.5
New Zealand	56.6	56.4	56.8	50.7	49.0	51.1	75.7
Philippines	80.8	82.2	79.4	81.9	79.6	81.4	80.3
Singapore	82.0	80.2	83.7	80.8	74.2	79.6	93.3
Thailand	77.3	79.2	75.4	92.8	59.7	79.1	77.7
United States	43.0	46.3	39.7	37.9	39.1	42.2	52.9

Notes: [a] The ratios reported in this table represent the frequency with which a country has failed to commit to liberal trade measures under the General Agreement on Trade in Services (GATS). The higher the number, the more the restrictions.
[b] Each mode represents a different way for services to be transacted internationally. Mode 1 = cross-border supply; Mode 2 = consumption abroad; Mode 3 = commercial presence; Mode 4 = presence of persons.
Source: Tony Warren, *The Political Economy of Services Trade Policy: Australia, Japan and the United States* (Ph.D. Thesis ANU, forthcoming).

The table provides a number of measures of the extent to which APEC economies have not committed to liberal trade under the GATS. The most important finding is that listed for all commitments. This is the average level of impediments for each country across all industries and all modes. The United States is the most liberal in terms of this score, Japan is second and Australia is third. It is interesting to note that Japan is the most liberal in terms of market access, the US in terms of national treatment.

industrial countries (Lawrence, 1987; Balassa and Noland, 1988) and it is frequently argued that non-official barriers limit access to the Japanese market for these goods. 'Hidden barriers' to trade, the argument runs, are endemic in Japanese corporate organization and business structures and the 'peculiar' features of the Japanese market effectively exclude foreign competition.

This survey focuses on the question of how market structure and different corporate organizational forms might affect access to the Japanese market for industrial goods. The question is how and whether *keiretsu* corporate structures in Japan constitute an important unofficial barrier in access to the Japanese market for manufactured goods.

This is an important issue.

The premise that 'hidden' barriers to trade explain Japan's low manufactured goods trade shares and international price differentials has gained currency in policy circles and come to provide a rationale for so called 'results-oriented' trade strategies, including the application of Section 301 (of the 1974 United States Trade Act) (Robinson and Houghton, 1989) and attempts to set numerical import targets, sector by sector, for the volume of American goods that Japan and (potentially) other foreign countries are expected to buy (Passell, 1989; Altman, 1994; Bergsten and Noland, 1993; Bhagwati, 1994).

The latest and most threatening expression of this thinking was in the contretemps between the United States and Japan over the American share of the Japanese automobile market (Kantor, 1995b; Clinton, 1995).

First, I review briefly the literature which contests the importance of Japanese barriers to trade in manufactured goods. Then, I explore the link between corporate structures and closed markets, identifying two analytically separate arguments which suggest that *keiretsu* corporate structures exclude foreign competition in the market for manufactures. Three types of *keiretsu* corporate structure are defined—financial *keiretsu*, vertical *keiretsu*, and distribution *keiretsu*. All are vertical organizational structures, in the sense of the literature on industrial organization. I explore the argument that these structures are 'anti competitive' and that they constitute a 'hidden barrier' to trade. I draw attention to a study of Japanese investment in Australia which has been cited widely as evidence of the closedness of Japanese markets. Finally, I review the implications for policy.

Many other facets of developments in trans-

Pacific economic diplomacy are worthy of review—the macroeconomic context which has brought the bilateral trade balance into sharp political focus in the United States; Japan's trade and current account surpluses, as a lightning rod for tensions in the management of the relationship with the United States; the dynamics of trade and foreign economic policy developments between Japan and the United States; the transition in the structure of economic power in Asia and the Pacific and its impact on policy substance and posture; the effect of these trends in trade policy between the two largest economic powers on the international trade policy environment. Some of these issues I have reviewed elsewhere (Drysdale, 1989).

But understanding whether *keiretsu* corporate structures constitute a 'hidden barrier' to trade is central to assessment of the strength of the intellectual foundations, and therefore of the good sense, of the new trade policy strategies towards Japan. That is not to say, of course, that the strategies would have no impact even if they were premised on false intellectual foundations. As always, the question is whether they are likely to contribute to international welfare, not just redistribute income, for example, in favour of particular American producers and factors of production. There is also a broader scholarly interest in the effect of corporate organizational structures on the nature and operation of international markets—a big question which is illuminated somewhat, but is not in the spotlight of attention in the literature surveyed here.

Barriers to Trade in Manufactures

A number of studies have explored the low propensity in Japan to import manufactured goods and sought to confirm the contention that Japanese institutions, or reliance on a variety of informal barriers to trade, is its cause (Balassa, 1986; Lawrence, 1987; Balassa and Noland, 1988; Krugman, 1991; Lawrence, 1991a; Fung, 1991; Lawrence, 1991b; Bergsten and Noland, 1993). These studies compare Japan's imports of manufactured goods with those of other industrial countries and conclude that Japan is an 'outlier', with a lower share of manufactured goods imports and intra-industry trade in this sector. On the other hand, evidence provided by other studies of Japan's trade dependence and trade structure, such as those of Saxonhouse (1986), Saxonhouse (1988, esp. p.240), Saxonhouse and Stern (1989),

Goto, F (1991), Weinstein and Yafeh (1993), and Saxonhouse (1993) suggests that there is no significant difference between Japan's trade structure and that of other industrial countries, when account is taken of cross-national differences in factor endowments, including capital, labour and a variety of natural resources, as well as distance in the international marketplace.

Sazanami, Urata and Kawai (1995) attempt to overcome the problems associated with 'indirect' assessment of the barriers to Japanese imputs of manufactured goods by measuring directly the price wedge between Japanese products and similar imported goods. There have been other price comparison studies but they are far less rigorous (US Department of Commerce and Japan Ministry of International Trade and Industry, 1989). Very few countries collect data that allow ex-factory prices to be compared directly with the import prices of 'comparable' products at the required level of disaggregation; Japan is one of them. Unit value (price) differences are assumed to reflect the effect of official barriers to trade—which are measurable or observable—or non-official 'hidden' barriers to trade. Studies of differentials *over time* would be more robust to this criterion.

Although Sazanami, Urata and Kawai (1995, p.14) exclude 26 product categories (among them automobiles) from their study because of product heterogeneity revealed in sensitivity analysis of the data, their findings reveal large differentials in the prices of 'comparable' domestically produced and imported products. These differentials reflect official barriers to trade (272.5 per cent for the food and beverages product category) but, in other cases are not satisfactorily explainable by official barriers to trade (34.5 per cent for cotton yarn and 282.2 per cent for clothing) and are attributed to 'hidden' or non-official barriers to trade. While the authors are careful not to attribute these measured price differences to Japanese corporate practices, their evidence has been used with less caution to support the interpretation that corporate practices in Japan are their cause (Bergsten and Noland, 1993, pp. 279–97).

There are two significant problems with this study, despite its being the most comprehensive and rigorous of its kind thus far. First, as Sazanami, Urata, and Kawai admit (1995, p.12) there is a real question about whether like is being compared with like in the price comparisons. Take the case of clothing product price comparisons. There are substantial quality differences between clothing made in Japan and imported clothing from China and other developing economies (which constitute the bulk of imports in this category). Imports service a different segment of the market for clothing from Japanese made clothing. The price differential for this product category is not a credible measure of the difference in price of the *same* goods produced domestically and produced abroad. Even for foodstuffs, the problem of matching product categories is serious: 12 canned and bottled Japanese products are 'matched' with 42 imported items (p.8), but how can they be, reliably? Second, there is the endemic problem with studies of this kind (Kravis, and Lipsey, 1971 pp.42–3) that measures of price differentials reflect continuous disturbance and adjustment in dynamic markets (the forces of competition itself) at least as much as, and probably more than, the presence of restrictions—official or non-official—in the market.

This problem is extreme in a study which seeks to measure price differences between Japanese products and imported products in the period 1985 and uses price indices to project differentials in 1989 (a period over which there was a sharp appreciation of the Japanese currency and huge change in the structure of Japanese trade), the share of manufactured goods imports almost doubling over the period (Drysdale, 1989).

These elementary practical and analytical issues are also ignored in other studies which interpret price differentials as evidence of 'hidden' barriers to trade and relate these barriers to Japanese corporate practice (Krugman, 1991; Lawrence, 1993).

Corporate Structure and Closed Markets

The idea that *keiretsu* corporate structures in Japan are associated with 'closed' Japanese markets has wide currency in American policy and business circles (ACTPN 1993, USTR 1995; Bergsten and Noland, 1993).

There are two elements in the idea.

The first is that Japanese corporate organizational structures facilitate collusion and predatory pricing behaviour in Japanese markets and internationally. Cartels and collusive trade practices constitute barriers to entry and an 'unfair' impediment to trade.

The second analytically separable element relates to the nature of inter-firm ties and relational transactions which appear to typify manufacturing assembly in Japan. Dore (1986, p. 248)

makes the point: 'Imports penetrate into markets, and where there are no markets, only a network of established "customer relationships", it is hard for them to make headway'. An ancillary issue is the 'exclusionary' system whereby intermediate and final products are distributed in the Japanese market.

Monopolistic behaviour, were it distinctively prevalent, would certainly limit market access. And undoubtedly there are markets in Japan in which monopolistic behaviour is a concern, such as construction or glass (McMillan, 1990; Sazanami, Urata and Kawai, 1995). But the question is whether *keiretsu* corporate structures can be presumed synonymous with monopolistic behaviour as the first element in the idea that Japanese corporate structures serve to close markets suggests.

Access to markets which are 'closed' because they are internalized through the vertical integration of firms (historically a common pattern in the United States) or because they are characterized by long-term contracting, relational dealings or 'partial' vertical integration (the pattern observed more commonly in Japan) is another matter altogether. How such market structures are ordered reflects the choice of firms in defining the boundaries of their operations (Coase, 1937; Williamson, 1975; Alchian and Demsetz, 1972; Jensen and Meckling, 1976; Fama, 1980; Cheung, 1983; Williamson, 1985; Sheard, 1993; Sheard 1994). It is not clear that there is a policy role where competitive pressures encourage this choice to be made efficiently. Firms (both domestic and foreign) have a strategic interest in how other firms make the choice about the boundaries of their operations but government intervention in this area is more likely to reduce efficiency and welfare than it is to enhance it.

Keiretsu may be associated with 'closure of markets' in the sense that the location and nature of transacting at the boundaries of intermediate product markets is endogenously determined in the organization of industry, but this is a completely different sense of closure from its meaning in the context of trade policy where closure results from exogenously imposed trade barriers.

In policy discussion the two elements in the idea that *keiretsu* corporate structures exclude foreign competition are routinely confused. There is also a deal of confusion in the academic literature, especially that which relies on secondhand knowledge of the institutions and how they operate. The language of trade practices and competition policy—collusion, exclusionary practices, closed markets—is applied indiscriminately and inappropriately to both elements in the idea. The first step is to clarify the nature of *keiretsu* corporate structures to establish a sounder foundation for the analysis of their impact on access to the Japanese market.

This is not so simple a task as it may seem. Others (Saxonhouse, 1993; Sheard, 1994) have observed that, even in technical discourse, the term *keiretsu* is used loosely in Japan to describe a wide range of corporate affiliations and the corporate groups which they define. There is an endless literature in Japanese (Sheard, 1986) and a growing literature in English which helps to clarify the issues (Goto, A, 1982; Abbeglen and Stalk, 1985; Sheard, 1991; Saxonhouse, 1991; Gerlach, 1992; Fruin, 1992; Gibson and Roe, 1993; Saxonhouse, 1993; Aoki, Patrick and Sheard, 1994; Sheard, 1994).

Sheard (1994) distinguishes three kinds of *keiretsu* structures. The first—financial *keiretsu*—comprises corporate groups, each representative of a wide range of industrial sectors and associated through cross-shareholdings and financial transactions with one of Japan's major city (or commercial) banks. There are six main-bank corporate groups—Mitsui, Mitsubishi, Sumitomo, Fuji (deriving from the pre-war *zaibatsu*), Sanwa and Daiichi Kangyo (formed in the high growth period after the war). These *keiretsu* groups are linked through the financing relationships with the main bank and other financial institutions, interlocking shareholdings, association with a general trading company, supply relationships, and membership of one or more 'presidents' clubs, which provide an opportunity for senior management to meet regularly. Only 8 per cent of listed firms on the Tokyo Stock Exchange belong to these clubs but the source used by Sheard (Keizai Chosa Kyokai, 1992) classifies 59 per cent of non-financial firms listed on the exchange as being affiliated in some way with one or another of these main-bank groups. The average level of the intragroup shareholding of these groups is around 18 per cent, so too is the average level of intra-group bank and insurance financing. On average only 9 per cent of purchases and 8 per cent of sales are with other group firms, although for the general trading companies intra-group business is as high as two thirds of total business (Sheard, 1994, pp. 8–9).

Financial *keiretsu* are vertical structures, in the sense of the literature on industrial organization. Main bank and co-insurance networks resemble a partially internalized capital market and the vertical linkages prominent in vertical *keiretsu* in intermediate commodity markets.

The second—vertical *keiretsu*—comprises large assembly and manufacturing firms and their networks of subsidiaries and affiliated suppliers upstream in the production chain. Toyota is typical in the automobile industry. Matsushita, Hitachi, and Toshiba are typical in the electrical goods industry. Sheard (1994, p.9) identifies 40 major 'pyramid-style') *keiretsu* groups like this, each with an average of over 190 subsidiaries or associated companies (Toyo Keizai Shimposha, 1991, p.54). One study of Toyota affiliates identifies 168 first-tier suppliers with, in turn, 5437 indirect or second-tier suppliers and a further 41 702 lower level or third-tier suppliers (Fruin, 1992, p.271).

Toyota's 41 most important direct suppliers and subcontractors, for example, accounted for 75 per cent of total inputs in 1991. These firms are not totally dependent on Toyota, which on average held about 25 per cent of their shares and accounted for around 43 per cent of their sales (Sheard, 1994, pp.10–11, 44–5).

The third—distribution *keiretsu*—also involves vertical ties, but downstream in the production and distribution process, not upstream as in the case of vertical *keiretsu*. Most large firms have some kind of distribution system. Affiliated dealer networks or chain store outlets are common in final goods markets. The nine Japanese passenger vehicle producers, for example, have almost 4000 affiliated leaders and over 17 000 outlets. In many cases the dealerships are exclusive, but producer ownership links vary considerably. For intermediate products 'special agency contracts', management and other assistance to agents is common (Sheard, 1994, pp.11–12).

These three types of *keiretsu* structure are not mutually exclusive. As Sheard (1994, p.13) points out, 'leading industrial firms in financial *keiretsu* are typically parent firms in their own supplier networks, distribution networks and subsidiary groups.' Clearly *keiretsu* membership cannot be defined on a single dimension and it is much more ambiguous even than this helpful taxonomy suggests.

Saxonhouse (1993, p.37) draws attention to the variety of definitions of *keiretsu* and consistent classification systems available from Japanese sources. Dodwell Marketing Group, Nihon Keizai Shimbunsha, Toyo Keizai Shimposha, Keizai Chosa Kyokai are four of the most prominent sources and data from these sources can differ widely. Weinstein and Yafeh (1993) show that none of the five most commonly used definitions are closely correlated (the highest coefficient being 0.32) and Saxonhouse (1993, p.37) points out that classifications change arbitrarily even in the one source year by year. The Dodwell Marketing Group classification, on which Lawrence (1991a) bases his work, lists 9 vertical *keiretsu* in 1986, but three years later the number jumps to thirty-three. Arbitrary classification is obviously a product of different understandings of the nature of *keiretsu* and muddies analysis of their role in the operation of the Japanese economy.

On top of the problem of the classification of *keiretsu* structures consistently, Japanese firms do change their corporate affiliations, much more frequently than is generally understood. Horiuchi, Packer and Fukuda (1988) report that more than 25 per cent of firms listed on the Tokyo Stock Exchange changed their main-bank or financial *keiretsu* affiliation between the 1970s and 1980s. *Keiretsu* corporate structures are clearly a more plastic economic variable than many research analysts and most policy commentators realize.

However, suppose that *keiretsu* affiliations can be described unambiguously in the three dimensions set out by Sheard (1994). At least at one point in time, using the one data source (Sheard chose Keizai Chosa Kyokai) this is practicable.

What are their implications for access to the Japanese market?

Do Japanese financial *keiretsu* allow more monopoly power in Japanese manufacturing activity than there is in American or European manufacturing, and consequently limit foreign access to the Japanese market, thereby affecting the welfare of Japanese consumers and international producers in a way that distinguishes corporate behaviour in Japanese markets from that in other industrial countries?

Does the presence of vertical *keiretsu* lead to exclusion of competitive foreign suppliers from the Japanese market for manufactures?

Does the prevalence of distribution *keiretsu* lock out competition in final or intermediate goods markets?

Financial Keiretsu *and Competition*

The suggestion that financial *keiretsu* are harbingers of monopoly power to a peculiar extent can be dispatched quickly.

As the literature on industrial organization makes clear (Jacquemin and Slade, 1989; Tirole, 1988), cartels or anti-competitive and collusive practices involve price-fixing or coordination in the same product markets. Firms in Japanese financial *keiretsu* (and, for that matter in vertical or distribution *keiretsu*) cannot collude or form cartels by virtue simply of their *keiretsu* affiliations because *keiretsu* firms from the same group do not operate in the same product market. Financial *keiretsu* are sometimes described as 'horizontal' structures, but they are not in the sense in which the term horizontal (as in 'horizontal merger') is used in the literature on industrial organization. They are horizontal structures only in the sense that they involve operations in different product markets across a whole range of corporate activities. This is the 'oneset' phenomenon identified by Miyazaki (1967).

The fact that there are six major financial *keiretsu* in Japan, it might reasonably be argued, intensifies competition in different product markets rather than reduces it. Participation in most markets is high and the threat and ease of entry great. These *keiretsu* groups as well as independent firms are players in most important markets which are consequently less concentrated than markets in many other industrial countries. Moreover, the trading companies, which are a mainstay of financial *keiretsu*, are very competitive and active in each other's markets. There are particular markets characterized by a large degree of concentration and monopoly or oligopolistic behaviour in Japan and it is also theoretically conceivable, but not practically credible (Sheard, 1994, pp.7–18), that *keiretsu* groups may facilitate multi-market collusion (Tirole, 1988). But most studies of market concentration across industrial countries do not reveal Japan as an outlier (Caves and Uekusa, 1976). Indeed, for most sectors, market concentration is relatively low in Japanese manufacturing. There are nine automobile producers in Japan in contrast to the big three in the United States, and while concentration ratios have limited value as an indicator of competition in product markets, the Japanese automobile industry, for example, appears intensely competitive (Smitka, 1991).

Sheard (1994, p.16) exposes the confusion in the literature on *keiretsu*, competition and market access in Lawrence's influential study (1991a). Lawrence concludes (p.329):

> While antitrust motivations should be punished, there are cases where *keiretsu* relationships

improve efficiency. As might be expected, these efficiencies tend to be associated with vertical rather than horizontal linkages. Given the complexity and pervasiveness of vertical *keiretsu*, it is difficult to support extreme approaches that would either entirely ban these linkages or outwardly tolerate them. Instead vigilance and a 'rule of reason' approach, which pays a particular attention to horizontal linkages, seems more appropriate.

The horizontal linkages Lawrence has in his sights here, as Sheard points out, have nothing to do with monopoly potential but are cross-market rather than within-market conglomerate-like structures involving vertical linkages in the sense of the literature on industrial organization.

Financial *keiretsu* do not offer scope in themselves for collusion and exclusionary market practices in the way that policy discussion and policy-driven academic discussion suggests.

Vertical Keiretsu *and Market Access*

Most of the political rhetoric and policy energy surrounding the *keiretsu* issue focuses on the way in which vertical *keiretsu* are said to discriminate against 'outsiders'. There is a large number of anecdotes from journalists, businessmen and politicians about 'cosy relationships' between upstream and downstream producers in almost every part of manufacturing. These anecdotes are about discriminatory or preferential vertical relationships in the market for intermediate goods and supplies.

There are two puzzles about the claim that long-term contracting in vertical *keiretsu* discriminates against competitive foreign suppliers of intermediate products in Japanese manufacturing. The first has to do with why Japanese assembly firms, like automobile manufacturers, would wish to handicap themselves by maintaining inefficient suppliers when they have to operate in a competitive international final product market. In the industrial organization literature, this observation relates to the 'rule of reason' that vertical relationships are acceptable provided that the relationships are formed in contestable markets. This does not mean that such markets adjust immediately to new competitive pressures. Indeed, such corporate dealings may contain a conservative bias, delaying the emergence of intermediate goods imports beyond the time when they initially appear to have become competitive (Drysdale,

1969; Saxonhouse, 1988, p.234; Drysdale and Garnaut, 1993). But such lags in the process of market adjustment are not unique to Japanese corporate structures. It took several years for German and Japanese steel producers to sell their cheaper steel to General Motors in the United States after American steel became uncompetitive (Drysdale, 1989). As Cooper's (1975) study of North American markets for metals in the 1970s shows us, the lagged response to relative price change is an appropriate response in dynamic and competitive markets. Long-term contracting has a similar effect in the Australian resource trade (Smith, 1979).

The second puzzle is why vertical relationships—which would attract no attention in trade practice law and policy if they were conducted within fully integrated corporate operations—are an object of policy interest if practised between two firms that are not fully integrated. General Motors purchases 25 per cent of its imports from outside suppliers, compared with Toyota's outside purchases of some 75 per cent (Aoki, 1986). Why, asks Saxonhouse (1993, p.38), is formal vertical integration in the United States better (or fairer) than informal integration in Japan? In fact, it may be less efficient as well as no fairer, as trends in North America in the last decade or so seem to confirm (Smitka, 1991; Smitka 1993). Dyer (1993) provides data suggesting that Japanese automobile parts markets are as open to arms-length supply as those in the United States. As Weinstein and Yafeh (1993) demonstrate, the higher the proportion of *keiretsu* firms in a Japanese industry, the lower the price-cost margins, a phenomenon consistent with intense competition among *keiretsu* groups.

There is an extensive analytical literature on discriminatory vertical relationships in industrial organization (Perry, 1989). The findings in the literature support scepticism about such relationships being instruments of collusive behaviour: as Sheard (1994) observes, what to outsiders may appear as 'cosy relationships' may be characterized alternatively as 'value adding partnerships' (Johnston and Wallace, 1988).

The central question is whether vertical *keiretsu* are plausibly cast as instruments of market foreclosure, where a firm at one stage of production 'closes off' another stage of production to its rivals (Sheard, 1993; Sheard, 1994).

Vertical foreclosure can take two forms, depending on whether the purchasing firm is upstream or downstream. Downstream foreclosure occurs when an upstream firm enters into contracts with downstream firms with the aim of shutting out other upstream firms from the output market (the downstream input market). Upstream foreclosure occurs when a downstream firm enters into contracts with upstream firms with the aim of disadvantaging other downstream firms in its output market by raising the costs of supply of inputs … a traditional concern in the anti-trust literature involves the case of a downstream monopolist foreclosing entry to its market by denying the potential entrant access to an essential input that it controls (Sheard, 1994, p.24).

The concern about foreclosure through vertical *keiretsu* would be relevant, as Sheard (1994) also points out, only under very unlikely circumstances. Downstream foreclosure would require, for example, that suppliers of inputs like steel or glass in the automobile industry tried to exercise market power by locking up downstream automobile producers' input markets against other suppliers of steel or glass, domestic or foreign. It is hardly probable that it will be in the interests of automobile manufacturers to allow upstream firms to monopolize their input markets, potentially raising their costs and lowering quality and competitiveness. Technically, this is not a Nash equilibrium and so is an unlikely outcome—parties to this type of agreement have incentives not to abide by it. The other possibility is upstream foreclosure by Japanese automobile manufacturers. This strategy would aim at excluding rivals from supply networks, but the issue of Toyota or other Japanese auto-makers denying American makers access to their affiliated suppliers so that American makers are disadvantaged is not an issue that is really on the agenda.

Firms enter into long-term contracts in competitive markets because they generate value—lowering costs, improving quality, securing supply channels—through doing so. The way in which a firm organizes its input purchases is an important choice in a market economy. It is one of the decisions to be made about using corporate resources and strategic opportunities. Manufacturers compete with one another more or less successfully in this dimension as in others. To represent this process in terms of closure of markets is misleading.

The Distribution System

The arguments about the way in which the Japanese distribution system limits access to the Japanese market may have more substance. Yet, here too, it is important to distinguish the effect of distribution *keiretsu* from other factors affecting access in final goods markets.

The analysis of potential foreclosure in the distribution of final or intermediate products is analogous to the case of intermediate product markets; if 'distribution' is seen as another kind of input used in delivering output. From this perspective, the distribution system presents an opportunity for upstream foreclosure by Japanese manufacturers using distribution channels to disadvantage domestic and foreign competitors by denying them access to a needed input. This is the essence of the United States complaint about restraints in marketing American automobiles in Japan.

Because distribution has many of the characteristics of a non-traded good—at least some of the inputs must be acquired locally—there may appear a special opportunity for foreclosure in this market. However, the conditions under which foreclosure will succeed are strict in theory (Hart and Tirole, 1990) and remote in practice (Sheard, 1994, pp. 27–8). There is always the option of a firm mobilizing its own distribution facilities—presuming the right of establishment and entry. If the right of establishment and entry is denied, that is likely a problem of the regulatory system, not a problem of the corporate structures involved.

Moreover, and more tellingly, downstream firms will have an incentive to enter contracts with upstream suppliers of final products only if such contracts lower their costs, or enforce quality in delivery, and only so long as other upstream suppliers (including those from abroad) cannot supply a competitive alternative.

In the automobile market, this circumstance will be recognized by Australian readers familiar with the entry of Japanese suppliers into the Australian passenger vehicle markets in the 1960s and 1970s. As the competitiveness of Japanese automobiles was established, exclusive dealerships for the products of American owned firms crumbled, but only after a time.

There are other more important reasons why American trade negotiators put much effort into opening up Japan's distribution system. Regulatory controls, not distribution *keiretsu*, limit outlets and increase distribution costs for a range of products both domestic and foreign. Hence, reform of Japan's Large Scale Retail Store Law was an important target in the Structural Impediments Initiative negotiations (Terada, 1994). The effect of these regulatory controls is formidable and embedded in social structures (such as the appeal of 'mom and pop stores' in retailing) so that inertia to reform and change may be great.

An Australian Connection

Australian policy makers and corporations with extensive dealings in Japan are knowledgeable about the restrictions and regulatory systems that affect access to the Japanese market, especially over a wide range of the agricultural and services trades. Australia is not a leading exporter of manufactures to Japan, although Japan is Australia's second largest single export market for manufactured goods after New Zealand (APEG, 1995). New entrants to the Japanese market, of vehicle components, for example, are familiar with the time-consuming processes involved in establishing a beachhead and market share.[3] But, significantly, the issues of corporate behaviour and practice reviewed in this paper have not been conspicuous in Australian business or policy discussion of access to the Japanese market.

Yet, oddly, there is an important Australian connection in the literature.

The purchasing behaviour of Japanese firms in Australia has been cited prominently to substantiate the claim that Japanese practices are exclusionary, limiting access by foreign suppliers to Japanese companies at home and abroad (Lawrence, 1991b, p.21).[4]

The principal evidence on this matter is presented in a survey by Kreinin (1989) of 62 companies in Australia, of which 20 were Japanese, 22 were American, and 20 were European. On the basis of responses to his questioning, he suggests that Japanese subsidiaries in Australia 'are highly controlled by the respective parent company, procure their equipment mainly from Japan and use and operate mainly Japanese machinery' (Kreinin, 1989, p.540). Kreinin's conclusion is very strong and his interpretation of his findings unequivocally links this behaviour to peculiar Jap-

anese corporate practice. His work is cited widely in policy circles in the United States and provided early credence to the notion that *keiretsu* corporate structures constituted a major 'hidden' barrier in accessing the Japanese home market.[5] Yet his questionnaire appears open-ended, there is no summary statistical reporting of his findings whereby it is easy to assess his impression of the evidence, and he makes no comparison between his findings and those of others, including the regular surveys by responsible Japanese and American agencies.

Kreinin reports that in 15 out of 20 Japanese companies surveyed either all or over 80 per cent of the equipment was of Japanese origin (p.535). Only five firms used international competitive bids for purchasing standardized equipment, compared with 21 of the 22 American-owned subsidiaries for machinery or materials not available for Australia. He did note that a few Japanese firms intended to move to open tendering but this observation did not qualify the interpretation of his findings. Kreinin's study of Japanese foreign direct investment in Australia is consistent with the general impression of Japanese corporate use of own suppliers of parts and components in Japanese investments elsewhere, in North America and East Asia.

There is a valuable reference point to Kreinin's work and general impressions in the classic study of American investment in Australia by Brash (1966). Brash undertook a careful survey of the sales and purchasing of American investors in Australia in 1962. Interestingly, Kreinin appears unaware of Brash's earlier study or its relevance to his own work.

Brash's work reveals that American subsidiaries he surveyed were unlikely to purchase equipment or components from Australian suppliers, even if they were cheaper than equipment and materials sourced from affiliated or parent companies (pp.203–11). Most of the imports of American-owned companies were purchased from or through American affiliated firms with wholly owned firms having a higher dependence on imports than joint ventures. Significantly, Brash's data (p. 205) suggest that the more recently established American subsidiaries imported a much higher proportion of their equipment and material requirements than older established forms. Meas-

---

[3]One Australian manufacturer of components for the vehicle industry reported to me a requirement that his consignment to Japanese agents be delivered in non-branded packaging so as to disguise the switch in purchases by assemblers (interview, Sydney, 1994).

[4]The material in this section is drawn from Drysdale, 1993.

[5]Kreinen's study is cited as justification for import targeting policy strategies by American officials (Interview, USTR, December 1990).

ured as a proportion of total sales (rather than purchases, for which data were not readily available), the import ratio for all firms was 18.7 per cent, but for firms established in the previous five years it was 29.5 per cent.

On the basis of both the impressionistic and the more comprehensive statistical evidence that Brash provides on American subsidiary purchasing behaviour in Australia, it would seem difficult to conclude that Japanese firms differ significantly in this respect from their American counterparts. There is, in fact, a deal of published quantitative evidence that can be turned to analyzing the purchasing behaviour of Japanese and, to a lesser extent, American subsidiaries in Australia. I have reviewed this evidence in some detail elsewhere (Drysdale, 1993, pp. 33–4).[6]

It is clear from this evidence that Japanese subsidiaries imported a higher proportion of intermediate goods and equipment from the home country than their American counterparts in the 1980s. It is also clear that there was a significant change in the pattern through the decade. Imports from Japan were consistently and significantly declining as a proportion of intermediate goods purchases over these years. Whatever drives this pattern of purchases, it is not a permanent feature of Japanese corporate behaviour.

Kreinin's findings can be explained rather on grounds that have little to do with discriminatory or exclusionary practices by Japanese firms or *keiretsu* corporate structures (Saxonhouse, 1991). Most Japanese manufacturing operations in Australia are of recent origin. The bulk of these investments in the past were designed to produce substitutes for products that were previously imported to Australia from Japan. Japan continues to have a strong comparative advantage in what Japanese affiliates in these sectors are producing in Australia (in automobiles, for example). By contrast, most of the American and European firms with which Kreinin makes comparison are decades old, producing goods in which the home country has lost much of its comparative advantage. It is hardly surprising that the sourcing pattern of Japanese manufacturing firms in Australia is as it is. This has historically been typical also of the sourcing patterns of American manufacturing firms in Australia. The evidence reinforces Saxonhouse's observation that Krein-

in's Australian study is entirely consistent with the histories of multinational corporations more generally (Wilkins, 1975; Chen and Drysdale, 1995). It does not suggest distinctive Japanese trade practices. This issue is endemic in the experience of multinational corporations and host countries as is attested by the prevalence of local content requirements in the national regulation of direct foreign investment throughout the world.

Implications for Policy

This paper set out to explore how market structure and different corporate organizational forms might affect access to the Japanese market for manufactured goods. The argument that *keiretsu* corporate structures in Japan are collusive and exclusionary has been used to justify American trade policy strategies, such as calling for import targets in Japanese markets for manufactured goods, which would treat Japan differently from other industrial countries and seek to manage trade flows in ways which are not consistent with the principles to which GATT has appealed in the past and which are embodied in the WTO.

This is no trivial issue. American trade policymakers pushed this argument strongly in the recent attempt to 'open' Japanese automobile and automobile parts markets. Significantly, there was widespread unease in international policy circles about this American trade policy approach. This paper provides argument which reinforces this unease.

Keiretsu corporate structures are not accurately characterized as 'collusive', 'cartel-like', 'anti-competitive' or 'exclusionary' in the antitrust sense of the term.[7] Financial *keiretsu* are more likely to increase competition in final product markets than they are to reduce it, other things being equal. Vertical *keiretsu* reflect efficient relational dealings in intermediate product markets rather than restrictive trade practices. Even in the case of distribution *keiretsu*, an area of more concern on the surface of it, vertical foreclosure is not the main issue. The main issue is regulatory controls which inhibit or facilitate entry to final product markets, and they are the relevant target of policy attention.

The argument for trade policy strategies which

---

[6]A recent study by Nicholas (1995) provides a rich new source of data on the characteristics and behaviour of Japanese affiliates in Australia.

[7]As Sheard (1994, p.32) points out, the notion of 'exclusion' as an aspect of long-term contracting or the dynamics of repeated transactions needs to be carefully distinguished from 'exclusion' in the context of antitrust.

seek to break down 'hidden barriers' to trade resulting from *keiretsu* corporate structures through the imposition of import targets and managed trade arrangements is intellectually flawed—built on loose logic and incomplete information about the nature of the institutional arrangements which are the object of policy. If Japanese policy makers had yielded to this argument, Japan would, incidentally, have signed on to a policy of re-regulation against the thrust of domestic and international interest in Japan's liberalization and economic reform agenda.

This is not, of course, to suggest that there are not problems of access to the Japanese market for manufactured goods. In some industries, industry associations provide a potential vehicle for collusive practices. Regulatory systems impact on these markets, as they do on other markets in Japan, such as in the agricultural and services sectors. However, the direct effect of regulatory systems on manufactured goods markets is circumscribed. For example, in the case of automobile product markets, American negotiators focused attention on Japan's motor vehicle inspection system (*shaken*) as a restraint on import trade. The inspection agency arrangements effectively cut suppliers of imported parts out of the market. This provides ground for legitimate complaint and is accepted as such by Japanese negotiators. These regulations affect foreign supplier access and the welfare of Japanese consumers. In the Section 301 move on the automobile products trade against Japan, American officials (Kantor, 1995a) were careful to confine the formal complaint, which triggered action, largely to the issue of the so-called 'after-parts' market for automobile products. But this market is tiny in relation to the entire automobile products market, control over which was more broadly and publicly contested between Japan and the United States (Kantor, 1995b; Clinton, 1995).

Here, there is not the space to analyze developments in trans-Pacific automobile products trade in detail. Suffice it to observe that this market will undergo further rapid change over the next decade, as it has over the past decade; that there will be a significant increase in Japan's intra-industry trade, as the competitiveness of manufacturing automobiles in Japan peaks and Japanese firms adjust to the new competitive circumstances of their operations in Japan, North America and elsewhere; and that these changes will be largely driven by competitive forces in the market, not by policy posture in North America.

Markets that appear closed to new entrants because of *keiretsu* corporate ties are markets that need to be opened by business, not government negotiators. Japanese firms have no sensible interest in sheltering their suppliers from foreign competition. They do not need Japanese or US government officials to guide them to make cost-minimizing import purchase decisions. There may be good reasons to increase foreign access to the Japanese market. The justification for these actions, however, must lie other than in the anti-competitive and market foreclosure rhetoric in which they are clothed (Sheard, 1994, p.41).

It needs to be added, nonetheless, that the threat of reprisals and aggressive unilateral trade policy action by the United States can have impact, however flawed its intellectual foundations. Australian exports of vehicles and components to Japan have been stagnant over the past year while imports from other sources in Europe, and even North America, have grown.[8] This may be simply a product of the structure of import adjustment during a deep recession. On the other hand, it could also be related to the gathering threat of American trade action. Detailed analysis is needed to assess whether American trade policy threats affected procurement strategies by the Japanese industry over this period and what effect they might have in the future. There is enough circumstantial evidence to warrant active research interest in this area.

REFERENCES

Abbeglen, J. and Stalk, Jr G. (1985), *Kaisha: The Japanese Corporation*, Charles E. Tuttle, Tokyo.
Advisory Committee for Trade Policy and Negotiations (ACTPN) (1993), *Major Findings and Policy Recommendations on US–Japan Trade Policy*, Washington D.C., January.

[8] Japanese imports of Australian-made motor vehicles and components fell by 8 per cent between April 1994 and March 1995, while imports from the United States grew by 53 per cent. Imports from all sources grew by 35 per cent. Imports of Australian-made components fell by 13 per cent, while imports of American-made components increased by 22 per cent. Australia's exports of motor vehicle parts and components to Japan were $A207.4 million in 1994, in total exports of these products were $A1.54 billion. (Data on imports of automobile products into Japan are from Nikkei Telecom Database, Australia–Japan Research Centre, and data on Australian exports are from the Australian Bureau of Statistics.)

Alchian, A. and Demsetz, H. (1972), 'Production, information costs, and economic organization', *American Economic Review* **77**, 388–401.

Altman, R. (1994), 'Why pressure Tokyo?', *Foreign Affairs* **73** (3), May/June.

Aoki, M. (1986), 'Horizontal vs. vertical information structure of the firm', *American Economic Review* **76**, 971–83.

— Patrick, H. and Sheard, P. (1994), 'The Japanese main bank system: an introductory overview', in M. Aoki and H. Patrick (eds), *The Main Bank System: Its Relevancy for Developing and Transforming Economies*, Oxford University Press, Oxford.

Asia Pacific Economics Group (APEG) (1995), *Asia Pacific Profiles*, Australian National University.

Balassa, B. (1986), 'Japan's trade policies', *Weltwirtschaftliches Archiv* **122**, 754–90.

— and Noland, M. (1988), *Japan in the World Economy*, Institute for International Economics, Washington D.C.

Bergsten, C.F. and Noland, M. (1993), *Reconcilable Differences?*, Institute for International Economics, Washington D.C.

Bhagwati, J. (1994), 'Samurais no more', *Foreign Affairs* **73** (3), May/June.

Brash, D. (1966), *American Investment in Australian Industry*, Australian National University Press, Canberra.

Caves, R. and Uekusa, M. (1976), 'Industrial organization' in H. Patrick and H. Rosovsky (eds), *Asia's New Giant: How the Japanese Economy Works*, Brookings Institution, Washington D.C.

Chen, E. and Drysdale, P. (eds) (1995), *Corporate Links and Foreign Direct Investment in Asia and the Pacific*, Harper Educational, Sydney.

Cheung, S. (1983), 'The contractual nature of the firm', *Journal of Law and Economics* **26** (1), 1–21.

Clinton, W. (1995), White House statement on Japanese trade talks, 28 June.

Coase, R. (1937), 'The nature of the firm', *Economica*, n.s. **4**, 386–405.

Cooper, R. (1975), 'Natural resources and national security', *Resources Policy* **1** (4), June.

Dore, R. (1986), *Flexible Rigidities: Industrial Policy and Structural Adjustment in the Japanese Economy 1971–80*, Stanford University Press, Stanford.

Drysdale, P. (1969), 'Japan, Australia and New Zealand: The prospects for Western Pacific economic integration', *Economic Record* **45** (111), September, 321–42.

— (1989), 'Japan's trade diplomacy: yesterday, today, tomorrow', *Pacific Economic Papers*, No. 178, December.

— (1993), 'Japanese direct foreign investment in Australia in comparative perspective', *Pacific Economic Papers*, No. 223, September.

— and Garnaut, R. (1993), 'The Pacific: An application of a general theory of economic integration', in C. F. Bergsten and M. Noland (eds), *Pacific Dynamism and the International Economic System*, Institute for International Economics, Washington D.C.

Dyer, J. (1993), 'The Japanese vertical keiretsu as a source of competitive advantage', mimeo, University of Pennsylvania.

Fama, E. (1980), 'Agency problems and the theory of the firm', *Journal of Political Economy* **88**, 288–307.

Fruin W. M. (1992), *The Japanese Enterprise System: Cooperative Structures and Competitive Strategies*, Clarendon Press, Oxford.

Fung K. C. (1991), 'Characteristics of Japanese industrial groups and their potential impact on US–Japan trade', in R. Baldwin (ed.), *Empirical Studies of Commercial Policy*, University of Chicago Press, Chicago.

Gerlach, M. (1992), *Alliance Capitalism: The Social Organization of Japanese Business*, University of California, Berkeley.

Gibson R. and Roe, M. (1993), 'Understanding the Japanese keiretsu: overlaps between corporate governance and industrial organization', *Yale Law Journal* **102**, 871–906.

Goto, A. (1982), 'Business groups in a market economy', *European Economic Review* **19**, 53–70.

Goto, F. (1991), 'Is the Japanese market really closed? a critical review of the economic studies', *Studies in International Trade and Industry*, No. 8, Research Institute of International Trade and Industry, Tokyo.

Hart, O. and Tirole, J. (1990), 'Vertical integration and market foreclosure', *Brookings Papers: Microeconomics 1990*, 205–76.

Hashimoto, R. and Kantor, M. (1995), Joint announcement regarding autos and auto parts, 28 June.

Horiuchi, A., Packer, F. and Fukuda, S. (1988), 'What role has the "main bank" played in Japan?' *Journal of the Japanese and International Economies* **2** (2) June, 159–80.

Jacquemin, A. and Slade, M. (1989), 'Cartels, collusion and horizontal merger', in R. Schmalensee and R. Willig (eds), *Handbook of Industrial Organization*, Vol. 1, North Holland, Amsterdam, 415–73.

Jensen, M. and Meckling, W. (1976), 'Theory of the firm: Managerial Behavior, Agency Costs and Ownership Structure', *Journal of Financial Economics* **3** (4), 305–60.

Johnston, K. and Wallace, P. (1988), 'Beyond vertical integration: the rise of the value-adding partnership', *Harvard Business Review*, July–August, 94–101.

Kantor, M. (1995a), 10 May, *US to file WTO Trade Complaint Against Japan Auto Policy*, Press Statement.

— (1995b), Text of press conference, 28 June.

Keizai Chosa Kyokai (1992), Nenpo 'Keiretsu no kenkyu' daishu (1992), Daiichibu jojo kigyohen, No. 32.

Kreinin, M. (1989), 'How closed is the Japanese market? Additional evidence', *The World Economy* **11** (4), 529–42.

Kravis, I. B. and Lipsey, R. E. (1971), *Price Competitiveness in World Trade*, NBER, Columbia, New York.

Krugman, P. (1991), 'Introduction', in P. Krugman (ed.), *Trade with Japan: Has the door opened wider?*,

University of Chicago Press, Chicago.

Lawrence, R. (1987), 'Imports to Japan: Closed markets or closed minds?', *Brookings Papers on Economic Activity* **2**, 517–52.

— (1991a), 'Efficient or exclusionist? The import behavior of Japanese corporate groups', *Brookings Papers on Economic Activity* **1**, 311–41.

— (1991b), 'How open is Japan?', in P. Krugman (ed.), *Trade with Japan: Has the door opened wider?*, University of Chicago Press, Chicago.

— (1993), 'Japan's different trade regime: An analysis with particular reference to keiretsu', *Journal of Economic Perspectives* **7** (3), Summer, 3–19.

McMillan, J. (1990), '*Dango*: Japan's price fixing conspiracies', *Economics and Politics* **3** (3), 201–18.

Miyazaki Y. (1967), 'Rapid economic growth in postwar Japan: with special reference to "excessive competition" and the formation of "keiretsu" ', *The Developing Economies* **5** (2), 329–50.

Nicholas, S. (1995), 'Japanese investment in Australia: the investment decision and control structures in manufacturing, tourism and financial services', Public Seminar, Australia–Japan Research Centre, 17 July.

Passell, P. (1989), 'Economic scene: managed trade or open trade?', *The New York Times*, 5 April.

Perry, M. (1989), 'Vertical integration: determinants and effects', in R. Schmalensee and R. Willig (eds), *Handbook of Industrial Organization*, Vol. 1, North Holland, Amsterdam, 183–255.

Robinson, J. and Houghton, J. (1989), *Analysis of the US–Japan Trade Problem*, Report of the Advisory Committee for Trade Policy and Negotiations, Washington D.C., February.

Sazanami, Urata, and Kawai (1995), *Measuring the Costs of Protection in Japan*, Institute for International Economics, Washington D.C.

Saxonhouse, G. (1986), 'What's wrong in the Japanese trade structure?', *Pacific Economic Papers*, No. 137, July.

— (1988), 'Differentiated products, economies of scale and access to the Japanese market', Seminar Discussion Paper No. 288, Research Seminar in International Economics, University of Michigan.

— (1991), 'Comment' in P. Krugman (ed.) (1991), *Trade with Japan: Has the door opened wider?*, University of Chicago Press, Chicago.

— (1993), 'What does Japanese trade structure tell us about Japanese trade policy?', *Journal of Economic Perspectives*, Vol. 7(3), Summer, 21–43.

— and Stern, R. (1989), 'An analytical survey of formal and informal barriers to international trade and investment in the United States, Canada and Japan', in R. Stern (ed.), *Trade Relations Among the United States, Canada, and Japan*, University of Chicago Press, Chicago.

Sheard, P. (1986), *Corporate Organisation and Struc-*

tural Adjustment in Japan, Ph.D. thesis, Australian National University.

— (1988), 'On the economic organization of the firm', Seminar, Department of Economics, 25 February.

— (1991), 'The economics of Japanese corporate organization and the "structural impediments" debate: a critical review', *Japanese Economic Studies* **19** (4), 30–78.

— (1993), '*Keiretsu* and closedness of the Japanese market: an economic appraisal', Working Paper Series No. 93–5, Centre for Japanese Economic Studies, Macquarie University, April.

— (1994), '*Keiretsu*, competition, and market access', Discussion paper 94–17, Osaka University, Faculty of Economics, December.

Smith, Ben (1979), 'Security and Stability in Mineral Markets: The Role of Long Term Contracts', in *The World Economy* **2**, No. 1, January.

Smitka, M. (1991), *Competitive Ties: Subcontracting in the Japanese automobile industry*, Columbia University Press, New York.

— (1993), 'The decline of the Japanese auto industry: domestic and international implications', paper for The Japan Economic Seminar, East Asian Institute, Columbia University, New York, February.

Terada, T. (1994), 'Political economy of the large-scale retail store law: transforming 'impediments' to entering the Japanese retail industry', *Pacific Economic Papers*, No. 237, November.

Tirole, J. (1988), *The Theory of Industrial Organization*, MIT Press, Cambridge MA.

Toyo Keizai Shimposha (1991), Kigyo keiretsu soran 1992 Nenban (Corporate affiliation directory), Tokyo.

United States Department of Commerce and Japan Ministry of International Trade and Industry (1989), *The Joint DOC/MITI Price Survey: Methodology and Results*, Washington D.C., December.

United States Trade Representative (USTR) (1995), *National Trade Estimates*, Washington D.C.

Warren, T. (forthcoming), *The Political Economy of Services Trade Policy: Australia, Japan and the United States*, Ph.D. thesis, Australian National University.

Weinstein and Yafeh (1993), 'Japan's corporate groups: collusive or competitive? An empirical investigation of keiretsu behavior', Harvard Institute of Economic Research Discussion Paper No. 1623, Harvard University.

Wilkins, M. (1975), *The Maturing of Multinational Enterprise: American Business Abroad, 1914–1970*, Harvard University Press, Cambridge Massachusetts.

Williamson, O. (1975), *Markets and Hierarchies: Analysis and Antitrust Implications*, Free Press, New York.

— (1985), *The Economic Institutions of Capitalism*, Free Press, New York.

[8]

Cambridge Journal of Economics 1993, 17, 131–157

The political economy of industrial policy in Korea

Ha-Joon Chang*

The rapid growth and structural change of South Korea (henceforth referred to as Korea) during the last three decades has spawned a large body of literature, which is becoming almost impossible to keep track of.[1] With the accumulation of research, it has been revealed that the state played an important role, and the proponents of Korea as a free market have been on the defensive for the last several years. The 'alternative' literature emphasising the role of the state in the Korean developmental experience is still in its infancy, despite some important contributions by Jones and Sakong (1980), Luedde-Neurath (1986), and most notably Amsden (1989). The present article provides some additional empiricial support to this alternative literature, and consolidates its theoretical basis by using some recent developments in economic theory such as the New Institutionalist Economics.

In sections 1 and 2 of the article we review some mainstream interpretations of the Korean developmental process. It is argued that these explanations, which try to dismiss the role of the state in the Korean developmental process, have a weak theoretical and empirical basis. In section 3 we examine *how* state intervention works in Korea. In section 4 we attempt to explain *why* state intervention works in Korea. The concluding section draws out some of the implications of our discussion for a new view of the Korean developmental experience and for economic development in general.

Manuscript received 11 May 1990; final version received 23 March 1992.

*Faculty of Economics and Politics, University of Cambridge. I thank Bob Rowthorn for his willingness to discuss and clarify many difficult questions which emerged in the process of writing this paper. Continuous discussions with Hawon Jang, Mushtaq Khan, and Jong-il You were also crucial in formulating many ideas in this paper. Peter Nolan and Terence Moll read two earlier versions of the paper and made detailed and enlightening comments. Pranab Bardhan, Geoff Harcourt, Alan Hughes, Paul Kattuman, Michael Landesmann, Nathan Rosenberg, Helen Shapiro, Ajit Singh, John Sender, and Richard Wright made helpful comments on various earlier versions of the paper. I also want to thank two anonymous referees of the *Journal* for some important suggestions.
[1] Between 1965 and 1986, Korea's annual per capita GNP growth was 6·7%, compared to 2·9% for the developing countries as a whole. Korea's manufacturing growth rate between 1965 and 1980 was 18·7%, compared to 13·2% for Singapore, 9·6% for Brazil, 9·5% for China, 7·4% for Mexico, and 4·3% for India. Between 1980 and 1987, the corresponding figure was 10·6% in Korea, compared to 12·6% in China, 8·3% in India, 3·3% in Singapore, 1·2% in Brazil, and 0·0% in Mexico (World Bank, 1988). This rapid growth was accompanied by major structural change. The production structure in Korea, which looked more like that of low-income countries like India and Kenya in the 1960s, had become more like that of upper-middle income countries like Argentina, Brazil, and Spain by the mid-1980s.

0309–166X/93/020131 + 27 $08.00/0

132   H.-J. Chang

1. A free market?

Although the formerly common interpretation of the Korean developmental experience as a free-market and a free-trade economy (e.g. Ranis and Fei, 1975; Balassa, 1982) is rapidly losing its popularity, it is useful to discuss briefly its argument, since the more recent mainstream interpretations (examined below) can be seen as attempts to rescue the conclusions of the early interpretation.

According to the free-market view, the Korean economy was stagnating in the late 1950s after it had depleted the possibility of 'easy import substitution' in non-durable consumer goods. This 'inward-looking' strategy was inefficient because of the 'distortions' generated by excessive state intervention in various markets. Such 'chaotic' import substitution with multiple exchange rates behind the wall of across-the-board protection, largely using discretionary quantitative restrictions rather than universal tariffs, allowed inefficient firms to survive and discouraged export activities. This, in turn, added to foreign exchange shortage and hence to the pressure for more import restrictions.

The phenomenal growth of the economy, the argument goes, started with the transition from an inward-looking, or import-substituting industrialisation, strategy to an outward-looking, or an export-led growth, strategy. The turning point in this transition was a series of policy reforms around 1965, whose most important ingredients included (i) the introduction of a unified, realistic exchange rate régime; (ii) trade liberalisation involving cuts in tariffs and the abolition of most quantitative restrictions; and (iii) a substantial increase in real interest rates. These policies are regarded as having radically improved the performance of the economy for the following reasons. First, realistic exchange rates, by making export activities as profitable as they should be, allowed Korea to follow her comparative advantage in labour-intensive industries, and therefore to reap the gains from foreign trade. Second, trade liberalisation improved the efficiency of the economy by exerting competitive pressures on domestic producers. Finally, the rise in interest rates enabled the economy to invest more by mobilising more savings, on the one hand, and to use capital more efficiently by restoring the relative price of capital to near its 'realistic' level, on the other.

In the words of Ranis and Fei (1975, p. 56), '[s]tabilisation plus dismantling of the various existing direct control measures, on trade, interest rate and foreign exchange ... created a more market oriented economy most conducive to access for large numbers of domestic entrepreneurs seeking efficient utilisation of the economy's relatively abundant resources via embodiment in labour-intensive industrial exports'.[1]

There is abundant empirical evidence, however, which runs counter to these explanations. Concerning trade-related reforms, Luedde-Neurath (1986) shows that such reforms were not as thorough as is usually presented and were implemented half-heartedly.[2] First, tariffs were still quite high after the 'liberalisation' and the bureaucracy retained the power to impose 'emergency tariffs' (for items with 'excessively' fast import growth) without changing the relevant laws. In the second place, quantitative restrictions, usually under the name of various 'special laws' and import area diversification regulations, were still pervasive after the 'liberalisation'. As late as 1982, 93% of total imports (in value terms) were subject to one or more of such restrictions (see Luedde-Neurath, 1986, p. 156,

---

[1] It is interesting to note that one of the authors has, by emphasising the importance of 'institutional/organisational changes orchestrated by the governments' in Korean and Taiwanese developments, in effect denied most of what they said earlier (see Ranis, 1989).

[2] Although there has been more 'trade liberalisation' since Luedde-Neurath's study all of the following 'invisible' import restrictions are still in operation.

Political economy of industrial policy in Korea 133

Table 1. *Real interest rates in Korea, 1960–1984 (percent)*

Period	Curb market[a]	Deposits[b]	Export loans
1960–1964	31·1	−6·7	n.a.
1965–1969	44·4	26·9	n.a.
1970–1974	28·2	−0·2	−16·3
1975–1979	24·0	−4·5	−12·5
1980–1984	19·7	2·4	1·3

Source: adapted from Dornbusch and Park (1987), p. 419, table 14.
[a]Nominal interest rates less consumer price inflation.
[b]Nominal interest rates less inflation of the GNP deflator.

table 14.4). Third, prohibitive inland taxes were often used virtually to ban importation of luxury consumer items which were subject only to non-prohibitive tariffs.[1] Fourth, there was extensive state support for import substitution: for example, subsidised credits to the import-substitutors and to the purchasers of some domestic products (especially machinery), which in effect acted as import restrictions. Lastly, and most importantly, there was widespread foreign exchange rationing, which meant that often the importation of a certain item was impossible, not because it was illegal but because it was impossible to get the foreign exchange to pay for it.

The effect of financial reform has also to be reinterpreted (for a detailed discussion, see Harris, 1987). As may be seen in Table 1, the post-reform high interest rates did not last more than a few years, and real interest rates were negative until the 1980s owing to inflation. Nevertheless, savings ratios have showed a rising trend for the last three decades, up from less than 10% in the 1950s and the early 1960s to more than 30% in the late 1980s. That is, 'Korea's saving responds little to interest rates. Overall, the Korean experience suggests that there is no need for high positive real interest rates to mobilise saving through the financial system; as long as large negative real interest rates are avoided, the real interest rate is relatively insignificant' (Dornbusch and Park, 1987, pp. 418–9).[2]

Even if 'liberalisation' in Korea was as comprehensive as the proponents of free markets insist, it is not necessarily true that a 'more market oriented economy' is more efficient even in the neoclassical sense, as the above quote from Ranis and Fei implies. As the theory of second best tells us, the removal of market distortions in some, but not all, markets does not guarantee that the economy achieves higher allocative efficiency (Lipsey and Lancaster, 1956). Moreover, even if it is true that the move to a 'more market oriented' economy improved the *static* allocative efficiency of the economy by moving it closer to its comparative advantage, it does not explain why Korea *grew faster* (also see Bruton, 1989, p. 1616). There is very little economic theory which supports the view that conforming more closely to comparative advantage leads to higher growth, as even the leading neo-classical trade theorists admit (e.g. see Krueger, 1980). More importantly, when growth

[1] For instance, the domestic price of imported Scotch whisky, whose tariff was 100%, was over nine times that of the c.i.f. price after various inland taxes, e.g. liquor tax, luxury consumption tax, and VAT (Luedde-Neurath, 1986, p. 130).

[2] In other words, '[b]y paying depositors low real interest rates and by controlling capital outflows, the government implicitly taxed depositors, then channelled the proceeds to favoured sectors for investment' (Dornbusch and Park, 1987, p. 418).

134   H.-J. Chang

involves innovation, there may exist a conflict between the achievement of static allocative efficiency and growth. As Schumpeter (1987, ch. 8) emphasised, under conditions guaranteeing perfectly free entry and thereby allocative efficiency, there will be little incentive for innovation, because any monopoly rent, or what he calls 'entrepreneurial profits' in his earlier work (Schumpeter, 1961, ch. 4), will be instantly competed away. As far as innovation is important for growth, this means that growth may be damaged by an improvement in the static allocative efficiency of the economy (also see subsection 4.1).

2. Market-preserving state intervention?

Evidence shows that state intervention has been pervasive in Korea during its rapid industrialisation period. As Bhagwati (1987) correctly argues, '[t]he key question then is not whether there is governmental action in the Far Eastern economies, but rather how have these successful economies managed their intervention and strategic decision making in ways that dominate those of the unsuccessful ones' (p. 285). And, naturally, some neoclassical economists, including Bhagwati himself, have put forward explanations of the Korean experience which try to reconcile the existence of an interventionist state with rapid growth of the economy.

One such argument is the theory of the virtual free trade régime, which suggests that various measures of state intervention in Korea cancelled each other out to produce a neutral incentive structure (Little, 1982; Lal, 1983; Word Bank, 1987). Another is the theory of prescriptive state intervention, which argues that state intervention in Korea does not hinder growth because it leaves room for 'private initiatives' (Bhagwati, 1985, 1987, 1988). In effect, these theories argue that, whatever state intervention there may have been in Korea, it did not affect the workings of the market mechanism, because it was either self-cancelling (virtual free trade) or porous (prescriptive state intervention). Below, we examine these arguments in turn, and argue that they are neither theoretically convincing nor empirically correct.

2.1. Self-cancelling state intervention?

According to the proponents of the theory of virtual free trade régime, in Korea there existed widespread price distortions due to one set of state interventions (e.g. import protection), but these were cancelled out by another set of interventions (e.g. export subsidies), producing a neutral incentive structure between production for export and production for the domestic market. They emphasise the fact that Korean exporters had free access to imported inputs at world market prices, and consequently by-passed various import restrictions (Lal, 1983). The economic crisis in the early 1980s following the heavy and chemical industrialisation (HCI) drive during the 1970s (in 1980, Korea experienced negative growth for the first time since the industrialisation drive began in the early 1960s) is presented as proof that a departure from incentive neutrality was a disaster (Lal, 1983; for a different interpretation of the early 1980s crisis, see Chang, 1987).

At the theoretical level, it is not clear how meaningful it is to call the import-substitution-cum-export-incentives régime a virtual 'free trade' régime, because there is no reason why the structure of relative prices under this trade régime should be the same as the one under genuine free trade (Yusuf and Peters, 1985, p. 18, n. 49). And, if the relative price structures under the two régimes are different, we cannot say that the incentive structure under the former is 'neutral', because what matters in determining the relative attractiveness of export and production for the domestic market is the relative price structure, and not the 'average' incentive (for a more detailed discussion, see Wade, 1990, ch. 5).

Political economy of industrial policy in Korea   135

Table 2. *Korea's comparative industrial performance, 1979–1988 (annual real growth rates of production)*

	Brazil	Chile	Greece	Korea	Mexico	South Africa	Spain
Heavy industries[a]	0·6	1·6	−0·8	17·2	2·7	0·4	2·1
Chemical industries[b]	2·6	0·6	2·2	7·5	3·4	1·3	0·8
Light industries[c]	1·5	2·6	0·3	7·8	1·8	2·7	1·6
Manufacturing	1·5	2·7	0·4	11·7	2·1	1·6	1·5
1986 per capita GNP (dollars)	1810	1320	3680	2370	1860	1830	4860

Source: UN, *Industrial Statistics Yearbook* (1983, 1984, 1990).

Notes: [a]Includes the following industries: iron & steel, non-ferrous metal, metal products, machinery not elsewhere classified, electrical machinery, transport equipment, and professional goods.

[b]Includes the following industries: industrial chemicals, other chemicals, petroleum refineries, petroleum & coal products, rubber products, and plastic products not elsewhere classified.

[c]Includes the following industries: food products, beverages, tobacco, textiles, apparel, leather & leather products, footwear, wood products, furniture & fixtures, paper & paper products, printing & publishing, pottery & china, glass & glass products, non-metal products, and all other industries.

All figures are weighted averages unless otherwise stated. The weights are 1980 (except for South Africa, which is for July 1980–June 1981) output at producers' prices (including indirect taxes and excluding subsidies), except for Greece, South Africa, and Spain, which are at factor values (excluding indirect taxes and including subsidies).

Moreover, at the empirical level, it is not true that Korean exporters could freely get inputs (raw material and machinery) at world market prices. Luedde-Neurath (1986, ch. 4) shows that only raw materials can be described as relatively, but not absolutely, 'freely-importable' in the Korean trade régime. The importation of machines was heavily controlled to promote the domestic machinery industry, which was seen as the vital ingredient in building a well-integrated economy (see below). Credits were usually refused to the importers of domestically available machines and, instead, subsidised credits, which often amounted to 90% of the product value, were provided to the purchasers of domestic machinery (KDB, 1981, pp. 473–4).

Moreover, it is quite incorrect to assert that the promotion of the heavy and chemical industries through a departure from the incentive neutrality was a failure. Table 2 compares the performance of Korean three industry groups—that is, light, chemical, and heavy industries—between 1979 and 1988 with those of some countries at comparable levels of development and, except for Brazil, of a similar size. While Korean performance in all industry groups has been far better than that of other countries, the difference is especially pronounced in the heavy industries, where Korean performance was truly spectacular.

The advance of the heavy and chemical industry products was not confined to the domestic market. Table 3 shows trade performance for commodities at 1-digit and 2-digit levels between 1977 and 1987. Almost all the items promoted through HCI—which roughly comprise Standard International Trade Classifications (SITC) 5, 67, 68, and 7—show (often dramatic) improvements in trade balances during this period. The export–import growth differentials [which show the rate at which the sectoral trade deficit (surplus) decreases (increases)] of these items are mostly higher than that between the overall exports and imports, although, again, the performance of chemical products does

Table 3. *Trade performance by commodity groups in Korea, 1977–1987*

SITC	Commodities	Trade balance (1977)	Trade balance (1987)	Export growth	Import growth	Differential
0	Food and live animals	1·1	0·5	8·2	8·5	−0·3
1	Beverages and tobacco	0·4	n.a.	−1·7	n.a.	n.a.
2	Crude materials, excluding fuels	−7·9	−6·2	4·3	11·7	−7·4
3	Mineral fuels (e.g. petroleum, petroleum products)	−9·9	−6·0	20·4	10·7	9·7
4	Animal, vegetable oil and fat	n.a.	n.a.	n.a.	5·0	n.a.
5	Chemicals and related products	−3·7	−3·7	19·6	16·6	3·0
6	Basic manufactures	7·2	4·5	12·9	15·2	−2·3
61	Leather, dressed fur, etc.	−0·5	−0·4	23·7	15·4	8·3
62	Rubber manufactures n.e.c.	n.a.	0·6	16·3	n.a.	n.a.
63	Wood and cork manufacture n.e.c. (e.g. plywood)	n.a.	n.a.	−14·1	n.a.	n.a.
64	Paper products	0·2	0·1	16·5	19·8	−3·3
65	Textile yarn, fabric, etc.	3·5	3·0	14·1	15·2	−0·9
66	Non-metal mineral manufactures n.e.c. (e.g. cement, glass)	1·0	0·2	8·5	22·2	−13·7
67	Iron & steel	−1·1	0·5	19·6	11·7	7·9
68	Non-ferrous metals	−0·8	−0·8	27·3	18·4	8·9
69	Metal manufacture n.e.c. (e.g. tools, cables, cutlery)	2·1	1·2	10·7	15·5	−4·8
7	Machines & transport equipment	−3·6	3·2	24·7	16·9	7·8
71	Power generating equipments	−1·5	−0·7	31·7	12·0	19·7
72	Machinery for special industries (e.g. textile machinery)	−2·0	−2·1	22·6	17·0	5·6
73	Metal working machinery	n.a.	n.a.	n.a.	11·2	n.a.
74	General industrial machinery n.e.c. (e.g. furnaces, pumps)	−2·4	−1·9	35·6	15·5	20·1
75	Office machinery (e.g. computers)	−0·0	0·8	39·3	28·5	10·8
76	Telecommunication & sound equipment (e.g. TV, phone)	1·2	4·4	25·4	15·3	10·1
77	Electric machinery n.e.c. (e.g. transformers, microchips)	−0·2	−0·0	23·6	22·6	1·0
78	Road vehicles	−0·4	3·1	48·2	18·5	29·7
79	Other transport equipment (e.g. ships, aircrafts)	1·2	0·4	35·3	10·3	25·0
8	Miscellaneous manufactured goods	14·7	14·9	16·2	19·6	−3·4
9	Goods not classified by kinds	n.a.	n.a.	n.a.	n.a.	n.a.
Total		−3·8	7·0	16·8	14·3	2·5

Source: UN, *International Trade Statistics* (1980, 1987).

Notes: ªAll figures are measured in per cent.

ᵇData for each commodity group appear only if the value in each year is greater than or equal to 0·3% of the total trade for that year.

ᶜTrade balance for commodity i is $(X_i - M_i)/\sum(X_j + M_j)$, where $X_i(M_i)$ is exports (imports) of commodity i and $X(M)$ is total exports (imports).

ᵈExport and import growth rates are average annual growth rates between 1977 and 1987 in current value terms.

ᵉThe differentials are the differential between the export and import growth rates.

Political economy of industrial policy in Korea   137

not particularly stand out. A detailed cost-benefit analysis of the HCI programme is beyond the scope of this paper, but the above evidence suggests that the HCI programme, far from being a failure, produced impressive growth and trade performance, especially in the heavy industries.

2.2. Porous state intervention?

The theory of prescriptive state intervention proposed by Bhagwati (1985, 1987, 1988) tries to resolve the (neoclassical) dilemma of an interventionist state in a rapidly growing economy by characterising the Korean state as 'prescriptive' (one which identifies a number of 'dos'), in contrast to a 'proscriptive' state (one which declares a number of 'don'ts'), such as that of India. According to this theory, state intervention in Korea does not hinder growth because it is less 'stifling'. According to Bhagwati (1988), 'although a prescriptive government may prescribe as badly as a proscriptive government does, a proscriptive government will tend to stifle initiative, whereas a prescriptive government will tend to leave open areas (outside of the prescriptions) where initiative can be exercised' (pp. 98–9)—that is, state intervention in Korea does not hinder growth because it is porous.

At a superficial level, it is hardly questionable that an obstructive state will not be very helpful for business and, by implication, economic growth. However, on closer examination, we find the theory both theoretically and empirically unconvincing.

In a world with scarce resources (and therefore with opportunity costs), doing something means not doing something else. In this world, saying 'do' A is equivalent to saying 'don't' do 'not A'. And there can be no presumption that saying 'do' A (= 'don't' do 'not A') will allow more initiatives than saying 'don't' do A (= 'do' 'not A'). A prescriptive state can be as 'stifling' as a proscriptive one, since it can make private enterprises do so many things against their will that they are left with few resources to do what they want, even if these activities are not explicitly forbidden. Likewise, a proscriptive state may allow a lot of initiative if it proscribes only a few things. In fact, if we adopt the Liberal concept of negative freedom, that is, 'freedom from' (on the different notions of freedom, see Berlin, 1969), we may say that one has less freedom under a prescriptive state than under a proscriptive one, because private enterprises with government prescription are coerced to execute the prescription, whereas the private enterprises with a state proscription are not coerced into any particular action and therefore can choose the best option from whatever is not forbidden by the state (and thereby exercise 'initiatives').

The Korean state's prescriptions were certainly 'stifling' in many ways. The Korean state prescription for private firms to invest in heavy and chemical industries in the 1970s was a proscription against investing in less risky and often more profitable consumer goods industries. The best example in this regard is the shipbuilding industry, which has grown literally from scratch to the world's second biggest in less than a decade.[1] The Korean shipbuilding industry was set up in direct response to a personal 'command' from the then president Park Chung Hee, against the will of the Hyundai group, the boldest of the Korean business groups, who are famous for their boldness (Jones and Sakong, 1980, pp. 119–20, 357–8). Moreover, if private firms could not be made to do something, the Korean state did not hesitate to set up public enterprises, making the share of public enterprises in GDP almost equal to that of India (Jones and Mason, 1982, pp. 22–3). In a country like

---

[1] The Korean shipbuilding industry raised its share of world shipbuilding output from nil in 1973 (when the first modern shipyard started production) to 4% in 1980 and then to 21·6% in 1986. Korea is now the second largest shipbuilding nation in the world (next to Japan), and produces more ships (in gross tonnes) than Western Europe as a whole, whose world production share was 12·2% in 1986 (NRI, 1988, pp. 162–4).

138   H.-J. Chang

Korea where private firms depend heavily on the state-run banking sector for their investment funds, the state's channelling of money into public enterprises can have a very visible
impact on 'private initiatives'.

Moreover, the degree of proscriptive intervention by the Korean state has not been so
minimal as to warrant the description 'prescriptive' without serious qualifications. In
addition to the restrictions on prices of foreign exchange and credit, there was legally
implemented direct price control over all marketed products up to 1973. And even after
1973, the state reserved the right to impose a price ceiling when necessary. No price
change is conceivable without formal and/or informal state permission, except in some
unimportant markets.[1] In addition to price controls, most important Korean industries
have had restrictions on entry and capacity (see subsection 3.2). Frequently, the Korean
state 'reorganises' industries which it thinks have 'too many' firms, through state-led
mergers and market-sharing arrangements (see subsection 4.1). It is not clear to us what
could be more 'stifling', if so many firms have so little freedom to decide what and how
much to produce at what price.

3. How does state intervention work in Korea?

Some mainstream explanations of the Korean developmental experience were discussed
above. Their attempts to play down the role of the state in Korea are clearly unconvincing,
on theoretical and empirical grounds. In this section, we present an alternative account of
the role of the state in the Korean developmental process. This account tries to draw both
from the 'revealed' and the 'stated' policy objectives, which are found in various policy
documents, and have hardly been investigated by researchers outside Korea.[2] The
account will be highly stylised, partly due to lack of space, but mainly due to the fact that
this article aims to raise new issues for future research, rather than to be a comprehensive
and conclusive case study.

3.1. Themes of Korean state intervention

The basic theme of state intervention in Korea has been the making of an 'independent
economy' (Jarip Gyongjé) (see various Five Year Plan documents and EPB, 1982). Until
recently, the dependence on foreign savings for financing of investments was seen as the
major economic problem by Korean policy-makers. They regarded the ultimate solution
to this problem to be the construction of an economy with sufficient technological
capability to permit a reasonable living standard without a chronic balance of payments
deficit. It was believed that the cause of the balance-of-payments problems lay in the
underdevelopment of capital and intermediate goods industries, and therefore that 'a shift
towards heavy and chemical industries is imperative in order to increase the independence
of the Korean economy' (WP, 1970, p. 340)—a principle known in Korea (and Japan) as
'upgrading' the industrial structure (also see, 2nd FYP, pp. 9–10; 3rd FYP, p. 1).

To Korean policy-makers, economic development required giving priority to investment, which was 'essential for growth' (WP, 1968, p. 48). Therefore, macroeconomic
policy was geared towards the need to create an expansionary environment—if necessary
through inflationary measures—which was seen as vital for a sustained high level of

---

[1] Reading Korean newspapers, one usually finds that 'the government has allowed', and not that 'firm A has
decided on', a certain percentage price rise of a product.

[2] The most important policy documents include various Five Year Plan (FYP) documents and the White
Paper on the Economy (WP), annually produced by the Economic Planning Board (EPB), the super-ministry
with *both planning and budgeting authorities*. The 1st FYP (1962–1966) was issued in 1961, and was revised in
1964. Some of the later FYPs, for example, the fourth and the sixth, were also revised during the plan period,
but the changes are mainly in macroeconomic forecasting, rather than in policy themes.

Political economy of industrial policy in Korea   139

investment. Until the late 1980s, of course, there existed a persistent savings gap, which had to be filled by foreign savings. Although the filling of the savings gap was believed to depend ultimately on rising income levels (a Keynesian savings assumption), serious attempts were also made to repress consumption demand through policy measures, expressed in unashamedly paternalistic terms like 'the need to establish a sound consumption pattern (4th FYP, p. 27). The state-owned banks were instructed not to make consumer loans. The heavy reliance on indirect taxes was also justified (against the accusation that they are less equitable than income taxes) in terms of its discouraging effect on consumption (3rd FYP, p. 16). The control was even stricter when it came to consumption which involved foreign exchange expenditure. For example, foreign holidays were banned until the late 1980s, and imports of 'luxury' goods have been either banned or subject to high tariffs and inland taxes (see section 1). One outcome of such anticonsumption policies is low passenger car ownership, discouraged until recently by high taxation and restrictions on consumer loans. Despite being citizens of a major exporter of passenger cars, Koreans until very recently owned far fewer passenger cars than other developing countries at a comparable income level. In 1985, there were 73·5 people per passenger car in Korea, whereas the corresponding figures in 1983 were 27·0 in Taiwan, 21·8 in Chile, 16·3 in Malaysia, and 15·2 in Brazil (see NRI, 1988, p. 190, table 9·8). Given such a clear (stated and revealed) anticonsumption bias, Korean macroeconomic policy may be more appropriately understood as 'investment management' rather than as 'aggregate demand management'.

Maintaining a high investment level through 'investment management' was, however, seen by the Korean policy-makers as necessary but insufficient to upgrade the industrial structure in a short period of time. Macroeconomic policy measures were seen as ineffective for the rapid upgrading of the industrial structure, owing to their uncertain impact on specific sectors, and were consequently given a status secondary to industrial policy. It was explicitly stated that 'the market mechanism cannot be entirely trusted to increase competitive advantage of industries', and therefore sectors with high productivity growth potential had to be identified by the state and designated as 'promising strategic industries' (WP, 1984, p. 123), or 'priority' sectors, and given custom-designed financial, technical, and administrative support (see later for details). Although macroeconomic constraints often set severe limitations on the conduct of industrial policy, the latter has been actively used whenever deemed necessary and practical. When the aim of macroeconomic stability clashed with the aim of upgrading the industrial structure, the latter was usually allowed to dominate, as testified to by the fact that preferential (subsidised) loans directed to the 'priority' sectors increase faster than general (non-subsidised) loans during recession periods, when the availability of financing can be a matter of life and death for firms (Ito, 1984; Chang, 1987). That is, even when the increase in the overall money supply is contained, the priority sectors are guaranteed financing, at the cost of non-priority sectors. The 'unfair' nature of such a policy has been subject to criticisms inside and outside Korea, but the dominant attitude in policy-making circles has been that being unfair in the short run is justified in the long run by the greater benefits generated by the priority sectors in the form of faster growth and more efficient structural change.

In moving towards high productivity sectors, the biggest concern for Korean policy-makers was that these industries are often characterised by large-scale economies. (e.g. WP, 1968, p. 174).[1] The strong emphasis on scale economies is exemplified by EPB (1982), which diagnoses the cause of the troubles in the heavy and chemical industries

---

[1] WP (1968) states that 'it is needless to say that the attainment or otherwise of efficient production scale is the most fundamental determinant of productivity' (p. 174).

140   H.-J. Chang

in the early 1980s—an example which is often thought to be the classic case of overly ambitious investments (e.g. Lal, 1983)—as 'the lack of scale economies due to the participation of too many firms in each industry' (p. 222).

The prevalence of scale economies in many priority sectors posed two challenges to Korean policy-makers. One was that individual firms in these sectors needed to be large, in order to obtain the minimum efficient scale of production. Firms were often instructed by the state to build plants of efficient production scale, which compelled them to start exporting as soon as possible in order not to incur losses due to low capacity utilisation. And when firms were thought to be smaller than the minimum efficient scale, state-initiated or state-subsidised mergers were often implemented. The most dramatic example of this was the 1980 'industrial reorganisation' (see subsection 4.1). The mergers of two automobile producers in 1965, of five PVC firms in 1969 (see KDB, 1981) and the mergers within fertiliser, shipping, and overseas construction industries in the 1980s (see subsection 4.1; also Leipziger, 1988) are other examples. The other challenge from the presence of large scale economies was the high possibility of 'excessive competition', a term used among Korean (and Japanese) policy-makers to describe the well-known propensity of industries with large sunk costs to engage in price wars. As a result, serious attempts were made to restrict entry and regulate capacity expansion in such industries (see subsection 3.2).

The apparent antitrust implication of the above policies (merger, entry restriction, etc) was regarded as secondary, because the Korean policy-makers thought that 'excessive competition' can result in 'social waste' (e.g. WP, 1968, p. 173). In traditional textbook economics, where it is believed that large numbers guarantee competition and small numbers hamper it, the notion that there can be 'excessive competition' and that it can result in 'social waste' may not be readily accommodated.[1] However, as has been suggested by the Austrian/Schumpeterian economics and the New Institutional Economics, competition is not a costless process in the presence of 'specific assets' which may not be redeployed without serious loss in value in cases of investment failures (on the notion of asset specificity, see Williamson, 1985).

Although they were not able to articulate this idea very clearly in theoretical terms, Korean policy-makers have regarded competition as a means to achieve efficiency rather than as an end in itself (on the different notions of competition, see Hayek, 1949; McNulty, 1968; O'Driscoll, 1986). This view is exemplified by the 6th FYP document, which states that collusive behaviour should be allowed, and even encouraged, in 'promising industries' which need to 'increase R & D, improve quality, attain efficient production scale' and to 'declining industries' which need to 'scale down their capacities' (p. 79). Likewise, the antitrust law (the Law for the Regulation of Monopoly and for Fair Trade), which came into being in 1981 after four abortive attempts at legislation (in 1964, 1966, 1969, 1971), aimed to regulate anticompetitive *behaviour*, rather than market concentration itself, although the growing criticism of the concentration of economic power into the hands of conglomerates brought about an amendment (in 1986) with stronger restrictions on cross-investments between members of the same conglomerate (see Paik *et al.*, 1988, pp. 28–9, 40–2).

Another related theme of Korean state intervention is the policy-makers' attitude towards foreign firms. Korean policy-makers regarded assimilation of advanced technology by

---

[1] Of course, the mainstream economists have not been unaware of the possibility that competition can be 'wasteful'. The recent growth of the literatures on 'wasteful R & D' (for a survey, see Tirole, 1988, ch. 10) and 'sunk cost' (for a survey, see Pindyck, 1991) attest to a growing disillusion with the traditional concept of competition even among mainstream economists. However, it seems fair to say that such developments have not been fully incorporated in the mainstream theory of competition in general.

Political economy of industrial policy in Korea   141

domestic firms as a vital condition for an effective industrial upgrading (for the issue of technology assimilation, see Rosenberg, 1982). To them, this meant tight state control over foreign direct investment.[1] Of course, the persistent savings gap had to be filled, but Korean policy-makers preferred (state-guaranteed) foreign loans to foreign direct investment. As a result, the share of foreign direct investment in total foreign capital inflow (except foreign aid) between 1962–83 was a mere 5% (see Amsden, 1989, p. 92, table 5).

Although such restrictions have been weakening recently, even the latest version of the Law for Importation of Foreign Capital (amended 1988), which is regarded as a 'liberal' one by Korean policy-makers, specifies that foreign direct investment is subject to restrictions in 'priority' industries, infant industries, industries with high imported raw material contents, (especially luxury) consumer goods industries, polluting industries, and agriculture and fishery—which can mean practically all industries, if the state so wishes. Even when foreign direct investment was allowed, foreign majority ownership was practically banned, with some rare exceptions, outside the Free Trade Zones. The fact that only 6% of MNCs in Korea are wholly-owned subsidiaries, compared to 50% in Mexico and 60% in Brazil, suggests a substantial degree of state control over foreign direct investment in relation to ownership (Evans, 1987, p. 208). Even technological licensing, which was preferred to foreign direct investment whenever feasible, was put under heavy restrictions. For example, the latest version of the Law for Importation of Foreign Capital clearly states that technological licensing is banned in industries where local technological capability is deemed to be promising—which, again, can effectively mean any industry.

3.2. Industrial policy

As suggested above, the dominance of industrial policy with a view to 'industrial upgrading' has been the most distinctive feature of Korean state intervention (for the seminal work in this line, see Amsden, 1989). The Korean state has chosen several industries at a time as the 'priority' sectors and provided massive support to them. Most of Korea's major industries were designated as priority sectors at some stage and were developed through a combination of massive support and heavy controls from the state. The 'designated' industries had priority in acquiring rationed (and often subsidised) credits and foreign exchange, state investment funds, preferential tax treatments (e.g. tax holidays, accelerated depreciation allowances) and other supportive measures, including import protection and entry restrictions. In return for these supports, they became subject to state controls on technology (e.g. production methods, products), entry, capacity expansion, and prices. The most important tool of such policy was the use of 'policy loans' [i.e. loans with subsidised interest rates and/or priorities in the (ubiquitous) credit rationing], which accounted for 57·9% of total bank loans made between 1962 and 1985 (Lee et al., 1987, p. 53, table III-1).[2]

The practice of giving priority to certain industries identified as important originated in the very early years of Korean development, with the designation of cement, fertiliser, and

[1] Of course, this does not necessarily mean that it is impossible to develop national technological capability by inviting multinationals in. For example, Singapore has developed a sophisticated technological capability with a large multinational presence (see Evans, 1987, pp. 208–9). Likewise, there has been a substantial technological diffusion through subcontracting by multinationals in the Malaysian electronics industry in Penang (see Rasiah, 1990). The important question, then, seems to be what kind of policies are necessary to promote technological transfer by multinationals.

[2] Credit availability becomes very important given the high leverage of Korean firms. The average equity participation ratio (as a proportion of total assets) of Korean manufacturing firms was 22·7% during 1971–1979 (Cha, 1983, table V-30). The same figure for 1986 was 22·2%, which is even lower than the Japanese figure for the same year (28·3%). Compare this with 47% of American firms (1986) or with 46·8% of Taiwanese firms (1985) (see Paik et al., 1988, p. 43, table I-6).

142   H.-J. Chang

oil refining in the first FYP (1962–1966) as 'basic' industries.[1] In the second FYP (1967–1971), chemical steel, and machinery were designated as 'priority' sectors. And during the third and fourth FYP periods (1972–1981), especially through the HCI programme (announced in 1973), non-ferrous metals, shipbuilding, and electronics were added to the list of 'priority' sectors. The practice continued in the fifth and the sixth FYP periods (1982–1991), during which machinery, electronics, automobile, chemical, shipbuilding, and various high-tech industries (semiconductor, new materials, biotechnology) were designated 'priority' sectors.

Details of such support and control measures can be seen in Table 4, which summarises the measures employed in some selected Promotional Laws, enacted in the late 1960s and early 1970s (except for textiles) to provide legal backing for support for and controls over 'priority' sectors. The Korean policy-makers' concern for 'excessive competition' and the resulting 'social waste' (see subsection 3.1) is reflected in the laws in the form of entry restrictions and regulations on capacity expansion. Violators of such restrictions could be heavily punished with revocation of license, fines, and, in some serious cases, prison sentences. Another interesting feature of these laws is the tight performance monitoring system. The monthly export performance monitoring by the Korean state is already famous (see, e.g. Sakong and Jones, 1980, p. 97), but all firms in the 'promoted' industries were required to report on not just export performance but also on performance in other areas. The failure of regular reporting and/or false reporting could be punished with fines and prison sentences. Such a system provided the Korean state with up-to-date and detailed information concerning the state of business in priority sectors, something which is absolutely essential for an effective industrial policy.

More recently, various Promotional Laws were integrated into the Industrial Development Law (enacted in 1986). The novelty of the Industrial Development Law (IDL), compared to the Promotional Laws, is its emphasis on 'rationalisation programmes' with *limited*, albeit extendible, lifetimes (usually 2–3 years). The rationalisation programmes are custom-designed to the needs of individual industries and aim to provide temporary boosts for industries which need import substitution, capacity upgrading, and improvements in international competitiveness, on the one hand, and temporary protection for 'declining' industries which need a smooth phasing-out, on the other. Rationalisation programmes based on IDL may be implemented on application from the industry, but may also be implemented by the government *without any such application*.

The measures employed by the IDL can be divided into three groups (for details, see Kim, 1989, pp. 36, 62; Paik *et al.*, 1988, pp. 46–47; Lee, 1989, pp. 64–73). In the first place, there are protective measures to ease the adjustment process, which include import restrictions on competing products, reductions in tariffs for raw materials, price controls, and outright subsidies. Second, there are measures related to the attainment of optimal production scale and the prevention of 'excessive' competition. These include restrictions on entry and capacity expansion, state-initiated mergers, co-ordinated capacity scrapping and/or exit, and market-sharing arrangements (i.e. subdivision of markets into non-overlapping segments). Third, there are measures which aim to raise productivity. These include provision of subsidised credits for such activities as capacity upgrading (or capacity scrapping for 'declining' industries), import substitution of inputs (e.g. machine parts), subsidies for expenditures on R & D and training programmes, and joint research programmes between private firms and government-funded research institutes. As we can see, except for the introduction of limited lifetimes for rationalisation programmes, absent

---

[1] The concept of 'basic' industries was also used in the early French planning practice (Cohen, 1977).

Political economy of industrial policy in Korea   143

Table 4. *Major content of promotional laws*

Major content (year of enactment)	Machinery (1967)	Shipbuilding (1967)	Electronics (1969)	Petro-chemicals (1970)	Iron & Steel (1970)	Non-ferrous metals (1971)	Textiles (1979)
Regulations							
Entry restriction	x	x	x	x	x	x	x
Capacity regulations	x	x					
Setting up facility standard							
Capacity expansion approval		x	x	x	x		x
Incentives to use domestically produced facilities	x						
Production regulation							
Regulation of material imports	x		x		x	x	
Production standard and its inspection	x	x	x	x	x	x	
Restrictions on technology imports	x			x	x		
Price control			x	x	x		
Reporting and inspection	x	x	x	x	x	x	x
Rationalisation							
Rationalisation programmes	x	x	x	x			x
R & D support							
Subsidies to R & D	x	x	x	x	x		
Joint R & D projects			x				
Financial support							
Special purpose fund	x	x	x		x	x	x
Financial assistance	x	x	x		x	x	x
Subsidies							
Direct subsidy	x				x	x	
Reduced public utility rates	x				x		
Tax preferences							
Special depreciation	x	x	x	x		x	
Tax reduction/exemption	x		x	x	x	x	x
Special industrial complex	x		x				
Administrative assistance							
Facilitating overseas activities			x		x		
Purchase of raw materials					x	x	
Producers' association	x	x	x		x	x	x

Source: Kim (1989), p. 34, table 3.1; S. H. Lee *et al.* (1989), pp. 52–9.

144   H.-J. Chang

in the Promotional Laws, the major characteristics of Korean industrial policy have changed very little with the introduction of the IDL. The policy measures used are virtually the same, and the discretion of the bureaucracy remains as great as before (because the eligibility criteria are deliberately made vague enough to entitle any industry). The custom-designed nature of individual programmes also remains strong.

Since the enactment of the IDL in 1986, cars, coal-mining, dyeing, ferro-alloys, fertilisers, heavy construction machinery, heavy electrical equipment, naval diesel engines, and textiles have undergone such rationalisation programmes (for details, see Lee, 1989, pp. 64–72; Kim, 1989). As we have mentioned before, the rationalisation programmes were custom-designed for the different needs of different industries. For industries which needed technical upgrading involving large sunk investment (cars, ferro-alloys, heavy construction machinery, heavy electrical machinery, and naval diesel engines), the emphasis was on creating a more stable environment for major new investments and R & D activities, supported by state-led arrangements for market-sharing along product line (among existing producers), entry restrictions, and subsidies to investment and R & D. For the textiles and dyeing industries, which were identified as industries with satisfactory technological capabilities but aging capital stocks, the priority was capacity upgrading, and therefore subsidies were given to producers for scrapping old machines and installing new ones. For the (largely state-owned) fertiliser industry, where the local technological capability was already substantially developed, the programme aimed to introduce more competition in the product market, by granting sales licenses to more distributors and by reducing tariffs on fertiliser imports (but at the same time reducing tariffs on raw material imports). Coal-mining, which was identified as a 'declining' industry, had been under a phasing-out programme, which involved restrictions on entry and capacity expansion, subsidised capacity scrapping, price controls, and import restrictions.

4. Why does state intervention work in Korea?

In the previous section, we gave an account of how state intervention works in Korea. One interesting thing which emerges from this discussion is that the policy measures used by the Korean state are not radically different from those often associated with economic failures in developing countries. This is contrary to the widespread belief that the Korean state's role, 'apart from the promotion of shipbuilding and steel . . . has been to create a modern infrastructure, to provide a stable incentive system, and to ensure that government bureaucracy will help rather than hinder exports' (Balassa, 1988, p. S286), unlike the Latin American countries, where 'there are pervasive controls of investment, prices, and imports and decisions are generally made on a case by case basis, thereby creating uncertainty for business decisions' (Balassa, 1988, p. S287). Why does the seemingly disastrous recipe of heavy-handed intervention work in Korea and not in other countries? In this section, we attempt some answers to this difficult question, although a full response to it would require a comparative study of the role of the state in different countries.

4.1. State-created rents and industrial development

Schumpeter (1987) emphasised that those who are starting 'new things' (p. 87), or innovating, need to be provided with 'profits far above what is necessary in order to induce the corresponding investment', or what he called entrepreneurial profits, which provide 'the baits that lure capital on to untried trials' (p. 90). According to him, this is because of the riskiness of innovative activity which is 'like shooting at a target that is not only indistinct but moving—and moving jerkily at that' (p. 88). Schumpeter argued that entrepreneurial profits, or what modern economics calls '(quasi-) rents' may sometimes be provided by the

Political economy of industrial policy in Korea   145

difficulty of imitating the new technology (or organisation), but sometimes would have to be secured through 'restraints of trade' like cartel arrangements (p. 91). The thrust of Schumpeter's argument is, then, that entry barriers of one form or another are necessary to provide incentives for innovation because it means doing 'new things'.

Establishing an industry in a late-developing country may not involve doing anything 'new' from a global point of view, but poses a similar incentive problem, because it still is a 'new thing' for the nation. In order to set up an industry, a late-developing country has to import technology, but making the imported technology work requires a period of 'learning', which is often a costly activity with highly uncertain returns (Rosenberg, 1982; Abramovitz, 1986; Dore, 1989). Such risk means that those who are starting new industries in a late-developing country have to be provided with some form of entry barrier and the resulting rents. Now, in the context of late development, the market mechanism may not provide such rents, if only because the firms who are borrowing technology from someone else cannot, by definition, set up an entry barrier with the help of the technology, as innovators on the frontier are able to do. Therefore, in a late-developing country, the state, as the ultimate guarantor of property rights, has to create some 'restraints of trade' and provide rents to those who are developing new industries (or even set up those industries itself). And this is exactly what the states in many late-developing countries, from Germany and Japan down to Korea and other currently developing countries, have tried to provide through tariff protection and other forms of state-created rents like subsidies and preferential loans.[1]

Of course, as the opponents of industrial policy correctly point out, there are certain dangers associated with industrial promotion through state-created rents. First of all, there is the risk of policy failure due to lack of information, because the state may not have the information necessary to 'pick the winners' (e.g. Burton, 1983; Grossman, 1988). Second, as the currently popular theory of rent-seeking argues, the existence of state-created rents can lead to 'social waste' by diverting entrepreneurial activities from productive activities into unproductive activities like lobbying (see, e.g. Krueger, 1974; Buchanan *et al.* (eds), 1980; Colander (ed.), 1984). Third, state-created rents, once implemented, are not easy to remove, unlike market-created rents. The existence of 'infant' industries which refuse to grow up is a testimony to such a danger (for some evidence on infant industry performance, see Bell *et al.*, 1984). Korea, like other countries, had to face all the above problems. Korean policy-makers, naturally, made mistakes. The abuse of bureaucratic power, political favouritism, and corruption are hardly rare in Korea. And the country by no means lacks stories of rent-seeking activity. The puzzle is to explain, then, why in the case of Korea these dangers did not inhibit rapid industrial development.

---

[1] From a purely static point of view, the states in late-developing countries should not deliberately seek to develop new industries, because it means, *ceteris paribus*, a less efficient use of resources. This was perhaps what was in their minds when various international lenders, including the World Bank and KISA (Korea International Steel Associates)—a consortium formed by steel-makers from the US, West Germany, the UK, and Italy—turned down Korea's three applications for loans to build an integrated steel mill in the 1960s (Amsden, 1989, p. 295; Watanabe, 1987, p. 69) or when the Bank of Japan was fiercely opposing MITI's effort to develop the car industry in the 1960s (Magaziner and Hout, 1980, p. 55). However, in a world where there is learning, the fact that an industry is unprofitable in a developing country at present prices does not mean that it should not be promoted, as the spectacular successes of Korea's (state-owned) steel mill and the Japanese car industry testify. After the above-mentioned three unsuccessful attempts to raise money for the steel mill, the Korean state was finally successful in securing funds through the war repatriation from the Japanese government and the loans from Japanese Ex-Im Bank (EPB, 1982, pp. 92–4). Ten years after it started operation, the state-owned steel mill (POSCO) became the fourth largest and one of the most cost-efficient steel makers in the world (Amsden, 1989, pp. 298–9). The success of the Japanese car industry is too obvious to merit further discussion.

146   H.-J. Chang

The informational problem, we agree, is often a very serious one, especially in developing countries where basic statistics and other information, which are routinely acquired in developed countries, are not available. However, we would argue that the informational problem can be exaggerated and that it is solvable.

First of all, it is simply not true that private firms operate on the basis of perfect knowledge while bureaucrats know nothing about business. Private firms themselves often operate on the basis of 'informed guesses' or 'animal spirits' when they make major investment decisions, especially in new industries. In addition, large private firms, and not just the state, suffer from informational problems in controlling their divisions and subsidiaries. And when the state maintains an efficient information network of its own, as in the case of Korea, the informational gap between the private sector and the state may be virtually non-existent. The Korean state has kept very close track of priority industries through the obligatory reporting system (see subsection 3.1). In some respects, the state may often be better informed than the private sector, as exemplified by the important role played by the information collected by Korean state agencies, including the diplomatic service and, more importantly, KOTRA (Korean Trade Promotion Corporation) in the penetration of new export markets by Korean firms (see Sakong and Jones, 1980, p. 97).

Further, the difficulties of identifying 'sunrise' industries is not as great as is often made out by opponents of industrial policy, except perhaps on the very frontier of technological development. There usually exists a widespread consensus as to which industries are 'sunrise' industries. For example, we all know that, say, the car and microelectronic industries are going to be important in the conceivable future.[1] Especially, in 'catching up' situations, it is fairly easy to identify which sectors to favour and what kind of support is required for success (Dore, 1986, p. 135). The fact that the Korean economic bureaucracy has been traditionally manned by lawyers (at least until the 1970s) also suggests that 'expert' knowledge in the conventional sense may not be necessary for solving the informational problem.[2]

Recently, the proponents of rent-seeking arguments pointed out that industrial policy may, by opening up opportunities to acquire wealth through unproductive activities such as influence-peddling, divert entrepreneurial efforts away from productive activities. However, if the 'waste' from rent-seeking activities has been an obstacle to growth in Turkey or India (e.g. Krueger, 1974; Mohammad and Whalley, 1984), why has this apparently not been the case in Korea?[3]

---

[1] The reaction of the Korean conglomerates to the recent move by the Korean state to increase specialisation among them is instructive in this regard. In 1991, the Korean state forced the top 30 conglomerates to choose three 'core' lines of activity, which are to be exempted from the credit restrictions imposed on the member firms of top conglomerates in 1984 (in a move to mitigate the increasing concentration of economic power) in return for higher investments in technological development. Twelve of the top 30 conglomerates, for example, chose petrochemicals as their core businesses. Cars and electronics were also a common choice (*Financial Times*, 23 April, 1991). This shows that there exists a broad consensus on which industries are 'sunrise' industries.

[2] In terms of their theoretical sophistication, the earlier Korean planning documents do not compare with, say, the Indian ones, which were based on such advanced models as the Mahalanobis model.

[3] Bhagwati (1988) has suggested that 'prescriptive governments provide fewer inducements for such unproductive activities, because the prescriptions leave large areas open for initiatives' (p. 100). Nevertheless, prescriptive policy is no less prone to rent-seeking activities, because the logic of rent-seeking activities is such that, even if there are large areas open for private initiatives, individuals will engage in such activities if their rate of return is higher than in those areas which are 'open for initiatives'. For example, it is well known in Korea that obtaining subsidised credits (by being a producer in a 'priority' sector) is a very profitable business in itself, because one can divert that money into the curb market where real interest rates can be more than 40% points higher than that of the subsidised credit (see Table 1).

Political economy of industrial policy in Korea   147

Rent-seeking costs are fundamentally 'transaction costs' expended in the process of *seeking* rents (which will involve activities like information collection, influence-peddling, and bargaining), and have to be strictly differentiated from the rent itself, which is a pure transfer (Chang and Rowthorn, 1990 and Chang, 1991, ch. 1). Therefore, the mere existence of state-created rents—and therefore the *opportunity* of rent-seeking—does not mean that resources will *actually* be spent on rent-seeking. The *realised* magnitude of rent-seeking costs in a society will depend on how state-created rents can be obtained (Khan, 1989). For example, it has often been suggested that less resources are spent on influencing the state in Korea, because there is not much point in spending resources to influence a 'hard' state (in the Myrdalian sense) like that of Korea (e.g. Bardhan, 1984). One difficulty with this view is that, as is well known to anyone familiar with Korean politics and business, the country by no means lacks stories of huge corruption scandals, a sign that the Korean state certainly *is* subject to influence, if less so than other, 'softer' states.[1] The explanation has to be more sophisticated.

We think one solution to this puzzle lies in the fact that the Korean state is subject to influence, but mainly to influence from a small, exclusive group of agents, that is, the *chaebols*.[2] Although this practice has produced some undesirable distributional consequences, it seems to have reduced rent-seeking costs in Korea in several ways. First, when a small number of people have exclusive access to rents, rent-seeking activities will be less frequent and of lesser magnitude, because others may not join the rent-seeking contest, knowing that they have little chance of success in influencing the state (this is what Bhagwati, 1988, calls the 'brother-in-law theorem'). Second, since the *chaebols* as a group have exclusive access, they need to spend few resources on finding out what kind of agent the present opponent is (e.g. his/her strategy and belief), because they are frequently confronted by the same adversaries in different rent-seeking contests. Third, the fact that the *chaebols* are conglomerates, with stakes in multiple markets, also reduces rent-seeking costs by the 'bundling of issues'. A bargaining solution can be more easily devised if there are other related bargains which allow more room for arranging side-payments (see Schelling, 1960, pp. 32–3).[3]

Moreover, rent-seeking costs are often of a once-and-for-all nature, because once a rent is granted, there will be an 'entry barrier' into the 'rent market' which will discourage the potential entrants from spending resources to dislodge the incumbent. The more serious danger associated with the use of state-created rents is that state intervention may protect or even encourage inefficient producers or production methods, with long-lasting consequences for efficiency. This problem is not explicitly discussed in the rent-seeking literature, which normally assumes that all rent-seeking agents are identical and use optimal production methods. However, in the real world, there is no guarantee that someone who is competent (or even lucky) at seeking rents is equally competent as a producer, although this may well be the case, if rent-seeking takes the form of franchise

---

[1] The head of one of the country's largest companies is reported to have recently complained that '[t]he government has all the power and you have to purchase approval . . . [and as a result] we pay as much in extortion—legal, semi-legal and illegal extortion— as we do in legitimate taxes' (FEER, 30 May 1991, p. 54).

[2] A *chaebol* is a diversified conglomerate which is usually controlled by one or two families, although professional managers have been becoming more influential recently. It is similar to the pre-war Japanese *zaibatsu*, except that it does not have its own bank, banks being mainly owned by the state in Korea.

[3] In the 1980 industrial reorganisation, for example, Daewoo, the third largest *chaebol*, remained in the passenger car market as one of the duopolists, but was forced to exit from the diesel engine industry and to specialise in a cheaper variety of product in the electronic switching system industry; Hyundai, the second largest *chaebol*, remained in the passenger car industry in return for forced specialisation in diesel engines and heavy electrical machinery.

148   H.-J. Chang

bidding. In Korea, the assumption of 'equal competence' of agents is paradoxically met due to the limitation of access to state-created rents to the *chaebols* which, as conglomerates, are able to operate in almost any line of business equally well. That is, state-created rents in Korea may generate a certain amount of once-and-for-all 'transaction costs' (rent-seeking costs), which are likely to be small for reasons we provided above, but generates little long-lasting production inefficiencies (for a seminal argument in this line, see Khan, 1989).

Probably the most serious problem with industrial policy is that, once implemented, state-created rents may be difficult to withdraw owing to *political* pressure from the recipients of such rents. As was powerfully argued by Marx's theory of 'surplus profit' (1981, e.g. pp. 373–4) and Schumpeter's theory of 'entrepreneurial profit' (1961, ch. 4), the beneficial role of rents, as a means to lure (positive rents) and force (negative rents) firms into more productive activities, hinges on the fact that no rent accruing to 'the innovator' is permanent. In a situation where rents are created by the state, these rents may cease to be transitory and become semi-permanent, if the state is unable to withdraw them when necessary.[1]

Indeed, Korea is no different from other countries in that industrial policy has created many inefficient firms. However, what differentiates Korea from other countries is that the Korean state has been willing and able to withdraw support whenever performance has lagged (Khan, 1989; Amsden, 1989; Shapiro and Taylor, 1990). Such state discipline, when combined with the strategy of 'industrial upgrading' (which involves creation of new and often bigger rents in more productive industries), has acted as a powerful incentive for the firms to enhance their technological capabilities. The imposition of such discipline, of course, has not been a purely technocratic procedure whereby the impartial bureaucrats teach non-performers a lesson, nor has it been a smooth and consensual procedure. It has been, rather, a painful process of continuous bargaining and conflict between the state and the private sector, which, as we shall see below, sometimes had to be solved by forceful measures which are difficult to imagine in other countries.

In 1969, the proliferation of inefficient firms after the massive investment boom in the late 1960s prompted the Korean state to set up a task force accountable only to the Blue House (the presidential residence) to deal with the problem. Between 1969 and 1972, the task force forced dozens of inefficient firms (exact numbers not released) into mergers, sales, and liquidation (sometimes sweetened by debt roll-overs by the Korea Development Bank). The programme eventually ended with the notorious 8–3 Decree (after the date of its announcement, August 3, 1972) involving a total freeze on all curb market loans which were eating into the profits of many firms under financial distress, with subsequent reduction in their interest rates and/or in debt-equity swaps (for details, see Lee, 1985).

After the investment boom of the late 1970s, which led to temporary excess capacity in some major industries, the Korean state again stepped in with the Reorganisation of Heavy and Chemical Industries programme (for more details, see Chang, 1987). Four existing companies in the power-generating equipment industry were merged into Korea Heavy Industries and Construction Co. (KHIC), which was subsequently nationalised, on the ground that the state support needed to make KHIC profitable was too big to be

---

[1] The introduction of limited lifetimes for rationalisation programmes, with the implementation of IDL, may be understood as an attempt to increase the 'transitory' nature of rents.

Political economy of industrial policy in Korea   149

given a single private firm.[1] In the passenger car industry, one of the three existing producers (Kia) was forced to exit and specialise in trucks and buses with a promise that it would be allowed in again when the demand condition improved (this actually occurred).[2] One of the three companies in the naval diesel engine industry (Daewoo) was forced to exit, and the other two were forced to split the market into two segments and specialise (Hyundai in over-6000 h.p. engines and Ssangyong in under-6000 h.p. ones). In the heavy electrical machinery industry, which consisted of eight companies, three (Hyosung, Ssangyong, Kolon) were merged into one (Hyosung) and allowed to produce only highly specialised and expensive products. A subsidiary of Hyundai was asked to produce only for its sister companies. Four other minor companies were forced to produce only less sophisticated and cheaper products. Each of the four companies in the electronic switching system industry (Samsung, Gold Star, OPC, and Daewoo) was forced to specialise in a different product. The two companies in the copper smelting industry were merged by forcing one to buy the other's equity, which was supported by equity participation of KDB and a moratorium on bank loans repayment.

Another round of state-led mergers and liquidations of inefficient firms occurred between 1984 and 1988 (see Lee *et al.*, 1988, pp. 60–2). This time, the shipping, overseas construction, and fertiliser industries, which were identified as declining industries, formed the focus of the programme. In 1984, three fertiliser producers were liquidated, and 63 shipping companies were merged into 17. In 1986, a major reorganisation of the overseas construction industry was implemented. And between 1986 and 1988, 82 inefficient firms (23 of them in shipping and overseas construction industries) were forced into liquidation and mergers.

What is notable in the conduct of such 'reorganisation' programmes is that even the economically and politically powerful conglomerates, *chaebols*, as individual *conglomerates*, were not immune to state discipline, although, as *a group*, they were certainly privileged in their access to various rents. To the Korean policy-makers, it seems to matter less who runs a business than that it is run efficiently. If a particular *chaebol* runs a plant well, fine; otherwise, the ownership has to be transferred to another *chaebol* or even to the public sector (e.g. nationalisation of KHIC). The fact that the *chaebols* as conglomerates are potentially able to move into any line of business (on the basis of their activities in related lines) makes it difficult for a *chaebol* to keep a particular industry as its fiefdom. Unless it

---

[1] In addition to rolling over KHIC's debt (details not released), that state tried to boost its activities by giving it monopoly rights to produce certain power-generation components and certain heavy construction equipment (FEER, 2 June 1983, pp. 67–8).

[2] The history of the passenger car industry characteristically shows how the Korean state shapes up a targeted industry (the following account is based on KDB, 1981, pp. 501–6). The Korean passenger car industry started in 1962 as assemblage of imported semi-knock-down (SKD) kits. In 1965, there was a state-led merger between the two existing passenger car makers (Senara and Shinjin) into one (Shinjin). In 1968, there were two more entries (Hyundai and Asia), and, thereafter, new entry was banned until 1972, when a lorry producer, Kia, was allowed to enter. In 1974, the government announced the Long-term Plan for Promotion of Automobile Industry to develop local passenger car models [at this point, passenger car producers were still assembling complete-knock-down (CKD) kits from Toyota, Ford, GM, and Fiat], and forced Asia, which failed to submit a plan for a development of local passenger car models, to exit and its capacities to be bought by Kia. From 1974, local models were developed (Kia's Brisa in 1974, Hyundai's Pony in 1975, GMK's Gemini in 1977). In the mean time, Shinjin withdrew from GMK (its joint venture with GM since 1972) owing to a sales crisis in the newly introduced Chevrolet models. Shinjin's stake was bought by the Korea Development Bank (KDB) (hence a KDB-GM joint venture), which ultimately sold it to Daewoo in 1978 (hence a GM-Daewoo joint venture until 1992). In the 1980 reorganisation of the sector, the original plan was to force Kia to exit and to merge Hyundai and Daewoo, but it was aborted because the policy-makers would not accept Daewoo's plan to abandon local models in favour of GM 'world car' models. The market was maintained as a duopoly between Hyundai and Daewoo until 1987, when Kia was allowed in again.

150   H.-J. Chang

remains reasonably efficient, other *chaebols* can easily persuade the state that they can do a better job and get state support in the next round of capacity expansion in that industry. Therefore, the *chaebols* had a powerful incentive to remain efficient, especially when the loss of state support can mean a sharp downturn in business in a few years' time, given the state control of credit and the high leverage of Korean firms. Many *chaebols* which lost state favour (for political and/or efficiency reasons) went into oblivion or were disbanded and their carcasses were distributed to other *chaebols*, as exemplified by the fact that only two of the ten biggest *chaebols* in 1966 were among the top ten in 1974; only five out of the 1974 top ten were in the 1980 top ten; only six of the 1980 top ten were in the 1985 top ten (Paik *et al.*, 1988, p. 352, table 35).

4.2. *The bases of state power: history, politics, and economics*

The Korean state played a central role in the country's economic development through its cunning use of state-created rents as an instrument for industrial development. Of course, such a result was only possible because the Korean state was a strong state which could discipline firms.[1] What was the basis for such state power?

It has often been suggested that the Korean state could become strong because the country's historical development left a social structure with no powerful social classes to contest state power (Hamilton, 1983; Lim, 1985; Evans, 1987; Amsden, 1989, ch. 2). The landed class was eliminated through land reform at the time of the Korean War, and the incipient political organisations of the working class and the farmers were also crushed during the war and the subsequent domination of Cold War politics. Moreover, it is argued that the country's Confucian tradition produced a society where the state commands the moral high ground and draws on the best talents (e.g. Luedde-Neurath, 1985).[2] The long tradition of centralisation in Korean history seems to have been another factor serving to legitimatise the power possessed by the central bureaucracy.[3]

We think these historical factors are extremely important, and perhaps what differentiates Korea most from, say, India or Latin America (on India, see Datta-Chaudhuri, 1990; on Latin America, see Fishlow, 1990, and Shapiro and Taylor, 1990). The weakness of social classes was certainly important in deciding the balance of power between state and society in Korea. The Confucian belief in the state as a legitimate social institution (if not necessarily in particular governments and individual political leaders), often lacking in other developing countries, also seems to have been an important factor in making state intervention effective in Korea.

However, we think that such historical factors are, in themsleves, not enough to bring about a strong state. For example, if social classes had been weak since the end of the

---

[1] The power of the Korean state has frequently been underrated, especially by some neoclassical economists (e.g. Balassa, 1988), on the ground that the 'size' of Korean state (defined in terms of public sector expenditure) is relatively small (but see Sachs, 1987, for some evidence to the contrary). However, what matters for the effectiveness or otherwise of state intervention is not where the boundary of the state as a legal entity lies, but how far it can exercise its influence. Public sector expenditure as usually defined is a very poor measure of this.

[2] However, Confucianism in itself is not necessarily beneficial to economic development. Its contempt for commercial and industrial pursuits (the merchant and the craftsman occupied the two lowest castes in the traditional Confucian social hierarchy) could have acted as an obstacle to industrialisation. In fact, Confucianism, often hailed currently as the reason for the Korean success, was often blamed for the relatively poor economic performance in the 1950s.

[3] Korea has traditionally been even more centralised than other Confucian countries. The Japanese feudal system was fairly decentralised until the Meiji Restoration, and the Chinese system, owing to the sheer size of the country, had a strong tendency to dissolve into a decentralised one except in the prime time of a dynasty.

Political economy of industrial policy in Korea   151

Korean War, why was the Korean state so weak and incompetent in the 1950s? Again, if Confucianism is conducive to a strong and competent state, why was the Kuomintang government before 1949 so weak and incompetent? Although a full discussion of the subject is beyond the scope of this article, we would argue that the strong state should be at least partly understood as an outcome of the conscious actions taken by the military régime of General Park Chung Hee, which fundamentally shaped the political economy of the country for decades to come. The strong Korean state was, as we shall see soon, as much, if not more, an outcome of calculated political moves and institutional innovations as of historical conditions and culture.

The political ideas of the top political decision-makers of the military régime were fundamentally shaped under the shadow of the Japanese variety of corporatism.[1] In terms of their economics, the early Korean top political decision-makers were no fans of the free market, although they had to pay constant lip service to the 'free enterprise economy', given the critical importance of US support for the political survival of the régime.[2] In addition, whatever little economic knowledge the early Korean economic bureaucracy had was not neoclassical economics but the economic theories of Friedrich List, Joseph Schumpeter, and Karl Marx, which dominated Japanese academia and policy-making circles in the first half of the twentieth century (see Morris-Suzuki, 1989). The major themes of Korean economic policy-making, for example, the concern with 'social waste' from 'excessive competition', the emphasis on scale economies (and large firms), the obsession with capital accumulation (reflected in the anticonsumption bias), and the desire to develop heavy and chemical industries, make more sense when we understand the intellectual background of the economic bureaucracy. Given such a background, it is more than natural that the political-economic agenda of the Park régime was summarised as 'guided capitalism' (Gyodo Jabon-Jui), where the state plays a guardian role.

As soon as it came to power, the Park régime moved siwftly to prepare some institutional ground for its political-economic agenda. One of the first moves of the Park régime was to nationalise all the banks, and therefore to gain control over the financial flows in the economy. Subsequently, new state-owned banks (e.g. the Korean Exchange Bank, the Bank for Medium and Small Firms, the Ex-Im Bank) were set up over a period of time, resulting in full state control over investment loans.[3] At the same time, the Park régime imprisoned many prominent businessmen on the charge of having accumulated wealth through 'illicit' means (e.g. using political connections) and later released them in return for their promises to 'serve the nation through enterprise', which basically meant building new plants in state-designated industries (the so-called 'Illicit Wealth Accumulation' episode; see Jones and Sakong, 1980, pp. 69–70, 281–2). With these two major political

---

[1] Park was a fierce nationalist strongly influenced by corporatist ideas. His education in the Japanese military academy in Manchuria, which he joined after a brief career as a school teacher, left him deeply influenced by the Japanese variety of corporatism, as is testified by his naming the 'October Restoration' in 1972, his own mid-career political coup to guarantee himself a lifetime presidency, after the Meiji Restoration. He was also strongly influenced by Communism. His brother was an influential local Communist leader, and he himself was sentenced to death (but earned an amnesty by publicly denouncing Communism) as one of the leaders of a Communist mutiny within the Korean army in 1949.

[2] With the growing acceptance of 'private initiative', later policy documents (especially the fifth and the sixth FYP documents) emphasise the government's commitment to the 'private-led economy', but this testifies to the persisting dominance of the state (if the economy was already 'private-led', no comments of this sort would have been necessary).

[3] Short-term working capital, given credit rationing, was mainly provided either by small non-bank financial institutions or by the curb market.

152   H.-J. Chang

blows, the business community suddenly became, morally, like criminals on parole on condition that they 'served the nation through enterprise', and, economically, a paper tiger with little power to make investment decisions—the ultimate capitalist prerogative.

Another important institutional innovation made by the Park régime was the centralisation of economic policy-making power in the hands of the super-ministry headed by the deputy prime minister, namely, the Economic Planning Board (EPB) (see Whang, 1991, pp. 86–7). The integration of *both planning and budgeting authorities* within the EPB eliminated the conflict of interests, if at the cost of concentration of power within the government (which may be objected to on other grounds), between the planning and industrial ministries (which are usually more interested in long-term investments) and the finance ministry (which is usually more interested in short-term stability). Elimination of such conflict made the implementation of industrial policy in Korea more effective than in other 'industrial policy states' like Japan and France where such conflict has been a problem (see Johnson, 1982, for Japan; see Hall, 1987, for France).

Even the much-vaunted cultural and ideological homogeneity of Korean society was not purely a historical bounty which the nation accidentally stumbled on. The Park régime mobilised the nation with the ideology of 'Renaissance of the Nation' through the building of 'Jarip Gyongjé' (independent economy). Workers were described by the state-controlled media and state-issued school textbooks as 'industrial soldiers' fighting a patriotic war against poverty (although the labour movement was brutally suppressed) and businessmen were given medals for their achievement of export targets as if they were generals who won major battles. Farmers were mobilised into semi-compulsory (unpaid) labour for rural infrastructural development à la Mao Tse Tung, through the 'Sémaul (New Village) Movement' (Michell, 1982, pp. 205–8). Although not all such ideological mobilisations were successful (for example, the Sémaul Movement was much resented) and some may criticise them as 'militarising' society (e.g. Halliday, 1980), it is undeniable that they were important in promoting that society's ideological homogeneity.

The Korean state has continued to occupy the economic and moral commanding heights throughout the country's developmental period. State control over credit, which has been the most effective means of controlling private firms, given their high leverage (see above), continued, although some of the state-owned banks (the so-called 'city banks') were partially 'privatised' in 1982. Despite privatisation, the independence of these banks is almost nil, given their over-exposure to highly-borrowed firms and their consequent dependence on the central bank, which is under full control of the state.[1] Indeed, following the 'privatisation', the share of 'policy loans' has actually *increased*, from 56·0% (1962–1981) to 67·6% (1982–1985), making it very difficult to argue that state control over the banking sector has loosened. In addition to their freedom to make loan decisions, the banks' freedom to set interest rates has also been severely limited. Despite the legal deregulation of rates on loans and long-term deposits in December 1988, it is still reported in 1991 that '[i]nterest rates are still strictly controlled by guidance from the Bank of Korea and the Ministry of Finance, despite the legal deregulation' (FEER, 30 May, 1991, p. 52).

In addition to its control over domestic financial flows, the Korean state has maintained tight foreign exchange controls. The buying and selling of foreign exchange has been tightly regulated and, up to a few years ago, it was illegal (and subject to a prison sentence)

---

[1] 'The government [as of 1988] appoints senior bank officials and major credit allocation decisions have traditionally been cleared with government authorities' (FEER, 21 April, 1988, p. 58).

Political economy of industrial policy in Korea   153

to possess foreign exchange except for business purposes. The state's control over foreign loans and foreign direct investments has been near-absolute. Although foreign borrowing and, to a lesser degree, foreign direct investment has not been discouraged, the state has had the final say in deciding whether a certain loan or foreign direct investment would be permitted, and on what terms.

Albeit far less important than the control over financial resources, the state's control over material resources through public enterprises should not be ignored. The Korean state has owned various strategic industries, including oil, coal (partly), gas, fertilisers, steel, and electricity. The fact that such crucial intermediate inputs like oil, coal, gas, electricity, steel and fertilisers (used as a means to control farmers) are supplied by public enterprises is another important factor contributing to the power of the state.

Of course, the regular threat by the Korean state that it is going to use this power to discipline non-performers (e.g. that it will restrict loans to firms which do not comply with a particular policy) is not always carried out, partly because large business firms have a strong influence on policy formation and implementation. Nevertheless, such a threat is not an idle one and is often realised, as exemplified by the freezing of bank credit (on 8 May, 1991) to 14 subsidiaries of eight conglomerates that had not complied with state pressure to sell non-business land (EIU, 1991, p. 20). A still more dramatic example is the Kukje group incident in 1985, when the state deliberately bankrupted the inefficiently run Kukje group, then the seventh largest conglomerate in the country, by ordering its major lending bank not to honour its cheques (for details, see FEER, 21 April, 1988, pp. 58–60). Although it is believed that the decision to let Kukje go under was in part motivated by its lukewarm attitude in meeting the ruling party's financial demands, this is a good example of how far the Korean state can go, if it chooses.

Conclusion

The Korean experience shows first that a development strategy is a complex set of inter-related policies rather than a simple matter of trade regime, as is often implied by debates between the proponents of 'outward-looking' and of 'inward-looking' strategies. Without doubt, trade strategy is a crucial ingredient in a developmental strategy, especially because, as we have seen in the Korean case, the fastest way to build up an advanced industrial base in a developing country is to earn foreign exchange to import advanced technologies and the machines which embody them. Nevertheless, the Korean success was based on a conception of economic development which encompassed far more than mere trade strategy. Development strategy is a multidimensional problem involving such wide-ranging areas as the establishment of long-term targets for growth and structural change, investment in productive facilities and infrastructure, the supply of an adequate labour force with industrial competence and discipline, and technological catching-up and development. Development strategy should no longer be discussed in terms of the mis-conceived dichotomy between export-led (or outward-looking) and import-substituting (or inward-looking) strategies.

Second, the Korean experience shows the importance of a long-term dynamic perspec-tive in managing industrial transition. The industrial transition in Korea was achieved not mainly through the attainment of short-term static efficiency ('getting the prices right'), but through the pursuit of long-term dynamic efficiency through the state's constant creation of rents (or Marxian/Schumpeterian profits). A constant upgrading of the industrial

154   H.-J. Chang

structure based on the development of local technological and managerial capabilities was seen by Korean policy-makers as the surest way to achieve sustained growth and efficient structural change, and hence higher living standards. The state's control over technological transfers and foreign direct investments, and the state's commitment to long-term lending through state-owned banks and various special investment funds, have been vital in this respect. Many individual instances of intervention in Korea might have appeared inefficient and sometimes even megalomanic from a short-term static point of view (e.g. the establishment of steel and shipbuilding industries), but when viewed from a long-term dynamic point of view, most, if not all, make sense.

Third, the Korean experience suggests that a rethinking of the concept of competition is necessary. Until recently, the obsession of Korean (and other, notably Japanese) policy-makers with 'excessive competition' and the resulting 'social waste' has, unfortunately, been regarded as a sign of the stupidity of the bureaucrats who lack a good education in economics. However, as we have pointed out earlier (subsection 3.1), such concerns are more than legitimate in a world with asset specificity, because, in such a world, competition is not a costless process. Ultimately, competition is a means to achieve efficiency, and not an end in itself. We value competition because it can produce more than it costs, and not simply because it is categorically good. And, if the technological and institutional conditions are such that there is going to be 'excessive competition', suppressing competition may be desirable. The Korean experience comes as a serious challenge to the mainstream conception of competition, which is unable to explain why the Korean policy-makers could use all those blatantly 'anti-competitive' (in the neoclassical sense) policies to generate some of the most rapid growth rates and structural change ever seen in human history.

Last but not least, the Korean experience may be 'unique' in the sense that it was supported by a set of idiosyncratic institutions, but this does not mean that it is irrelevant for other countries which have different histories.[1] Practically all successful industrialisation after the British one was based on conscious efforts to import and modify more advanced nations' institutions. Korea, and its predecessor, Japan, are classic examples of such 'institutional learning'. Even when an institution is not transplantable, it is often possible to create some, at least partial, functional equivalent for it.[2] And, if all else fails, there is still the possibility of institional innovation through conscious design. For example, the famous Swedish 'concensus' between labour and capital was constructed from the most contested industrial relations systems in Europe of the 1920s (Korpi, 1983, ch. 3). Moreover, the construction of a new and well-functioning institution need not take a long time. The famous Japanese lifetime employment is basically a postwar creation (Johnson, 1982, p. 14). The French state, once regarded as one of the most 'archaic' in Europe, transformed itself into one of the most 'modernising' states in the world soon after the Second World War (Cohen, 1977, ch. 4). And, as we have tried to show, Korea is another example of how a well-functioning system can be constructed in a reasonably short period of time through conscious action.

---

[1] For a rare attempt to consider the importance of the idiosyncratic factors in the developmental experience of East Asian NICs in general (Korea, Taiwan, Singapore, and Hong Kong), see Nolan (1990).

[2] For example, the Swedish system of state-guaranteed employment and Japanese lifetime employment are radically different from each other in many respects, but in so far as they create positive attitudes among workers towards the introduction of more mechanised (and hence generally more productive) technology, they are functionally equivalent to one another. It is no coincidence that these two countries are the most robotised economies in the world.

Political economy of industrial policy in Korea   155

Bibliography

Amsden, A. 1989. *Asia's Next Giant*, New York, Oxford University Press

Balassa, B. 1982. Development strategies and economic performance, in Balassa, B. *et al.*, *Development Strategies in Semi-Industrial Economies*, Baltimore, Maryland, The Johns Hopkins University Press

Balassa, B. 1988. The lessons of East Asian development: an overview, *Economic Development and Cultural Change*, vol. 36, no. 3, Apr. 1988, Supplement

Bardhan, P. 1984. *The Political Economy of Development in India*, Oxford, Basil Blackwell

Bell, M., Ross-Larson, B. and Westphal, L. 1984. Assessing the performance of infant industries, *Journal of Development Economics*, nos. 1/2

Berlin, I. 1969. Two Concepts of Liberty, in Berlin, I. *Four Essays on Liberty*, Oxford, Oxford University Press

Bhagwati, J. 1985. Foreign trade regimes, in Bhagwati, J. *Dependence and Interdependence*, Oxford, Basil Blackwell

Bhagwati, J. 1987. Outward orientation: trade issues, in Corbo, V., Khan, M. and Goldstein, M. (eds), *Growth-Oriented Structural Adjustment*, Washington DC, IMF and World Bank

Bhagwati, J. 1988. *Protectionism*, Cambridge, Massachusetts, MIT Press

BOK (Bank of Korea) 1987. *National Accounts*, Seoul, BOK

BOK (Bank of Korea) 1988. *Economic Statistics Yearbook 1988*, Seoul, BOK

Bruton, H. 1989. Import substitution, in Chenery, H. and Srinivasan, T. (eds), *Handbook of Development Economics*, vol. 2, Amsterdam, Elsevier Science Publishers

Buchanan, J., Tollison, R. and Tullock, G. (eds) 1980. *Toward a Theory of the Rent-Seeking Society*, College Station, Texas A&M University Press

Burton, J. 1983. *Picking Losers . . .?: The Political Economy of Industrial Policy*, London, Institute of Economic Affairs

Cha, D. S. 1983. 'Öja Do-ip ui Hyokkwa Boonsok' (The Effects of Foreign Capital Inflow), Seoul, Korea Institute for Economics and Technology (KIET)

Chang, H-J. 1987. 'Crisis of Capital Accumulation in South Korea, 1979–82—An Analysis of Policy Solutions', unpublished M.Phil. thesis, Faculty of Economics and Politics, University of Cambridge

Chang, H-J. 1991. 'The Political Economy of Industrial Policy—Reflections on the Role of the State Intervention', unpublished Ph.D. dissertation, Faculty of Economics and Politics, University of Cambridge (forthcoming from Macmillan)

Chang, H-J. and Rowthorn, R. 1990. 'Rent-Seeking, Transaction Costs, and State Intervention—Towards a New Institutionalist View of State Intervention', mimeo., Faculty of Economics and Politics, University of Cambridge

Cohen, S. 1977. *Modern Capitalist Planning: The French Model*, 2nd edition, Berkeley, California, University of California Press

Colander, D. (ed.). 1984. *Neoclassical Political Economy*, Cambridge, Massachusetts, Ballinger Publishing Co.

Cumings, B. 1987. The origins and development of the Northeast Asian political economy: industrial sectors, product cycles, and political consequences, in Deyo, F. (ed.), *The Political Economy of the New Asian Industrialism*, Ithaca, Cornell University Press

Datta-Chaudhuri, M. 1990. Market failure and government failure, *Journal of Economic Perspectives*, vol. 4, no. 3

Dore, R. 1986. *Flexible Rigidities: Industrial Policy and Structural Adjustment in the Japanese Economy 1970–80*, London, The Athlone Press

Dore, R. 1989. Latecomers' problems, *European Journal of Development Research*, vol. 1, no. 1

Dornbusch, R. and Park, Y. 1987. Korean growth policy, *Brookings Papers on Economic Activity*, no. 2

EIU (Economist Intelligence Unit) 1991. *South Korea—Country Report*, no. 2

EPB (Economic Planning Board) 1982. Gaebal Nyondae ui Gyong-je Jonngchek (Economic Policy in the Developmental Era), Seoul, EPB

EPB (Economic Planning Board) 1989. *Major Statistics of Korean Economy*,1989, Seoul, EPB

Evans, P. 1987. Class, state, and dependence in East Asia: lessons for Latin Americanists, in Deyo, F. (ed.), *The Political Economy of the New Asian Industrialism*, Ithaca, Cornell University Press

FEER *(Far Eastern Economic Review)*, various issues

156   H.-J. Chang

Fishlow, A. 1990. The Latin American state, *Journal of Economic Perspectives*, vol. 4, no. 3

FYP (Five Year Plan) various years. Seoul, Republic of Korea Government

Grossman, G. 1988. Strategic export promotion: a critique, in Krugman, P. (ed.), *Strategic Trade Policy and the New International Economics*, Cambridge, Massachusetts, The MIT Press

Hall, P. 1987. *Governing the Economy*, Cambridge, Polity Press

Halliday, J. 1980. Capitalism and Socialism in East Asia, *New Left Review*, no. 124

Hamilton, C. 1983. Capitalist industrialisation in East Asia's four little tigers, *Journal of Contemporary Asia*, 1983, no. 1

Harris, L. 1987. Financial reform and economic growth: a new interpretation of South Korea's experience, in Harris, L. (ed.), *New Perspectives on the Financial System*, London, Croom Helm

Hayek, F. 1949. The meaning of competition, in Hayek, F. *Individualism and Economic Order*, London, Routledge & Kegan Paul

Ito, K. 1984. Development finance and commercial banks in Korea, *The Developing Economies*, vol. 22, no. 4

Johnson, C. 1982. *MITI and the Japanese Miracle*, Stanford, Stanford University Press

Jones, L. and Mason, E. S. 1982. Role of economic factors in determining the size and structure of the public-enterprise sector in less-developed countries with mixed economies, in L. Jones (ed.), *Public Enterprise in Less-Developed Countries*, Cambridge, Cambridge University Press

Jones, L. and Sakong, I. 1980. *Government, Business and Entrepreneurship in Economic Development: The Korean Case*, Cambridge, Massachusetts, Harvard University Press

KDB (Korea Development Bank) 1981. 'Palship Nyondae ui Jonryak Sanup' (Strategic Industries of the 1980s), Seoul, KDB

Khan, M. 1989. 'Clientelism, Corruption, and Capitalist Development: An Analysis of State Intervention with special reference to Bangladesh', Unpublished Ph.D. Thesis, Faculty of Economics and Politics, University of Cambridge

Kim, J. H. 1989. 'Korean Industrial Policies for Declining Industries', Korea Development Institute (KDI) Working Paper no. 8910, Seoul, KDI

Korpi, W. 1983. *The Democratic Class Struggle*, London, Routledge & Kegan Paul

Krueger, A. 1974. The political economy of the rent-seeking society, *American Economic Review*, vol. 64, June

Krueger, A. 1980. Trade policy as an input to development, *American Economic Review*, 1980, Papers and Proceedings

Lal, D. 1983. *The Poverty of Development Economics*, London, The Institute of Economic Affairs

Lee, S. H. 1985. Gookka, Kyegup mit jabon chookjok (The state, classes and capital accumulation), in Choi, J. J. (ed.), *Hangook Jabonjui wa Gookka* (Korean Capitalism and the State), Seoul, Hanwool

Lee, S. H., Kim, S. D. and Hahn, S. H. 1989. *Hangook ui Sanup Jongchek—Sanup Goojo Jongchek Gwanryon Jaryojip* (Korean Industrial Policy—Policies concerning Industrial Structure), Seoul, Korea Institute for Economics and Technology (KIET)

Lee, Y. S., Lee, J. H. and Kim, D. H. 1987. *Sanup Goomyoong Jongchek ui Hyoyool-hwa Bang-ahn* (A Proposal for Improving the Efficiency of Industrial Financing Policy), Seoul, Korea Institute for Economics and Technology (KIET)

Leipziger, D. 1988. Industrial restructuring in Korea, *World Development*, vol. 16, no. 1

Lim, H-C. 1985. *Dependent Development in Korea*, Seoul, Seoul National University Press

Lipsey, R. and Lancaster, K. 1956. General theory of the second best, *Review of Economic Studies*, vol. 24, no. 63

Little, I. 1982. *Economic Development*, New York, Basic Books

Luedde-Neurath, R. 1985. State intervention and exported-oriented development in South Korea, in Wade, R. and White, G. (eds), *Development States in East Asia*, Brighton, IDS

Luedde-Neurath, R. 1986. *Import Controls and Export-Oriented Development; A Reassessment of the South Korean Case*, Boulder and London, Westview Press

Maddison, A. 1989. *The World Economy in the 20th Century*, Paris, OECD

McNulty, P. 1968. Economic theory and the meaning of competition, *Quarterly Journal of Economics*, vol. 82, November

Marx, K. 1981. *Capital*, vol. 3, Harmondsworth, Penguin Books

Michell, T. 1982. South Korea: vision of the future for labour surplus economies? in Bienefeld, M. and Godfrey, M. (eds), *The Struggle for Development: National Strategies in International Context*, New York, John Wiley & Sons Ltd

Political economy of industrial policy in Korea 157

Mohammad, S. and Whalley, J. 1984. Rent seeking in India: its costs and policy significance, *Kyklos*, vol. 37, no. 3

Morris-Suzuki, T. 1989. *A History of Japanese Economic Thought*, London and New York, Routledge

Nolan, P. 1990. Assessing economic growth in Asian NICs: some thoughts on the conclusions drawn from their experience, *Journal of Contemporary Asia*, 1990, no. 1

NRI (Nomura Research Institute) 1988. *Sekai ni Hiyakusuru Kankoku Sangyo* (Korean Industries are Joining the World Class), Tokyo, NRI; Korean language edition, Seoul, Panmun Book Company

O'Driscoll, G. 1986. Competition as a process: a law and economics perspective, in Langlois, R. (ed.), *Economics as a Process*, Cambridge, Cambridge University Press

Paik, N. K., Chang, S. I. and Lee, D. H. 1988. *Hangook ui Sanup Jongcheck—Sanup Jojick Jongchek Gwanryon Jaryojip* (Industrial Organisation Policies of Korea), Seoul, Korea Institute for Economics and Technology (KIET)

Pindyck, R. 1991. Irreversibility, uncertainty, and investment, *Journal of Economic Literature*, vol. 29, no. 3

Ranis, G. 1989. The role of institutions in transition growth: the East Asian newly industrialising countries, *World Development*, vol. 17, no. 9

Ranis, G. and Fei, J. 1975. A model of growth and employment in the open dualistic economy: the cases of Korea and Taiwan, in Stewart, F. (ed.), *Employment, Income Distribution and Development*, London, Frank Cass

Rasiah, R. 1990. 'Electronics Industry in Penang', mimeo., Faculty of Economics and Politics, University of Cambridge

Rosenberg, N. 1982. The international transfer of technology: implications for the industrialised countries, in Rosenberg, N., *Inside the Black Box: Technology and Economics*, Cambridge, Cambridge University Press

Sachs, J. 1984. Comment on C. Diaz-Alejandro, Latin American debt: I don't think we are in Kansas anymore, *Brookings Papers on Economic Activity*, 1984, no. 2

Sachs, J. 1987. Trade and exchange rate policies in growth-oriented adjustment programs, in Corbo, V., Khan, M. and Goldstein, M. (eds), *Growth-Oriented Structural Adjustment*, Washington DC, IMF and World Bank

Schelling, T. 1960. *The Strategy of Conflict*, Cambridge, Massachusetts, Harvard University Press

Schumpeter, J. 1961. *The Theory of Economic Development*, London, Oxford University Press

Schumpeter, J. 1987. *Capitalism, Socialism, and Democracy*, 6th edition, London, Unwin Paperbacks

Shapiro, H. and Taylor, L. 1990. The state and industrial strategy, *World Development*, vol. 18, no. 6

Tirole, J. 1988. *The Theory of Industrial Organisation*, Cambridge, Massachusetts, The MIT Press

UN (United Nations) various years. *Industrial Statistics Yearbook*, New York, UN

UN (United Nations) various years. *Trade Statistics Yearbook*, New York, UN

Wade, R. 1990. *Governing the Market*, Princeton, New Jersey, Princeton University Press

Watanabe, T. 1987. *Venture Capitalism* (translated from Japanese), Seoul, The Korea Economic Daily

Whang, I. J. 1991. Government direction of the Korean economy, in Caiden, G. and Kim, B. W. (eds), *A Dragon's Progress—Development Administration in Korea*, West Hartford, Connecticut, Kumarian Press

Williamson, O. 1985. *The Economic Institutions of Capitalism*, New York, The Free Press

World Bank 1987. *World Development Report 1987*, New York, Oxford University Press

World Bank 1988. *World Development Report 1988*, New York, Oxford University Press

WP (White Paper on the Economy) various years. Seoul, Economic Planning Board (EPB)

Yusuf, S. and Peters, R. 1985. 'Capital Accumulation and Economic Growth: The Korean 'Paradigm', Washington, DC, World Bank Staff Working Paper no. 712

[9]

Overview of Results _____

Throughout the 1970s, until the spring of 1979 when it announced the Comprehensive Stabilization Program, the Korean government carried out the heavy and chemical industry (HCI) policy to promote the development of certain important or key industries, which included iron and steel, nonferrous metal, shipbuilding, general machinery, chemicals, electronics, and others as designated by the president. Tax and trade policies, as well as credit and interest rate policies, were mobilized to promote the development of the heavy and chemical industries.

The tax system provided numerous incentives for the qualified firms in these industries, among the major ones tax holidays, special depreciation rates for fixed capital, and temporary investment tax credit. The legal bases for the preferential treatment were provided by various laws promoting the development of important industries that were already in place at the beginning of the 1970s, and the Tax Exemption and Reduction Control Law that underwent a major revision in line with the HCI policy in late 1974.

The effective tax rates on the marginal return to capital for firms in various industries, estimated under the assumption that firms take full advantage of the major incentives provided by the tax system, clearly shows the substantial differences in the tax treatment afforded between the industries favored by the HCI policy and other manufacturing industries.[1] From the mid-1970s until the early 1980s, the effective tax rate for the "favored" industries taking advantage of tax incentives was below 20 percent on the marginal return to capital, while the effective tax rate for other industries remained close to 50 percent (see Table 4-1 and Figure 4-1). Although these estimates are not the actual tax rates, they clearly illustrate the large bias the tax incentives gave to the favored industries. Subsequent to the reform of the tax system in 1981, the preferential tax treatment had nearly disappeared by 1982.

Table 4-1. Effective Corporate Tax Rate (in percentage)

Industry	1970	1971	1972	1973	1974	1975	1976	1977	1978	1979	1980	1981	1982	1983
Policy favored	39.2	34.9	27.7	33.5	29.9	15.9	18.0	17.5	16.9	18.3	18.3	20.6	47.1	40.4
Chemicals	38.3	34.2	29.5	33.6	33.8	16.9	19.1	19.3	18.2	21.6	17.2	19.5	47.0	41.0
Primary metals	39.9	33.1	24.8	30.8	33.7	12.4	11.9	11.9	11.0	10.6	15.0	16.4	47.5	40.0
Machinery/transport equipment	39.5	37.3	28.8	36.1	22.3	18.3	23.1	21.3	21.6	22.7	22.8	26.0	46.8	40.3
Others	39.4	34.7	29.8	38.6	37.7	52.1	51.0	49.5	48.4	48.5	48.8	51.1	48.2	42.2
Food and beverages	41.9	37.6	32.7	38.3	39.1	52.8	52.3	50.0	48.9	49.1	49.5	51.3	48.8	42.8
Textiles and clothing	38.8	33.1	28.1	38.0	35.6	51.4	50.4	48.8	47.1	46.8	48.0	50.2	47.2	41.3
Wood and furniture	40.2	33.7	28.7	38.1	37.5	52.1	50.8	50.0	48.3	48.4	48.7	52.0	49.0	42.9
Paper and printing	41.7	36.8	33.5	40.0	38.5	53.0	51.6	49.3	48.6	49.3	49.1	51.4	48.4	42.4
Nonmetallic minerals	41.6	38.0	31.7	38.9	37.4	52.0	50.8	50.5	49.7	49.3	48.7	51.0	48.1	42.1
Miscellaneous industries	32.3	29.2	24.1	38.1	37.8	51.3	49.9	48.6	47.6	48.2	49.0	50.6	47.9	41.9

Source: Taewon Kwack, Depreciation and Taxation of Income from Capital (Seoul: Korea Development Institute, 1985), reproduced with permission.

64

The Economic Development of Northeast Asia IV

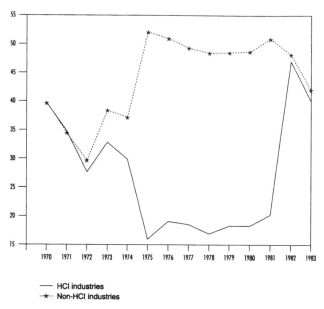

— HCI industries
··★·· Non-HCI industries

Figure 4-1. Effective Tax Rates on the Marginal Returns to Capital

Trade policy was another tool used to assist the favored industries. During the 1970s imports that were thought to compete with the output of the favored industries were severely limited, in a reversal of the import-liberalizing trend that began in the mid-1960s. In 1967 the positive list system of import approval, under which only those items on the list could be imported, was changed to a more liberal negative list system, under which imports required no prior government approval unless listed. At the same time the number of items on the negative list was reduced. As the data in Table 4A-1 show, the import liberalization ratio for the manufacturing sector in 1966 stood at under 8 percent; by 1970 it had risen to 42 percent.[2] During the 1970s, the ratio for the manufacturing sector as a whole declined, albeit marginally, to 40 percent in 1978. Note also that the decline was primarily due to the large drop in the liberalization ratios for the policy-favored industries. As part of the industrial policy, protection for the favored industries was increased by putting some products back on the negative list so that such imports once again required prior government approval. It became virtually impossible for anyone, with the exception of exporters, to import foreign products if domestic firms produced similar or substitute goods in the designated key industries.[3]

66 Industrialization and the State

The most powerful tool the government used to implement its industrial policy was the allocation of investment funds. Through the National Investment Fund, established in 1974, the government directly allocated investment funds among various manufacturing industries and even among individual investment projects. The commercial banks, largely owned by the government at the time, were also directed to make loans to these investment projects. The loans to heavy and chemical industries and others—so-called policy loans—were offered at preferentially low interest rates. During the HCI period, the policy loans expanded to take on an increasingly large share of the domestic credit.

Table 4-2 shows the shares in total domestic credit to the private sector of three different kinds of policy loans for the 1970–1985 period. One is for foreign trade, which was available primarily for the purpose of financing exports. The other may be called "earmarked," and it includes the loans for the agricultural sector, small- and medium-sized firms, home construction, and some others. These two kinds of loans were available only for specified purposes and were not directly related to the HCI policy. The third is simply the remainder of the policy loans, and it is labeled "unearmarked" in Table 4-2. This was the source of investment funds available to the HCI projects. In 1971 various policy loans accounted for half of all domestic credit to the private sector. By the late 1970s and early 1980s, this share rose to 60 percent, and by 1985 its share fell back to about one-half. This rise and fall in the share of all policy loans is almost entirely due to the change in the share of unearmarked loans. From the mid-1970s to the end of the decade, the share of such loans rose approximately six percentage points, from 27 percent to around 33 percent. Then it declined to around 25 percent by the mid-1980s. Thus, at one point, the government had 60 percent of all domestic credit under its control, and more than half of it went to the projects favored by the industrial policy.

The significance of the credit policy can be better appreciated by looking at the interest rates on the policy loans in Table 4-3. While the loans for foreign trade always enjoyed the lowest interest rate, the favor conferred on loans for HCI investments was substantial. This is clear from a comparison of the interest rate in column 3 charged by the Korea Development Bank on loans to finance the investments in capital equipment in the key industries and the discount rate charged by the commercial banks on commercial bills in column 1. The rates reported in column 3 were 5 to 10 percentage points lower in the first half of the 1970s and about three percentage points lower in the second half; except for one year, they were always lower than the inflation rate (column 4), so that in effect the key industries were charged a negative real interest rate.

Table 4-2. Share of Policy Loans in Domestic Credit (in percentage)

	Unearmarked (1)	Foreign Trade (2)	Earmarked (3)	All Policy Loans (4)
1970	29.67	5.56	12.18	47.41
1971	30.25	6.11	11.91	48.27
1972	26.74	6.71	20.33	53.79
1973	25.54	10.53	19.37	55.44
1974	23.87	11.32	17.48	52.66
1975	27.18	9.01	16.57	52.76
1976	26.29	9.99	16.15	52.43
1977	29.25	10.41	16.18	55.84
1978	32.32	10.81	17.52	60.66
1979	33.43	10.63	14.97	59.03
1980	34.05	11.50	14.23	59.78
1981	31.30	12.73	14.64	58.67
1982	29.61	12.27	12.50	54.38
1983	27.99	12.68	14.03	54.70
1984	26.47	12.72	14.81	54.00
1985	25.12	12.85	14.79	52.77

Notes: "Domestic credit" includes all loans and discounts to the private sector by deposit money banks (commercial banks and special banks), the Korea Development Bank, and the Korea Export-Import Bank.
  "Unearmarked" includes loans funded by the National Investment Fund and government fund, loans in foreign currency, and all loans by the Korea Development Bank.
  "Foreign trade" includes the loans for foreign trade by deposit money banks and all loans by the Korea Export-Import Bank.
  "Earmarked" includes the loans for agricultural industries, small- and medium-sized firms, and home building.
Source: Economic Planning Board, *Korean Economic Indicators* (1986), and Bank of Korea, *Economic Statistics Yearbook* (various issues).

In early 1979, the government estimated that 74 percent and 82 percent of all fixed investments made in the manufacturing sector in 1976 and 1979, respectively, went to the heavy and chemical industries.[4] This was primarily the result of the government's intervention in the allocation of investment funds, but because the preferential loans carried negative real interest rates, strong incentives were also in place for the private sector to invest in the favored industries. Trade policy, by strengthening the bias of the incentive structure, played an important role in complementing other policy measures. By guaranteeing the market for domestic firms, which effectively reduced their risk and artificially raised their profitability, trade policy made the private sector a willing partner of the HCI policy.

Evolution of Korean Manufacturing Industries, 1966–1985

During the 1970s, Korea's manufacturing sector grew very rapidly, with widely varying rates across different industries. This section describes the salient features of this experience, especially those facets that relate to the

68 Industrialization and the State

Table 4-3. Interest and Inflation Rates (in percent per annum)

	Commercial Banks' Discount on Bills (1)	Interest Rate for Loans for Foreign Trade (2)	Interest Rate on Loans for Equipment to Key Industry (3)	Consumer Price Index (4)
1970	24.30	6.00	12.00	16.01
1971	23.00	6.00	12.00	13.51
1972	17.79	6.00	11.17	11.51
1973	15.50	6.67	10.00	3.20
1974	15.50	8.83	10.00	24.48
1975	15.29	7.67	12.00	25.20
1976	16.33	7.42	12.42	15.27
1977	17.25	8.00	13.00	10.17
1978	18.02	8.58	14.17	14.46
1979	18.75	9.00	15.00	16.26
1980	23.33	12.00	20.50	28.70
1981	19.50	12.00	18.00	21.30
1982	12.38	10.75	12.75	7.25
1983	10.00	10.00	10.00	3.38
1984	10.27	10.00	10.31	2.30
1985	10.75	10.00	9.56	2.47

Notes: The interest rates are weighted averages, with weights equal to the number of months the interest rates were in use in a given year. When source data are given as a range, the midpoint is shown in this table.
Source: Bank of Korea, *Economic Statistics Yearbook* (various issues).

HCI policies of the 1966–1985 period.[5] Manufacturing industries have been aggregated into two groups. The first, referred to as the HC group, consists of industries favored by the HCI policy; the second, referred to as the Light group, covers those not favored by the HCI policy measures. (For a more detailed explanation of the industry groupings, see Appendix 4A.)

Growth of Value-Added

The most outstanding feature in the evolution of the manufacturing sector from the 1970s was its rapid growth, at times exceeding 20 percent per annum in real terms (Table 4-4). However, the pace of growth slowed considerably in the last few years of the 1970s, and output declined in 1980. During the 1980s, the sector's growth partly recouped its earlier speed.

Two other notable features were that the industries belonging to the HC group grew faster than those in the Light group and that for the manufacturing sector in general the double-digit growth rate plunged below 10 percent after 1978. In the 1970–1978 period, the average annual growth rate of the HC group was about 30 percent, twice that of the Light group. The HC group, comprising basic metals, various machineries, including transport equipment, and chemicals, doubled its real value-added every

Table 4-4. Growth in Value-Added and Employment (in percentage change)

	Total Manufacturing	Heavy and Chemical	Light	Electric Machinery	Clothing and Footwear
Value-added					
1966–1970	21.0	23.2	17.8	29.5	18.0
1970–1973	20.2	32.2	19.2	56.4	32.8
1973–1975	13.8	25.0	11.5	19.5	19.6
1975–1978	20.0	31.2	15.7	38.9	16.1
1978–1980	4.8	3.6	5.2	3.7	−5.2
1980–1983	8.0	12.8	6.4	13.8	8.0
1983–1985	9.2	13.5	6.6	12.3	4.0
1970–1978	18.5	30.0	15.9	39.9	23.0
1978–1985	7.4	10.3	6.1	10.4	2.9
Employment					
1966–1970	8.8	11.8	8.2	22.5	0.0
1970–1973	9.6	15.5	8.2	33.1	12.4
1973–1975	15.6	18.0	15.1	21.6	18.6
1975–1978	8.4	13.5	7.0	18.5	8.1
1978–1980	−1.0	2.5	−1.8	3.3	−6.7
1980–1983	2.7	8.3	0.6	3.7	−3.5
1983–1985	2.:	5.1	0.8	4.6	3.0
1970–1978	10.6	15.4	9.4	24.6	12.2
1978–1985	1.4	5.7	−0.1	3.9	−2.6

three years or less. During the 1978–1985 period, the growth rates dropped sharply. The HC group again grew at much faster rates than the Light group, except between 1978 and 1980. As a result, the relative size of these groups changed considerably. In real terms, the value-added of the HC group was only a third as large as the Light group in the early 1970s but became seven-tenths as large by 1985.

Employment Growth
The second half of the 1960s saw a rapid employment growth in the manufacturing sector. It accelerated further during the 1970–1978 period (Table 4-4), to reach an average annual rate of nearly 11 percent. But the rate fell to about 1.4 percent per annum for the period 1978–1985. Although this sharp drop in employment growth is observed for both HC and Light groups, it was more pronounced for the clothing and footwear industries, where employment had surged in the first part of the 1970s and declined in the 1978–1980 period.

Capital Accumulation
Capital accumulation in the manufacturing sector also showed a pattern of rapid growth followed by a sudden slowdown (Table 4-5). The slow- down began in the early 1980s, somewhat later than it did in employment growth. The table also shows that the HC and the Light groups had contrasting

70 Industrialization and the State

Table 4-5. Rates of Capital Accumulation (in percentage change)

	Total Manufacturing	Heavy and Chemical	Light	Electric Machinery	Clothing and Footwear
1966–1970	11.6	11.0	11.8	22.1	14.4
1970–1973	21.7	23.6	20.2	35.1	23.8
1973–1975	18.9	32.0	14.3	71.8	27.8
1975–1978	14.6	21.6	11.5	16.1	25.8
1978–1980	12.9	13.1	12.8	13.6	6.3
1980–1983	7.9	10.1	6.2	11.1	7.2
1983–1985	8.5	10.4	7.2	24.5	7.5
1970–1978	18.3	24.9	15.4	35.5	25.5
1978–1985	9.5	11.0	8.3	15.5	7.1

experiences in terms of capital accumulation in the mid-1970s. Until the early 1970s, capital accumulation proceeded at roughly the same rate in the two groups, but then capital accumulation accelerated in the HC group while decelerating in the Light group. During the 1973–1978 period, the average annual rate of capital accumulation was more than twice as high in the HC group as in the Light group. This could be the consequence of a response by the private sector to the different rates of return to investment in the two groups, a phenomenon little influenced by the HCI policy. But given that the HCI policy greatly favored the HC group and that the 1973–1978 period almost exactly coincided with the duration of the policy, it is highly likely that the contrasting capital accumulations in the two groups reflect the effect of HCI policy.

Changes in Capital Intensity
The capital intensity of production, measured as a ratio of capital stock to the number of workers employed, is bound to change as employment grows and capital accumulates. As we shall see, the change in capital intensity seems to reflect the effect of the HCI policy more closely than capital accumulation did. Table 4-6 shows that the capital intensity of the manufacturing sector as a whole increased sharply in two different periods. The first was in 1970–1973, when capital intensity increased at an average annual rate of 11 percent. With capital accumulating at about 22 percent per annum, capital intensity jumped even while employment increased by 9.6 percent per annum. The second sharp rise took place in 1978–1980. In contrast to the first episode, capital accumulation was much slower, increasing only by 13 percent, but capital intensity rose faster mainly because the associated levels of employment declined.

Underneath these changes for the manufacturing sector as a whole lay quite distinct movements of capital intensity for the Light and HC groups. A close look at Table 4-6 reveals that the capital intensities of the two groups twice moved in opposite directions, in the 1966–1970 period and again in 1973–1975. This could not have happened if they faced the same wage-rental ratio, because the capital intensity, an increasing function of the wage-rental ratio, must rise or fall in response to a rise or fall in the wage-rental ratio.

Of the two episodes, the 1966–1970 one, when the capital intensity rose for the Light group and declined for the HC group, was more apparent than real. Of twenty-three individual manufacturing industries, seven experienced a decline in capital intensity (see Tables 4A-2 and 4A-3). Of these seven, five were in the Light group and two in the HC group. Thus, the decline in the capital intensity was more widespread among the Light industries than among the HC industries, and a common feature of these industries was that their outputs were rising faster than the manufacturing average (see Table 4A-10). In response to the rapid increase in demand, firms must have temporarily been increasing labor inputs faster than their capital inputs.

On the other hand, in the 1973–1975 episode, where the capital intensity of the Light group declined at an annual rate of 0.7 percent while that of HC group was rising at 12 percent per annum, the contrast was highly unusual. Excluding the group "other manufactures" (see Table 4A-2), which had an inexplicably rapid rise in capital intensity, the capital intensity of the Light group declined by 2.3 percent annually between 1973 and 1975. Textiles, the largest industry in the Light group in terms of value-added and employment, experienced a decline in capital intensity of 18 percent a year. Unlike the 1966–1970 period, in none of the HC industries did capital intensity decline.

Two immediate causes can be posited for the contrasting experience of the two groups over the period 1973–1975. First, the HC group's capital accumulation, at an annual rate of 32 percent, was more than twice as fast as that observed for the Light group, at 14 percent per annum. The second was the employment surge, already noted, in the Light industries. Employment grew at an annual rate of 15 percent for the Light group, a near doubling of the growth rate over the previous period. (The growth rate of employment also rose for the HC group, from 15.5 percent over 1970–1973 to 18 percent over 1973–1975, but this acceleration was relatively modest compared to what happened in the Light group.)

Thus, during the 1973–1978 period, capital intensity rose faster in the HC group than in the Light group. From the late 1970s, as the HCI policy came to an end, this relative speed between the two groups was reversed: the capital intensity rose faster for the Light than for the HC group. For

72 Industrialization and the State

Table 4-6. Capital Intensity

	Total Manufacturing	Heavy and Chemical	Light	Electric Machinery	Clothing and Footwear
Capital-labor ratio (in million 1980 won/worker)					
1966	3.9	6.9	3.1	2.3	0.3
1970	4.3	6.7	3.5	2.3	0.6
1973	5.9	8.2	4.8	2.4	0.8
1975	6.2	10.2	4.7	4.8	0.9
1978	7.4	12.5	5.3	4.5	1.4
1980	9.6	15.3	7.0	5.5	1.9
1983	11.1	16.0	8.3	6.7	2.6
1985	12.6	17.7	9.4	9.5	2.8
Percentage change in K/L ratio					
1966–1970	2.5	-0.7	3.3	-0.3	14.4
1970–1973	11.1	7.0	11.1	1.5	10.2
1973–1975	2.8	11.9	-0.7	41.2	7.7
1975–1978	5.7	7.1	4.2	-2.1	16.4
1978–1980	14.1	10.3	14.9	10.0	14.0
1980–1983	5.1	1.7	5.6	7.1	11.1
1983–1985	6.3	5.1	6.4	19.0	4.4
1970–1978	7.0	8.2	5.4	8.8	11.8
1978–1985	7.9	5.0	8.4	11.2	10.0

example, in the 1978–1980 subperiod, the capital intensity for the Light group rose much faster, at an average annual rate of 15 percent, as compared to the annual increase of 10 percent observed for the HC group. This more rapid rise in capital intensity continued well into the mid-1980s.

Factor Market Distortion

One can safely infer from the contrasting changes in capital intensity between the HC and Light groups that the two groups faced wildly different wage-rental ratios. During the 1973–1978 period, the wage-rental ratio must have been rising for the HC group but falling or rising very slowly for the Light group. For the 1978–1985 period, almost the opposite must have been the case: the wage-rental ratio was rising for both groups, but the rise must have been faster for the Light than for the HC group.

The wage-rental ratio for the HC and the Light groups would diverge if the rental rates the two groups faced diverged. Since there was no government attempt to fix wages at different rates for the two groups, it seems safe to assume that both faced the same labor market. The key to the explanation must be the effect of HCI policy measures on rental rates, which strongly favored investments in the industries in the HCI group during the 1970s. Various incentives and direct government involvement in credit allocation lowered the capital cost for the HC group but raised it for the Light group. The high cost of capital for the entrepreneurs in the latter group could have simply taken the form of unavailable investment funds from the banks at the government-controlled interest rates or high interest rates in the curb market. Thus, in the 1973–1978 period, the HCI policy must have lowered the wage-rental ratio for the Light group while raising that for the HC group. The decline in the Light group's capital intensity over the period 1973–1975, especially for textiles, suggests a high probability of an absolute fall in the wage-rental ratio for the group.

For the 1978–1985 period, however, the capital intensity of the Light group rose faster than that of the HC group, indicating that the wage-rental ratio rose faster for the former group of industries than for the latter. This could have been brought about by the denominator of the wage-rental ratio's (the rental rate) falling faster for the Light group than for the HC group if the two groups are again assumed to face the same labor market. This was indeed what happened. As one can see in Table 4-3, the interest rates on ordinary commercial loans (column 1) were three to four percentage points higher than the rates for the key industries (column 3), in the late 1970s and early 1980s, that is, toward the end of the HCI policy period and immediately after. By the mid-1980s, the difference almost disappeared. Thus, for the 1978–1985 period, the wage-rental ratio must have risen faster for the Light group than for the HC group.

The Effect of Resource Allocation: Capital Efficiency

This section assesses the effect of the HCI policy on resource allocation by estimating capital efficiency of the manufacturing industries and comparing the estimates. Capital efficiency, that is, the rate of return to capital employed in individual industries, was estimated under the assumption that there were only two factors of production—capital and labor—and that the wage rate was competitively determined.

If diminishing returns prevail, a capital efficiency estimate of the HC group higher than or equal to that of the Light group may be regarded as evidence that the HCI policy improved resource allocation. Since the policy had directed and encouraged investments to the HC group, the capital efficiency of the group would have been still higher than the estimates even without the policy. It must have been that the policy allocated the resources to the industries with higher rates of returns—an improvement in resource allocation and increase in output. Higher capital efficiencies in the HC group than in the Light group could also result if the investments

74 Industrialization and the State

under the HCI policy had the effect of shifting the technology of the HC group to a new, higher level. If this were the case, still greater incentives should have been given to the HC group so that still more capital may have been allocated to the group. On the other hand, if the capital efficiency in the HC group is estimated to be lower than in the Light group, it would indicate that the HCI policy induced excessive investment in the HC group, an evidence of resource misallocation.

This approach is motivated by the simple optimization rule that output is maximized when a resource is allocated so that its marginal product is equalized among different uses. It is also based on the recognition that the HCI policy affected primarily the allocation of capital among the manufacturing industries. Although the approach is clearly founded in comparative static, the estimates of capital efficiencies over the period 1966 to 1985 will shed light on the dynamic effects on resource allocation of the HCI policy.

Estimation Method of the Capital Efficiency
Although the concept of capital efficiency is fairly straightforward, its estimation here encountered a number of statistical problems. The first problem was the availability of value-added data. In order to estimate an industry's capital efficiency, it was necessary to have the constant-price value-added broken out into the components (for example, compensation to labor and indirect taxes). The constant-price value-added originating from individual manufacturing industries was available as part of the national income estimates by the Bank of Korea. However, this source did not break it down into its components. The breakdown was available only in current prices in the input-output (I-O) tables, also estimated by the Bank of Korea. Thus, the proportions of the labor compensation and indirect taxes in constant-price value-added were assumed to be the same as those in current-price value-added obtainable from the I-O tables.

Second, the reported value-added of an industry, in both current and constant prices, included indirect taxes, some of which may have been shifted to the buyers of a firm's output or to the suppliers of intermediate inputs. Hence, not all of the indirect taxes may represent value-added by the factors. Furthermore, how the burden of tax that was not shifted was shared between capital and labor is not known. No attempt was made to estimate the parameters needed in order to clarify these unknowns. Instead, two kinds of capital efficiency estimates were made: one under the assumption that all indirect taxes were shifted, that is, no part of the indirect taxes was value-added created by the factors, and the other under the assumption that half of the indirect taxes were not shifted but borne by capital. Thus, under the latter assumption, half of the indirect taxes were counted as the value-added created by capital.

Third, the compensation to labor reported in the I-O tables was that made to paid workers. Since there are unpaid workers—self-employed and family workers—the reported labor compensation understates the value-added created by labor. The value-added created by all workers in an industry was estimated by using the numbers of paid and unpaid workers that I-O tables provided. The reported compensation was first divided by the number of paid employees, and the quotient was multiplied by the total number employed. The result is taken to be the compensation that would have been made to all workers, had the unpaid workers gotten on average the same wage as the paid employees. This imputed compensation is assumed equal to the value-added created by the labor.[6]

Fourth, there was a valuation problem. Value-added in constant price, denoted as VA, as estimated by the Bank of Korea, consists of three elements, as follows:

$$(4.1)$$

$$VA = VA^*_e + VA_d + T,$$

where VA^*_e and VA_d are the parts due to export sales and due to domestic sales, respectively, and T represents indirect taxes. The valuation problem arises because prices need not be the same in the domestic and international markets when the former is protected. In Korea, value-added in producing exports can be taken as being reflective of international prices, since imported inputs for exports faced few nontariff barriers and were available at international prices, thanks to the tariff rebate system. On the other hand, protection of an industry tends to raise the domestic prices of the industry's outputs and value-added. Hence, the sum in equation 4.1 represents a sum of two items valued in different prices.[7]

Initially ignoring this valuation problem, two kinds of capital efficiency are estimated. The first, denoted as $q1$, was estimated under the assumption that all indirect taxes were shifted forward or backward and were not borne by the capital, as follows:

$$(4.2)$$

$$q1_i = \frac{VA_i (1 - t_i - s1_i)}{K_i},$$

where the subscript i denotes the ith industry, K stands for capital stock, and $s1$ and t are, respectively, the proportions of imputed labor compensation and indirect taxes in the current-price value-added.

76 Industrialization and the State

Second, capital efficiency was estimated under the assumption that half of the indirect taxes were borne by the capital. The resulting measure of capital efficiency, $q2$, is defined as:

(4.3)

$$q2_i = \frac{VA_i\,(1 - 0.5t_i - s1_i)}{K_i}.$$

These two measures of capital efficiency, $q1$ and $q2$, do not yet take into account the fact that domestic sales and exports are valued under two different price regimes. Thus, a third measure, taking this into account, was estimated under the assumption that all indirect taxes were shifted away, the same assumption used in the estimation of $q1$. First, an industry's constant-price value-added less indirect taxes was divided into the proportion due to exports and that due to domestic sales, VA^*_e and VA_d, as follows:

(4.4)

$$VA^*_e = VA\,(1 - t)\,sx$$

(4.5)

$$VA_d = VA\,(1 - t)\,(1 - sx)$$

where sx is the proportion of exports in an industry's current-price gross output less indirect tax, and the subscripts are suppressed. (See Table 4A-7 for sx.)

Then VA_d was deflated by the effective rate of protection and summed with the VA^*_e to yield a measure of value-added in international prices. From this sum, labor's imputed incomes were subtracted, and the result was divided by the industry's capital stock to obtain the third measure of capital efficiency:

(4.6)

$$q3 = \left[VA^*_e + \frac{VA_d}{(1 + z)} \right]\left(1 - \frac{s1}{1 - t} \right),$$

where z is the effective rate of protection, and $s1/(1 - t)$ is the share of labor income in the current prices value-added after subtracting indirect taxes. Because indirect taxes are subtracted from the value-added, labor's share expands by a factor of $1/(1 - t)$. This measure of capital efficiency was estimated for the years 1970, 1975, 1978, and 1983, when effective protection estimates were readily available.[8] (See Table 4A-8 for z.)

Estimation Results

The estimated capital efficiency, $q1$, of individual industries is shown in Table 4A-4; Figure 4-2 shows the results for the HC and Light. We also report estimates for a new industry group, which consists of the HC group but excludes the electric machinery sector, while estimates for $q2$ are shown in Table 4A-5 and Figure 4-3. Finally, Figure 4-4 shows the estimates for $q3$ for industry groups. (The full details are set out for individual industries in Table 4A-6.)

As expected, $q2$ was greater than $q1$, since the former regarded half of indirect taxes as created by capital. In addition, notice that in Figures 4-2 and 4-3 the difference in capital efficiency between the HC and Light groups as measured by $q2$ is wider than that measured by $q1$. The reason was that indirect taxes made up for a greater proportion of the value-added in the light industries than in the heavy and chemical industries. Hence, the margin by which $q2$ is greater than $q1$ is greater for the Light group than for the HC group. Leaving this difference aside, the two estimates show similar trends.

There were two salient features in the estimated capital efficiency. One was common to Light and HC groups, and the other revealed a difference between the two groups. The common feature was the general trend revealed by the estimates of $q1$ and $q2$ for the entire period under study. In the 1966–1973 period, the capital efficiency rose steeply; for the remainder of the 1970s, the rise stopped or decelerated; and in the 1980s the efficiency fell below the level observed in the 1970s. Estimates of $q3$, though available only for four years, tend to confirm this trend.

The rapid increase in the capital efficiency in the 1966–1973 period was, of course, the result of the returns to capital increasing faster than the capital stocks. The manufacturing sector value-added, including returns to capital, increased at an average annual rate in excess of 20 percent during the period. On the other hand, the average annual rates of growth for employment and capital accumulation were 8.8 percent and 11.6 percent, respectively, in the 1966–1970 period, accelerating to 9.6 and 21.7 in the 1970–1973 period. It appears that until the early 1970s, industry was in a transition, with employment of labor and capital stock at lower levels than those considered to be desirable by firms, and the factor inputs to growth accelerated to catch up with output growth. The rapid increase in capital efficiency in the 1966–1973 period appears to be a reflection of this stock adjustment process, which could not continue indefinitely.

The second feature that the estimates reveal is that capital efficiency was estimated to be higher in the Light group than in the HC group from

78 Industrialization and the State

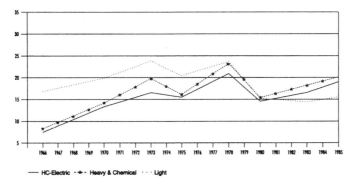

Figure 4-2. Capital Efficiency, q*1*

the mid-1960s until the end of the 1970s. This efficiency difference between the two groups is of interest because it tells us if the HCI policy improved resource allocation. According to the estimates of $q1$ and $q2$, the difference remained unchanged in the 1966–1973 period, but it seems to have narrowed for the rest of the 1970s, and in the 1980s the efficiency in the HC exceeded that in the Light.

Resource Misallocation

What do these estimation results imply regarding the effect of the HCI policy on resource allocation? Consider first the estimates for the second half of the 1960s. The capital efficiency was much higher in the Light group than in the HC group, and the efficiency was rising in both groups. This could not have much to do with the HCI policy, although industries belonging to the HC group were somewhat favored during the 1960s by the many promotional laws in place even then. The incentives to invest in heavy and chemical industries could not have been as strong in the second half of the 1960s and 1970s. As we have seen, the difference in the effective corporate tax rates between the HC and the Light groups began to widen after 1973. Similarly, direct government intervention in credit allocation in favor of the heavy and chemical industries did not begin in earnest until the mid-1970s. Thus, the HCI policy cannot explain the higher capital efficiency of the Light group compared to the HC.

The rising capital efficiency must have been a phenomenon in a transitory period. An industry's capital efficiency rises only if the value-added rises faster than capital input. The second half of the 1960s was likely such a period. The explosive export expansion that accelerated the

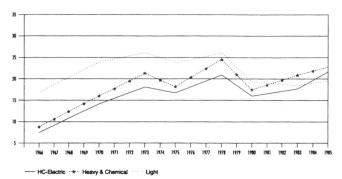

Figure 4-3. Capital Efficiency, q2

growth of Korea's manufacturing sector began in the early 1960s. By 1966, the first year when the capital efficiencies were estimated, only several years had passed. At the time firms must have been increasing employment of factors as fast as they could but still not fast enough to keep up with the rapid rise in value-added, causing the capital efficiency to rise.

Why, then, was the capital efficiency lower in the HC group than in the Light group while it was rising in both groups? The answer must have something to do with the fact that exports of the industries belonging to the Light group accounted for nearly all of Korea's export growth in the 1960s. Hence, the Light group's value-added and its capital efficiency must have begun to increase earlier than the HC group's. Thus, it is not surprising that the capital efficiency of the Light group was higher than that of the HC group while both were rapidly rising during the transitory period.

This transitory period would normally end as the capital efficiency of the Light group leveled off while that of the HC group kept rising so that the efficiency of the two groups became roughly equal. This indeed appears to have taken place (see Figures 4-2 and 4-3). Especially in Figure 4-2, by the late 1970s the capital efficiency of the HC group slightly exceeded that of the Light group.

Before accepting this conclusion, we note that it makes a considerable difference in the efficiency estimate whether electric machinery is counted as a part of the HC group. Excluding electric machinery from the HC group considerably lowers its efficiency, especially in 1978 (see Figures 4-2 and 4-3). Electric machinery was an industry favored by the HCI policy, and this is the reason that it is included in the HC group. However, its high capital efficiency in the 1970s may be as much a consequence of the changing pattern of Korea's comparative advantage

80 Industrialization and the State

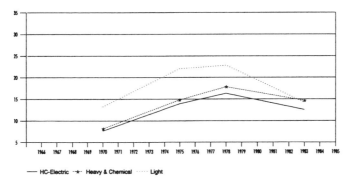

Figure 4-4.   Capital Efficiency, q3

dictated by the industry's production characteristics as the effects of the favors of the HCI policy. As noted earlier, electric machinery is more capital intensive than clothing but less so than textiles (see Table 4A-2). As a rising wage rate shifts the comparative advantage away from labor-intensive industries such as clothing to more capital-intensive ones, electric machinery is likely to become competitive at an earlier point in time than other HC industries. Electric machinery, with its value-added nearly as large as clothing's, was already one of the most rapidly growing industries in the 1960s and 1970s. If electric machinery is excluded from the HC group (see Figures 4-2 and 4-3), the conclusion that the efficiency gap between the HC and Light groups narrowed during the 1970s is not very convincing.

In addition, it should be recognized that protection raises the prices of an industry's output and inputs above the free-trade levels. Hence, the part of an industry's value-added due to domestic sales often increases in value and does not reflect the true value to the society of the factor services rendered in producing it. This artificial increase in value due to protection under the HCI policy has to be deflated before true capital efficiency can be obtained.

The third measure of capital efficiency, $q3$, deflates value-added by the effective rates of protection, as shown in equation 4.6. According to this measure, the margin by which the capital efficiency of the Light group was greater than that of the HC group was five percentage points in the 1970s. This difference widened to seven percentage points in 1975, falling back to five percentage points in 1978 and virtually disappearing by 1983.

Consider the implication of the above on the effects of the HCI policy under the assumptions that the production functions of the manufacturing industries are linearly homogeneous and that the labor compensation equals its marginal product. Under these assumptions, the estimated capital efficiency may be taken as the marginal product of capital, expressed in percentage terms, since under a linearly homogeneous production function, output is exhausted by the products of factor inputs multiplied by their marginal products.

The discussion of the capital efficiency estimates indicates that the marginal product of capital was lower in the heavy and chemical industries favored by the HCI policy than in the light industries during the 1970s. Static optimum allocation of a scarce resource requires equalization of its marginal product among different uses at a given point in time. The marginal product of capital in the two industry groups could have been brought more in line with each other had capital accumulation been slower in the favored HC industries and faster in the Light industries under diminishing returns—that is, if there had not been the HCI policy.

In a dynamic sense, optimum allocation does not require the returns to capital of different industries to be equalized every year. In an industry, the return may be low at first if subsequently it becomes large enough to make up for the earlier low levels. However, it has to justify the low capital efficiency estimates in the 1970s for the HC group on this ground. While a big surge in capital efficiency is required later in time for the justification, instead the group's efficiency declined in the 1980s (see Figures 4-2 through 4-4). The surge may take place in the 1990s or even later. But the later it happens, the greater the efficiency surge has to be for the early low levels to be justified. Given that the capital efficiency or real rate of return to manufacturing capital was as high as 20 percent, which may be regarded as the discount rate to use in obtaining the present value of future returns, it seems hard to justify the excessive investments in the HC group.

Export Competitiveness

The previous section estimated the capital efficiency of the manufacturing industries in an attempt to assess the effect of the HCI policy on resource allocation. The estimation results of high capital efficiency for the Light group and low efficiency for the HC group, and the efficiency gaps between the two groups failing to narrow during the 1970s, suggest that the policy resulted in misallocation of resources. This section considers another effect of the HCI policy: the effect on export competitiveness, determined by examining Korea's share in world exports.

Table 4-7 shows two measures of Korea's market share in world exports: a percentage share in the total world exports (labeled "world exports") and total world exports less OPEC exports (labeled "adjusted world exports"). In this measure, OPEC exports are excluded from the world total to control the effects of the oil price rise, which reduces a nonoil exporter's market share. However measured, Korea's share in world exports, which was rising rapidly, peaked in 1978 and fell over the following two years before rising again. This unmistakable drop in Korea's market share indicates that there must have been other reasons for the drop besides the oil price rise.

It is possible that the drop in Korea's market share was caused by a shift in world demand away from Korea's export products. In order to see if this was indeed the case, Korea's share in world exports is compared with the sum of the shares of six countries whose export products composition was most similar to Korea's in the late 1970s.[9] In contrast to Korea's share, the combined share of these competitors continued to rise in the latter half of the 1970s (Table 4-7). Hence, a shift in world demand could not have been the reason for the decline in Korea's share in world exports. The reason must have been a deterioration of competitiveness, and the cause lay inside Korea.

Thus, Korea's market shares were examined in the world exports of both the HC and Light product groups (Table 4-8). Although these groups cover only the major export goods of the industries, they accounted for 80 percent or more of all exports of manufactures, as shown in the last column of the table. Korea's shares in these world exports show very distinct trends.

Korea's share in the world exports of HC products continued to rise throughout the 1970s and in the 1980s. The only exception to this trend was the drop in 1975, the year of the world recession. On the other hand, regarding Korea's share in Light products, the trend in the first half of the 1970s was a relatively smooth and rapid expansion in market share, while toward the end of the 1970s the market share virtually stood still or declined.

There are reasons to believe that the impact of the HCI policy explains the contrasting experience of the two export products groups. As we saw, there was a considerable slowdown in capital accumulation in the Light group, which produced the traditional major export goods. According to Yoo, a 1 percent increase in production capacity had the effect of reducing the export price of heavy and chemical industry products by 0.37 percent and the export price of light industry products (very close to the definition of Light group used here) by a full percentage point.[10] The estimation, based on quarterly data from the first quarter of 1972 to the third quarter of 1982, suggests that the export products of

The Economic Development of Northeast Asia IV

Table 4-7. Market Shares in World Exports (in percentage)

	Korea's Share		Competitors' Share in World Exportsc
	World Exports[a]	Adjusted World Exports[b]	
1970	0.296	0.315	3.682
1971	0.337	0.364	3.970
1972	0.431	0.465	4.257
1973	0.615	0.669	4.327
1974	0.578	0.690	4.101
1975	0.639	0.745	3.935
1976	0.854	1.007	4.493
1977	0.965	1.129	4.435
1978	1.059	1.206	4.658
1979	0.988	1.153	4.898
1980	0.937	1.121	5.183
1981	1.157	1.367	5.474
1982	1.271	1.461	5.540
1983	1.462	1.637	5.776
1984	1.654	1.826	6.442
1985	1.697	1.854	6.625
1986	1.749	1.856	6.611

[a]Sum of exports from all countries.
[b]Sum of exports from all non-OPEC countries.
[c]Competitors are Hong Kong, Israel, Portugal, Spain, Taiwan, and Yugoslavia.
Sources: International Monetary Fund, *International Financial Statistics* (various issues); United Nations, *Yearbook of International Trade Statistics* (various issues).

light industries could have been more competitive had there been more fixed investment in the sector.

The difference in the behavior of the two groups of export products may also be related to the overvaluation of the won in the latter half of the 1970s. The exchange rate was kept constant at 484 won/US$ from 1974 to 1979, although the domestic inflation rate exceeded that of Korea's trading partners, resulting in overvaluation of the won. This period almost exactly overlaps with the period when Korea's share in world exports stopped expanding or even declined for the light industries. However, in order to explain the contrasting experience between the two groups regarding the market share with the fixed exchange rate, one has to believe that the overvaluation of the won does not affect the competitiveness of the HC products, while having a damaging effect on the competitiveness of the Light products. The more probable explanation would be that the effect of the won overvaluation reinforced the HCI policy on the competitiveness of the light industries' export products and, ultimately, of total exports in the late 1970s. Furthermore, a main reason that the fixed exchange rate was maintained during the HCI regime was to lighten, in local currency terms, the repayment burden of foreign debt that financed the policy-favored investments in the HC industries. In this

84 Industrialization and the State

Table 4-8. Korea's Market Shares in World Exports of HC and Light Products
(in percentage)

	HC Products[a]	Light Products[b]	Share of Manufactured Exports Accounted For
1968	0.03	1.35	83.18
1969	0.07	1.50	81.66
1970	0.07	1.83	87.24
1971	0.09	2.13	88.05
1972	0.20	2.45	87.83
1973	0.33	3.52	84.69
1974	0.42	3.44	84.46
1975	0.33	4.13	84.23
1976	0.48	5.51	84.38
1977	0.54	5.56	80.32
1978	0.70	5.92	83.93
1979	0.71	5.52	82.72
1980	0.80	5.27	82.67
1981	1.04	6.40	82.19
1982	1.25	6.10	83.36
1983	1.60	6.23	85.00

[a]Includes chemical elements and compounds (SITC 51); petroleum products (SITC 332); iron and steel (SITC 67); nonferrous metals (SITC 68); nonelectrical machinery (SITC 71); electrical machinery (SITC 72); and transport equipment (SITC 73).
[b]Includes rubber products (SITC 62); plywood (SITC 631); textiles (SITC 65); travel goods (SITC 83); clothing (SITC 84); footwear (SITC 85); and miscellaneous manufactures (SITC 89).
Sources: UN, *Yearbook of International Trade Statistics* (various issues), and authors' calculations.

sense the exchange rate policy was part of the HCI policy, and the effects on export performance should be regarded as part of the cost of that policy.

The 1979 Stabilization Program and the Policies in the 1980s

Thus far, our attention has focused on the HCI policy and its influence on the manufacturing sector. This section considers the overall performance of the economy and the background of the government decision in the spring of 1979 to discontinue the HCI policy. It also briefly discusses the direction of new industrial policy that emerged in the 1980s.

Data on the economy's performance over the period 1971 through the mid-1980s are presented in Table 4-9. Inflation, which had subsided after the first oil crisis, reemerged toward the end of the 1970s. The nominal wage, which had risen at an approximate annual rate of 30 percent from the mid-1970s, marginally decelerated in 1979. In foreign trade, real export growth sharply decelerated in 1977 and declined absolutely in 1979. Economic growth slackened, resulting in negative 4.8 percent growth in 1980.

The negative growth is often attributed to several unfavorable external developments. Above all, the second oil crisis in 1979, which adversely affected the world economy and international trade, is cited as a major reason. Others allude to the political uncertainty following the assassination of President Park in late 1979. In 1980, the unusually cool weather during the summer severely reduced the agricultural output in the fall. Although all of these factors influenced economic developments, they could not have been responsible for the worsening economic performances in the preceding years, 1978 and 1979, or for the rapid slowdown in real export growth that began as early as 1977.

In the late 1970s, it became apparent that the accumulated effects of the industrial policy were beginning to overwhelm the growth momentum generated and sustained since the early 1960s. Fortunately, the seriousness of the situation was recognized, and substantial changes began to be introduced in economic policy during the spring of 1979. In April 1979, the government announced the Comprehensive Stabilization Program, which attempted to redress the excesses of the HCI policy of the 1970s. The program was based on the recognition that the industrial policies had caused havoc in all aspects of the country's economic life: management of macroeconomic policies; management of small- and large-scale firms, in both the favored sectors and other industries; competitiveness in the export markets; and credit standing in the international financial market. Rather than set the general framework for industrial development, macroeconomic policies had become a hostage held by the industrial policies.

The stabilization program cited the following problems as being directly related to the excessive investment in the favored heavy and chemical industries: the increase in investment that outpaced the increase in the supply of skilled labor or the capacity to absorb the related technology, development of bottlenecks in the supply of light industry products, and low rates of capacity utilization. The extent of the capacity utilization problem is easily seen in Table 4-10, which was included in the announcement of the Comprehensive Stabilization Program. The major contents of the program included:

- Restrictive budget management with expenditure cuts and deferral of public investment projects.
- Restrictive monetary policy with particular attention given to improving the operation of preferential policy loans and interest rates.
- Plans to adjust investments in the heavy and chemical industries.
- Measures to facilitate the supply and stabilize the price of daily necessities.

86 Industrialization and the State

Table 4-9. Selected Economic Indicators, 1971–1986 (in percentage change)

Year	Gross National Product	Wholesale Price Index	Consumer Price Index	Wages	Real Exports	Trade Balance ($ millions)
1971	9.1	8.6	13.5	16.2	29.45	– 1,045.9
1972	5.3	13.8	11.7	13.9	50.22	– 573.9
1973	14.0	6.9	3.1	18.0	57.20	– 566.0
1974	8.5	42.1	24.3	35.3	9.26	– 1,936.8
1975	6.8	26.5	25.3	27.0	22.76	– 1,671.4
1976	13.4	12.2	15.3	34.7	35.79	– 590.5
1977	10.7	9.0	10.1	33.8	19.06	– 476.6
1978	11.0	11.6	14.1	34.3	14.36	– 1,780.8
1979	7.0	18.8	18.3	28.6	–0.96	– 4,384.1
1980	4.8	38.9	28.7	22.7	11.39	– 4,384.1
1981	6.6	20.4	21.3	20.1	17.65	– 3,628.3
1982	5.4	4.7	7.2	14.7	6.43	– 2,594.4
1983	11.9	0.2	3.4	12.2	16.29	– 1,763.5
1984	8.4	0.7	2.3	8.1	15.66	– 1,035.9
1985	5.4	0.9	2.5	9.9	7.56	– 19.4
1986	11.7	1.5	2.8	9.2	12.98	+4,205.9

Source: Economic Planning Board, *Major Statistics of the Korean Economy, 1987* (Seoul: Economic Planning Board, 1987).

• Measures to prevent real estate speculation.
• Measures to support low-income groups.

The monetary and fiscal policies envisaged in the program were being implemented when, later in the year, the government switched to a reflationary policy package in response to the second oil crisis and the recession abroad. Nevertheless, the program was a turning point that set the economic policy off in a new direction, expressed at that time as the pursuit of a private-sector led economy as opposed to a government-led economy. The basic tenet that became more firmly established over the following years consisted of attaining price stability, establishing an unbiased incentive structure, and promoting competition within the domestic market and from abroad. The emphasis shifted from the promotion of particular industries to overall economic efficiency and from the intervention at the industry and firm level to greater reliance on the market.

Conservative management of fiscal and monetary policies succeeded in reducing the double-digit inflation rate to under 3 or 4 percent a year by 1983 (Table 4-9). The effort to bring inflation under control was helped by the decline in international crude oil prices and other raw materials, for which Korea heavily depended on imports. As inflation declined, the government reduced the subsidy elements in the preferential policy loans

Table 4-10. Capacity Utilization Rates of Selected Industries (in percentage)

Industry	1978	1979
Industrial machinery	62	60
Shipbuilding	28	29
Color television	54	26

Source: Economic Planning Board, *Comprehensive Stabilization Program* (April 1979).

by lowering the interest rates on nonpreferential policy loans faster than the rates on policy loans, with the result that the differential between the two types of loans largely disappeared in the early 1980s. Government-owned stocks of commercial banks were sold to the public as a measure to increase the banks' independence of government influence.

In order to counterbalance the increased concentration of economic power that had occurred under the HCI policy, the Anti-Monopoly and Fair Trade Act was enacted toward the end of 1980, and a Fair Trade Commission was created. The act also reduced the number of products whose prices had been under government control on the grounds that they were monopolistic or oligopolistic items. Establishment of small- and medium-sized firms was encouraged, and various support measures for them were devised in recognition of the reality that they could not compete with the giant conglomerates on an equal footing. Over the years there had been increasing dissatisfaction with the plethora of special laws purported to promote particular industries. These laws were either abolished altogether or replaced in 1986 by the Industrial Development Law, which was based on the principle that policy supports to specific industries should be abandoned in favor of functional supports.

Import liberalization measures were extended as an essential remedy against inflation and the distorted incentive structure. The government removed an increasing number of importables from the negative list (those that needed prior government approval to be imported) despite broad public opposition. The import liberalization ratio rose even during the late 1970s and early 1980s when the balance of payments was in severe deficit.

Conclusion: An Assessment of the Role of the Korean Government

Until recently the Korean government's intervention in the economy had been extensive, and at times pervasive. Although the two decades of the 1960s and the 1970s did not differ much in terms of the extent of government intervention, the content of the economic policies that were followed differed significantly. In the 1960s, the primary goal of nearly all economic policies was export expansion; in the 1970s, changes in the international economic and noneconomic scenes led the government to build a more advanced industrial structure, similar to those found in the advanced industrial countries. To pursue that goal, the government became directly and extensively involved in resource allocation at the sectoral, industry, and even firm levels. Thus, the decades of the 1960s and 1970s are fairly distinct in the content of government policies, while the 1980s are distinct from the two previous decades in that government intervention declined substantially.

The economic policies in the 1960s worked much better than the policies of the 1970s in terms of export development. Although protection of domestic industries was substantial, the main policy emphasis in the 1960s was to encourage the private sector's exports through a variety of incentives. This approach seems to have had two advantages over the industrial policy in the 1970s. First, the policy was results oriented. Under the policy in the 1960s, it was the private sector that made the efforts to achieve increased exports. In contrast, the policy in the 1970s was pro-cess oriented, which in no way abandoned the goal of export expansion but attempted to achieve the goal by promoting certain industries.[11] Under this approach, the government was deeply involved in picking the "right" industries and supplying them with the needed investment funds and complementary factors at the "right" price, time, and place. In effect, it was the government that tried to achieve the results.

The second advantage the export promotion policy of the 1960s had over the industrial policy in the 1970s is related to the effects the policy had on the incentive structure. In the 1960s, the government implemented export promotion policies on top of the protective measures of domestic production in the 1950s. The net effect was that numerous export incentives offset the bias against exports that had been engendered by the protection of domestic industries. One study concludes, after quantification of the effects of various policy measures at the time, that the incentives for firms to sell their products in the domestic market or to export were almost equal in the late 1960s.[12]

If this was, in fact, the case, the incentive system could not have remained neutral under the industrial policy of the 1970s, which had a strong import-substitution focus, with a bias in favor of domestic sales. Not surprisingly, exports expanded faster, and the economy performed better in the 1960s when the private sector faced a neutral incentive system than in the 1970s when the government attempted to substitute itself for the private sector and created a bias for domestic sales.

It is possible to disagree with this assessment of the effect of government intervention and call attention to the rapid export expansion and economic growth in the 1980s, arguing that the industrial policy in the 1970s laid the ground for the strong economic performance in the late 1980s. This argument sounds plausible in that the increases in Korea's exports in the 1980s were most visibly seen in such products as various kinds of consumer electronics, semiconductors, other computer-related products, telecommunications equipment, and passenger cars. These are the products of "heavy" industries that were promoted under the HCI policies. Should the economic policies of the 1970s, no matter how wrong they may appear now, be credited with the success of the 1980s? Is the rapid economic growth of the 1980s proof of the desirability of an industrial targeting policy? Before reaching any conclusion, it is necessary to consider the reasons for the rapid export expansion and economic growth and ask some counterfactual questions.

First, the increase in Korean exports was largely due to circumstances that could not have been anticipated in the 1970s when the industrial targeting policy was formulated or implemented. Most of the rapid increase in Korean exports in the 1980s was due to exports to the United States. From 1980 to 1987, Korean exports increased by $30 billion. Of this increment, nearly half went to the United States. The big increase in Korean exports to the United States was a part of the surge in U.S. imports, which resulted primarily from the failure of the U.S. government to close its fiscal deficit. Korean exports also benefited from the depreciation of the real effective exchange rate, due to an 8 percent depreciation of the won/dollar exchange rate in 1985 and the steep appreciation of the Japanese yen and German mark since that time.

Second, much of the rise in Korean exports was due to U.S. restrictions on imports from Japan, which created a market for Korean products at the cost of imports from Japan. These developments were especially favorable to the exports by the industries targeted by the industrial policy of the 1970s. These exogenous external developments contributed to the rapid increase in Korean exports to the United States and the rest of the world and were, of course, unforeseen by the policymakers who set forth the industrial development agenda of the 1970s.

One could argue that the industrial policies should get some credit, although their economic benefit may have been for unanticipated reasons. Two counterfactual questions seem important in this regard. First, what would have been the result if the government had persisted in its policy of promoting certain industries at the expense of others? There seems to be little doubt that the state of the economy would have worsened if the Comprehensive Stabilization Program of the 1979 had not corrected economic policy. This was exactly the reason that the same government that vigorously pursued the industrial targeting policy reversed its policy with the announcement of the program. If the industrial policy had been continued, the economy would have been seriously damaged, at least over the short term, and could not have benefited from the external developments that contributed so much to the export expansion in the 1980s. It is easier to create a heavy manufacturing capacity than it is to ensure that such capacity can compete internationally.

The second counterfactual question to ask is, What would have happened if the government had not promoted the heavy and chemical industries during the 1970s? If the current economic conditions in the 1980s are better than a plausible answer to the counterfactual question, then one could argue that government policy had desirable effects even though the effects were due to unanticipated reasons. To answer this question directly in a satisfactory fashion is very difficult. One possible solution is to look at the performance of Taiwan, an economy that was similarly situated in the mid-1970s but did not adopt the same kind of industrial policy. While any such comparison is fraught with statistical difficulties, it is clear that neither Taiwan's exports nor its income growth suffered as a result of following a different development strategy. To the contrary, Taiwan's exports expanded faster than Korea's. Although the composition of Taiwan's exports remains heavily concentrated on labor-intensive exports, Korea's exports have moved strongly to capital-intensive products.[13] The difference in the change in the commodity structure reflects the difference in the development strategy. Unlike Korea, Taiwan did not engage in a deliberate effort to change the structure of its industrial sector. Korea, like Taiwan and other newly industrialized economies, did not need an HCI policy to take advantage of the expanding export opportunities that had developed in the United States and other parts of the world. Only the product composition of Korean exports would have been different without the policy.

Finally, were the structural changes observed in Korea over the 1970s in any sense unusual, or were they the result of the transformation expected as income per capita rises? Comparing the changes in both industrial structure and export composition for six rapidly growing countries—Brazil,

Korea, Malaysia, Mexico, Philippines, Taiwan, and Thailand—provides little statistical evidence that the structural transformation in Korea was significantly different from those observed in other rapidly developing countries, once changes in per capita income are taken into account.[14] Although the HCI policies accelerated the changes in industrial structure and export composition and moved the economy away from labor-intensive production and exports, they did not dramatically alter the process of development.

The government's actual role in the experience of Korean economic growth was very different from the popular perception, inside and outside Korea, that the phenomenal increase in its exports and economic growth was due to industrial targeting. The government was not successful in the area of industrial policies, through which it attempted to create an advanced industrial structure in a short time period. When the economy performed well under extensive government intervention, as in the 1960s, the net effect of intervention was a neutral incentive system. The case in support of the Korean government's role in economic development seems stronger when its policies were not actively interventionist, such as policies that controlled inflation through conservative management of fiscal and monetary policies, maintained the trade regime that provided Korean exporters with access to foreign intermediate goods at international prices, liberalized imports, or corrected the overvaluation of the exchange rate. In many ways, the government's greatest contribution was its willingness to reconsider policies once they were found not to work. The ultimate criterion of policy decisions was economic performance, and the economic policy flexibly adapted to changing domestic and international circumstances. Ironically, the flexibility in economic policy was a product of an authoritarian government. Having come into power with questionable legitimacy, the Park Chung Hee and Chun Doo Hwan governments relied heavily on the performance of the economy to build and maintain their legitimacy, and the power elite left economic decision making largely in the hands of the technocrats. In general, Korean technocrats and bureaucrats have not had strong vested interests in the welfare of certain social classes, certain sectors, or certain industries of the economy. Their policy choices were more generally guided by a concern for overall economic performance. This is not to say that the political system or the bureaucracy was immune to the influence of interest groups or was corruption free. However, decisions on the details constituting the overall policy framework, especially those not materially affecting general economic performance, were more likely to have been influenced by pressures from interest groups.

92 Industrialization and the State

Appendix 4A: Description of the Data

Value-Added

Value-added for the manufacturing industries is estimated as part of the national income estimates by the Bank of Korea. It was available in 1980 won at the three-digit Korean Standard Industrial Classification (KSIC) level.

Labor and Labor Share

The numbers of laborers employed in the manufacturing industries were obtained from employment tables, part of the input-output tables estimated by the Bank of Korea. The employment tables distinguish two groups of laborers: paid employees and unpaid workers, which includes the self-employed and family members. The number of laborers used in this study is the simple sum of the two groups.

Capital Stock

Pyo's estimates of capital stocks are used.[15] Included in these estimates are buildings and structures, machinery and equipment, and transportation equipment. Employing the polynomial-benchmark method, Pyo made use of investment data from two national wealth surveys for the years 1968 and 1977: the census and annual surveys of the mining and manufacturing sectors. He made two series of capital stock estimates: gross and net. The estimates were available at the three-digit KSIC level.

This study uses Pyo's estimates of gross capital stock in 1980 constant prices. Some adjustments on the estimates were made before using them. In a few instances, Pyo estimated the combined capital stock of two three-digit KSIC industries.[16] In these instances, the estimated capital stocks were split into two, one for each component industry, in the following way. First, Pyo's capital stock for 1973 was split into two by referring to the component industries' book values of capital stocks reported in the mining and manufacturing census for the same year. The splitting was done according to the component industry's share in the sum of the book values of the capital stocks. In the second step, annual increments in Pyo's capital stock were again split into two. This time, an increment was split according to the component industry's share in the sum of the acquisition of new capital stocks. In the last step, to obtain a new time series of capital stock for a component industry, the split increment of capital stock was added to the split capital stock for the years after 1973 or was subtracted from it for the earlier years.

Industry Grouping

The manufacturing sector consists of twenty-seven three-digit KSIC industries. At this level of aggregation KSIC is identical to the International
Standard Industrial Classification (ISIC). Two industries—plastic products
(KSIC 385) and industries not elsewhere classified (KSIC 356)—are omitted
from the analysis for lack of data. These two activities accounted for
about 1.5 percent of total manufacturing value-added in 1970 and less
than 3 percent in 1985. In all the analysis the phrase "manufacturing total"
is to be taken as excluding these two industries.

The analysis divides manufacturing into two groups: those that were
favored by the HCI policy and those that were not. The favored group
contains eight three-digit KSIC industries:

Industrial chemical (KSIC 351)
Oil refining (KSIC 353)
Iron and steel (KSIC 371)
Nonferrous metals (KSIC 372)
Metal products (KSIC 381)
Nonelectrical machinery (KSIC 382)
Electrical machinery (KSIC 383)
Transport equipment (KSIC 384)

The other seventeen industries are:

Food products (KSIC 311 and 312)
Tobacco (KSIC 314)
Textiles (KSIC 321)
Clothing (KSIC 322)
Leather and fur products (KSIC 323)
Footwear (KSIC 324)
Wood products (KSIC 331)
Furniture (KSIC 332)
Paper (KSIC 341)
Printing and publishing (KSIC 342)
Other chemicals (KSIC 352)
Petroleum and coal products (KSIC 354)
Rubber products (KSIC 355)
Pottery, china, and earthenware (KSIC 361)
Other nonmetallic mineral products (KSIC 369)
Other manufactures (KSIC 390)

94 Industrialization and the State

In order to facilitate the analysis, the industries favored by the HCI policy, excluding oil refining, are aggregated and labeled the heavy and chemical industry group or (HC group). Oil refining was excluded because developments in this sector were strongly affected by the oil crisis in the late 1970s. In addition, because the industry is dominated by a few firms, it is more than likely that its value-added was exaggerated by monopoly profits. The seventeen industries not favored by the HCI policy were aggregated into the light industry group (Light group). This grouping excluded the tobacco sector, which was a government monopoly until March 1986 and a monopolistic public enterprise since then. The relevant data at the individual industry levels are shown in the following tables.

Table 4A-1. Import Liberalization Ratios by Manufacturing Industries
(in percentage)

Industry	1966	1970	1976	1980	1983	1985
1. Food	14.5	13.2	22.4	37.5	34.1	55.9
2. Beverages	0.0	0.0	0.0	0.0	13.0	19.6
3. Tobacco	0.0	0.0	0.0	0.0	9.1	9.1
4. Textiles	2.3	23.7	25.2	74.7	75.4	86.9
5. Clothing	0.0	16.7	16.7	70.6	44.8	95.7
6. Footwear	12.9	25.8	35.5	70.8	74.6	93.5
7. Wood	7.7	53.8	64.1	93.1	96.2	100.0
8. Furniture	0.0	14.3	14.3	0.0	60.5	95.6
9. Paper	2.9	40.0	20.0	63.2	88.5	88.0
10. Printing	0.0	27.3	54.5	90.9	100.0	100.0
11. Chemicals[a]	18.9	38.5	35.0	25.7	46.6	66.6
12. Other chemicals	8.3	43.3	51.7	54.9	59.6	66.4
13. Oil refining[a]	12.5	6.3	12.5	12.5	51.2	53.5
14. Petroleum products	27.3	100.0	100.0	100.0	100.0	100.0
15. Rubber	0.0	35.3	52.9	88.2	92.7	92.9
16. Nonmetallic minerals	5.7	71.4	65.7	77.3	80.1	83.6
17. Iron and steel[a]	4.9	64.6	67.1	84.2	93.3	95.6
18. Nonferrous metals[a]	4.9	64.6	67.1	84.2	93.3	95.6
19. Fabricated metals[a]	3.3	33.3	33.3	70.4	91.5	94.6
20. Nonelectrical machinery[a]	14.1	56.3	33.8	47.6	64.4	76.5
21. Electrical machinery[a]	0.0	23.5	17.6	31.0	46.9	64.5
22. Transport equipment[a]	0.0	65.0	13.8	44.4	58.8	69.2
23. Miscellaneous manufacturing	8.1	41.7	40.1	56.6	64.1	77.1

[a]Industries favored under the HCI policy regime.

Source: Kwang Suk Kim, *The Economic Effects of Import Liberalization and Industrial Adjustment Policy* (Seoul: Korea Development Institute, 1988), appendix table 1, reproduced with permission.

96 Industrialization and the State

Table 4A-2. Capital Intensity (in million 1980 won/worker)

	1966	1970	1973	1975	1978	1980	1983	1985
Light industries								
Food	2.6	2.6	3.7	4.4	5.6	6.4	7.8	9.8
Beverages	7.9	5.8	6.9	7.3	8.2	12.5	12.5	19.3
Tobacco	15.3	13.8	14.1	13.9	11.0	29.7	42.5	49.1
Textiles	5.2	4.5	8.2	5.5	6.1	8.6	10.1	11.2
Clothing	0.3	0.5	0.6	0.7	1.1	1.4	1.9	2.0
Footwear, leather	1.2	1.4	2.3	1.7	3.3	4.1	5.0	6.9
Wood	8.1	5.5	4.9	6.7	5.9	9.2	11.5	11.7
Furniture	0.8	2.8	2.8	2.2	2.1	2.9	3.7	4.7
Pulp, paper	7.9	6.6	6.9	6.9	7.9	9.7	11.5	13.8
Printing	4.9	5.1	6.4	8.4	10.7	12.2	11.5	12.9
Other chemicals	2.2	2.8	2.7	3.0	3.7	4.5	5.0	6.0
Petroleum and coal products	2.1	3.8	5.3	6.0	6.1	7.5	9.2	11.8
Rubber products	2.6	3.9	4.9	5.1	5.8	6.3	6.5	6.0
Nonmetallic minerals	4.1	9.0	10.2	11.5	13.6	16.6	18.8	22.3
Other manufactures	1.1	1.0	1.5	4.2	3.9	5.2	6.3	7.2
Heavy and chemical industries								
Industrial chemicals	47.9	31.4	29.2	35.4	36.0	42.9	65.2	71.7
Oil refining	50.9	51.1	112.9	118.2	124.3	137.4	109.7	128.5
Iron and steel	5.3	6.8	14.8	22.8	34.6	37.6	37.7	38.0
Nonferrous metals	4.2	4.3	8.7	12.6	12.2	14.0	12.6	12.8
Fabricated metals	2.0	3.0	4.4	5.9	9.1	10.7	9.5	11.2
Nonelectrical machinery	3.0	4.9	6.6	7.9	13.2	14.7	14.3	14.2
Electrical machinery	2.3	2.3	2.4	4.8	4.5	5.5	6.7	9.5
Transport equipment	4.5	5.2	7.5	7.8	12.0	19.8	18.3	20.1

Table 4A-3. Changes in Capital Intensity (average annual percentage change)

	1966–1970	1970–1973	1973–1975	1975–1978	1978–1980	1980–1983	1983–1985	1970–1978	1978–1985
Light industries									
Food	0.2	12.1	9.2	8.7	6.2	7.0	10.3	10.1	7.7
Beverages	-7.4	6.3	2.3	4.0	23.6	0.0	24.1	4.4	13.0
Tobacco	-2.6	0.8	-1.0	-7.4	64.2	12.7	7.5	-2.8	23.8
Textiles	-3.4	21.8	-17.8	3.2	19.1	5.5	5.1	3.7	9.1
Clothing	18.0	7.7	8.6	12.8	14.1	11.6	1.8	9.8	9.4
Footwear/leather	3.7	18.6	-13.5	23.4	12.6	6.6	17.1	11.2	11.2
Wood	-9.2	-3.5	16.9	-4.4	25.2	7.9	0.8	0.9	10.4
Furniture	37.2	-0.4	-10.2	-2.0	16.9	8.6	12.8	-3.5	12.1
Pulp, paper	-4.1	1.4	-0.	4.5	10.6	6.0	9.3	2.2	8.2
Printing	0.7	8.1	14.2	8.6	6.3	-1.8	5.8	9.8	2.6
Other chemicals	7.2	-1.5	5.0	7.0	10.4	3.8	9.5	3.2	7.3
Petroleum and coal products	15.8	12.2	5.7	0.9	10.9	6.7	13.4	6.2	9.8
Rubber products	10.2	7.6	2.5	4.2	4.7	0.6	-3.4	5.0	0.6
Nonmetallic minerals	21.9	4.3	5.9	5.8	10.7	4.1	9.1	5.3	7.3
Other manufactures	-2.8	15.4	66.5	-2.6	15.2	6.3	7.5	18.7	9.1
Heavy and chemical industries									
Industrial chemicals	-9.8	-2.4	10.1	0.6	9.2	14.9	4.9	1.7	10.3
Oil refining	0.1	30.3	2.4	1.7	5.1	-7.3	8.3	11.8	0.5
Iron and steel	6.1	30.0	23.8	15.0	4.2	0.1	0.4	22.6	1.4
Nonferrous metals	0.9	26.3	20.0	-1.0	7.0	-3.4	0.7	13.8	0.7
Fabricated metals	9.7	14.5	15.5	15.2	8.6	-3.7	8.4	15.0	3.1
Nonelectrical machinery	12.8	10.7	9.3	18.4	5.4	-0.7	-0.3	13.2	1.1
Electrical machinery	-0.3	1.5	41.2	-2.1	10.0	7.1	19.0	8.8	11.2
Transport equipment	3.4	13.2	.3	15.3	28.5	-2.6	4.8	11.2	7.7

98 Industrialization and the State

Table 4A-4. Capital Efficiency (*q*1) (in percentage)

	1966	1970	1973	1975	1978	1980	1983	1985
Light industries								
Food	26.9	34.3	26.1	22.1	22.2	14.5	13.9	15.3
Beverages	18.4	31.	44.5	42.1	41.0	19.8	17.8	19.1
Tobacco	13.7	39.2	55.5	35.5	33.1	14.9	8.2	5.6
Textiles	7.5	9.3	14.0	11.8	17.1	11.5	10.8	11.7
Clothing	68.5	65.4	119.2	80.7	43.7	22.1	12.3	24.4
Footwear, leather	41.1	44.5	68.7	74.4	62.0	27.3	9.1	19.4
Wood	7.7	8.1	13.1	10.3	17.2	-2.8	7.4	6.7
Furniture	6.2	21.7	- 2.3	21.1	28.1	-1.7	21.0	14.4
Pulp, paper	11.1	14.0	19.5	17.9	21.8	15.3	16.2	15.3
Printing	10.9	11.0	9.0	11.3	10.3	9.0	8.8	7.8
Other chemicals	39.9	36.7	77.9	69.0	78.3	57.7	54.5	52.3
Petroleum, coal products	74.4	56.6	62.3	51.1	53.5	65.1	44.6	44.3
Rubber products	5.7	12.1	17.4	14.7	19.6	18.2	12.9	15.4
Nonmetallic minerals	17.5	16.0	22.8	18.8	20.0	14.6	15.7	15.5
Other manufactures	17.7	44.7	31.3	22.7	20.4	12.2	10.4	8.6
Heavy and chemical industries								
Industrial chemicals	2.5	12.6	18.7	15.9	30.1	26.3	27.3	27.6
Oil refining	32.1	41.3	28.5	23.2	48.3	28.6	30.1	32.6
Iron and steel	16.6	13.3	18.5	13.2	14.8	15.8	16.6	19.4
Nonferrous metals	20.9	21.5	21.0	16.4	25.9	13.6	31.2	38.7
Fabricated metals	14.6	11.3	15.9	15.2	21.0	8.9	10.6	13.8
Nonelectrical machinery	16.1	11.7	15.5	23.0	26.9	14.0	14.6	18.2
Electrical machinery	26.5	26.4	50.8	21.1	38.8	22.7	29.4	25.2
Transport equipment	11.3	16.2	10.3	13.7	15.7	6.3	10.8	13.6
Industry groups								
All manufacturing	14.9	20.0	23.7	19.7	24.5	15.8	16.6	18.1
Heavy and chemical	8.5	14.3	19.8	16.3	23.4	15.7	18.4	20.2
Light	16.9	19.9	23.8	20.7	23.5	15.2	14.5	15.6
Clothing and footwear	60.2	60.9	105.7	78.7	50.6	24.1	11.0	22.4
HC-Electric machinery	7.6	13.4	16.5	15.4	20.9	14.5	16.5	19.0

Note: Assumption: No indirect taxes borne by capital.

Table 4A-5. Capital Efficiency ($q2$) (in percentage)

	1966	1970	1973	1975	1978	1980	1983	1985
Light industries								
Food	30.0	39.5	29.1	26.0	24.5	21.2	20.3	21.4
Beverages	33.9	62.4	77.1	84.0	86.2	62.1	63.0	63.9
Tobacco	34.5	82.3	93.4	86.5	96.4	80.6	70.2	69.3
Textiles	8.7	10.9	14.7	13.4	17.4	12.4	11.7	12.5
Clothing	69.4	66.7	121.1	84.6	43.7	28.5	19.4	29.9
Footwear, leather	42.2	48.7	72.8	77.3	62.0	29.8	10.3	21.0
Wood	8.2	8.9	13.8	11.8	17.2	−1.1	9.0	7.6
Furniture	6.9	26.3	4.5	24.7	32.5	6.0	29.8	19.6
Pulp, paper	11.7	15.4	20.5	19.9	22.0	16.8	18.0	16.5
Printing	11.2	11.2	9.2	11.7	10.5	9.9	9.5	8.4
Other chemicals	43.4	42.4	80.4	74.0	81.3	63.3	61.1	57.8
Petroleum, coal products	76.5	59.8	63.5	55.5	54.6	65.5	45.4	45.1
Rubber products	16.1	12.5	17.9	15.9	19.7	19.6	14.6	16.6
Nonmetallic minerals	18.5	17.2	23.8	20.2	20.2	15.7	16.9	16.1
Other manufactures	18.4	46.1	32.3	24.3	20.8	13.8	11.9	9.8
Heavy and chemical industries								
Industrial chemicals	2.6	12.8	19.4	17.5	30.1	28.5	30.0	29.4
Oil refining	49.5	82.9	46.3	40.9	68.6	56.4	44.2	46.3
Iron and steel	17.1	13.8	18.9	14.5	15.0	16.3	17.1	19.7
Nonferrous metals	22.4	23.5	22.7	17.8	26.1	14.6	32.9	39.6
Fabricated metals	15.1	12.9	16.1	24.2	27.2	15.3	16.0	20.0
Nonelectrical machinery	28.1	32.8	57.2	27.5	47.3	28.6	36.5	29.7
Electrical machinery	28.1	32.8	57.2	27.5	47.3	28.6	36.5	29.7
Transport equipment	12.1	20.9	12.8	16.0	17.2	8.6	13.0	16.7
Industry groups								
All manufacturing	18.3	26.1	27.9	24.6	28.1	20.9	21.3	22.4
Heavy and chemical	8.9	16.0	21.2	18.7	24.9	17.7	20.7	22.3
Light	19.7	23.9	26.4	24.4	25.9	19.2	18.6	19.4
Clothing and footwear	61.2	62.8	108.2	82.3	50.6	29.0	15.8	26.4
HC-Electric machinery	7.9	14.7	17.5	17.0	21.3	15.9	18.1	20.7

Note: Assumption: One-half of indirect taxes borne by capital.

100 Industrialization and the State

Table 4A-6. Capital Efficiency (*q3*) (in percentage)

	1970	1975	1978	1983
Light industries				
Food	13.2	13.1	30.3	20.3
Beverages	36.5	52.8	39.1	18.3
Tobacco	41.2	51.5	19.1	5.5
Textiles	7.6	13.3	17.1	10.5
Clothing	63.6	124.7	23.8	10.5
Footwear, leather	34.1	60.3	63.9	9.4
Wood	4.3	7.8	18.0	6.9
Furniture	9.3	14.8	23.3	22.8
Pulp, paper	12.6	18.2	16.3	13.4
Printing	14.9	16.2	10.7	9.9
Other chemicals	12.7	43.0	54.2	40.7
Petroleum, coal products	29.5	149.3	24.6	44.7
Rubber products	6.6	13.7	20.6	12.8
Nonmetallic minerals	11.6	19.7	18.0	12.7
Other manufactures	14.0	18.3	20.0	10.7
Heavy and chemical industries				
Industrial chemicals	10.6	20.5	22.6	17.9
Oil refining	81.7	– 1.4	38.9	6.0
Iron and steel	5.0	4.8	12.3	13.5
Nonferrous metals	16.7	10.3	20.4	26.0
Fabricated metals	6.6	18.0	19.6	10.6
Nonelectrical machinery	6.4	26.5	19.5	12.1
Electrical machinery	12.4	18.3	25.9	24.0
Transport equipment	4.9	10.8	13.4	10.2
Industry groups				
All manufacturing	15.7	19.1	21.3	14.1
Heavy and chemical	8.3	14.9	17.9	14.8
Light	13.3	22.0	22.9	14.3
Clothing and footwear	57.2	104.3	45.3	10.1
HC-Electric machinery	8.0	14.2	16.6	13.3

Note: Assumption: Based on international price of value-added.

Table 4A-7. Export Shares in Gross Output (*sx*) (in percentage)

	1966	1970	1973	1975	1978	1980	1983	1985
Light industries								
Food	7.3	5.8	8.6	13.3	8.3	4.1	3.2	3.4
Beverages	1.7	0.8	3.4	3.7	2.4	0.5	1.0	1.9
Tobacco	10.2	0.2	0.4	0.2	0.1	0.7	2.7	2.0
Textiles	12.9	24.9	37.0	34.0	33.4	31.5	35.9	33.0
Clothing	18.5	31.3	66.4	48.5	61.6	55.8	70.4	82.4
Footwear, leather	4.6	6.6	26.3	44.6	52.8	53.0	58.3	33.1
Wood	35.7	39.4	67.4	42.6	36.5	33.9	13.4	9.5
Furniture	3.6	11.9	52.9	23.7	31.4	10.3	11.0	11.6
Pulp, paper	1.0	1.3	13.8	6.4	3.4	1.6	1.3	1.3
Printing	1.0	1.3	13.8	6.4	3.4	1.6	1.3	1.3
Other chemicals	0.2	2.5	4.5	3.6	3.3	5.8	5.6	6.8
Petroleum, coal products	0.0	0.0	0.1	0.2	1.6	0.4	1.4	1.0
Rubber products	17.5	23.3	48.4	54.2	49.3	58.5	67.1	64.0
Nonmetallic minerals	5.9	4.0	4.0	4.5	4.0	7.9	21.8	11.8
Other manufactures	24.7	54.9	54.3	59.9	66.0	55.2	55.6	64.6
Heavy and chemical industries								
Industrial chemicals	1.9	4.1	7.9	4.3	13.6	17.0	13.2	13.9
Oil refining	11.5	12.1	7.5	7.3	5.7	1.6	8.1	13.1
Iron and steel	9.2	4.6	24.8	15.8	14.7	22.3	21.3	18.1
Nonferrous metals	12.2	11.9	10.7	6.4	11.9	11.9	12.7	11.0
Fabricated metals	10.2	13.4	38.6	29.7	41.6	46.3	40.3	44.5
Nonelectrical machinery	8.9	3.2	24.9	10.0	10.0	11.0	9.1	7.6
Electrical machinery	10.6	23.3	50.2	41.4	35.4	38.9	40.2	46.1
Transport equipment	1.6	2.0	7.2	20.5	35.9	31.2	48.9	41.6
Industry groups								
Heavy and chemical	6.9	7.3	25.3	18.8	24.2	26.6	28.2	29.3
Light	8.3	14.0	26.0	24.8	26.1	23.9	28.0	26.4

Note: *sx* = [exports/(output − indirect taxes)]. Computed from the relevant input-output tables estimated by the Bank of Korea.

102 Industrialization and the State

Table 4A-8. Effective Rate of Protection (z) (in percentage)

	1970	1975	1978	1983[a]
Light industries				
Food	190.5	86.5	−28.8	−32.6
Beverages	− 13.9	− 20.8	4.8	−4.1
Tobacco	− 4.8	− 31.1	73.7	50.0
Textiles	29.4	− 15.1	0.2	5.3
Clothing	4.1	− 51.5	142.7	93.8
Footwear, leather	33.5	51.8	−6.1	−2.4
Wood	323.9	67.9	−9.4	9.1
Furniture	182.6	65.5	36.1	−8.8
Pulp, paper	11.5	− 1.3	36.2	22.9
Printing	−26.4	− 31.7	− 3.6	−11.7
Other chemicals	202.7	64.0	46.4	36.5
Petroleum, coal products	91.8	− 65.8	121.6	−0.2
Rubber products	145.6	16.5	−9.6	2.0
Nonmetallic minerals	38.6	− 5.0	12.2	32.3
Other manufactures	−290.9	95.4	5.9	−5.9
Heavy and chemical industries				
Industrial chemicals	19.5	− 23.2	40.7	65.8
Oil refining	− 52.7	−798.8	26.1	681.9
Iron and steel	190.9	303.2	24.7	31.5
Nonferrous metals	32.5	65.7	31.6	23.6
Fabricated metals	90.4	− 20.7	12.8	0.0
Nonelectrical machinery	88.9	− 14.9	44.2	23.6
Electrical machinery	223.6	29.4	105.4	44.8
Transport equipment	248.2	36.3	30.4	12.4
Industry groups				
Heavy and chemical	94.4	9.5	43.2	32.7
Light	56.1	−8.2	3.6	−0.3

[a]ERP estimates for 1982.
Sources: Data for 1970 and 1975 are from K. S. Kim and S. D. Hong, *The Long-term Changes in the Structure of Nominal and Effective Rate of Protection* (Seoul: Korea Development Institute, 1982). Data for 1978 and 1982 are from Yoo Jung-hoo, *The Basic Task of Industrial Policy and the Reform Proposals of Industrial Assistance* (Seoul: Korea Development Institute Press, 1982). Reproduced with permission.

Table 4A-9. Proportion of Paid Workers among All Workers (in percentage)

	1966	1970	1973	1975	1978	1980	1983	1985
Light industries								
Food	86.5	88.6	87.5	90.3	89.7	90.6	87.9	86.5
Beverages	89.0	92.7	93.5	95.1	95.7	95.9	94.9	94.0
Tobacco	100.0	100.0	100.0	100.0	100.0	100.0	100.0	100.0
Textiles	94.5	96.7	96.9	98.0	97.7	97.4	97.1	97.2
Clothing	88.0	93.1	93.1	93.1	92.9	92.1	92.1	93.1
Footwear, leather	90.5	92.4	92.6	99.2	94.6	96.0	92.5	98.0
Wood	93.5	95.7	95.9	98.7	97.0	97.6	97.7	97.9
Furniture	60.7	87.1	87.0	93.0	92.7	93.8	92.5	94.1
Pulp, paper	94.1	95.7	95.9	98.7	97.0	97.6	97.7	97.9
Printing	95.2	96.9	96.8	96.9	96.9	96.5	96.6	96.0
Other chemicals	96.4	98.0	98.5	98.7	99.0	98.8	98.5	98.8
Petroleum, coal products	92.1	94.1	95.5	95.8	96.1	97.8	98.3	98.1
Rubber products	98.7	99.2	99.7	99.8	99.9	99.4	99.5	99.5
Nonmetallic minerals	91.7	94.2	95.2	96.2	96.9	97.7	97.1	97.1
Other manufactures	94.1	92.0	92.1	90.8	91.6	91.3	91.5	96.7
Heavy and chemical industries								
Industrial chemicals	97.5	98.9	99.5	99.6	99.7	99.5	98.5	98.7
Oil refining	100.0	100.0	100.0	100.0	100.0	99.7	99.6	99.5
Iron and steel	98.9	99.3	99.6	99.6	99.5	99.5	99.6	99.6
Nonferrous metals	96.7	98.2	98.7	99.0	98.3	98.4	98.5	96.7
Fabricated metals	87.0	88.0	89.1	97.6	90.3	93.0	94.2	95.8
Nonelectrical machinery	82.0	93.9	96.6	97.2	95.6	96.7	97.8	97.5
Electrical machinery	97.3	98.6	99.4	99.7	99.6	99.5	99.3	98.9
Transport equipment	96.6	97.3	97.7	97.8	97.6	98.1	99.2	99.1
Industry groups								
Heavy and chemical	92.3	96.0	97.3	98.7	97.6	98.1	98.3	98.3
Light	90.1	93.3	93.4	95.3	94.9	94.9	94.4	95.0

Table 4A-10. Rate of Growth of Manufacturing Value-Added (in average annual percentage changes)

	1966–1970	1970–1973	1973–1975	1975–1978	1978–1980	1980–1983	1983–1985	1970–1978	1978–1985
Light industries									
Food	15.8	9.9	5.3	11.6	10.6	7.1	10.9	9.4	9.2
Beverages	17.1	14.3	12.8	10.8	7.7	4.5	6.0	12.6	5.8
Tobacco	22.8	12.1	13.7	8.8	7.0	7.2	2.9	11.3	5.9
Textiles	22.2	29.3	13.3	14.2	7.0	5.0	3.1	19.4	5.0
Clothing	20.0	30.3	16.9	11.6	-1.7	9.1	5.8	19.7	5.0
Footwear, leather	10.1	43.7	28.5	27.4	-12.3	5.1	-1.2	33.5	-1.9
Wood	21.0	18.2	5.4	19.5	-12.8	-1.7	-2.6	15.3	-5.3
Furniture	20.9	-6.0	16.1	27.5	4.0	15.7	1.1	11.1	8.0
Pulp, paper	15.1	18.0	9.3	19.4	7.8	7.7	5.0	16.3	6.9
Printing	5.5	11.0	9.7	15.3	7.8	4.1	5.3	12.3	5.5
Other chemicals	24.2	24.4	16.3	23.5	4.2	9.2	10.3	22.0	8.1
Petroleum, coal products	4.8	10.6	2.3	7.2	9.8	3.2	10.1	7.2	7.0
Rubber products	9.7	34.4	17.1	28.6	16.4	7.1	13.1	27.7	11.4
Nonmetallic minerals	24.6	20.0	6.7	18.6	6.7	9.2	5.3	16.0	7.4
Other manufactures	38.9	11.6	11.5	21.7	-2.2	2.6	8.7	15.3	2.9
Heavy and chemical industries									
Industrial chemicals	47.9	28.5	27.5	22.5	9.8	4.9	6.8	26.0	6.8
Oil refining	43.6	11.7	0.6	19.5	5.9	-4.4	8.5	11.6	2.1
Iron and steel	25.6	41.5	22.4	22.3	19.9	10.8	5.4	29.2	11.7
Nonferrous metals	7.0	24.7	29.5	28.3	10.9	27.9	7.2	27.2	16.8
Fabricated metals	12.1	18.8	24.2	41.8	-0.6	10.0	10.0	28.3	6.9
Nonelectrical machinery	7.1	38.4	19.2	41.5	-7.1	15.6	15.8	34.4	8.6
Electrical machinery	29.5	56.4	19.5	38.9	3.7	13.8	12.3	39.9	10.4
Transport equipment	21.8	11.5	37.7	26.9	-8.2	20.3	31.7	23.4	14.3

NOTES

1. Taewon Kwack. *Depreciation and Taxation of Income from Capital* (Seoul: Korea Development Institute, 1985). The estimates take into account statutory tax rates and various tax incentives, as well as inflation.
2. The measure of import liberalization used here is defined as the ratio of import items that require no prior government approval, except for imports restricted on the grounds of health or safety standards, to the total number of import items used by the industry.
3. Exporters continued to have access to foreign goods at international prices through the tariff rebate system.
4. Economic Planning Board, *Comprehensive Stabilization Program* (Seoul: Economic Planning Board, April 17, 1979).
5. Data are shown only for years when the Bank of Korea prepared interindustry tables. The availability of such tables restricts the number of observations.
6. It is assumed that unpaid workers created the same amount of value-added as paid workers. However, it is likely that in the manufacturing sector, a self-employed or family worker creates, on average, less value-added than a paid employee. If so, the estimated returns to capital and the capital efficiencies are likely to be underestimated. The extent of this underestimation would be greater, the greater the proportion of unpaid workers. As shown in Table 4A-9, the proportion of unpaid workers was higher in the Light group than in the HC group by three to four percentage points during the period under review. On this ground, the capital efficiency of the Light group is likely to have been underestimated by more than that of the HC group.
7. Although the value-added used in this section is in constant prices, the difference in their valuation is a problem, given the Bank of Korea's method of estimating the value-added in constant prices. It first obtained the ratio of value-added to output in current prices and multiplied the constant-price output by the ratio to obtain the value-added in constant price. The value of an industry's output was a simple sum of exports and domestic sales that did not take into account the difference between domestic and international prices. Likewise, the value-added was a sum that did not recognize the price differences.
8. For the 1983 *q3*, the 1982 effective rates of protection were used. The effective rates for 1970 and 1975 were available in Kwang Suk Kim and Sung Duk Hong, *The Long-term Changes in the Structure of Nominal and Effective Rate of Protection* (Seoul: Korea Development Institute, 1982). Those for 1978 and 1982 are Jung-ho Yoo's estimates reported in *The*

106 Industrialization and the State

Basic Task of Industrial Policy and the Reform Proposals of Industrial Assistance (Seoul: Korea Development Institute Press, 1982). These effective rates are reported in Table 4A-8.

9. The countries were Hong Kong, Israel, Portugal, Spain, Taiwan, and Yugoslavia. After excluding natural resource–based products, the product composition of the forty-seven largest trading countries' manufacturing exports of the late 1970s were compared with exports from Korea at the two-digit level. Austria, Italy, and India had compositions more similar to Korea's than to Yugoslavia's, Portugal's, or Spain's, designated here as competitors. However, they were not included as competitors on the ground that their per capita incomes were very different from Korea's.

10. Jung-ho Yoo, "Estimation of Some Disaggregate Export and Import Functions," *Korea Development Review* (Fall 1984).

11. See Chapter 5 for a discussion of the relationship between export development and the success of selected HCI projects.

12. L. E. Westphal and Kwang Suk Kim, "Korea," in B. Balassa et al., eds., *Development Strategies in Semi-industrial Countries* (Baltimore: Johns Hopkins University Press, 1982). For a more general discussion of export promotion and import substitution policies, see A. O. Krueger, "Trade Policy as an Input to Development," *American Economic Review* 70, no. 2 (May 1980).

13. See J. J. Stern, "Korea's Industrial Policy and Changing Industrial Structure," *Development Discussion Paper 352* (Cambridge: Harvard Institute for International Development, July 1990).

14. Ibid.

15. Hak-kil Pyo, "Estimates of Capital Stock and Capital/Output Coefficients by Industries for the Republic of Korea (1953–1986)," *Korea Development Institute Working Paper 8810* (Seoul: Korea Development Institute, 1988).

16. The pairs of industries for which capital stock was combined were apparel (KSIC 322) and footwear (KSIC 324); industrial chemicals (KSIC 351) and other chemical products (KSIC 352); petroleum refining (KSIC 353) and petroleum and coal products (KSIC 354); and iron and steel (KSIC 371) and nonferrous metals (KSIC 372). These industries were either individually interesting or, as in the case of petroleum refining and industrial chemicals, an industry favored by the HCI policy (industrial chemicals) lumped with one nonfavored (petroleum refining).

[10]

Government Intervention, Rent Distribution, and Economic Development in Korea

As part of their economic development strategies, most governments in developing countries intervene in the market to affect resource allocation. In the process, economic rent is created. The creation of economic rent and its distribution provide government with perhaps its greatest leverage for affecting the economic behavior of the private sector. In every economy, developing or industrialized, economic rent is created and rent seeking is ubiquitous. The difference among economies may be the relative size of rent created and the way it is distributed—and this seems to have important consequences for the performance of the economy.

Korea is a country where government intervention in the market, especially in the financial market, was extensive, and where substantial economic rent was created and allocated in the course of economic development. However, the areas where major rent was created and the rules by which it was distributed changed over time, with the changes in political regimes and economic policy goals. In retrospect, this brought remarkably different outcomes in the course of Korea's postwar economic development. In the 1950s, rent was created mainly in relation to import restriction and overvalued foreign exchange rates. The sale of government assets, which had been owned by the Japanese during the Japanese occupation period (1910–45), to the private sector also entailed substantial rent. During this period, the government did not have a clear vision for economic development and the development goal was overshadowed by the political agenda related to nation-building. Thus, the creation and distribution of rent was done largely with political considerations in mind rather than clear economic goals.

Change occurred in the 1960s and 1970s in the main area where rent was created. As the Korean government shifted to an export-oriented development strategy, the rent involved with overvalued exchange rates almost disappeared and that involved with the restriction of import quotas diminished. Instead, rent was created mainly in relation to financial allocations—allocation of domestic bank loans as well as foreign loans to priority sectors (e.g., the export sector in the 1960s and the heavy and chemical industries in the 1970s). The government, during this period, created rent with a clear vision of providing incentives to the priority sectors (mainly exports), thereby striving to accelerate economic development. It had a comprehensive development strategy in which credit policies were well coordinated with other economic policies. Although the amounts of rent created and distributed were equally substantial in both periods, the economic performance in the 1960s and 1970s differed widely from that of the 1950s.

This chapter discusses how economic rent was created and distributed in the course of the economic development of Korea, and how the government used this rent to achieve its economic goals. In discussing rent, the chapter focuses mainly on government intervention in the financial market. This study thus attempts to shed some light on the role of government in the early stages of economic development.

The first section briefly discusses the main features of Korean economic policies during the aforementioned periods and the main policy instruments used to achieve economic goals. In this context, it focuses on the areas where economic rent was created and how it was distributed during the 1950s, 1960s, and 1970s. The experience of the 1950s is contrasted with that of the 1960s and 1970s in order to highlight how the areas of rent creation and methods of distribution can have significantly different consequences on economic performance. Section 7.1 also attempts to estimate the relative size of this rent over time. Section 7.2 attempts to assess whether or not government intervention in the market (i.e., the creation and distribution of rent intended to affect industrial behavior) can have a positive impact on economic development in its initial stages by examining the Korean experience. The chapter concludes with brief summary remarks.

7.1 RENT CREATION AND DISTRIBUTION OVER TIME

The 1950s: Import Restriction and Foreign Exchange Allocation

With the end of World War II, Korea gained independence from the Japanese occupation (1910–45). Soon thereafter, it was divided into the two countries of North Korea and South Korea (hereafter, "Korea" refers to the latter). The first Korean government was led by President Rhee Syng-Man. Rhee devoted much of his agenda to building the nation, securing a United States military commitment to ensure Korean security, guiding the country's involvement in the Korean war (1950–53), stabilizing war inflation, and securing US grants for the war-devastated economy.

In the 1950s, the government did not have a comprehensive economic development strategy and economic policy during this time was characterized by an assortment of government regulations that lacked a clear vision or set of policy goals. Since the government's economic policy came under strong US influence, the government did not systematically intervene in the market, and a relatively independent central bank was established following the model of the US Federal Reserve Board, resulting in the private control of banks. Although interest rate regulations and preferential credit programs existed, bank operations were not subject to much government regulation.

However, the government did enact strong regulations with respect to external transactions. It maintained import restrictions and highly overvalued exchange rates. The import restriction policy was adopted not necessarily in accordance with an industrial development strategy, but rather in consideration of the shortage of foreign exchange and the political agenda. Korea did not have any significant exports and the major source of foreign exchange at that time was foreign aid and the local expenditures of the US ground forces. Korea also maintained restrictions on imports, as did most developing countries at that time, for nationalistic reasons. In particular, the government rejected the purchase of Japanese manufactured products. Thus, the government had to ration the scarce foreign exchange mainly to alleviate the shortage of daily necessities and to build factories to produce them. In order to maximize foreign exchange revenues derived from the local expenditures of the US ground forces, the Korean currency remained highly overvalued.

The allocation of import quotas under the strong import restriction that accompanied foreign exchange allocation entailed substantial rent. Importers received windfall gains and prospered; some of the Korean *chaebol* operating in the 1990s were established during this period as major recipients of this rent. The amount of rent that accompanied foreign exchange allocation is estimated to have been roughly 10–14 per cent of annual GNP during this period (see Table 7.1).[1]

In the 1950s, the government had no comprehensive economic development strategy and did not create rent to drive private business in the direction of its economic policy goals. There were no established rules for the allocation of rent or for the explicit and formal institutions in charge of making decisions regarding allocation. The ruling political party and strong political figures intervened in the allocation process. Consequently, there was no clear link between rent distribution and economic considerations for development (Yoon 1991). The allocation of rent was mainly discretionary, and those who received these allocations benefited from windfall gains, portions of which were shared with politicians and bureaucrats.

The 1960s: Rent Creation and Distribution through Credit Market Intervention

Korea's rapid economic growth began in the 1960s. In May 1961, Park Chung Hee, a military general, grasped control of the government in a *coup*

TABLE 7.1 Exchange Rate of the US Dollar and Economic Rent in Relation to Overvalued Exchange Rates (million won, %)

Year	Official Rate[a]	Parallel Market Rate[a]	Total Rent (A)[b]	A/GNP
1953	18.00	37.90	6,873.5	14.3
1954	18.00	43.60	6,228.5	9.3
1955	50.00	96.40	15,841.0	13.6
1956	50.00	96.60	17,992.3	11.8
1957	50.00	103.30	23,569.3	11.9
1958	50.00	118.10	25,755.4	12.4
1959	50.00	125.50	22,936.9	10.4
1960	65.00	145.30	27,583.1	11.2
1961	130.00	150.10	6,535.6	2.1
1962	130.00	134.00	1,687.2	0.5
1963	130.00	174.50	24,933.4	5.1
1964	255.77	290.07	13,870.9	2.0
1965	271.78	323.68	24,050.5	3.0
1966	271.18	302.58	22,495.0	2.2
1967	274.60	305.70	30,981.8	2.5
1968	281.50	309.00	40,229.8	2.6
1969	304.45	339.85	64,555.4	2.6
1970	316.65	348.75	63,686.4	2.5

Notes: [a] Exchange rates are averaged on an annual basis.
[b] Total rent = total imports × exchange rate gap. Imports are valued at CIF and the exchange rate gap is the gap between the official rate and the parallel market rate.
Source: Bank of Korea.

d'état; in 1963, he became president in a popular election. His regime continued until his assassination in 1979. When Park took power, he—and many other Koreans—harbored little confidence in the free market system. He and his economic staff believed the government should guide important prices, such as interest rates, and oversee the allocation of resources. But they gradually began to see the merits of price reforms that allowed important prices such as interest rates and the exchange rate to become closer to market prices. So they implemented price reforms that strengthened guidance in resource allocation.

In the early 1960s, Park's military government established new priorities for Korea's economy by shifting its policy stance from stabilization to growth and from import substitution to export promotion. The overvalued exchange rate was devalued by approximately 100 per cent. Consequently, rent associated with foreign exchange allocation in the 1950s almost disappeared, as indicated in Table 7.1.

The government believed it could accelerate economic growth by taking the lead in mobilizing and allocating resources. In pursuit of this goal, the

212   *Government Intervention and Rent Distribution: Korea*

government launched its first five-year economic development plan and implemented two measures to strengthen state control of the financial market: nationalizing commercial banks, and amending the Bank of Korea (BOK) Act to subordinate the central bank under the government. In addition, it introduced three significant policy reforms: the overhaul of the export credit program, the reform of interest rates, and the facilitation of foreign capital inflow. The government strengthened its control over the financial system and used credit allocation as the major industrial policy instrument. However, it also streamlined relative prices to correspond more closely to market levels during this period; interest rates were substantially increased and the exchange rate overvaluation was corrected.

The rent generated in relation to credit allocation was substantial during the 1960s, not necessarily because the government heavily repressed interest rates, but because the total volume of credit (both bank loans and foreign loans) to be allocated expanded as a result of interest rate reform and government effort to mobilize foreign borrowing.

Expansion of Export Credit Programs

An export credit program to support the export industry was in place as early as the 1950s, but the size of loans then was negligible. When the military government initiated the export-led strategy for economic growth, it naturally strengthened export credit programs to support exporters. Until the mid-1980s, when Korea ran a current account surplus,[2] the system of export financing played a critical role in promoting the export industry.

The short-term export credit system was streamlined in 1961. The essence of the new system was the "automatic approval" of loans by commercial banks to prospective borrowers holding export letters of credit (L/C). Initially, the program covered certain portions of the production costs of goods slated for export. Its coverage expanded rapidly, extending to sales to United Nations forces in Korea in 1961; to exports on a documents-against-payment (D/P), documents-against-acceptance (D/A), or consignment basis in 1965; to construction services rendered to foreign governments or their agencies in 1967; to imports of raw materials and intermediate goods for export-related use or to purchases from local suppliers in 1967; and so on. In each case, the expanded coverage was intended to promote the exploration of new export opportunities and the diversification of export items. These new programs were established after close consultation between the government and exporters.

General trading companies were introduced in the new export-financing system and were provided with financing on the basis of their export performance. To be eligible for financing, these companies had to exceed a specified level of exports which increased year to year, thus linking their export performance to their access to credit. The general trading companies had favorable access to export credit but were required to renew their licenses each year. Those whose exports did not exceed the specified level had their licenses revoked.

The interest rate on export loans was subsidized heavily. When the 1965 interest rate reform was implemented with the doubling of nominal rates (see below), the interest rate on export credit remained untouched. Consequently, the gap between export loans and general loans widened sharply. Interest rates on loans to exporters remained at 6.5 per cent while the general loan rate rose to 26 per cent (see Table 7.2). The rent associated with export credit alone is estimated to have been about 0.5–1.0 per cent of GNP during the 1960s, and about 2–3 per cent of GNP during the 1970s (see Table 7.3).

Interest Rate Reform

The government drastically changed its interest rate policies in 1965. Overnight, it raised the nominal interest rate on (one-year) time deposits from 15 per cent per year to 30 per cent, and the general loan rate from 16 to 26 per cent. However, the reform only partially helped draw the interest rates offered by the banks closer to market rates. Loan-rate increases were selective, excluding export-related, agricultural, and many other categories of investment loans. This action was intended to spur domestic saving to finance ambitious investment programs for economic development. To protect industrial firms from increasing costs incurred from overborrowing, a "negative interest margin" was introduced. At the same time, to protect the profitability of banks, the central bank provided cheap credit to commercial banks, which depended heavily on this credit in the extension of loans to firms.[3] On the other hand, the central bank placed high reserve requirements on commercial banks to contain inflationary pressure due to the expansion of its credit, but it paid interest on this reserve to protect commercial banks' profitability.

The reform successfully attracted private saving. In the first three months, the level of time and savings deposits increased by 50 per cent; over the next four years the level grew at an annual compounded rate of nearly 100 per cent. The stock of M2 relative to GNP increased from 8.9 per cent in 1964 to 31.8 per cent in 1971. Total bank loans increased by an equivalent amount. The annual growth rate of bank loans rose from 10.9 per cent during 1963–64 to 61.5 per cent during 1965–69.

More importantly, the reform helped shift funds from the unregulated informal sector to the banking sector, over which the government tightened its control. This allowed the government to increase controls on financial flow. It increased the total volume of capital to be distributed under government influence. Despite the interest rate reform, bank interest rates were still substantially lower than market rates (Table 7.2). Thus, the allocation of bank credit was accompanied by substantial rent. The rent associated

TABLE 7.2 Comparison of Various Interest Rates and Rent Created in the Financial Sector (%)

Year	Bank Loan Rate General Loan (A)	Bank Loan Rate Export Loan (B)	Curb Market Rate (C)	Corporate Bond Rate	Inflation[a]	A – B	C – A	Rent/GNP[b]	Rent/GNP[c]
1968	25.8	6.0	55.9	—	16.1	19.8	30.1	5.6	—
1969	24.5	6.0	51.2	—	14.8	18.5	26.7	5.5	—
1970	24.0	6.0	50.8	—	15.6	18.0	26.8	7.0	—
1971	23.0	6.0	46.3	—	12.5	17.0	23.3	6.3	—
1972	17.7	6.0	38.9	22.9	16.7	11.7	21.2	6.1	1.5
1973	15.5	7.0	39.2	21.8	13.6	8.5	23.7	7.2	1.9
1974	15.5	9.0	37.6	21.0	30.5	6.5	22.1	8.7	2.2
1975	15.5	7.0	41.3	20.1	25.2	5.8	25.8	9.5	1.7
1976	17.5	8.0	40.5	20.4	21.2	8.5	23.0	8.0	1.0
1977	19.0	9.0	38.1	20.1	16.6	10.0	19.1	6.3	0.4
1978	19.0	9.0	41.7	21.1	22.8	10.0	22.7	8.2	0.8
1979	19.0	9.0	42.4	26.7	19.6	10.0	23.4	9.2	3.0
1980	20.0	15.0	45.0	30.1	23.9	5.0	25.0	10.8	4.4
1981	16.4	15.0	35.4	24.4	17.0	1.4	19.0	8.8	3.7
1982	10.0	10.0	33.1	17.3	6.9	0.0	23.1	11.8	3.7
1983	10.0	10.0	25.8	14.2	5.0	0.0	15.8	8.4	2.2

Notes: [a] GNP deflator.
[b] Rent = total loans × (curb market rate – bank loan rate).
[c] Rent = total loans × (corporate bond rate – bank loan rate).

Source: Bank of Korea.

TABLE 7.3 Rent Created in Export Loans (billion won, %)

Year	Export Loans[a] (A)	(A) × Interest Gap[b] (B)	Rent (B)/GNP
1963	3.9	1.4	0.3
1964	10.0	4.6	0.7
1965	12.1	4.0	0.5
1966	16.6	5.4	0.5
1967	32.4	9.8	0.8
1968	43.4	13.1	0.8
1969	80.7	21.5	0.9
1970	161.6	43.3	1.7
1971	248.5	57.9	1.8
1972	231.8	49.1	1.3
1973	416.2	98.6	2.0
1974	652.6	144.2	2.1
1975	1,042.7	269.0	3.0
1976	1,511.5	347.6	2.9
1977	2,616.0	499.7	2.9
1978	3,764.8	854.6	3.7
1979	5,642.8	1,320.4	4.5
1980	6,957.4	1,739.4	4.7
1981	6,957.4	1,321.9	2.9
1982	8,192.0	1,892.4	3.7
1983	9,232.6	1,458.8	2.5

Notes: [a] Outstanding loans at the end of the year.
          [b] Interest gap = curb market rate – export loan interest.
Source: Bank of Korea, *Economic Statistics Yearbook*, various issues.

with domestic credit allocation is estimated to have been around 4–6 per cent of GNP in the 1960s when bank interest rates were significantly high.[4] Real interest rates were very positive in the 1960s. However, interest rates were reduced to support the heavy and chemical industries in the 1970s, and accordingly the rent generated also increased to 6–12 per cent of GNP (Table 7.2).

The interest rate reform of the 1960s has been described by many economists as financial liberalization.[5] This is correct in the sense that the degree of government repression on the interest rate level was substantially reduced. In price terms, therefore, it was substantial liberalization that brought rapid growth of the financial sector. However, as mentioned earlier, liberalization in fact helped to enhance government influence over the total financial flow of the economy by expanding the formal banking sector, which was already under tight government control. Funds shifted from the informal credit market, which lay beyond government control. Therefore, the interest rate policy in the 1960s can be assessed as one of financial restraint.[6] On the other hand, government policy in the financial sector

216   *Government Intervention and Rent Distribution: Korea*

shifted toward more financial repression in the 1970s, as the government reduced interest rates, tightening its control over credit allocation.

However, financial repression in Korea was somewhat different from that usually found elsewhere or that defined in Chapter 6 by Hellmann, Murdock, and Stiglitz in this volume. In Korea, financial repression was not the mechanism for the nonproductive transfer of wealth from the household sector to the government. Rather, that mechanism was the implicit taxation of depositors to subsidize priority industrial sectors. Cheap credit for industrial firms was supported by interest rate control on deposits and the central bank's cheap credit to commercial banks, which sometimes reached 20–30 per cent of the latter's total lending. The interest rates on these loans were very low in order to sustain the profitability of banks.[7]

Most of the central bank credit to commercial banks was to support the policy-based lending of commercial banks such as export bills. In Korea, a substantial part of policy loans was supported by the expansion of high-powered money rather than fiscal funds, as was the case in postwar Japan. This was a fundamental reason why Korea had a relatively unstable inflation rate compared to Japan or Taiwan, despite its conservative fiscal stance. The financial resources to support industrialists in the priority sector were mobilized through implicit taxation on depositors. In Korea, through this implicit taxation, the transfer of wealth took place within the private sector rather than from the private to the public sector as was the case in many other developing countries.

Facilitating the Flow of Foreign Capital

The Korean saving rate remained very low in the 1960s. In order to compensate for the shortage of domestic capital and declining foreign aid, the government normalized its relations with Japan in 1965 and amended the Foreign Capital Inducement Act in 1966, allowing state-owned banks to guarantee foreign borrowing by the private sector. This measure prompted a large inflow of foreign capital, especially from Japan. Since few Korean firms had direct access to foreign borrowing in the 1960s, the government's repayment guarantees to private borrowers through state-owned banks facilitated and reduced the cost of private foreign borrowing. Because domestic interest rates were high, private firms perceived foreign borrowing as a very attractive alternative. Yet each foreign loan had to be approved and allocated by the government, and foreign loans were used selectively to support industrial policy goals. The *ex post* rent associated with foreign loans fluctuated with changes in exchange rates but was quite substantial (Table 7.4). Estimations are presented in Table 7.5.

Rent Distribution in the 1960s

Following the creation of substantial rent in relation to credit allocation, rent distribution was used more effectively as an industrial policy instru-

TABLE 7.4 Cost of Foreign Loans and Domestic Market Rates (%, % point)

Year	Cost of Foreign Loans		Bank Loan Rate	Curb Market Rate (C)	Corporate Bond Yield (D)	C − A	D − A	C − B	D − B
	Nominal (A)[a]	Effective (B)[b]							
1968	7.13	15.28	25.8	55.9	—	48.77	—	40.62	—
1969	10.06	14.07	24.5	51.2	—	41.14	—	37.13	—
1970	6.57	24.61	24.0	50.8	—	44.05	—	26.19	—
1971	5.81	12.70	23.0	46.3	—	40.49	—	33.60	—
1972	6.19	5.84	17.7	38.9	22.9	32.71	16.71	33.06	17.06
1973	10.03	31.79	15.5	39.2	21.8	29.17	11.77	7.41	-9.99
1974	10.19	10.19	15.5	37.6	21.0	27.41	10.81	27.41	10.81
1975	6.63	6.63	15.5	41.3	20.1	34.67	13.47	34.67	13.47
1976	5.38	5.38	17.5	40.5	20.4	35.12	15.02	35.12	15.02
1977	7.50	7.50	19.0	38.1	20.1	30.60	12.60	30.60	12.60
1978	12.31	12.31	19.0	41.7	21.1	29.39	8.79	29.39	8.79
1979	14.44	50.78	19.0	42.4	26.7	27.96	12.26	-8.38	-24.08
1980	16.75	22.90	20.0	45.0	30.1	28.25	13.35	22.10	7.20
1981	14.81	21.59	16.4	35.4	24.4	20.59	9.59	13.81	2.81
1982	9.50	15.85	10.0	33.1	17.3	23.60	7.80	17.25	1.45
1983	10.06	13.86	10.0	25.8	14.2	15.74	4.14	11.94	0.34

Notes: [a] Libor-based cost of borrowing.
[b] Nominal cost adjusted for the annual fluctuation rate of the exchange rate.
Source: Bank of Korea.

218   *Government Intervention and Rent Distribution: Korea*

TABLE 7.5 Rent Created in Foreign Loan Allocation (million $US, %)

Year	Total Foreign Loans (A)	B × A[a]	C × A[b]	D × A[c]	E × A[d]
1968	1,199	584.8	—	487.0	—
		(11.2)	—	(9.3)	—
1969	1,800	740.5	—	668.4	—
		(11.2)	—	(10.1)	—
1970	2,277	1,003.0	—	596.4	—
		(12.6)	—	(7.5)	—
1971	2,984	1,208.2	—	1,002.7	—
		(12.9)	—	(10.7)	—
1972	3,580	1,171.0	598.2	1,183.6	610.8
		(11.1)	(5.7)	(11.2)	(5.8)
1973	4,257	1,241.8	501.0	315.4	−425.3
		(9.2)	(3.7)	(2.3)	(−3.1)
1974	5,955	1,632.3	643.7	1,632.3	643.7
		(8.8)	(3.5)	(8.8)	(3.5)
1975	8,457	2,932.0	1,139.2	2,932.0	1,139.2
		(14.1)	(5.5)	(14.1)	(5.5)
1976	10,635	3,735.0	1,597.4	3,735.0	1,597.4
		(13.0)	(5.6)	(13.0)	(5.6)
1977	12,649	3,870.6	1,593.8	3,870.6	1,593.8
		(12.3)	(5.1)	(12.3)	(5.1)
1978	14,823	4,356.5	1,302.9	4,356.5	1,302.9
		(8.4)	(2.5)	(8.4)	(2.5)
1979	20,287	5,672.2	2,487.2	−1,700.7	−4,885.7
		(9.1)	(4.0)	(−2.7)	(−7.8)
1980	27,170	7,675.5	3,627.2	6,003.9	1,955.6
		(12.7)	(6.0)	(10.0)	(3.2)
1981	32,433	6,678.0	3,110.3	4,478.7	911.1
		(10.1)	(4.7)	(6.8)	(1.4)
1982	37,083	8,751.6	2,892.5	6,396.7	537.6
		(12.6)	(4.2)	(9.2)	(0.8)
1983	40,378	6,355.5	1,671.6	4,822.6	138.8
		(8.4)	(2.2)	(6.3)	(0.2)

Numbers in parentheses are ratio to GNP.
Notes: [a] B = curb market rate – nominal Libor (London interbank offer rates) rate.
    [b] C = corporate bond yield – nominal Libor rate.
    [c] D = curb market rate – effective Libor rate.
    [d] E = corporate bond yield – effective Libor rate.

ment in the 1960s than in the 1950s. Credit allocation (both domestic and foreign), especially export credit allocation, was linked with the performance of rent seekers: those who were more successful in the export market were rewarded with more allocated credit. In the 1950s, harboring close ties with government officials or politically powerful figures often proved to be enough to receive rent allocations. However, such practices and conditions changed in the 1960s. In addition, industrialists were required to prove they could perform in the international market and meet the criteria set by the government. If they did not perform up to the standards, they faced the revocation of favorable treatment. In the 1950s, the volume of items to be allocated with rent (i.e., foreign exchange) was quite small, but the price subsidy (degree of overvaluation) was significant and the rules for distribution were not clear. In the 1960s, however, the degree of the price subsidy was reduced, the volume of items to be allocated credit (both domestic and foreign) was large, and rent distribution was more closely linked to the performances of rent seekers.

The 1970s: Intensified Rent Creation Associated with Development of the Heavy and Chemical Industries

In the 1970s, the government reverted to lower interest rates while intensifying its controls on credit allocation. Credit policies were made more "selective." This reversion was marked by a Presidential Emergency Decree in 1972, which bailed out many financially insolvent firms by placing an immediate moratorium on all loans in the informal credit markets, and reduced the bank loan rate from 23 per cent to 15.5 per cent.[8] Furthermore, approximately 30 per cent of short-term high-interest commercial bank loans to businesses were converted into long-term loans with concessional terms for repayment on an installment basis, over a five-year period, at an 8 per cent annual interest rate, with a three-year grace period. The lapse back to more repressive financial policies was motivated by the policy shift toward the promotion of the heavy and chemical industries (HCI), which required enormous amounts of cheap financing and constituted a significant departure from the export-oriented, non-sectoral-biased strategy adopted throughout the 1960s.

The government adopted two other important measures to support the HCI drive: it established the National Investment Fund (NIF), and it expanded BOK discounts. HCI development required a large amount of term financing. In December 1973, the government established the NIF to finance long-term investments in HCI plants and equipment.[9] The NIF was mobilized from a combination of funds from private financial intermediaries and the government, but predominantly from the former. Although the NIF did not comprise a large share of total bank loans, it provided more than 60 per cent of term financing for HCI equipment investment in the years 1975–80 (Cho and Kim 1995). BOK also expanded its rediscount facility to support the HCI. Considering the long maturation period of investments in the HCI, BOK also increased the maximum loan period for equipment investment. Furthermore, BOK brought out the "Guide to

Bank Loans," adding HCI to the list of high-priority industries for financial support to induce more lending by banks to the HCI. The Guide curbed, or in some cases prohibited, some service industries from receiving bank financing (Cho and Kim 1995).

As the government pursued HCI development, rent was generated through the restriction on entry and selection of manufacturers in specific industries (since there were economies of scale in production for most HCI) in addition to the allocation of credit. Choosing market entrants and providing financial support were packaged. Since great uncertainty accompanied HCI investment, in the opening stages of the HCI drive, industrialists were reluctant to enter these industries, even with the large rent generation. Later, when the government's determination to stand behind selected market entrants at whatever cost was confirmed, these industrialists competed fiercely to receive selection as HCI manufacturers.

In accordance with the nature of this kind of industrial policy, rent distribution became more discretionary in the 1970s than it had been in the 1960s. Although most selected entrants were already established industrialists (and thus their management capability was proven), there was no explicit criterion for the selection of a specific industrialist or *chaebol* as an entrant to a specific industry. There was substantial room for the discretionary allocation of rent and favoritism. Since the HCI required an immense scale of investment, most of the firms that entered these industries with strong government support, in terms of credit allocation, were the already well-established *chaebol*. Consequently, rent distribution in the 1970s increased the degree of economic concentration in the Korean economy, later becoming a serious burden on economic policy.

7.2 DID GOVERNMENT INTERVENTION AND ECONOMIC RENT PROMOTE RAPID DEVELOPMENT?

In Korea, as discussed earlier, government intervention in the financial market was extensive: the government controlled interest rates and supervised the allocation of bank credit. Economic rent associated with credit allocation (and foreign exchange allocation) was substantial, and its distribution constituted the major government tool for corporate governance and industrial policy. The export drive in the 1960s and the HCI drive in the 1970s were supported by various preferential credit programs and the government's discretionary allocation of credit.

To what extent, then, did credit spur growth in the priority sectors and/or support industrial development? A direct answer to this question is not possible. Since credit supports were provided in conjunction with other incentives, it is not easy to isolate the impact of the credit supports from the other incentives. Thus, we can address this issue only in an indirect manner.

We can first examine the impact of credit supports on the take-off of exports in the 1960s; second, we can discuss the impact of credit supports on the HCI in their rapid growth during the 1970s, to determine their merit and whether rent allocation had occurred.[10]

The Impact on Export Growth

In order for exporters to respond to foreign demand, they should have access to the trade financing necessary to fill export orders (Rhee 1989). In many developing countries, financing mechanisms that are taken for granted in industrial countries, such as short-term money markets and bill discount markets, are rudimentary or nonexistent; such was the case in Korea in the 1960s. Thus, one way to provide a market for bill discounts to exporters was to establish the central bank's rediscount facility (Rhee 1989). Although exporters in Korea in the 1950s received some selective credit supports through lending by the central bank, export credit programs were formalized only in the 1960s. The total amount of credit supported by export credit programs increased from 4.5 per cent of total bank credit in the years 1961–65 to 7.6 per cent (1966–72), and further to 13.2 per cent (1973–81). In addition, as shown in the previous section, interest rate subsidies for export credits were substantial. In the years 1966–72, the interest rate for export credit was 17.1 per cent lower, on average, than the general loan rate. Exporters also received support from various other credit programs (such as equipment funds for export industries) and favorable credit allocations in conformity with government directives or administrative guidance. During Korea's export expansion period, credit subsidies comprised the major component of total export subsidies (Figure 7.1), which peaked in 1967 when the total interest rate subsidy was 2.3 per cent of the total value of exports,[11] far exceeding the fiscal subsidy of 1.0 per cent in the same year.

The extent to which credit subsidies contributed to the take-off of Korean exports in the 1960s is unclear (Figure 7.2 shows the export growth rate throughout the economic development period). A competitive exchange rate (with a major devaluation of the won in 1964) and various institutional supports also contributed to export growth. The expanded accessibility of credit (subsidized by low interest rates) was crucial in enabling Korean exporters to fill foreign orders and to explore foreign markets. In general, access to credit seems to have been more essential for supporting the continuous growth of exports than were interest rate subsidies. But, because export marketing requires substantial fixed costs in the initial stages and involves tremendous externalities,[12] government subsidies may also have made a large contribution because private efforts and investment in the exploration of external markets might not have been sufficient to fuel rapid growth. Alternatively, export marketing could have been subsidized

222   *Government Intervention and Rent Distribution: Korea*

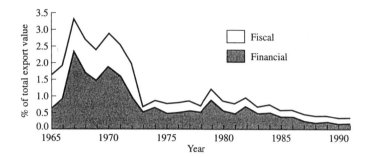

FIG. 7.1 Subsidies to Export, 1965–1991
Note: The amount of financial subsidies is the size of export-related loans
       multiplied by the interest rate differential between the average loan rate
       for the manufacturing industry and interest rates for export-related loans.
       The tax subsidy ratio is the total amount of tax subsidies from export
       reserves and special depreciation systems divided by the total value of
       exports. If the amount of the financial subsidy were based on the gap
       between the market interest rate and the export loan rate, the credit
       subsidy would be much larger. The tax subsidy from the export reserve
       system is the amount of tax savings that comes from corporate tax exemp-
       tions on the export reserve in a given year. That is, it is calculated by
       subtracting the net present value of the deferred tax on the export reserve
       that would be paid over a three-year period after a two-year grace period
       from the tax on the export reserve that should have been paid in a given
       year. The tax subsidy from a special depreciation system is the net present
       value of the tax savings from the added depreciation that is allowed within
       30 per cent of the normal depreciation on fixed assets purchased by an
       exporter.

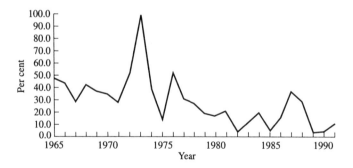

FIG. 7.2 Growth of Exports, 1965–1991

by the budget. But given the poor budgetary situation in the 1960s when
total tax revenue fell within the range of 6.8–12.4 per cent of GNP (as
discussed earlier), the use of fiscal subsidies was clearly limited. It was also
true that using subsidized credit through implicit taxation on the banking
system (and consequently on depositors) was politically easier.

Cho 223

Impact on HCI Development

As discussed in the previous section, bank loans were allocated favorably to the HCI in the 1970s. The manufacturing sector received 46.1 per cent of total domestic bank loans in 1970 but contributed only 21.3 per cent to GDP.[13] Within the manufacturing sector, the HCI received 22.6 per cent of total bank loans but contributed only 8.6 per cent to GDP. In 1980, after a decade of the HCI drive, the share of bank credit to the HCI increased further to 32.1 per cent, while its contribution to GDP also rose to 16.5 per cent.

The NIF was the major credit support program for the HCI, providing preferential maturities and interest rates. Credit support was provided not only by explicitly designated credit programs such as the NIF, but also by government directives to banks to provide more credit. The allocation of foreign loans was also a large part of total credit support. In the years 1972–76, for example, industries in the manufacturing sector claimed 66.1 per cent of the total amount of foreign commercial loans. Of this amount, 64.1 per cent went to the HCI (Table 7.6 provides a breakdown of the composition of foreign commercial loans).

The massive credit support made it possible to invest heavily in the HCI during the 1970s. During the late 1970s, almost 80 per cent of all fixed investment in the manufacturing sector went to the HCI. Consequently, the industrial structure and export composition of Korea changed drastically (Table 7.7). The expansion of the HCI in the 1970s is striking. Within a decade, the HCI share of total industrial output grew more than two and half times, and their share of exports tripled. Moreover, HCI shares of bank

TABLE 7.6 Composition of Public and Commercial Loans by Industry (%)

Year	Type of Loan	Agriculture, Forestry, & Fisheries	Manufacturing		Service[a]	Total
			HCI	Light		
1959–66	Public	7.5	11.7	8.3	72.5	100.0
	Commercial	22.3	43.4	31.4	2.9	100.0
1967–71	Public	42.2	6.8	1.6	49.4	100.0
	Commercial	3.6	31.6	23.9	40.8	100.0
1972–76	Public	18.2	6.1	0.0	75.8	100.0
	Commercial	2.2	42.4	23.7	31.7	100.0
1977–82	Public	17.0	1.5	0.3	81.2	100.0
	Commercial	0.6	46.0	10.6	42.8	100.0
1959–82	Public	19.0	3.0	0.4	77.6	100.0
	Commercial	1.6	43.6	15.4	39.5	100.0
	Total	9.6	24.9	8.5	57.0	100.0

Note: [a] Service includes construction, electricity, transportation, etc.
Source: Cha (1986).

224   *Government Intervention and Rent Distribution: Korea*

TABLE 7.7 Industrial Structure and Export Composition: HCI Trends, 1970–1988 (%)

	1970	1975	1980	1985	1988
Industrial Structure					
Agriculture/fisheries	17.0	12.8	8.3	7.7	6.3
Mining	1.1	0.9	0.8	0.7	0.6
Manufacturing	40.3	50.4	51.0	50.0	52.7
Light	28.4	29.5	24.7	21.7	21.4
HCI	11.9	20.9	26.3	28.3	31.3
Petrochemical	5.9	10.8	12.6	11.4	10.0
Basic metal	2.0	3.4	5.1	4.9	5.3
Metal/machinery	4.0	6.7	8.6	12.0	16.1
Power/gas/construction	9.8	7.7	10.2	10.4	9.3
Service	31.8	28.2	29.7	31.2	29.4
Total	100.0	100.0	100.0	100.0	100.0
Composition of Exports					
Light	49.4	45.6	35.2	30.0	29.1
HCI	12.8	29.0	38.3	47.5	51.4
Petrochemical	5.4	9.2	9.9	12.4	11.0
Basic metal	1.5	4.0	8.1	5.8	5.1
Metal/machinery	5.9	15.8	20.3	29.3	35.4

Source: Bank of Korea, "Input-Output Tables," various issues.

credits, output, and exports within the manufacturing sector also expanded rapidly over time (see Figure 7.3). It is obvious that without government intervention in the allocation of credit, the quick transformation of the industrial composition and discrete jump in the level of industrial development would not have been possible.

Impact on Overall Economic Growth

Did the growth of these credit-supported sectors contribute to the rapid economic growth of Korea? In response to this question, we can only make tentative conclusions. In a sense, it is too early to answer, since Korea is still undergoing economic development and may not yet have fully realized the costs or benefits of financial policies. One solid conclusion pertains to the growth of exports, which was the main engine of rapid growth in Korea during the 1960s and 1970s. To the extent that credit support was indispensable to export growth, credit support, in turn, must have acted as the catalyst for rapid economic growth; but whether the extent of the subsidization implemented was necessary to propel the growth of exports remains questionable. However, the impact of credit support on the HCI drive and its subsequent effect on growth remains controversial (e.g.,

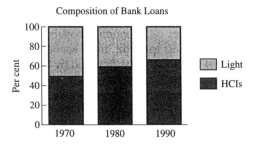

Composition of Bank Loans

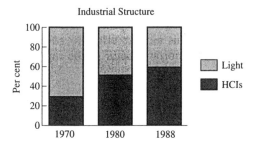

Industrial Structure

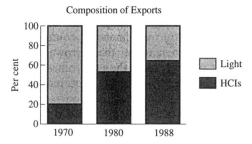

Composition of Exports

FIG. 7.3 Significance of the HCI and Light Industries in the Manufacturing Sector: Trends

Amsden 1989; Stern et al. 1992; Leipziger and Petri 1992; and World Bank 1987a). Although credit supports were influential in spurring the rapid development of the HCI, credit allocation might have been more efficient had it been allocated more equitably between the HCI and light industry— particularly given the labor endowment in the 1970s.[14] However, by the mid-1980s, the HCI did become the leading export industries in Korea; currently, HCI exports such as steel, metal, general machinery and equipment, electrical and chemical products, etc. constitute 66.1 per cent of Korea's total exports.

226   *Government Intervention and Rent Distribution: Korea*

The Effectiveness of Credit Policy as an Industrial Policy Instrument

The impact of credit policies on economic growth is not limited to their effect on the cost of and access to credit. In an economy such as Korea's, in which the expansion of investment was financed by bank credit and foreign loans, the financial structure of firms was highly leveraged. By controlling financing, the government could become an effective risk partner for industrialists and motivate the latter's development of risk ventures and entrepreneurship. It could induce industrialists to adopt long-term business perspectives, while a competitive financial market might have prompted firms to take a shorter-term view (Cho and Hellmann 1993). In other words, by controlling financing, the government established a government-industry-bank coinsurance scheme to protect industrial firms from any unexpected circumstances. This indirect effect of government credit policy may also have been an important factor in the rapid industrialization of Korea.

Credit Policy as an Instrument for Corporate Governance

In Korea, state control over financing was the most powerful tool for inducing cooperation and compliance among businesses in the promotion of exports and industrialization. One of the distinct advantages of credit supports over other policy measures, such as fiscal subsidies, is that it gives the government greater leverage for implementing industrial policy (Cho and Hellmann 1993). Control over financing confers on the government some explicit right of governance over the borrowers for the entire period of their loans. Credit policies allow the government to allocate subsidies flexibly, according to the performance of supported firms or industries. In turn, such control extends to refinancing decisions—whether or not existing debt should be rolled over or new debt extended, and, if so, under what conditions. Well-measured refinancing decisions provide incentives: good performance can be rewarded with continued or expanded support; or inappropriate use of funds can be punished with a reduction in or even termination of support, an action that could make a firm's survival untenable. This carrot-and-stick policy underlying credit programs makes them effective tools of government industrial policy, being more effective than fiscal incentives, which stem from legislative initiation and are subject to the rigidity of the implementation process.[15]

But credit policies carry their own risk—the "risk of government failure." In Korea, the government's continuous communication with business leaders and close monitoring of firms through various channels (such as monthly export promotion meetings) helped reduce its risk of failure. Moreover, by controlling the banks, the government created incentives for firms to maximize their assets and growth, rather than to strive for immediate profitability. As long as they satisfied the government by expanding exports and successfully completing the construction of plants, firms ensured their continued credit support and survival. The government thus mitigated the risk of failure by adopting a sounder, more stable investment environment.

Credit Control as an Instrument for Risk Management

Industrial investment in Korea was financed largely by debt, especially during the period of rapid economic growth. Fiscal incentives and low interest rates allowed some firms to accumulate retained earnings, but, in the absence of a well-functioning domestic equity market, huge investment requirements for rapid industrial expansion had to be financed largely with

TABLE 7.8 Growth of the Financial Sector (%)

Year	M2/GNP	M3/GNP	Financial Intermediation Ratio[a]	Domestic Saving Ratio to GNP[b]
1968	26.4	—	—	15.1
1969	32.7	—	—	18.8
1970	32.2	10.0	2.22	15.8
1971	31.7	37.4	2.23	14.7
1972	34.6	40.2	2.36	16.3
1973	36.8	44.5	2.43	22.2
1974	32.4	40.1	2.29	20.2
1975	31.1	38.5	2.26	18.7
1976	30.3	38.1	2.18	24.0
1977	33.0	42.2	2.28	27.4
1978	33.0	42.4	2.28	29.3
1979	32.0	43.3	2.29	28.8
1980	34.0	48.7	2.56	24.8
1981	34.3	51.4	2.71	25.1
1982	39.7	59.6	3.04	26.3
1983	36.9	61.3	3.07	29.6
1984	34.8	64.4	3.72	32.1
1985	36.0	69.9	3.94	32.4
1986	36.4	77.1	3.83	35.9
1987	36.7	85.3	3.79	38.5
1988	37.3	91.6	3.79	40.0
1989	39.6	104.0	4.25	36.8
1990	38.5	111.0	4.33	36.4
1991	39.1	113.9	4.40	36.7
1992	40.3	123.5	4.67	35.4
1993	42.5	132.4	—	35.3

Notes: [a] Domestic stock of financial assets/GNP (at current prices).
          [b] Domestic saving ratio = GDP − final consumption expenditure.
Source: Bank of Korea.

bank loans and foreign debt. In the years 1963–71, the debt ratio of the Korean manufacturing sector increased more than fourfold, from 92 per cent to 394 per cent. Even in the 1990s, Korean firms remain highly leveraged, although their debt ratio in the second half of the 1980s declined somewhat with the expansion of the stock market. Consequently, Korean firms became more vulnerable to internal and external shocks.[16] In fact, Korea could have undergone several financial crises had the government not become actively involved in risk management through credit intervention.

The government implemented major corporate bail-outs in 1969–70, 1972, 1979–81, and 1984–88 to ride out recessions and avoid major financial crises. In the credit-based economy, the government made these bail-outs by intervening in credit markets. The government's involvement in restructuring firms and industries and in redistributing losses made risk sharing possible among the members of the economy. Depositors usually incurred the lion's share of this cost, but were also beneficiaries, reaping subsequent rewards from the steady economic growth, increased job opportunities, and higher wages (Woo 1991). The overall size of the financial sector and the total saving rate grew rapidly in Korea although the banking system, subject to heavy government intervention, remained stagnant (Table 7.8).

7.3 AN OVERALL ASSESSMENT

In Korea, government intervention in the financial market was extensive during the process of economic development. The government owned the banking institution, controlled its interest rates, and directed a substantial portion of its loans. This allocation of credit was accompanied by substantial rent, and it constituted a major industrial policy instrument and tool for government control of industrial firms. This strategy— often called financial repression—is viewed by most economists as an ineffective way to achieve high economic growth. It is true that this policy stance in Korea also caused many problems. From time to time it led to the allocation of large amounts of credit to unsuccessful ventures, forcing the government to bail out firms and banks through monetary expansion. It inhibited the development of an efficient banking system and fostered economic concentration. However, the Korean government targeted industrialization and achieved it by allocating cheap credit to large industrialists, forcing them to build industries and increase their exports, while threatening to withdraw the credit if they did not perform up to par. As an additional result, depositors were paid lower rates of return on their deposits but they were rewarded as wage-earners with the expansion of job opportunities and the increase in real wages. Rapid income increases contributed to the accumulation of domestic savings and the subsequent expansion of the financial market. What made this approach work in Korea, while similar policy initiatives led to unsuccessful developmental experiences elsewhere?

This question cannot be answered completely. Only a tentative conclusion can be asserted based on observations on the thrust of policy measures and the overall economic environment prevailing during the process of Korea's economic development. From the observations in this chapter, it is quite obvious that government intervention and the creation of economic rent as such does not contribute to rapid economic development. It could simply nurture widespread corruption in relation to rent-seeking behavior and help sustain economic backwardness, as was manifested in Korea in the 1950s. However, government intervention through the creation and distribution of rent could also be an effective industrial policy measure to help spur economic development, when it is managed carefully as part of a comprehensive economic development strategy with a clear vision.

The major difference between the experiences of Korea in the 1950s and those in the 1960s lay in the areas where rent was created (i.e., import versus export) and the ways it was distributed (i.e., discretionary versus rule based). Providing subsidy (rent) to the export sector, the development of which presented substantial externalities to the economy through the rapid upgrading of technology, etc., can contribute positively to growth in the early stages of development. Rent distribution linked to the performance of exporters in the international market helped expose domestic firms to international competition and encouraged mobilization of high-powered human as well as physical capital in the export sector. Despite the fact that interest rate control entailed substantial subsidies, the level of interest rates remained positive in real terms, and this allowed the rapid growth of financial savings in the 1960s. Although the government's intervention in the financial market and its control over financial institutions afforded it discretion in decision making on rent distribution, the criterion of distribution was monitored reasonably according to the economic development goals. However, when the focus of industrial policy was shifted to HCI development in the 1970s, more room was created for the discretionary allocation of rent, and the extent of rent (or financial repression) was also increased with the widened gap between controlled interest rates and the market rate. This also increased the cost of government intervention. The government was able to partially compensate for the consequently negative impact on financial sector growth by allowing the expansion of nonbank financial institutions and the securities market, which were less regulated during the 1970s.

Overall, what contributed most to the effectiveness of government intervention from the economic development standpoint seem to be effective economic management and the competitive business environment. In Korea, close consultation between government and business and the government's risk partnership with business made what could have been a very

230   *Government Intervention and Rent Distribution: Korea*

distorted investment approach into quite an effective developmental strategy. When the risk capital market was poorly developed, the Korean government controlled banks and effected a close relationship between government, banks, and industry, and thereby made itself an effective risk partner with industry. This implicit coinsurance scheme among the government, industries, and banks allowed the credit-based economy and its highly leveraged corporate firms to explore risky investment opportunities and to operate without the danger of major financial crisis.

However, the Korean experience also suggests that the cost of this approach can be substantial and can be exacerbated as economic development advances. The Korean policy strategy fueled rapid industrialization, but it also dampened efforts to develop an efficient banking system. The government's risk partnership with industrial firms placed a heavy burden on the banking system, loading it with large nonperforming loans, and raised social equity issues. Extensive government intervention in financing, especially in relation to low interest-rate ceilings, slowed the growth of financial savings. Korea was able to overcome this negative impact of government intervention by relying heavily on foreign borrowing. Korea's special relationship with the United States and Japan gave the country access to foreign loans. Furthermore, the perpetuation of strong government intervention in credit allocation when the industrial sector was well established and when economic organizations had become sophisticated placed Korea at greater risk of distorting the allocation of financial resources. The coinsurance scheme among government, industries, and banks fostered a moral hazard for banks and firms, despite contributing to the development of entrepreneurship and the expansion of industrial investment. Consequently, the government became captive to a vicious cycle of intervention. It also became captive to its own bureaucratic interests.

The overall lesson from the Korean experience is that it is possible for governments to intervene productively and effectively in the early stages of economic development. The balance between the role of government and market forces should reflect the financial market, industrial organization, market structure, and political and international environment that face the country. But as economic development advances, the role and scope of government intervention must be reappraised with a view toward fostering greater reliance on market forces.

NOTES

I am grateful for helpful comments from Masahiko Aoki, Hyung-Ki Kim, Masahiro Okuno-Fujiwara, and participants of seminars held for this project in Tokyo and Stanford.

[1] This estimate, however, should be qualified. In a sense, it is purely indicative because there is some doubt whether parallel market rates were at the equilibrium rate. Furthermore, import restrictions allowed importers to monopolize the supply of certain goods, entailing additional rent.

[2] The export credit program has been substantially reduced since the mid-1980s.

[3] Central bank credit to commercial banks constituted 20–30 per cent of total loans extended by the latter during the 1970s.

[4] Again, the rent estimate here may have been exaggerated because it is doubtful that the curb market rate was the equilibrium rate when the financial market was liberalized.

[5] For example, McKinnon (1973) and Shaw (1973).

[6] See Hellmann, Murdock, and Stiglitz, Chapter 6 in this volume.

[7] For instance, the central bank's rediscount rate for export bills was 3.5 per cent in the years 1964–75.

[8] See Cho and Kim (1995) and Kim (1990, 1994) for detailed discussion on the two impacts of the decree.

[9] According to Nam, then Minister of Finance, he was compelled to establish the NIF, given the importance of the heavy industry program, for project financing, thereby attempting to minimize the burden on banking operations.

[10] This part relies on the analysis by Cho and Kim (1995).

[11] Here, the export subsidy is estimated based on the gap between average bank loan rates and the export loan rate. If it was estimated based on the gap between the curb market rate and the export loan rate, as done in this volume by Hellmann, Murdock, and Stiglitz (see Chapter 6), the amount of the subsidy would be much higher.

[12] It is asserted that since Korean export growth was based on the expansion of manufactured exports, the technological effect of export marketing and the informational externality was substantial (see Kim and Roemer 1979, World Bank 1987b).

[13] This reflects the fact that the Korean government's credit allocation favored the manufacturing sector over other sectors.

[14] But in terms of dynamic efficiency, heavy HCI investment might have had some merits.

[15] However, the benefits of the flexibility of credit policies cannot be taken for granted. In particular, poor information on behalf of creditors may turn their potential effectiveness into a large hazard, because renegotiations and refinancing decisions involve delicate trade-offs. In order to use credit effectively as a selection and incentive device, creditors should have the ability to understand two crucial aspects of a firm's performance. First, in order to provide an effective incentive scheme, the creditor should be able to distinguish external factors from managerial performance. Second, in order to make effective selection decisions among external factors, creditors should be able to distinguish cyclical influences from structural ones; in particular, they should have good information on whether financial distress is due to temporary or permanent problems.

[16] This is, to some extent, the result of the government-led industrial financing strategy.

232   *Government Intervention and Rent Distribution: Korea*

REFERENCES

AMSDEN, A. (1989), *Asia's Next Giant: South Korea and Late Industrialization*, Oxford University Press, Oxford.

CHA, D.-S. (1986), *Waekuk Jabon Doyip Hoykya eui Bunseok* (An analysis of the effect of foreign capital inflow), Korean Institute for Economics and Technology, Seoul.

CHO, Y. J. and KIM, J.-K. (1995), "Credit Policies and Industrialization of Korea," World Bank Discussion Papers, No. 286.

——and HELLMANN, T. (1993), "Government Intervention in Credit Markets in Japan and Korea: An Alternative Interpretation from the New Institutional Economics Perspective," PRE Working Paper Series No. 1190, World Bank, *Seoul Journal of Economics*, 7(4).

KIM, C.-Y. (1990), *Hankuk Kyungje Jeongchaek Samship yeon sa* (A 30-year history of Korean economic development policy: a memoir), Seoul Joong-ang and Ilbo-sa, Seoul.

——(1994), "Policy Making on the Front Lines: Memoirs of a Korean Practitioner, 1945–1979," EDI Retrospectives in Policy Making, World Bank, Washington.

KIM, K. S. and ROEMER, M. (1979), *Growth and Structural Transformation*, Harvard Institute for International Development, Cambridge, Mass.

LEIPZIGER, D. M. and PETRI, P. A. (1992), "Korean Industrial Policy: Legacies of the Past and Directions for the Future," unpublished manuscript.

McKINNON, R. (1973), *Money and Capital in Economic Development*, Brookings Institution, Washington.

NAM, D.-W. (1979), "Korea's Economic Take-off in Retrospect," paper presented at the Second Washington Conference of the Korea-America Association.

RHEE, Y.-W. (1989), "Trade Finance in Developing Countries," Policy and Research Series, No. 5, World Bank.

SHAW, E. (1973), *Financial Deepening in Economic Development*, Oxford University Press, New York.

STERN, J. *et al.* (1992), *Industrialization and the State: The Korean Heavy and Chemical Industry Drive*, Harvard Institute for International Development, Cambridge, Mass.

WOO, J.-E. (1991), *Race to the Swift: State and Finance in Korean Industrialization*, Columbia University Press, New York.

World Bank (1987a), *Korea: Managing the Industrial Transition*, World Bank, Washington.

——(1987b), *World Development Report 1987*, Oxford University Press, Oxford.

YOON, Y.-J. (1991), "Hankuk eui Kyungje Sungjang Kwajung aesu ei Jungbu Gaeyip Jidae Chuku Hwaldong ae kwanhan Yeonku" (A study on government intervention and rent-seeking behavior in Korean economic development), master's thesis, School of Public Administration, Seoul National University, Seoul.

[11]

[Asian Economic Journal 1997, Vol. 11 No. 1]   1

Taiwan's Industrial Policy in the 1980s:
An Appraisal*

Heather Smith

Australian National University

In the early 1980s, Taiwan embarked on a development programme designed to shift the economy away from reliance on labour-intensive industries towards the development of technology-intensive products and industries. While continuing to pursue ongoing trade liberalization, the government simultaneously adopted a sectoral policy of identifying and promoting "strategic industries" in order to further industrial development and restructure industry. This assessment suggests that the success of this strategy has at best been debatable.

I. Introduction

The rapid postwar economic growth of Taiwan has raised many questions relating to its possible causes. While populist debate on the relationship between industrial policy and economic growth has traditionally dwelt on the Japanese experience, there has been a progressive shift towards examining the role of government in the economic growth of other East Asian economies.

This paper focuses on Taiwan's industrial policy during the 1980s and the government's attempt to shift the economy away from a reliance on labour-intensive industries towards the development of technology-intensive products and industries. Though widely used, the term "industrial policy" has no standard definition. Yue (1993, pp. 16–17) provides a broad definition of industrial policy as one that aims to promote new and/or sunrise and strategic industries, protect adjustment assistance of ailing and declining industries, upgrade existing industries and promote technological development, exports, regional dispersion, and so on. A narrower definition sees industrial policy as targeting or "picking winners". In reviewing Taiwan's industrial policy, this paper employs the latter definition.

* I am gateful to Ross Garnant, Peter Drysdale, Richard Pomfret and an anonymous referee for helpful comments and suggestions.

ASIAN ECONOMIC JOURNAL   2

1.1 The Structuralist Model

During the 1980s two sources of heterodoxy – the governed-market model and
new trade or strategic trade model – emerged to challenge the mainstream neoclassical explanation of East Asian development.[1] According to the governed-
market model, East Asia's rapid industrialization has "resulted from the state
deployment of a range of industrial promotion policies, including ones to intensify the growth of selected industries" (Wade, 1990a, p. 370). Wade argues that
in Taiwan, as well as in Northeast Asia generally, governments have guided or
governed market processes of resource allocation so as to produce production
and investment outcomes different from those that would have occurred in a free
market. Government intervention of a "leadership" kind is considered to have
focused on industries which are capital intensive, or which use technology that
must be imported from a small number of potential suppliers (Wade, 1990a,
p. 303). The state is thought to have anticipated shifts in comparative advantage
and intervened aggressively to develop national champions for international
markets (Wade, 1984, p. 65). Leadership is thus applied to a shifting band of
industries (Wade, 1990b, p. 249). In turn, sector-specific interventions are supported by a certain kind of organization of the state and the private sector. In
particular, the corporatist and authoritarian political arrangements of East Asia
are said to have provided the basis for market guidance.

    In the case of Taiwan, it is argued, Taiwan's industrial policy since the 1950s
has been characterized as having had two objectives – encouraging exports and
promoting infant industries (Wade, 1990a, 1990b). Exports have been promoted
using policies largely thought to be neutral (Lee and Liang, 1982), exhibiting an
absence of differential effects on the allocation of resources among activities
relative to free trade. Non-neutral policies have focused on promoting infant
industries. In so far as government policies have affected economic outcomes,
improved industrial performance and export growth are believed to have resulted from the coordinated use of both kinds of policy. While asserting the
object of industrial policy has been quite different in each development phase,
the governed-market model argues that, in general, it has worked to change
comparative advantage in anticipation of changing market conditions. In the
1980s, Taiwan's government is considered to have continued its role as facilitator
of industrial growth in response to the pressures of technological upgrading.
Implicit then is a rejection of the notion that government became less dirigiste
as industrialization proceeded, at least at this stage of development.

    On this view, an emphasis on trade considerations is secondary to technologi-
cal ones in searching for an understanding of industrialization that is relevant to
policy making. When technological change rather than trade is emphasized as
the centrepiece of industrialization, an economic rationale for selective industrial
promotion then follows for two reasons. First, because comparative advantage
is not simply the result of given endowments, but also rests on the accumulated

---

1. For a survey of the competing models see Smith (1995).

capital and skills which can be enhanced by a long-term national strategy. Secondly, because some sectors and products are more important to the economy's future growth prospects than others (Wade, 1988, pp. 152–153). Industry policy interventions are thought to have been motivated by the belief that shifting the industrial structure towards increasingly sophisticated sectors would increase the opportunities for capturing dynamic scale economies that result from learning. The presence of externalities or "spillover" effects is thought to have provided the grounds for industry-specific interventions so that the incentive structure was correcting for such market failures.

Similarly, Amsden (1990), in arguing that Taiwan represents a successful case of etatism, has also emphasized the role that state capitalism played in the emergence of Taiwan's economy. It is suggested that the reason East Asian economies have grown faster than other late-industrializers is not because of markets operating more freely and because they "got relative prices right", but rather that governments have intervened more effectively.[2] These economies are thus thought to have succeeded by "getting relative prices wrong", by deliberately distorting prices with a variety of subsidies when extensive currency devaluations and other policies to liberalize the price mechanism failed to create competitiveness (Amsden, 1990).

While the government market model was gaining prominence, some economists were developing a new theoretical rationale for active intervention by government to pursue a "strategic trade policy". Krugman (1984, 1987) sought to encapsulate empirically what Givens (1982) referred to as the Japanese "narrow moving band". The government, it was said, targets a series of new industries in succession, leaving subsidies in place just long enough for long-run competitiveness to be assured. In this way, industries are "sliced off" one after another. Baldwin and Krugman (1988) suggest that this policy may have been adopted by Japan as a means of overcoming the "early start" advantage of the United States semiconductor industry and enabling Japan's industry to become a significant exporter of the 16K random access memory chip. Other East Asian economies are said to have used similar policies to establish export industries.

From the mid-1980s, much of the more informal academic discussion of strategic trade theory increasingly emphasized externalities as a reason for protecting or promoting strategic sectors. Krugman (1992, p. 436) and other, predominantly US, academics raised the possibility that a country could advance its standard of living at the expense of other countries by systematically promoting industries subject to external economies of a particular kind.[3] They cited the

---

2. The impressive body of empirical research on trade and industrialization undertaken in the 1970s by Little, Scitovsky and Scott (1970), Balassa (1971), Krueger (1978) and Bhagwati (1978) related the economic success stories of the export-oriented East Asian NIEs, noting that their development accelerated as they liberalized their foreign trade regimes and adopted an outward-looking strategy of export promotion.
3. But proponents of the more recent theoretical literature are not dogmatic on the issue of intervention to capture technological externalities. In arguing that the presence of externalities in high

ASIAN ECONOMIC JOURNAL   4

importance to modern industrial competition of economies of scale, of learning-by-doing, and of externalities stemming from research and development. These "dynamic effects" associated with the development of "strategic" high-technology industries were said to provide productivity-enhancing spillover effects. Such industries were also said to show rapid growth in productivity, to be marked by rapid reductions in cost over time, to exhibit high value added per worker, and to have substantial barriers to late entrants and first-mover advantages which tend to create imperfectly competitive market structures. Support for industries possessing these characteristics was therefore crucial if a country was to stay at the technological frontier (Tyson, 1990).

Much of this research emerged from the United States at a time of increasing American fears of an East Asian challenge in trade and technology. A number of authors argued that the Japanese government's targeting of industries on the basis of their technological potential was the foundation of Japan's dramatic competitive success in world markets (Dosi, Tyson and Zysman, 1989, pp. 3–34). Other East Asian governments were considered to have been accomplished practitioners of such policies through the course of their industrialization (Tyson, 1992, p. 4). Richardson (1991, p. 38) in a survey of the new trade literature and its relevance to the Pacific region notes that

> American and European perceptions are that selected Asian technological protectionism and trade-policy activism have actually succeeded . . . [they] have come to believe that Japan, Korea, and probably Singapore and Taiwan as well, have been the most accomplished practitioners of new-view trade policies. Out of that perception comes the desire to establish new ground rules, to "even the playing field".

New trade theories, emphasising the role of scale, learning, and market structure, have also been said to be more relevant to the developing countries, because of their small and imperfect markets, than to the industrialized world for which most of the writing on them has been intended (Krugman, 1986; Rodrik 1988). Yet while increasingly being applied in the context of developing countries, the theoretically-based new trade literature has by and large not focused on the debate surrounding East Asian industrial development. The governed-market model on the other hand has sought support for selective government intervention, by drawing on the insights of the new trade literature.[4]

I.2   The Neoclassical Model

In characterizing East Asia's experience, the mainstream neoclassical approach has been to argue that, while interventionist at varying stages, these economies

technology industries may provide a legitimate case for intervention, some new trade theorists have stressed that the circumstances giving rise to such externalities are likely to be very limited.
4. See, for example, Wade (1990a) and Komiya, Okuno and Suzumura (1988).

ensured their trade regimes were more neutral between import substitution and export activities than most economies. This facilitated specialization on the basis of comparative advantage. In other words, local prices of traded goods, on average, departed much less from world prices than in other developing regions, even though there were substantial variations for some individual items and for some countries. Neoclassicists stressed that the economically successful economies were by and large those that had "got their prices right" and had not greatly inhibited market signals driving resource allocation. Great importance is attached to the ongoing process of trade liberalization and strengthening of the market mechanism in maintaining the growth momentum.

On this view, government industrial policy interventions are not the *sine qua non*. Rather good macroeconomic management is thought to account for superior economic performance. Specifically, the soundness of underlying policies – fiscal, monetary, financial, trade, labour and infrastructure – determined the speed, sustainability and equity of growth (Hughes, 1993).

In highlighting the disadvantages of interventionist industrial policy the neoclassical school did not argue that the state had no role to play in the process of economic development. Mainstream neoclassical economists stressed that "dynamic" effects, such as learning-by-doing and externalities arising from R&D, provided the strongest, if not the only valid, reason for promoting industrialization in the sense of allocating resources between industries on a discriminatory basis (Corden, 1974). Functional measures, such as across-the-board R&D incentives, provision of training facilities and incentives to develop a broad-based venture capital market, were advocated rather than industry and firm-specific interventions (Baldwin, 1969).

In the case of Taiwan, Ranis and Mahmood (1992, pp. 116–117) contend that the government has been active in the creation of a favourable environment for economic growth, but has successfully resisted the temptation to push growth beyond its "natural levels", maintaining policy flexibility in response to changing economic conditions. Fiscal and monetary policy remained restrained and flexible, with the government refraining from intervening heavily and, to the extent that it did intervene, exhibiting political courage by relying on overt rather than covert means of transferring resources either to itself or private interest groups. The end result was not only a consistent increase in Taiwan's external orientation, but also much higher average rates of growth, achieved with an egalitarian distribution of income.

The market guidance by the Taiwan government was thus of a special form. This involved: guiding the market economy in response to world demand and supply changes by maintaining control over the money supply and avoiding deficit spending; maintaining a proper exchange rate, enabling market forces to equilibrate around a pegged rate; and the continual encouragement of economic structural change to help deployment of resources, again in accordance with market forces.

While the initial choice of appropriate labour-intensive technologies and sectors in response to relatively undistorted price signals was important in increasing both output and employment in the early decades of rapid growth, the ability to adjust to a rapidly growing capital to labour ratio, growing real wages and changing international product markets, required considerable flexibility. The shift to new industries characterized by more capital- and technology-intensive processes and the adoption of new technologies was facilitated by a simultaneous growth in the level of education (Pack, 1992, p. 102).

According to both the new-trade and governed-market models, the role of the state in Taiwan during the 1980s was one of orchestrating the technological upgrading of the economy. To evaluate this proposition, this paper focuses on the Taiwan government's adoption in the early 1980s of a "strategic industrial policy" designed to provide preferential finance to high technology industries. This is used to assess whether the incentive structure was specifically designed to promote strategic industries? Was the allocation of resources to the "strategic" industries important in influencing this sector's development? Answering these questions can in turn provide an insight into whether the Taiwan government became more or less *dirigiste* over the 1980s.

Section II of this paper discusses the structure of incentives to industry over the 1980s. The Taiwan government's policy response to changing economic circumstances was quite different from that of past decades as it came under increased external pressure to liberalize, and was faced with the domestic problem of declining industries. While addressing these concerns via a programme of trade liberalization, the government also sought to foster specific industries to shift the economy away from a reliance on labour-intensive industries towards the development of technology-intensive industries. This section discusses this dual policy, evaluates the effectiveness of preferential fiscal and financial measures directed to industry during the 1980s and assesses whether the incentive structure discriminated among traded-goods industries. Section III then evaluates the government's implementation of a strategic industrial policy. This provides an interesting test case for the evaluation of the propositions put forth by new-trade theory. In Section IV the Taiwan experience is drawn on to highlight the practical limitations and shortcomings of new-trade theory when various policy implications are taken into account. In particular, the problems associated with identifying what constitutes a high technology and strategic industry are considered, as are the criteria used by the government to select strategic industries. This discussion informs the question of whether the government's policy possessed a forward-looking rational view on how the industrial structure should evolve. Conclusions follow in Section V.

II. Evaluation of Trade and Industrial Incentives

Despite rapid export expansion in the 1960s and 1970s, by the early 1980s the Taiwan economy was facing a number of structural pressures. Persistent trade surpluses were placing heavy upward pressure on the exchange value of the New Taiwan (NT) dollar and intensifying trade friction with the United States.

In response to US pressure and several other factors, such as US retaliatory actions against Japan, the passage of the US Omnibus Trade and Competitive Act in 1988, and withdrawal of Generalized System of Preference (GSP) trade concessions treatment, Taiwan announced in 1989 the adoption of an official policy of diversifying its export trade away from the United States.[5]

However, Taiwan's trade surpluses have created pressures to liberalize quite separately from US pressure. Haggard (1988) notes that the surpluses gave new impetus to trade liberalization on purely economic grounds and that Taiwan became a target of US attention precisely as a result of domestic policies that contributed to external imbalance. Hence the adjustment process demanded went beyond exchange rate adjustments to encompass broader reforms.

By the 1980s the industrial sector was subject to a number of domestic pressures. A labour shortage had been gradually apparent in the manufacturing sector since the late 1970s, and more so after the mid-1980s, resulting in firms relocating industrial activities offshore to mainland China and Southeast Asia. Labour costs rose as a result of this labour shortage, following the introduction in 1984 of the Labour Standard Laws, which were designed to improve working conditions. The average monthly wage, which increased in real annual terms by 6.5% during 1981–86, increased by 11.4% between 1986 and 1990. Rising living standards led to a greater community awareness of environmental concerns with the government imposing increasingly stringent pollution control standards. Requirements on firms in polluting industries to meet these standards also contributed to cost pressures.

In addition to domestic pressures, a number of external factors were affecting the industrial sector. Developing countries in Southeast Asia and mainland China began to move into producing light industrial products, placing pressure on Taiwan to upgrade its export composition. In the early 1980s, rising protectionism in US markets towards Taiwan's exports of textiles and consumer goods induced Taiwan to change the composition of its exports and diversify its markets by seeking other trading partners. This, in turn, required Taiwan's export industries to increase competitiveness without the burden of protection and subsidies to inefficient industries.

In recognizing that structural adjustment of the economy required a more liberal environment, the government in 1984 announced its intention to promote a strategy of economic liberalization and internationalization of the economy (see Schive, 1994, 1995). A trade surplus reduction programme was announced. This included the relaxation of foreign exchange and interest rate controls, the lifting of foreign investment restrictions and tariff reductions. These measures

5. Up until 1992, Taiwan had been named in seven cases for investigation under Section 301 of the Trade Act of 1974 (as amended). Four of these cases were in manufacturing, two in agriculture and one covering intellectual property rights. Three of the seven cases led to explicit threats of retaliatory measures by the United States. Friction centred mostly on market access for major agricultural and food products, including wine and cigarettes, and intellectual property rights (Bayard and Elliott, 1992).

ASIAN ECONOMIC JOURNAL   8

were aimed at ensuring that domestic demand, rather than foreign demand, became the driving force behind future industrial development.[6]

The rapid development of science-based technology in developed countries meant that industrial upgrading required a more liberal policy with regard to direct foreign investment. As an increasing number of domestic producers became foreign subsidiaries, the rationale for protecting domestic producers no longer held. Policies to support domestic producers could end up supporting foreign subsidiaries, contrary to the government's desire to increase technology transfer as a means of enhancing indigenous technological capabilities. Table 1 shows how technology-intensive industries gradually took over the role of traditional industries in exports with this trend accelerating after 1986.

II.1   Trade Policy Measures

Although a policy of economic liberalization was announced in 1984, actual implementation took several years to gain momentum. Under the pressure of excess foreign exchange reserves and the threat of US "Super 301" retaliatory action, the process of trade reform speeded up after 1986.[7] The reduction of tariffs and removal of remaining import restrictions was considered necessary to smooth trading relationships, to foster the upgrading of the industrial structure and to strengthen international competitiveness. On the other hand, the tariff structure has at times been adjusted fragmentarily in response to foreign pressure with little attempt to revise and simplify the entire tariff structure based on a clear conception of the economic rationale in view (Lee et al., 1975). Trade liberalization measures have also met with resistance from various interest groups, particularly from within the agricultural sector and sectors within manufacturing, such as the automobile industry (Tu and Wang, 1988).

Table 2 indicates that the average nominal tariff rate remained above 40% throughout the 1950s, 1960s and 1970s. Despite gradual liberalization, tariff rates in fact still remained relatively high until the mid-1980s. In 1974 the average nominal tariff rate for all importables was 55.7% . The pace of liberalization accelerated after 1985 with the nominal rate falling from 30.8% to 8.9%

6.   Financial liberalization was also accelerated, whereby interest rates were decontrolled and a new Banking Law, enacted in 1989–90, removed all interest rate restrictions. Foreign exchange controls were lifted on trade-related transactions and residents were allowed to hold and use foreign currencies after July 1987 (although remittances of foreign exchange were still subject to quantitative limitations).

7.   The accumulation of foreign exchange reserves increased from less than US$11 billion in 1981 to over US$73 billion in 1990. Appreciation of the US dollar in the first half of the 1980s made the US market relatively attractive to Taiwan exports. From 1980 to 1986 the percentage of exports to the United States rose from 34 to 48%. Since 1985, the US dollar has fallen against the NT dollar, the yen, and other major currencies. The US share in Taiwan's exports has declined throughout this period following the appreciation of the NT dollar by 40% against the US dollar in the period 1986–88.

Table 1   Distribution of Exports by Industry, Taiwan: 1982–94

Year	1982	1983	1984	1985	1986	1987	1988	1989	1990	1991	1992	1993	1994
Total	100	100	100	100	100	100	100	100	100	100	100	100	100
Agriculture, Forestry and Fishing	2.2	2.1	1.8	1.7	1.7	1.4	1.6	1.0	0.8	0.9	0.9	0.8	0.7
Processed Food	5.0	4.5	4.0	4.3	4.7	4.5	3.7	3.6	3.5	3.6	3.3	3.2	3.2
Beverages and Tobacco	0.1	0.1	0.0	0.0	0.0	0.0	0.0	0.0	0.0	0.0	0.1	0.1	0.1
Energy and Minerals	0.0	0.1	0.1	0.1	0.1	0.1	0.1	0.1	0.1	0.0	0.0	0.1	0.0
Construction Materials	0.7	0.8	0.6	0.5	0.4	0.3	0.4	0.3	0.2	0.2	0.2	0.2	0.1
Intermediate Products A*	8.8	7.9	7.5	8.7	7.4	6.9	8.7	9.0	9.5	9.5	9.4	10.0	11.3
Intermediate Products B*	25.7	26.5	26.4	26.8	26.0	26.5	27.7	31.0	34.9	37.0	39.1	41.2	43.5
Consumer Non-Durable Goods	35.5	35.7	36.5	35.5	35.3	33.3	29.7	27.4	23.7	22.0	19.8	17.0	14.6
Consumer Durable Goods	12.3	12.7	11.6	10.3	11.7	11.9	11.2	10.3	8.9	8.5	8.0	7.8	7.3
Machinery	6.5	7.6	9.8	10.3	10.8	13.1	15.4	15.5	16.3	16.1	17.2	17.4	16.8
Transportation Equipment	3.2	2.0	1.7	1.7	1.9	1.9	1.5	1.9	2.1	2.1	2.0	2.3	2.3
Share of Technology-Intensive Exports	25.3	26.0	27.2	27.0	27.6	30.0	33.7	33.9	35.9	36.3	37.9	40.1	42.1

Notes: Intermediate products A are products that can be used for consumer goods or producer goods after processing.
Intermediate products B are products that can be used for consumer goods or producer goods without processing.

Source: The Republic of China; Department of Statistics, Ministry of Finance, Taipei. *Monthly Statistics of Exports and Imports, Taiwan Area*, Table 7; February 1992, pp. 327–328; October 1995, pp. 353–354.

ASIAN ECONOMIC JOURNAL   10

Table 2   List of Tariff Changes, Taiwan (percentages)

Year	Average Nominal Tariff Rate (%)			Amended Items			Average Tariff Burden
	Column I Countries		Column II Countries	Reduction	Free	Increase	
1955	..	..	..	..	..	..	38.2
1965	..	..	..	..	..	..	16.5
1970	..	..	..	..	..	..	16.1
1971	..	..	..	242	39	171	14.1
1972	..	..	..	415	0	53	12.1
1973	..	..	..	94	4	16	12.6
1974	..	55.65	..	202	2	7	11.7
1975	..	52.69	..	71	0	13	9.9
1976	..	49.13	..	44	11	19	11.4
1977	..	46.17	..	159	4	14	10.4
1978	..	43.58	..	996	16	119	11.3
1979	..	39.14	..	432	21	16	11.6
1980	35.96	n.a.	31.17	1604	23	10	9.0
1981	35.96	n.a.	31.17	0	0	0	7.5
1982	35.95	n.a.	31.04	106	5	124	7.6
1983	35.95	n.a.	31.04	0	0	0	7.6
1984	35.95	n.a.	30.81	281	2	23	7.7
1985	32.79	n.a.	26.46	1058	35	1	7.9
1986	31.77	n.a.	22.83	777	25	11	7.7
1987	..	n.a.	19.37	1599	15	6	7.5
1988	..	n.a.	12.57	3377	142	..	6.2
1989	..	n.a.	9.73	4738	..	..	5.1
1990	..	n.a.	8.90	..	..	..	5.9

Notes: 1. Average tariff burden is defined as the collected tariff revenue weighted by total import value.
2. Column I countries refer to those countries that do not grant preferential tariffs to Taiwan, while Column II countries do grant preferential tariffs to Taiwan.
3. .. not available.
4. n.a. – not applicable.

Sources: a. Table 4, Kuo (1991, p. 135). Derived from Customs Import Tariff Table, The Inspectorate General of Customs, Ministry of Finance, Republic of China.
b. Table 2, Tu and Wang (1988, p. 67).
c. Figures for 1990 are from Hsueh (1992, p. 9).

between 1985 and 1990 for the so-called Column II countries.[8] The average tariff burden (total tariff revenue as a percentage of the total value of imports)[9] fell from 7.9% to 5.9% over the same period (Hsueh, 1992, p. 9). As a result, 96% of tariff rates on industrial items were lower than 15% by 1990 compared with 34% in 1986. Moreover, 58% of the rates were lower than 5%. Under the government's "Four-Year (1989–92) Tariff Reduction Plan", the effective real tariff rate was further reduced to 4.2%, which is the average of the OECD countries.

Non-tariff barriers began to be lowered from the early 1970s. The percentage of permitted import items, or the import liberalization ratio, rose from 57.1% in 1970 to 97.0% by the late 1980s. However, as Table 3 shows, of the permissible imports, only 11% were free from import licences, with many other items subject to other forms of import restriction.[10] After 1985 items free from import licences increased to 31.4%, reaching 65.7% by 1991. Also, the number of items restricting applicants who could qualify, and the origin of the imported products criteria, were sharply reduced over the period. While non-tariff barriers are no longer used as instruments to protect domestic industries, some restrictions still apply to particular sources of origin, and the status of applicants.

In the past Taiwan has imposed local content requirements which have affected parts of such industries as machinery (tractors), electrical equipment (colour televisions, video recorders and refrigerators), and transport equipment (motorcycles, bicycles and heavy sedans). These restrictions were designed to foster linked parts and components industries but have also resulted in the maintenance of higher prices and lower quality relative to imports (Wu, 1991). From 1989, local content requirements have applied only to the automobile industry.

II.2 Fiscal Incentives

The most influential fiscal incentive scheme for investment was the Statute for the Encouragement of Investment (SEI). Available to both domestic and foreign firms, the SEI was in force between 1961 and 1990, during which period it was revised several times. The primary purpose of this statute was to encourage and

8. From 1980, Taiwan adopted a two-column tariff schedule. Column I countries refer to those countries that do not grant preferential tariffs to the ROC, while Column II countries do grant preferential tariffs to the ROC. Column II preferential rates apply to goods imported from most countries, with 119 countries or areas eligible for applying the Column II preferential rates.

9. As is well known, averaging tariffs by means of import values introduces a downward bias since high tariffs are given a small weight and low tariffs a large weight. The simple average of tariffs will also be overstated because of the various tax exemptions and the tax rebate system, with the same true of the frequency distribution of actual tariffs.

10. Imported commodities are classified into three groups: one, commodities that may be imported but only under strict controls; two, commodities that may be imported but only with the consent of certain branches of government or with restrictions imposed on the qualifications of importers or country of origin; and three, commodities that cannot be imported at all by private importers.

ASIAN ECONOMIC JOURNAL   12

Table 3   Type of Permissibel Imports, Taiwan

Year	Total Permissible Imports		Free of Import Licences		Restricting Applicants' Qualifications		Restricting Origins of Imported Products	
	No. of items	% of total	No. of items	% of total	No. of items	% of total	No. of items	% of total
1983, 8	25,640	96.4	2,805	10.5	628	2.4	1,610	6.1
1983, 12	25,827	97.1	2,986	11.2	372	1.4	124	0.5
1984, 12	25,968	97.1	2,937	11.0	339	1.3	125	0.5
1985, 12	26,065	97.4	8,412	31.4	330	1.2	99	0.4
1986, 12	26,270	98.1	11,477	42.9	271	1.0	64	0.2
1987, 12	26,426	98.3	11,457	42.6	226	0.8	58	0.2
1988, 12	26,472	98.5	11,454	42.6	165	0.6	58	0.2
1989, 1	8,519	97.0	5,849	66.6	93	1.1	41	0.5
1989, 3	8,610	97.3	5,887	66.5	86	1.0	42	0.5
1989, 12	8,715	97.2	5,928	66.2	43	0.5	51	0.6
1991, 1	8,758	97.3	5,918	65.7	43	0.5	46	0.5

Notes: 1. There was a change of classifications in January 1989.
       2. Since January 1990, import licences have been abolished.
Sources: a. Table 6, Kuo (1991, p. 138), Derived from the Board of Foreign Trade, Ministry of
             Economic Affairs, Republic of China; and Kuo (1991).
         b. Table 1, Tu and Wang (1988, p. 66).

channel investment into areas considered important for economic development. The emphasis of the statute in the 1960s was to encourage the establishment and enlargement of exporting industries; in the 1970s to encourage capital-intensive industries; and in the 1980s to encourage technology-intensive industries. Over time, however, the objectives and incentive measures available under the SEI have become more complex, with the statute serving as a policy instrument guiding enterprise economic behaviour in such areas as export, pollution control, R&D and energy conservation. As a result of these additions, the targets for encouragement have continuously been increased and the items receiving encouragement have been enlarged, resulting in a complicated tax reduction system.

Under the statute, a "productive enterprise" conforming to certain categories of, and criteria for, encouragement were eligible for several major fiscal incentives during the 1980s. "Newly established" and "newly expanded" productive enterprise could choose from either a tax exemption of four or five years respectively, or accelerated depreciation on machinery and equipment. Under the accelerated depreciation option offered, an enterprise could reduce the service life of machinery and equipment to five years for machines whose service life was more than ten years, or by half for those whose service life was less than ten, and by one-third for buildings, construction, communications and transportation facilities.

The accelerated depreciation option served as an alternative to tax exemption, but very few enterprises chose to take it up. Prior to 1987 only twenty-one enterprises applied for accelerated depreciation, while thousands of enterprises applied for tax exemption (Chung-hua Institution for Economic Research, 1987). While the accelerated depreciation option was expected to become more popular as the economy underwent industrial restructuring and more capital and technology-intensive production techniques were adopted, the number of applicants did not increase significantly. This option was obviously beneficial for a firm engaged in capital-intensive production with heavy investment in long-service-life machinery or equipment. However, most enterprises in Taiwan are small and medium-sized enterprises, operating under labour-intensive production technology.

The income tax rate for "ordinary" productive enterprises was reduced in 1977 from 30% to 25% and since 1987 "important productive enterprises" have been eligible for an income tax ceiling of 20%.[11] A productive enterprise could also apply for a tax credit for the purchase of machinery and equipment ranging from 5% to 20%. The tax credit was introduced in 1981 and discontinued between 1984 and the first half of 1985. The effectiveness of the tax credit was somewhat controversial and the measure was discontinued in 1990.

In addition, a productive enterprise could be exempted from import duties or had the option to use an instalment plan for paying duties on machinery purchased from abroad.[12] This helped enterprises to lower capital costs to some extent when import duties were high, but the importance of the measures diminished as tariff rates and other surcharges were progressively lowered (Chou and Wu, 1991, p. 13).

Other tax benefits included incentives: for research and development; for promoting the rationalization of enterprises through merger and consolidation; for acquisition of land for industrial use; and for the purchase of machinery and equipment for energy conservation.

In 1987 the Taiwan government initiated a long-term research project to evaluate the effectiveness of the SEI.[13] Research institutions were contracted to conduct a series of studies on Taiwan's industrial organization, to evaluate industrial policy measures and to review government incentive schemes. The study

11. The income tax rate for all "other" enterprises was reduced to 35% in 1975, to 30% in 1985, and to 25% in 1986.
12. The size of rebates expanded as the items covered expanded and exports grew. Rebates have applied to customs duties, the defence surtax on customs duties, harbour construction dues, commodity taxes and the salt tax. These rebates made up 1.2% of total relevant tax receipts in 1955, 30% in 1964, and 62% in 1972. In 1983, as part of the trade liberalization strategy, the government announced a five-year programme to abolish tax rebates. By 1986, their level had fallen to 21% (Wu, 1991, p. 319).
13. This study was undertaken by the Industrial Development Bureau (IDB) and the Chung-Hua Institution for Economic Research. The IDB is the major governmental agency dealing with industrial development. The IDB is responsible for initiating industrial policies and strategies for overall industrial development, as well as for specific industries such as electronics, information, aviation and automotive.

ASIAN ECONOMIC JOURNAL   14

concluded that, while extensive tax relief might have been useful in speeding up economic development in the past, it was no longer suitable for a maturing economy. The intervention was seen as resulting in distorted resource allocation, and it was considered highly questionable whether the results of government intervention justified the costs in lost taxes. The report concluded that:

• excessive tax exemptions and deductions were causing an unfair distribution of the tax burden;
• complications of the law were creating insurmountable difficulties in tax administration;
• the incentives had created entrenched interest groups that were hampering the establishment of a fair tax system; and
• the correlation between favoured enterprises and their productivity and profitability was low (Chung-Hua Institution for Economic Research, 1987).

The majority of the tax revenue losses due to the enforcement of the SEI occurred during the 1980s. This tax revenue loss of NT$290.5 billion was equivalent to 6.8% of the total tax revenue collected over the period 1981–90.[14]

More specifically, the report noted[15] that in the initial stages of industrial development the statute was quite effective in encouraging an increase in investment but that the effectiveness of tax reductions had lessened overtime. While the five-year tax exemption was estimated to have reduced the investment costs for firms by some 20%, and the number of firms benefiting from tax exemptions or reductions had increased, the growth rate of total investment had not been obviously enhanced. Moreover, measures used to accelerate depreciation were found not to be as effective as tax exemptions and reductions, while measures to encourage business mergers, R&D and environmental protection were also all thought to have had limited effectiveness for the following reasons:

• the motivation behind encouraging R&D was based on the potential for expected development and the pursuit of profit-making, so that preferential tax reductions and exemptions had not been a major element;
• the motivation behind merging of enterprises, in seeking to reduce expenses, coordinate manpower and technology, and control access to marketing, had little to do with tax reductions and tax exemptions;
• the effect of encouraging the prevention of industrial pollution had not been significant, given that the equipment for curbing pollution was not capital that generated profits;
• measures for encouraging energy saving were considered insignificant since the price of energy still did not reflect real cost; and

14. Tax revenue includes taxes collected at all levels of government, but excludes monopoly revenue.
15. The following findings are taken from the work of Yu (1988), which in turn has been taken from the Summary Report: An Evaluation of the Statute for the Encouragement of Investment, Chung-Hua Institution for Economic Research, August 1987.

- investment credits, while stimulating investment, particularly during a period of recession, could not be employed as a long-term instrument (Yu, 1988).

At the time of promulgation the basic philosophy underlying the SEI was that an economy will undergo certain stages of development, and at each stage there are certain key industries which through various linkages will bring about development of the entire economy. This strategy assumed government officials knew what those key industries were and what policy measures should be adopted to develop those industries (Hou, 1988, p. 48). In recent years, though there has been an increasing awareness among government officials that it is difficult to pick the right industries or winners, if indeed such winners can be identified in advance; and that selective protective measures may not be effective. This view has been reinforced by several other studies into government incentives to industry. One study, for example, based on input–output tables for the 1970s and 1980s, found no significant relationship between tariff protection and growth rates of industries when industries are classified according to market orientation (for export or for the domestic market) or according to value added (Hou, 1988, p. 49).[16] Another study (Sun, 1985) suggested that government measures designed to encourage investment in certain selected industries had little effect. Rather it was found that investment decisions were primarily determined by persistent increases in sales which government officials were not in a position to determine beforehand. Interest burden and tax deductions were found to be insignificant in influencing investment decisions.

Consensus was reached by the Taiwan government in 1990 that the encouragement of targeted products and industries should be discontinued. A substantial modification was made to the system of fiscal incentives and the more function-oriented Statute for the Upgrading of Industry (SUI) was adopted in 1990 to replace the specific industry-oriented SEI. The SUI does not single out any specific industry for special tax treatment, but provides tax benefits to all industries for certain generic types of investment, such as R&D, manpower training and anti-pollution measures. Hence it is not a targeting measure, since all benefits are available to all industries. The following incentives are available under the SUI:

- industries using selective technologies are eligible for accelerated depreciation and tax credits of 5 to 20% relating to R&D, manpower training, pollution control, industrial equipment, energy conservation and international marketing;
- in the case of merger or consolidation, a company is exempted from stamp tax and deed tax;
- tax benefits are available for acquisition of land for industrial use;
- exemption is allowed from personal income tax for royalties derived from patents or computer software;

---

16. Based on Hou's (1988) study on the problem of Taiwan's trade surplus by a research team at the Chung-Hua Institution for Economic Research.

- companies which invest overseas may set aside a tax free reserve of up to 20% of their total outward investment to cover investment losses; and
- tax incentives are provided for the encouragement of purchase of machinery and equipment for energy conservation.

II.3   Financial Incentives

The Taiwan government has also at various times adopted selective credit rationing policies to accommodate the financing needs of some specific industries, economic activities or borrower groups, in order to promote economic growth or to equalize to some extent the availability of bank loans among borrower groups (Yang, 1990, p. 19). The most important of these have been the export financing policy[17] and the strategic industry financing policy. The export financing policy is discussed briefly below while the strategic industry financing policy is discussed in greater detail in the following section.

Since the 1960s, export activities have been granted special low interest loans to provide pre-shipment finance and for the importation of raw materials.[18] The difference between the export loan rate and the minimum interest rate for secured loans is illustrated in Table 4. With continuous trade surpluses and accumulated foreign exchange reserves, the interest rate differential has narrowed over the past decade and the margin of preference for exports has diminished. Other forms of finance available to exporters have also been considerably wound back since the mid-1980s.

But while the financial system in Taiwan is considered to have effectively mobilized domestic savings, its performance in allocating funds during the 1980s was subject to criticism. It was claimed that collateral was emphasized rather than profitability of the firm in determining allocation of funds; that public enterprises and large firms were favoured, while private enterprises and medium and small enterprises were discriminated against; and that exporting industries enjoyed privileged access to bank loans and preferential loans, compared with import-competing industries and the non-tradables sector (Shea and Yang, 1990, p. 13).

In testing these criticisms, and in determining which industries have been favoured, Shea and Yang (1990) estimated a "bank finance equation" by applying

---

17. As McKinnon (1991, p. 37) notes, although some financial repression existed in the form of preferential interest rates for exporters, these rates were generally kept positive and substantial in real terms; nor was this commitment to finance exporters sufficient to undermine the central bank's control over the monetary base.

18. As Wu (1991, p. 319) in quoting Lin (1973) notes, credit has generally been of the revolving, short-term type; for example, for three months covering the period between receipt of letter of credit and shipping. The letters of credit were discounted by the central bank at a lower rate than a commercial bank would charge, if the bank would even advance money at all. This provided firms, especially small and medium-sized ones, with needed working capital to fill orders without resorting to the high-cost black market, and thus promoted smaller enterprises as well as exports.

Table 4   Export Loan Subsidy, Taiwan

Year	Export Loan Rate (%) (1)	Minimum Interest Secured Loans (%) (2)	Interest Rate Difference (%) (3)=(2)-(1)	Export Loans of Manuf. Industries by Domestic Banks (millions of NT$) (4)	Exports of Manuf. Industries (millions of NT$) (5)	Export Loans Subsidy (%) (6)=((3)*(4))/(5)
1963	7.50	14.94	7.44	..	..	..
1964	7.50	14.04	6.54	..	..	..
1965	7.50	14.04	6.54	..	..	..
1966	7.50	14.04	6.54	..	..	..
1967	7.50	13.63	6.13	..	..	..
1968	7.50	13.32	5.82	..	28,460	..
1969	7.50	13.32	5.82	..	38,252	..
1970	7.50	13.30	5.80	..	53,429	..
1971	7.50	12.25	4.75	3,983.14	75,019	0.2522
1972	7.50	11.63	4.13	6,200.25	113,869	0.2249
1973	8.17	11.81	3.64	8,304.08	162,744	0.1857
1974	10.99	15.89	4.90	8,094.75	207,104	0.1915
1975	7.80	13.48	5.68	6,761.58	190,804	0.2013
1976	7.00	12.83	5.83	8,934.83	296,727	0.1755
1977	6.62	10.91	4.29	9,924.00	339,278	0.1255
1978	6.50	10.50	4.00	10,750.58	453,043	0.0949
1979	8.75	11.89	3.23	12,609.42	563,724	0.0722
1980	10.53	13.50	2.97	12,597.08	693,953	0.0539
1981	11.55	14.19	2.64	15,345.67	807,134	0.0502
1982	9.79	11.18	1.39	19,151.67	843,147	0.0316
1983	8.05	8.60	0.55	20,981.75	979,856	0.0118
1984	7.86	8.31	0.45	20,593.25	1,178,811	0.0079
1985	7.41	8.08	0.67	20,422.08	1,197,951	0.0114
1986	5.79	7.20	1.41	17,427.67	1,475,760	0.0167
1987	5.50	6.75	1.25	15,162.33	1,674,866	0.0113
1988	5.50	6.87	1.37	16,374.00	1,731,804	0.0129

Note: 1. .. not available.

Sources: a. Table 19, Shea and Yang (1990, p. 45). Derived from *The Central Bank of China, Financial Statistics Monthly, Taiwan District, The Republic of China.*

b. Department of Statistics, Ministry of Finance, *Monthly Statistics of Exports and Imports, Taiwan Area, The Republic of China,* 1988.

ASIAN ECONOMIC JOURNAL   18

pooling data of twelve manufacturing industries over the period 1974–87. Their results provide support for the claim that larger firms have found it easier to obtain financing from financial institutions, while the smaller the asset scale of a firm, the greater the dependence on curb market finance. Thus, to the extent that export finance has been regarded as stimulating exports and economic growth, it has also distorted the fund allocation among exporting, import-competing, and the non-tradables sectors, and contributed to the problem of large trade surpluses in recent years.

The study found also that food and beverage, paper, printing and publishing, chemicals, basic metals, and transport equipment have been favoured in applying for access to loans, while wood and bamboo products, non-metallic mineral products, fabricated metal products, electrical and electronic machinery and equipment, and miscellaneous products have been discriminated against. The preference order of bank financing to manufacturing industries was found to be unrelated to the order of production growth rates of manufacturing industries, suggesting that the financial institutions have not allocated loans according to the growth potential of industries.

II.4 Informal Credit Markets

The curb market (informal financial system) is composed of all markets where borrowing and lending activities occur without being subject to the supervision and regulation of financial authorities. It is generally believed that the active curb market, which the government has never tried to suppress vigorously, has played an important role in Taiwan by attracting household saving and financing the investment needs of private enterprises.

Table 5 shows that curb market finance (enterprises and households) grew from 20% of total domestic financial assets in 1965 to more than 30% in 1980, and then fell to around 17% by the end of the 1980s. At its peak in 1980, curb market finance was roughly equal to that of all regulated financial institutions taken together, indicating a very large diversion of savings from the regulated financial institutions to the unregulated curb market.

During the period 1964–87, financial institutions provided the business sector with 58% of total financing from the financial system, while the informal curb market, capital market and money market accounted for 25%, 14% and 7% respectively. Between 1981 and 1987, financial institutions provided 51% of financing, while the curb, capital and money market contributed 26%, 14% and 9% respectively (Shea and Yang, 1990, p. 30). Over the period 1964–87 public enterprises obtained 95% of their borrowings from financial institutions and 2.1% of their borrowings from the curb market. This compared with private sector shares of 60% and 30% respectively. Over the sub-period 1981–87, public enterprises' share of borrowings from financial institutions was 88.7%, compared with 3.7% from the curb market. Private enterprises' share was 53.5% and 35.2% respectively (Shea and Yang, 1990).

Table 5   Composition of Domestic Financial Assets, Taiwan, 1965–89 (percentages)

	1965	1970	1975	1980	1985	1989
Loans by:						
Financial Institutions	31.1	28.5	36.8	33.0	32.7	43.0
Enterprises and Households	19.6	29.0	28.6	32.2	26.8	16.6
Government Agencies	9.7	4.6	1.7	1.7	1.7	0.9
Securities:						
Government Enterprises	2.6	2.7	0.8	0.6	1.2	2.2
Long-term	35.4	32.3	28.6	26.1	28.0	29.8
Short-term	0.0	0.0	0.0	2.1	3.5	1.9
Other Domestic Assets (net)	1.5	2.9	3.5	4.3	6.1	5.6
Total	100	100	100	100	100	100

Note: Loans made by enterprises and households include suppliers' credits as well as direct borrowing from households through various informal financial channels.
Source: Derived from the Central Bank of China, *Flow of Funds in Taiwan District*, December
(1990, Table 1, pp. 115, 125, 135, 145, 155, 163).

Table 6 compares various types of bank interest rates with a curb market interest rate and consumer price inflation rate. In real terms, the bank deposit rate yielded a fairly consistent and positive rate of return (except for high inflation years). However, compared to the returns that seem to have been available in the curb market – the loan rate minus an undetermined, presumably high, profit margin – the bank deposit rate was probably not very attractive for many savers (Cheng, 1986).

Export loans were extended by banks at interest rates lower than the savings deposit rate. A special rediscount facility at the central bank made this possible and effectively meant that the central bank financed exports while commercial banks collected a fee for initiating and servicing the loans and bearing the credit risk. Cheng (1986, p. 151) notes that these separate arrangements created a three-tiered credit market.

Exporters enjoyed a heavily subsidized loan rate, other privileged borrowers (mostly large enterprises) paid the bank loan rates, and the rest sought high-cost finance in the curb market. Given the significant size of the curb market, the average cost of capital in Taiwan was probably much higher than indicated by the bank loan rates.

III.   Other Measures for Industrial Upgrading

III.1   Technology Policy

While over the course of the 1980s Taiwan continued to maintain competitiveness in some of the labour-intensive industrial sectors, the government, in recognizing the need for industrial restructuring, announced in 1979 the adoption

ASIAN ECONOMIC JOURNAL   20

Table 6   Interest Rates and Inflation rates in Taiwan: 1956–89 (percentages)

Year (end)	Bank Rates			Curb Market Unsecured Loans	Consumer Price Inflation
	Savings Deposits*	Unsecured Loans	Export Loans		
1956–62	17.00	20.90	11.20	41.10	8.35
1963–73	10.10	14.10	7.70	25.40	3.40
1974	13.50	15.50	9.00	29.30	47.47
1975	12.00	14.00	7.00	26.40	5.24
1976	10.75	12.75	7.00	27.60	2.50
1977	9.50	11.50	6.50	25.60	7.04
1978	9.50	11.50	6.50	27.20	5.77
1979	12.50	15.25	10.50	30.10	9.75
1980	12.50	16.20	10.50	31.30	19.01
1981	13.00	15.25	11.00	30.10	16.34
1982	9.00	10.75	8.25	27.70	2.96
1983	8.50	10.25	8.00	26.80	1.35
1984	8.00	10.00	7.75	25.90	−0.02
1985	6.25	9.50	6.25	24.48	−0.07
1986	6.25	9.00	5.50	21.96	0.70
1987	6.25	9.00	5.50	21.60	0.52
1988	6.25	9.00	5.50	21.00	1.28
1989	6.25	12.00	6.50	21.96	4.41

Note: * One-year savings deposits.
Source: Data for 1956–84 are from Cheng (1986, p. 151, Table 11.6). Data for 1985–89 are from
        Tsai (1993, p. 56, Table 5). Derived from the Central Bank of China, *Financial Statistics
        Monthly*, various issues; and Council for Economic Planning and Development, *Taiwan
        Statistical Data Book*, 1990.

of a Science and Technology Development Programme. The programme, which
was later integrated into the Eighth Four-Year Economic Plan (1982–85), sought
to raise R&D expenditure and focus attention on private sector technology
development. A further sub-plan in 1982 called attention to the development of
the following eight strategic areas: information, automation, materials science,
energy, optoelectronics, food processing technology, biotechnology and hepatitis
prevention. This was followed in 1984 by the formulation of the Ten-Year
National Science and Technology Development Plan (1986–95), a major goal of
which was the improvement of the general environment for science and development. The government's aim was to raise R&D expenditure by 1995 to 2%
of GNP – 40% from government (including public enterprises) and 60% from
private enterprises. The government also established the Hsinchu Science-based
Industrial Park in 1980 to attract high technology industries with high R&D
content.

    The heavy dependence on the government to finance R&D activities is due to
the lack of research capabilities of small and medium-sized enterprises (SMEs).
But investment in private domestic R&D has become essential for the mainten-

ance of future competitiveness. R&D expenditure as a percentage of GNP rose from 0.7% in 1978 to 1.4% by 1989 (compared with 1.9% for Korea and 2.7% for Japan). Between 1978 and 1989, the government accounted for between 50 and 65% of total R&D spending (35 to 47% by government agencies, 10 to 25% by public enterprises). By 1989, nearly 50% of R&D spending was being undertaken by private enterprise, indicating that the government was achieving its aim of increasing private sector R&D. However, private sector spending on R&D as a percentage of sales was only 0.1% in 1978, compared with 2% and 3% in the United States and Japan respectively. By 1989 this had risen to 0.7%, but was still much lower than that of Korea (1.9%) and Japan (2.7%). Throughout the 1980s, R&D spending by the foreign sector has largely remained under 1%.

III.2 Strategic Industry Financing Policy

In 1982, in order to promote industrial development and restructure industry, the Taiwan government adopted a policy of identifying "strategic" industries and products for promotion. Apart from factors already mentioned, the policy was largely adopted as a means of addressing the structural imbalance apparent in the manufacturing sector since the early 1980s, and the associated reliance of Taiwan on Japan for imported intermediate goods of machinery and equipment.

Selection of strategic industries was based on the following six criteria, as identified by the government (Council for Economic Planning and Development, 1981): high technology intensity, high market potential, high rate of value added, low energy intensity, low pollution, and large linkage effects. The selected products were drawn from the mechanical, information and electronics industries in the original promulgation. The list was revised four times during the 1980s, with additional products added after 1986 to include biotechnology and material technology industries.

The government offers two measures to subsidize strategic industries – preferential medium- and long-term low interest loans, and technology and management guidance. The interest-rate difference between the strategic loans and the prime rate is around 1.75–2.75%. The loans are managed by the government's development bank, and were disbursed in five phases from 1982 to 1991. The actual amounts extended are listed in Table 7. By the end of 1988, 32% of the total preferential loans, were directed to the strategic industries. In addition to financing strategic industries, preferential loans have been expanded to finance the purchase of automated equipment, domestically produced machines and pollution prevention equipment, the production of exports and the development of new products (Yang, 1990, p. 2). Under the technology and management guidance incentives, the government subsidizes 60% of total consulting expenses of firms, up to NT$1 million. Strategic industries were also eligible for the incentives contained under the SEI.

Since implementation, the strategic loan policy has been subject to two major criticisms. The first relates to its distortionary effects. The second is that the

Table 7   Medium- and Long-Term Low-Interest Loans for Strategic Industries and Major Industries and Loans for Strategic Projects, Taiwan

Credit Type	Period	Size of Loan	Interest Rate	Function of Project	Approved Loans No. of Applicants	Amount
Phase I	May 1982–Dec 1983	NT$10 billion	Av. interest rate minus 2%	1. Production of Strategic Industry 2. Procurement of Local Made Machinery and Equipment 3. Project Approved by the CEPD.	433	NT$10 billion
Phase II	Jan 1984–June 1985	NT$20 billion	"	Supplementary Project: Procurement of Automatic Machinery	451	NT$22 billion
Phase III	July 1985–June 1987	NT$20 billion	Prime Rate minus 1.75% to 2.75%	Supplementary Project: Procurement of Pollution-Control Equipment	465	NT$24 billion
Phase IV	July 1987–Aug 1988	NT$20 billion	"	Supplementary Project: 1. Production of Pollution-Control Equipment and Plant Relocation 2. Implementation of Good Manufacturing Process Project	447	NT$28 billion
Strategic Investment Project Phase I	March 1989–Feb 1990	NT$20 billion	Prime Rate minus 1.75%	Supplementary Project: 1. Procurement of the Energy Conservation Equipment 2. Parking Lot Construction	245	NT$25 billion
Phase II	Aug 1990–Dec 1991	NT$30 billion	Prime Rate minus 2%	Supplementary Project: Procurement of Mass Transportation Vehicles	236	NT$26 billion
Total		NT$120 billion				

Source: 1) Compiled on request of author by the Loan Department, Bank of Communications 1992.
2) Table 1, Bank of Communications (Chiao Tung) *Annual Report* (1991, p. 11).

various criteria used by government to determine what constitutes a strategic product are inconsistent with each other and lack a clear rationale.

A study by Yang, Jen and Chou (1990) is the only research to date which has sought to review the effectiveness of the policy.[19] Based on questionnaire data sent to some 3,000 firms, of which 357 responded, the authors attempted to answer the following questions:

- To what extent has government intervention changed the pattern of investment from what free market prices would have generated, so as to carry out a planned pattern of sectoral growth?
- To what extent has government intervention made for faster economic growth?
- To what extent have the processes of and measures for executing policy been effective in improving the investment position and performance of firms?

The authors' sample included firms which had acquired strategic preferential loans, firms which acquired technical and management assistance, and firms in the mechanical, information and electronic industries which did not receive preferential loans.

The authors then applied principal component analysis[20] to test the following hypotheses:

- the characteristics of the firms influence the probability of their receiving the loans;
- strategic loans cause a greater level of fixed asset accumulation in subsidized firms than in non-subsidized firms;
- strategic loans help decrease the interest burden of firms; and
- strategic loans increase the operational performance of subsidized firms compared with that of non-subsidized firms.

Five OLS regression equations were estimated based on the following dependent variables representing the various hypotheses – subsidize or not, interest burden, growth of fixed capital, operational efficiency, and productive efficiency. The explanatory variables included the aforementioned plus technology level, scale of firm, sufficiency of funds, investment mood, and credibility.

The results of this research indicated that the most significant item influencing the availability of preferential loans was the firm's investment mood, evaluated on the basis of the following categories – frequency of firm investment, the depth of the evaluation employed in the investment decision-making process, and the importance of investment in the firm's growth. Other factors, such as technology level, scale, sufficiency of funds and credibility (evaluated by the availability of short-term, medium and long-term credit to the firm) were shown

---

19. See Smith (1994) for subsequent research into the effectiveness of this policy.

20. Principal component analysis involves combining several variables that represent each characteristic of the firms to form a representative variable. For example, the growth of sales and profitability are combined to form a term to represent operational performance, and the variables of productivity of labour and capital are combined to represent productivity performance.

ASIAN ECONOMIC JOURNAL   24

not to be important factors in the issuance of loans. In the electronic, information and mechanical products industry preferential loans were also found not to significantly influence interest burdens, or to stimulate fixed capital formation or operational performance (Yang, Jen and Chou, 1990).

The effects of technological and management guidance on the firms' operational performance were also evaluated. Higher technology firms were found to rely more heavily on non-government support than on government assistance. It was shown also that government aided in the dissemination of technology, but not in the upgrading of technology. Thus, whether a firm obtained assistance through government or other institutions was not a key factor influencing the production performance of firms. The study also found that most subsidized firms would have continued with their investment projects and would have sought funds from other institutions in the absence of preferential support from the government.

IV. Policy Lessons from the Taiwan Experience

IV.1   The Identification Problem: Defining a High Technology Industry

High technology usually refers to those technologies at the cutting edge of science which have a great potential for commercial use or are already involved in commercial production. However, a comparison of country classifications reveals that there is neither a uniform standard nor a formula for identifying what constitutes a high technology industry. Some classifications relate to standard industry codes; other high technology industries, particularly in OECD classifications, cover many standardized products. Japan, for example, lists the following nine high technology industries: industrial robots, integrated circuits, office automation, new industrial materials, biotechnology, computers, information, optoelectronics and aerospace. It is often unclear though how these industries have been chosen.[21] Some industries, such as new industrial materials and biotechnology, are still at the development stage, without mass production, yet the technological and market potential is thought to have been thoroughly analysed. There are also "strategic-transformative" technologies or industrial technologies which are not necessarily bonded to any specific product. Thus there is a problem of how to distinguish among the many high technology industries and their sub industries.

In popular discussions, the delineating aspects of a strategic industry are rarely identified. The attitude of many observers is that they know one when they see one (OECD, 1991, p. 36). Strategic industries are considered "good" industries for a nation to have or defined as industries that a country feels "it has

---

21.   Accordingly, MITI used the following criteria in determining key industries for promotion in the 1960s and early 1970s: productivity growth, income elasticity, and employment relatedness (Okuno-Fujiwara, 1992).

to have". Within the literature there would appear to be at least some consensus that major positive externalities and large economies of scale based on learning by doing should be involved. But some industries are regarded as strategic by all governments, not only in the static sense of oligopolistic games as suggested by new trade theory, but also in terms of their dynamic potential for future growth. The problem thus remains of how to identify the industries in which opportunities for dynamic gain may exist. The examples are largely based on ex post identification, and the theoretical models do not suggest a strong definition of the required characteristics of such industries.

IV.2   The Information Problem

It seems doubtful that, in designing policy, bureaucrats are particularly conscious of the mechanism behind the criteria. The Taiwan government, for example, identifies strategic industries as "industries that have to grow at an accelerated pace in order to promote improvements or breakthroughs in the present industrial structure", while key industries are identified as being "indispensable to continued economic growth" (Council for Economic Planning and Development, 1981, p. 8). Thus when the policy was first announced the information industry was considered a strategic industry, whilst its software component was not. Basic metals and metal products on the other hand are considered to be key industries but not strategic industries.

As mentioned previously, government selection of a strategic industry was judged according to the criteria of great market potential and linkages, high technology intensity and value-added ratio, a low level of energy consumption and low pollution. While each criterion may have some economic justification, together they appear to have little consistency.

As the priority accorded to each criterion has not been explicitly spelt out, it is difficult to identify which industries meet all the criteria, given that any industry may exhibit one or more of the characteristics. In practice, though, there would appear to be few oligopolistic-type firms which readily conform to all the characteristics put forth by the theory. Schive and Hsueh (1987, pp. 150–151), in assessing the criteria applied by the government in Taiwan, point out that encouragement of investments with great market potential is redundant if the market signal is clear. A similar argument can be applied to the low energy requirement. A high value-added ratio reveals nothing about the efficient use of resources, as is true for the rule for high technology intensity. As far as linkages are concerned, though more investment can be induced by the initial investment if there are linkages, there is no guarantee of success of such an investment. Moreover, the failure of the investment of great linkages implies that the negative impact upon other industries will be greater. There also exist great difficulties in determining the positive spillovers that may accrue to end users and related industries.

ASIAN ECONOMIC JOURNAL   26

IV.3   Implementation

By the end of March 1987, of the 199 strategic products defined and eligible for
preferential loans, only 72 had asked for technological assistance in production,
and 46 for management consulting. Only 82, less than half of the total, applied
for preferential loans. Two results concerning the distribution of preferential
loans are worth mentioning. First, the ratio of transmitted loans for the strategic
industries – machinery and information – over total funds at the end of March
1987 was around 21%. The ratio rises only to 31% when the electrical and
automobiles and parts industries are added. Second, the highest ratio of funds
went to the textiles industry, which received 28.6% of total loans transmitted.
From this information, it is somewhat difficult to determine the theoretical
rationale behind the strategic industry policy where the textile industry enjoyed
the largest share of preferential loans originally designed for high technology
industries. Though a comprehensive empirical study is necessary for a thorough
evaluation of the policy, preliminary findings show that implementation of the
policy is far from satisfactory (Schive and Hsueh, 1987, p. 131). In particular, it
appears that changes in the incentive structure during this period were not concerned with directing resources towards the development of high technology
"strategic" industries.

IV.4   Was the Policy Necessary?

It could be argued that the preferential loans are too small to have a significant
impact, and incentives should be chanelled directly to R&D activities, instead of
production, as far as the externalities are concerned. This then begs the question
of whether the policy was necessary at all.

Small and medium-sized enterprises (SMEs) are generally regarded as having
provided the backbone for economic development in Taiwan. These SMEs have
made a greater contribution to the development of foreign trade than have the
larger enterprises and, unlike the larger firms, have not on the whole been major
recipients of government protection and incentives.[22] Almost 99% of total manufacturing enterprises are SMEs, employing in 1986 around 68% of the manufacturing workforce (compared with 43% in 1966), and contributing almost 45%
of manufacturing output in 1989 (compared with 27% in 1971). Table 8 shows
that, economy-wide, large enterprises on average exported 37% of their production
between 1976 and 1988. SMEs, however, exported more than 64% during the
same period.

The contributions of SMEs to Taiwan's economic development can also be
illustrated by the export shares of SMEs in manufacturing. The share of SME
exports in manufacturing ranged from 62.5% to 73.5% between 1981 and 1988,

22.   Yen (1984) has calculated the percentages of loanable funds of the whole banking system
extended to SMEs between 1977 and 1981. While SMEs accounted for 95% of all firms in the
economy, they received around 32.5% of preferential total loans in 1981 (28% in 1977).

Table 8   Export Ratios of Small and Medium Enterprises (Economy-Wide), Taiwan (percentages)

Year	Large Enterprises	Small and Medium Enterprises
1976	39.1	56.8
1977	36.8	53.5
1978	40.9	56.7
1979	40.2	59.0
1980	40.1	66.7
1981	41.9	74.8
1982	39.3	75.9
1983	35.0	73.3
1984	36.6	71.8
1985	34.2	70.0
1986	32.4	66.5
1987	32.3	61.9
1988	32.5	47.0
Annual average		
1976–88	37.0	64.2
1981–88	35.5	67.7

Sources: Table 10, Lee (1992, p. 47). Derived from *Industrial Financial Situation Survey*, (various issues).

with precision instruments, textiles, plastic products, leather and electrical machinery and appliances as the major export industries. However, since 1982, SMEs have experienced a decline in their export contributions, indicating that they have been under fairly competitive pressures.

Small and medium-sized enterprises are by and large price takers, being heavily influenced by, and adapting to, the overall environment rather than relying on their individual strategies or efforts. In the past, SMEs have shown considerable flexibility and adaptability in response to changing market decisions, though this challenge has become more difficult since the early 1980s as product cycles have shortened. But the predominantly labour-intensive SMEs have gradually been losing their international competitiveness as a result of increases in production and marketing costs. Moreover, maintenance of traditional practices of operating on small profit margins with attention to costs and cost adjustment have become more difficult as capital deepening and technology have grown more important in maintaining niche markets and market shares both domestically and abroad.

In responding to this challenge, SMEs have either changed their traditional lines of business or invested abroad. While flexible in meeting market demand, the SMEs are still characterized as having labour-intensive technologies and thus being largely incapable of conducting intensive R&D other than basic

ASIAN ECONOMIC JOURNAL   28

research, as having lower capabilities in marketing and after sales service, and as having few brand name products (Kuo, 1992). Thus how these firms undertake restructuring in response to both domestic and global pressures is seen as crucial to Taiwan's future industrial development. The bottleneck to further industrial upgrading though is not seen as being one of capital *per se* but acquisition of design and processing technology. Over the 1980s the SMEs have adopted the following strategies in seeking to overcome these limitations: overseas mergers, outward investment, joint efforts for the upgrading of technology, technology alliances in acquiring design and processing technology and a mixture of economy of scale and economy of scope approaches.

A question not sufficiently dealt with in the new trade literature then is whether the anticipated benefits of high technology can be realized through foreign direct investment (FDI) rather than strategic policies. The fundamental rationale for FDI lies in the transfer of firm- and industry-specific intangible assets, such as the knowledge embodied in both new products and new processes and man-agerial skills. A related question concerns the strategic benefits of FDI by domestically-owned producers. Often the presumption is that domestically-owned firms are necessary to obtain the national strategic benefits of high technology production. However, in this respect Taiwan has always had an open door policy towards foreign investment. This has been particularly fruitful for the electronics industry, where local electronic firms are importers and distributors of foreign high-tech products, and as an industry where Taiwan firms are becoming more international in design, production and marketing. Between 1952 and 1988, of the US$8.5 billion total of FDI realized by foreign nationals and overseas Chinese, 28% of this went into the electronics industry – the majority in the latter half of the 1980s. This foreign investment has been an important channel for the rapid diffusion of technology into these export industries as well as for industrial upgrading.

The Taiwan government has also played a major supportive role in developing high technology industries through the provision of training, equity loans, research support and science parks, and in providing the institutional structures for technical support. Such policies are not concerned with picking winners, but have created support by offering better information conditions, reducing uncer-tainties and sustaining organizational change and skill formation. It is thus dif-ficult to see how strategic policies have been the main force behind this sector's rapid growth.

The Taiwan case thus reveals a significant paradox in the actual emergence and growth of domestic strategic industrial policies and their theoretical foun-dations, given that the "domestic" firms at which such policies are aimed are becoming increasingly global, are themselves involved in so-called "strategic alliances", and are increasingly sourcing on an international scale "strategic" science and technology inputs.

A major constraint on the effectiveness of strategic policies then is the emer-gence of the multi-domestic corporation, where governments cannot be sure of the domestic competitive effects. The trend among major players in so-called "strategic sectors" is to strengthen their competitive position, share the burden of R&D costs, or gain access to foreign markets via an intricate web of joint ventures, cooperative agreements and so on. This has further blurred the distinction between "home" and "host" country, and complicated any definition of national economic interest. National technology policy to support specific firms or activities may thus become increasingly meaningless given the leakages, in terms of both financial advantages and research results, to foreign enterprises (OECD, 1991, p. 100). Industrial policy measures to support domestic production may end up supporting foreign production facilities and subsidizing foreign subsidiaries while programmes to increase domestic production may subsidize goods that have largely been produced abroad through offsets and subcontracting arrangements. Investment incentives and domestic policies may thus in fact transfer income to trading partners and help strengthen rival industries. Moreover, policies to isolate and build technology through domestic strategies may in fact slow progress by reducing the scale of the market and blocking cross-fertilization of ideas.

V. Conclusion

In focusing on Taiwan's industry policy in the 1980s, this paper has highlighted the special form of liberalization that took place, whereby general trade liberalization, including the winding back of export incentives, occurred in conjunction with an industrial policy of identifying and favouring certain industries over others. This latter policy was gradually abandoned in response to various studies showing the policies to be inefficient and difficult to implement successfully. In fact, the considerable progress in trade liberalization that took place after 1985 suggests that industrial upgrading appeared to be driven largely by economic forces (both internal and external) rather than by industry policy initiatives. This suggests that the government became less rather than more *dirigiste* over the period.

A survey of the available evidence does not support the view that strategic policies were a major factor in furthering Taiwan's industrialization during the 1980s. Most of the changes in the incentive structure over this period were not concerned with the promotion of strategic industries. It is important to distinguish the economic impact from changes in the internal economic environment in the 1980s – such as the exchange rate appreciation and the policy of economic liberalization including reductions in tariffs and import controls – from the impacts due to the selective fiscal and financial incentives and measures. The former provided the opportunity for the mechanism of comparative advantage to operate and is the crucial factor explaining the industrialization and structural change during the past four decades of Taiwan's development. The latter, in discriminating between traded goods industries, led to the distortion of resource allocation. In fact, the policy of allocating funds to strategic industries in order to

ASIAN ECONOMIC JOURNAL   30

stimulate economic growth contradicts the objective of equalizing the availability of bank loans among borrower groups based on equity considerations. It is also contrary to the liberalization programme announced in 1984 and to Taiwan's progress in trade liberalization as a prelude to admission to GATT.

This paper has also sought to highlight that the circumstances under which strategic policies might pay off are difficult to detect in practice. Given Taiwan's industrial structure, composed predominantly of small and medium-sized enterprises, with a reliance on informal channels of financing, it is doubtful whether the policy was significant in furthering industrial growth over the period. Moreover, it is difficult to determine the economic rationale behind the implementation of the policy given that the high technology "strategic" industries did not appear to be the major recipients of preferential finance. In implementing the policy, it is not apparent that the government had a clear perception on how the industrial structure should be evolving. It is thus difficult to determine the rationale behind the government's designing of the policy. An assessment of the extent to which the government appeared to be directing resources to "strategic" industries finds that incentives were not important in this sector's development and, in fact, it appears that the government did not possess a "strategic" view on how this sector should be evolving.

References

Amsden, A., 1990, *Taiwan in International* Perspective. Paper presented at the Columbia University Conference on Taiwan, New York, September.

Baldwin, R. and P. R. Krugman, 1988, Market access and international competition: a simulation study of 16K random access memories. In R. Feenstra, Ed., *Empirical Methods for International Trade*. MIT Press, Cambridge, Mass.

Baldwin, R. E., 1969, The case against infant-industry tariff protection. *Journal of Political Economy*, 77, pp. 295–305.

Balassa, B., 1971, *The Structure of Protection in Developing Countries*, Johns Hopkins University Press, Baltimore.

Bank of Communications, 1981, 1982, 1989, *Annual Report*, various years, Taiwan.

Bayard, T. O. and K. Elliott, 1992, Aggressive unilateralism and Section 301: market opening or market closing? *The World Economy*, 15(6), pp. 685–706.

Bhagwati, J. N., 1978, *Foreign Trade Regimes and Economic Development: Anatomy and Consequences of Exchange Control Regimes*. Ballinger Press, Cambridge, Mass.

Brander, J. and B. Spencer, 1985, Export subsidies and international market share rivalry. *Journal of International Economics*, 18, pp. 83–100.

Cheng, Hang-Sheng, Ed., 1986, Financial policy and reform in Taiwan, China. In *Financial Policy and Reform in Pacific Basin Countries*. Lexington Books, Lexington, Mass.

Chou, Ji and De-Min Wu, 1991, The cost of capital and the effective tax rate in Taiwan: 1961–1985. Chung-Hua Institution for Economic Research Discussion Paper No. 9110, Taiwan.

Chung-Hua Institution for Economic Research (CIER), 1987, *An Economic Cost–Benefit Analysis Evaluation of Regulations to Encourage Investment*. Taipei (in Chinese).

Cole, D. C. and H. T. Patrick, 1986, Financial development in the Pacific Basin market economies. In A. H. H. Tan and B. Kapur, Eds, *Pacific Growth and Financial Interdependence*. Allen and Unwin, Sydney.

Corden, W. M., 1974, *Trade Policy and Economic Welfare*. Clarendon Press, Oxford.

Council for Economic Planning and Development (CEPD), 1981, *Four-Year Economic Development Plan for Taiwan, Republic of China (1982–1985)*, Taiwan.

Deardorff, A. and R. Stern, 1987, Current issues in trade policy: an overview. In R. Stern, Ed., *US Trade Policies in a Changing World Economy*. MIT Press, Cambridge, Mass.

Dixit, A., 1984, International trade policy for oligopolistic industries. *Economic Journal* (supplement), **94**, pp. 1–16.

Dosi, G., L. D. Tyson and J. Zysman, 1989, Trade technologies and development: a framework for discussing Japan. In C. Johnson, L. D. Tyson and J. Zysman, Eds, *Politics and Productivity: the Real Story of Why Japan Works*. Ballinger Press, Mass.

Givens, N. L., 1982, The U.S. can no longer afford free trade. *Business Week*, **15**, November 22, p. 11.

Grossman, G. M. and J. D. Richardson, 1985, Strategic US trade policy: a survey of issues and early analysis. *Princeton University Special Papers in International Economics*, No. 15, April.

Haggard, S., 1988, Policy, Politics and Structural Adjustment: the U.S. and the East Asian NICs. Paper presented at the Columbia University Conference on Taiwan, New York, September.

Helpman, E. and P. Krugman, 1985, *Market Structure and Foreign Trade*. MIT Press, Cambridge, Mass.

Helpman, E. and P. Krugman, 1989, *Trade Policy and Market Structure*. MIT Press, Cambridge, Mass.

Hou, Chi-ming, 1988, Relevance of the Taiwan Model of Development. Paper presented at the Conference on Successful Economic Development Strategies of the Pacific Rim Nations, Taiwan, 14–18 November.

Hou, Chi-ming, 1992, Strategy for Economic Development in Taiwan and Implications for Developing Countries. Paper presented at the Conference on the Economic Development Experience of Taiwan and its Role in an Emerging Asia–Pacific Area, Vol. II., Academia Sinica, Taiwan, 8–10 June.

Hsueh, Li-Min, 1992, Taiwan's industrial policies for industrial restructuring in the 1990s. Proceedings of the Joint Conference on the Industrial Policies of the ROK and ROC, Korea Development Institute, Seoul, 2–3 April.

Hughes, H., 1993, *Is There an East Asian model?* Economic Division Working Papers No. 4, Research School of Pacific Studies Canberra, The Australian National University.

Johnson, C., 1982, *MITI and the Japanese Miracle: The Growth of Industrial Policy, 1925–1975*. Stanford University Press, Stanford.

Komiya, R., M. Okuno and K. Suzumura, Eds., 1988, *Industrial Policy of Japan*. Academic Press, Tokyo.

Krueger, A. O., 1978, *Foreign Trade Regimes and Economic Development: Liberalization Attempts and Consequences*, Vol. 10. National Bureau of Economic Research, Ballinger Press, New York.

Krugman, P. R., 1984, Import protection as export promotion: international competition in the presence of oligopoly and economies of scale. In H. Kierzkowski, Ed., *Monopolistic Competition and International Trade*. Oxford University Press, Oxford.

Krugman, P. R., Ed., 1986, *Strategic Trade Policy and the New International Economics*. MIT Press, Cambridge, Mass.

Krugman, P. R., 1987, The narrow moving band, the Dutch disease, and the competitive consequences of Mrs Thatcher. *Journal of Development Economics*, **27**, pp. 41–55.

Krugman, P. R., 1992, Does new trade theory require a new trade policy? *World Economy*, **15**(4), pp. 423–441.

Kuo, Wen-Jeng, 1991, *Effects of External Protectionism and Internal Liberalisation: the Case of Taiwan*. Paper presented at the Conference on the Industrial Policies of The ROC and ROK, Taiwan, 8–9 April.

Kuo, Wen-Jeng, 1992, The marketing of small and medium enterprises in Taiwan. Paper presented at the Seminar on the Development of Small and Medium Enterprises in the ROC, Chung-Hua Institution for Economic Research, Taiwan.

ASIAN ECONOMIC JOURNAL 32

Lee, C. J., 1992, *The Role of Small and Medium Enterprises in the Process of Economic Develop-ment*. Paper presented at the Conference on Economic Restructuring and Growth, Chung-Hua Institution for Economic Research, Taiwan, 1–2 May.

Lee, T. H., Kuo-shu Liang, Chi Shive and Ryh-song Yeh, 1975, The structure of effective protection and subsidy in Taiwan. *Economic Essays*, **6**, pp. 55–175.

Lee, T. H. and Liang, Kuo-shu, 1982, in Balassa, B. et al. Ed., *Development Strategies in Semi-industrial Economies*, Johns Hopkins University Press, Baltimore.

Liang, Kuo-shu, 1992, *Evolution of Foreign Trade from Protection to Liberalization in Taiwan, the Republic of China*. Paper presented at the Conference on Economic Restructuring and Growth, Chung-Hua Institution for Economic Research, Taiwan, 1–2 May.

Liang, Kuo-shu, 1993, The evolution of Taiwan's economy in the emerging Asia–Pacific century. *Industry of Free China, LXXX(3)*, pp. 33–48.

Lin, Ching-yuan, 1973, *Industrialization in Taiwan, 1946–72*. Praeger, New York.

Little, I., T. Scitovsky and M. Scott, 1970, *Industry and Trade in Some Developing Countries*. Oxford University Press, London.

McKinnon, R. I., 1991, *The Order of Economic Liberalization*. Johns Hopkins University Press, Baltimore.

National Science Council, 1989, *Science and Technology Yearbook*. Taipei.

National Science Council, 1991, *Indicators of Science and Technology*. Republic of China Taiwan.

OECD, 1991, *Strategic Industries in a Global Economy*. OECD, Paris.

Okuno, M. and K. Suzumura, 1986, The economic analysis of industrial policy: a conceptual frame-work through the Japanese experience. In H. Mutoh et al., Eds., *Industrial Policies for Pacific Economic Growth*. Allen and Unwin, Sydney.

Okuno-Fujiwara, M., 1992, Industry policy in Japan. In P. R. Krugman, Ed., *Trade with Japan*. University of Chicago Press, Chicago.

Pack, H. 1992, New perspectives on industrial growth in Taiwan. In Ranis, Ed., *Taiwan: From Developing to mature Economy*. Westview Press, Boulder.

Pai, Pei-Ying, 1991, *Tax Policy and Economic Development in the Republic of China*. Paper pre-sented at the CIAT Technical Conference on the Role of Tax Policy and Tax Administration in the Course of Economic Development, 21–25 Taiwan, October.

Ranis, G. and S. A. Mahmood, 1992, *The Political Economy of Development Policy Change*. Blackwell, Cambridge, Mass.

Reidel, J., 1992, International trade in Taiwan's transition from developing to mature economy. In G. Ranis, Ed., *Taiwan: From Developing to Mature Economy*. Westview Press, Boulder.

Richardson, J. D., 1989, Empirical research on trade liberalization with imperfect competition: a survey. *OECD Economic Studies*, No. 12, Spring, pp. 7–50.

Richardson, J. D., 1991, *"New" Trade Theory and Policy a Decade Old: Assessment in a Pacific Context*. Paper presented at the First Australian Fullbright Symposium, *Managing International Economic Relations in the Pacific in the 1990s*, Australian National University, Canberra, 16–17 December.

Rodrik, D., 1988, Imperfect competition, scale economies, and trade policy in developing countries. In R. E. Baldwin, *Trade Policy Issues and Empirical Analysis*. National Bureau for Economic Research, University of Chicago Press, Chicago.

Schive, C., 1994, How did Taiwan solve its Dutch disease problem? In M. Dutta and R. Shiratori, Eds, *Asian Economic Studies, Vol. V, Asia-Pacific Economies: 1990s and Beyond*. JAI Press, London.

Schive, C., 1995, *Taiwan's Economic Role in East Asia*. The Center for Strategic and International Studies, Washington, D.C.

Schive, C. and Kuang-tao Hsueh, 1987, *The Experience and Prospects of High-tech Industrial Development in Taiwan, R.O.C. – The Case of the Information Industry*. Paper presented at the Joint Conference on the Industrial Policies of the ROC and the ROK, 16–17 February; and Chung-Hua Institution for Economic Research, Occasional Paper No. 9001, Taiwan.

Scott, M., 1979, *Foreign trade*. In W. Galenson, Ed., *Economic Growth and Structural Change in Taiwan: The Postwar Experience of the Republic of China*. Cornell University Press, Ithaca.

Shea, J. D. and Ya-Hwei Yang, 1990, *Financial System and the Allocation of Investment Funds*. Chung-Hua Institution for Economic Research, Taiwan.

Simon, D. F., 1992, Taiwan's strategy for creating competitive advantage: the role of the state in managing foreign technology. In N. T. Wang, Ed., *Taiwan's Enterprises in Global Perspective*. M. E. Sharpe, New York.

Smith, H., 1994, *The Role of Government in the Industrialization of Taiwan and Korea in the 1980s*. Unpublished PhD dissertation, The Australian National University, Canberra.

Smith, H., 1995, Industry policy in East Asia. *Asia Pacific Economic Literature*, 9(1), pp. 17–39.

Sun, Keh-nan, 1985, An economic evaluation of the Statute for Encouraging Investment. Chung-Hua Institution for Economic Research Economic Papers No. 17, Taiwan (in Chinese).

Tsai, Chi-yuan, 1993, The causes of Taiwan's current account surplus in the 1980s. *Industry of Free China, LXXX(3)*, pp. 49–83.

Tu, Chaw-hsai and Wen-thuen Wang, 1988, Trade liberalisation in the Republic of China and the economic effects of tariff reductions. In *Industrial Policies of Korea and the Republic of China*. Korea Development Institute, Seoul.

Tyson, L. D., 1990, Managed trade: making the best of the second best. In R. Z. Lawrence and C. L. Schultze, Eds. *An American Trade Strategy*. Brookings Institution, Washington, D.C.

Tyson, L. D., 1992, *Who's Bashing Whom*? Institute for International Economics, Washington, D.C.

Wade, R., 1984, Dirigisme Taiwan-style. *Institute of Development Studies Bulletin*, 15(2), pp. 65–70.

Wade, R., 1988, The role of government in overcoming market failure: Taiwan, Republic of Korea and Japan. In H. Hughes, Ed., *Achieving Industrialisation in East Asia*. Cambridge, Cambridge University Press.

Wade, R., 1990a, *Governing the Market: Economic Theory and the Role of Government in East Asian Industrialization*. Princeton University Press, Princeton.

Wade, R., 1990b, Industrial policy in East Asia: does it lead or follow the market? In G. Gereffi and D. Wyman, Eds., *Manufacturing Miracles, Paths of Industrialization in Latin America and East Asia*. Princeton University Press, Princeton.

Wu, Hui-lin and Tein-chen Chou, 1988, Small and medium enterprises and economic development in Taiwan. *Industry of Free China*, Council for Economic Planning **LXXIX** (3), pp. 15–30.

Wu, Rong-I, 1991, Taiwan: adjustment in an export-oriented economy. In H. Patrick and L. Meissner, Eds, *Pacific Basin Industries In Distress*. Columbia University Press, New York.

Yang, Ya-Hwei, 1990, *The Influence of Preferential Policies on Strategic Industries: an empirical study of Taiwan*. Chung-Hua Institution for Economic Research Discussion Paper No. 9003, Taiwan.

Yang, Ya-Hwei, Li-Chung Jen and Rong-Chien Chou, 1990, An evaluation of the effects of preferential policies for strategic industries. *CIER Modern Economic Studies Series*, No. 17, Taiwan (in Chinese).

Yen, Gi-il, 1984, *Industrial Policies as They Relate to SMBs – a Financial Perspective*. Paper presented at the Joint Conference on the Industrial Policies of the ROC and the ROK, Chung-Hua Institution for Economic Research, Taiwan, 27–28 December.

Yu, Tzong-shian, 1988, *The Role of Government in Industrialization*. Paper presented at the Columbia University Conference on Taiwan, New York, September.

Yue, Chia Siow, 1993, *The Dynamics of East Asian Growth – Reform and Government Management*. Paper presented at *Sustaining the Development Process, A Festschrift Seminar held in honour of Helen Hughes*, Australian National University, Canberra, 19–20 August.

[12]

Industrial Policy in a Laissez-Faire Economy
The Case of Hong Kong

Edward K.Y. Chen and Kui-wai Li

Industrial development in Hong Kong began in the early 1950s. There were several factors that contributed to this development. The communist take-over of China in 1949 gave rise to a huge influx of capital, entrepreneurs, and labour into Hong Kong. Traditional industries could not absorb the new employment. In the early 1950s the trade embargo imposed on China by the major Western powers as a result of communist rule and the Korean War not only reduced Hong Kong's entrepot trade, but also brought more foreign capital flowing into Hong Kong (especially from Southeast Asia) because of its stability relative to neighbouring countries. On the international level, the booming post-war global economy enabled the advanced economies to absorb greater amounts of low-cost exports from developing economies such as Hong Kong. It was against this background that Hong Kong went through its industrialization in the 1950s and 1960s.

Hong Kong's industrial structure consolidated further in the 1970s. Faced with increasingly protectionist trade policies by overseas importers and a rather flexible domestic industrial structure, the manufacturing sector diversified from the low-cost textile, transistor radio, and wig industries to electronics, clothing, toys, and watches and clocks.

In the 1980s the industrial scene underwent another significant change. China's open-door policy and economic reform permitted Hong Kong industrialists to escape rising production costs at home by establishing manufacturing bases in southern China where land and labour costs were substantially lower. The consequent contraction in Hong Kong's manufacturing sector led to a new dimension in the industrial development agenda: the diversification emphasis of the 1970s gave way to concern with quality and technological improvement in the 1980s and early 1990s.

By the mid-1990s, the economy of Hong Kong has become service-oriented. The tertiary sector has overtaken manufacturing as the one having the largest employment and the highest growth. However, a large portion of the economic activity in the tertiary sector depends on the continued success of the manufacturing sector. Industrial investments in southern China created the need for services in the banking, wholesale, and supporting sectors. Furthermore, those manufacturing industries that chose to stay in Hong Kong have opted for higher quality and technological improvements.

In the mid-1990s, there has been a renewed call for a more concrete industrial policy, but the focus has changed considerably. Instead of institutional support, industrialists have become more concerned with technological development and with potential co-operation with institutions in China in the post-1997 economy.

TRADITIONAL ROLE OF THE GOVERNMENT IN INDUSTRIAL DEVELOPMENT

The role of the Hong Kong Government in industrial development differed in both nature and approach from other newly industrialised economies in the Asian region. The nature of industrial policy in Hong Kong is described by three "i's": investment in human capital, infrastructure, and institutional. The government's key approach to industrial policy has been to maintain Hong Kong's locational advantages which are its political stability, simple government regulations, a trained work force, and good infrastructure. This contrasts greatly with industrial policy based on fiscal and financial incentives given in other Asian countries. For example, the governments of other Asian economies approach industrialization by influencing the allocation of resources among particular industries. The Hong Kong Government has provided neither fiscal nor financial incentives to influence the allocation of industrial resources. (See Appendix 4.1 for a list of major industrial policies in Hong Kong.) Loans were provided to statutory boards for infrastructure and land development, not to private enterprises.[1]

Industrial support given by the Hong Kong Government has been indirect and aimed at creating a conducive environment for investment and business. The government has not selected any single industry for development. Rather, it has provided supporting services and physical infrastructure to the manufacturing sector in general. If the Hong Kong Government can be said to have undertaken industrial policy, it falls under the broad definition of industrial policy.[2] Industrial policy in the narrow sense has never been considered by the Hong Kong Government.

Nature

Instead of having an industrial policy, the Hong Kong Government prefers to promote an "industrial development policy", which rests on four major assumptions:

- Hong Kong's prosperity depends ultimately on its ability to export;
- the manufacturing sector remains a major employer and exporter;
- Hong Kong will continue to face severe competition from other Asian economies; and
- the pattern and level of demand for manufacturing outputs are changing.

The aim of Hong Kong's industrial development policy is "to improve the real earnings of employers and employees in manufacturing by helping them to improve real output per head" (Director General of Industry 1993, p. 8).

Industrial development policy involves providing infrastructure and developmental support that enables the manufacturing sector to function more efficiently. Direct investment in manufacturing is left entirely to the private sector. Infrastructure support is aimed at the factors of production by ensuring an adequate supply of industrial land, manpower, transportation and communication, water, electricity, fuel and raw materials, and financial and other business services. Developmental support includes: encouraging the manufacturing industry to increase productivity growth and improve quality by adopting various management and technical services and systems, by innovating through the application of industrial design, and by emulating and absorbing useful technologies brought into Hong Kong by overseas investors.

It is noteworthy that although foreign direct investment (FDI) is important in Hong Kong's manufacturing production, the government does not use fiscal incentives other than a relative low tax system to attract FDI. Hong Kong's investment-promoting activities are mainly institutional. The Hong Kong Industry Department (HKID) has set up overseas investment promotion offices in major cities worldwide. The investment unit of HKID provides "one-stop" service to potential investors because it can deal with most questions on statutory and other aspects of investment in Hong Kong.

Approach

The Hong Kong Government's approach to industrial policy is "diffusion-oriented" (D-O) as opposed to "mission-oriented" (M-O) (Dasgupta and Stoneman 1987). Under the D-O approach to industrialization, the government is less active and less intervening. Its role is to provide a flexible industrial structure to enhance production and technological diffusion. It aims to facilitate changes rather than give directions. The industrial policy of Hong Kong has four major characteristics which follow from the D-O approach:

- Industrialization is almost entirely private-sector driven.
- There is no strategic industry in Hong Kong. Techno-economic case studies of individual industries are undertaken by various organizations (e.g., Trade Development Council, Productivity Council, trade associations) for the purpose of keeping up the comparative advantage of Hong Kong.
- There is very little public sector R&D, and no extra or specific fiscal incentives are used to encourage private sector firms to undertake research.
- No subsidies are ever provided. Even services rendered by such organizations as the Trade Development Council, the Productivity Council, and the Vocational Training Council are operated on cost-recovery basis by charging fees or imposing levies.

THE INSTITUTIONAL FRAMEWORK AND FORMATION OF INDUSTRIAL POLICY

Despite the indirect nature of Hong Kong's industrial policy, a large number of agencies including government departments, statutory bodies, and trade associations are involved in supporting and promoting industrial development. In Hong Kong, there are two types of actors which influence the formulation of industrial policy. They are individual actors and institutional actors.

Individual actors are mainly persons either appointed to the Executive Council or elected to represent functional constituencies in the Legislative Council. Other than the ex-officio members from the government, the Executive Council is composed of citizens who are distinguished in their particular business, industry, or profession. Their views and ideas are communicated directly to the Governor.

A central policy unit, commonly known as the 'think tank', is composed of invited individuals who specialize in particular policy areas. It undertakes in-depth examinations of policy matters and suggests recommendations and solutions. Policy issues, specified on a case-by-case basis, are assigned by the Governor, Chief Secretary, and Financial Secretary. These issues have a long-term, strategic nature, and relate to more than one policy branch or government department.

There are two groups of institutional actors that formulate industry policy in Hong Kong. (The responsibilities of these institutions are described in Appendix 4.2.) One group, led by the Industry and Technology Development Council and the Industry Department, relates to industries and technology, while the other group, including the Hong Kong Trade Development Council, relates to the service sector (Hong Kong Government 1994, 1995). Other important associations include the Hong Kong Management Association, the Hong Kong Exporters' Association, the American Chamber of Commerce, the Indian Chamber of Commerce, and the Hong Kong Japanese Chamber of Commerce and Industry. Associations and unions established within individual industries and services often present their views either publicly or through government channels. For example, associations have been established for the restaurant industry and the taxi industry. Recently, it has been suggested to establish an association of real estate agents which will examine the quality and standards in that industry. Associations for professional services, such as law, accountancy, and the medical profession, have already been established.

The process of policy formulation usually begins with the commissioning of an industrial study by the government. The study aims to identify both the determinants and the constraints of growth and to recommend ways and means of building on strengths and overcoming weaknesses. The study report will be examined in detail and recommendations made to the Industry and Technology Development Council concerning the kinds of infrastructure and developmental supports that might be needed.

In general, government departments in Hong Kong formulate policies for the Governor who has the ultimate direction of the administration. The Executive Council offers advice to the Governor on important matters of policy. Decisions are arrived at by consensus and the Executive Council is collectively responsible for the decisions made by the Governor in Council. The major functions of the Legislative Council are to enact laws, debate policy issues, and control public expenditure. The government is responsible for submitting legislative and public funding proposals to the Legislative Council for consideration. Legislation is enacted in the form of bills, but a bill passed by the Legislative Council does not become law until the Governor gives his assent to it. Legislative Council members may question the government on policy issues. A total of eighteen panels, including a trade and industry panel, have been set up by the Legislative Council to examine and monitor government policy matters. Panel members hold sessions with government officials and interest groups to solicit their views.

Once a policy on infrastructure or developmental issues is passed, its implementation rests with various government departments and institutions. The responsibility for monitoring the adequacy of provision, however, rests with the Industry Department.

The Industry Department of the Hong Kong Government provides information on available industrial support services through its Industrial Extension Service and carries out regular studies on major manufacturing industries. The techno-economic case studies aim at identifying and remedying the weaknesses of individual industries and investigating their potential for development. The Hong Kong Productivity Council is the government's principal agent to help the manufacturing sector improve productivity and move up the value-added ladder.

THE CHANGING STRUCTURE OF HONG KONG'S MANUFACTURING INDUSTRIES

In the past decade, the manufacturing sector has fallen to second place as employer and even lower place as contributor to GDP in Hong Kong (Table 4.1). Manufacturing's share of employment fell from 46.0 percent in 1980 to 17.1 percent in 1994, while its contribution to GDP fell from 23.0 percent in 1980 to 9.3 percent in 1994. In contrast to the situation of the 1950s and 1960s, low labour cost is no longer the economic comparative advantage of Hong Kong. With the rising domestic cost of production and the opening-up of China's abundant labour and land resources, Hong Kong industrialists have set their eyes on southern China since the mid-1980s. Investments in China were matched with the migration of manufacturing plants. In place of labour-intensive manufacturing, Hong Kong now excels in quality, services, communication networks, and international connections. The tertiary sector became the largest employment sector and biggest generator of income in Hong Kong in the 1980s.

One might imagine that in consequence of the massive relocation to China, Hong Kong has no more manufacturing sector and it is therefore unnecessary to discuss industrial policy in Hong Kong, unless one is thinking of the future. However, the truth is that despite the relocation of

TABLE 4.1
Composition of Employment and GDP for Major Economic Sectors, 1980–94

Sector	1980	1983	1985	1987	1989	1991	1993	1994
				% Share of GDP				
Wholesale, retail. export, import trades, restaurants and hotels	21.4	20.5	22.8	24.3	25.0	25.9	27.0	27.0
Finance, insurance, real estate, and business services	23.0	17.7	16.1	17.9	19.5	22.7	25.8	26.1
Community society and personal services	12.1	16.0	16.8	14.5	14.1	14.9	15.7	15.6
Manufacturing	23.7	23.0	22.1	22.0	19.3	15.4	11.1	9.3
Transport, storage, and communications	7.4	8.2	8.1	8.6	9.0	9.6	9.5	9.7
Other	12.4	14.6	14.1	12.7	13.1	11.5	10.9	12.3
				% Share of Employment				
Wholesale, retail, export, import trades, restaurants and hotels	23.1	25.2	27.2	28.0	31.1	35.4	38.7	41.0
Finance, insurance, real estate and business services	6.5	7.8	8.3	9.1	10.2	11.6	13.6	14.1
Community society and personal services	8.6	9.3	9.4	9.2	9.6	10.5	11.1	11.4
Manufacturing	46.0	41.4	39.2	37.8	33.0	26.4	20.5	17.1
Transport, storage, and communication	3.9	4.3	4.4	4.5	5.1	5.3	6.2	6.5
Other	11.9	12.0	11.6	11.5	10.9	10.8	9.9	9.9

Source: Industry Department, 1995. *Hong Kong's Manufacturing Industries.* Hong Kong Government.

manufacturing activities over the past fifteen years Hong Kong has re-mained a manufacturing centre of the region. There are two reasons for this.

First, the relocation of industries has been largely an incomplete one. In most cases, although labour- and land-intensive production processes have relocated, other activities such as product design and development, quality control, procurement, group management, and marketing remain in Hong Kong. It has become difficult to distinguish a manufacturing activity from a service. This also explains why Hong Kong has not encountered any serious problems resulting from "hollowing out".

Second, while some industries, notably textiles, clothing, toys, and plastics, have been declining, other manufacturing industries are on the rise. For example, Hong Kong has become a printing centre for the region. In 1994, the printing industry comprised 9.7 percent of total manufacturing employment and 2 percent of total domestic exports. Unlike other manufacturing industries in Hong Kong, printing supplies mainly the local market. Industrial machinery, jewelry, food and beverages, and packaging are also growing rapidly.

Hong Kong's seven largest manufacturing industries are: textiles (including knitting), wearing apparel (except knitwear and footwear), paper products, printing and publishing, basic and fabricated metal products, machinery and equipment, and electrical and electronic products. Plastic products, which was among the top five industries in the 1980s, has fallen behind since 1990. Gross output of all manufacturing industries declined slightly between 1989 and 1993, but value added has increased considerably reflecting the increasing emphasis on quality in manufacturing output (Table 4.2). Between 1981 and 1991, industries with the fastest growth in terms of value added included tobacco manufactures (up 12.4 times), paper and paper products (up 4.6 times), machinery (up 3.8 times), food manufactures (up 3.7 times), and printing and publishing (up 3 times).[3]

The pursuit of an open door policy by mainland China since 1978 has given rise to new opportunities for Hong Kong manufacturers. In recent years, more and more local manufacturers have engaged in outward processing activities in China. They produce some of their product lines in China and then ship the finished goods back to their Hong Kong facilities for distribution and sale. Sales of goods which have been produced by outward processing arrangements are recorded as "resale of goods in the same condition as purchased". Comparison of resales as a percentage of total sales indicates the extent to which individual industries are involved in outward processing. Between 1981 and 1991 the electrical appliances and electronic toys, plastic products, radio, television and communication equipment, watches and clocks, photographic and optical goods, scientific equipment industries have become extensively involved in outward processing activities.

As labour-intensive production processes are relocated to China, products which are still manufactured in Hong Kong are mostly those having a greater skill content and thus higher value added. Consequently, the value added content of gross output has increased with the increase in

TABLE 4.2
Gross Output and Value Added of Broad Industry Groups, 1989–93
(HK$ millions)

Industry	Value of Gross Output					Value Added				
	1989	1990	1991	1992	1993	1989	1990	1991	1992	1993
Clothing	81,625	81,954	85,095	85,164	79,761	23,949	23,922	23,105	24,746	21,246
Electronics	61,208	60,272	55,487	61,518	58,290	12,476	12,665	12,275	13,943	13,313
Textiles	33,662	32,617	32,153	32,162	26,603	9,227	9,053	9,329	9,593	7,944
Watches & clocks	20,454	20,494	19,837	20,459	18,596	3,792	3,720	3,256	3,297	3,093
Printing	13,020	16,194	17,130	18,389	20,998	5,561	6,842	7,049	7,815	9,065
Plastic	24,795	19,204	16,318	15,865	11,026	6,931	5,923	5,238	4,824	3,804
Metal products	16,015	14,754	15,914	15,403	14,244	4,704	4,651	4,790	5,056	4,536
Food & beverages	10,929	12,725	13,599	14,811	15,087	3,417	4,139	4,705	5,196	5,598
Industrial machinery	7,649	9,093	10,352	10,415	9,686	2,792	3,558	3,652	957	3,751
Jewelry	11,103	8,610	9,021	8,419	10,408	2,281	2,150	1,917	1,955	2,329
Toys	12,607	9,182	6,488	6,907	4,427	3,473	2,884	2,195	2,161	1,674
Household appliances	5,260	5,214	5,426	3,666	—	1,181	155	1,471	883	—
Photographic & optical goods	3,026	2,431	3,113	3,852	3,545	771	760	911	949	921

Source: Industry Department. 1995. *Hong Kong's Manufacturing Industries*. Hong Kong Government.

outward processing. For example, the value added content of gross output of the radio, television, and communication equipment industry rose from 20 percent in 1981 to 24 percent in 1991 (having dropped to 15 percent in 1988).

One constant feature of Hong Kong's industrial structure has been its dominance by small firms. Over 96 percent of manufacturing establishments in Hong Kong engage fewer than fifty persons (Table 4.3). And these small-sized manufacturing enterprises employ 51 percent of the total manufacturing work force. The increase in outward processing exacerbated this tendency. According to the review by the Census and Statistics Department (1993), average employment per establishment in the manufacturing sector as a whole decreased from 21 persons in 1981 to 15 persons in 1991. The greatest declines in employment were in those industries most extensively involved in outward processing: radio, television and communication equipment (–74%), electrical appliances and electronic toys (–62%), plastic products (–56%), and the watches and clocks, photographic and optical goods, scientific equipment category (–55%). Industries that recorded positive growth in the number of persons

100   EDWARD K.Y. CHEN & KUI-WAI LI

TABLE 4.3
Number of Establishments and Number of Persons Engaged, by Size of Establishment, 1989–94

Size of Establishment	Number of Establishments						Number of Persons Engaged (1,000s)					
	1989	1990	1991	1992	1993	1994	1989	1990	1991	1992	1993	1994
1–9	34,802	35,915	33,888	31,261	29,818	25,979	129.6	131.0	121.9	111.8	101.6	87.8
10–19	7.270	6.366	5,980	5.120	4,564	3,870	97.7	87.0	80.2	68.6	61.0	51.8
20–49	4,735	4,219	4,018	3,501	3,032	2,703	145.1	136.1	122.6	106.2	91.8	82.0
50–99	1,919	1,520	1,430	1,221	1,110	934	131.4	113.7	96.8	82.5	75.8	64.7
100–199	741	668	602	524	450	356	100.3	91.3	81.6	70.3	60.8	48.5
200–499	346	302	284	249	199	170	103.2	91.3	87.7	74.6	59.0	50.7
500–999	88	77	56	45	45	41	58.6	50.2	37.0	30.7	30.3	28.4
1000+	26	20	18	17	19	15	36.9	29.7	26.9	26.5	28.0	24.5
Total	49,926	49,087	46,276	41,937	39,238	34,068	803.0	730.2	654.7	571.2	508.1	438.4

Source: Industry Department. 1995. *Hong Kong's Manufacturing Industries*. Hong Kong Government.

engaged include tobacco manufactures (+55%), food manufactures (+31%), printing and publishing (+19%), machinery (+14%), and paper and paper products (+12%). With the exception of food manufactures, these increases in the number of persons engaged were accompanied by an increase in the number of establishments.

During the 1980s, local manufacturers became increasingly subject to the pressures of a tight labour market, rising production costs, and keen competition from other newly industrialised economies (particularly Singapore, South Korea, and Taiwan) in overseas markets. One step that Hong Kong manufacturers took to contain production costs and improve export competitiveness was to raise productivity by investing in physical capital. Between 1981 and 1991, for example, the retained imports of industrial machinery for manufacturing use recorded an average annual growth rate of 7.8 percent in real terms.

The ratio of value added to the number of persons engaged is a crude indication of labour productivity. For Hong Kong's manufacturing sector as a whole, this ratio trended upward practically throughout the 1980s. The improvement in productivity was partly attributable to increased investment in machinery and equipment. Furthermore, with the relocation of labour-intensive production processes across the border, local manufacturers concentrated on more capital- and skill-intensive activities, which raised the productivity of the manufacturing sector. The industries which recorded the highest annual productivity growth during the 1980s were tobacco manufactures (24 percent), paper and paper products (18 percent), and office and computing equipment (17 percent). Higher productivity growth was also recorded in the chemical and chemical products, watches and clocks, photographic and optical goods, scientific equipment, and electrical appliances and electronic toys industry groups — all with an average annual growth rate of about 16 percent. The increase in productivity in most of these industries was due to a combination of increased investment and relocation of labour intensive production processes to China between 1981 and 1991.

Despite rising production costs, most Hong Kong manufacturing industries were able to improve their profit margins during the 1980s. Industries that were more successful in raising profit margins included tobacco manufactures, food manufactures, transport equipment, and paper and paper products. These industries were also successful in reducing non-labour costs as reflected by a significant decrease in the percentage component of raw materials and other expenses between 1981 and 1991. For those outward-processing oriented industries, the percentage of employee compensation in 1991 was lower than 10 years earlier.

Recent empirical studies found that service industries such as wholesale, import/export trade, and business services had expanded in terms of the number of establishments and employment as a result of Hong Kong's outward investment to southern China. Tuan and Ng (1994) confirmed that Hong Kong's industrial sector underwent a structural change in the mid-1980s in their estimates of a Cobb-Douglas production function for various manufacturing industries with a dummy variable to distinguish the period 1978–86 from the period 1987–91. Since 1987, the share of labour in Hong Kong's manufacturing has declined due both to the shift of manufacturing to China and to the expansion of the tertiary sector.

THE CHANGING ROLE OF GOVERNMENT

The traditional attitude of the Hong Kong government has been not to intervene in industrial development. Industrial policy in Hong Kong has concentrated on educational, infrastructure, and institutional developments which promote industrial development indirectly.[4]

In the 1960s and early 1970s there were occasional calls by industrialists for a more active government role in helping Hong Kong industries, but in the latter half of the 1970s there was a definite call for government promotion of industrial diversification. In the mid-1970s the growth of Hong Kong's economy and her industrial survival were threatened by the increasing pressure of textile trade protection and competition from other newly industrializing countries, such as South Korea, Taiwan, and Singapore. An advisory committee on diversification was set up in late 1978, and a report was published in December 1979. It probably was the first official document on industry policy in Hong Kong.

Chaired by the Financial Secretary, the main task of the committee on diversification was to advise "whether the process of diversification of the economy, with particular reference to the manufacturing sector, can be facilitated by the modification of existing policies or the introduction of new policies" (Advisory Committee on Diversification 1979, p. 2). Among the forty-seven recommendations made in the report, nine were related to industrial and trade development. All nine of these recommendations called for the establishment of more institutions providing further support to industrial development.

The report on diversification became outdated as soon as it was published. The opening up of China in 1979 created new opportunities for Hong Kong industrialists to integrate themselves with the Guangdong economy. Also, entrepôt trade and financial activities were sufficient to sustain the high rate of growth of the economy. Enthusiasm to upgrade Hong Kong's technological infrastructure and technological capability was losing steam.

Instead of support for specific industrial sectors, the Hong Kong Government has made an increasing effort to provide supporting services and technical backup services to industry. Since 1979, the Hong Kong Productivity Council (HKPC) and the Hong Kong Industry Department (HKID) have widened their scope of operation from providing training and consulting to include developing supporting industries (such as plastic conversion and metal and light engineering) and upgrading traditional ones (such as electronics, textiles, and garments). A CAD/CAM sub-committee was set up in 1984 to monitor the development and application of CAD/CAM technology for electronic production. The "United Approach" programme of the HKPC, set up in 1985, provides industries with advice and assistance to achieve vertical integration. The Primary Standards Laboratory, the Hong Kong Product Standards and Calibration Laboratory, the Product Standard Information Bureau, and the Hong Kong Laboratory Accreditation Scheme, which were established in 1980, 1983, 1984, and 1986 respectively, provide services on standards testing and quality control. The Plastic Technology Centre, established in 1987 at Hong Kong Polytechnic University, has been providing technical assistance to the plastic conversion industry. Finally, the Hong Kong Design Innovation

Company Limited, established in 1986, provides industries with comprehensive product innovation, design, and development services.

In early 1992, the Industry and Technology Development Council (ITDC) replaced the former Industry Development Board and the Committee on Science and Technology. The aim was to ensure that Hong Kong could respond to the rapidly changing technological environment and to emphasize the vital connection between industry and technology. Within the ITDC, a Technology Committee advises the Government on the technology issue, while the Technology Review Board advises on the direction of technology development. The Hong Kong Quality Agency was established in 1992 to ensure the greater use of quality assurance in manufacturing through a Quality Awareness Campaign. In June 1993, the Hong Kong Industrial Technology Centre Corporation was established to facilitate the promotion of technological innovation and the application of new technology in domestic industries. The Centre also acts as an incubator for start-up technology-based companies. A second centre is now under consideration.

In educational development, the government allocated 16.6 percent of its expenditures in 1989–90 to educational and vocational training, a higher share than in Singapore or Taiwan (Hong Kong Government 1994). The Open Learning Institute was established in 1990 to provide off-the-job learning opportunities. The new Hong Kong University of Science and Technology started in October 1991 to meet the growing demands for engineers and scientists. From 1990 to 1995, institutions of higher education doubled their enrollment. The New Technology Training Scheme launched in June 1992 by the Vocational Training Council, provides financial assistance to employers to train technicians and managers who are considered to be strategic for the industrial and economic development of Hong Kong. In June 1993, the government injected an additional capital sum of HK$50 million into this scheme, on top of the original HK$55 million.

The argument for a greater involvement of the government in technology and industry has been raised again recently, but this time the context is the wider implication of technological and industrial co-operation between Hong Kong and mainland China after July 1997 when the sovereignty of Hong Kong will be returned to China.

The small scale of Hong Kong's manufacturing firms became one area of concern and of potential government intervention. The flexibility of small firms to switch from one line of production to another is an advantage in an environment of changing export demand and rising protectionism when uncertainty of future orders is high. However, small firms also usually lack significant research capability and they usually withdraw from unstable situations. The political and economic reality in the 1980s suggested that Hong Kong would need industrial firms that could carry out research and development on their own, firms that were large enough to persist after the 1997 change of sovereignty, firms that could maintain headquarters in Hong Kong while utilizing the low production cost in China, and firms that would allow owners free movement of capital and personal emigration on the one hand and on the other permit them to maintain their base of business in Hong Kong. Hong Kong's industrial structure, dominated as it was by small firms, might not be suited to the future.

In the early 1990s "industrial amalgamation" was suggested as a way to reorganize Hong Kong's industry to meet this challenge (Li 1990, and Li and Lo 1993). Groups of small firms would amalgamate into industrial conglomerates, sharing ownership among the original partners. Such conglomerates would be large enough to face instability and at the same time flexible enough to undergo rapid changes in industrial structure. However, realizing industrial amalgamation in Hong Kong is easier said than done. First, the Hong Kong Government cannot be expected to direct industrial development or to involve itself with the ownership pattern of firms. It is unlikely that the government would help to create conditions for amalgamation. More important, the strong entrepreneurial attitudes of Hong Kong industrialists are not likely to make them amenable to sharing decision making with partners. Industrial amalgamation will not take place in Hong Kong unless it emerges from the needs of small firms themselves.

Aside from this proposal for strengthening the ownership structure of Hong Kong's manufacturing sector, there have been various other projections regarding the future of the Hong Kong industrial sector. With continued economic growth in Guangdong and the deepening of economic reform in China, Hong Kong manufacturers will continue to exploit the lower production costs across the border. Short of government intervention, industrial development in Hong Kong will soon establish an "office-factory" relationship with the Guangdong economy. The "New York of China" or "Manhattanization" are other suggested models for Hong Kong after 1997.

The Hong Kong Government has asserted repeatedly that there is not going to be a deliberate industry policy in Hong Kong. A 1991 statement on industrial policy said:

the government's industrial policies aim at maintaining
an infrastructure which enables manufacturing businesses to
function efficiently and providing services which enable industry to become more competitive through productivity growth,
quality improvement, and product innovation. The government encourages technology transfer through an inward investment promotion programme. (Hong Kong Government
1991)

However, rapid changes in the industrial sector have brought a strong
reaction from various institutions and interested groups. The Hong Kong
Government has come to recognize a need to secure Hong Kong's manufacturing sector so that industrial employment can be stabilized. According to a 1994 statement, the government's position is to

facilitate industrial and trade activities within the framework of
a free market. It neither protects nor subsidises manufacturers.
It recognises, however, a responsibility to provide an accept-
able industrial infrastructure, particularly in terms of land and
manpower, and to make available services which enable industry to become more competitive through productivity growth,
quality improvement and product innovation. It also encourages technology transfer through an inward investment promotion scheme. (Hong Kong Government 1994, p. 85, italics
added for emphasis).

The wave of industrial relocation to southern China in the 1980s finally
culminated in severe structural unemployment in Hong Kong becoming a
top issue in 1993–94 when unemployment exceeded two percent. By mid
1995, the official unemployment figure reached 3.5 percent. Labour unions claimed the rate was much higher when under-employment was
considered. Most of the unemployed are factory workers although unemployment in some service industries such as restaurants and hotels is
higher than the overall trend. Employers claimed that wages were too high
and that local workers were not willing to accept lower wages. Trade
unions, on the other hand, claimed that employers deliberately shied away
from employing local workers. They urged the government to prohibit the
import of labour. The government's response was instead to promote
industrial retraining. The government supported retraining because surplus workers from the manufacturing sector cannot readily be re-deployed

106   EDWARD K.Y. CHEN & KUI-WAI LI

to the sectors that are experiencing a shortage of labour such as finance, commerce, and on-site construction.

CONCLUSION

The Hong Kong Government has never intervened directly in the industrial sector. Rather, it has contributed to the development of the manufacturing sector through indirect assistance including establishing suitable institutions, promoting relevant infrastructure support, and easing the cost of production by providing low-cost industrial land. The situation facing Hong Kong today, however, calls for the government to be more responsive to technological needs. The Hong Kong economy is undergoing unprecedented, rapid structural change. It is difficult to envisage that market forces left all to themselves will restore equilibrium within a reasonable period of time. Although, in the past, the Hong Kong economy prospered as a result of positive non-interventionist industrial policy, the Hong Kong economy can probably only survive the current transformation through the positive intervention by the government. There are three areas in which government policy is needed.

First, the government needs to facilitate the upgrading of Hong Kong's technological base. Hong Kong falls far behind other economies at a similar level of development in its expenditure on R&D. Hong Kong spends only about 0.5 percent of GDP on R&D while other NIEs spend close to 2 percent. For the time being, the rapid development of commercial and financial services is preventing the hollowing out of the Hong Kong economy, but in the longer run the economy needs to develop the sophisticated industries and services which serve the tertiary sector (telecommunications, regional headquarters activities, investment banking, and information services). These industries can be labeled as "fourth" sector activities and they require a sound technological base. Furthermore, in a mature stage of economic development Hong Kong cannot as in the past rely entirely on its flexible entrepreneurs and labour; it needs technological capability to become resilient to external economic and technological changes. It is therefore imperative for Hong Kong to spend much more on R&D. Government expenditure in this regard has increased, though the overall fiscal allocation has remained unchanged.

Second, the government must increase Hong Kong's investment in human capital and reformulate its manpower capabilities. Hong Kong's investment in education, especially in primary and secondary education, falls below that of many developing countries in Asia. The share of education expenditure in GDP is currently 3.2 percent in Hong Kong but it is over 4 percent in South Korea, Taiwan, Singapore, and Thailand. An aggressive training and retraining strategy must be formulated to deal with Hong Kong's severe structural unemployment situation. Today, the mismatch of jobs in Hong Kong occurs not only between manufacturing and trade but also within a single trade due to a mismatch of skills. The structural unemployment situation is exacerbated by the 150 people who immigrate legally each day from China but who are not adapted to Hong Kong's working environment. Also, many workers have become unemployable because of quality improvement in certain industries.

Third, the government needs to consider formulating a comprehensive competition policy. The export-oriented manufacturing sector, which was subject to the competitive pressures of the global market place, is declining in importance and the non-tradable sector is becoming more important in Hong Kong's economy. Monopolistic tendencies have emerged in many service sectors, such as broadcasting, telecommunications, banking, and supermarket chains. Hitherto, any policies regarding competition had been ad hoc and piecemeal. But the situation now requires policy makers in Hong Kong to enact competition laws and establish fair trade commissions such as exist in South Korea and Taiwan. Despite this need, however, competitive policy is not expected to become an important part of industrial policy in Hong Kong because the notion that such policy is anti-business and anti-market remains deep-rooted.

Notes

[1] The one exception, which was very short-lived, was the Loans for Small Industrial Scheme (1972–75).

[2] See the introductory chapter to this volume and Caves (1986), Okuno and Suzumura (1986), and Wong (1991) for definitions of industrial policy.

[3] In September 1993, the Census and Statistics Department of Hong Kong conducted a special review on the changing structure of the manufacturing sector. The review compared value added and gross output figures, resale value as a percentage of total sales, the number of establishments and employment, and investment structure in 1981 and 1991. The data in this and the following paragraphs comes from this review.

[4] For a long time the government has been involved in the provision of industrial land. The development of new towns had multiple objectives, but facilitating industrial development was certainly one of them.

108   EDWARD K.Y. CHEN & KUI-WAI LI

APPENDIX 4.1

Major Industrial Policies of Hong Kong, by Category, 1979–94
(Updated December 1995)

Year	Policy

Non-Fiscal Incentives

1988	Governor's Award for Industry
1989	Awards to consumer product design and machinery equipment design
1989	Awards to productivity growth and excellence in quality
1992	The number of awards was increased to 6 categories (2 extra awards for environmental performance and export marketing)

Financial Assistance

1972–75	Loans for Small Industries
1989/90	Technology Loan Fund (to encourage training in new technologies)
1992/1993	New Technology Training Scheme (to train technicians & managers in new technologies)
1994	A revolving fund providing financial support for projects recommended by the Industry and Technology Development Council to enhance industrial and technological development

Industrial Selection

1973	New Industrial Land Policy (to accommodate capital- and technology-intensive industries)
Since 1983	Industry Department conducted techno-economic and market research studies on the 4 major industry sectors: textiles and clothing, electronics, plastics, and metals/light engineering. Individual industries studied at 4-year intervals
1991	Study on the development potential of the chemical processing industry
1993	Study on the metals and light engineering industries
1994	Consultancy studies on local software, electronics, and plastics industries

| 1994 | Biotechnology directory produced by the Industry and Technology Development Board (to facilitate networking and collaboration among research institutions and overseas businesses) |

Research and Development Policy

Since 1983	The Industry Department (ID) commissioned techno-economic studies on selected industries, for example:
1982	electronics
1984	watches and clocks and textiles and clothing
1986	plastics conversion and optics and photo-graphics
1983	metals and light engineering industries
1987	plastics conversion
1988	textiles
1989	electronics
1990	plastics conversion
1982–85	Industrial research projects funded by the Industry Development Board to promote industry-university link:
1982	fabrication and analysis of integrated circuits (University of Hong Kong)
1983	CAD of electronic systems (Hong Kong Polytechnic)
1983	integrated circuit technology and semi-conductor devices (Chinese University of Hong Kong)
1985	CAD/CAM system for the Hong Kong manufacturing sector (University of Hong Kong)
1989	Hong Kong Technology Centre Feasibility Study Final Report to the Hong Kong Government Industry Department
1990	Provisional Hong Kong Technology Centre Company Limited formed
1992	Study commissioned to examine the case for establishing a science park
1992	Industry and Technology Development Council formed (to replace the Industry Development Board and the Committee of Science and Technology)
1993	Hong Kong Industrial Technology Centre Corporation established to promote technological innovation and application of new technologies in local industries
1995	Plan to establish an Applied Research Centre to promote joint projects with China's leading research institutes

110   EDWARD K.Y. CHEN & KUI-WAI LI

Land Development

1973	New Industrial Land Policy (gave special preference to capital- and technology- intensive industries)
Since 1974	New Towns Programme (e.g., Tsuen Wan, Shatin, Tuen-Mun, and Tsing Yi)
1977	Hong Kong Industrial Estates Corporation (HKIEC) (sold land at concessional prices to high technology industries that cannot operate in multi-storey factory buildings)
Since 1977	Market town planning and engineering (develops industrial estates for light and high technology industries e.g., Tai Po Industrial Estate and Yuen Long Industrial Estate)
1979	Development of Shatin's 3 light industrial zones to Fo Tan, Siu Lek Yuen and Pak Shek
1981	The HKIEC started to build standard factory blocs to suit a wide range of factory requirements
1991	Began construction of the third industrial estate at Tseung Kwan O (first phase opened in 1994)
1993	Tin Shui Wai new town opened
1997	First phase of 9th new town at Tung Chung and Tai Ho on northern Lantau Island ready

Technical Support and Services

Since 1980	The Hong Kong Productivity Council (HKPC) widened scope to provide a wide range of support and technical backup services to industries
1980	Primary Standards Laboratory of the Industry Department
1981	Hong Kong/Japan Business Co-operation Committee
1983	Industry Development Board (IDB)
1983	Hong Kong Standards and Calibration Laboratory of the IDB
1984	Product Standards Information Bureau of the IDB
1984	The IDB set up a CAD/CAM sub-committee to monitor the development and application of CAD/CAM technology
1986	Hong Kong Laboratory Accreditation Scheme
1986	Hong Kong Design Innovation Co., Ltd. (government-backed institution to improve design and product innovation capabilities)

1987	Plastics Technology Centre at the Hong Kong Polytechnic (provides technical assistance to plastics conversion industry)
1988	The HKPC prepared formation of Clothing Technology Demonstration Centre
1988/89	HKPC established a Textiles and Apparel Division
1988/89	Expansion of the Metals Development Laboratory
1988/89	Expansion of the CAD/CAM Centre for the electronics industry
1989	The Surface Mount Technology (SMT) Laboratory (provides technical assistance and training in SMT)
1989	The Radio Frequency and Digital Communication (RF/Digicom) Laboratory (helps the firms acquire knowledge and expensive equipment on the design of communication products)
1988	HKPC's new Productivity Enhancement Services
1989	HKID's Industrial Extension Services (IES). (Engineers and researchers provide direct information, advice, and technical assistance to medium- and small-sized factories.
1989/90	HKID's Quality Awareness Campaign
1989/90	Hong Kong Quality Assurance Agency (HKQAA) (assist and encourages manufacturers to adopt quality management and production)
1990	HKPC established 3 wholly-owned limited liability subsidiaries (to corporatise and privatise industry support activities)
1991	Force calibration service for the construction industry
Since 1990	HOKLAS reached agreements with similar testing authorities overseas
1992	HOKLAS accredited several laboratories on environmental testing
1993	HKQAA signed a memorandum of understanding with the British Standard Institutions (Quality Assurance)
1993	HKPC invited local companies to form consortia to facilitate the transition to high valued-added production
1993	HKPC set up a Guangzhou Liaison Office (to strengthen the capabilities by using specialist resources in China)

112   EDWARD K.Y. CHEN & KUI-WAI LI

1989	ID outlined environmental measures in 1989 *White Paper on Pollution* (e.g., Water Pollution Control and Waste Disposal Ordinances)
1992	ID commissioned consultancy study on support to industry on environmental matters
1993	ID assessed operational and financial effects of current and planned legislation and measures on manufacturing industries
1994	ID's Centre for Environment Technology Limitd (provided specific guidance for texture bleachers & dyers, electroplaters and printed circuit board manufacturers)
1994	ID operates information hotline and a directory of pollution control and prevention equipment

Industrial Training

1982	Vocational Training Council (VTC)
1983	Engineering Graduate Training Scheme of the VTC
Up till 1987	Hong Kong has 8 technical institutions to train craftsmen and technicians and 8 training centres to provide basic off-the-job training for major sectors (such as metals and electronics)
1988	The VTC organized a training scheme to train engineers in the design of applications — specific integrated circuits
1989	The HKPC offered training and consultancy services on two advanced production management techniques: Just-In-Time (JIT) and Total Quality Management (TQM)
1990	VTC's Precision Tooling Training Centre
1990	Application Specific Integrated Circuit (ASIC) Training Centre
1990	Training centre for the wholesale/retail and import/exports trades
1992	VTC converted the Chai Wan Technical Institute into a Technical College and built a new Technical College at Tsing Yi
1992	A Statutory Employees Retraining Board
1994	VTC organized an internship programme for biotechnology industry

Basic Education and Skills Training

1978	White Paper on the '*Development of Senior Secondary and Tertiary Education*' (expanded and developed secondary schools and technical institutes)
1978	Government introduced 9-year free schooling (upgraded general education of craft students, operatives and unskilled workers)
1978	More practical and technical subjects introduced into secondary schools
1984	City Polytechnic of Hong Kong
1987	HK Polytechnic Rehabilitation Engineering Centre
1987	Hong Kong Polytechnic CAD/CAM Research and Education Centre
1987	Computer Education Centre (training and resource centre for teachers)
June 1990	Open Learning Institute
Oct. 1991	Hong Kong University of Science and Technology
Since 1991	Tertiary education expanded to meet manpower needs
1990	The HK Council for Academic Accreditaticn
1990	Education Commission Report No. 4. (curriculum development, assessment systems and language in education)
1991	HK University of Science and Technology
1992	Education Commission Report No. 5. (recommendations on the status, training and workloads of teachers)
1994	The HK Institute of Education
1994	University status for City Polytechnic of HK, HK Polytechnic, and Baptist College

Infrastructure (examples)

Since 1974	The government started to build up infrastructure of new towns and industrial estates e.g., Tsing Yi Bridge linked Tsing Yi with Kwai Chung, the two new locations for industrialists. A 12-year programme started in 1978 to develop dockyards on Tsing Yi Island
1990/91	Sino-British discussion on financing and implementing the Port and Airport Development Project
1990	Shing Mun Tunnel opened
1991	Tate's Cairn Tunel opened

114   EDWARD K.Y. CHEN & KUI-WAI LI

1991	Container Terminal 8 officially commissioned (completed in 1995)
1991	Feasibility study on Container Terminal 9 at Southeast Tsing Yi completed
Since 1991	Construction of the Airport Core Programme began (including new airport and related transportation network)
1993	Consultative paper presenting findings of the Railway Development Study
1994	Second Ap Lei Chau Bridge opened
1994	Government announced the Railway Development Strategy (plans for future development)
1997	Completed construction of the first phase of the new airport

Foreign Direct Investment Policy (FDI)

Hong Kong government offers foreign investors freedom of ownership, employment, and movement of capital and goods. No preferences and no fiscal incentives given to FDI

Supporting Services to facilitate FDI

1981	Promotion Consultancy Division (PCD) of the Industry Department
1982	The PCD set up overseas investment promotion offices in Tokyo, London, Stuttgart, and San Francisco
1983	The PCD set up a one-stop investment unit in Hong Kong, in support of overseas investment promotion offices
1985	The PCD opened New York overseas investment promotion office
1989/90	Consultancy services in Italy and Switzerland to encourage FDI from Europe
Since 1990	Aimed to bring in foreign investment to upgrade technology levels and expertise in local industries, for example:
1990	Manufacture of organic photo-conductive drums for photocopier, and the recycling of lubricating oil
1991	Manufacturing of semi-processed plastic pellets, and the recycling of paper
1992	Manufacture of polystyrene and compact discs
1994	Hong Kong signed investment promotion and protection agreements with Denmark and Sweden

APPENDIX 4.2

Institutions Supporting Industry and Technology

Hong Kong has altogether seven institutions and agencies that are involved in industrial and technological support services:

Industry and Technology Development Council (ITDC)   The ITDC advises the Secretary for Trade and Industry. Members of the ITDC include prominent industrialists and businessmen, academics, representatives of major industries and relevant officials.

Industry Department (ID)   The ID facilitates the development of manufacturing industries. Its major functions are to: a) promote inward investment and operate overseas Industrial Promotion Units; b) facilitate access to relevant technologies and encourage applied research and development; c) conduct periodic studies of manufacturing industries regarding their technology levels and market trends; and d) identify constraints on industrial development. The Industry Department established an independent organisation known as the Hong Kong Quality Assurance Agency to audit factories which have adopted a quality management system specified by the international standard ISO9000. The ID also operates the Hong Kong Government Standards and Calibration Laboratory which provides a calibration service and measurement standards for manufacturers, the Product Standards Information Bureau which gives advice on international standards, and the Hong Kong Laboratory Accreditation Scheme whose aim is to improve the standard of testing and management in laboratories for toys, textiles, electrical and electronic goods, food, and construction materials. The Applied Research Council was established in 1995 with an initial funding of $50 million and aims to promote joint projects with China's leading research institutes. By the end of August 1995, two out of three applications, with a total of HK$11 million, had been approved (1995 Policy Address: 223). A Hong Kong science park was proposed in 1992 to enhance the manufacturing capabilities of specific sectors. A feasibility study was completed in 1995 and consultation with various interested parties is expected to be complete by early 1996.

Hong Kong Industrial Estates Corporation (HKIEC)   The main task of HKIEC is to ensure an adequate supply of land. It develops and manages industrial estates and offers land, at cost, to companies with new or improved technologies and processes. There are altogether three industrial estates in the New Territories — Tai Po (73 hectares), Yuen Long (67 hectares) and Tseung Kwan O (28 hectares).

116   EDWARD K.Y. CHEN & KUI-WAI LI

Vocational Training Council (VTC)   The VTC provides technical education and industrial training in two technical colleges, seven technical institutes, and twenty-four industrial training centres. The Council runs a New Technology Training Scheme which provides financial assistance to employers to train their technicians and managers.

Hong Kong Productivity Council (HKPC)   Established by statute in 1967, the HKPC acts as the agent for technology transfer and promotes industrial productivity. It is financed by an annual government subvention and by fees earned from its services. It is staffed by experts from a wide range of industrial disciplines. It provides a variety of training programmes, industrial and management consultancies, and technical support services to assist industry in manpower, product, and process development. The HKPC represents the government in the Asian Productivity Organization (APO) on industrial productivity issues. It has a total of 17 operational divisions.

Hong Kong Applied R&D Fund Company Limited   The main duty of this government-owned company is to run the Applied R&D Scheme. The Scheme aims to develop the technological capabilities and competitiveness of industries and can fund up to half the cost of an applied R&D project, or a total of $10 million for a single company or organization.

Hong Kong Industrial Technology Centre Corporation (HKITCC) The HKITCC was established in 1993 by statute to promote technological innovation and application of new technologies. It has three primary functions to provide incubation and accommodation for technology-based businesses, technology transfer services, and product design, development, and support services. A grant of $250 million was provided by the government, but the HKITCC is required to conduct its business according to prudent commercial principles.

Institutions Supporting the Service Sector

Hong Kong has four main institutions relating to the industrial policy of service industries such as trade and tourism. In addition, various trade and industrial associations exist to facilitate industries and exports. The four major institutions are:

Hong Kong Trade Development Council (HKTDC)   The HKTDC was set up by statute in 1966 to promote and expand trade. Its major functions include exploring new markets for Hong Kong exporters, organising trade fairs for all major Hong Kong industries, providing information to local manufacturers and traders about foreign buyers, promoting Hong Kong as the most effective gateway to China and to the markets of the Asia-Pacific region, gathering information on foreign buyers for the council's global corporate database which can be accessed by Hong Kong traders and manufacturers, and working intensively with companies in Hong Kong to upgrade the quality and design of their products. The HKTDC has a total of 40 overseas offices in 27 countries. Nine more offices are scheduled to open in 1994–1995.

Hong Kong Export Credit Insurance Corporation (HKECIC)   This is a statutory corporation set up in 1966. It provides insurance protection to exporters against the risk of loss arising from non-payment by their overseas buyers for goods exported and services rendered on credits not normally covered by commercial issuers. The HKECIC is a member of the International Union of Credit and Investment Insurers (the Berne Union), and has ready access to confidential and updated economic and market information on other countries as well as credit reports on overseas buyers. Three main categories of services are provided to exporters: indemnification of policy-holders for up to 90 percent of their losses; credit advisory services, and risk management and advice when policy-holders encounter payment problems.

Consumer Council   The Consumer Council is a statutory body established in 1974. Its major responsibility is to protect and promote the interests of consumers of goods, services, and immovable property. The Council engages in a wide spectrum of consumer protection activities including: developing consumer protection initiatives; conducting studies on the state of competition and trade practices of various business sectors; mediating in disputes between consumers and businesses; conducting product testing and surveys on goods and services; disseminating consumer information and advice on consumer awareness; promoting consumer well-being and sustainable consumption lifestyles; and pursuing research on the competitive environment in the domestic market. The Council works closely with the government through the Trade and Industry Branch and is consulted on major policies affecting the interests of consumers. It is a council member of the International Organisation of Consumers Union.

Hong Kong Tourist Association (HKTA)   The HKTA was established in 1957 to develop the territory's tourism industry. The association works to increase the number of visitors to Hong Kong, promotes the improvement of visitor facilities, secures overseas publicity for Hong Kong, co-ordinates the activities of the tourism industry, and advises the government on industry-related matters.

In addition to these organizations, there are a number of other trade and industrial organizations representing the interests of industry and commerce. The long established and more influential associations include:

Federation of Hong Kong Industries   The Federation is a statutory body established in 1960 to promote and protect the interests of Hong Kong's manufacturing industry. It provides services on the certificate of origin, the Hong Kong Quality Mark Scheme, a custom-built multi-risk insurance policy, consultancy work on quality assurance, trade marks and copyrights, trade enquiries and economic research. It serves the Hong Kong Toys Council, the Chemical and Pharmaceutical Industries Council, the Transport Services Council, the Hong Kong Watches and Clocks Council, the Hong Kong Electronics Industry Council, the Hong Kong Plastics Industry Council, and the Hong Kong Mould and Die Council. It also runs the annual Young Industrialist Awards of Hong Kong, and is responsible for organising the consumer product design award category of the Governor's Award for Industry.

Chinese Manufacturers' Association of Hong Kong (CMA)   The CMA was established in 1934. It is authorized by the government to issue certificates of origin and it provides trade information, handles trade enquiries, and organises missions, fairs, and exhibitions. The CMA Testing and Certification Laboratories provide technical backup services, including materials and product testing, pre-shipping inspection, and technical consultancy services. The CMA operates two pre-vocational schools to provide technical education and training. Since 1989, the CMA has been responsible for the organization of the machinery and equipment design award category of the Governor's Award for Industry.

Hong Kong General Chamber of Commerce   Founded in 1861, the chamber organises trade and good-will missions overseas and receives inbound delegations. It handles trade enquiries and is authorized by the government to issue certificates of origin. It represents Hong Kong in the International Association Temporarie Admission Carnets. The Chamber is represented on a wide range of official advisory committees and bodies. It established the Hong Kong Article Numbering Association, the Hong Kong Coalition of Service Industries and the Hong Kong Franchise Association; and sponsors the Hong Kong Committee of the Pacific Basin Economic Council.

Chinese General Chamber of Commerce   Established in 1900, it represents local Chinese firms. Its activities include the certification of origin, the organization of seminars, exhibitions, trade missions and other trade promotional activities, and the maintenance of close links with trade organizations both in Hong Kong and China. Recently, a world wide network on different Chinese-related chambers of commerce was established to widen the business interest in various Chinese societies.

References

Advisory Committee on Diversification. 1979. *Report of the Advisory Committee on Diversification.* Hong Kong Government.

Caves, R.E. 1986. "Industry Policy and Trade Policy: A Framework". In *Industrial Policies for Pacific Economic Growth.*, ed. Mutoh, Sekiguchi, Suzumura, and Tamazawa. London: Allen and Unwin.

Census and Statistics Department. 1993. "Structural Change in Manufacturing Sector, 1981–1991". *Hong Kong Monthly Digest of Statistics* September, pp. 113–23.

Chen, Edward K.Y. and Kui-Wai Li. 1991. "Industrial Development and Industrial Policy in Hong Kong". In *Industrial and Trade Development in Hong Kong*, ed. Edward K.Y. Chen, Mee-Kau Nyaw, and Teresa Y.C. Wong. University of Hong Kong: Centre of Asian Studies.

———— and Kui-Wai Li. 1994. "Manufactured Export Expansion in Hong Kong and Asian-Pacific Regional Co-operation". In *Manufactured Exports of East Asian Industrializing Economies,* ed. Shu-Chin Yang, pp. 103–34. New York: M.E. Sharpe.

Dasgupta, P. and P. Stoneman, eds. 1987. *Economic Policy and Technological Performance.* Cambridge: Cambridge University Press.

Director General of Industry. 1993. *1992/93 Departmental Report.* Hong Kong Government.

Hong Kong Government. 1991. *Hong Kong 1991.*

————. 1994. *Hong Kong 1994.*

————. 1995. *Hong Kong 1995.*

Kwok, Raymond H.F. and Kui-Wai Li. 1991. "Generalized System of Preference Graduation and Hong Kong's Export Performance". Seoul *Journal of Economics* 4 (June): 173–87.

Li, Kui-Wai. 1990. "Industrial Amalgamation". *Intellectus.* Bulletin of the Hong Kong Institute of Economic Science 16 (October–December).

————. 1991 "Positive Adjustment against Protectionism: The Case of the Textile and Clothing Industry in Hong Kong". *The Developing Economies* 29, no. 3 (September): 197–209.

———— and Kenneth W.K. Lo. 1993. "Trade and Industry". In *The Other Hong Kong Report,* ed. Po-king Choi and Ho Lok-sang, pp. 109–26. Hong Kong: Chinese University Press.

120   EDWARD K.Y. CHEN & KUI-WAI LI

———— and Carson Chan. 1994. *Matching Investment Opportunities and Relocation of Industries: The Experience of Hong Kong*. Division of Industry, Human Settlements and Environment, United Nations Economic and Social Commission for Asia and the Pacific. Bangkok, Thailand (May).

Okuno, M. and K. Suzumura. 1986. "The Economic Analysis of Industrial Policy: A Conceptual Framework through the Japanese Experience". In *Industrial Policies for Pacific Economic Growth*, ed. Mutoh, Sekiguchi, Suzumura, and Tamazawa. London: Allen and Unwin.

Tuan, Chyau and Linda Fung-Yee Ng. 1994. "A Study of the Turning Point of Hong Kong Manufacturing in Phase of Outward Investment to Pearl River Delta". International Conference on "Four Little Dragons Economic Development and Transformation". Chinese University of Hong Kong, Department of Decision Sciences and Managerial Economics (June).

Wong, Teresa Y.C. 1991. "A Comparison of the Industrial Policy of Hong Kong and Singapore in the 1980s". In *Industrial and Trade Development in Hong Kong*, ed. Edward K.Y. Chen, Mee-Kau Nyaw, and Teresa Y.C. Wong. University of Hong Kong: Centre of Asian Studies.

C
Technology Policy

[13]

Industrial Policy Instruments for High Technology

Going into the last quarter of the twentieth century, U.S. companies completely dominated the so-called high-tech fields, just as U.S. producers had once dominated the old-line manufacturing sectors. The United States, postwar birthplace for nearly all high-tech industries, held a commanding lead in such areas as semiconductors, computers, aerospace, telecommunications, new materials, and biotechnology. Most of the innovative breakthroughs that gave birth to glamorous new industries were made in the United States: the integrated circuit, vacuum-tube computer, microprocessor, digital switching equipment, fiber optics, nuclear fission, and recombinant DNA, among others. Even today, most of the leading corporations in these fields are American: IBM (semiconductors and computers), AT&T (telecommunications), Boeing and McDonnell-Douglas (commercial jet aircraft), and Lockheed, Martin Marietta, Rockwell, and Hughes (aerospace).

Not long ago, the same could be said of the old-line manufacturing sectors. From the end of the Second World War until the late 1960's, U.S. producers of automobiles, steel, and color televisions led the world in market share, technology, and profitability. Both the car powered by an internal combustion engine and the color television set were invented in the United States, and the names of leading U.S. corporations were almost synonymous with the product itself: General Motors and Ford (automobiles), U.S. Steel, and RCA and Zenith (color televisions).

By 1970, however, Japanese latecomers had caught up with and overtaken U.S. front-runners in steel, automobiles, and consumer electronics. The speed with which the Japanese closed the gap and opened up a widening lead of their own startled everyone, including the Japanese themselves. Japan's capacity to overcome what had seemed, at one time, like an insurmountable disadvantage has been attributed, at least in part, to the momentum imparted by Japanese industrial policy.[1] How else could a country come from so far behind so swiftly?

For years, even while U.S. producers of cars, steel, and consumer electronics were receiving a sound thrashing in their own marketplace, U.S. front-runners in high technology could take comfort in the thought that their industries were not as vulnerable as those in the smokestack sectors. Unlike steel and automobiles, which played to Japan's strengths in mass production and standardized process technology, competitiveness in semiconductors, computers, and other high-tech industries depended on new product innovation, state-of-the-art design, creative software applications, and complex systems integration—areas in which the Japanese were thought to be weak. The pivotal importance of innovation thus lulled some Americans into a false sense of security. Semiconductors and computers seemed safe from Japan's commercial offensive; high technology was the last bastion of U.S. comparative advantage.

The sense of security did not last long. By 1988, leading U.S. corporations found themselves embroiled in a raging war against Japanese corporations on virtually all fronts of high technology, from lasers to pharmaceuticals. The battle in semiconductors seemed especially fierce and decisive in the eyes of the combatants. It was a battle Americans seemed to be on the verge of losing. By 1986, at any rate, Japan had surpassed the United States to become the world's largest producer of semiconductors, with 45.5 percent of world market share, compared to the United States' 44 percent; only eight years earlier, in 1978, U.S. companies had held 56 percent of the world market whereas Japanese firms accounted for only 28 percent.[2] Of the world's top ten semiconductor companies, six, including the top three, were Japanese. In certain standard, high-volume products, like dynamic random access memory chips (DRAMs), the Japanese had come to command 90 percent of world market share. Even in the technologically more complex products, such as microprocessors, microcontrollers, and applications specific integrated circuits (ASICs), the Japanese were making swift and significant enough inroads to set off warning sirens (if not Cassandra-like prophecies of doom) in Silicon Valley.

How has Japan done it? How has it managed to confound skeptics in fields where it was thought to be weak? In the minds of many non-Japanese, the answer resides in the effectiveness of MITI's industrial policies for high technology.[3] Specifically, MITI is believed to have given the Japanese semiconductor industry a powerful thrust

Industrial Policy Instruments   57

forward by applying some of the same instruments of industrial policy that had been used for the old-line sectors: namely, industrial targeting, infant industry protection, controls over foreign direct investment, close government-business collaboration, access to cheap capital, encouragement of excessive competition, R&D subsidies, buy-Japanese programs, dumping and predatory pricing in overseas markets, and other unfair trade practices. Against the advantages conferred by industrial policy targeting, the small, innovative, and market-driven firms in Silicon Valley, operating without the benefit of government support and protection, appeared hopelessly overmatched. Like steel and auto producers, many felt they could not compete against "Japan, Inc."

The view summarized above, however, gives Japanese industrial policy more credit (or, depending on one's point of view, more blame) for the development of the semiconductor industry than it deserves.[4] Although it did play an indispensable role in the emergence of the steel industry (as pointed out in Chapter 1), Japanese industrial policy has contributed less to the success of high-tech industries.[5] MITI has applied a less extensive set of policy instruments, one more attuned to the different functional needs of high-technology endeavors. Recognizing that a world-class semiconductor industry could emerge only from the crucible of market competition and that, for the long-term health of the industry, the government should hold interventionist impulses in check, MITI refrained from using several strong instruments that had been applied to accelerate the growth of the steel industry: investment guidance, production targets, antirecession and rationalization cartels, extensive involvement in upstream activities, stringent standards of approval for technology transfers, strict controls over foreign direct investment, and mergers to achieve economies of scale. MITI did try to promote mergers in the computer industry, but in the face of private-sector resistance the idea died an early death.

In choosing policy instruments to fit the needs of specific high-tech industries, MITI has demonstrated a capacity to deftly adapt industrial policy to varying circumstances and to resist the temptation to intervene beyond the point of usefulness. It realizes that overzealous attempts to wean an industry can create perverse incentives, which can undermine rather than strengthen an industry's competitiveness. The combination of restraint, selective intervention, and respect for the discipline of market forces has made for an effective formula. This chapter will examine the concrete policy measures that MITI chose to administer, given the functional needs of high technology and the

58   *Industrial Policy Instruments*

range of policy instruments available. Let us begin with an analysis of the functional requisites.

Functional Requisites

Industrial Dynamics

Although high technology differs fundamentally from smokestack industry, the two sectors share some characteristics. In both cases, manufacturing is a key ingredient of latecomer catch-up and commercial success. In both cases, attention needs to be paid to the upgrading of process technology; this, in turn, ensures that product quality will be continually improved. For standard high-tech products, as for most products of heavy manufacturing, the longer the production run, the lower the per-unit costs of production. The advantages gained from volume production suggest that it is vital to take a global view of markets and to export aggressively, especially to large overseas markets. Concerning such basics, high technology and heavy manufacturing have much in common.

The two differ, however, in the scope of technological change, the uncertainties, risks, and costs of research and development, the length of product life cycles, the complex relationship to downstream applications and end-user demand, and the structure of industrial organization. On each of these dimensions, the difference is one of degree, not of kind; but the amplitude of variation is so wide that the differences in degree add up to a difference in kind. At least the differences require the administration of distinct policy instruments.

None of the differences is more striking than the potential for technological change. The opportunities for technological advancement are much greater in high technology, because know-how is at an earlier stage of maturation. In older industries like steel, the chances of developing revolutionary new products—products that transform the very nature of competition—are exceedingly low. In the semiconductor industry, by contrast, major new products, like the microprocessor, have emerged at fairly regular intervals to alter the basic direction of industry, and no end is in sight. This gives small, entrepreneurial companies opportunities to find and exploit niche markets that are constantly opening up. In heavy manufacturing, pursuing a strategy of product differentiation is harder because there is less leeway to bring new products to market.

Because products, manufacturing processes, and competitive dynamics change constantly, companies must sink substantial resources

Industrial Policy Instruments   59

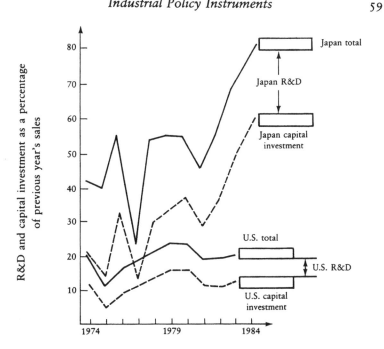

Fig. 2.1. R&D and capital investment in the semiconductor industry: United States and Japan, 1974–1984. Source: Dr. Yoshio Nishi.

into research and development. Over the years, Japanese semiconductor companies have ploughed back about 20 percent of their revenues into R&D (Fig. 2.1), an extraordinarily high rate compared to most old-line industries, which typically invest 3 percent or less. If companies fail to sustain high investment levels, they run the risk of falling hopelessly behind and of being forced out of the race altogether. To survive in the marketplace, high-technology companies must stretch themselves to the limit in R&D resource allocations. The level of R&D spending is, in fact, one way of defining the difference between old-line and high-technology industries.

Although the functional imperative of sustaining high levels of R&D investment is clear, the risks and uncertainties of R&D are substantial, and the investment of large sums by itself is no guarantee of success. The ratio of cost to commercial yield rises as companies strive to push beyond the frontiers of knowledge. Over time, the uncertainties and the rising ratio of costs to commercialization can strain the financial resources of competing corporations, since they must also simultaneously sink even larger sums into new plant facilities (see Fig. 2.1).

The cost problem is exacerbated by the fact that state-of-the-art R&D in high technology is close to and even overlaps the frontiers of knowledge in the basic sciences. Most companies feel they must have a firm foundation at both ends of the R&D process—upstream in basic science and prototype research, and downstream in applied development. The problem is that the farther one pushes upstream, the more research takes on the properties of a collective good; it is an inexhaustible collective resource to which everyone has access and for which no one is willing to pay.[6] Since upstream research has to be done—without it, applied development will eventually bump against the limits of knowledge—the question of who pays is problematic. Corporate budgets already tend to be overstretched by investments in new plant facilities and downstream product development.

For companies, the uncertainties and costs of R&D are aggravated by the shortening of product life cycles. Even when R&D investments yield commercial products, the period of time during which companies can capture rents and recoup the upfront costs of R&D has become shorter and shorter. Unlike steel products, which may sell for more than a decade, or car models, which may sell (with slight modifications) for several years, the typical life cycle for a DRAM might last less than a year and a half. The brevity of the product life cycle thus increases the costs and risks of R&D. The problem of sustaining heavy capital investments is especially acute during cyclical downturns in business demand.

The character of high technology also gives rise to diverse and complicated industrial structures. In the United States, where the semiconductor industry began, a multilayered structure of firms has emerged, consisting of giant captive (in-house) corporations, like IBM and AT&T, with full downstream capabilities, diversified merchant companies (which sell semiconductor devices to other companies), like Motorola and Texas Instruments, with considerable system-design expertise, nondiversified merchant producers, like Intel, Advanced Micro Devices, and National Semiconductor, with little or no downstream capability, and small, specialized niche producers, like LSI Logic, VLSI Technology, and Cypress, that concentrate on fairly narrow niche markets.[7] Rounding out the U.S. structure are a group of small, independent semiconductor equipment makers, which supply vital know-how in process technology, and large military houses, which purchase semiconductor components for installation in sophisticated weapons systems. Overall, the multitiered structure has met the functional imperatives of innovation in the growing semiconductor industry very well, though questions have been raised about the continuing viability of the structure as it is presently constituted.

The structure of the Japanese semiconductor industry poses a sharp contrast. The largest producers are big, vertically integrated, systems-oriented corporations, like NEC and Toshiba, that manufacture for in-house use and for external sales and also buy from rival producers. Smaller consumer electronics companies, like Sanyo and Sharp, similarly manufacture for in-house use and external sales and also purchase from the outside market. The stratum of small merchant producers, which has contributed so much to new product design and innovation in the United States, does not exist in Japan. There are many small semiconductor equipment manufacturers, but the most prominent of them are closely tied to the large systems houses through equity holdings and other ties of interdependence. Just as the heterogeneous industrial structure has served the needs of the U.S. semiconductor industry, so too the less heterogeneous, more vertically integrated structure has met Japan's needs as a latecomer, especially with respect to technological catch-up and worldwide market share expansion.

As the semiconductor industry reaches technological and commercial maturity, and as fierce competition continues unabated, the advantages and disadvantages of each industrial structure will become more apparent and certain adjustments may have to be made. In the United States, the mid-sized merchant houses, lacking the deep pockets, diversified product portfolios, and extensive marketing and service networks of the large Japanese corporations (and of giant U.S. captives), may feel most acutely the squeeze of competitive pressures. All U.S. companies will feel the effects of a decline in the market position of the small equipment manufacturers, especially in the area of process technology. Thus, the long-term trends may be moving in the direction of industrial restructuring, greater market concentration, vertical integration (though there will be room for small niche producers), and downstream diversification.

For Japan, the challenge ahead will center on the need to be innovative at the frontiers of both new product design and process technology. To date, Japan's structure of large, vertically integrated corporations has not lent itself to new product innovation as readily as America's multilayered structure. Even though size can mean deeper pockets for R&D investment, it frequently gets in the way of research flexibility and quick turnaround. One structural adaptation in Japan has been the "hiving off" of R&D to small, subsidiary companies and subcontractors, a pattern that Masahiko Aoki calls, in a broader context, "quasi-disintegration."[8]

Another structural response, involving both Japanese and U.S. companies, has been the proliferation of international alliances, such as joint ventures, mergers, acquisitions of foreign firms, venture capital investments overseas, original equipment manufacturing, and cross-licensing agreements. Strategic alliances have sprung up everywhere, reflecting the severity of global competition. There is no sign yet that the proliferation will come to a halt. So long as the functional requisites of high technology remain demanding, the internationalization will continue.

For Japanese and U.S. companies alike, the functional requirements of high technology are challenging and clear. They revolve around the need to advance technology beyond the frontiers of knowledge. To do so requires access to financial and human resources, sustained investments, simultaneous pursuit of new product design and process technology, the assumption of high risks and uncertainties, sufficient production experience to move along steep learning curves, the formation of international strategic alliances, and ongoing adaptations in industrial structure.

Government Requisites

In order to facilitate efforts by the private sector to meet these challenging functional requirements, national governments must do what they can to create a supportive business environment. Thus, in parallel with, and closely related to, private-sector requirements, there are government requisites that must be met if countries want to maximize their chances of achieving world competitiveness in high technology.

As most high-technology products have high demand elasticity, macroeconomic policy measures aimed at generating greater aggregate demand are bound to quicken the growth rate of high-technology industries. Similarly, low inflation levels, stable exchange rates, and sound fiscal management not only are vital ingredients of a healthy economy but also serve to cushion downturns in business cycles. Because investment levels in high-technology industries are sensitive to cyclical movements, anything the government can do to flatten out the dips in business demand will help companies maintain high levels of capital investment. Thus, sound macroeconomic policies are essential to the creation of healthy high-tech sectors.

Leaving aside macroeconomic measures, the government must also overcome the collective goods problem associated with basic research. If no one is willing to assume the costs of basic research, and progress in high technology hinges on breakthroughs in basic knowledge, then the government must find ways of supporting basic R&D. It can either allocate public funds or offer incentives for private-sector investment.

The government can facilitate the development of commercial R&D by offering tax incentives, organizing cooperative projects, furthering research economies of scale, relaxing antitrust provisions, eliminating needless duplication, and transferring technology from government laboratories to the private sector. Moreover, in Japan, the system of career-long employment tends to erect de facto barriers to the diffusion of technology between firms, a problem that does not beset more mobile labor markets, like the United States', where the movement of workers from company to company serves to diffuse know-how. From an economic point of view, the diffusion of technology is at least as important as product innovation, for it is only through the processes of diffusion that economic growth and commercial development take place.

High-technology industries are also dependent on the quality and quantity of technical human resources available. Here again, the burden of assuring that the human resource needs are met falls, in part, on the government's shoulders. The government's responsibilities include public education and vocational training, though the private sector can be expected to play a role as well. The Ministry of Education is in charge of Japan's educational system; and MITI, since it is not involved in curricular planning, has not been able to adjust the distribution of university students in various disciplines to match human resource needs within industry. Nor has it had much input in discussions of how to go about reforming the educational system in ways that bring out greater creativity in Japanese students (in keeping with the national need for innovation in high technology). MITI is involved in certain areas of vocational training, such as the establishment of minimum standards for certification in software programming.

Where MITI's industrial policy has had an impact is on the employment preferences of college graduates. When MITI promulgates its long-term "vision" for Japan's industrial future, Japanese graduates can identify the high-growth industries of the future. With this knowledge, choosing what industries and companies to enter can be easy. Over time, the best and brightest from Japan's finest institutions of higher learning have tended to gravitate en masse to jobs in rapidly growing industries: steel until the late 1960's, automobiles until the mid-1970's, electronics and the information industries since the mid-1970's.

In the United States, by contrast, the best and brightest tend to scatter in all directions. The most capable graduates appear to make more individualistic, short-term decisions (owing, in part, to the very mobile labor market). There is less responsiveness to industry-specific trajectories. It would be risky to forecast, for example, that there will be a swelling tide of graduates entering high technology; such traditional fields as law and finance, offering big bucks to young professionals, continue to skim more than their share of the cream off the United States' college crop. In neither the United States nor Japan does the government make a concerted effort at steering students directly into fields of study on the basis of the anticipated needs of the economy.

An area in which the government is expected to play an active role, however, is international trade. Since trade in high technology can engender serious conflicts, the government must try to resolve trade disputes that arise between domestic producers and foreign competitors. This task can take many forms: bilateral and multilateral negotiations, trade agreements, enforcement of fair rules and procedures, information gathering, and adjudication of grievances.

In all the above areas—demand stimulation, technology push, and trade mediation—the Japanese government has felt an especially strong sense of responsibility, owing to the nature of the country's finely meshed industrial system, which functions on the basis of competition and cooperation, market and hierarchy, public- and private-sector coordination, structural interdependence, "no-exit" relationships, and integrative consensus. Without government support, the high-technology industries in Japan would have a harder time meeting the demanding functional requirements of commercial success in competitive world markets.

Industrial Targeting

U.S. industrial and government leaders have voiced strong objections to MITI's practice of what they call industrial targeting: that is, the identification of strategic industries and their promotion through preferential treatment, funneling of large subsidies, infant industry protection, export promotion, and buy-Japanese programs.[9] The effect of MITI targeting, according to some U.S. critics, is that it creates a playing field tilted unfairly in Japan's favor, since the U.S. government does not engage in similar interventionist practices. High-tech companies in the United States are left to fend for themselves.

Although Japanese government officials dislike the term *targeting* because it carries connotations of unfair state intervention, they do not deny that they select certain industries for preferential promotion. The U.S. International Trade Commission (USITC) defines industrial targeting as "coordinated government actions taken to direct productive resources to help domestic producers in selected industries become more competitive."[10] A number of countries around the world engage in the practice, so defined, but with varying degrees of success. To engage in targeting is no guarantee of competitive advantage. Even Japan, regarded as the most successful, has made its share of mistakes, pointed out in the last chapter.

In semiconductors, for example, MITI has not always exercised good judgment. In 1953, when a small company called Tōkyō Tsūshin Kōgyō sought permission to purchase Western Electric's transistor technology for $25,000, MITI was reluctant to grant approval, citing a shortage of foreign currency. The use of scarce foreign currency for a technology with uncertain commercial applicability appeared to be a poor risk, particularly since the company making the application was a small start-up without much of a track record.

Only after a contract had been signed with Western Electric did MITI, in 1954, authorize the transfer of transistor technology.[11] That small start-up, subsequently renamed the Sony Corporation, went on to revolutionize the field of consumer electronics by successfully installing the transistor in small, portable radios and television sets. Thus began the process of miniaturization, which caught the fancy of consumers with its low cost and the convenience of compactness.

Imagine the enormous opportunity costs to the Japanese electronics industry if Tōkyō Tsūshin Kōgyō had not gone ahead to sign the transistor patent agreement, which it presented to MITI as a fait accompli. The episode belies the myth of MITI's prescience. It also brings to light the fact that some of Japan's most successful export industries—consumer electronics, cameras, watches, and other precision equipment—have managed to grow up strong and healthy outside MITI's incubator for targeted infant industries.

What about the charge of unfairness? Do the instruments of industrial targeting tilt the playing field unfairly in Japan's favor? To answer this question requires an in-depth examination of Japanese industrial policies for high technology, comparing them wherever possible to those of the United States and Western Europe. The miscellaneous measures will be grouped under three broad categories: technology push, other facilitating measures, and demand pull. An effort will be made to assess the relative importance of these policy instruments with respect to the development of Japan's high-technology sector.

Technology Push

National R&D Systems

Before analyzing the concrete measures taken to accelerate the pace of technological change, it might be useful to compare briefly, as background, the R&D systems of the United States and Japan. Probably the biggest differences lie in the scope of military R&D, the proportion of government expenditures, and the links between universities, industry, and government.[12] Japan has the luxury—enjoyed by no other large industrial economy—of being able to concentrate almost exclusively on commercial R&D. By contrast, the United States bears the onerous responsibility of providing for the common defense of the Western alliance. The ramifications of this disparity in defense burdens are far-reaching.

Japan's purely commercial orientation is a major asset because it permits the government to make cost-effective use of the country's R&D resources. Few of its scientists and engineers, and only a small portion of its budgetary resources, have to be diverted to military R&D projects. Since the commercial spillover from narrowly specialized military R&D projects tends to be limited, the diversion of finite resources means that substantial opportunity costs are incurred by the United States, France, and other countries spending large amounts for military purposes.

To be sure, the U.S. military-oriented R&D system has served as the womb of nearly all high-technology industries during the postwar period. The U.S. government's role as R&D contractor and guaranteed first customer has fostered the growth of one high-tech industry after another. Following infant nurturance, each industrial offspring has reached maturity and independence with the expansion of commercial demand in the U.S. market, the largest in the world.[13] The U.S. R&D system has thus functioned like no other in the world to create

whole new industries of enormous economic and technological significance—semiconductors, computers, supercomputers, telecommunications, and many others.

The same R&D system, however, so admirably suited to the creation and early development of high-technology industries, has had
trouble coping with the latecomer challenge posed by Japan. This is
because there appear to be hard trade-offs between military and commercial R&D. Military and commercial technologies, which overlap
during gestation and the early years, tend to separate as fledgling
industries mature. Zero-sum investment choices have to be made.

The inefficiencies, rigidities, and commercial opportunity costs built
into the U.S. military R&D system may render the overall R&D system less adaptable than Japan's, at least in the commercial realm. If
the strength of the U.S. system lies in its pioneering character, the
strength of Japan's system lies in its capacity to convert breakthroughs
in basic knowledge swiftly into tangible products on store shelves.
Japan's commercially oriented and market-driven R&D system is
based on painstaking consensus building, government-industry cooperation, an emphasis on advancing the not very glamorous but commercially decisive area of process technology, cost-effective resource
allocation, information sharing, technology diffusion, and a singular-
ity of focus on commercial applications.

Until the 1980's, the Japanese R&D system was geared to latecomer
catch-up, and the above-mentioned features contributed to Japan's
remarkable capacity to close the gap with front-runner countries.
However, as Japan reaches the frontiers, it is striving hard to adapt its
latecomer system to one better suited to pioneering breakthroughs,
while retaining its strengths in process technology. The shift from
latecomer to pioneer will not be easy. To innovate at the frontiers,
Japan must overcome some glaring deficiencies, such as the lack of
synergistic interaction between universities, corporations, and the government. This will require Japan to upgrade its upstream activities in
basic scientific research and precommercial development. This, indeed, is what has prompted the Japanese government to organize an
ambitious series of national research projects aimed at pushing Japan
beyond the frontiers of technology.

National Research Projects

From the standpoint of cost-effectiveness, national research projects
gathering together talent from the leading companies and government
laboratories represent an ideal way of leapfrogging ahead. The trouble

is that few countries are capable of organizing them effectively. Either the companies are not sufficiently competitive, or the distrust between them is too deep-seated to be overcome; more often than not, the disincentives outweigh the incentives to cooperate, and sometimes antitrust is too strictly enforced.

Japan is one of the few countries in the world that has demonstrated that it can organize national projects successfully. The reasons are too complex to go into here, but perhaps the concentration of R&D talent in a manageable number of leading firms and a relationship of trust between government and industry can be cited as noteworthy reasons.[14] National projects for the information industries began in earnest in the early 1970's; the 3.75 Series Computer Development Project (1972–76) was Japan's response to IBM's development of a third-generation computer. A flurry of national projects followed in rapid succession, the best-known of which have been the very large scale integrated (VLSI) circuits and Fifth Generation Computer projects.

It is no coincidence that the number of R&D projects increased markedly at just the time when Japan was feeling the force of foreign pressures to liberalize its import tariffs and investment barriers. MITI officials and industry leaders, fearing that liberalization would expose the weaknesses of Japan's information industry, felt that the level of Japanese technology had to be advanced through a crash program of national R&D projects. The dismantling of tariff and investment barriers thus forced Japan to turn to national projects as a vehicle for technologically leapfrogging ahead. Fortunately for Japan, the information industry had already developed to a point where it was poised to make a great leap forward. Had it lagged further behind, national projects might not have been enough to advance it to its present level of competitiveness.

The focus of all national research projects in Japan is on basic, precommercial technologies of such seminal importance that interfirm cooperation makes eminent sense. The projects reveal several common characteristics: (1) the development of precommercial prototype products, (2) long gestation periods, (3) high uncertainties and risks, (4) heavy capital outlays, (5) research economies of scale, (6) steep learning curves, (7) the promise of advancements in process technology, and (8) potential commercial utility across an array of industries. They have to focus on upstream technologies that are so costly and risky that individual companies, left to their own calculations of cost-effectiveness, would probably not make the investment. The govern-

ment must step in where market incentives alone might not be sufficient to promote the collective interests of priority industries and of
the national economy. Projects must also hold out the promise of
multiplier-effect benefits.

MITI feels a public and national responsibility to do whatever it can
to give domestic producers a competitive edge over foreign companies.
The organization of national projects provides tangible evidence that
it is doing something of high visibility and strategic value to promote
both Japanese industry and the public well-being. Such projects also
offer MITI a concrete and effective mechanism for shoring up its
power, consolidating ties with the private sector, and coaxing more
money out of the Ministry of Finance. Such secondary effects should
not be dismissed as incidental by-products of national research
projects inspired by more noble aspirations. In the ongoing struggle
for power, ministries will seize upon any mechanism that can give
them an edge against rival bureaucracies.

By identifying seminal technologies for the future and providing
seed money, national projects can also help research directors at various companies build a consensus about research directions and R&D
priorities. When a critical mass of leading *kaisha* (large Japanese corporations) decides to pursue a basic technological course, other companies are likely to follow. An entire industry can be mobilized. By
dividing up the research labor, moreover, national projects can prevent wasteful duplication, without crowding out parallel research efforts in company laboratories. Making project patents available to all
companies on a nondiscriminatory basis also ensures that key technologies will be widely diffused, overcoming the barriers to cross-
pollination resulting from Japan's relatively low labor mobility.

MITI has organized a variety of national research projects, covering
everything from opto-electronics to bioelectronic engineering (see Fig.
2.2). As national projects have proliferated, foreign competitors have
expressed concern about the lack of openness and transparency and
the asymmetrical advantages conferred on Japanese corporations.
This concern implies that national research projects have been and
will continue to be highly successful undertakings. Some foreign analysts give them credit for catapulting Japan to the technological
forefront.[15] Other see them as vehicles for "unfair" competition, tangible evidence of "Japan, Inc." in action.[16] Many fear that Japan will
surge ahead in most fields of high technology, once the multiple
projects on the drawing boards or currently under way are completed.

Leaving aside the media attention and expressions of foreign con-

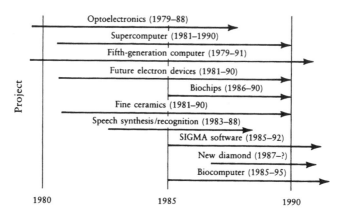

Fig. 2.2. MITI joint R&D projects. Source: DATAQUEST.

cern, how much have national research projects actually accomplished? Probably not as much as foreign Cassandras fear. Such projects, to begin with, are intended to complement, not to replace, corporate R&D. The largest and most important research effort continues to be conducted within the laboratories of individual companies.[17] What national projects provide is a foundation of basic knowledge on which applied commercial development can be conducted. Applied development is still the main driving force behind Japan's commercial competitiveness.

While government subsidies relieve companies of some of the burdens of continuous R&D investment, leading companies are not always enthusiastic about participating in national projects; often they feel they possess more advanced technology than their competitors and believe they have little to gain from joining. Successful organization of national projects is thus dependent on the relatively even distribution of technological capabilities among participating firms. There must also be the expectation that the project will yield substantial collective benefits with regard to foreign front-runners. The paucity of national projects in chemicals, pharmaceuticals, and machine tools—all important high-technology endeavors—can be understood in terms of the absence of one or more of these conditions.

None of the national research projects have yet achieved momentous breakthroughs in state-of-the-art technology. Some have failed to reach even modest objectives. The 3.75 Series Computer Development Project, the first of its kind, was considered a failure from a technical standpoint. Likewise, the Software Development Project (1976–80) failed to fulfill the specific mission for which it had been organized: the development of computer-written applications software. Although an effort was made to cast the results in a positive light by referring to the "library of working aids for programmers" that had been developed, no amount of window dressing could disguise the fact that the project had fallen short of the goals that had been set. Only about 20 percent of the software packages developed during the six-year project have turned out to be commercially useful.[18]

The VLSI project, trumpeted as Japan's greatest triumph, advanced the state of semiconductor technology, particularly Japanese capabilities in process technology (electron beam lithography, silicon crystal growth and processing, device testing, and so forth). But the VLSI project failed to make state-of-the-art breakthroughs, except for its work in the use of liquid crystals.[19] Some people believe that most of its developments would eventually have taken place anyway. All the VLSI project did was to hasten the process, a noteworthy but not earthshaking contribution.

The project's most heralded achievement—collaborative research at four cooperative laboratories involving five participating companies and specialists from MITI's Electrotechnical Laboratories—took several years of administrative massaging by the project's executive director before it could get on with the business of joint research. For the first several years, mutual suspicion and fears about leaking proprietary information impeded the free exchange of information. "What I actually did [the] last four years," says the executive director, "was nothing but to chat with the staff over sake" to create the kind of atmosphere that would be conducive to joint research.[20] The fact that collaboration could be achieved at all should not be denigrated; but whether it was worth the years of trial and error and administrative massaging, or whether the lessons learned can be applied to future projects, is not clear.

The research being done at the Institute for New Generation Computer Technology (ICOT), the central laboratory for Japan's Fifth Generation Computer Project, suggests that meaningful collaboration is repeatable.[21] But since the project is still several years from completion, it is too early to tell whether a major breakthrough will take place. The same holds true of most of the other ambitious projects currently under way. An objective assessment of the technological value of national projects must therefore await the outcome of the current generation of research activities.

Nevertheless, on the basis of the track record so far, some tentative conclusions can be drawn. National research projects have made the biggest contributions in the following areas: (1) identifying the seminal technologies on which R&D cooperation can take place; (2) promoting extensive generation and exchange of information between industry, government, universities, and the financial community; (3) allocating more R&D expenditures and subsidies for private companies, which are especially helpful during cyclical downturns; (4) helping companies commit themselves to the long-term development of vital precommercial technologies; (5) transferring know-how from government to corporate laboratories; (6) encouraging and facilitating close contact among scientists and engineers; (7) diffusing precommercial technology throughout an economy where career-long employment limits the speed and scope of diffusion; and (8) equalizing technological capabilities among leading firms and intensifying the race to develop new products and process technologies. Of these contributions, the last four have been of particular importance.

The list suggests that, quite apart from the question of breakthroughs, national research projects appear to serve a variety of instrumental functions. Indeed, the value of national projects may reside as much in their secondary effects—corporate commitments, technological diffusion, and stepped-up market competition—as in their primary goals—advances in state-of-the-art technology. Assessments of their long-term effectiveness must take both primary and secondary effects into account.

Although national research projects have hastened the pace of latecomer catch-up, it is far from clear that they will continue to impart as much impetus in the future. When Japan was a latecomer, the research directions to take were fairly clear. All that was required was to observe the successes and false starts of the front-runners. Now that Japan has come to the frontiers of technology, the natural paths to take are no longer clear. If MITI sets industry off in pursuit of the wrong set of technological goals, or charts the wrong pathways to discovery, the miscalculations might be exceedingly costly—not only in terms of the investment of financial and human resources but also in terms of lost time and forgone commercial opportunities. Setting technological targets has thus come to involve greater uncertainties and risks.

The risks of moving in false directions, however, are more effectively minimized in Japan's system of industrial policy-making than in most other countries, owing to the scope and depth of government consultations with the private sector. As pointed out in the last chapter, MITI engages in painstaking discussions with scientists and engineers, research scholars, industry leaders, and financial analysts—the people in the know—to find out where technology is headed and where the most promising commercial opportunities lie. The information it collects and processes is about as thorough as could be obtained. National research projects thus emerge from an ongoing process of national consensus building based on extensive give-and-take between government and the private sector.

NTT-Related Research

The visibility of national projects should not cause one to lose sight of important research simultaneously going on elsewhere in Japan, at such places as Nippon Telegraph and Telephone's (NTT) four large laboratories, the Electrotechnical Laboratories (ETL), the Science and Technology Agency, and other research institutes. From the standpoint of research in microelectronics, these government and public corporation laboratories—working in close contact with researchers from the private sector—have probably done more to raise the level of Japan's technological capabilities than any national project completed as of 1988. In the early 1950's, the Electrical Laboratory (Denki Shikenjo), ETL's predecessor, and the Electrical Communications Research Laboratory (Denki Tsūshin Kenkyūjo), forerunner of the NTT labs, laid much of the groundwork for Japan's introduction of transistor technology. The first transistor ever made in Japan, the point contact transistor, was developed at the communications lab in October 1951.[22]

NTT operates four major laboratories, employing over 3,000 scientists, engineers, and researchers, and is planning to establish another research lab in the Kansai region. NTT had a budget of ¥94 billion in 1983, or about $400 million.[23] Of that amount, NTT spent about ¥35 billion ($146 million) for four major projects: information processing (¥12 billion), digital switching (¥8.1 billion), large-scale integrated circuits (¥8.7 billion), and satellites (¥6.4 billion). Owing to its superb research facilities, large R&D budget, and prestige, NTT has been able to attract top-notch college graduates and conduct research of the highest quality in such fields as integrated circuits, electronic switching, power transmission, and data processing. Its laboratories have played a central role in advancing Japan's technology; NTT holds over 8,000 patents.

During the early decades of the postwar period, the quality of NTT research in microelectronics was a cut above that conducted in corporate laboratories. NTT worked closely with family firms across a broad spectrum of technical tasks, contracting out research, exchanging information, and joining forces with them on certain technical problems. Over the years, a number of NTT research specialists, like higher civil servants, "descending from heaven" (*amakudari*) into high-level positions in the private sector, have left NTT to assume positions of high responsibility in the R&D divisions of leading NTT family firms. The close relationship has thus functioned as a conduit for the transfer of technology from NTT to the private sector and vice versa, enriching the state of knowledge on both sides.

Japan's capacity to overwhelm U.S. manufacturers of mass memory chips has been due, in no small measure, to joint research conducted by NTT family firms with NTT and the diffusion of NTT technology. NTT laid important groundwork in the development of the 64K random access memory (RAM), the 256K DRAM, and the 1M read only memory (ROM), covering device designs and production technology. Japanese manufacturers could not have come from so far behind in such a short time without NTT's diffusion of technology.

To get a notion of what NTT has meant to the Japanese microelectronics industry, imagine the impetus U.S. companies would have received if AT&T had purchased all its supplies from the merchant market and if U.S. firms had been given the same opportunity to work closely with Bell Laboratories as Japanese firms had with NTT labs. Because AT&T's needs were met internally by Western Electric, its captive supplier, however, the direct benefits for the U.S. electronics industry turned out to be small. Nor did Bell Labs work in as close physical proximity with leading private companies as NTT did, even though top researchers left Bell Labs to join private-sector companies.

To be sure, Bell Labs had to make its patents freely available at reasonable fees as part of the 1956 antitrust consent decree. The effect of this transfusion of technology on the growth of the U.S. telecommunications, semiconductor, and computer industries can scarcely be overstated. But Bell Labs' compulsory licensing not only invigorated the U.S. information industries but also facilitated the growth of Japan's fledgling information industry, because Bell patents were also available for international transfer, and Japan took full advantage of the available know-how.[24]

The consequences of the divergence of U.S. and Japanese telecommunications structure and antitrust policies—each put in place independently on the basis of domestic considerations, with little or no thought being given to the international repercussions—were entirely fortuitous but far-reaching. AT&T's structure and the international diffusion of Bell technology kept the barriers to new entry low not only for U.S. companies but also for Japanese and other foreign latecomers. NTT's structure, particularly the absence of a counterpart to Western Electric and the intimate give-and-take relationship between NTT labs and private Japanese companies, provided Japan's private producers with the opportunity to speed up the process of industrial catch-up. Japan benefited from the United States' open structure and strict antitrust enforcement. Had the situation been reversed, with Japan and NTT the pioneers and the United States and AT&T the latecomers, the U.S. information industries would have had a much harder time overtaking the Japanese front-runners.

The flow of benefits has not been entirely one-way. NTT family firms have shared proprietary technology with NTT. One Japanese company, which shall be called Daimaru, started work on fiber optics and gallium arsenide during the late 1960's, when most companies were hesitant to invest in these unproven technologies. The early start and sustained attention put Daimaru well ahead of everyone else. When fiber optic and gallium arsenide products became commercially feasible, Daimaru willingly shared its know-how with NTT on a confidential disclosure basis. Then, with its circle of family firms, NTT succeeded in developing the vapor axial deposition (VAD) fiber optic production method, considered the most advanced in the world.[25] To standardize fiber optic cables, NTT licensed all Japanese cable makers to use VAD, thus diffusing the technology.

Daimaru was willing to disclose what it had learned through fifteen years of painstaking research because its relationship with NTT was of overriding importance. The relationship can be accurately described as give-and-take reciprocity based on mutual trust and long-term commitment, an illustration of the infusion of organization linkages into market transactions.[26] Like other family firms, Daimaru knew NTT would safeguard the confidential information, even though it realized that some portion would eventually be recycled to competitor firms. To begrudge information out of short-run fears of leakage would have violated the spirit of trust and obligated reciprocity on which NTT–family firm relationships are based.

Here is an illustration of what is organizationally fairly common in Japan, a long-term strategy of variable-sum cooperation.[27] Obligatory

Industrial Policy Instruments

reciprocity is common among firms that are bound together by ties of structural interdependence, such as parent corporations and subcontractors and keiretsu companies.[28] What is unusual is that confidentiality and trust also extend to relations between the private and public sectors.

In addition to its bilateral interactions with individual firms, NTT also organizes its own version of multifirm research projects. In the mid-1970's it sponsored its own VLSI project in parallel with the better-known MITI undertaking by the same name. NTT's VLSI project was oriented toward applications in telecommunications equipment while MITI's concentrated on computer applications. NTT has coordinated R&D efforts in key areas of telecommunications technology such as digital switching systems, an area requiring large R&D outlays, high risks, common standards, and the development of compatible equipment.[29]

Until NTT's privatization, the old system of NTT-related R&D may have given more momentum to the development of microelectronics technology than MITI's national research projects. NTT family firms became very competitive under NTT's auspices. For the microelectronics industry as a whole, the old system reduced risks, lowered costs, and set very exacting standards that helped to upgrade overall quality in Japan's commercial marketplace.

The combination of NTT and national research projects, together with research conducted at other government laboratories (like those at Tsukuba), has helped to compensate for past shortcomings in Japan's university-based system. What is striking about both NTT and the national projects is the synergism—not simply the spillover benefits—produced by the interplay between joint R&D efforts in the public and private sectors. Through such interaction, public and private interests converge and the collective good is advanced.[30]

Government Financing

As pointed out earlier, one of the key functional requisites of high technology is that companies sustain high levels of capital investment, including the escalating costs and risks of R&D. As part of its strategy of "technology push," the Japanese government has tried to lighten the burden of high-tech companies by making low-cost capital available. During the 1950's and 1960's, when investment capital was in short supply, the government played a pivotal role in allocating capital to the high-priority industries. But the importance of this role has decreased over time as investment capital has become plentiful.

The proportion of funds available to industry through the Fiscal Investment and Loan Program (FILP), the main source of public funding (from postal savings and insurance funds), has declined steadily since the early 1950's. FILP funds accounted for nearly 30 percent of the total capital available to industry in the early 1950's, but its share in the 1980's has fallen below 10 percent, with only a tiny portion of that going to high technology. According to one estimate, the government's share of plant and equipment investments in the electronics equipment industry came to only 2.5 percent during the early 1960's and a mere 0.8 percent in the late 1970's.[31] Compared to the amount the French government is pouring into its electronics industry, this is modest indeed.

Since Japan's cup of investment capital is now running over, there is much less need to channel public funds to priority sectors. Even the practice of indicative lending—the funneling of small amounts of public funds to targeted industries, prompting private institutions to follow suit—has diminished as an instrument of capital allocation. Leading corporations in targeted sectors are fully capable of meeting their own needs through a combination of retained earnings, bank loans, and stock and bond issuances.

Research Subsidies

In what forms, and to what extent, has the Japanese government subsidized research in the information industries? The perception outside Japan is that the subsidies have been huge—far out of line with what governments in other countries provide. Some believe that a case could be made that Japan has violated the Subsidies Code of the Tokyo Round agreement.[32] Is this the case? Does the Japanese government give larger subsidies than the governments of other countries?

In providing funds for research, the government can draw upon several sources: special grants allocated by the Ministry of Finance (MOF) for national research projects, internal allocations from MITI's own budget (including "hidden" funds available from energy-related taxes and bicycle racing proceeds), and support from other government ministries (Science and Technology, Education, Posts and Telecommunications, and the Japan Defense Agency). Let us calculate the total by adding up the known categories of expenditures, beginning with the budgets for national research projects.

Government subsidies for national projects can be grouped into two periods: the era of frenetic catch-up (1970–79) and the period of

78   *Industrial Policy Instruments*

TABLE 2.1

Government-Supported Research Projects in Japan, 1966–1980

Period	Project	Amount (million $)
1966–71	High-performance computer R&D	$42
1972–76	3.75 Series Computer development	228
1971–80	Pattern information processing system	115
1976–80	VLSI development	150
1976–80	Software development	30
TOTAL		$565

SOURCE: Personal interviews.

state-of-the-art development (1980–90). Government outlays from 1966 to 1980 amounted to around $565 million, or roughly $43 million per year; this represented less than 10 percent of the total R&D expenditure for the information industry, the rest of which was shouldered by private enterprise. The main research projects of this period are listed in Table 2.1. Public funds were small, whether they are measured in the aggregate, averaged out on an annual basis, or calculated as a proportion of total R&D in the information industry.

In the United States, the government has funneled far larger aggregate, annual, and percentage sums into R&D. In 1957, for example, the Air Force, Army, and National Aeronautics and Space Administration (NASA) provided $518 million for electronics and communications equipment, or roughly 70 percent of the total spent on this industry. Even as late as 1968, the U.S. government accounted for about $1.5 billion, or roughly 60 percent of total R&D.[33] It should be pointed out, of course, that the U.S.-Japan comparison is a bit misleading, given the fact that the United States served as the technological pioneer and Japan as the follower. For firstcomers, the costs of R&D are usually far higher than for latecomers, if only because the level of initial uncertainty is so much greater; failures and false starts are almost unavoidable. Latecomers, knowing what has worked and what has not, have a decided advantage in that they deal with less uncertainty. Often key patents can be obtained at a fraction of the cost that would have been incurred. Nevertheless, the comparison brings to light the relatively modest sum of subsidies provided by the Japanese government from the mid-1960's to 1980.

The small sum shrinks ever further when one notes that most of the early subsidies were conditional loans, or *hojokin*, repayment of which was contingent on the success of the project. Although conditional loans would seem to create perverse incentives to "cheat" on repayments—what Oliver Williamson calls "opportunism" or "self-seeking with guile"[34]—a surprisingly high percentage of loans have been repaid. Of the hojokin grants made by MITI's Agency for Industrial Science and Technology (AIST) over the five-year period 1974–78, nearly half, or 43.6 percent, had been repaid by 1982.[35] This record of repayment thus reduced the net R&D subsidy to an unspecified amount well below the aggregate figure cited for national research projects. (The reduction cannot be specified because the data on repayment are not broken down by research project, making it impossible to ascertain which of the information industries projects had been repaid.) The amount can be estimated roughly in terms of the unpaid principal plus the uncharged commercial interest rates.

MITI chooses which projects to organize and subsidize very carefully, in close consultation with industry. To qualify for government assistance, a project must meet four criteria: (1) the proposed project must be of seminal importance to Japan's technological development and future economic well-being; (2) the research must be of a pre-commercial nature so that participating companies do not gain a decisive commercial headstart over excluded firms; (3) government assistance must be indispensable for the project to get under way and be completed; (4) the time frame for the project's completion must be realistic. Government financing provides the critical missing ingredient for launching projects of high capital costs and risks, relatively long gestation, fundamental technological importance, and broad commercial applicability.

MITI prefers to put up only a portion of the total capital necessary to finance a national project.[36] Usually the sum is less than half the total cost. The rationale is that the subsidy should represent seed money, a sum that makes the project feasible but requires industry to put up its own capital. If MITI bore the full costs and risks, it might dampen industry's incentive to be efficient. MITI might then be strapped with the same problems that plague DOD research in the United States: padded expenses, unanticipated delays, huge cost overruns, and failure to meet strict technical specifications and development targets. Other things being equal, therefore, MITI's clear preference is to insist on cost sharing through the extension of hojokin, low-interest loans repayable from the profits made on commercial products.

Industrial Policy Instruments

TABLE 2.2

Government-Supported Research Projects in Japan, 1980's

Period	Project	Amount (billion ¥)
1979–83	Software for VLSI hardware	22.5
1976–82	Software production technology	6.6
1979–86	Optoelectronics applied system	18.0
1981–89	Fourth Generation high-speed computer	51.5
1981–91	Fifth Generation computer	10.5*
1981–90	Next-generation industries technology	25.0
1977–84	Flexible manufacturing	13.0
Continuous	Important technology	2.1
1983–90	Critical work robot	17.5
TOTAL		¥ 166.7

SOURCE: U.S. Embassy, Tokyo, unclassified telegram, May 1982, cited in Arthur D. Little, Inc. (Japan), "Summary of Major Projects in Japan for R&D of Information Processing Technology," unpublished study, 1983.
  *Amount for 1981–84 only.

Having closed the gap with U.S. front-runners in most areas of high technology, the Japanese government turned its attention to the organization of more ambitious national research projects aimed at achieving state-of-the-art breakthroughs. The 1980's have witnessed the organization of nine major projects related to the information industries, all designed to propel Japan beyond the frontiers of knowledge (see Table 2.2).

Unlike most national projects during the catch-up phase, many of the state-of-the-art projects listed in Table 2.2, with the notable exception of the Fourth Generation computer project, involve the government's assumption of all expenses. Such financing, referred to as *itakuhi*, is akin to contract research in the United States. Itakuhi has come to be used more than hojokin because state-of-the-art projects are by definition substantially more costly, riskier, more uncertain, and of longer gestation. Private companies are more hesitant to commit their own resources.

For several of these ambitious projects, MITI has had to take the initiative, instead of simply responding to industry demands. Had it not done so, the projects might never have been launched. Private firms would not have been willing to take the initial step of bearing the full costs of precommercial research. An employee of one of the companies that agreed to participate in the Fifth Generation project explained the financial arrangements from the private sector's point of view:

Industrial Policy Instruments   81

At first, MITI wanted to support this project at only 50 percent for the first three years, with private firms supplying the other 50 percent of the funding, but we in the companies said no. We can't afford to support such a high-risk project, even at 50 percent, plus contribute researchers' time. When they saw we meant it, they agreed to support it 100 percent, at least for the first three years. After that, we'll see.[37]

The shift from hojokin to itakuhi has increased the actual amount of subsidies significantly. Over 60 percent of R&D subsidies from 1976 to 1982 were hojokin, subject to eventual repayment. But for the nine projects listed in Table 2.2, itakuhi support has come to surpass hojokin by a wide margin.

The government's willingness to underwrite the full cost of a number of the frontier R&D projects, however, should not be misinterpreted. It does not mean that all private companies are eager to jump on the bandwagon and reap the benefits of the government's free ride. Consider the case of the Fifth Generation project; several firms had to be coaxed into participating, and several groused openly about it. On their visits to Japan, Edward A. Feigenbaum and Pamela McCorduck observed that "resentment and hostility are hardly strong enough to describe the attitudes of another firm's managers toward the Fifth Generation. They told us frankly that they had not wanted to participate and only under duress (whose nature we couldn't ascertain) did they finally contribute their researchers to ICOT."[38]

Quite apart from having to divert research personnel, Japanese corporations often have the same reservations about itakuhi as U.S. companies do about federal contract research: reams of paperwork, minute and irritating regulations, rigid accounting procedures, constant government monitoring, strict technical specifications, no guaranteed markets for commercializable products, and so forth. Sometimes it does not seem worth the hassle.

On top of the bureaucratic red tape, contracting companies in Japan are usually not allowed to retain proprietary rights over the research results. Patents automatically revert to the sponsoring government agency, which makes them available on a nondiscriminatory basis to all nonparticipating companies for the cost of a patent license fee. Despite full financial coverage, therefore, itakuhi is not as attractive to private companies as the term *free ride* might suggest. The administrative costs alone are hardly trivial.

The aggregate sum for all Japanese national research projects—

82   *Industrial Policy Instruments*

¥166 billion spread over more than ten years—sounds enormous, and
the figure does not include costs for the second half of the Fifth Generation computer project. Nor does it include internal MITI funds
requiring no Ministry of Finance authorization, such as revenues from
bicycle racing and special energy tax revenues. In 1982, for example,
MITI was able to allocate around ¥2 billion (about $8.5 million)
from its regular budget for high-tech R&D support. In addition, discretionary funds are available every year from revenues gained from
regulated gambling at bicycle races. The amount varies from year to
year, depending on the amounts gambled, but in 1982 it came to
around ¥27 billion (about $112 million), or slightly more than 5
percent of MITI's budget. Most of that money is used to support
miscellaneous activities such as trade fairs, public relations activities,
and trade associations, but some can be expended to underwrite research in advanced technology.

From MITI's standpoint, the advantage of drawing on bicycle racing revenues, instead of special grants from the Ministry of Finance, is
that administrative entanglements can be averted. MITI does not have
to go through the time-consuming process of submitting formal budget proposals; there is flexibility in the choice of technological focus,
and companies are not saddled with bothersome reporting requirements. MITI has a free hand. In 1982, it allocated ¥800 million
(about $3.3 million) for research in computer software and data pro-
cessing, an area of pressing need in which Japanese companies were
lagging behind U.S. pacesetters.

The real value of discretionary funds is not so much the incremental
amounts that are available, but the flexibility they bestow. MITI drew
on these funds, for example, when the Ministry of Finance balked at
the idea of underwriting the risky Fifth Generation computer project.
By putting up its own funds, MITI was able to get the project
launched. Once its feasibility and long-term value had been demonstrated and both momentum and excitement had been generated, the
project received substantial funding from the Ministry of Finance.
Without the discretionary funds at MITI's disposal, the Fifth Generation computer project, Japan's best-known and perhaps most important project to date, might never have moved beyond the planning
stage.

If we include a portion of NTT's R&D expenditures, the grand total
for research subsidies over a ten-year period comes to ¥516 billion
(roughly $2.3 billion at an exchange rate of 230 yen to the dollar, the

official rate in September 1985). Although the figure seems enormous, it averages out to only ¥51.6 billion per year over a ten-year period ($230 million per year). For any given year, that figure represents only a fraction of national R&D expenditures. Compared with Bell Laboratories' 1983 budget of $2 billion[39] or IBM's yearly budget of over $1.6 billion,[40] Japan's $230 million seems modest; keep in mind also that the latter figure includes the principal of conditional loans that have to be repaid and thus overestimates the actual subsidy. This brings us back to the point made earlier: the purpose of government subsidies is to compensate for market imperfections by serving as catalysts, not substitutes, for private-sector investment in basic and precommercial research.

U.S. and European Research Subsidies

What about the U.S. government's support for R&D in the information industries? How does it compare with Japan's? Let us look at only a few of the federal government's most highly publicized projects, most of them sponsored by the Department of Defense (DOD). The very high speed integrated circuit (VHSIC) project, launched in 1980 and scheduled for completion by 1989, calls for DOD to put up an estimated $500 million in contract research.[41] In partial response to Japan's Fifth Generation project, DOD has also launched its own Strategic Computer Project, designed to advance the frontiers of artificial intelligence, software, and computer architecture, with a projected budget of around $600 million for the first five years, and perhaps another $900 million for the final five years. Two other DOD projects of note are a $100 million program for the development of gallium arsenide circuits and a seven-year, $250 million project called Software Initiative. The allocations for just these four projects and U.S. government financing come to $2.35 billion, roughly the same as the aggregate sum in Japan, including the Japan Development Bank, MITI, and NTT. Since virtually all the money is in the form of contract research (none of it in repayable loans), the actual amount of the subsidies in the United States for the four projects may exceed Japan's total over a ten-year period. If subsidies for all other projects were included (for which full statistics are not available), the U.S. level would exceed Japan's by several times.

The U.S. government accounted for over 18 percent of total R&D expenditures in the category of office machinery (SIC code 357) and 40 percent in communications equipment (SIC code 361–64, 369) in

1980.[42] These figures exceed those in Japan by a big margin. But it should be pointed out that most of the U.S. government money goes to support military-related R&D projects, with only limited spillover benefits for commercial applications. From a purely commercial point of view, therefore, the U.S. government total is not nearly as cost-effective as Japan's; to the extent that it is not, the dollar amounts of federal subsidies should be discounted. Nevertheless, U.S. and European criticisms of Japanese subsidies—even allowing for low commercial spillovers—sound hollow or hypocritical.[43]

Certain countries in the European Community also provide larger research subsidies than Japan. Take, for example, semiconductor research: state financing in the United Kingdom topped Japan's.[44] The government in France has also subsidized its electronics industry more heavily. Under President François Mitterrand, the French state embarked on an ambitious crash program to upgrade France's capabilities in electronics and other high-tech industries. It set aside $1 billion for investment in France's electronics industry over a five-year period, 1982–86, with $600 million earmarked for R&D and $400 million for expanding manufacturing facilities.[45] The $1 billion was only a fraction of the massive $17 billion package in public and private funds that Mitterrand has committed to the development of electronics. Nor is that all. The troubling inability of the French computer industry to compete effectively against U.S. and Japanese companies has prompted the French government to take the ultimate step: nationalization of major parts of the computer industry and its organization into four autonomous subsidiaries under the control of one holding company, Compagnie des Machines Bull.[46]

On top of subsidies supplied by individual countries, the European Commission (EC) has launched a major five-year research project called Esprit, which is aimed at raising Europe's level of technology in microelectronics, software, artificial intelligence, office automation, and computer-aided design and manufacturing (CAD/CAM).[47] The EC is also seeking to streamline research across the European continent in order to achieve the benefits of scale economies and to curtail the waste that results from excessive duplication of R&D. By one estimate, the total amount of money, public and private, invested in European R&D in 1982 was more than double that invested by Japan.[48] Should projected spending levels stay on track until 1990, the gap will widen. Such spending levels are high relative to the overall size of Europe's electronics industry. Europe's share of the world market for integrated circuits in 1982 came to a mere 7 percent, and

European-built computers accounted for only 10 percent of world production. State subsidies in Europe as a percentage of total electronics output, therefore, surpass those in Japan by a wide margin.

Whether measured domestically, in terms of total investment, or internationally, in comparison with U.S. and European outlays, Japanese government subsidies cannot be considered abnormal. It is, however, difficult to standardize measures for international comparisons. How can Japan, the United States, and Europe be compared when there is not even agreement on what constitutes a subsidy? Is it best to add up loans, outright grants, and contract research? How does one adjust for differences between military and civilian research or for interest rate differentials? How can adjustments be made for fluctuations in official exchange rates?

Even the measure referred to as the "marginal subsidy equivalent"—the value obtained when a company produces an additional unit of output as a function of a given subsidy input—is beset with problems.[49] What we are left with, then, is rough, aggregate data that provide only crude evidence of government R&D assistance. The weight of the evidence indicates that the Japanese state is hardly alone in thinking that the market mechanism must be supplemented with subsidies if society is to reap the full fruits of innovation and growth in high-technology industries.

If anything, the level of Japanese subsidies is located toward the lower end of the bell-shaped curve of world distribution, with the United States, France, and the United Kingdom nearer the higher end. It is too early to tell whether the massive government and EC subsidies will propel Europe to the technological forefront. If past patterns hold true, the likelihood is that simply pumping more subsidies into the R&D effort will not remedy whatever it is that ails Europe. Although technology push by the government appears to be a necessary condition of leadership in high technology, it is clearly not a sufficient condition. Commercial competitiveness hinges on far more than the amount of government largess made available. Indeed, the cost-effectiveness of subsidies can no doubt reach a point of diminishing returns. Used to excess, they may even dull incentives to compete.

The effectiveness of government subsidies depends less on their size than on the intangible factor of the private sector's capacity to convert public assistance into technological progress and commercial competitiveness. Japanese industry has demonstrated time and again that it possesses the capacity to derive the most from government assistance.

Industrial Policy Instruments

In many contexts and in a variety of industries, the Japanese have demonstrated an unsurpassed talent for collective learning, an ability to organize themselves effectively for such diverse tasks as research, production, and marketing.[50] It is this collective learning capacity, not the size or number of subsidies, that accounts for Japan's success at making the most of government seed money.

All governments in advanced industrial countries subsidize their high-tech industries in one form or another; only the nature and scope of subsidization vary. The need for government support can be understood in the context of the characteristics and functional requisites of high technology, discussed earlier, and the very high stakes riding on the outcome of international competition. For lagging countries, reliance on research subsidies might be preferable to import protection. Recall that, in Japan's case, R&D subsidies rose substantially when foreign pressures forced a lowering of tariff and investment barriers. When faced with a hard choice between subsidizing and protecting domestic producers, many governments will opt for subsidization as the less costly, more palatable course of action, particularly in terms of the norms of free trade. The problem is that some governments may feel compelled to combine subsidies with trade protection.

Other Policy Instruments

Tax Policies

For most governments, taxation is perhaps the most readily available instrument of industrial policy. Tax provisions that discriminate between sectors, for example, offer an immediate means of providing special encouragement to priority industries. From a political standpoint, the virtue of taxation is that it requires no direct or visible drain on government budgets. This means that it can be shielded from the glare of public scrutiny and more effectively insulated from the pressures of political accountability. It is a ubiquitous tool of industrial policy, politically easier to use than most line-item, zero-sum budget allocations, for which special-interest lobbying can be ferocious.

The danger is that tax policies, indiscriminately used, can become the handmaiden of political expediency, with short-term concessions to vested interest groups exacting heavy costs in terms of long-run economic efficiency. The problem is particularly acute when the interest groups with the most political clout also happen to be among the most inefficient economically, as is often the case in advanced industrial countries. Old-line industries, which employ large, unionized labor forces, tend to maintain their political influence long past their economic prime. There is a lengthy time lag between the retention of political power and the loss of economic viability, an "iron law of rigidity,"[51] so to speak, restricting the ability of advanced industrial economies to adapt their industrial structures to changes in the international division of labor.

The power of old-line industries helps to explain why, in the United States and most European states, intersectoral tax burdens are heavily skewed in favor of economically inefficient sectors. Reflecting the organized strength of old-line interest groups, uneven tax burdens have the effect of channeling resources to the declining sectors of the economy. This distorts the government's revenue base and shifts the weight of taxes onto the shoulders of the most efficient and promising sectors, a perverse reward for efficiency and growth.

Even when the U.S. Congress is moved to pass generous tax provisions for high-tech-related R&D, such as capital gains, investment credits, and accelerated depreciation allowances, the provisions can lead to unforeseen and sometimes undesirable consequences. To begin with, Congress is apt to extend such provisions to other sectors in order to avoid the appearance of playing favorites. Even if it does not, certain non-targeted interest groups, like real estate, may wind up reaping the biggest windfall benefits; this may represent a substantial cost to the U.S. economy in terms of lost tax revenues, rising real estate prices, and allocative distortions caused by misinvestments in the less productive sectors.

There is, thus, the danger that the legislative branch will treat inefficient industries overgenerously on two fronts: (1) through the uneven distribution of corporate tax burdens, and (2) through the extension of special tax incentives, which benefit the less productive sectors disproportionately. A potentially effective tool of industrial policy, therefore, can turn out to be a blunt and harmful instrument for high-tech industries.

The relative weakness of the legislative branch in Japan and MOF's policy-making authority over tax measures have produced a more coherent, less distorted set of tax policies. The declining, inefficient industries have failed to secure blatantly inequitable tax concessions. The corporate tax burden is more evenly distributed among industrial sectors in Japan than in either the United States or the United Kingdom.[52] The even distribution means that the targeted sectors receive less preferential treatment than is commonly presumed. But, since old-line industries also receive less favorable treatment, the high-tech sectors may be better off overall, by virtue of the smaller distortions caused by preferential tax policies.

According to a study by Gary Saxonhouse, the effective rate of capital taxation in Japan in 1973 ranged from 34.7 percent (nonferrous metals) to 49 percent (electrical machinery); in the United States, the variation was much wider, ranging from 19.7 percent (petroleum) to 131.2 (electrical machinery).[53] Yet the average corporate tax rate, including state and local levies, was roughly the same in both countries: 53.2 percent in Japan, compared to 51.2 percent in the United States. Thus, targeted taxation is, in some senses, practiced less widely in Japan than in the United States; the declining and inefficient sectors tend to be the biggest beneficiaries of preferential tax treatment in the United States. The differences can be attributed largely to regime characteristics, particularly the greater power exercised by the legislative branch in the United States.

In Japan, the two key bureaucracies, MOF and MITI, enjoy greater insulation from the pulling and hauling of interest-group politics. Every year, MOF and MITI negotiate an aggregate ceiling for special tax measures, freeing MITI to grant special tax exemptions in whatever amounts it deems appropriate for industries of its choosing (so long as it stays within the limits of the agreed-on aggregate ceiling). Various divisions and bureaus within MITI vie with one another to win special tax provisions for industries under their jurisdiction. The contending claims are aggregated, hard trade-offs are made, and a unified package of special exemptions is worked out within the ministry. The Business Behavior Division (Kigyō kōdōka) of the Industrial Policy Bureau (Sangyō Seisakukyoku) decides which industries deserve to receive tax exemptions, and in what amounts, after consulting with all the sector-specific divisions and bureaus and huddling with the Accounting Division (Kaikeika) and the General Coordinating Division (Sōmuka) of the Minister's Secretariat (Daijin Kanbō).

In aggregating competing interests within MITI, special tax provision are one of four related policy instruments; the others are subsidies, legislation, and administrative guidance. The General Coordinating Division tries to blend all four ingredients, in appropriate measure, into a recipe that meets the needs and peculiar circumstances of each industry. Thus, declining industries may get a stronger dose of administrative guidance and subsidies, while for high-tech industries, tax incentives and research support may receive more weight. Whatever the mix, MITI sees the four elements as related and to some extent interchangeable parts of a whole.

The virtue of Japan's system is that it (1) keeps a cap on the estimated losses due to special tax incentives; (2) forces all industries to
compete with each other for special tax treatment on the basis of what
is in the best interest of the industrial economy as whole; (3) gives
MITI the leeway and authority to determine the optimal uses of special tax incentives; (4) holds parochial politicking in check; and (5)
balances the use of tax measures with other tools of industrial policy.
Tax targeting is thus subsumed within the broad framework of other
policy measures, not utilized in isolation as an elastic solution to short-
term political lobbying. That Japanese industrial tax policies come out
bearing fewer signs of obvious inconsistencies than U.S. policies is
therefore hardly surprising.

With respect to specific tax incentives, such as the one for R&D
investments—a matter of obvious importance for high-tech industries—the stereotype of unfair Japanese tax provisions is again belied
by comparisons with the United States. Japan grants tax credits of 20
percent for all R&D expenditures that exceed the highest annual rate
in a corporation's past, up to a ceiling of 10 percent of the corporation's taxes. The United States, by contrast, allows tax credits of 25
percent for all R&D expenditures exceeding the *average* over the preceding three years; there is no ceiling on the amount that is deductible
and the tax credit can be carried over a fifteen-year period. Japanese
corporations saved ¥27 billion (roughly $122 million) in 1981,
thanks to this R&D tax credit; no comparable data were available for
the United States, but given the higher tax credits and the larger
amount of R&D investment, the figure surely exceeded that.

In the United States, high-tech industries also receive investment tax
credits of up to 6 percent of the value of new equipment on depreciation schedules as short as three years, and up to 10 percent for
equipment with a longer life. Japan offers nothing comparable. Such
provisions indicate that Japanese high-tech companies receive less
preferential treatment than is widely assumed. The situation fits with
Saxonhouse's findings about the comparatively low variation in tax
burdens across sectors.

This is not to say that high-tech companies in Japan enjoy no tax
advantages whatsoever over their U.S. competitors. The most significant advantage is that the effective tax rate on Japanese corporations,
taking into account national price factors, is lower than comparable
rates for U.S. companies, thanks to lower inflation rates.[54] The high
rate of inflation in the U.S. from the mid-1970's to the early 1980's
has had the effect of raising real corporate taxes. The negative inter-

action between inflation and taxes has also inhibited capital investment in the United States. However, the difference between Japan and the United States stems from macroeconomic, not industrial, policies and is systemic in nature, not the result of industrial targeting. In national tax policies, as in R&D subsidies and national research projects, industrial policy per se does not appear to confer outrageously unfair advantages on Japanese high-tech companies. To the extent that they exist, the discrepancies in Japan's favor can be better explained by reference to regime characteristics than to aberrant policy practices.

Antitrust

Two other areas in which Japan differs from the United States are the enforcement of antitrust laws and the use of administrative guidance as tools of industrial policy. Although antitrust is not usually considered a part of industrial policy, the strictness or laxity with which it is enforced has a bearing on the government's flexibility in making use of certain policy tools.

National research projects, for example, would pose greater problems of organization in the United States because of the stricter interpretation of antitrust and greater concerns about possible anticompetitive effects. Japan's Fair Trade Commission (FTC) seems to feel that national projects pose little threat to market competition as long as most of the major firms participate. If participation were limited to a single national champion (as in France and some of the smaller European states), the excluded companies might be placed at an insurmountable disadvantage; this could bring about unacceptable levels of market concentration and create formidable barriers to new entry.

Inviting most of the large corporations to participate, on the other hand, might give rise to a different set of problems. It might, for example, strengthen the hands of already dominant firms, accentuate oligopolistic patterns of behavior, and relegate other firms to second-class status. Why do the second-tier companies in Japan's information industries—like Sanyo, Sharp, and Sony—accept their exclusion from many national research projects? Why do they not voice objections or seek legal injunctions to prevent oligopolistic practices from taking place, as excluded companies in the United States would be apt to do? Are there not legal grounds for charges of collusion in restraint of trade?

If there are negative antitrust implications, the Japanese government does not appear to be too concerned. Levels of market concentration in high-tech sectors—though higher in some cases (such as semiconductors) than in the United States—remain sufficiently low that the FTC does not have to worry about the dangers of oligopoly. Since demand is still ascending steeply—with new products continually hitting the market and lots of leeway for both new venture start-ups and horizontal entry from companies in related industries—fears of excessive market concentration appear to be unfounded.

In its less stringent enforcement of antitrust, Japan resembles France, Sweden, and other European states more than it does the United States. The difference is that the domestic markets of the individual European states tend to be significantly smaller and the number of domestic producers in any given sector of high technology is usually small. Countries with tiny domestic markets and leeway for only one or two domestic producers feel they cannot afford the luxury of adhering to the strict standards of antitrust enforcement in the United States. It is all they can do to maintain the existence of one or two companies in niche markets. Neither the United States nor Japan has a problem with an undersized domestic market; yet Japan is not as fervent in the enforcement of antitrust as the United States, in part because its government is less preoccupied with the concept of individual consumer sovereignty and more concerned about the collective good.

The basic, precommercial nature of research also makes national projects palatable from an antitrust point of view. Similarly, the availability of patents on a nondiscriminatory basis to all firms neutralizes the most serious objections that excluded companies might raise. The principal advantages gained by participation in national projects are therefore confined to two areas: government funding, which can be used to supplement the firm's own R&D investments; and the benefits of hands-on laboratory experience and close contact with researchers from government labs and other firms, which far exceed the know-how obtainable through access to patent licenses. Although these advantages are certainly significant, they are not so decisive that firms gain an insurmountable edge by participating. Since the selection of participating firms is done on the basis of merit, the second-tier companies express few complaints about being excluded from the projects (though companies like Sanyo and Sharp have been included in some of the recent national projects).

It should be pointed out, furthermore, that U.S. antitrust policies do not rule out all forms of cooperative research. Every year a few dozen requests, usually involving small firms, to engage in joint research are approved. So long as cooperation does not seriously inhibit competition, joint research can be accommodated under the provisions of U.S. antimonopoly law. In DOD projects, collaboration is sometimes encouraged. The VHSIC project, for example, organized companies into several distinct contract teams in an attempt to bring about an efficient division of labor and encourage research cooperation. Hughes, RCA, and Rockwell standardized their computer-aided design system and exchanged information on mask designs, design rules, and patents as they worked to develop complementary metal oxide semiconductor/ silicon on sapphire (CMOS/SOS) technology.[55] Perkin-Elmer and Hughes Research Labs also joined forces in the development of electron beam lithography, exchanging very sensitive company information in order to achieve better results. Collaboration was also necessary to ensure compatibility for key technological systems such as the signal processor chip set. Thus, interfirm collaboration and cooperation do take place in the United States under the aegis of government projects, though far less extensively than in Japan.

What about interfirm cooperation in the nondefense sector? Although antitrust is more strictly enforced in the commercial domain, a potentially big step forward was taken when the Microelectronics and Computer Technology Corporation (MCC), a consortium of more than a dozen major U.S. companies, was granted permission to undertake joint research on advanced computer architecture, software, artificial intelligence, component packaging, and CAD/CAM technologies. MCC is, to some extent, an organizational response to the competitive challenge posed by Japanese national projects. Each member company sends researchers to MCC headquarters in Austin, Texas, where they work alongside representatives from other firms. The member companies bear the costs of research and share in its fruits.

MCC is the first consortium of its kind ever to be given the go-ahead to operate as a corporate entity. It performs some of the same functions as Japanese national projects: judicious identification of long-range technological objectives, mobilization of collective resources, research economies of scale, facilitation of information exchange and technological diffusion, and avoidance of wasteful duplication. The Justice Department has warned that it will monitor MCC's activities closely, and it may rescind approval if it uncovers evidence of anti-competitive consequences. Even in the commercial domain, therefore, cooperative research in the United States has been permitted, albeit under stricter constraints and closer monitoring than comparable projects in Japan.

The passage of special development laws in Japan to promote high-tech industries does exempt certain areas from antitrust prosecution. But the exemptions apply only to such matters as standardized specifications for electronics components. Special development laws, in effect for only a limited time, do not give high-tech industries license to engage freely in collaborative research, much less to divide up product and overseas markets, as some charge.[56] The VLSI project, for example, did not qualify for special exemption from antitrust; it fell into the standard category of "laws concerning public enterprise research associations."[57]

Antitrust leniency, based originally on the Law Concerning Temporary Measures for the Promotion of the Electronics Industry (1957), had a major impact on the creation of the Japan Electronic Computer Corporation (JECC) in 1961. JECC is a semigovernmental joint venture comprising Japan's seven leading computer manufacturers; it arranges favorable financing for computer rentals and purchases.[58] It has played a central role in shoring up the competitive power of Japan's computer industry, particularly during the 1960's and 1970's, when IBM threatened to take over Japan's domestic market. Something like JECC would be hard to envision in the United States. It probably would not pass either the Justice Department or the FTC. Here is an instance in which leniency in the application of antitrust law has had long-term consequences.

The overall picture is thus complicated: although antitrust policy in Japan has not permitted Japanese high-tech companies to collude in restraint of trade, it has given them more leeway for collaborative research than U.S. antitrust policy. Moreover, the creation of JECC has had a big impact on the development of the fledgling Japanese computer industry.

Administrative Guidance

One of the most talked-about instruments of Japanese industrial policy, one that has no counterpart in the United States, is administrative guidance (gyōsei shidō)—informal guidelines issued by MITI and other government ministries to help specific industries deal with vexing short-term problems that threaten to harm the collective interest. Unlike formal legislation, administrative guidance is not backed by legal sanctions, since it does not pass through the legislative branch for approval; yet it carries the weight of statutory law in terms of eliciting voluntary compliance. As with other policy decisions, thoroughgoing consultations take place prior to the issuing of administrative guidance. It seldom comes down from above as a unilateral decree, forcefully imposed on a surprised and recalcitrant private sector. Often, private industry approaches the government with the request that certain guidelines be issued.

For MITI, administrative guidance has served as a versatile tool for industrial fine-tuning, particularly during the era of high-speed growth.[59] It has offered MITI the flexibility with which to tailor policies to fit ever-changing circumstances without having to pass a batch of semipermanent laws in the Diet. Over time, the accumulation of such laws tends to clog and constrict the range of policy options. By avoiding heavy dependence on formal legislation, MITI has been able to protect industrial policy from partisan politicking. This has also enabled MITI to intervene selectively and then to pull back. The secret to the effectiveness of administrative guidance is the willingness of the private sector to abide by it, in spite of its nonbinding nature. Such informal guidelines would not work in the United States, where the distance and distrust between government and private enterprise are simply too great to permit coordinated patterns of compliance.

Like other tools of industrial policy, such as antirecession cartels, administrative guidance has come to be used less and less as Japan's economy has matured. For administrative guidance to work, several conditions have usually had to exist: (1) a relatively small number of companies in a given industry that have interacted over a period of time; (2) a clear opinion-leader or market-leader among them; (3) a fairly high degree of market concentration; (4) a mature stage in the industry's life cycle; (5) either a cohesive and strong industrial association or effective mechanisms of industrywide consensus formation; (6) a high degree of dependence on MITI, or at least a history of dependence; (7) common problems of sufficient severity to coax individual companies into cooperating, rather than "cheating," in order to advance collective interests.

Except for the last two, none of the above conditions pertain to the high-tech industries. Consider the software industry. There are literally thousands of companies competing against each other, with no clear leader or strong industrial association, in a dispersed market still in the early phases of growth. Under such conditions it is exceedingly difficult either to arrive at industrywide consensus or to close ranks in pursuit of common objectives. It is not surprising, therefore, that administrative guidance has been used relatively infrequently as a tool of industrial policy for high technology.

One exception is in the area of international trade. Owing to trade conflicts and pressures from foreign trading partners, MITI has had to negotiate a series of binding agreements with domestic companies on matters ranging from dumping to voluntary export restraints. Such agreements have taken the form of administrative guidance with respect to minimum prices, production volume, and export levels. Except for trade-related issues, MITI's reliance on administrative guidance has waned over time.

It is still used for sunset or declining industries that are beset by such structural problems as stagnant or severely fluctuating demand, serious plant overcapacity, and declining international cost-competitiveness. But even for sunset industries, the practice of issuing administrative guidance has been curtailed. In a landmark 1974 decision, the Tokyo High Court ruled that price fixing in the petroleum industry, which had resulted, in part, from private-sector responses to administrative guidance, was illegal. Although stopping short of declaring administrative guidance illegal, the Tokyo High Court noted that limits had to be imposed on its use. Hence, though well known as one of Japan's unique targeting tools, administrative guidance is no longer relied upon extensively, even for old-line industries. Like credit allocation and antirecession cartels, administrative guidance has receded in functional importance over the years, though it continues to be used as a low-key and informal policy instrument.

Industrial Location

Mention should be made, finally, of MITI's role in developing centers of high technology throughout Japan's archipelago. Working closely with local and prefectural governments, MITI has established a network of "technopolises" across the country.[60] The technopolis network is based on the notion that there are advantages to be gained from concentrating facilities for research and development, manufacturing, marketing, and service in compact centers of high technology, like Silicon Valley. The technopolis and companion "science city" provide the advantages of logistical convenience, close communications, close contact, and the synergy that emerges from the existence of a critical mass.

In remote or depressed regions, far removed from the major metropolitan centers (Tokyo-Yokohama, Osaka-Kyoto, and Nagoya), the idea of establishing such centers has struck a responsive chord. It holds forth the prospect of building an enduring infrastructure, ideally suited to the emerging era of high technology; such an infrastructure would produce revenue, employment, prosperity, and demographic balance. From a national standpoint, the technopolis networks would relieve Tokyo and Osaka of the enormous pressures of overcrowding. The desirability of deconcentration and regional relocation has long been recognized in Japan. Former Prime Minister Kakuei Tanaka once proposed a grand scheme for remodeling the Japanese archipelago in a book entitled *Nihon rettō kaizō-ron,* or *A Plan for Restructuring Japan.*[61]

For MITI, the technopolis concept has opened up an avenue for carrying out its responsibility to look after the economic interests of all regions of the country. Industrial location is a central focus of attention in the industrial policies of Great Britain, Italy, France, and West Germany—all countries that have had to grapple with the problem of declining industries in what have come to be known as regional "rust belts." It is also a concern of U.S. officials, even though the federal government has no comprehensive course of action or even a clear center of institutional authority for the development of a long-range plan; the initiative to do something about the regional imbalance has devolved, almost by default, on individual state governments.

In Japan, MITI has retained control over the problem of industrial location; it is an integral aspect of its overall industrial policy approach to high technology. Indeed, one reason for the alacrity with which MITI has grabbed hold of the issue is that it presents an opportunity to extend MITI's influence beyond Tokyo, where it tends to be concentrated, into the farthest reaches of the countryside. To help prefectural governors formulate and implement plans for industrial development, MITI now sends a number of its bright young bureaucrats to serve for short periods as special assistants. This has put MITI in a position to expand its influence in local areas (a position the Construction and Finance ministries have enjoyed for years). It is possible that the establishment of regional influence will serve as a local base for former MITI bureaucrats to run for election to the national Diet, just as the local tax offices serve as a springboard for former MOF officials to run for elective office. For MITI, the extension of its influence into the outlying regions has softened the blow of losing many of the key powers it once possessed.

What impact the technopolis networks and science cities (once they are completed) will have on the competitiveness of Japanese high technology is hard to say. The hope is that they will encourage greater investment; redistribute production, employment, and wealth; construct bigger and better facilities; and create a lasting national infrastructure that will allow Japan to make the transition smoothly from a smokestack to high-technology economy and to sustain itself well into the twenty-first century.

Demand Pull

Technological innovation, production efficiency, and healthy revenues—the sine qua non of competitiveness in high technology—can rest as much on demand pull as on technology push. Although the two are closely connected, some analysts give somewhat greater weight to demand pull.[62] Yet, except in the infant and declining stages of the industrial life cycle, the range and impact of industrial policy instruments for demand pull can be limited, especially if military expenditures are low, as they are in Japan. The available instruments of demand pull include government procurements, home market protection, "buy-national" programs, and export promotion. Yet, as in the case of technology push, the instruments of demand pull, if used unwisely, can distort market forces and cause serious long-term damage. Home market protection and buy-national programs are also capable of giving rise to trade frictions, including violations of GATT-based rules. And the dangers of corruption, fiscal overextension, and politicization loom large because of the sheer size of the public largess.

This suggests that with respect to market demand, the efficacy of industrial policy instruments is limited. Government is poised to make its biggest impact through the macroeconomic stimulation of aggregate demand. Other areas of indirect demand pull that fall into the category of industrial policy include import protection and buy-national campaigns to confine demand to domestic producers. Although such nonmarket measures may bolster the position of domestic producers in the short run, they usually turn out to be self-defeating over the long run because they thwart competition and breed inefficiency.

All sectors have benefited immensely from Japan's postwar growth, the fastest among the large industrial states. High-tech industries have been among the prime beneficiaries because of the high income elasticity of demand for most of their products. One can argue, therefore, that insofar as demand pull is concerned, Japan's high-tech sectors have advanced more as a consequence of sound macroeconomic management than of industrial policies.

Where guaranteed demand as an instrument of industrial policy can register a significant impact is in the early stages of an industry's or a new product's life cycle. The assurance of military procurements, for example, greatly facilitated early innovation in the U.S. microelectronics industry.[63] But the offer of R&D support, by itself, may not be sufficient to persuade companies to assume major investment risks; there must also be the lure of commercial markets. Government-sponsored R&D projects are enticing to some companies only if they are perceived to represent the first wave in what promises to be a second and much larger wave of commercial demand.[64]

Often, the lure of demand pull, combined with the momentum of technology push, is enough to reduce the costs and risks and make forays into the unknown acceptable.[65] The history of innovation in the U.S. semiconductor, computer, and telecommunications industries reveals that the government as guaranteed first purchaser and prime R&D contractor played a crucial initial role, only to be replaced by the subsequent expansion of commercial demand. Government procurement today accounts for only a fraction of aggregate demand in these industries.

MITI: The Lack of Procurements

One of the most striking and significant—but overlooked—features of Japanese industrial policy is the comparative slackness of demand-pull measures. Unlike the U.S. Department of Defense, MITI possesses practically no budget for public procurements. The Japan Defense Agency (JDA), the closest counterpart to DOD, does not make much of a dent on aggregate demand through weapons acquisition. The JDA has one of the world's smallest defense budgets—roughly 1 percent of GNP—of which only about 25 percent is earmarked for weapons acquisition. Of course, because Japan's GNP is so large, the 1 percent figure is not a trivial amount in absolute terms; but even when calculated in yen (rather than percentages), the amount falls far below that of the United States.

The implications of MITI's lack of procurement power are far-reaching. Among other consequences, MITI has had to rely more on a strategy of technology push; for demand pull, high-tech industries have had to rely on macroeconomic measures. Fortunately for them, Japan's domestic market is large enough, and overseas markets are sufficiently open, to allow them to develop without the stimulation of direct demand from the government. But in the absence of an assured customer base of government procurements, Japanese high-tech companies have had to enter consumer-oriented mass markets (such as hand-held calculators for mass memory chips) to recoup the upfront costs of R&D. They established an early foothold in consumer electronics and only recently have moved toward more sophisticated systems applications. The lack of procurement powers has thus forced Japanese companies to compete vigorously in mass consumer markets, a necessity that has caused them to be lean and efficient. The absence of large procurement programs has also spared MITI from excessive political interference, the by-product of corporate lobbying to carve up slices of the public largess.

Whereas MITI lacks the funds for large-scale procurements, other government agencies have substantial purchasing power. The Ministry of Construction presides over a very large budget for public works, and the Ministry of Transportation has drawn on procurement funds to stabilize the ups and downs of shipbuilding demand. There is no doubt that having control over large procurement budgets gives these ministries significant leverage over the private sector; however, such power comes at the price of having to accept a high level of political interference. The ministries of Construction and Transportation, as pointed out in Chapter 4, are among the most politicized bureaucracies in Japan.

Like governments elsewhere, Japanese agencies have tried to bolster domestic companies by purchasing domestically made computers and other high-tech equipment for use in the myriad local, prefectural, and central government offices, public corporations, and public schools. Until 1975, IBM and other foreign manufacturers had been excluded from the circle of companies receiving procurement orders. But in trying to bolster the position of domestic producers, Japan is not different from France or Britain, which gives preferential procurements to national companies. American computer companies in the United Kingdom have gone to court to protest the British government's discriminatory procurement practices.[66] What is noteworthy about Japan is that the level of demand generated by all public procurements is relatively small, accounting for less than 4 percent of the number of computers sold in 1980, and less than 14 percent of the total value of all computers used in Japan.[67]

NTT Procurements

The sole exception to the pattern of limited procurements has been NTT, the public telephone monopoly under the authority of the Ministry of Post and Telecommunications and one of the few public corporations with substantial demand-generating power for the information industries. In 1981, NTT's procurement budget came to about $2.7 billion. For Nippon Electric Corporation (NEC), NTT's largest supplier, procurements exceeded $500 million, representing 12 percent of total company sales. Assured annual sales of telecommunications equipment allowed NTT family firms (especially Hitachi, Fujitsu, NEC, and Oki) to reap valuable benefits, such as economies of scale, greater learning by doing, advances in process technology, large revenues to plow back into R&D, hands-on experience to apply to related technologies, and the capacity to raise more capital.

Until 1981, the procurement bonanza had been closed to foreign bidders; however, under heavy foreign pressure, NTT agreed to open up its procurement system. In 1984, three years after liberalization, foreign manufacturers had managed to win less than 5 percent of NTT procurements, and that mostly in the lower-value-added products, not the higher-value-added areas, like systems integration, in which foreign companies excel. Foreign competitors believe that the closed system bestowed de facto subsidies on Japanese companies; they believe that the competitive ramifications have been felt not only in telecommunications but also in such related fields as semiconductors and information processing.

Demand for telecommunications equipment is expected to keep climbing through the end of the century as NTT implements an ambitious plan to expand and upgrade the nation's entire telecommunications infrastructure through the Information Network System (INS).[68] Over a twenty-year period, INS is expected to generate upward of ¥30 trillion in procurement demand—roughly $230 billion (at the late 1987 exchange rate of 130 yen to the dollar), or an average of over $10 billion per year. If Japanese companies garner all but a small share, the commercial and technological impetus imparted could be enormous for voice recognition and storage, high-speed and mass-volume information processing, and facsimile equipment.

The combination of NTT and JDA demand may facilitate bolder risk-taking and state-of-the-art breakthroughs by Japanese corporations in the future. Large demand stimulation may serve to reduce the risks and costs of new product development and may facilitate innovation in process technology. But defense-related R&D is likely to remain relatively small for the foreseeable future, and the conversion of NTT from a public to a private corporation has transformed the relationship between NTT and its former family firms.[69] The old organizational arrangements for joint R&D have been abandoned, and

Industrial Policy Instruments

NTT procurements have shifted from a closed system of guaranteed demand for NTT family firms to an open system of competitive bidding and price-sensitive market transactions. The change opens up opportunities for foreign companies and international consortia to participate in the booming demand expected to be generated by the growth of Japan's telecommunications industry.

Indirect Demand Stimulation

Without the power of procurements, MITI has had to rely on a variety of indirect instruments to stimulate demand: special tax incentives, export promotion, support for rental and leasing, and home market protection. Until 1983, MITI used special tax incentives to encourage Japanese manufacturers to purchase and install robots, numerically controlled (NC) machine tools, and other automated assembly-line equipment. Although the primary objectives were to raise productivity levels and reduce hazardous working conditions, the switch to automated equipment had the effect of boosting demand for high-tech products. Companies buying robots and NC machine tools received a 13 percent tax credit on the purchasing price, on top of regularly scheduled depreciation allowances.

MITI has also exhorted domestic producers to move down the learning curve by exporting to open overseas markets. Unlike exports of traditional products, like steel, which are sold overseas by giant trading companies, the export of high-tech equipment tends to be handled by the producer companies themselves. Most high-tech products, like computers, require specialized technical knowledge on the part of overseas sales forces and conscientious after-sales service for customers; large trading companies are not particularly well suited to providing the full range of services, from marketing and distribution to customer aftercare. The burden for exporting thus falls squarely on high-tech companies. The Japanese government, through organizations like Japan External Trade Research Organization (JETRO), provides valuable information about overseas markets and sponsors a variety of meetings, conferences, and trade exhibitions. MITI also helps to make arrangements for export financing and insurance through the Japan Export-Import Bank. Since the mid-1980's, when Japan's trade surpluses hit embarrassing highs, MITI has also tried to facilitate industry efforts to find suitable opportunities for direct foreign investment in manufacturing plants abroad.

Lacking the budget to purchase high-tech equipment, MITI has come up with clever ways of accomplishing the next best thing:

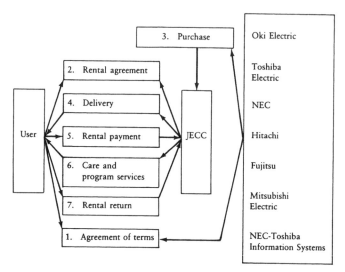

Fig. 2.3. JECC rental system

namely, the organization of nonprofit companies to purchase, rent, or lease costly and continually changing high-tech products. The JECC, created in 1961 as a semigovernmental joint venture involving the seven leading computer manufacturers, is perhaps the best-known example (see Fig. 2.3). Drawing on a pool of funds, including low-interest loans from the Japan Development Bank, JECC had purchased a cumulative total of over $7.25 billion worth of computer equipment by 1981, with rental revenues of $5.6 billion. Its role in helping Japan's computer industry establish a secure foothold in the expanding leasing market was critical, especially during the early years, when IBM appeared to be on the verge of taking control of the Japanese market and Japanese computer firms lacked the resources to compete individually.[70]

The Japan Robot Leasing Company (JAROL), organized in 1980, is another joint venture (comprising 24 robot manufacturers, 10 insurance companies, and 7 general leasing firms) that leases robots to small and medium-sized companies. As of 1982, it had leased nearly 800 robots worth over $25 million. Furthermore, the Small Business Finance Corporation, a government institution, provided loans to small and medium-sized companies for robot installation. Thus, even without a procurement budget, MITI has not been completely hand-cuffed on demand-pull measures. It has made full use of various indirect policy instruments. While these instruments have not had as much impact as large-scale procurements, they have helped to boost demand in ways that would not otherwise have been possible.

Home Market Protection

Another indirect instrument of demand stimulation on which MITI has relied in the past (but much less since 1980) is the protection of home markets against foreign competition through the imposition of formal import duties, quotas, restrictions on foreign direct investment, and an assortment of nontariff barriers. Formal tariffs, which used to be high as part of Japan's infant industry strategy, have been brought a long way down since the mid-1970's. In 1963 dutiable imports carried a 20.9 percent average levy; by 1983, this had fallen to 4.3 percent. Import duties for high-tech products have also come tumbling down. From 1972 to 1983, computer peripheral duties fell from 22.5 percent to 6 percent; computer mainframe duties fell from 13.5 percent to 4.9 percent; duties on semiconductors dropped from 15 percent to 4.2 percent and all the way down to zero in 1987. Such reductions have brought Japanese duties in line with U.S. levels, and well below those of the European Community.

It can be argued, of course, that it took years of banging on the door before the Japanese government responded and that the barriers came down only after Japanese producers had reached a position of rough parity with foreign manufacturers. Even after liberalization, a variety of nontariff barriers remain, including the unintentional ones of language, business culture, and industrial organization.[71] The thick, tightly integrated network of long-term relationships binding buyers and suppliers, parent corporations and subcontractors, member companies in keiretsu groupings, distributors, financial intermediaries, government, and industry makes Japan an especially difficult market to penetrate (quite apart from other barriers to entry). The difficulties of breaking into the organizational nexus are particularly frustrating for foreign producers of high-tech intermediate goods, because the enclosed and long-term nature of relations between buyers and suppliers alters the character of spot-market, arms-distant transactions.[72]

The barriers to outside entry are also evident in the maze of intercorporate stockholdings that tie Japanese companies together. It may be that the willingness of the Japanese government to accede to foreign pressures to dismantle formal barriers stemmed, in part, from the realization that unintentional structural barriers would still impede full foreign access to Japan's lucrative market. Hiroshi Okumura draws attention to the fact that the impact of capital liberalization, which took place during the late 1960's, has been neutralized by developments within the realm of intercorporate stockholding:

> While the government went about liberalizing capital, Japanese companies were busily implementing their own plans for keeping foreign capital out by means of stock-securing maneuvers. As mentioned, these involved the placement of a large bloc of the stock issued by one company in the hands of other companies—typically its bank and leading partners. The companies thus entrusted with stock did not accept it merely because they were asked to. They became stockholders to enhance intercorporate cohesion and to bind the group together more firmly. The main reason almost no Japanese companies have been absorbed by foreign capital is that each corporate group met the capital liberalization program with its own stock-defense program.[73]

The government encouraged the trend toward intercorporate stock concentration. Loose antitrust enforcement permitted corporate entities to expand their shares of outstanding stocks to over 70 percent, and occasional administrative guidance facilitated the process.

Not only has this obstructed foreign acquisitions and takeovers, an easy path to establishing a physical presence in overseas markets; it has also contained foreign penetration of Japanese markets because of the tight, long-term bonds of structural interdependence between companies in Japan. Buying and selling intermediate goods within a self-contained circle of Japanese companies that own stock in one another makes sense from the standpoint of implicit, long-term contracts and what Oliver Williamson calls "low transaction costs" and what Harvey Liebenstein refers to as "x-efficiencies."[74] The logic of business in such a setting is different from that of spot-market transactions. Purchasing intermediate goods from subsidiaries, closely affiliated subcontractors, or members of the same keiretsu can almost be considered quasi-internal transactions. Considering the structure of Japanese home markets, therefore, it is hardly surprising that foreign companies have had difficulty breaking in.

Sales of foreign-made intermediate goods are limited further by the structure of Japanese kaisha as vertically integrated, diversified companies. Instead of meeting all their needs on the merchant market, Japanese computer companies make their own semiconductors and sell what they do not use. Captive, in-house production thus imposes limits on the expansion of foreign shares in Japan's semiconductor market. U.S. semiconductor companies complain that Japanese customers tend to purchase only those highly sophisticated components that they themselves cannot make, such as state-of-the-art microprocessors and custom-made logic devices.[75] Once Japanese companies learn how to produce the advanced devices themselves, the demand for U.S.-made products plummets.

Frustrated American business executives suspect that a well-orchestrated "buy-Japanese" policy lies behind their inability to expand exports. They point out that when they compete with Japanese companies in neutral third markets, such as Europe, they often win the competition and garner larger market shares. But there are other plausible explanations, involving the greater vertical integration among Japanese companies and the self-enclosed nature of Japanese industrial organization. Whatever the reason, the fact is that foreign producers have had a much harder time breaking into, and expanding their shares of, the Japanese market than Japanese producers have had in penetrating the U.S. and European markets.

Japanese electronics companies conduct business within a clear hierarchy of corporate customers, based on the length, magnitude, and overall importance of the business relationship. Priority in terms of financing, services, and supplies is given to corporate customers with which the supplier has had long-standing and extensive relations. Should there be shortfalls of supplies—for example, of 256K DRAMs—Japanese corporations will distribute available supplies in accordance with their hierarchical priorities; companies near the bottom of the hierarchy receive smaller rations. It is not a matter of open bidding or of a neutral, first-come-first-served arrangement. Price is only one factor, and sometimes not the decisive one.

Japanese industrial organization emphasizes the importance of extramarket factors, especially the strong preference for stable, predictable, long-term business relationships based on mutual obligation and trust. This has had the effect of raising the barriers to entry from the outside, whether by foreign manufacturers or by non-mainstream Japanese producers. Such nontariff barriers, deeply embedded in the structure of the industrial economy, are not directly connected to Japanese industrial policy. But their existence, whether by design or by accident, serves basically the same function as formal measures of home market protection—only more effectively, because they do not diminish the vigor of market competition between domestic producers.

Conclusions

There is no alchemy involved in MITI's formula for successful industrial policy. Most of its policies can be found on any standard list compiled by states seeking to promote their high-tech industries. The dosage and mix vary according to specific circumstances and particular needs, but the prescription is fairly standard. MITI's formula can be broken down into three basic elements: technology push, demand pull, and other facilitating measures. Of these, MITI has placed the heaviest emphasis on technology push, featuring national research projects, R&D subsidies, support for basic research, and efforts at technology diffusion. The emphasis comes from the readier accessibility of policy instruments for technology push. It is not derived from a belief that technology push is inherently more efficacious than demand pull. MITI has tried various ways of generating demand, but without a budget for public procurements, its efforts have been limited. Insofar as demand pull is concerned, the Ministry of Finance's macroeconomic measures have registered a far greater impact than MITI's industrial policies.

Nearly all policy instruments that MITI uses in Japan are also employed extensively by governments in other industrial states. As we have seen, Japan is not abnormal in either their adoption or level of use. The only difference is that Japan has somehow managed to wring higher yields from such policy instruments. One reason for the higher yield is that MITI has exercised moderation in its use of all three categories of industrial policy tools—technology push, demand pull, and other facilitating measures. When used to excess, all three categories are capable of doing serious damage to market efficiency.

In coming up with its own formula, MITI has altered the mix of industrial policy instruments that had been applied successfully to the development of old-line industries. It has carefully chosen only those instruments that fit the functional requisites of high technology. Such old-line instruments as structural consolidation and antirecession cartels have been largely abandoned because they are considered too blunt and unwieldy to meet the subtle needs of high technology. The adjustment from smokestacks to high technology is by no means automatic. That Japan has managed to make the transition is a reflection of MITI's capacity to fine-tune market intervention to match the circumstances and goals of specific industries.

Other states have failed to make as smooth a transition. The French government has bought major shares of the stock of high-tech companies like Bull, just as it had in certain areas of banking and heavy manufacturing. State-controlled companies in Italy, like the Istituto per la Riconstruzione Industriale (IRI), hold equity control over key organizations in high technology, just as they do in the old-line sectors. In Britain, the government has entered into venture capital investment, an area restricted to private risk-taking in the United States and Japan. Although the effects of government involvement are not yet clear, the continuing problems of high-tech sectors in Europe suggest, at the very least, that state underwriting is no guarantee of success. Indeed, recent trends toward privatization in England and the sale of government stocks in France may be an admission that extending old industrial policy measures to new sectors of the economy has been a failure.

Selective Omission

Comparing Japanese industrial policy with the policies of other industrial states, one cannot help but notice the absence of certain policy measures that have figured prominently elsewhere. Mention has already been made of the absence of large defense procurements, extensive state ownership of corporate stocks, and state investments in new venture activities—all of which have had costly consequences in terms of economic efficiency in other countries. There are other conscious omissions that have helped Japan to avoid serious economic and political pitfalls.

Although Japanese industrial policy has had the effect of promoting the growth of certain big, blue-chip companies in priority sectors, MITI has not followed a strategy of cultivating one or two "national champions" as France and the small European states have. In large part, as pointed out earlier, this is attributable to differences in size. Japan has a much larger domestic market, population base, and manpower pool, with which it can support more than one or two world-class companies across a spectrum of economic activities. It does not need to concentrate finite resources on the cultivation of a national champion in a few carefully chosen sectors.

If the government attempted to cultivate a national champion for each targeted sector, the effort would violate deeply held norms of fairness and impartiality (not to mention antimonopoly laws); it would also trigger an outburst of outraged opposition. But no such attempt needs to be made. Like the United States, Japan possesses the factor endowments to let a number of strong companies fight it out in the marketplace. The ferocity of the competition strengthens efficiency and the international competitiveness of Japanese firms.

Because it entertains no superpower aspirations in the political-military sphere, Japan has also managed to sidestep another serious pitfall: namely, the disproportionate mobilization of resources for

highly visible projects of great pomp and national prestige, but of
limited commercial value. Those nations caught up in the "big power"
game—the United States, France, and Great Britain—have all suc-
cumbed at various times to the temptation of placing national prestige
above more mundane considerations of commercial cost-effectiveness.
France's program to build a supersonic jet, the Concorde, is an illustration of a high-visibility national project that yielded paltry commercial benefits.

The U.S. Strategic Defense Initiative (SDI) project, the Reagan Administration's ambitious program to build a missile defense system in
space, is different from the supersonic jet and airbus projects in its
military orientation, but it emerged from the same "big power" syndrome and will probably be as costly in its absorption of finite R&D
resources and crowding out of commercial opportunities. Japan has
averted such costly mistakes by maintaining a low political-military
profile and eschewing big, splashy projects that would thrust it mo-
mentarily into the world spotlight. Japan has remained single-minded
in its pursuit of only those projects that hold forth the promise of
long-run, cost-effective commercial opportunities.

As an ally of the United States, Japan has agreed to abide by the
COCOM rules restricting the export of dual-purpose technology to
the Communist bloc countries. Except for the Toshiba Milling Machine Company's much-publicized violation in 1987, Japan has ad-
hered fairly faithfully to the letter of the COCOM agreement by not
engaging in direct sales to Communist countries. But some U.S. government officials believe that the Japanese have been lax about selling
technology to third countries that resell it in turn to the Communist
bloc. The U.S. government takes a much tougher stance toward domestic companies trying to circumvent the COCOM guidelines
through third-country sales. Indeed, as the military standard-bearer
for the Western alliance, the United States administers a restrictive and
cumbersome set of controls over the sale of products incorporating
sensitive dual-purpose technology of any kind. Chafing under the
weight of costly paperwork and frustrating delays, U.S. companies
complain that government regulations are handcuffing them in their
competition against Japanese firms for lucrative export markets.[76]
Here again, the lightness of Japan's military burden looms as a major
asset.

Of the selective omissions, however, none is of greater importance
than MITI's refusal to cave in to demands that the structurally depressed industries be accorded formal protection against foreign im-

ports. When textile, steel, and automobile producers in the United States could no longer compete, they lobbied the government and persuaded it to pressure foreign producers (especially the Japanese) to accept a series of voluntary export restraints (VERs) that imposed quantitative export ceilings. VER agreements have come to function as vital, life-support systems for many old-line industries in the United States, even though they were originally designed to provide only temporary relief. The problem with VERs is that they erode the GATT framework of trade, delay structural adjustments to the ever-changing international division of labor, and cause serious distortions in the allocation of capital and labor. High-tech industries cannot escape the indirect and multiplier effects of the distortions.

The fact that Japan has not resorted to the imposition of VERs to prop up its declining sectors is of significant indirect benefit to its high-tech industries. It means that they do not have to bear the costs of inflation and inefficiency that semipermanent protection for old-line manufacturers causes. Of course, as pointed out in Chapter 4, the high-tech industries in Japan have incurred costs from the protection of other inefficient sectors, like agriculture; but because steel and car makers are still competitive, Japanese high-tech companies have a healthy set of downstream industries on which to rely for the consumption of their intermediate goods. In an economy of complex interdependence, the benefits of efficiency can be passed along, just as the costs of inefficiency are bound to be transmitted in the form of indirect multiplier effects.

From a long-term, economy-wide perspective, the United States' imposition of a succession of VERs on Japan has had a boomerang effect. It has pushed Japan steadily up the ladder of higher value added in the composition of its exports to the United States. When VERs were placed on textiles, Japan stepped up its sale of steel; when VERs were placed on steel, Japan expanded its market shares of cars and consumer electronics; and when VERs were placed on cars and consumer electronics, Japan shifted to the export of high-technology products. Throughout, total export volume has continued to rise. By clamping down on one product category (old-line manufacturing), the United States merely accelerated Japan's speed in moving into the production and export of more sophisticated and expensive goods (high technology). In a very real sense, therefore, U.S. protectionism in the declining, old-line sectors has had the perverse effect of making the Japanese more competitive in high technology.

Although Japan has not forced other countries to swallow VERs, textile producers in China and steel and automobile companies in Korea have complained about being shut out of Japanese markets. They believe Japan is relying on hidden nontariff barriers instead of VERs to protect domestic producers in old-line sectors. Whether and to what extent this allegation is true is hard to determine. If it is true, and if the scope of protection is as far-reaching as they claim, then Japan is apt to suffer the same boomerang effects as the United States.

There is, however, a significant difference between Japan and the United States: namely, that the Japanese government has coordinated comprehensive plans to cut back plant capacity in the structurally depressed sectors. Nearly 50 percent of total plant capacity has been scrapped in old-line industries like shipbuilding, aluminum smelting, certain areas of textile production, and petrochemicals. Steel and other old-line industries are similarly undergoing structural reductions and automated upgrading. Moreover, with the yen's sharp upward revaluation, Japanese old-line manufacturers are investing in offshore production facilities through the vehicle of joint ventures with indigenous partners. Seeing the handwriting on the wall, many are also diversifying into higher-growth fields; a number of textile companies, for example, have entered into the field of biotechnology.[77] Through "positive adjustments," therefore, Japan is relieving some of the pressures that would otherwise mount for the protection of inefficient old-line industries. Here, as in other respects, Japan bears a striking resemblance to the small European states, which feel they have no choice but to bow to the forces of the international economy.[78]

Assessment

Although most instruments of Japanese industrial policy are neither unique nor abnormal, a few take distinctive form in Japan. Although they serve the same functions as policy instruments in other industrial states, they have no precise equivalent elsewhere. Administrative guidance, special temporary development laws for promoting priority industries, the old NTT family setup, and positive adjustment policies for the scrapping of excess plant capacity fall into this category. All have contributed something to the overall effectiveness of Japanese industrial policy. The old NTT family system for cooperative research and procurement and positive adjustment policies designed to streamline surplus plant capacity have been especially constructive and distinctive policy instruments.

Japan has also had some measure of success, where others have experienced nothing but failure, in the organization of national re-

Industrial Policy Instruments   III

search projects, the encouragement of both competition and cooperation, the insulation of industrial policy from politicized forces, the limitation of damage by the distortion of market forces, the comparative coherence of MITI's industrial policy, and the relative absence of irreconcilable conflicts between industrial and macroeconomic policies. These represent considerable achievements when compared to industrial policy in most other countries. Being able to keep industrial policy from falling into the hands of politicians, for example, is a rare feat; the same holds true for all the other achievements listed above. Few other countries have managed to replicate Japan's accomplishments, in spite of using most of the same instruments of industrial policy.

Why is it that countries using basically the same set of industrial policy instruments should experience such divergent results? The question suggests that the policy measures themselves are not the sole factors determining the success or failure of industrial policy. Although unwise, market-defying measures will surely subvert economic efficiency, market-conforming measures will not always produce successful results. In other words, the selection of sound measures may be a necessary but not sufficient condition of an effective industrial policy. Effectiveness depends on other factors, especially the characteristics of market organizations and the structure of political institutions.

In Japan's case, the relative efficacy of the policy instruments used for the promotion of high technology has depended on the distinctive nature and structure of Japan's political economy. Sound instruments were chosen and then made to work because of the existence of such systemic factors as the consensual mode of policy-making, the extensive information gathering and analysis on which consensus is based, and the tradition of close government-business relations—all of which emerge from the strengths of Japan's political economy. To understand why industrial policy has not created more problems than it has solved in Japan—when it has given rise to a multitude of problems in countries like Italy and Britain—requires that we move the focus of our analysis beyond the repertoire of policy instruments. At a higher and more abstract level, we must analyze the regime characteristics of Japan's political economy, especially the organization of its private sector and its relationship to the institutions and processes of the political system. It is to an analysis of these subjects that we turn in Chapters 3 and 4.

Chapter Two

1. Eugene Kaplan, *Japan: The Government-Business Relationship* (Washington, D.C.: U.S. Department of Commerce, 1972).

2. Daniel I. Okimoto, Henry Rowen, and Michael Dahl, *National Security and the Declining Competitiveness of the American Semiconductor Industry*. Occasional Paper (Stanford, Calif.: Northeast Asia–United States Forum on International Policy, 1987).

3. Semiconductor Industry Association, *The Effect of Government Targeting on World Semiconductor Competition* (Cupertino, Calif.: Semiconductor Industry Association, 1983).

4. Michael Borrus, James Milstein, and John Zysman, *U.S.-Japanese Competition in the Semiconductor Industry* (Berkeley: Institute of International Studies, University of California, 1982).

5. Daniel I. Okimoto, "Political Context," in Daniel I. Okimoto, Takuo Sugano, and Franklin B. Weinstein, eds., *Competitive Edge: The Semiconductor Industry in the U.S. and Japan* (Stanford, Calif.: Stanford University Press, 1984), pp. 78–113.

6. Mancur Olson, *The Logic of Collective Action* (Cambridge, Mass.: Harvard University Press, 1965).

7. Okimoto, Rowen, and Dahl.

8. Masahiko Aoki, "The Japanese Firm in Transition," in Kōzō Yamamura and Yasukichi Yasuba, eds., *The Political Economy of Japan*, vol. 1, *The Domestic Transformation* (Stanford, Calif.: Stanford University Press, 1987), pp. 282–86. See Aoki's article "Innovative Adaptation Through the Quasi-Tree Structure: An Emerging Aspect of Japanese Entrepreneurship," *Zeitschrift für Nationalökonomie*, suppl. 4 (1984): 177–98.

9. Semiconductor Industry Association.

10. United States International Trade Commission, *Foreign Industrial Targeting and Its Effects on U.S. Industries, Phase I: Japan* (Washington, D.C.: U.S. Government Printing Office, 1983), p. 17.

11. Nakagawa Yasuzō, *Hihon no handōtai kaihatsu* (The development of semiconductors in Japan) (Tokyo: Daiyamondosha, 1981), pp. 57–60.

12. Daniel I. Okimoto and Gary R. Saxonhouse, "Technology and the Future of the Economy," in Kōzō Yamamura and Yasukichi Yasuba, eds., *The Political Economy of Japan*, vol. 1, *The Domestic Transformation* (Stanford, Calif.: Stanford University Press, 1987), pp. 385–419.

13. Daniel I. Okimoto, *Pioneer and Pursuer: The Role of the State in the Evolution of the Japanese and American Semiconductor Industries*. Occasional Paper (Stanford, Calif.: Northeast Asia–United States Forum on International Policy, 1983), pp. 3–20.

14. Daniel I. Okimoto and Henry K. Hayase, "Organizing for Innovation," unpublished paper prepared for High Technology Conference, Honolulu, Hawaii, Jan. 1985.

15. United States International Trade Commission, p. 77.

16. Semiconductor Industry Association.

17. Makoto Kikuchi, *Japanese Electronics* (Tokyo: Simul Press, 1983), p. 6.

18. Interview with MITI official, Jan. 1984.

19. Daniel I. Okimoto, Takuo Sugano, and Franklin B. Weinstein, eds., *Competitive Edge: The Semiconductor Industry in the U.S. and Japan* (Stanford, Calif.: Stanford University Press, 1984), pp. 38–39.

20. Masato Nebashi, "VLSI Technology Research Association," unpublished paper, 1981; interview with Masato Nebashi, June 24, 1982.

21. Edward A. Feigenbaum and Pamela McCorduck, *The Fifth Generation: Artificial Intelligence and Japan's Computer Challenge to the World* (Menlo Park, Calif.: Addison-Wesley, 1983).

22. Nakagawa, pp. 22–32.

23. United States International Trade Commission, p. 111.

24. Arthur D. Little, "Summary of Major Projects in Japan for R&D of Information Processing Technology," unpublished study, 1983.

25. Interview with Daimaru executives, Dec. 1983 and Feb. 1987.

26. Oliver E. Williamson, *Markets and Hierarchies: Analysis and Antitrust Implications* (New York: Free Press, 1975).

27. Masahiko Aoki, *The Cooperative Game Theory of the Firm* (Oxford: Oxford University Press, 1984).

28. Ronald P. Dore, *Flexible Rigidities: Industrial Policy and Structural Adjustment in the Japanese Economy, 1970–80* (Stanford, Calif.: Stanford University Press, 1986).

29. Okimoto and Hayase.

30. Charles L. Schultze, *The Public Use of Private Interest* (Washington, D.C.: Brookings Institution, 1977).

31. United States International Trade Commission, p. 90.

32. Semiconductor Industry Association, pp. 99–101.

33. Okimoto, *Pioneer and Pursurer*, p. 4.

34. Williamson, pp. 26–31.

35. United States International Trade Commission, p. 105.

36. Interviews with MITI officials, Sept. 1983.

37. Feigenbaum and McCorduck, p. 109.

38. Ibid.

39. "Bell Labs: The Threatened Star of U.S. Research," *Business Week*, July 5, 1982, p. 47.

40. "A Research Spending Surge Defies Recession," *Business Week*, July 5, 1982, p. 54.

41. Glenn R. Fong, "Industrial Policy Innovation in the United States: Lessons from the Very High Speed Integrated Circuit Program," unpublished paper presented at the annual meeting of the American Political Science Association, Chicago, Sept. 1–4, 1983.

42. National Science Foundation, "Industrial R&D Expenditures in 1980 Show Real Growth for Fifth Consecutive Year," *Highlights*, Dec. 31, 1981, pp. 81–331.

43. Robert W. Wilson, Peter K. Ashton, and Thomas P. Egan, *Innovation, Competition, and Government Policy in the Semiconductor Industry* (Lexington, Mass.: D.C. Heath, 1980), p. 154.

44. Nico Hazewindus with John Tooker, *The U.S. Microelectronics Industry* (New York: Pergamon Press, 1982), p. 121.

45. Keith Jones, "French and U.S. Interests Intertwine Around ICs," *Electronic Business* 8, no. 7 (1983): 88.

46. Keith Jones, "Nationalized French Computer Industry Sparks Controversy," *Electronic Business* 9, no. 4 (1983): 37–38.

47. "Europe's Desperate Try for High-Tech Teamwork," *Business Week*, May 30, 1983, p. 45.

48. United States International Trade Commission.

49. Ibid.

50. Thomas P. Rohlen, "Learning: The Mobilization of Knowledge in the Japanese Political Economy," unpublished paper prepared for the Japan Political Economy Research Conference, Tokyo, Jan. 6–10, 1988.

51. Robert Michels, *Political Parties: A Sociological Study of the Oligarchical Tendencies of Modern Democracy* (New York: Dover, 1959).

52. Gary R. Saxonhouse, "Japanese High Technology, Government Policy, and Evolving Comparative Advantage in Goods and Services," unpublished paper, 1982.

53. Ibid.

54. United States International Trade Commission, p. 76.

55. Fong.

56. Interviews with Silicon Valley executives, Sept. 1982, Apr. 1986, June 1987.

57. Interview with Masato Nebashi, former executive director, VLSI project, Tokyo, June 24, 1982.

58. Nihon Denshi Keisanki Kabushiki Kaisha, *JECC Computer Handbook* (Tokyo: Nihon Denshi Keisanki Kabushiki Kaisha, 1983).

59. Chalmers Johnson, *MITI and the Japanese Miracle: The Growth of Industrial Policy, 1925–1975* (Stanford, Calif.: Stanford University Press, 1982).

60. Sheridan Tatsuno, *The Technopolis Strategy: Japan, High Technology, and the Control of The 21st Century* (Englewood Cliffs, N.J.: Prentice Hall, 1986).

61. Tanaka Kakuei, *Nihon rettō kaizō-ron* (A plan for restructuring Japan) (Tokyo: Nikkan Kōgyō Shinbun, 1972).

62. Morton I. Kamien and Nancy L. Schwartz, *Market Structure and Innovation* (Cambridge, Eng.: Cambridge University Press, 1982), pp. 35–48.

63. Richard Levin, "The Semiconductor Industry," in Richard R. Nelson, ed., *Government and Technical Progress* (New York: Pergamon Press, 1982), pp. 9–100.

64. Interview with Elliott Levinthal, formerly of the Defense Advanced Research Project Agency, U.S. Department of Defense, Sept. 1983.

65. Richard R. Nelson, "Government Stimulus of Technological Progress: Lessons from American History," in Richard R. Nelson, ed., *Government and Technical Progress* (New York: Pergamon Press), pp. 471–72.

66. Robert L. Muller, "U.S. Computer Firms in Britain Suspect U.K. Agencies Favor Home Companies," *Wall Street Journal*, Aug. 12, 1982.

67. Nihon Jōhō Shori Kaihatsu Kyōkai, *Conpyuuta hakusho, 1981* (Computer white paper) (Tokyo: Nihon Jōhō Shori Kaihatsu Kyōkai, 1981), pp. 95–105.

68. Yasusada Kitahara, *Information Network System: Telecommunications in the Twenty-first Century* (London: Heinemann Educational Books, 1983), pp. 80–103.

69. Okimoto and Hayase.

70. Nihon Denshi Keisanki Kabushiki Kaisha.

71. Daniel I. Okimoto, "Outsider Trading: Coping with Japanese Industrial Organization," *Journal of Japanese Studies* 13, no. 2 (1987): 85–116.

72. Williamson.

73. Hiroshi Okumura, "The Closed Nature of Japanese Intercorporate Relations," *Japan Echo* 9, no. 3 (1982): 61.

74. Williamson; Harvey Liebenstein, "The Japanese Management System: An X-Efficiency-Game Theory Analysis," in Masahiko Aoki, *The Economic Analysis of the Japanese Firm* (Amsterdam: North-Holland, 1984), pp. 331–53.

75. Interviews with Silicon Valley executives, 1983 to 1987.

76. Interview with Art Hausmann, former chairman of Ampex Corporation, June 1984.

77. Gary R. Saxonhouse, "Industrial Policy and Factor Markets: Biotechnology in Japan and the United States," in Hugh T. Patrick, ed., *Japanese High Technology Industries* (Seattle: University of Washington Press, 1986).

78. Peter J. Katzenstein, *Small States in World Markets: Industrial Policy in Europe* (Ithaca, N.Y.: Cornell University Press, 1985).

[14]

Science and technology policy and its influence on economic development in Taiwan

Otto C.C. Lin

1 INTRODUCTION

In the period since the early 1970s, the Republic of China in Taiwan has made remarkable economic achievements despite formidable difficulties. This success can be attributed to many factors, of which progress in technology has been crucial. Supporting this remarkable progress was an early national commitment in developing science and technology.

The advances in science and technology of Taiwan, and of other East Asian newly emerging economies – Korea, Singapore and Hong Kong – illustrate one of the main themes of this book: the high learning capacity of the peoples in the area with deep Chinese culture. The speed of their technological advances during this period is perhaps the most rapid in history. The various ways in which this was accomplished provide important lessons for developing countries throughout the world.

These countries had what, paradoxically, has come to be seen increasingly as an advantage: a lack of land and raw materials. They were compelled to develop other vehicles to achieve prosperity. Science and technology became a logical choice. Unlike other production factors such as land, minerals or labor, science and technology is an acquired resource. It is markedly different from natural resources in the ability of regeneration and accumulation. Countries with limited natural resources such as Japan, the Netherlands and Switzerland have become prominent economic players owing largely to the motivation to use technology to upgrade the values of their goods and services.

This chapter focuses on the role of science and technology in Taiwan's industrialization, especially in the last two decades. The key question addressed is how Taiwan, under extremely difficult circumstances, was able to use science and technology to achieve economic growth.

2 TAIWAN'S PERFORMANCE: FROM LABOR-INTENSIVE TO TECHNOLOGY-INTENSIVE OUTPUT

Taiwan's industrial growth in this period can be characterized as a "take off". In 1972, the GNP was approximately US$7.9 billion, in current

186   *Otto C.C. Lin*

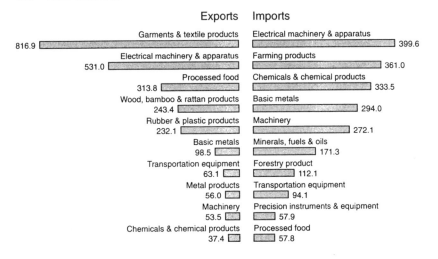

Figure 9.1 Taiwan: major goods traded, 1972 (US$ million)
Source: Monthly Statistics of Exports and Imports, Taiwan Area, R.O.C.

dollars, and the per capita income was $522. In 1992, the GNP had increased to US$210.7 billion, with per capita income reaching a landmark at $10,202. Industrial output had soared from a meager US$2.7 billion to $69.3 billion, and manufacturing industry had become increasingly high-technology. In 1972, for example, the exports of labor-intensive industries, including clothing and textiles, food processing and bamboo and wood products, totaled US$1.4 billion, while exports of machinery and electrical products, as well as plastic products, were only US$760 million. By 1992, the former was US$9 billion and the latter had jumped to US$35 billion. The shift of Taiwan's industries from labor-intensive to technology-intensive can also be shown by the composition of imports and exports during the period 1972–92 (see Figures 9.1 and 9.2).

Industrialization was realized in two parts: the establishment of new hi-tech industries and the upgrading of traditional industries. These reinforced each other and transformed Taiwan's industrial structure.

3 THE EARLY STRATEGIC PROBLEM: HOW TO MAKE RAPID TECHNOLOGICAL PROGRESS

Taiwan, and the other East Asian NICs, had many liabilities and certain assets in the early days, i.e., the period after the stabilization of power by the ruling parties. All four had achieved stability by the mid-1960s – although much earlier for Taiwan. But their liabilities were numerous. One was poverty. The average per capita income of Taiwan was only

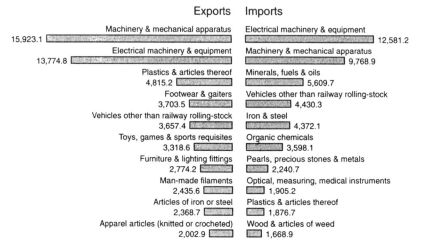

Exports   Imports

Machinery & mechanical apparatus   Electrical machinery & equipment
15,923.1   12,581.2

Electrical machinery & equipment   Machinery & mechanical apparatus
13,774.8   9,768.9

Plastics & articles thereof   Minerals, fuels & oils
4,815.2   5,609.7

Footwear & gaiters   Vehicles other than railway rolling-stock
3,703.5   4,430.3

Vehicles other than railway rolling-stock   Iron & steel
3,657.4   4,372.1

Toys, games & sports requisites   Organic chemicals
3,318.6   3,598.1

Furniture & lighting fittings   Pearls, precious stones & metals
2,774.2   2,240.7

Man-made filaments   Optical, measuring, medical instruments
2,435.6   1,905.2

Articles of iron or steel   Plastics & articles thereof
2,368.7   1,876.7

Apparel articles (knitted or crocheted)   Wood & articles of weed
2,002.9   1,668.9

Figure 9.2 Taiwan: major goods traded, 1992 (US$ million)
Source: EURO-ASIA Trade Organization

US$202 in 1964. Its industrial products were far behind those of the United States, Japan, and West Germany in performance, quality, and technical sophistication. Although the workforce was educated by the standards of the developing world, and school enrollments were high, the educational level lagged behind that of the advanced countries. Taiwan also faced competitive pressure from the low labor costs of other emerging countries, such as South Korea, Thailand, and the Philippines. And Taiwan had to import over 90 percent of its raw materials and energy.

Later on, Taiwan suffered an experience the others did not: the breaking of diplomatic relations by the US in 1979. Previously, Taiwan had lived under a US security umbrella. The unilateral action by the Carter Administration made painfully clear to the people of Taiwan that they had to depend on themselves for survival. The sense of crisis precipitated efforts in many sectors; it became an important impetus for the development of science and technology.

All through the 1980s Taiwan had other important assets besides the motivation to survive. The society was peaceful and the government was effective in supplying basic services. Its education effort was rapidly building human resources. The talented young graduates, of all levels, were increasing skills and productivity on the job. Equally important, the Chinese cultural tradition had created a strong work ethic. This disciplined and energetic labor was inexpensive compared with that in the advanced countries. After the end of the military turmoil in the Taiwan Strait in the 1950s, and in the relatively tranquil post-Korean War environment, Taiwan was at peace; it was not involved in the Vietnam conflict. On the Chinese mainland, the Cultural Revolution had distracted the leadership

188   *Otto C.C. Lin*

and largely paralyzed the economy. The People's Republic of China was weak in international commerce at that time.

The challenge in upgrading technology was how to move from a condition of little know-how, inadequate institutions (private and public), and an under-supply of trained scientists and engineers. After post-war reconstruction, Taiwan had proceeded through a phase, common in the developing world, of import substitution. Given its low technological level and low-cost labor, it concentrated on such products as textiles, toys, and hand tools, a familiar phase in the international product cycle, in which labor-intensive products migrate among countries driven by relative wages. Taiwan could not live long making such products; their production would migrate sooner or later to Thailand, Indonesia, and beyond. The key problem was how to keep upgrading the technological content of the country's products.

There were four key components to the overall strategy:

- Building human resources;
- Acquiring technology from the more advanced countries;
- Creating science and technology capacities;
- Converting research results to commercial products.

4 BUILDING HUMAN RESOURCES

The human resource is Taiwan's most valued asset. The emphasis on learning and education is a deep tradition of the Chinese culture, perhaps the most profound influence of Confucius' teachings. It is expressed in the Constitution of the Republic of China, Article 164, which proclaims that no less than 15 percent of the national budget shall be appropriated for education, culture and science; and so shall be 20 percent of the provincial budget and 25 percent of the county budget. Article 18 of the Second Constitution Amendment in 1993 has further outlined the roles of science and technology in national developments.

The building of human resources had several elements. The education system is the foundation. Since the early 1960s, strengthening education has been a national priority. By the 1990s, over 99 percent of school-aged children received primary education and over 85 percent of the students advanced to senior high, technical and vocational schools. Today there are almost 5.3 million students, about 25 percent of the total population, enrolled in various levels and types of education (see Table 9.1).

This has resulted in a large pool of well-trained university and technical college graduates. The number of science and engineering degree holders also increased significantly over the years. Table 9.2 shows the achievement of Taiwan and other NICs in training engineers by the late 1980s. Along with Japan, Korea and Singapore, Taiwan had more engineering

Science and technology policy in Taiwan   189

Table 9.1 School enrollments in Taiwan: historical

	Percent of school-aged children in elementary schools	Percent of elementary school graduates in junior high schools	Percent of junior high school graduates in senior high schools	Percent of senior high school graduates in schools of higher education
1960–61	95.59	52.24	75.88	43.41
1970–71	98.01	78.59	82.66	41.92
1973–74	98.09	83.71	67.90	37.92
1980–81	99.72	96.14	65.16	44.64
1983–84	99.81	97.95	69.55	46.40
1990–91	99.89	99.77	84.70	48.58
1992–94	99.89	99.53	87.78	65.48

Source: Ministry of Education

Table 9.2 Engineering graduates per 10,000 population (bachelor degree level), 1989

South Korea	6.70
Japan	6.62
Singapore	4.84
Taiwan	4.00
Mexico	3.32
France	2.97
US	2.70
West Germany	1.55
China (1992)	1.30
India	0.34

Source: UNESCO, Statistical Yearbook 1994

graduates than other advanced industrial countries, such as the US and West Germany or developing countries such as China and India.

Recognizing the need to learn from the outside world, the government encouraged students to go abroad for post-graduate studies. Government programs were set up for the selection of candidates and for their financial support. During this period, various scholarships, fellowships, assistantships and loans by major US universities were extremely helpful; most Chinese students could not otherwise have afforded such education. After the 1970s, the number of students going abroad, mostly to the US, increased steadily, and with increased affluence in the 1980s, more of them were supported on family or personal resources. Furthermore, the easing of travel restrictions has enabled students to go out of Taiwan through many non-education channels. After 1990, government statistics covered mainly students supported by government scholarships. This is shown in Figure 9.3, Curve A.

190   *Otto C.C. Lin*

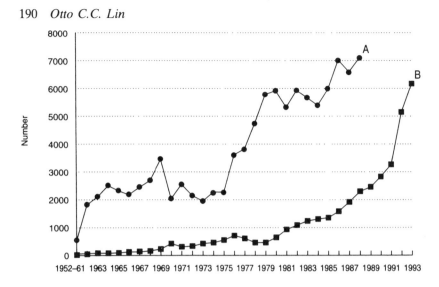

Figure 9.3 Students studying abroad (A) and students returning to Taiwan (B)

After finishing post-graduate studies, many students found jobs abroad, mostly in the US, since opportunity in Taiwan was limited. Not until the late 1980s did the number of returning students start to climb (Figure 9.3, Curve B). The contribution of these expatriate scholars to development in Taiwan is a factor unmatched in most other developing countries. The Industrial Technology Research Institute (ITRI) was an important channel for returning experts because of its early engagement in cutting edge technology. With technology transfers from ITRI to industries, some of these professionals also moved with them. As the development of hi-tech industries progresses, more returning professionals are going directly into industry.

After the mid-1980s, science education, scientific instrumentation, and general research in universities greatly increased. Academic departments involved with national research and development (R&D) projects received additional funding. The government set up a "key research institute" and "center of excellence" at each of the four national universities: National Taiwan, National Tsing-Hua, National Chiao-Tung, and National Cheng-Kung, in the fields of applied mechanics, materials science, information technology, and aviation and aerospace technology, respectively. Technical presentations at international conferences and publications in refereed journals numbered in the thousands every year. In the 1990s, technical contributions from researchers in Taiwan were listed among the top 20 countries in the world (Table 9.3), ahead of Singapore, South Korea, and Hong Kong.

Table 9.3 Scientific publications in several East Asian countries, 1988 and 1993

	1988		1993	
	Number	*Rank*	*Number*	*Rank*
Sciences				
Taiwan	2001	30	5164	21
South Korea	1683	33	2431	32
Hong Kong	904	38	1632	34
Singapore	653	40	1435	36
Engineering				
Taiwan	918	16	2399	11
South Korea	380	28	1249	16
Hong Kong	153	37	383	33
Singapore	208	36	651	22

Source: Scientific Citation Index and Engineering Index, as reported by National Science Council, Republic of China.

5 ACQUIRING TECHNOLOGY FROM THE MORE ADVANCED COUNTRIES

The industrial structure of Taiwan has a large number of small- and medium-sized firms and a few large ones. In the 1950s over half of Taiwan's industrial output was from the relatively large state-owned firms, but this proportion rapidly shrank with the expansion of the private sector. These small firms are family-run and remarkably nimble in the marketplace. Thus it has a very different structure from that of Korea, with large conglomerate firms, or that of Singapore, with many multinational corporations. Because these small firms find it difficult to be expert in a wide range of technologies, cooperation between them and their suppliers and customers, and between them and government laboratories, is very important for acquiring needed technologies.

Taiwan's technologies originally came mostly from Japan and the US. By establishing linkages backward with materials and technology suppliers, domestic and foreign, and forward with buyers and customers, most of them foreign corporations, the industry slowly developed niches of advantage. This strategy succeeded in developing a strong position in consumer electronics, small machineries, footwear and textiles, bicycles and other sporting goods, and other fast-growing industries.

Progress in information products illustrates the process. Taiwan began by making simple transistor radios and black-and-white TVs in the 1950s and 1960s, moved to color TVs in the 1970s, and in the 1980s to monitors, VCRs, and computers. By the early 1990s, much of Taiwan's consumer goods and other lower technology products had moved on to the Mainland and elsewhere. Although some firms, such as Ta Tung and Acer became large (each achieving sales of over $1 billion by 1990), in 1985 the average electronics firm had only 24 employees, even less than in Hong Kong.

192   *Otto C.C. Lin*

In 1989, there were 3,700 exporters of computers, of whom 650 were manufacturers and most of the rest were companies dealing with parts, components and trades.

In the late 1950s and early 1960s, multinational firms from Japan and the US found Taiwan's good and low-cost labor force to be attractive. Early firms included Sanyo, Sony, Sharp, Matsushita, Philips, NCR, DEC, General Instruments and Texas Instruments. In the long run, the financing they supplied was far less important than the technology they brought. The pattern became one of the Japanese firms forming joint ventures, initially to supply the local market and later exporting, while American firms produced for export to the US. Local firms in Taiwan relied heavily on licensing agreements and improvements by reverse engineering. And, as noted above, many experienced ethnic Chinese from the US and elsewhere brought valuable technical, management and marketing skills.

The government increasingly began to influence this process by, on the one hand, discouraging further labor-intensive investments by foreign multinationals and, on the other, by supporting Taiwan's own science and technology buildup. Increasingly, local firms were making more sophisticated products. In doing so they increased their technology inputs, offered more advanced designs, and moved into higher value-added niche markets. They became innovators. The development of high definition television (HDTV) using digital image processing technology is a good example. The project was formed by a consortium which consisted of ITRI and domestic manufacturers such as Proton, Ta Tung, Sam Po and others. Although the targeted HDTV will not be in the market until 1997–98, its intermediary technologies have contributed to the manufacturing of camcorders, projection TV and other high value consumer electronics.

6 CREATING SCIENCE AND TECHNOLOGY CAPACITIES: ORGANIZATIONS

The science and technology system has three principal parts: basic research, industrial technology, and manufacturing and marketing. Basic research covers all the academic institutes and universities, as well as the Academia Sinica. Funding of the institutes and universities comes from the Ministry of Education and National Science Council. The Ministry of Education funds training of students at all levels and the National Science Council supports basic research.

The organization for applied research and industrial technology is more complicated. Since applied research and technology development requires more funds, closer coordination with government policies is needed. In telecommunication, for example, the Ministry of Communication has direct supervision of the Telecommunication Laboratory. In agriculture, the Council of Agriculture directs the operation of the Taiwan Swine-Raising Experimental Station and various fishery laboratories. In manufacturing, the Ministry of Economic Affairs supports about 14 to 15 non-profit R & D organizations such as ITRI, the Institute for Information Industry (III), the Metal Industry Development Center (MIDC), the Center for Biotechnology Development (CBD) and the China Productivity Center (CPC), etc. The backbone of R&D for the manufacturing industry is formed by ITRI and its 11 research laboratories and centers.

Commercial manufacturing comprises both state-owned and private firms. In the 1970s, government-owned enterprises, such as China Steel, Chinese Petroleum, China Petrochemical Development, Taiwan Power and Taiwan Sugar accounted for about 15 percent of national industrial output. Private enterprises were mostly medium- and small-sized. Among them, Formosa Plastics, Far Eastern and Ta Tung were among the leading groups.

In the early 1970s, little R&D was done. In basic research, researchers were few, funds were limited and projects scattered loosely. A similar situation existed in the manufacturing industry. Overall R&D expenditure by industry was less than 0.4 percent of revenue, far below that in the industrialized countries; in the US it was common for R&D expense to account for 3 percent of sales revenue. By comparison, Taiwan's total R&D spending, public and private in 1985, was about at the level of Digital Equipment Company, which then ranked number ten among US companies for R&D investment. Shown in Table 9.4 is a summary of total R&D expenditure expressed as a percentage of business revenue in Taiwan in the decade 1982–92.

When ITRI was founded in 1973, it had about 450 employees; it grew slowly in the first decade. But, with the inception of major R&D projects, it grew rapidly in the 1980s. By 1994, ITRI had about 6,000 employees, of whom 4,250 had bachelor's or higher degrees, and 560 held doctorates. Its research scope covered semiconductors, computers and communications, opto-electronics, advanced materials, machinery, chemicals, energy and resources, industrial measurements and standards, pollution prevention, industrial safety, and, civil aviation and aerospace.

ITRI is now the largest industry-oriented research institution in Taiwan. It has established technology relations with more than 20,000 manufacturing companies. It receives contracts from the government to develop

Table 9.4 Taiwan: R&D expenditure as a percentage of business revenue

Industry	1982	1986	1990	1992
Total manufacturing industry	0.56	0.47	0.92	0.95
Textile	0.21	0.23	0.52	0.40
Chemicals and Materials	0.38	0.16	0.88	1.08
Plastic Products	1.53	1.07	0.86	1.24
Machinery and Equipment	2.08	0.36	0.44	0.60
Electric and Electronic	1.14	0.86	2.53	2.05
Precision Instrument	0.50	0.48	0.39	1.27

Source: Indicators of Science and Technology, National Science Council, Taiwan

194   *Otto C.C. Lin*

generic technologies and transfer the results to industry in a non-exclusive manner. It conducts short-term R&D projects in cooperation with private sponsoring organizations, generally to improve product performance and process efficiency. Adhering to the principle of fairness and openness, it transfers technology to industrial companies through many channels. It has systems for strategic planning, performance evaluation, human resource development and total quality management. ITRI's mode of operation has become a model for similar organizations in the world.

7 CREATING SCIENCE AND TECHNOLOGY CAPACITIES: SCIENCE AND TECHNOLOGY POLICY

Developing science and technology has been a major national effort since 1980 (see Figure 9.4).

In 1968, the National Advisory Committee on Long-Term Science Development outlined a 12-year "National Science Development Plan" with two key elements. One was strengthening science education and personnel training at college and university levels; the second was outlining the need for research and development in all fields of science and technology.

The First National Science and Technology Conference in 1978 named energy, materials, information technology and industrial automation as national thrust R&D objectives. (It was also at this time that diplomatic relations between Taiwan and the United States were severed; this sent shocks across Taiwan and quickened the pace of science and technology development.)

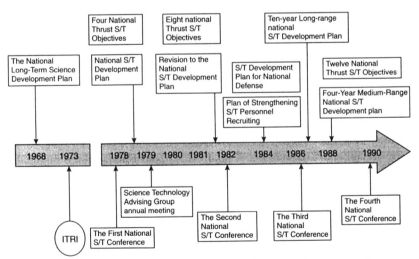

Figure 9.4 Taiwan: schematic diagram showing the key milestones in science and technology development

The second such conference in 1982 raised R&D expenditures from 0.6 percent to 1.0 percent of GNP and added four more objectives: bio-technology, opto-electronics, food science and hepatitis prevention. Together they became known as the "Eight Thrust Objectives of Science and Technology." The "Plan of Strengthening Technical Personnel and Recruiting Senior Professionals" and "Science and Technology Development Plan for National Defense" also took shape. Science and technology development grew rapidly after 1984, with Government spending on R&D, excluding national defense, moving from NT$7.8 billion in 1984, to $32.9 billion in 1993, an average growth rate of 17.3 percent for the decade.

The third conference in 1986 adopted a ten-year plan with a R&D investment target of NT$90 billion for 1996 (making it 2.2 percent of GNP), with 12 percent of the total R&D expenditures earmarked for basic research. It also set a target of 60 percent of all R&D to be performed in the private sector by 1996. It called for the continued development of Hsin-Chu Science Based Industrial Park, as well as of ITRI's hi-tech R&D projects.

In 1988, the government put forth a "Four-Year Medium Range Plan for Science and Technology Development." Natural disaster prevention, synchrotron radiation, ocean science and technology, and environmental science and technology were added to form a total of twelve "Thrust Science and Technology Objectives."

These twelve thrust projects are mixed in nature. Some are designed to strengthen basic national competencies, such as energy and materials. Some are related to timely issues such as hepatitis prevention and environmental and other disaster prevention. Others are related to economic development such as automation, opto-electronics and information technology. Still others are futuristic such as bio-tech, synchrotron radiation, ocean science and technology. Over half of them were targeted to support hi-tech industry.

The fourth conference in 1991 increased the GNP percentage of R&D expenditure, from 1.32 in 1989 to a goal of 2.8 in the year 2002. It also proposed to strengthen the protection of intellectual property rights.

Overall R&D spending by the central government increased significantly between 1984 and 1994 (see Figure 9.5), but in recent years the growth rate has declined. For fiscal year 1993 and 1994, it was 6.6 percent and 4.4 percent, respectively. In 1995, the central government R&D spending saw no real growth.

Many private organizations have also been active. For instance, the Modern Engineering Technology Seminar sponsored by the Chinese Institute of Engineers, held alternatively in Taiwan and in the United States annually, has become an important forum for information and personnel exchanges.

196   *Otto C.C. Lin*

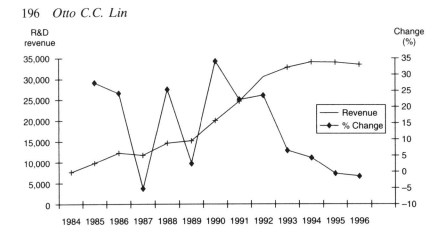

Figure 9.5 Taiwan: government (non-defense) R&D budget, 1984–96 (NT$ million)

8 CONVERTING RESEARCH RESULTS TO COMMERCIAL PRODUCTS: THE GROWTH OF HI-TECH INDUSTRY

The beginning of high-tech industry in Taiwan can be traced back to the 1970s when the China Steel Corporation (CSC), Chinese Petroleum Corporation and China Petrochemicals Development Corporation (CPDC) were part of the Ten National Construction Projects under President Chiang Ching-Kuo. China Steel built its fully integrated production line and became an important factor of the national infrastructure. It now has a 5.5 million-ton per year capacity of carbon steel. CSC has branched out recently to form a joint venture with US partners to make silicon semiconductors. The naphtha-cracking plants of CPC, along with CPDC's acrylonitrile and terephthalic acid plants, have supported Taiwan's petrolchemical, plastic, and synthetic fiber industries. The polymers produced by private enterprises such as FPG, China General and Chi Mei are highly regarded in the world market.

Taiwan's participation in the emerging hi-tech industries progressed rapidly after the mid-1980s. There are three major contributing elements.

The establishment of the Hsin-Chu Science Based Industrial Park

This was set up by the National Science Council, under the leadership of Dr S. S. Shu, Chairman of the NSC, in 1978. It started operations in 1983 with about 35 participating companies and has attracted hi-tech companies and seasoned scientists and engineers from overseas. By 1993, the number of companies had reached 150, providing employment for 30,000 and had a total business revenue of NT$130 billion, accounting for 2 percent of

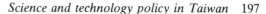

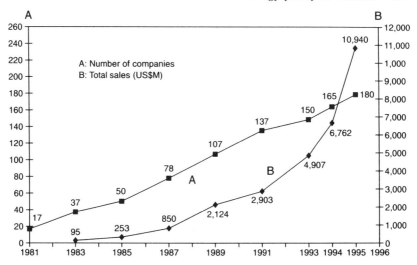

Figure 9.6 Taiwan: growth of the Hsin-Chu Science-Based Industrial Park
Source: SIPA

that year's GNP (see Figure 9.6). Presently its most difficult problem lies in acquiring more land for expansion at the Hsinchu site. Thus, a similar park is being planned in Taiwan.

Technological assistance offered by industrial research institutes and academic circles

Among the eight national thrust projects, five having direct impacts on hi-tech industry were managed by ITRI. Between 1983 and 1994, about 25 percent of the central government's non-defense projects were carried out by ITRI contributing to the commercialization of many hi-tech products. During this period, intellectual property rights and their protection were emphasized. Patents awarded to ITRI, both domestic and international, increased rapidly in the decade (see Figure 9.7).

In 1993, ITRI transferred 209 technologies to 297 companies. Several major companies in the Hsin-Chu Park are ITRI spin-offs, including UMC (1980), TSMC (1987), MIRLE Automation (1988), the Taiwan Mask Co. (1989), as well as the recently-founded VSIC (1994), which will manufacture 16 megabyte DRAM and other sub-micron devices. About 50 percent of the companies in the Park have established technical relationships such as joint R&D, technology transfer, and technical services, with ITRI. Many universities have also taken active parts in various R&D and training projects of the Park's companies and ITRI.

Hi-tech industries have, in recent years, increased their R&D spending to about 5 percent of sales revenue, about 5 times the average R&D

198   *Otto C.C. Lin*

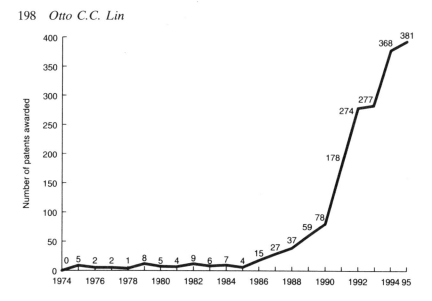

Figure 9.7 Taiwan: patents awarded to ITRI

expenditure of the manufacturing industry. Many companies outside the industrial park, in areas such as specialty alloy, stainless steel, super-fine fiber, optical fiber, light emitting diodes, fine ceramics and bio-tech, are also engaged actively in product R&D as well as in marketing development.

Entrepreneurship

Taking advantage of government support, many start-up companies prospered. Firms found synergies with each other and with R&D institutions, forming an integrated network, as is shown most clearly in the information industry. As a result, Taiwan passed Britain as the world's fifth largest producer of semiconductors by 1993. The total output value of information industry products in 1995 was nearly US$20 billion, making Taiwan one of the top three exporting countries of information products. Personal computers made in Taiwan, for instance those made by Acer, Mitac and Ta Tung, are now competitive with those made in the US and Japan. Many peripheral products have gained top market shares in the world, such as monitors (57 percent), computer mouse devices (70 percent), and printed circuit boards (65 percent). In addition, the satellite communication products of MTI and consumer electronics of TECO and Taiwan Philips are well-received in the world market. The software industry, although smaller than the hardware industry, is also developing rapidly.

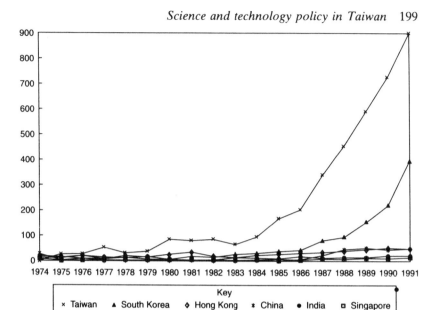

Figure 9.8 US patents granted to inventors from emerging East Asian economies

A measure of technology progress is the number of US patents awarded to Taiwan inventors: individuals, institutions and industries. These have increased rapidly in the last decade and outnumbered all other East Asian emerging economies, including South Korea, Singapore and Hong Kong (see Figure 9.8).

Hi-tech advances have not been limited to electronics and information products, they included such areas as chemicals, speciality materials and machinery. For example, advances in high-speed fiber spinning and ultra-fine fibers technologies have made possible the development of high-value textile products. Structural and functional ceramics have contributed to the development of electro-mechanical end-uses. Another important development was the establishment of the China Engine Corporation in 1995 for manufacturing of a common automotive power train, the result of a R&D consortium consisting of ITRI, four domestic manufacturers – Yue Loong, Chung Hwa, San Yang and Yu Tien – and the British Lotus Engineering Co. This was a pioneering effort in establishing an indigenous automobile engine manufacturing capacity.

While there is uncertainty, Taiwan's hi-tech sector basically has a bright future. In 1990, the Executive Yuan put forward a Six-Year National Development Plan, which identified ten emerging industries and eight key high technologies. These are sectors with demonstrated technology foun-dation, manufacturing capability and sales experience. If successfully

200 *Otto C.C. Lin*

implemented, total sales could reach US$60 billion by the late 1990s, about 25.5 percent of all manufacturing. The added value will be 40 percent, and export value will total US$34 billion, accounting for 32 percent of the total export value of manufacturing. This was the vision for the economic development of Taiwan.

9 CONVERTING RESEARCH RESULTS TO PRODUCT COMMERCIALIZATION: THE UPGRADING OF TRADITIONAL INDUSTRY

Traditional enterprises are the mainstay of manufacturing. They consist mainly of small and medium-sized companies with assets under NT$40 million and account for 98 percent of all manufacturing firms. The number of employees of a typical small company may be as few as ten, or as many as hundreds. In total, they account for approximately 75 percent of Taiwan's industrial employment. Restricted by limited capital and production scale, they are susceptible to such disturbances as labor shortages, skyrocketing land prices, energy shortages, environmental protection laws, labor–management disputes, exchange rate fluctuations, tariff changes, and criminal underworld threats.

The government tries to help these firms through the Bureau of Industrial Development and the Medium and Small Enterprises Service. The state-owned Chiao Tung Bank has established funds for industrial automation and for improving pollution controls. Besides various ITRI laboratories, the China Productivity Center helps to improve management quality. The Metal Industry Development Center, Textile Research Development Center, Food Industry Research and Development Institute, and Bio-tech Development Center, etc., all have responsibilities for technical support.

There are four fundamental elements of industrial technology: design, material, processing, and quality. By improving these elements, the product value and manufacturing cost can be significantly upgraded. One example is the use of carbon fiber composite materials in bicycles and other sports equipment. In the 1970s, the average price of a Taiwan-made bicycle was under US$50. In 1984, ITRI, working with Giant Manufacturing Corporation, started to develop a carbon fiber/epoxy resin system for bicycle frames. After four years, the designed carbon fiber bicycles were introduced and rapidly became popular all over the world market, with a 20–30 fold increase in unit price. Similar composite materials technology has also been used in tennis rackets, golf clubs, and other sporting goods. Taiwan has become the largest exporter in the world of these products.

Other examples of upgraded traditional industries include programmable logic control, precision mould design, optimized materials layout, electroless plating of plastics, chemical process improvement, processing and recycling of metals and plastics, chemical and bio-chemical treatment of waste water, dehumidifying air conditioning, loss control, risk analysis and management, total quality improvement, industrial metrology and ISO-9000 certification, etc.

In 1991, ITRI began to develop the technology for making components and parts for aircraft, with the aim of helping small- and medium-sized companies enter the aviation and aerospace markets. More that 30 enterprises have since received certifications and become qualified suppliers.

In the national quality contests in 1992 and 1993, over 70 percent of the silver and gold prize winners had technical cooperative relations with ITRI. These winners were awarded the "Made-in-Taiwan" and "Mark of excellence" emblems. Thus increasingly more traditional enterprises have recognized the importance of improving technology and have regarded R&D as a crucial means for strengthening competivity in the world market.

10 A REVIEW OF SOCIAL AND CULTURAL FACTORS

Success factors

(A) Rich human resources

Both the quantity and quality of human resources have been crucial. The commitment to achievement through learning and hard work has been at the base of these accomplishments.

(B) Clear and Compelling Missions

All along, it has been evident that Taiwan had to succeed. In the late 1970s, various diplomatic setbacks raised the sense of crisis and provided further motivation for developing science and technology for national survival.

(C) Good Organizational Structure

The R&D establishment supporting the industrial growth has operated satisfactorily. Each R&D organization has largely focused on a defined area of responsibility in basic research, applied research, or commercial manufacturing. A small but healthy overlap among institutions provides channels of communication and creates a good competitive spirit. The role each plays is also subject to adjustment at different stages of industrial growth and technological development.

(D) Delivering on Key Projects

The eight thrust science and technology projects have set specific goals, with good market orientations, and have been analyzed for economic

202   *Otto C.C. Lin*

feasibilities. And most have been well managed. In the early stages the government was aggressive in providing the needed resources. A case in point is information technology. Since the early 1980s, about 45 percent of the government R&D expenditure has been dedicated to electronics and information-related projects. This has helped in nurturing technology, cultivating personnel and building infrastructure. The results as shown by the phenomenal growth of the information industries in Taiwan, were impressive. Recently, the introduction of more thrust projects has diluted national focus and distorted resource allocation and project management. Since 1995, R&D expenditure from the Central Government has declined and development has suffered. It is worth noting that most advanced countries have continuously budgeted 2–3 percent of GNP as R&D expenditure over several decades. Consistency and perseverance in R&D investment is very important for long-term results.

(E) Technology Diffusion

Diffusion of the technology is as important as its development. There are numerous ways to do this, including direct technology transfer, technical consulting, technical services, cooperative R&D, personnel training, strategic alliances, seminars and exhibits, and spin-off companies. As an example, ITRI makes several hundred technological transfers yearly (see Table 9.5).

(F) Cooperation among Enterprises

Since the 1970s, Taiwan's industry has accumulated much marketing and management experiences. Firms have gradually built up foreign distribution and sales channels, and, up- and down-stream cooperation. Supply networks have formed, especially in electronics-related industries. When a new technology is developed by a research organization, the business community can readily follow up by manufacturing the product and marketing it worldwide.

Table 9.5 Taiwan: technology diffusion of ITRI

		1992	*1995*
Technology transfers	Projects	143	280
	Companies	262	418
Contracted research/joint R&D	Cases	411	1,004
Conferences and Exhibitions	Sessions	643	880
Patents approved	Cases	274	368
Seminars/workshops/technical training programs	Attendees	40,150	59,492
	Cases	37,141	50,944
Technology services	Companies	21,943	27,061

(G) Establishing the Hsin-Chu Science Based Industrial Park

The Park had remarkable successes in nurturing hi-tech start-up companies.

(H) Professionalism of Entrepreneurs and Researchers

Taiwan's industries have encountered severe pressure in natural resources, technical capacities, environmental restrictions, and foreign competition, but entrepreneurs have carried on business successfully, opened up new markets and have created new lines of business. Researchers in Taiwan, often somewhat isolated due to adverse political circumstances in the scientific community worldwide, have maintained high professionalism and dedication. This has resulted in a gradual narrowing of the gap between Taiwan and advanced countries in many fields of science and technology.

(2) Negative factors

In the 1990s, Taiwan's political and social environment has seen major changes, some of which have been negative for science and technology development.

(A) Resistance from environmental activists

Earlier, economic growth and employment opportunities were regarded as high priority. Because environmental protection and industrial safety issues were not adequately addressed, heavy pollution and industrial hazards have created adverse public reactions. The skepticism and caution of environmental activists today are, by and large, justifiable. But constructive criticism should not be confused with negative resistance and misused with political motives. The ten-year delay for the construction of the fourth nuclear power station of TPC is a classic case.

(B) Weakening of Government Functions

Changes in the political and social environment have taken their toll on policy priorities and governmental efficiency. Land profiteering, traffic jams, labor shortages, illegal underground influence, and erosion of public powers have confronted the business community. A deterioration of the infrastructure, in both hardware and software, has surfaced. As a result, the momentum of rapid industrial development has slowed. The commitment of the government to science and technology has been hurt.

204   *Otto C.C. Lin*

(C) Excessive Speculation of the Stock Market

A properly functioning stock market increases the efficiency of an economy by bringing together investors and entrepreneurs. In recent years, however, the stock market in Taiwan has seen excessive speculative activity. This has created undue tensions, heightened risks and uncertainties and has dampened the entrepreneurism of industrialists.

(D) Disorderly Outflow of Businesses

Recently, owing to the changes of the business environment, many manufacturers have reacted by moving investments abroad. Under normal circumstances, business moves offshore to lower manufacturing cost or to better serve the marketplace. This type of globalization is appropriate. However, if Taiwan's firms fail to upgrade their technical capability as they globalize, they are likely to have troubles at both ends.

(E) Outdated Regulations for Science and Technology

There have been alarming signals that some government agencies were losing efficiency and policy focus. The Legislature, on the other hand, was often paralyzed by excessive politicking. Many laws and codes have failed to keep pace with the advancements of science and technology and the impacts they have shown on the society at large. In the hands of bureaucrats who would insist on enforcing outdated regulations, the consequences can be grave with innovation smothered. The Fourth National Science-Technology Conference in 1990 resolved to submit draft legislation to help science and technology; however, some agencies fumbled and stumbled on actions.

11 CONCLUDING REMARKS

The rise to international prominence of Taiwan in economic development from the early 1970s is a remarkable story. Many cultural, social and organizational factors have contributed. Technologically, the Taiwan story illustrates the progress from a low level of skills through multiple paths of learning to high achievements. Two components have been key: the development of industrial technology and the nurturing of the business environment, both bolstered by an increasingly competent scientific and technological establishment.

Industrial technology is the bridge connecting scientific research to product commercialization. It consists of many linkages: applied research, product development, process development, technology diffusion and pilot trials. Strengthening these components is the responsibility of the R&D establishment.

Creating a favorable environment is the responsibility of the government. This includes a system of laws, tax and monetary measures, the supply of land, labor, energy and transportation, rational environmental protection regulations, work safety rules and a safe and orderly society. It is understandably difficult to achieve complete control of these components.

In Taiwan, after an initial period of import substitution, the government adopted a strategy of acquiring technology from foreign sources followed by building domestic competencies. Government R&D policy bet on certain broad sectors, but much of the implementation was left to professionals, technocrats and the private sector. The government created ITRI and the Hsin-Chu Science-Based Industrial Park complex, as a mini-environment, to nurture hi-tech industries. As the start-ups and the spin-offs grew, they were encouraged to move and to multiply outside the fence; hopefully, a maxi-environment conducive to the growth of high-tech business can be generated throughout. This approach has proven successful and has served as a model throughout the Asia/Pacific region. However, there is no guarantee of success if the ingredients are not adjusted for time and place. It should be noted that success brings changes in the environment which, in turn, require changes in future actions.

In the national comparisons conducted by the International Management Development Institute/World Economic Forum (IMD/WEF), Taiwan has been ranked high since the turn of the 1990s, with science and technology recognized as a competitive strength. Among the emerging Asian economies, Taiwan and Singapore have alternated in being number 1 in science and technology in the study. For 1995, Taiwan was ranked number 5 in science and technology worldwide in the IMD/WEF competitiveness report. Although the policy and practices of the NIC East Asian economies – South Korea, China, Hong Kong, Taiwan, and Singapore – in science and technology have differed, all have succeeded in varying degrees. Overall, the ability to synchronize business, government, and technology circles will continue to be the key to reaching national goals.

ACKNOWLEDGMENTS

In the course of preparing this chapter, I received valuable information, references, and suggestions from Mr Hsu Chi-sheng and Ms Hou Yu-chen of the Industrial Technology Research Institute. During the final stages of preparation, Mr George Wilson, Ms Nancy Wong and especially, Ms Betty Hsieh have offered valuable assistance in finalizing the manuscript. I extend my sincere thanks to them.

206   Otto C.C. Lin

REFERENCES

Chinese-language sources

Council for Economic Planning and Development, *Summary of the Income Statistics of the Taiwan Region*, Taipei, 1992.

Hsiao F.S., *Industrial Policy and Industrial Developments in R.O.C.*, Far Eastern Economics Research Publisher, Taipei, 1994.

Industrial Technology Research Institute, *A Synopsis of Twenty Years' Research and Development at ITRI*, 1993.

Industrial Technology Research Institute, *1993 Annual Report*, 1994.

Lin, Otto C.C., *Twelve Fleeting Years of R&D*, The Central Daily News, Taipei, April 18, 1994.

Lin, Otto C.C., in *The Taiwan Experience: Past and Future*, Kao and Lee, eds, Chapter 7, Commonwealth Publishing Co., Taipei, 1995.

Ministry of Economic Affairs, *Synopsis of the Industrial Science and Technology Development of R.O.C.*, 1992.

National Science Council, *Science and Technology Development Yearbook of the Republic of China*, Taipei, 1992.

National Science Council, *Guidelines of Scientific and Technological Statistics*, Taipei, 1993.

English-language sources

Hobday, M., *Innovation in East Asia: The Challenge to Japan*, Brookfield, Vt, Edward Elgar, 1995.

IMD/DEF, World Competitiveness Reports, 1992–95.

Lin, Otto C.C., in *Development and Transfer of Industrial Technology*, in Lin, Shih and Yang, eds, *Advances in Industrial Engineering*, vol. 20, Elsevier Science, 1994.

UNESCO, Statistical Yearbook 1994, UNESCO, 1994.

US National Science Foundation Report No. 95–309, 1995.

[15]

Charting Taiwan's Technological Future: The Impact of Globalization and Regionalization

Denis Fred Simon

There is now general agreement among observers of international economic and technology affairs that the world has entered a period characterized by the interplay of two potent and possibly dialectical forces – globalization and regionalization. Globalization, which is clearly manifested in the changing nature of competition in industries ranging from textiles to telecommunications, is being driven by a combination of diverse forces, including the communication and transportation revolutions, the growing trends towards liberalization, privatization and de-regulation, and the rapid diffusion of technologies around the world.[1] Multinational companies (MNCs) have become the principal purveyors of globalization as they seek out new markets and search the world for access to critical R&D, production and distribution assets irrespective of where they may be found.[2] Regionalization, on the other hand, has primarily been driven by macro-political forces, with governments as the initiating agents, as in the case of the formation of the European Union and the North American Free Trade Association. Where regionalization is driven by explicit and overt government actions and policies it can more often than not be seen as an anathema to globalization; politically-induced regionalization in these cases is driven, in large part, by concerns about loss of national competitiveness and a decline in economic welfare.[3]

The major exception to this characterization of the nature and thrust of regionalization can be found in the Pacific Rim. From a comparative perspective, regionalization in the Asia-Pacific region has been primarily a market-driven phenomenon with cross-border investment, technology flows and trade being vehicles for expanded regional integration. Intra-regional trade now accounts for over 40 per cent of the total trade of these economies and the largest sources of foreign investment continue to come from within rather than outside the region.[4] While the governments, via such entities as APEC and PECC, are trying to give some degree of formality to efforts at regional co-operation, the process of institutionalization has been slow. In a world where the imperatives of global competition have not abated so far as most industries are concerned, most of the economies in the region see little virtue in moving too far too fast for fear of inducing greater fragmentation of global markets and industries. Simply put, Asian economies would be the big losers in a world

---

1. Denis Fred Simon (ed.), *Corporate Strategies Towards the Pacific Rim* (London: Routledge, 1996).
2. Rosabeth Moss Kanter, *World Class* (New York: Simon and Schuster, 1995).
3. See Kenichi Ohmae, *The End of the Nation State: The Rise of Regional Economies* (New York: The Free Press, 1995).
4. Edward Chen and Peter Drysdale (eds.), *Corporate Links and Foreign Direct Investment in Asia and the Pacific* (Pymble, Australia: Harper Collins, 1995).

where regionalization thwarted the forces of market openness and liberalization associated with the increasingly borderless globalizing international economy.[5]

Another reason why greater formalization of this process in the Pacific Rim might not be in the interest of its economies is that the manufacturing and R&D assets of the leading firms in the region have come to assume a steadily more critical role in global competition, especially in industries such as microelectronics, computers, telecommunications and more recently aerospace and software development.[6] This indicates that the technological assets within the region will only become more important in the years ahead as multinational firms from around the globe seek out reliable and capable partners from among companies such as Samsung (Korea) and Acer (Taiwan) as well as Hitachi and Toshiba.[7] In fact, one of the consequences of the steadily improving technological base among the Pacific Rim economies is the growing proliferation of strategic alliances between OECD-member companies and Asian firms. These alliances can be viewed as part of the globalization process as firms from the United States, EC and Japan seek, for example, a hedge against actual and potential competition from domestic as well as foreign competitors.[8]

Collaborative agreements between Taiwan and the world's leading MNCs seem to be growing quite rapidly, raising many questions about the evolving pattern of competition and co-operation in the Asia-Pacific region. Moreover, as the number of these agreements increase, they could reach some critical threshold in terms of Pacific Rim regionalization. Will expanded industrial and technological co-operation between Taiwan and American or EC firms, for example, serve as a bulwark against Japanese companies both inside and outside the region? Are there enough technological assets on Taiwan to add substantial competitive advantage to the capabilities of OECD firms? Even more provocative is the possibility that expanded technological collaboration with Taiwan will serve as an impetus for a fundamental re-thinking by Japanese firms of their technology transfer policies towards the island, especially if Japanese companies view competition for access to Taiwan's manufacturing and R&D assets in a more strategic fashion.[9] This has already occurred to some degree among firms such as Matsushita, Canon, Sony and Fujitsu, all of whom have moved away from their traditionally hierarchical approach to foreign investment and technology transfer in respect of Taiwan. The recent collaborative agreement between Nan Ya Plastics and Oki Electric in the semiconductor field reflects the beginning of a new Japanese perspective.[10]

5. C. Fred Bergsten and Marcus Noland (eds.), *Pacific Dynamism and the International Economic System* (Washington, DC: Institute of International Economics, 1993).

6. Michael Hobday, *Innovation in East Asia* (Brookfield, VT: Edward Elgar, 1995).

7. Denis Fred Simon, "The international technology market: globalization, regionalization and the Pacific Rim," *Business in the Contemporary World*, Spring 1993.

8. Denis Fred Simon (ed.), *The Emerging Technological Trajectory of the Pacific Rim* (Armonk, NY: M.E. Sharpe, 1995).

9. "Technology transfer policy to Taiwan revised," *Sankei shimbun*, 23 July 1991, p. 11.

10. "Survey: Japan needs higher profile in Asia," *Nikkei Weekly*, 25 April 1992, p. 28.

This article examines the emerging architecture of Taiwan's growing technological prowess, aiming to highlight the implications in terms of globalization and regionalization within the Pacific Rim. The case of Taiwan's microelectronics industry is examined to underscore the growing role of the island's technological assets in international business. The general argument focuses on those emerging economic and technological factors – within the context of global competition – that are driving Taiwan companies to seek more substantial partnerships with foreign firms and vice versa. It is argued that these technological alliances hold much more strategic value in terms of the evolving patterns and thrust of globalization than they do for regional integration. In other words, technological collaboration with Taiwan must first and foremost be viewed as product of globalization, as both Taiwan and MNCs seek to enhance their respective positions in the larger international division of labour. Taiwan firms remain committed to playing a more central role in global competition, and view co-operation with MNCs primarily as a means to acquire needed technologies – thereby enhancing their own self-reliance – and to offset Japanese technological influence over Taiwan industry.

Charting Taiwan's Emerging Technological Trajectory

One of the most notable aspects of Taiwan's economic experience over the last four decades has been its ability to re-invent and re-engineer itself to respond to the changing demands of the domestic and international economy.[11] Starting from the ravaged state of the Taiwan economy in the immediate aftermath of the Communist takeover of the Chinese mainland in 1949, the government has been able to orchestrate a number of critical transitions in economic orientation and emphasis. In the 1950s, with the help of the U.S. Agency for International Development, Taiwan officials put in place a successful programme of import substitution.[12] During this period, beginning with the launching of the Ten Major Development Projects in 1973, a new economic infrastructure was constructed, including roads, ports, power plants and communications. In the 1960s and 1970s, the government helped to initiate and implement a programme of export promotion.[13] This provided the backdrop for the upgrading of Taiwan's manufacturing firms and the achievement of quality standards that helped make the export drive a success. It also served to stimulate the initial influx of foreign investment, which has proved to be a critical

11. Gustav Ranis (ed.), *Taiwan: From Developing to Mature Economy* (Boulder: Westview Press, 1992).
12. Thomas Gold, *State and Society in the Taiwan Miracle* (Armonk, NY: M.E. Sharpe, 1986).
13. Walter Galenson (ed.), *Economic Growth and Structural Change in Taiwan* (Ithaca: Cornell University Press, 1979).

factor in further areas such as technology transfer and management training.[14]

The 1980s, however, brought a broad array of problems so far as Taiwan's ability to compete in overseas markets was concerned. A principal problem was that the low-cost labour that had at one point been a major source of competitive advantage for the island's numerous manufacturers was no long available. With improvements in living standards among the island's residents and a continued strengthening of the overall economy, prices and wages both rose, thereby detracting from the attractiveness of Taiwan as a site for foreign investment.[15] In addition, questions arose about the overall business environment, especially with respect to such matters as intellectual property protection, labour turnover and government bureaucracy. Taiwan's private sector also revealed an apparent hesitancy to make new capital investments in the face of an uncertain political future. Lacking the technological wherewithal to compete head-on with the leading firms from the OECD nations and deprived of the cost advantages that in the past had helped drive exports and attract appreciable levels of American and Japanese foreign investment, many questions arose about the ability of the Taiwan economy to sustain any appreciable growth in the future. Add to this economic situation the growing isolation of Taiwan in international affairs engendered, in large part, by the policies of the People's Republic of China (PRC) government, and it becomes clear why a quasi-crisis atmosphere began to emerge in Taiwan at this time.[16]

The beginning of the 1990s brought into sharp relief a set of new economic and technological imperatives that had begun to make their presence felt during the latter part of the previous decade. In particular, as the dynamics of international competition shifted away from a variable-cost to a fixed-cost model – where technology rather than the "variable costs" of production inputs became more critical in determining overall competitiveness – and as the era of the energy-intensive economy began to give way to the era of the information economy, Taiwan officials recognized that another new economic foundation would have to be built.[17] Fortunately, the crisis of Taiwan's faltering sovereignty was abated by the continued, wide-scale participation of MNCs within the island's economy.[18] Although a combination of diplomatic manoeuvring and other factors had seemingly weakened the Taiwan state internationally, the reality in terms of domestic and foreign economic and technology relations seemed just the opposite. The government on

14. Chi Schive, *The Foreign Factor: The Multinational Corporation's Contribution to the Economic Modernization of the Republic of China* (Stanford: Hoover Institution Press, 1990).

15. Robert Wade, *Governing the Market: Economic Theory and the Role of Government in East Asian Industrialization* (Princeton: Princeton University Press, 1990).

16. Denis Fred Simon and Michael Y.M. Kau (eds.), *Taiwan: Beyond the Economic Miracle* (Armonk, NY: M.E. Sharpe, 1992).

17. Maurice Estabrooks, *Electronic Technology, Corporate Strategy, and World Transformation* (Westport, CT: Quorum Books, 1995).

18. N.T. Wang (ed.), *Taiwan's Enterprises in Global Perspective* (Armonk, NY: M.E. Sharpe, 1992).

Taiwan was able to weather the apparent storm and initiate a shift into new, knowledge-intensive industries as exemplified by the opening and operation of the Hsinchu Science and Industry Park in 1979 and the emergence of Taiwan as a major player in the global computer and microelectronics industry.[19] A key factor in this regard was the ability of the government on Taiwan to continue its quest to attract prominent MNCs to the island to make substantial investments in areas consistent with the shifting needs of the local economy.[20] In particular, the government was adept at facilitating and upgrading the transfer of technology into Taiwan by MNCs. Over time, this has led to a consolidation and further enhancement of Taiwan's place within the evolving international division of labour.

Taiwan's Evolving Technology Strategy

The key technological challenges faced by Taiwan are in two principal domains. First, Taiwan officials must establish a viable industrial structure and set of support mechanisms to move the economy further into the knowledge-intensive age. This requires assisting local firms to shift from dependence on traditional, labour-intensive industries as well as creating a vibrant R&D system capable of meeting the growing technological needs of both large, and small and medium enterprises (SMEs) on the island.[21] The second challenge is the need to devise a strategy for managing external technology relationships, especially with the world's leading corporations (see below). Taiwan officials must establish a pattern of relationships that will allow local firms, both big and small, the maximum room for manoeuvre with respect to the deployment of local R&D and manufacturing resources and capabilities. In other words, the government on Taiwan must strive for higher levels of technological sophistication domestically so that it remains attractive to MNCs as a collaborative partner.[22]

Taiwan's attempt to create a capable and responsive R&D and manufacturing infrastructure reflects the common effort in the Asian newly industrialized economies (NIEs) to strengthen indigenous science and technology resources.[23] Initially, Taiwan officials have adopted a two-pronged strategy for promoting rapid and sustained technological development. One element has been to use the process of technological upgrading as part of a strategy for building what David Teece has called

19. Russell Flannery, "Taiwan companies switch to hi-tech," *Asian Business*, April 1991, pp. 52–54.

20. See the articles by Thomas Gold and Denis Fred Simon in Edwin Winckler and Susan Greenhalgh (eds.), *Contending Approaches to the Political Economy of Taiwan* (Armonk, NY: M.E. Sharpe, 1988).

21. See the article by Gee San on Taiwan in Richard R. Nelson (ed.), *National Innovation Systems: A Comparative Analysis* (Oxford: Oxford University Press, 1993).

22. Even though he does not specifically address the Taiwan case, the work of Harvard Business School economist Michael Porter is relevant here. See Michael Porter, *The Competitive Advantage of Nations* (New York: Free Press, 1990).

23. Dieter Ernst and David O'Connor, *Technology and Global Competition: The Challenge for Newly Industrializing Economies* (Paris: OECD Development Centre, 1989).

"technological complementarities" with key high technology companies from around the world.[24] In many ways, the essence of this has been to enhance the island's linkages with major MNCs as well as with some critical second-tier firms in a range of priority technology fields. Heretofore, rather than competing head-on with firms from the industrialized world, as has been the case for South Korea, Taiwan adopted a strategy that essentially seeks to build products designed and offered by foreign firms. The strategy has been developed in recognition of the limited willingness of many local firms to invest an appreciable percentage of their revenues in R&D. Ideally, through this variety of linkages with MNCs, Taiwan officials have hoped to stimulate the diffusion of technology that will eventually, albeit gradually, strengthen local capabilities.[25] A recent example of such a relationship involves the decision by Boeing to set up a US$48 million quality assurance laboratory on Taiwan to test aircraft components.

The second prong of Taiwan's technology strategy is to increase the island's self-sufficiency in this area through industrial and technological deepening. To accomplish this goal, the government on Taiwan has offered a large number of financial and tax incentives to local companies to expand their R&D investments. These include accelerated depreciation allowances, investment tax credits, deferral of income tax payments, and duty-free import of selected machinery and equipment. The overall design of the strategy rests in the hands of the Science and Technology Advisory Group (STAG) under the Executive Yuan. The STAG, which was founded in 1979, is responsible for assessing global trends in science and technology and formulating relevant policies in conjunction with the National Science Council, the Council for Economic Planning and Development, and the Industrial Bureau of the Ministry of Economic Affairs.[26]

While the 1990s have witnessed the coming together of the various strands of a so-called overall technology strategy, the reality is that many of the policies in place today have their roots in the late 1970s when Li Kwo-ting, then a minister without portfolio, assumed responsibility for designing an entirely new industrial architecture for the island.[27] One of the key goals was to enlarge total R&D spending, which in 1978 was about US$111 million, representing only 0.48 per cent of GNP. At the time, the government provided approximately 56 per cent of the total, while the private sector contributed between 30 and 35 per cent. Most important, within the private sector, R&D spending averaged only 0.12 per cent of sales for domestic firms compared with 2–3 per cent in Japan and the United States, reflecting the generally small size of local firms

24. David Teece (ed.), *The Competitive Challenge* (Cambridge: Ballinger Publishers, 1989).
25. Denis Fred Simon, "Taiwan, technology transfer and transnationalism," Ph.D. dissertation, Berkeley, 1980 (unpublished).
26. Interviews conducted by author in 1991–92 in Taipei as part of research project under the auspicies of the Fujitsu Research Institute in Japan.
27. K.T. Li, *The Evolution of Policy Behind Taiwan's Development Success* (New Haven: Yale University Press, 1989).

and their tendency to ignore the potential, long-term value of R&D. By 1984, things began to improve when national R&D expenditure apparently reached the 1.0 per cent of GNP mark (US$540 million). By 1990, it represented 1.65 per cent of GNP and has continued to grow, reaching 1.79 per cent of GNP in 1992 and 1.82 per cent in 1994.[28] Starting from 1983, the growth of R&D spending has surpassed 15 per cent per annum on average, slower than South Korea but faster than Japan. The goal stated in the Ten-Year Science and Technology Development Plan (1986–95) was to reach the 2.0 per cent mark by 1995, though this was not attained.[29]

In June 1995, the government released its first White Paper on science and technology affairs. It is focused on matching together world technological trends with Taiwan's S&T policies and programmes, and is conspicuous by the ambitious nature of its R&D spending goals. According to the 12-year national S&T development plan now in effect, R&D spending will reach 2.8 per cent of GNP in 2002, reflecting a 14.2 per cent growth over the ten-year period starting in 1992. The release of the plan coincided with a new initiative designed to attract more young engineers into careers in the government. Young engineers may skip their compulsory military service if they make a six-year commitment to work within government-sponsored research institutes and think-tanks.

While increasing the overall level of expenditure allocated for R&D has been an important goal, to make an appreciable difference in the orientation of the economy there must also be a concomitant shift in the role of the private sector. Based on data from the National Science Council, the government provided 61.2 per cent of R&D funds in 1983. That amount declined to 45.8 per cent in 1990, but has grown to 52.2 per cent in 1992. Unlike South Korea, where the private sector has assumed almost 80 per cent of the expenditure for R&D, Taiwan still suffers somewhat from an industrial structure dominated by small and medium-sized firms. In 1982, Taiwan's SMEs accounted for 69.7 per cent of the island's exports, but by 1994 that percentage had decreased to 52.6; at the same time, SMEs have accounted for over 96 per cent of all the firms on Taiwan. The shift in the role of SMEs in exports reflects their inability to compete technologically from their present situation and the decision among a growing number to move their operations to places such as the PRC, Vietnam and Malaysia rather than invest in technological upgrading.[30]

Nevertheless, this acknowledged, the impact of the industrial structure has helped to create a unique R&D system on the island, but one that should not necessarily be thought of despairingly because it departs from

28. "Taiwan business highlights – R&D requirement," *China Economic News Service*, 1 June 1996.

29. According to government statistics, R&D spending on Taiwan was up over 400% between 1985 and 1995. See "Taiwan: R&D spending up 400% in decade," *China Economic News Service*, 22 December 1995.

30. See several of the articles in Hellmut Schutte (ed.), *The Global Competitiveness of the Asian Firm* (New York: St. Martin's Press, 1994).

the private sector model present in most industrialized nations. The government on Taiwan has had to adopt a more activist role to overcome the specific inadequacies that continued to affect the potential for innovation on the island. At the core of government efforts to promote innovation is the Industrial Technology Research Institute (ITRI) located in Hsinchu, the site of the Hsinchu Science and Industry Park.[31]

The role of ITRI, which was founded in 1973, resembles that of the Korean Advanced Institute for Science and Technology (KAIST) insofar as its main purpose is industrially oriented research and development. It has a budget of about US$500 million and a staff of 6,000. Even though ITRI is not considered to be a government organization, it receives government assistance to a far greater extent than KAIST. Additionally, it is less independent than KAIST in the sense that contract research and revenues from royalties form a much smaller percentage of overall revenue.[32] ITRI's most important role is as a partner in high priority government-inspired projects.[33] For example, in the late 1970s, the Electronics Research Service Organization (ERSO), which is one of the ITRI laboratories, was the local recipient in a major microelectronics technology transfer project with RCA of the United States. Once ERSO had received and absorbed the technology from RCA, it worked with a local firm to diffuse that technology into the local market. United Microelectronics Corporation was the prime beneficiary. It was formed as a local joint venture involving ERSO's technology and a 25 per cent equity position from the government's Bank of Communications, in keeping with the government's role of sometime facilitator and sometime initiator.[34]

While ITRI is composed of several functionally distinct institutes, the most important is ERSO. ERSO has become the premier research institute on the island in terms of Taiwan's current and future advances in integrated circuits and other complex microelectronics components. It provides technical support to over 40 local integrated circuit manufacturers and wafer makers on Taiwan. Even more critical, ERSO serves as the training ground for young engineers, some of whom eventually leave the organization to start up their own firms. In many ways, this informal training and technology transfer function may have a more profound effect on the development of the integrated circuit industry in Taiwan than one of the more explicit programmes of activity occurring within the ERSO laboratories.

The role of ERSO also can be appreciated by examining its involvement in the island's ongoing ultra-large scale integrated circuit development programme. The project also exemplifies the government's efforts simply to provide the spark for a range of activities with the expectation

31. Philip Liu, "ITRI at the crossroads," *Business Taiwan*, 4 September 1994.
32. Peter Gwynne, "Directing technology in Asia's dragons," *Research-Technology Management*, 4 March 1993, pp. 12–15.
33. "ITRI celebrates is 20th anniversary with symposium," *Business Taiwan*, 19 July 1993, p. 1.
34. See Simon, "Taiwan, technology transfer and transnationalism."

that the private sector will assume the larger responsibility once the viability of the endeavour is assured. In co-operation with the Ministry of Education, the National Science Council and several private companies, ERSO has set up a joint design centre in Hsinchu to help accelerate the development of Taiwan's semiconductor industry. More recently, it was the force behind the creation in 1987 of the Taiwan Semiconductor Manufacturing Corporation, which serves as a foundry for the manufacture of foreign and domestic designed application specific integrated circuits. The project involved an initial investment of US$206 million, the largest ever made in the domestic electronics industry. This corporation has become one of the largest and most profitable foundries in the world and is currently considering establishing its fourth fabrication facility to meet growing demand from both inside and outside Taiwan. The major foreign partner in the project is Philips of Holland (which owns 27.5 per cent of the equity in the project).

As mentioned, the centre for the high-technology push on Taiwan has been the Hsinchu Science and Industry Park.[35] Its development was led by Li Kwo-ting, the man who is most frequently cited as the principal architect behind Taiwan's economic growth in the 1960s and 1970s. Li's most important legacy, however, may be in the foundation that he created at Hsinchu for the re-structuring of the Taiwan economy. In its broadest sense, the park represents Taiwan's move into the next stage of economic development, where industries are characterized by their skill and knowledge intensity rather than their labour intensity. Just as the three export processing zones in Kaohsiung and Tainan served as the engines of Taiwan's export drive 20 years ago, the Hsinchu Park is now the new engine of growth.[36]

In its initial phase in the early 1980s, the idea of the park was primarily to attract high technology companies from abroad. As at December 1993, it was home to 165 companies which had been approved and were already in operation, with total revenues of US$6.7 billion (see Table 1). Some 40,600 people were employed, over 50 per cent of whom had college degrees with 12 per cent holding advanced degrees. At the beginning most of the firms entering the park were small in size, but more recently there has been a significant increase. Selection is based on a company's design, development and manufacturing capabilities. In the past, the goal was to attract firms with the plans and skills to improve products already developed in the industrialized nations rather than those planning to develop new technologies. Today, there is a greater concern with attracting the potential for innovation and new products. This is entirely in keeping with the philosophy in place when the park was established, namely to adjust and elevate the criteria for admission each year so that the park remains at the forefront of technological innovation

35. Philip Liu, "Hsinchu science-based industrial park," *Business Taiwan*, 28 October 1991.
36. Danielle Yang, "Industrial parks seen as engines of Taiwan economy," *Central News Agency*, 13 November 1995.

Table 1: **High Technology Industries in Hsinchu Park, 1994**

Industry	No. of plants	Sales (US$million)
Computers and peripherals	39	2,712
Integrated circuits	51	3,171
Telecommunications	28	555
Opto-electronics	23	178
Precision machinery	15	73
Biotechnology	9	14
Total	165	6,705

and development. In this regard, it is interesting to note that as of late 1993, the average ratio between R&D spending and production value among the firms inside the park was 5.4 per cent compared with around 1.0 per cent for firms outside the park (see Table 2).[37]

Another fundamental purpose of Hsinchu Park is to capture the spillover from the presence of high-tech firms in terms of training, technology transfer and direct co-operation with local firms. Taiwan officials hope that the private sector will view the presence of high technology firms in the Hsinchu Park as "opportunity creating," thus inspiring some of them to move into those industries that the government hopes will become Taiwan's future source of competitive advantage. The geographic setting of the park is important because of the agglomeration dynamics that are present; it is situated near three major universities and ITRI as well as the Chiang Kai-shek International Airport. Many of the high-technology entrepreneurs in Hsinchu Park were formerly employees at ITRI institutes.

The location of Hsinchu Park and its steadily improving infrastructure are some of the reasons it has become a catalyst in facilitating the return

Table 2: **R&D Spending Ratios in Hsinchu Park, 1993**

Industry	R&D spending	Production value	Ratio (%)
Computers/peripherals	1,580	38,638	4.1
Integrated circuits	1,950	30,310	6.4
Telecommunications	578	10,135	5.7
Opto-electronics	178	1,344	13.3
Precision machinery	133	1,270	10.5
Biotechnology	39	463	8.4
Total	4,458	82,160	5.4

Source:
National Science Council, Taipei, 1994

37. K.K. Chadha, "Taiwan science hits record year," *South China Morning Post*, 13 December 1994. p. 8.

of over 1,000 engineers and technicians who now work there. (Government officials estimate that in 1993 over 6,000 overseas Chinese returned to Taiwan to work in government and private companies; the National Science Council statistics indicate that between 1990 and 1994 some 23,000 Chinese returned with a Ph.D. or Masters degree.) According to Hsinchu Park officials, 73 of the enterprises in the park have been set up by returning overseas Chinese.[38] The reverse of the brain drain, while clearly not complete, has helped to facilitate the overall development of high technology industry on the island. It is estimated that there are over 200 ex-AT&T Bell Labs and over 150 ex-IBM former employees working at the Science and Industry Park.

There is now no more space available within the Hsinchu Park boundaries, but its success has led to the decision to establish a new US$600-million science and industry park near Tainan county.[39] The Tainan site was selected because the local farmers in the Hsinchu area were not willing to accept the level of compensation offered by the government to buy their land. In addition, Hsinchu Park has recently experienced shortages of electricity, water and land. The new park will have three special industry zones: biotechnology, semiconductors and precision machinery. The decision to move in this direction reflects the fact that Taiwan's microelectronics industry is poised to expand, with current investment plans calling for the establishment of 10–12 major new production facilities over the next three to five years.

The formation of these new parks is just one piece of a new concerted effort by Taiwan to bring the island into the 21st century with a bang rather than a whimper.[40] Numerous concerns have developed regarding the possible "hollowing out" of the economy. Things, however, seem to be improving. According to a survey of 5,975 local firms conducted by the Ministry of Economic Affairs in mid-1995, 54 per cent indicated that they had maintained their original level of operations even after they made an overseas investment, 22 per cent said they even expanded their domestic operations, while only 22 per cent said they scaled down their operations and 2 per cent indicated that they would close their local operations. Moreover, in 1995, capital-intensive and technology-intensive industries will account for 65.7 per cent of overall manufacturing, an increase from 59.3 per cent in 1991. For the first time in seven years, in 1995 Taiwan's industrial production growth is expected to exceed that of the service sector. To keep the economy moving in this direction, the Ministry of Economic Affairs, in conjunction with both the Executive Yuan and the National Science Council, has announced a number of new measures to strengthen manufacturing and upgrade the industrial technology base. These include adopting the so-called "Singapore model" of

38. "Taiwan: science park achieves record performance," *Business Taiwan*, 14 November 1994.
39. "Science park to be built in Tainan," *China Economic News Service*, 22 March 1996.
40. "Authorities predict Taiwan to be science-island in a decade," *China Economic News Service*, 5 May 1995.

training technology professionals, whereby the government will assist
financially the training of scientists, engineers and technicians by research
institutes; increasing R&D investments in government-run businesses
such as Taiwan Power and China Steel; opening access to the defence-
oriented Chung Shan Institute of Science and Technology so that local
industry can take advantage of existing equipment and expertise; and
expanding the overall scale and operation of technology development
projects.[41]

Taiwan's Emerging Informatics and Microelectronics Industries

The key to the new business environment is disintegration. After WWII, economists
promoted the theory of vertical integration in which manufacturers would take all the
stages of production, from processing the raw material to distributing the finished
item. This approach was popular with the corporations for forty years. However, the
current direction has turned, esp. for the IT industry. Now the emphasis is now on
continuous technological enhancement to make products that appeal to better educated customers who have an awakened sense of product quality.[42]

Today, Taiwan continues to exhibit ambitions to play a major role in
the global informatics and microelectronics industries. This is one of the
main reasons why the government and local industry have decided to
enter the semiconductor race, to ensure an even supply of microchips,
especially DRAMs, to the growing computer industry. In 1991, semiconductors surpassed crude oil to become Taiwan's largest import item with
a value of US$2.53 billion. By 1994, while oil imports reached US$2.7
billion, microchip imports shot up to US$7.2 billion. Estimates are that
chip demand in Taiwan totalled 6 per cent of the world market; domestic
producers turned out only US$3.1 billion and only supplied US$900
million to local end-users. Some suggest that the island's self-sufficiency
rate for semiconductors may be as low as 16 per cent.

This helps to explain why there are plans to build as many as 18 new
semiconductor facilities over the next few years, with a value of US$13
billion.[43] At present, while Taiwan is the fourth largest producer of
integrated circuits in the world, it holds only 2.3 per cent of the global
chip market. Even with its ambitious plans for chip production, *The
Financial Times* (London) suggests that the self-sufficiency level will
only reach 37 per cent by the year 2000. At that time, total semiconductor
production on Taiwan will top US$19 billion. Nevertheless, the momen-
tum is building and numerous projects are under way (see Table 3).
One of the most important is the joint venture initiated in 1989 between
Acer and Texas Instruments, in which 56 per cent is owned by the
Taiwan firm, 26 per cent by the American firm and 16 per cent by the
China Development Corporation. The two companies recently launched a

41. "Taiwan: government plan to boost R&D spending," *Business Taiwan*, 6 March 1995.
42. "On Asian competitiveness," *AsiaWeek*, 3 November 1995, p. 30.
43. "Taiwan wafer fabs are booming," *Electronic Buyers News*, 12 January 1996, p. 8.

Table 3: **Major Semiconductor Projects Planned for Taiwan**

Companies	Country	Project
Texas Instruments–Acer	United States	DRAM
Taiwan Semiconductor	Local expansion	Integrated circuit foundry
United Microelectronics–ATI	United States	Memory chips
Umax (Powerchip)–Mitsubishi	Japan	DRAM
Mosel–Vitelic–Mitsubishi	Japan	DRAM
Vanguard	Local	DRAM (sum-micron)
Nan Ya Plastics–Oki	Japan	DRAM
Macronix–Oki	Japan	Memory chips
Winbond	Local	SRAM, logic
Holtek	Local	Micro components
Hualon	Local	Micro components
Tatung	Local	Foundry??
Syntek	Local	Foundry

Source:
  The Financial Times, 15 May 1995.

second major facility on Taiwan to produce 16MB and 64MB DRAM chips based on 8″ wafers, the prevailing state-of-the-art. Another important project involves the start-up of a second major integrated circuit subcontractor that will compete with the Taiwan Semiconductor Manufacturing Corporation. In May 1995, the government approved the application of the Asia-Pacific Semiconductor Manufacturing Corporation to set up a facility in Hsinchu Park. The key local firm in the project is Syntek, a local integrated circuit design company

As a recent *Business Week* article suggested, "Taiwan isn't just for cloning anymore."[44] By early 1994, it ranked fifth in the world in terms of computer hardware product value, accounting for approximately 4 per cent of total world production, behind the United States and Japan. Total output value was about US$15 billion. Production of microcomputer systems climbed from about 1,440 in 1981 to 2.4 million in 1991. Taiwan is the largest supplier of computer monitors in the world with a 56 per cent share of the market. Manufacture of monitors for computers grew from 39,000 in 1980 to 8.4 million in 1991 and 24 million in 1994. It was expected to reach 30 million by the end of 1995. Two years ago, with the help of ITRI, eight of Taiwan's leading computer firms invested close to US$200 million to establish a CRT plant to develop a new generation of computer monitors that will diminish the dependence of the island's firms on Japanese technology. (The plant will also serve as a first step in the effort to get into the high definition television race.)[45] Low end manufacturing for monitors has already begun to move offshore; in 1994, offshore

44. "Taiwan's hi-tech race," *Business Week* (International Edition), 6 May 1996.
45. "Yin and Yang of flat panels," *Electronic Buyers News*, 29 May 1995, p. 2.

production of monitors grew 130 per cent, about 1.67 times the growth of domestic output.[46]

The most interesting feature of the industry, however, is its rapid growth over the last decade. Informatics exports have grown from less than 10 per cent of electronics exports in the early 1980s to over one-third in 1988. Moreover, over 96 per cent of the production value of informatics products is exported into the world market. Today, in addition to being the world's biggest exporter of colour monitors, Taiwan also leads in exports of keyboards, mouses and image scanners.

As suggested, in the electronics industry Taiwan has moved from being a technological imitator to an innovator. Total electronics production in 1994 was US$14.7 billion.[47] According to data supplied by the Institute for Information Industry in Taipei, for example, foreign invested firms account for less than 40 per cent of total exports. In addition, while many Taiwan firms got their primary start as OEM producers, more and more firms are manufacturing and marketing products under their own brand names, such as MITAC and Acer.[48] In 1992, for example, information products exported under local brand names grew to over 35 per cent of total exports, up from just 23 per cent two years earlier. A sort of division of labour seemed to be emerging between South Korea and Taiwan in the mid-1980s in this regard, with the latter seemingly focusing more on computer products and the former more on semiconductors. For example, in 1986 South Korea's exports of computers totalled US$707 million while Taiwan's exports exceeded US$2.1 billion. Yet in semiconductors, Korea's performance (US$1.3 billion) greatly surpassed that of Taiwan (US$707 million). More recently this seems to have faded with both economies vying for an increasing share of the highly competitive informatics market.[49] One major problem for Taiwan, however, is that it still imports almost 50 per cent of its personal computer components. In addition, markets are changing so fast that Taiwan is losing its job as a final assembler, especially as a result of the new manufacturing models adopted by American computer companies such as Compaq, Gateway and Dell.

The rapid changes in technology and markets have provided the main impetus for the decision by the Taiwan government to organize a consortium of semiconductor producers to advance the level of process technology on the island. ITRI will work with a range of local companies and universities in a research effort similar to the Sematech project in the

46. At the same time, some Japanese firms are arriving on the island to move into the higher end segment of the monitor industry. See "NEC ties up with Taiwan firm for CRT production," *Asian Economic News*, 15 April 1996, p. 1.

47. "A new view to the future: Taiwan special supplement," *AsiaMoney*, September 1995, pp. 14–29.

48. "What? You haven't heard of MITAC," *Business Week* (International Edition), 10 April 1995.

49. Brian Levy and Wen-jeng Kuo, "The strategic orientations of firms and the performance of Korea and Taiwan in frontier industries: lessons from comparative studies of the keyboard and personal computer assembly," *World Development*, Vol. 19, No. 4 (1991), pp. 363–374.

United States several years ago. The goal of the effort will be to develop key technologies and quickly diffuse them to local industry, so firms such as Acer-TI and United Microelectronics can develop the commercial processes. Towards the same end, the Taiwan government also announced in mid-1995 a programme to develop a "domestic" computer processing unit that will compete with Intel's pentium chips. Taiwan hopes to overcome Intel's dominance over microprocessors and diminish its growing influence in the areas of motherboard and chip set production. Taiwan officials hope to follow the United Microelectronics model for CMOS; utilizing project teams within ITRI and National Chiaotong University, they hope to transfer the "know-how" to local producers for domestic manufacture. This will help Taiwan overcome its present deficiency which means it has to ship over half its motherboards without processors.

Taiwan's Response to Global Competition: The Proliferation of Strategic Alliances

One of the notable response of firms in the globalizing industries has been the formation of strategic alliances with other firms – domestic and/or foreign – to share costs, minimize risks and combine complementary assets among themselves.[50] This new pattern of business strategy is most prevalent in industries with large economies of scale, shortened technology cycles and heavy R&D intensity. The semiconductor and aircraft industries are good examples.[51] According to Ohmae and others, the keys to success in such alliances seem to lie in four main areas: skill complementarities among the partners, co-operative corporate cultures, high compatibility of goals, and sharing commensurate levels of risk and return.[52]

Traditionally, the motives for international collaboration in most industries are threefold: access to markets, access to technology, access to capital. Standard forms of foreign direct investment and licensing are becoming less critical, especially in high-technology sectors. The growth in strategic alliances reflects the fact that companies are looking for new ways to compete in the current international business environment: share risks, reduce costs, exchange knowledge. They appear willing to accept a whole series of possible new business risks and managerial challenges to obtain the alleged benefits of these alliances, only to find out, in many cases, that they have selected the wrong partner or that their partner is not capable of performing its assigned tasks. Recent studies have suggested that less than 50 per cent of these alliances ever succeed from the perspective of both partners.[53] Still, firms seem willing to venture into

50. See the various articles in Harvard Business Review (ed.), *Global Strategies* (Boston: Harvard Business Review Press, 1994).

51. See Denis Fred Simon (ed.), *Techno-Security in an Age of Globalization* (Armonk, NY: M.E. Sharpe, 1996).

52. Kenichi Ohmae, "The global logic of strategic alliances," Harvard Business Review, March/April 1989, pp. 143–154.

53. Keith D. Brouthers *et al.*, "Strategic alliances: choose your partners," *Long Range Planning*, Vol. 28, No. 3 (June 1995), pp. 18–25.

these collaborative arrangements in increasing numbers as a way to help their organizations overcome inhibitions about risk-taking and resource sharing. While alliances cannot solve the problems of weak management or lack of strategic focus, they can provide a critical mechanism for companies to enhance their competitive position and acquire new knowledge.[54]

International aeronautics is an excellent example of an industry that has been shaped significantly by the forces of globalization.[55] Accordingly, it is no surprise to find a proliferation of strategic alliances among the major aeronautics firms from the United States, Japan and Europe in both the airframe and aeroengine segments. In fact, it would not be an exaggeration to suggest that the rules of the game have shifted from a pure "lone-ranger type" of competition to a new form characterized by higher and higher levels of inter-firm collaboration and co-operation.[56] The future survival of each of the key firms in the industry seems increasingly dependent on the nature and quality of the alliances it has or will form with other firms. Partnering – being able to identify, develop and sustain working partnerships with "quality" partners – has already become one of the critical success factors in this industry.[57]

In the case of industrial and technological collaboration involving Taiwan, similar forces have been important. For the MNCs, access to production assets and capital has been central to their thinking; for Taiwan firms, access to technology has been most important.[58] In response to what they see as increasing techno-nationalsim in the world, Taiwan firms, like their counterparts in Korea, feel that licensing and other forms of arms-length transactions in the international technology marketplace are becoming more limited.[59] They point to the fact that despite the claims about globalization of technology, in the early 1990s American based MNCs conducted only 12.7 per cent of their R&D abroad (up from 8.7 per cent in 1982). Companies such as Texas Instruments now generate sizeable revenues simply from enforcement of their patents rather than from actually creating the next generation technology.[60] The main problem for Taiwan, however, has not been the United States or EC; in fact, American and European firms had apparently become the main Taiwan hope. The real culprit is Japan. Heretofore, strategic alliances with firms from the United States or Europe have represented a means to reduce Taiwan's significant technological depen-

54. Peter Pekar and Robert Allio, 'Making alliances work – guidelines for success," *Long Range Planning*, Vol. 27, No. 4 (August 1994), pp. 54–65.
55. B. Bowonder, "Creating and sustaining competitiveness: an analysis of the world civil aircraft industry," *World Competition*, June 1993, pp. 5–47.
56. Ohmae, "The global logic of strategic alliances."
57. David Mowery (ed.), *International Collaborative Ventures in U.S. Manufacturing* (Cambridge: Ballinger Publishers, 1988).
58. For an interesting discussion of the attractiveness of Taiwan from a competitive perspective, see the forthcoming manuscript edited by George Yip, *Asian Advantage* (forthcoming, 1996).
59. Alan Tonelson, "The perils of techno-globalism," *Issues in Science and Technology*, Summer 1995, pp. 31–38.
60. Fred Warshofsky, *The Patent Wars* (New York: John Wiley & Sons, 1994).

dence on the Japanese.[61] Since the early 1980s, it has been the stated policy of the Taiwan government to engage the United States and Europe in a broad-based programme of technological co-operation with Taiwan firms.

Recently, however, the situation concerning Japan has begun to change. Faced with the appreciation of the yen and the need for fundamental re-structuring inside Japan, Japanese companies have re-focused their attention on economies such as Taiwan with respect to their higher value-added manufacturing operations.[62] During the first period of the endaka in the late 1980s, Japanese firms responded to their rising costs at home by re-locating much of their lower-end manufacturing to South-East Asia; a great deal of Japanese consumer electronics industry found a new home in the ASEAN economies. At present, however, Japanese firms have taken a dramatically different approach, perhaps in recognition of the achievements Taiwan has made in such industries as computers and peripherals.[63] The need to be near those firms that are actually designing and producing the components and final products in the information industry has stimulated a new Japanese strategy towards Taiwan.

Taiwan's technology linkages with the U.S. These are significant for Taiwan's pattern of technological development because American firms have been and will continue to be a primary source of advanced technology to local firms. In terms of overall dollar value, the United States also has been the principal source of foreign investment into Taiwan. And, from a technology transfer perspective, just as Taiwan has changed the central focus of its economic activity away from simple, low-cost labour assembly type operations and begun to concentrate on high-technology sectors such as informatics and microelectronics, the technological nature of American investments have shifted in the same direction. Many Taiwan firms have become enmeshed in the global sourcing and subcontracting of American multinational firms, serving as critical suppliers of key components and final products – often on an OEM basis.[64] World-class companies such as Hewlett Packard, NCR, Motorola and Texas Instruments have placed a great deal of emphasis on their Taiwan-based facilities and activities, seeing them as a central part of their overall global strategic operations.[65] In this context, the recent decision by AT&T/Lucent to set up two joint ventures on Taiwan is significant,

61. Kuo-shu Liang, "International strategic alliances and technology transfers," *Business Taiwan*, 22 March 1993, p. 1.

62. See the article by Denis Fred Simon and Yongwook Jun on Japanese foreign investment in Chen and Drysdale, *Corporate Links and Foreign Direct Investment*.

63. See United Nations Center for Transnational Corporations (ed.), *World Investment Report 1991* and *1993* (New York: United Nations, 1991, 1993).

64. See Poh Kam Wong, *Technological Development Through Subcontracting Linkages: A Case Study* (Tokyo: Asian Productivity Organization, 1991).

65. For a discussion of the global behavior of multinational firms and their subcontracting behaviour see John H. Dunning, *Multinational Enterprises and the Global Economy* (Reading, MA: Addison-Wesley, 1993).

as part of AT&T's strategic goal of generating 50 per cent of its revenues from overseas markets by the year 2000. One venture will utilize Taiwan's strong industrial design and manufacturing capabilities to develop new products and technology. The other will provide financial support to telecommunications firms in the Asia-Pacific region.

The American link is also significant because its market has been the traditional target for a large percentage of Taiwan exports. Even though local companies are diversifying away from dependence on the United States – approximately 50 per cent of Taiwan's exports in 1992 went to countries in the Asia-Pacific region – the fact remains that many of Taiwan's key exports are designed for use in the American market. The United States also receives a significant portion of overseas investment by Taiwan companies such as Formosa Plastics, which has invested in the American chemicals processing industry. Perhaps even more important, however, is the fact that within California's "Silicon Valley," many Taiwan entrepreneurs have either set up their own companies or made investments in existing companies. In some cases, the U.S.-based operations of these small, Taiwan-invested firms constitute high-technology listening posts for local firms on the island. Important technical and commercial information about new product developments and so on are frequently transmitted – legally and illegally – from California to Taiwan via these companies and their employees. In this context, it should also be remembered that the United States provides the main training ground for Taiwan's future engineers and scientists, a larger and larger percentage of whom now return home after receiving their education at the graduate level in America.

Taiwan's technology linkages with Japan. The impact of Taiwan's links with Japan on the island's technology orientation has been significant. Although 50 years have passed since the island was returned to China by Japan in the aftermath of the Second World War, the reality is that the Japanese continue to have a major influence on the Taiwan economy. If one looks simply at the total number of cases of foreign investment and formal technical co-operation agreements since the 1960s, Japanese firms have been predominant. As of 1994, even though the value of approved American investment on Taiwan has been approximately equal to that of Japan, Japanese companies have had more than twice as many cases of foreign investment. Statistics regarding technical co-operation agreements as of the end of 1993 reveal a similar pattern, with the number of Japanese cases exceeding American cases by almost a factor of three.

In almost all areas of the economy, the participation of companies from Japan has been critical to the growth of Taiwan exports, many of which entered world markets through the distribution channels of Japanese trading companies. Taiwan government officials and companies have often been critical of Japanese firms for their almost explicit efforts to forestall technology transfer. Since the 1960s, Japan has been said to transfer "show-how" but not "know-how," often refusing to provide or sell certain critical information or components to Taiwan companies that are seeking to minimize dependence on their Japanese counterparts. This is not to suggest that the contribution of Japanese industry has been negligible; in fact, Taiwan officials probably excessively play down its level, both formal and informal. Nevertheless, the fact remains that many opportunities for fruitful collaboration have been bypassed because potential Japanese partners were hesitant to transfer the desired levels of technology.

In this context, it is perhaps no accident that, until recently (apart from a few isolated examples), Japanese firms were conspicuous by their absence from important government initiatives such as the Hsinchu Science and Industry Park. While there is no evidence that this was the result of intentional discrimination, the reality is that given Japan's past track-record, the principal targets were the United States, Europe and overseas Chinese investors. The fact that Japan continues to run a tremendous trade deficit with Taiwan has not helped the situation; it reached almost US$15 billion in 1994. Taiwan firms have disproportionately relied on Japanese companies as the source for the equipment and components that are needed to upgrade the technological base of the economy. As one scholar remarked, "Taiwan's exports are mostly built on imports from Japan!" Japanese firms have not been in the forefront of purchasing Taiwan exports, except in such areas as processed foods and clothing. Manufactured goods exported to the United States in 1994, for example, constituted over 90 per cent of total Taiwan exports to that country, but for Japan, manufactured products accounted for less than 60 per cent of total exports. Even with the expansion of imports from the Asian NIEs in the aftermath of the Plaza Accords in 1985 and the tremendous growth of Japanese investment in East and South-East Asia, this situation did not change in any fundamental way.[66]

More recently, due to a combination of competitive considerations and political pressures, some Japanese companies are changing their attitudes about engaging in higher value-added operations on Taiwan (see Table 4).[67] Sharp, for example, has now set up an integrated circuit design centre for consumer appliances; a similar type of facility has also been set up by NEC. Matsushita is steadily expanding its R&D activities on the island, moving into computer software as well as engaging in design activities linked to its large joint venture in consumer electronics. Sony has established an international procurement centre on Taiwan. Other Japanese firms such as Mitsubishi are making major investments in Taiwan's semiconductor industry. In the Mitsubishi case, it appears the company wants to use the foundry at the Taiwan Semiconductor Manufacturing Company to provide capacity for memory production; Mitsubishi will serve as an intermediary between this company and Japanese chip producers. In February 1993, a high-level group of Taiwan and

---

66. "Who's NICst?" *The Economist*, 13 August 1994, p. 31.
67. This new thinking is part of the larger changing attitude of Japanese firms towards Asia. See "Survey: Japan needs higher profile in Asia," *Nikkei Weekly*, 25 April 1992, p. 28.

Table 4: **Recent Japanese High-Tech Initiatives on Taiwan**

Japanese firm	Taiwan partner(s)	Focus
Oki Electric	Nan Ya Plastics and Mosel-Vitelic	DRAM production
Mitsubishi	Umax-Elite Group/Powerchip	DRAM production
NEC	Taiwan Semiconductor Manufacturing Company	Chip subcontracting
Komatsu and Shin Etsu	NA	Silicon water materials
NKK	Macronix	Utilize production capacity in Japan

Japanese executives met to promote technology transfer from Japan to Taiwan's component industries. This followed an earlier visit in May 1991 by a 156-member delegation from the Keidanren to Taiwan to discuss trade and technology transfer issues. These activities suggest some change in the approach of Japanese companies to the island.

Taiwan's technology linkages with the PRC. The opening up of trade and commerce with the PRC has clearly helped to contribute to continued growth of the local Taiwan economy, though some important questions remain in terms of the impact on overall technological development. Because of rapidly rising labour costs and a shortage of workers for low-skilled jobs, many small and medium-sized Taiwan companies have transplanted their operations to Fujian and southern China, where labour is in ample supply and wages are considerably lower than Taiwan. China has also become an attractive market for Taiwan-made products, including consumer electronics, textiles, chemicals and computers. In addition, companies such as Formosa Plastics, faced with an increasingly hostile domestic situation in terms of activist environmental groups, have sought investment projects on the China mainland to bypass newly installed pollution laws.

The economic pulls from the Chinese mainland on the Taiwan economy are indeed very strong and ever present. They are part of the emergence of what some call "Greater China," a manifestation of the coming together of the economies of Hong Kong, the mainland and Taiwan. Government officials on Taiwan have made repeated efforts on several occasions to control, manage and even halt the expansion of investment and trade, but these have not succeeded as local companies have found numerous ways to sidestep official pronouncements and regulations. The reality is that the emergence of the mainland market for Taiwan has been a blessing in many ways, helping to offset the actual and potential loss of markets overseas and rising costs at home. Nevertheless, a number of critical issues have emerged. One problem is that while the opportunity to trade with and invest in the PRC has had some immediate positive effects, there is a danger that excessive focus on the Chinese mainland will pre-empt government efforts to upgrade the industrial technology base on the island. Over 10 per cent of Taiwan's total trade is with the PRC; as much as 15 per cent of its total exports may go to the Chinese mainland, primarily through Hong Kong. And while the mainland does provide some short-term relief for local firms, it could produce a degree of technological complacency that reduces rather than enhances these companies' interest in making new technological investments at home. This is especially true given the industrial structure on Taiwan, where small and medium-sized firms with limited capital availability continue to be predominant.

Another problem is related to larger firms, many of which see very lucrative opportunities opening up on the Chinese mainland – and only more and more bureaucratic entanglements at home. Of course, this does not only apply to the PRC but also to other parts of South-East Asia,

Eastern Europe and so on. Nevertheless, because of the historical and cultural links between Taiwan and the mainland, doing business in the PRC seems remarkably less complex – an irony in comparison with the experiences of many Western firms doing business in China. Thus these two problems – forestalling new investment in technological upgrading and siphoning off existing investment – could serve to damage government attempts to attract larger private sector involvement in Taiwan's high technology development programmes. Moreover, given the apparent technological gap that exists between the PRC and the United States, it remains to be seen whether the former can provide the same type of technological stimulation that the latter has and will continue to provide in the future.

This is not to deny that the potential for technological synergies does exist between the scientific and technical communities on Taiwan and the Chinese mainland. The decision in 1992–93 by the authorities on Taiwan to permit acquisition of technology from the PRC does open up some very interesting possibilities.[68] This is especially true when one considers the idea of "Greater China." Within areas such as biotechnology, computer software and materials, some collaborative activities have already begun on an informal basis. In August 1992, "the 1992 Workshop on Scientific and Technical Co-operation and Exchange Between Industries on Both Sides of the Strait" was held for two days in Beijing. Agreement was reached on five areas of co-operation, with special emphasis on computer science and information technology: protection of intellectual property rights; establishment of common information technology standards; joint technical development with regard to products distinctively related to Chinese fields of application; co-operative development of a large, possibly integrated, national information system; and establishment of a research and development centre and exchanges of skilled personnel. As a follow-up, the first science and technology delegation from the mainland since 1949 visited Taiwan in early 1993 to discuss possible areas of co-operation. And in October 1995, some 70 metrology experts from both sides met in Beijing to begin work on harmonization of standards.[69] In this regard, Taiwan would seem to hold the upper hand and greatest leverage since its interconnections with the West in high technology go far beyond those of the PRC. Recognition of this fact has prompted Taiwan authorities to caution local firms about providing technologies that could have military applications. Similarly, in fields such as information technology and consumer electronics, consideration must also be given to possible competition from PRC enterprises, many of which are anxious to enter an export market which is currently occupied, in part, by Taiwan companies.

---

68. "Taiwan government opens doors to technology transfers to/from China," *Nikkei Weekly*, 6 June 1992, p. 27.
69. "Mainland and Taiwan hold first joint metrology seminar," Xinhua News Agency, 30 October 1995.

Taiwan's technology linkages with the Asian NIEs. Although frequently grouped together for purposes of analysis, the four NIEs are highly competitive with one another over attracting foreign investment and technology and gaining an expanded market share in overseas markets. Unlike Taiwan's relationships with the United States, Japan and Europe, where there is a great deal of complementarity in terms of markets, technology capabilities, human resources and so on, the Asian NIEs are embarked on very similar paths of technological development. This requires careful understanding and constant monitoring of each of the economies. For example, just as Singapore and Hong Kong pushed ahead with their plans to serve as operational centres for the Asia-Pacific operations of many MNCs, Taiwan embarked on a similar course, having recently recruited Imperial Chemical Industries, AT&T and Microsoft to set up significant production and/or R&D facilities on the island. Philips, one of the world's leading electronics companies, has made plans to use Taiwan as its base for production of tubes for high definition televisions. While some might suggest that each of the Asian NIEs has developed its own particular areas of specialization in industries such as computers – with Taiwan focusing on monitors, Korea on semiconductors, Singapore on hard disk drives and Hong Kong on peripherals – there is little doubt that each hopes to move into higher value-added products even if is at the expense of its neighbours. Competition from the other Asian NIEs provides a healthy stimulus to Taiwan firms in terms of investing in R&D and new equipment, but it also adds an element of fragility to the situation, thus preventing even key players such as Acer and UMC from feeling secure for too long.

Taiwan's technology linkages with ASEAN. In many respects, the ASEAN represents an important outlet for the export of intermediate technologies and related equipment from Taiwan. With operating costs spiraling on the island, many Taiwan firms even in so-called high technology sectors have sought competitive refuge by investing in one or several of the ASEAN economies. This includes Acer, Taiwan's leading producer of personal computers, which has set up a factory in Malaysia to cut costs and provide needed capacity so that the Taiwan-based operations of the company can focus on higher value-added products. Acer's Malaysia operations now account for two-third of that company's total monitor output. Taiwan's investments in the ASEAN countries have proved to be of great significance in terms of building economic bridges, with Taiwan serving as a supplier of technology rather than as a recipient. Of course, Taiwan firms are well aware of the potential "boomerang effect" that could come from being too forthcoming in terms of technology transfer. Nevertheless, these relationships continue to expand, thus further integrating. Taiwan into the regional division of labour in the Pacific Rim (see Table 5).

Taiwan's other technology linkages. Technology ties between Taiwan and the EU, Eastern Europe and the former Soviet Union have been

Table 5: **Taiwan's Activities in South-East Asia**

Country	Amount invested	Major targets	Outcome
Vietnam	US$2.5 billion	Infrastructure	Low-cost labour but must face "red tape"
Indonesia	US$7.7 billion	Labour-intensive industry	Abundant cheap labour
Philippines	US$740 million	Labour-intensive industry	Poor infrastructure
Malaysia	US$7.3 billion	Computers/peripherals	Close to many MNCs
Thailand	US$5.1 billion	Electronics manufacture	Highly skilled labour but rising labour costs

Source:
Business Week, 6 November 1995.

growing as well. Taiwan officials have expressed a willingness to hire scientists and engineers from the former Soviet Union. Efforts are also under way to expand ties with Australia and New Zealand. Yet, in spite of these efforts, the fact remains that the shape of the Taiwan economy continues to be defined principally by the pushes and pulls associated with the five sets of linkages above. The benefits and dangers of becoming too involved in any one relationship have been identified, with the most significant danger coming from the growing pulls of the Chinese mainland. In some respects, therefore, an interesting four-sided dynamic is emerging: one set of forces that has the United States pulling at Taiwan – with a concerted push from several elements in the Taiwan government – to be a player in its global R&D and manufacturing networks; a second set that has the Japanese pulling to ensure that the Taiwan economy continues to articulate and move in tandem with the economic and technological re-structuring occurring in Japan; a third set, largely politically induced, that has the Chinese mainland pulling for closer economic and technological integration with Taiwan, perhaps even at the expense of short-circuiting expanded new local investment on the island; and a fourth set that involves competition with the other Asian NIEs as well as the pull of the ASEAN, with their attractive investment incentives and lower-cost labour. This situation could either contribute to the possible "hollowing out" of the Taiwan economy or accelerate the development of possible future competitors to Taiwan companies.

Challenges Ahead for Taiwan

Some scholars have suggested that one of the most significant phenomena affecting existing patterns of trade and technology intercourse in the international economy has been the "globalization of technology." As result of the expanded and extended diffusion of technology throughout the world, new, alternative centres of technological capability are springing up outside the traditional areas in the United States, Western Europe and Japan. The emergence of increasingly strong, indigenous manufacturing systems in places such as Taiwan has prompted greater interest in new types of collaboration with these economies. The global integration of capital markets together with the spread of information technologies and the development of global transportation links have further facilitated this collaboration. Within the realm of international business, there is some evidence to suggest that the traditional joint venture with its generally hierarchical character may have become a thing of the past, as it is replaced by new forms of network-oriented co-operation, such as those associated with strategic alliances.

If this is indeed what is happening in the world economy today, then there are important implications for the Taiwan economy. Simply put, Taiwan's technological assets are going to assume an increased importance in the playing out of global competition in the years ahead. This has already occurred to some extent in the new agreement between Acer and Texas Instruments to manufacture sophisticated computer memory chips.

It is also reflected in the emerging plan among Taiwan computer manufacturers to set up a computer-industrial zone in one of the EC countries
as a way to ensure a piece of the market in the coming years. As one
commentator in *The Economist* has suggested, "the multi-layered structure of the new computer industry and the large number of firms it now
contains, mean that any single firm, no matter how powerful, must work
closely with many others. Often this is to obtain access to technology or
manufacturing expertise. A web of a thousand joint ventures, cross-equity
holdings, and marketing pacts now entangles every firm in the industry."
Firms that are left out of these alliances and linkages will be hard pressed
to maintain their viability even over the short term.

The role of Japan in Taiwan's high technology development is likely
to become significant in this context as Japanese capital has already
begun to provide the cement for a more integrated East Asian regional
economy. Japanese firms are recognizing that Taiwan has an important
role to play in the regional emerging division of labour, perhaps not along
the lines of the now obsolete "flying geese model," but according to some
new model of interaction distinguished by technological complementarities rather than differential costs. Of course, Japanese firms will remain
cautious in their approach to Taiwan, but there is little doubt that Japan
can ill-afford to ignore the potential role that Taiwan firms can play in
terms of both regional and global competition. Taiwan will still maintain
its close relationship with the United States, but much depends on
whether American industry will respond in greater force to the new
dynamic situation in the Pacific Rim. Otherwise, concepts such as the
"Asianization" of the global semiconductor industry are likely to become
a reality.

In the world that is evolving, it is becoming clear that in order to attract
technology one already has to possess some technology. With respect to
industries such as microelectronics and informatics, this should prove to
be a great source of comfort for Taiwan, which is now finding that there
are indeed benefits from having made progress after all these years. At
the same time, however, there are many challenges to the future success
of Taiwan as it faces the rest of the 1990s and the next century. There are
growing barriers to entry into many of the high-technology industries that
are now the focal point of government officials and business leaders on
the island. For example, the cost of building a new state-of-the-art facility
for integrated circuit fabrication and production is now over ten times as
much as it was a few years ago. Based on current estimates to establish
a world-class facility to produce DRAM memory chips, the cost would
exceed US$1.0 billion. To offset some of these cost barriers, the govern-
ment has highlighted eight key technologies and ten high-growth industries in its new six-year economic plan (1990–96). It is clear, however,
that despite its huge foreign exchange reserves (US$96 billion), the
Taiwan government cannot absorb all the costs associated with these new
initiatives; foreign investment as well as private sector contributions are
required. Moreover, government initiatives are not always successful, as
demonstrated by the failed effort to organize a consortium to develop and

produce the first computer notebook on the island. Similar concerns also exist as a result of the failure of the aerospace industry initiative to yield the type of positive collaborative results in technological terms that the government anticipated.

Perhaps this is one reason why the Taiwan government decided in late 1993 to privatize the state-of-the-art semiconductor facility it operates in Hsinchu Park. The plant, which was created as part of the overall programme of high-technology investment orchestrated by the government, remains economically viable, and given the growing demand for memory chips throughout the island, clearly has the potential to be a very profitable venture. Taiwan imports a majority of the DRAMs it needs; unlike Korea which has focused primarily on DRAM production, Taiwan firms had tended to shy away from such projects because of the huge initial investment. This is now changing because of the rapid growth of the information industry. Quite frequently, the government has had to assume a major role to jump-start new high-technology initiatives. Once its mission has been achieved, as in the case of United Microelectronics and several other related projects, it may be appropriate for the government to remove itself from explicit involvement, either through equity ownership or direct managerial control. On Taiwan, there are legitimate concerns about whether private forces can muster the necessary political will and economic commitment to make something substantial happen.[70] This suggests that the government cannot simply abandon what it has accomplished, and must remain in some capacity with the industry, if only to give confidence to outside investors who want to identify the island's "pockets of excellence."[71]

Secondly, the ongoing efforts at technological re-structuring that are occurring on Taiwan are being inhibited to some degree by the general tightening up over access to advanced technology by many who feel threatened by the Asian NIEs.[72] This is especially true for settings such as Taiwan which continue to have a poor reputation as far as IPR protection is concerned. While the forces of globalization are at work, it should not be forgotten that significant forces of technological protectionism are also present. One of the major obstacles to the defunct deal with McDonnell Douglas was the inability of the two parties to agree upon the technology transfer provisions of their proposed collaboration.

Thirdly, there remain major questions in the United States, EC and elsewhere about the viability of a business strategy that relies too heavily on alliance-building in key high technology sectors. Strategic partnering has its advantages, but there are major questions of trust, cross-cultural understanding and politics that must be confronted in working to make these alliances truly mutually beneficial. Fourthly, there are major information and skills barriers in terms of the adoption and application of new

---

70. Julian Baum, "Mid-course correction," *Far Eastern Economic Review*, 15 July 1993, pp. 60–61.
71. Joel D. Auerbauch *et al.* (eds.), *The Role of the State in Taiwan's Development* (Armonk, NY: M.E. Sharpe, 1994).
72. See Simon, *Techno-Security in an Age of Globalization.*

technologies such as informatics.[73] This suggests that without an adequate infrastructure or training programmes, many Taiwan firms are going to have similar if not worse problems with assimilating many of the new technologies. It is estimated, for example, that by the latter part of the 1990s, the total number of engineers on Taiwan will be only be enough to fill 70 per cent of the projected needs, with the greatest dearth occurring in information engineering and computer science. Whether this shortage can be handled through the use of engineers from the PRC raises a very interesting and provocative question. And finally, it is one thing to desire to get beyond OEM status and enter into both product and process design in advanced industrial sectors on a regular basis, but it is another thing to succeed at doing them well. While there clearly is a strong foundation that suggests a high potential for Taiwan's success, with firms such as Acer, the reality is that the dynamics of global competition in all segments of the world economy call for a degree of responsiveness and flexibility that may or may not be present in view of the existing industrial structure in the local economy.[74] All these factors will weigh heavily on Taiwan as it seeks to establish a new position for itself in the still evolving international division of labour. Moreover, the confluence of these factors suggests that Taiwan companies as well as government officials must be extremely aware of the assorted pushes and pulls on the local economy, especially since they can ill afford to fall behind in those technologies that are providing the foundation for future growth.

73. See S.P. Bradley, J.A. Hausman and R.L. Nolan, *Globalization, Technology and Competition* (Boston: Harvard Business School Press, 1993).
74. Richard Schonberger, *World Class Manufacturing: The Next Decade* (New York: Free Press, 1996).

[16]

Government as a Learning Facilitator

"Here comes the Korean," once heralded *Newsweek* in its cover story on Korea's economic miracle and Korea's stampede into the international market. Many economists attribute Korea's success to the Korean government's developmental role,[1] concluding that the economic miracle stemmed from a policy miracle.[2] The government envisioned a miracle and provided a policy environment, but it was industry that made it reality.

The role of the government in industrialization is so complex and multifaceted that it cannot be adequately covered in a single chapter. Therefore, this chapter limits its discussions only to those facets directly or indirectly related to technological learning in Korea at the microeconomic level. Other writers have covered the government's developmental role in Korea more extensively, though mostly at the macroeconomic level.[3]

What can the government do to facilitate technological learning at individual firms under a dynamically changing global technology environment? Over the years, the Korean government has adopted an array of policy instruments designed to facilitate technological learning in industry and in turn strengthen the international competitiveness of the economy. This history can be better understood by analyzing it from three perspectives: market mechanism, technology flow, and time.

Market mechanism perspective includes both the demand side of technology development that creates market needs for technological change and the supply side of technology development that strengthens technological capability. The former is often referred to as industrial policy in a narrow sense of the term, while the latter can be thought of as science and technology (S&T) policy.

In other words, this perspective organizes policies related to technological development into three major components: policies designed to strengthen the demand side, creating market needs for technology, policies designed to strengthen the supply side, increasing S&T capabilities, and policies designed to provide effective linkages between the demand and supply sides, attempting to ensure that innovation activities are both technically and commercially successful.[4]

Unless there is a competitive market in which firms believe that innovation in products and processes is necessary to sustaining and raising market competitiveness, there is little investment in innovation activities, as innovation is usually uncertain and risky. Also, strong links to the market are needed to make sure public R&D efforts are effective and efficient. In this sense, science and technology policies should be an integral part of the overall industrial policies that shape market structure and industrial development.

However, even though the market calls for the introduction of new products and processes, countries without indigenous technological capabilities cannot be expected to grow industrially. Some economies have indigenous technological capabilities but still don't grow. To be commercially exploited, technological capabilities must be coupled with the right business capabilities.

Finally, despite the presence of both demand for innovation and supply of capabilities, few innovations can be realized unless there is good management of the R&D system, effectively linking demand with supply. The absence of this linkage explains why in some industrialized countries there is little innovation despite a strong demand for it and an adequate supply of technical capabilities. Some linkage instruments such as institutions to bridge the demand and supply sides of technology and tax and financial incentives for R&D efforts in developing countries are not effective in stimulating technological activities in the absence of demand and supply of technology.

Government policies related to technology development may also be assessed by the technology flow perspective. This perspective is mainly concerned with three key sequences in the flow of technology from abroad to catching-up countries: transfer of foreign technology, diffusion of imported technology, and indigenous R&D to assimilate and improve imported technology and to generate its own technology. The first sequence involves technology transfer from abroad through such formal mechanisms as foreign direct investment, the purchase of turnkey plants and machinery, foreign licenses, and technical services. Such transfer can facilitate the acquisition of technological capability in catching-up countries.

The effective diffusion of imported technology within an industry and across industries is a second sequence in upgrading technological capability of an economy. If a technology is transferred to a firm and its use is limited only to its original importer, it may give the firm monopoly power over other firms for a period of time; however, the broader economic effect of the technology may be considerably limited. To maximize its benefits, imported technology has to be diffused throughout its economy.

The third sequence involves local efforts to assimilate, adapt, and improve imported technology and eventually to develop one's own technology. These efforts are crucial to augmenting technology transfer and expediting the acquisition of technological capability. Technology may be transferred to a firm from abroad or through local diffusion, but the ability to use it effectively cannot. This ability can only be acquired through indigenous technological effort. Local endeavors can include self-directed attempts to copy or reverse-engineer foreign products and processes, those aimed at improving and adapting previously acquired technology, and one's own research and development. Such efforts become increasingly important as industrialization progresses. These activities are necessary to strengthen international competitiveness in the face of increasing pressure from other catching-up countries.

The two perspectives outlined here, market mechanisms and technology flow, may be combined as illustrated in Figure 2-1. The dynamic perspective dimension is added as the third dimension to indicate time, which is very important. The relative impact of the individual sequences of technology flow and the impact of different types of market mechanisms—demand, supply, and linkage—change as an industry advances through different stages of development over time

24 EVOLUTION OF PUBLIC POLICY

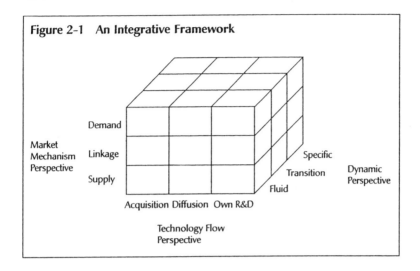

Figure 2-1   An Integrative Framework

(see Chapter 4 for detailed discussions). This integrative framework is used below to analyze and evaluate Korea's industrial and S&T policies.

GENERAL BACKGROUND

One of the most conspicuous characteristics of the industrialization of Korea is the strong government and its orchestrating role. The government steered the wheel and supplied fuel. It set ambitious goals and directed the private sector with sticks and carrots, and private firms, particularly *chaebols,* functioned as engines. What then made it possible for the government to become so strong in Korea? What made Korean technocrats smart enough to make their intervention relatively effective amid widespread and generally inefficient government intervention in most of the Third World? How has Korean government learned relatively effectively from Japanese experience?

First, when Park Chung Hee seized power in 1961, he was single-minded in his goal to industrialize Korea and transform its subsistent agricultural economy into an industrialized one in spite of the odds against it. Toward this end, he created a highly centralized, strong government to plan and implement ambitious economic development programs. The government was vested with power to license important business projects to private firms and set the direction of industrialization. Commercial banks were nationalized to allocate resources for industrial projects according to national priority. To push industrialization at the fastest possible speed, Park borrowed heavily from abroad rather than waiting patiently for domestic savings to be formed. This mechanism of channelling low-cost foreign finance to private firms further strengthened his centralized power. Then, with a small group of competent economists to advise him, he made all important decisions himself.[5] As a former army general, he was literally a field commanding general of Korea's industrialization drive.

Another important government means to consolidate its power over the private sector was in the handling of illicit wealth accumulation charges. The Park regime arrested thirteen leaders of large business conglomerates charging that they had engaged in illicit and illegal behavior in accumulating wealth during the corrupt Rhee years, 1948–1960, demonstrating that the government was in a powerful position to prosecute them. The government soon released most of the accused businessmen who promised to comply with the government in undertaking some of the major industrial projects, laying a ground rule of government dominance over the private sector during the Park regime through the 1970s.

Second, the centralized decision making by the president was relatively effective and efficient, compared with other developing countries, owing to competent technocrats who formulated and implemented development programs. Cultural values plus a selection process enabled the Korean government to staff its ministries in charge of industrialization programs with the most talented and best-educated young people. Confucian tradition, which imbued respect for scholars over farmers, craftsmen, and merchants and the civil service over all others, attracted well-educated young people to public service despite its low wages.[6] Except for political appointments at the cabinet level, examinations are used in selecting and in many cases promoting civil servants. Together with merit-based personnel evaluation, the system produced "meritocratic elites."[7] Successfully passing the highly competitive examination for the middle-level civil service is one of the most prestigious achievements for a young man in Korea. Such prestige enabled the government to recruit the cream of the leading universities.

Third, Korea had the broadest base from which to learn the Japanese experience effectively. Both Korea and Taiwan had been occupied by the Japanese, but Taiwanese leaders came from the mainland after 1949. In contrast, Korean political leaders and technocrats in the 1960s

26 EVOLUTION OF PUBLIC POLICY

and 1970s not only mastered the Japanese language but also acquired a significant understanding of Japan's culture and social system during the 1910–1945 Japanese occupation of Korea. President Park, for example, was one of a few who had been trained at the Japanese Military Academy. Many of his advisers and technocrats had also been educated in Japan or in Korea by Japanese during the occupation, studying the Japanese experience in detail. Even in 1990, 250,000 South Korean high school students were learning the Japanese language, accounting for about 70 percent of all non-Japanese high school students around the world studying Japanese.[8] A survey showed that the number of persons studying Japanese outside Japan had more than tripled in ten years to 1.62 million in 1993, and Koreans account for more than half of them.[9]

Although Alice Amsden concludes that on average American-trained Korean economists tend to accept the Anglo-Saxon model as the best solution to Korea,[10] no nation could profit more from an understanding of Japanese industrial success than Korea, given the geographical and cultural proximity and historical relations.[11]

Given the background, what policy mechanisms has the government used in facilitating technological learning in industry? How has the government role evolved in response to the rapidly changing economic environment?

INDUSTRIAL POLICY: DEMAND SIDE OF TECHNOLOGY

Korea's "developmental state" was at the wheel of its industrialization drive, at least through the 1970s.[12] In its efforts to create conditions for industrial growth and to ensure the transition from one stage to the next, the government used a complex web of direct and indirect policy instruments to define growth targets and discipline businesses to reach them. These instruments have largely been employed toward the following objectives: (1) the deliberate promotion of big business as an engine of technological learning, achieved through a systematic and comprehensive array of subsidies and incentives, (2) ambitious export-oriented industrialization, achieved by pushing the private sector into crises to reach imposed targets while providing incentives to make the crises creative rather than destructive, (3) the promotion of technologically advanced heavy and chemical industries, accomplished through even more critical crises, and (4) the repression of labor to maintain industrial peace, providing a conducive environment for learning.

Big Business

To overcome the disadvantage of a small domestic market and to exploit the stable nature of mature technologies on which initial industrialization strategy was to be built, the Korean government intentionally created large firms, *chaebols*. These organizations were deemed necessary to marshal the scale economies inherent in mature technologies, which would be used to attack government-designated strategic industries, producing export growth to fuel an advancing economy. A *chaebol* is a business group consisting of varied corporate enterprises engaged in diversified business areas and typically owned and managed by one or two interrelated family groups.[13]

The government helped the capital formation as well as the subsequent diversification of the *chaebols*. It sold Japanese colonial properties and state-owned enterprises to selected local entrepreneurs on favorable terms during the inflationary period, handing the local entrepreneurs windfalls. Owning all commercial banks in the early years, the government then provided these firms with scarce foreign currency and preferential financing at the official rates, both of which were only half the real market rate. The government also gave them large import-substitution projects and guaranteed the foreign loans. Foreign debt burdens resulting from currency devaluation were compensated with increased low-interest loans, further reducing the risks for these businesses.[14]

Their resulting huge growth enabled the *chaebols* to dominate Korea's industrial scene and stand out as world-class multinational corporations. Samsung, Daewoo, Ssangyong, and Sunkyong, as mentioned earlier, were among *Fortune* magazine's 100 largest industrial corporations in 1993. Including the two *chaebols*, Hyundai and LG, that did not reveal their group revenues all six rank in the top 100 global industrial enterprises.[15] Korea, sixth in the rank of firms included in the global 100, was preceded only by the United States, Japan, Germany, the United Kingdom, and France. This is especially noteworthy when Korea is compared with other Third World countries; only one state-owned petroleum corporation in each of Brazil, Venezuela, and Mexico made the list. Only Korea among these nations places private, nonpetroleum industrial corporations on it.[16] Six other *chaebols*, also among the global 500, have been powerhouses for Korea's industrialization.

The Korean government managed the *chaebols* relatively effectively compared with similar conditions in other catching-up countries. The government effectively disciplined the *chaebols* by penalizing poor performers and rewarding only good ones, a marked difference from big-business promotion efforts in other developing countries. Good performers were rewarded with further licenses to expand. The government rewarded entrants to risky enterprises with industrial licenses in more lucrative sectors, thus leading them to further diversification. In contrast, the government refused to bail out relatively large-scale, badly managed, bankrupt firms in otherwise healthy industries, appointing better managed *chaebols* to take them over.[17]

> President Park believed that even private projects in the First Economic Development Plan should be completed as scheduled so as not to make them turn into a burden to the government, because the government fully guaranteed the foreign loans. Personally, President Park checked and reviewed the development of all important projects, both public and private.[18]

In addition, *chaebols* that relied entirely on political collusion rather than on performance could not survive long, as they lost political support when power shifted from one hand to another. In contrast, better managed *chaebols* have endured and survived in a series of political power shifts.[19] As a result, only three of the ten largest *chaebols* in 1965—Samsung, LG, and Ssangyong—made the list in 1975. Similarly, seven of the ten largest in 1975 made the list in 1985. In fact, few of the original *chaebols* have survived. Most of them have evolved dynamically from small businesses in the midst of political turmoil, largely through rapid learning under effective strategic and organizational management.[20]

The *chaebols'* rapid growth and diversification have enormously affected industrial structure and market concentration in Korea. By 1977, 93 percent of all commodities and 62 percent of all shipments were produced under monopoly, duopoly, or oligopoly conditions in which the top three producers accounted for more than 60 percent of market share. The ten largest *chaebols* accounted for 48.1 percent of GNP in 1980, making Korean industry even more highly concentrated than that of Taiwan or Japan. Total factor productivity as well as output, however, grew faster in Korea's highly concentrated economy than in that of almost any other country.[21]

Chaebols played a crucial role in the rapid acquisition of technological capability in Korea. They were in the most advantageous position to attract the cream of the best universities. They had organizational and technical resources to identify, negotiate, and finance foreign technology transfer and assimilate and improve imported technologies. They also played a major role in drastically expanding and deepening R&D activities in Korea in the 1980s and 1990s. As a result, by the end of the 1970s, Korea had the largest textile plant, the largest plywood plant, the largest shipyard, the largest cement plant, and the largest heavy machinery plant in the world.

Export Promotion

The import-substitution policy played an important role in creating demand for foreign technology transfer.[22] Since there was no local capability to establish and operate production systems, local entrepreneurs had to rely completely on foreign sources for production processes, product specifications, production know-how, technical personnel, and components and parts. Studies in the electronics, machinery, steel, computer, and pharmaceutical industries demonstrate that import substitution under protection was one of the most powerful instruments that facilitated technology transfer from abroad, leading to the emergence of new industries and the introduction of more sophisticated products in existing industries.[23]

The export drive was a more important policy. The Korean government made exports a life-or-death struggle in order to achieve economic growth goals. The Korean government designated so-called strategic industries for import substitution and export promotion. Plywood, textiles, consumer electronics, and automobiles in the 1960s and steel, shipbuilding, construction services, and machinery in the 1970s are examples.

The strategic industries, which were created in violation of their static comparative advantage, had to suffer from high costs in addition to infant-industry growing pains. To help the industries overcome these problems, the government sheltered the domestic market from foreign competition. The average effective rate of protection was atypically high for the strategic industries. In some, protection was quickly lifted as firms accomplished a rapid rite of passage from infant to exporter. But in others, where technology was complex and marketing more elaborate, protection lasted relatively long, providing a lengthier period of incubation.[24] The United States benignly overlooked Korea's protected market well into the 1970s.

30 EVOLUTION OF PUBLIC POLICY

The government pushed firms with ambitious goals. It instituted the export-targeting system in the 1960s as a regular instrument to assess industrial success. Annual targets were assigned to major commodity groups, which were allocated to related industrial associations. They were also assigned by destinations, which were allocated to Korean embassies in respective countries. The Ministry of Trade and Industry maintained a situation room to monitor export performance. The data were then reported to the Monthly Trade Promotion Conference attended by the president of the nation, cabinet members, heads of major financial institutions, business association leaders, and representatives of major export firms. The conference served to solve many problems encountered by exporting firms through guidance and the president's final decisions.[25]

"Sticks" in the form of administrative guidance (a euphemism for Korean government orders) forced firms to reach its goals. If a firm did not respond as expected to particular goals, programs, or incentives, its tax returns were subject to careful examination or its application for bank credit was studiously ignored, or its outstanding bank loans were not renewed. Government agencies often showed no hesitation in resorting to command backed by compulsion. It usually did not take long for a Korean firm to learn that it would be better to get along by going along.[26] In other words, the role of the government was much stronger in Korea than in Japan and Taiwan, especially during the 1960s and 1970s. And it worked.

The government also cajoled firms with incentives, borrowing heavily from abroad and channeling the funds into export-oriented investments at below-market interest rates. Firms were granted unrestricted and tariff-free access to imported intermediate inputs and automatic access to bank loans for working capital for all export activities, even when the domestic money supply was being tightened. These firms also had unrestricted access to foreign capital goods and were encouraged to integrate vertically in order to sustain international competitiveness. These incentives operated automatically and constituted the crux of the Korean system of export promotion. Furthermore, the rationing of longer-term bank loans was used as a carrot to draw firms to new paths of exporting, encouraging diversification, and to export more than ever. These incentives, offered to all exporting firms, were particularly effective when combined with the greater organizational, financial, and political leverage of the *chaebols,* which grew even larger.[27] Exporters also benefited from a variety of tariff exemptions, accelerated depreciation, exemptions from value-added taxes, and duty-free imports of raw materials and spare parts. Tax holidays and reduced rates on public utilities further boosted corporate profitability. Assignment of lucrative import licenses was linked to export performance.[28]

With the government's sticks and carrots, Korea's total exports increased from a mere $175 million, or 5.8 percent of GNP, in 1965 to $1,132 million, or 12 percent of GNP, by 1971. With an average annual growth rate of 36.5 percent, Korea rose from number 101 in the rank of exporters in 1962 to fourteenth by 1986.[29]

How has the import-substitution and export-promotion policy affected technological learning in industry? While it created new business opportunities, it also created crises for firms to invest heavily in technological learning to acquire foreign technologies and assimilate and improve them in order to survive in the highly competitive international market.

As a result, firms in export-oriented industries (EOI) learned significantly more rapidly and in turn grew faster than firms in import-substituting industries (ISI). Likewise, countries with export-oriented industrialization grew faster than those with import-substituting industrialization. The average annual economic growth rate for EOI countries was 9.5 and 7.7 percent, respectively, for 1963–1973 and 1973–1985 compared with 4.1 and 2.5 percent for ISI countries. The real per capita income growth rate was 6.9 and 5.9 percent for the same periods for the former as compared with 1.6 and −0.1 for the latter, as the ISI group had a higher population growth rate.

Heavy and Chemical Industry Promotion

By the late 1960s, Korean government policymakers recognized the necessity of gradually restructuring the economy from labor-intensive light industries to more technology-intensive heavy industries. They understood the importance of developing the technological capability to do so, as Korea's competitive advantage in light industries was shifting to second tier catching-up countries, such as Thailand, Malaysia, China, and Indonesia.

A major change in international political conditions, however, prompted the Korean government to invest for the heavy and chemical industry program ahead of schedule. Frustrated by its protracted war in Vietnam, the U.S. government announced the Nixon doctrine in 1969, signaling its decision not to commit its ground forces in Asian future conflicts, and the Nixon administration withdrew one of two

U.S. Army divisions from Korea in 1971. President Park became ob-
sessed with acquiring a self-reliant national defense capability by developing heavy and chemical industries (HCIs) at a far greater intensity
and in a far shorter time than previously envisioned. $12.7 billion
was poured into HCIs, accounting for more than 75 percent of total
manufacturing investment in 1973–1979.[30] Steel, shipbuilding, heavy
machinery, petrochemical, industrial electronics, and nonferrous metal
industries were created by the HCI promotion. As a result, it took only
fifteen years for the ratio of value added in light industries over HCI
to fall from 4 to 1 in Korea, whereas the same shift took twenty-five
years in Japan and fifty years in the United States.[31]

   This hasty creation of HCIs on a gigantic scale without adequate
preparation in technological capability, more for military purposes
than for economic rationality, resulted in a rapid rise in foreign debt
from $2.2 billion in 1970 to $27.1 billion in 1980.[32] It also bred misallocation of resources, rapid inflation, wage increases far in excess of
productivity gains, and further concentration of economic powers in
several *chaebols* involved in HCIs.

   The most significant effect of the hasty HCI promotion, however,
was a major crisis in technological learning. Lacking capability, the
chaebols had to rely almost entirely on foreign sources for technology.
Tasks required to assimilate imported technology were so far beyond
the capability available at these firms that the HCI program imposed
a major crisis in setting up and starting up plants, let alone mastering
them. Firms were forced to assimilate technology very rapidly and
upgrade capacity utilization by expediting learning in order to survive.
Later chapters present more detailed discussions of how firms in these
industries expedited their technological learning to turn the crisis into
an opportunity.

Industrial Peace

"Economy is a tender flower. It does not flourish in the soil of war or
social unrest," said Paul Samuelson.[33] Likewise, the multinational firm
as a buyer, supplier, and investor considers industrial peace, among
other things, one of the most important factors in developing and
expanding businesses with firms in catching-up countries.

   In attempting to create a conducive environment, in which government's development goals could be achieved without interruptions,
the Korean government, as the central orchestrator for economic development and exports, also emerged as the responsible agency to
control labor movements and maintain industrial peace. The govern-

ment's leading role in repressing labor was a consistent policy through the late 1980s. Although the formal ban on unions had been lifted in the early 1960s, the legal framework in which unions could function was so restrictive that it virtually eliminated the possibility of organizing any genuine independent unions.[34] Furthermore, the government used the Korean Central Intelligence Agency (CIA) to spy on and repress labor as part of a broader economic strategy through the 1970s.[35] As a result, workers became exceedingly docile. For example, between 1979 and 1984, average lost workdays per 100 workers per year was only half a day in Korea compared with two in Japan and fifty in the United States.[36] A drastic shift toward political democratization in the late 1980s, however, triggered the explosion of labor unrest, which is discussed in Chapter 3.

Many intellectuals, in Korea and abroad, criticized the dreadful negative side of many of the government's practices to suppress labor movements, but it at least provided Korean firms with uninterrupted opportunities to learn cumulatively and discontinuously, making undoubtedly significant contributions to rapid industrialization. Such a repressive policy retarded the growth of trade unions and workers taking part in industrial democracy. Scandinavian and German experiences show that industrial democracy supports and encourages innovation.

In short, the government had been at the core of Korea's industrialization in the 1960s and 1970s. Some say that the government played the role of chairman in Korea, Inc., while *chaebols* functioned as its production units.[37] The government role included not only policy formulation but also the techniques of policy implementation, using an array of direct and indirect incentives and sanctions to harness the private sector in achieving rapid technological learning and, in turn, high growth.

Shift of Economic Environment and Public Policy

The economic environment for Korea, however, changed significantly in the 1980s, for several reasons. First, the world economy generally slowed down in the 1980s, particularly affecting outward-looking economies like Korea. Second, in the wake of rising trade imbalance, North America and Europe moved toward protectionist policies, making it increasingly difficult for Korea to sustain export growth in industries that led its export-oriented strategy in the past. Third, Korea lost its competitiveness in low-wage-based labor-intensive industries, as its real wage rose at an average annual growth rate of 5.8 percent in the

1960s and 7.5 percent in the 1970s. Concomitantly, other developing countries with much lower wage rates were rapidly catching up with Korea in these industries. Fourth, advanced countries, particularly Japan, were increasingly reluctant to transfer technology to Korea as it attempted to enter industries that they dominated. Fifth, Korea was forced to change its copyright and patent laws, preempting the imitative reverse-engineering of foreign products.

In the face of an increasingly unfavorable environment in the 1980s and 1990s, the Korean government set out on a major policy shift. It attempted to reduce government intervention and introduce market mechanisms and to undertake structural change toward the development of more technology-based industries. The policy shift included, among other things, antitrust legislation, trade liberalization, financial liberalization, promotion of small and medium-size enterprises, foreign investment liberalization, and shifting emphasis on innovation-related activities.

Antitrust and Fair Trade

The *chaebols'* increasing economic power gave rise to monopolistic abuses such as creating scarcities, price gouging, and predatory behavior in the domestic market. In response, the government shifted its policy on *chaebols* from promotion in the 1960s and 1970s to the regulation of their growth in the 1980s by adopting a policy of economic democratization. The Fair Trade Act of 1980, along the lines of American antitrust legislation, included, among other things, the prohibition of unfair cartel practices and mutual investment among the *chaebols'* affiliated companies, a ceiling on investment by and credit to large *chaebols*, and restrictions on their vertical and horizontal integration. The government also directed the thirty largest *chaebols* to restructure their sprawling businesses around three or fewer core sectors.

However, the *chaebols* continued to grow, with economic concentration increasing further until the mid-1980s and declining slightly thereafter; the number of affiliated companies of the ten largest chaebols increased from 77 in 1974 to 667 including 365 abroad in 1994.[38] and the combined sales of the five largest *chaebols* as a percentage of GNP increased from 12.8 percent in 1975 to 52.4 percent in 1984 and decreased slightly to 46.5 in 1993.[39] The number of *chaebols* designated by the government as dominating their respective markets increased from 105 in 1981 to 216 in 1985, but only ten were accused of having abused their economic power. Of 1,172 applications for vertical and horizontal integration, only two were rejected by the government.

Why? Although the antitrust policy made a small dent in the mid-1980s, the economic power of *chaebols* and their collusion with political power were so strong that the government could not implement some announced policy programs, showing a significant gap between what it intended to do and what it actually could do. In addition, the government bailed out insolvent enterprises to mitigate their impact on downstream sectors, not to tarnish the credibility of *chaebols* in the international market. As a result, some of them, anticipating a government rescue, expanded well beyond their evident financial capability and some postponed adjustments to market changes. In many cases, the government was under pressure to accept economic reality rather than fulfill economic justice.

Then, facing accelerating globalization in the 1990s, the government once again shifted its policy on *chaebols* from regulation to liberalization by revising the Antitrust and Fair Trade Act. Restrictions on the credit controls of the thirty largest *chaebols* were lifted, provided that their firms reduced internal ownership to less than 20 percent, raised capital-to-assets ratio above 20 percent, and offered more than 69 percent of its shares to the public. Such a liberalization policy was designed to enable *chaebols* to compete freely in the expanding global market. Although those firms' ownership and management structures have changed significantly in the past decade,[40] the new policy is expected to make significant progress in the separation of management and ownership in *chaebols*. LG Business Group, for instance, announced a plan to reduce its internal ownership (interfirm and family ownership combined) from 39 percent in 1995 to 19.5 percent by 1999 and family ownership from 5 percent to 3 percent during the same period.

In short, after promoting the formation and growth of *chaebols* during the first two decades and attempting unsuccessfully to regulate them in the 1980s, the government decided to limit protection and intervention and rely more on market mechanisms. *Chaebols* have been and will be the dominant factor in Korea's industrialization and globalization.

Trade Liberalization

In drastic contrast to the government's export-targeting system, the situation room, and heavy export subsidy programs in the 1960s, Korea's export trade was significantly liberalized during the 1970s.

36 EVOLUTION OF PUBLIC POLICY

Most of the ad hoc incentive measures used in the 1960s were abolished, and Korea's export trade was almost completely liberalized by 1982. The ratio of net export subsidies to the exchange rate dropped, for instance, from 36.6 in 1963 to 6.7 in 1970 to 0.4 in 1982.[41] In other words, although export-oriented industrialization continued in the 1980s and 1990s, Korean firms have been able to compete in the international market without government subsidies in these decades.

Import policies were also liberalized in the 1980s. The government promulgated the Tariff Reform Act in 1984, which was aimed to phase in general reductions in tariff levels. As a result, the import liberalization ratio—defined as the ratio of the number of unrestricted items to the total—rose from 51 percent in 1973 to 95.2 percent by 1988 and to 98.6 percent in 1994. The government also brought down the average tariff rate from 26.7 percent in 1984 to 7.9 percent by 1994. Nontariff barriers such as delay in custom clearance and tax examination of foreign car purchasers were also largely eliminated in recent years. As a result, imports increased, for instance, by 20.1 percent in 1989 compared with a 2.8 percent increase in exports, forcing Korean firms to compete, with little government assistance, against multinational firms not only in the export market but also in the domestic market.[42]

Financial Liberalization

In contrast to its monopoly of the financial sector in the 1960s and 1970s, the government has also taken major steps to liberalize the financial market. For example, the government reduced the regulation of nonbank financial intermediaries, many of which had long been controlled by *chaebols*, resulting in a significant rise in their share of total deposit liabilities in the 1980s. The denationalization of commercial banks led to a shift of significant share from government hands to the *chaebols*. The conversion of local short-term financing firms to either securities firms or commercial banks in 1990 marked another important step forward in restructuring the financial sector, thus allowing increased participation of private firms.

Although the government exercised its influence on financial institutions through its power to authorize the opening of new branch offices, it lost its teeth in allocating financial resources. Nevertheless, the protection of the local market from foreign financial institutions resulted in gross inefficiencies; Korean banks are loaded with nonperforming loans—8.8 percent of total credits in 1992.[43] The timetable has been set to completely liberalize the financial sector by 1997 in preparing to join the OECD, which requires Korea to make obligatory adjustments including complete financial liberalization.[44]

SME Promotion

A major government mistake in the 1960s and 1970s was neglecting to encourage balanced growth between large firms and small firms. It was the late 1970s when the government belatedly realized the importance of small and medium-size enterprises (SMEs) in healthy economic growth. The government began promoting SMEs, particularly technology-based small firms, to remedy the imbalance between the large- and small-business sectors. The government established sanctuaries for SMEs, designating 205 business territories where neither large corporations nor their affiliates can intrude. The Compulsory Lending Ratio program stipulates that the nationwide commercial banks should extend more than 35 percent of total loans and that regional banks offer more than 80 percent of their total loans to SMEs.

The government also took the initiative in establishing the venture capital industry as a means to advancing the emergence of technology-based small firms in which the private sector had no interest. Specifically, the government enacted a special law to establish the first venture capital firm, which was jointly funded by the government and a group of private firms. The government took a further step by enacting the Small and Medium Enterprise Formation Act in 1986, leading to the emergence of more than thirty venture capital firms, all jointly vested by the government and the private sector.

Preoccupied with *chaebols,* the government failed to learn from Japanese experience in developing an institutional framework for technology diffusion to SMEs. Only in 1979 did the government begin establishing several important institutions, such as Small and Medium Industries Promotion Corporations, Korea Trade Promotion Corporation, and SME-related R&D centers, as a way to support SMEs in developing technological capability and promoting their exports. The government also earmarked a significant portion of its investment fund, W (won) 2.5 trillion ($3.1 billion) in 1994, to promote SME modernization. Despite various support schemes, the number of SMEs that went bankrupt increased steadily over the years—6,156 in 1991 to 10,488 in 1994—due mainly to increasing imports from low-waged China and other Asian countries. The severe competitive rules set by the World Trade Organization will make it even more difficult for SMEs to survive.

38 EVOLUTION OF PUBLIC POLICY

Intellectual Property Rights

In Korea, as in other catching-up countries, imitative reverse engineering of existing foreign products was a backbone of industrialization
through the mid-1980s. Even advanced countries today rely heavily
on copying foreign products and refuse to honor copyrights until they
develop enough capability to stand on their own. The United States,
for instance, refused to join the Bern Convention on copyrights for
more than 100 years, saying that as a developing country it needed
to retain easy access to advanced foreign works, an argument still used
by many developing countries.[45] Japan and Switzerland refused to
recognize product patents until 1976 and 1978, respectively, when
they developed enough capability to innovate their own new materials.
For instance, they invented ninety-three and eighty-seven new materials, respectively, in the year they introduced product patent systems.[46]
Now the United States is the world's international property rights (IPR)
policeman, forcing ill-prepared catching-up countries to respect IPR.

Under U.S. pressure, Korea introduced new legislation in 1986 to
maintain IPR, preempting the reverse engineering of foreign products.
This hit all industries hard, particularly pharmaceuticals and chemicals.
The new statute also introduced an arbitration system for compulsory
licensing and increased penalties for infringement.

Enforcement of the law was not easy in Korea, where, as in other
Asian countries, people don't believe in owning an idea or thought
and consequently in paying for it. Frequent police raids in major
cities and lawsuits have, however, resulted in a rapid disappearance
of pirated products in the local market. The number of cases brought
to court by police and lawyers almost quintupled in four years, from
2,254 in 1989 to 10,423 in 1993.[47] Although Seoul's Itaewon Street
still draws foreign tourists for counterfeit goods produced by small
underground shops, a tide swept through major industries, eliminating
duplicative reverse-engineering practices to a large extent. Such forced
adoption of IPR resulted in significant upward pressure on costs of
Korean products because of increased royalties. On the other hand,
it forced Korean firms to intensify their technological efforts to innovate on their own.

Shifting Emphasis

The focus of industrial policy has shifted from the promotion of strategic sectors to promotion of innovation-related activities. In the 1960s
and 1970s, special incentives—tax concessions, custom rebates, access

to foreign exchange, and other forms of protection or enhancement—
were granted to strategic industries to make them competitive at a
world level. In contrast, the government abolished all industry-specific
promotion acts introduced in the 1960s and 1970s and instead legis-
lated a new Industrial Promotion Act in 1986 that ties all incentives
to special industrial activities such as R&D and human resource development. In the late 1980s, however, the government again designated
several high-technology industries, including information technology
and aircraft, for support, but its role in these industries is much more
limited than that in labor-intensive industries in the previous two
decades.

In short, the focus of industrial policy related to creating the demand for technological learning has shifted significantly. The earlier
policy period was marked by heavy government intervention. The
new period focuses on the introduction of market principles such as
enhancing competition through the control of *chaebols'* growth, trade
liberalization, financial liberalization, investment liberalization, and
support for innovation-related activities. In other words, government's
developmental role has substantially weakened over the years, but
some claim that the government still remains relatively powerful in
Korea compared with other countries.[48]

TECHNOLOGY POLICY: SUPPLY SIDE OF TECHNOLOGY

The government not only stimulates the demand side of technological
learning through industrial policy instruments but also gives rise to
the supply of technological capability through technology policy instruments.[49] The technology flow perspective—technology transfer,
technology diffusion, and indigenous R&D—provides insight into understanding how developing countries catch up with advanced countries.

Technology Transfer

Lacking technological capability at the outset of its economic development, Korea had to rely on foreign technology imports. However,
Korea's policies on foreign licenses (FLs) was quite restrictive in the
1960s. In the case of manufacturing, general guidelines issued in 1968
gave priority to technology that promoted exports, developed intermediate products for capital goods industries, or brought a diffusion effect
to other sectors. The guidelines also set a ceiling for royalties at 3
percent and duration at five years. This restrictive policy on licensing

40   EVOLUTION OF PUBLIC POLICY

strengthened local licensees' bargaining power on generally available mature technologies, leading to lower prices for technologies than would otherwise have been the case.[50]

The 1970s, however, saw a significant change in national policy. In an attempt to attract sophisticated technologies in response to the changing international environment, restrictions on foreign licensing were relaxed in 1970 and 1978, allowing, for one, a higher royalty rate. As a result, royalty payments for FLs increased significantly, as shown in Table 2-1, from $0.8 million during the first five-year economic development plan (1962–1966) to $451.4 million in the fourth one (1977–1981). This increase is insignificant compared with FLs in the 1980s. Most foreign licensing in the early years was associated with technical assistance needed to train local engineers to run turnkey plants.

Table 2-1   Foreign Technology Transfer to Korea, 1962–1993
(in millions of dollars)

Source	1962–1966	1967–1971	1972–1976
1. Foreign Direct Investment			
Japan	8.3	89.7	627.1
United States	25.0	95.3	135.0
All others	12.1	33.6	117.3
Total	45.4	218.6	879.4
2. Foreign Licensing			
Japan	–	5.0	58.7
United States	0.6	7.8	21.3
All others	0.2	3.5	16.6
Total	0.8	16.3	96.6
3. Capital-Goods Imports			
Japan	148	1,292	4,423
United States	75	472	1,973
All others	93	777	2,445
Total	316	2,541	8,841

SOURCES: Korea Industrial Technology Association for foreign direct investment and foreign licensing data; Korean Society for Advancement of Machinery Industry for capital-goods import data.

Continued overleaf

In contrast to the gradual relaxation of government control on foreign licensing, the government policy on foreign direct investment (FDI) saw a complete swing in the 1960s and 1970s. The FDI policy was quite free in the 1960s, permitting any form of bona fide foreign capital, including fully owned subsidiaries. But few foreign investments were made during the 1960s, primarily owing to questions about Korea's political stability and its uncertain economic outlook.

The government reversed its FDI policy in the 1970s, tightening its control. Joint ventures received higher priority than wholly owned subsidiaries. A general guideline was adopted setting three criteria: first, competition with domestic firms was seldom allowed in both domestic and international markets; second, export requirements were forced on FDIs; and third, foreign participation ratios were basically limited to 50 percent. Korea was one of the few countries with restric-

	1977–1981	1982–1986	1987–1991	1992–1993	Total
	300.9	876.2	2,122.3	441.1	4,465.5
	235.7	581.6	1,477.7	719.9	3,270.1
	184.0	309.6	2,035.9	777.8	3,472.9
	720.6	1,767.7	5,635.9	1,938.8	11,208.5
	139.8	323.7	1,383.6	619.1	2,529.9
	159.2	602.7	2,121.9	870.9	3,784.4
	152.4	258.5	853.9	307.0	1,592.1
	451.4	1,184.9	4,359.4	1,797.0	7,906.4
	14,269	20,673	54,641	25,337	120,783
	6,219	12,434	33,098	18,832	73,103
	7,490	17,871	33,213	22,983	84,872
	27,978	50,978	120,952	67,152	278,758

42 EVOLUTION OF PUBLIC POLICY

tive regulations on FDI when technology was not a critical element and necessary mature technologies could be easily acquired through mechanisms other than FLs or FDI, for example, reverse-engineering. Under this restrictive policy environment, Korea induced the FDIs, as shown in Table 2-1.

Consequently, the size of FDI and its proportion to total external borrowing were significantly lower in Korea than in other newly industrializing countries (NICs). For example, Korea's stock of FDI in 1983 was only 7 percent that of Brazil, 23 percent that of Singapore, and less than half that of Taiwan and Hong Kong. The proportion of FDI to total external borrowing was only 6.1 percent in Korea compared with 91.9 percent in Singapore, 45 percent in Taiwan, and 21.8 percent in Brazil.[51] The comparative figure reflects Korea's explicit policy of promoting its independence from multinationals in management control.

As a result, unlike these other countries, FDI had a minimal effect on the Korean economy. For example, FDI's contribution to the growth of Korean GNP in 1972–1980 amounted only to 1.3 percent, while its contribution to total and manufacturing value-added was only 1.1 percent and 4.8 percent, respectively, in 1971 and 4.5 percent and 14.2 percent, respectively, in 1980.[52]

Instead, Korea promoted technology transfer in the early years through the procurement of turnkey plants and capital goods. The rapid growth of the Korean economy required commensurate growth in investment for production facilities. However, government policy had been biased in favor of the importation of turnkey plants and foreign capital goods as a way to strengthen international competitiveness of industries using capital goods. Such a policy led to massive imports of foreign capital goods at the cost of retarding the development of the local capital goods industry. Protection of the machinery industry was relatively low until the first half of 1971, giving capital goods users almost free access to foreign capital goods. For example, chemical, cement, steel, and paper industries, established in the 1960s and early 1970s, all resorted to the purchase of turnkey plants and foreign capital goods for their initial setup. But Korean firms assimilated imported technologies so rapidly that they managed to undertake subsequent expansions and improvements with little assistance from foreigners.

The massive imports of foreign capital goods became a major source of learning through reverse-engineering by Korean firms.[53] Of the three categories of technology transfer listed in Table 2-1, capital goods imports far surpassed other means of technology transfer in terms of value through 1981. Capital goods imports were worth twenty-one times the value of FDI and seventy times the value of FLs. The total value of capital goods imports was sixteen times that of the other two categories combined. Although the values of different modes of technology transfer are not strictly comparable since they measure different things, they are useful indicators when compared with other countries. Among NICs, the proportion of capital goods imports to total technology transfer was highest in Korea, suggesting that Korea had acquired more technology from advanced countries through the importation of capital goods than through any other means when compared with such NICs as Argentina, Brazil, India, and Mexico.[54]

Various instruments also played an important role in lubricating the inflow of foreign capital goods to Korea. For example, the slight overvaluation of the local currency, tariff exemptions on imported capital goods, and the financing of purchases by suppliers' credits, which carried low rates of interest relative to those on the domestic market, all worked to increase the attractiveness of capital goods imports.

In short, Korea restricted FDI but promoted technology transfer through other means such as capital goods imports in the early years. Capital was acquired in the form of foreign loans. Such a policy, designed to maintain Korea's management independence from foreign multinationals, was effective in forcing Korean firms to take the initiative and a central role in learning, that is, acquiring, assimilating, and improving imported technologies, rather than relying entirely on foreign sources.

After two decades of restrictive policy toward foreign direct investment and foreign licensing, Korea liberalized its technology transfer policies in the 1980s and 1990s. Progressively more sophisticated foreign technologies were needed to sustain its international competitiveness in high value-added industries. The proportion of Korea's 999 industrial subsectors open to FDI rose from 44 percent in the 1970s to 66 percent in 1984 and to 90.6 percent by 1994. In response to complaints from foreign investors about extremely cumbersome bureaucratic redtape, in 1995 the government introduced the automatic approval system, the expansion of tax and other incentives for investment in strategic high technology sectors, and a one-stop service center.[55]

New FDI in manufacturing has, however, declined steadily in recent years from $1,069 million in 1991 to $527 million in 1993. In contrast, foreign investment in service sectors has significantly increased, accounting for 27.4 percent of the total investment in 1992 and 72.8 percent in the first seven months of 1994.[56] In the 1960s and 1970s, foreign companies invested in Korea to reap cheap labor costs. Now foreign companies are not so willing to collaborate with Korean companies in relatively more technology-intensive areas.

Foreign licensing has been completely open for all industries and for all terms and conditions. The approval system—obtaining prior consent from the government—changed to the reporting system— simply informing the government.[57] The government plans to abolish the reporting system in the near future, except for technologies related to the defense industry.[58] As a result, technology transfer through licensing has soared recently. FLs increased from 247 in 1981 to 707 in 1993, reflecting the liberalized public policy as well as the private sector's aggressiveness in acquiring more sophisticated foreign technologies. Slight drops in the early 1980s and 1990s reflect economic recessions in Korea.

Table 2-1 also reveals that Korea relied heavily on both Japan and the United States for technology. These two countries accounted for more than 80 percent of FDI and more than 70 percent of FLs and capital goods imports during the first two decades of Korea's industrialization. Japan in particular had been the major source of technology for Korea in those years. Korea acquired its mature technologies mainly from Japan and exported its products to the United States in the early years. But the U.S. share of technology transfer has increased significantly in the 1990s. The proportion of foreign licensing cases from the United States increased from 28.4 percent in 1991 to 42.8 percent in 1994. In contrast, FLs from Japan decreased from 47.6 percent to 28.9 percent during the same period, indicating Japanese reluctance to transfer sophisticated technologies to Korea and Korea's preference for U.S. technologies in emerging areas.[59]

Technology Diffusion

In upgrading the overall technological capability of the economy, the effective diffusion of imported technology across firms within an industry and across industries within an economy is as, if not more, important as the acquisition of foreign technology. If technology is transferred successfully to a firm and its use is limited only to its original importer, it may give the firm monopoly power over other firms for a time; however, the economic effect of the technology may be considerably limited. Government interventions that create necessary institutions would give rise to the firm's learning from the domestic community, resulting in the effective acquisition of knowledge available elsewhere in the economy.

There may be many specialized diffusion agents, such as capital goods producers, consulting engineering firms, and public research institutes, which the government could promote for the diffusion of technology within the economy. But these agents were not effective in Korea in diffusing technology in the 1960s and 1970s.

The government's plan to develop the capital goods sector was initiated in 1968 but not seriously implemented until the mid-1970s. The development of local consulting engineering firms was promoted by the Engineering Service Promotion Law of 1973, which stipulated that, if possible, all engineering projects should be given to local firms as major contractors with foreign partners as minor participants. Such a scheme was aimed mainly at stimulating the emergence of local engineering firms and providing local firms with opportunities to learn from experienced foreigners. But local infant engineering service firms were not capable of playing the role of diffusion agent in the early years of industrialization.

In 1962 the government established a scientific and technological information center as a linking mechanism for disseminating technical information, but its use by industry was quite limited in the early years because mature products were easily imitated through reverse-engineering without the need to consult technical literature. In 1966 the government established a public research institute as a diffusion agent. But Korean researchers, mostly from academic fields or R&D centers in advanced countries, lacked the manufacturing know-how that was in greatest demand during the early years and failed to serve as diffusion agents. The most important diffusion agents the government unintentionally created were the government enterprises established in the 1950s and 1960s. Engineers who accumulated modern production experience in state-owned fertilizer and machinery plants spun off later to head engineering and production departments of private enterprises.

Only in the 1980s did the Korean government introduce an extensive network of government, public, and nonprofit (private) technical support systems to promote technology diffusion within the economy, particularly among SMEs.[60] Some of the support systems dated back to the 1970s but flourished in the 1980s with the growing importance of technology. Figure 2-2 presents a schematic diagram of institutional arrangements related to technology diffusion systems.

46 EVOLUTION OF PUBLIC POLICY

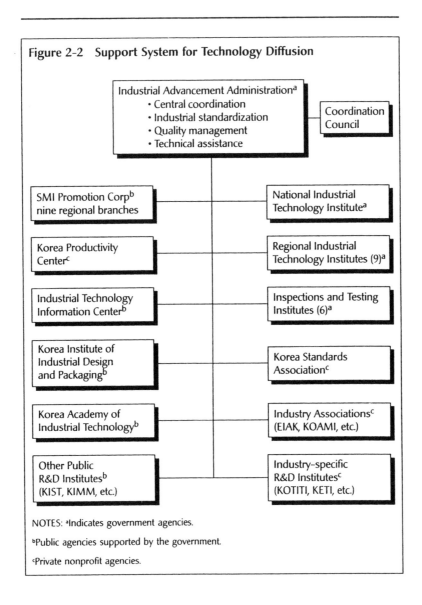

Figure 2-2   Support System for Technology Diffusion

Industrial Advancement Administration[a]
- Central coordination
- Industrial standardization
- Quality management
- Technical assistance

Coordination Council

SMI Promotion Corp[b]
nine regional branches

National Industrial Technology Institute[a]

Korea Productivity Center[c]

Regional Industrial Technology Institutes (9)[a]

Industrial Technology Information Center[b]

Inspections and Testing Institutes (6)[a]

Korea Institute of Industrial Design and Packaging[b]

Korea Standards Association[c]

Korea Academy of Industrial Technology[b]

Industry Associations[c] (EIAK, KOAMI, etc.)

Other Public R&D Institutes[b] (KIST, KIMM, etc.)

Industry-specific R&D Institutes[c] (KOTITI, KETI, etc.)

NOTES: [a]Indicates government agencies.

[b]Public agencies supported by the government.

[c]Private nonprofit agencies.

The Industrial Advancement Administration, a government agency, coordinates the functions of different technical support agencies for both large and small firms. The National Industrial Technology Institute and eleven regional industrial technology institutes, together with the Small and Medium Industry Promotion Corporation, constitute a national network of technical extension services, while the Korea Academy of Industrial Technology, together with other government R&D institutes (GRIs) and industry-specific R&D institutes under trade associations, comprise a core of an R&D network for technology diffusion. Several private, nonprofit technical support systems also play an important role in technology diffusion among SMEs. The Korea Standard Association with its national network and Korea Productivity Center promote technology diffusion among firms mainly through their educational and training programs on quality control, value engineering, physical distribution, and factory automation. In addition, the government introduced a scientific and technical information dissemination system by developing a data base in ten member institutions and integrating them through an on-line network.

In short, Korea developed, in the 1980s, an elaborate network of technical support systems for technology diffusion, which have evolved dynamically in response to changes in industries.

INDIGENOUS RESEARCH AND DEVELOPMENT

Korean firms acquired and assimilated foreign technology primarily through imitative engineering in the 1960s and 1970s, when relevant technology was readily available in a machine-embodied form and learning by doing was relatively easy. Consequently, none of the policy instruments to stimulate the country's own R&D were effective.

As Korea underwent structural adjustments and entered progressively more technology-intensive industries, the government focused more attention on indigenous R&D activities, primarily through two major mechanisms: direct R&D investment and indirect incentive packages. The government's direct investment is to develop the science and technology (S&T) infrastructure and to promote R&D at universities and GRIs. Its indirect incentive packages, including preferential finance and tax concessions, are aimed at stimulating increased industry R&D. Table 2-2 summarizes the foregoing discussions of industrial and science and technology policies as well as R&D policies discussed below.

Table 2-2   Industrial and Science and Technology Policies

Policies	1960s and 1970s	1980s and 1990s
Industrial Policies	Deliberate promotion of big businesses	Promotion of SMEs
	Export orientation	Export orientation
	Promotion of heavy and chemical industries	Antitrust and fair trade
	Repression of labor to maintain industrial peace	Trade liberalization
		Financial liberalization
		Intellectual property rights protection
		Shifting emphasis on R&D, manpower development
Science and Technology Policies	Restriction on FDI and FLs	Promotion of FDI and FLs
	Promotion of capital-goods import	Extensive diffusion networks
	Promotion of GRIs in lieu of university research	Promotion of university research
	Promotion of GRIs	Promotion of corporate R&D activities
		Promotion of national R&D projects

Science and Technology Infrastructure Development

Anticipating increasing demands for science and technology, the government established the Korea Institute of Science and Technology (KIST) in 1966 as an integrated technical center to support the industry's technological learning. As Korea's first multidisciplinary research institute, KIST covered a broad spectrum of activities in applied research ranging from project feasibility studies to R&D for new products and processes. KIST spent a large proportion of the nation's total R&D expenditure in its early years.

To keep pace with increasing sophistication and diversity, the government established several GRIs as spin-offs from KIST. Each was designed to develop in-depth capabilities in an area of high industrial priority: shipbuilding, marine resource, electronics, telecommunications, energy, machinery, and chemicals.

The government also created two science centers; Seoul Science

Park started in 1966 with three R&D institutes and three economic research institutes, but it failed to attract private R&D centers to the vicinity. Two of the three R&D institutes have been relocated. In contrast, Taedok Science Town, established in 1978 in an area 200 kilometers south of Seoul, boasts fourteen GRIs and three tertiary educational institutions and has attracted more than eleven corporate R&D laboratories. Eighteen more firms plan to establish their R&D laboratories in the town within a few years, making it the first high-technology valley in the country. But despite almost twenty years of existence, it has neither built a reputation for attracting world-class scientists, as Tsukuba has in Japan, nor become a bustling industrial park with technology-based SMEs that have large shares of world markets for personal computers and peripherals, as Hsinchu has in Taiwan.

The government also created an important milestone in 1975 by establishing a research-oriented graduate school of applied science and engineering, the Korea Advanced Institute of Science, offering both master's and Ph.D. programs, adding another in 1995. These schools draw the most highly qualified entrants by offering extraordinary incentives for students (e.g., full fellowships covering tuition, room, and board and exemption from military obligation).[61] These schools produce almost half of all Ph.D.s in science and engineering in Korea.

University R&D

Research endeavors in universities have been relatively underdeveloped. Their R&D expenditures increased significantly from W 572 million ($1.5 million) in 1971 to W 608 billion ($790 million) in 1994. While those institutions accounted for only 7.7 percent of the nation's R&D spending in 1994, they provided 33 percent of the nation's R&D manpower and 73.7 percent of its Ph.D.-level R&D personnel.

Government statistics indicate that basic research accounted for 14.4 percent, applied research for 23.8 percent, and development for the remaining 61.8 percent of the nation's total R&D expenditures in 1994. The statistics also show that the private sector accounted for 45.1 percent of the nation's basic research and 64.5 percent of applied research, while universities accounted for only 29.1 percent and 6.3 percent, respectively.[62] There is reason to doubt these figures for basic and applied research, particularly the share commanded by the private sector. Only fairly recently have the leading *chaebols* begun rather limited investment in applied research in their largest technology businesses such as semiconductors and information science. Basic research has been even less developed.

The Korean government's attempts to promote university R&D

activities began in the mid-1970s. Frustrated in its efforts to reform the undergraduate teaching-oriented tradition in education, the government conceived a dual system: since almost all universities under the Ministry of Education, public or private, were essentially teaching-oriented, the Ministry of Science and Technology (MOST) founded a research-oriented S&T school in 1975 and another in 1995, establishing a new research tradition in university education.[63]

The government also enacted the Basic Research Promotion Law in 1989, explicitly targeting basic research as one of the nation's top technological priorities. Emulating the U.S. experience, in 1989 the government introduced a scheme to organize science research centers (SRCs) and engineering research centers (ERCs) in the nation's universities. By 1993, fourteen SRCs and sixteen ERCs had been established, receiving government R&D subsidies of almost W 20 billion ($24.2 million) in 1993.

The lack of development in university research has been a major bottleneck in producing well-trained researchers. The government's recent efforts should result in significant reform in university R&D.

GRI R&D

Given the inadequacy of university research, GRIs have served as the backbone of advanced R&D in Korea. The government has made these institutes the major instruments in its Industrial Generic Technology Development Project (IGTDP), National R&D Project (NRP), and Highly Advanced National R&D Project. They have been the recipients of more than 90 percent of the research grants awarded by the government in new technology areas. GRIs undertake most of these projects in conjunction with private firms.

IGTDP concentrates mainly on current problems in existing technology areas with high economic externalities. Each year the Ministry of Trade, Industry, and Energy undertakes a survey to identify urgent R&D projects in industrial firms and offers financial support to GRIs and university laboratories to take on the projects jointly with private firms. Most of them are related to import substitution of Japanese components in the electronics and machinery industries. In 1989, for instance, 174 technologies were identified, 146 of which were designated as projects to be funded. For IGTDPs, the government earmarked W 11.5 billion ($17.2 million) in 1989, W 88.7 billion ($110.8 million) in 1993, about $118,000 per project in 1987 and $388,000 in 1993. These amounts are not substantial enough to solve critical problems.

In contrast, NRP projects focus primarily on future problems in new (to Korea) technology areas with a high risk of failure or with high economic externalities, thus warranting public support. MOST identified several target areas: localization of machinery parts and components, new materials development, semiconductor design, super-mini computer development, energy conservation technology, localization of nuclear energy fuel, new chemical development, biotechnology development, and basic research in universities. The government's total investment in NRPs increased significantly, from W 13.3 billion ($17.7 million) in 1982 to W 98.8 billion ($123.5 million) in 1993.

The most ambitious government vision is the Highly Advanced National R&D Project, also known as the G-7 Project, which is aimed at lifting Korea's technological capability to the level of G-7 countries by 2020.[64] The G-7 project has two parts: product technology development projects and fundamental technology development projects. The former includes new drugs and chemicals, broadband integrated services digital network, next-generation vehicle technology, and high-definition television (HDTV). The latter contains ultra-large-scale integrated circuit, advanced manufacturing systems, new materials for information, electronics, and energy industries, environmental technology, new functional biomaterials, alternative energy technology, and next-generation nuclear reactor. Jointly, the government, universities, and industries will invest $5.7 billion, about half of which will come from the private sector.

The $1.3 billion invested during the first three years involved more than 13,000 researchers and resulted in 2,542 patent applications, almost 2,000 academic articles, and three cases of technology export valued at $6 million. Notable outcomes include quinolon-based antibiotics, liver disease treatment medication, HDTV, and the completion of 256-mega dynamic random-access memory (DRAM) chip development.[65]

In the face of the rapid expansion of private R&D activities and increasing intensity in university R&D, reform of GRIs to redefine their roles has been discussed for some time. But inertia and the labor union of GRI members have made it difficult to implement the reform.

Military R&D

Given the threat of hostilities from North Korea, national security has been one of the major concerns in Korea. As a result, the home market for military technology is unusually sophisticated and demanding.

Seeking to lessen reliance on foreign weapon suppliers and to ensure military independence, the Korean government launched an ambitious program in the late 1970s to build local capability to develop modern weaponry, particularly nuclear warheads and missiles. Startled by Korea's bold move to develop its own defense capability, the U.S. government used carrots and sticks to persuade Korea to abandon the military R&D program.

As a result, the ambitious program was scaled back in the 1980s. Its budget dropped to $114 million in 1988, only 0.2 percent of that of the United States and 4 percent of that of France. The ratio of military R&D budget to total military expenditures was only 1.5 percent in Korea, compared with more than 10 percent in France and the United States. The nature of the R&D is confidential, and the R&D endeavors have been conducted almost strictly within the military: only 1.48 percent of the military R&D budget was allotted to universities in 1988.[66]

The isolated military R&D efforts have had little impact on the development of technological capability in the wider economy. The private sector is involved in manufacturing some traditional weaponry, but the spillover effects of such operations on industrial innovation appear to be negligible, except for improving the degree of precision in the machinery industry.

Indirect Support for Industry R&D

The government offered various tax incentives and preferential financing for R&D activities in the 1960s and 1970s, but during the 1970s the interest rate for R&D loans was one of the highest, reflecting the low priority of R&D in government policies. At the same time, these mechanisms were largely ignored by industry owing to the absence of a clearly felt need to invest in R&D and the relatively easy means of acquiring and assimilating foreign technologies then available from many sources. Only in the early 1980s did preferential R&D loans become the most important means for financing private R&D activities. Preferential financing amounted to W 671.6 billion ($848 million) in 1987, accounting for 94.3 percent of total corporate R&D financing funded by the government. In contrast, direct R&D investment by the government through NRPs and IGTDPs accounted for only 4 percent of the total and direct investment through venture capital firms accounted for 1.7 percent of the total.

Public financing (W 712.4 billion), mostly in the form of preferential loans, accounted for 64 percent of the nation's total R&D expenditure in manufacturing in 1987. In short, the government plays a major role in funding corporate R&D in Korea, primarily through allocation of preferential financing. The impact of this financing, however, may be overstated. With rates of preferential loans ranging between 6.5 percent and 15 percent, they conferred little advantage over financing terms available in markets outside Korea.[67]

Tax incentives are another indirect mechanism to make funds available for corporate R&D. In Korea, tax incentives may be classified into five categories, according to objectives to be served. Most important are tax incentives aimed at promoting corporate R&D investment, reduced tariffs on import of R&D equipment and supplies, deduction of annual noncapital R&D expenditures and human resource development costs from taxable income, and exemption from real estate tax on R&D related properties. The incentives also include a tax reduction scheme, Technology Development Reserve Fund, whereby an enterprise can set aside up to 3 percent (4 percent for high-technology industries) of sales in any one year to be used for its R&D work in the following three years. The private sector did not take advantage of this scheme in its early years, in the absence of the need for technological activities, but now considers it an important way to finance its R&D. Other tax incentives are aimed at reducing the cost of acquiring foreign technology, promoting technology-based small firms, reducing the cost of commercializing locally generated technologies, reducing the cost of introducing new products, and promoting the venture-capital industry.

In addition, the government introduced various indirect support programs for specific industrial R&D activities. For instance, the World Class Korean Products program, first instituted in 1986, is a government scheme to make selected Korean products world class. The government selected twenty-seven products involving fifty-nine manufacturers in the existing industries and offered preferential financing and other supports to improve the quality of the products, to develop innovative ideas for future development, and to energize overseas marketing strategies. Sports shoes, fishing rods, pianos, tires, bicycles, compact disc players, ultrasonic scanners, VCRs, and videotapes are examples.[68]

In 1993 the government introduced the New Technology Commercialization Program, in which the government offers preferential financing for activities related to R&D and commercialization of new (to Korea) technologies developed locally and designated by the government. The government certifies them as KT (Korea technology) or NT (new technology).

Realizing the importance of new technology venture firms, the

54   EVOLUTION OF PUBLIC POLICY

government introduced in 1992 the Spin-off Support program to encourage researchers in GRIs to spin off and establish new technology-
based small firms. Financial, managerial, and technical assistance are
offered to such prospective technical entrepreneurs.

R&D Investment

Facing the imperative to shift to higher value technology-intensive
products, R&D investment has seen a quantum jump in the past decades. Table 2-3 shows that total R&D investment increased from W
10.6 billion ($28.6 million) in 1971 to W 7.89 trillion ($10.25 billion)
in 1994. Though the Korean economy recorded one of the world's

Table 2-3   Research and Development Expenditures, 1965–1993
            (in billions of won)

	1965	1970
R&D expenditures	2.1	10.5
Government	1.9	9.2
Private Sector	0.2	1.3
Government vs. Private	61:39	97:03
R&D/GNP	0.26	0.38
Manufacturing Sector		
R&D Expenditures	NA	NA
Percent of Sales	NA	NA
Number of Researchers (total)[b]	2,135	5,628
Government/Public Institution	1,671	2,458
Universities	352	2,011
Private Sector	112	1,159
R&D Expenditure/Researcher (W 1,000)	967	1,874
Researcher/10,000 Population	0.7	1.7
Number of Corporate R&D Centers	0	1[c]

SOURCE: Ministry of Science and Technology (Korea), *1994 Report on the Survey of Research
and Development in Science and Technology* (Seoul: MOST, December 1994).

NOTES: [a] For 1976.
[b] The figures do not include research assistants, technicians, and other supporting personnel.
[c] For 1971.

Continued overleaf

fastest growth rates, R&D expenditure rose even faster than GNP. R&D increased its share of GNP (R&D/GNP) from 0.32 percent to 2.61 percent during the same period, surpassing that of the United Kingdom (2.12 percent in 1992). It should, however, be pointed out that there are many reasons to suspect bubbles in the R&D statistics, particularly those of the private sector.

The government has launched various programs to induce the private sector to establish formal R&D laboratories. These include tax incentives and preferential financing for setting up new laboratories and exemption from military service obligations for key R&D personnel. Owing partly to these programs and partly to increasing competi-

1975	1980	1985	1990	1994
42.7	282.5	1,237.1	3,349.9	7,894.7
30.3	180.0	306.8	651.0	1,257.1
12.3	102.5	930.3	2,698.9	6,634.5
71:29	64:36	25:75	19:81	16:84
0.42	0.77	1.58	1.95	2.61
16.70[a]	75.97	688.59	2,134.70	4,854.1
0.36[a]	0.50	1.51	1.96	2.55
10,275	18,434	41,473	70,503	117,446
3,086	4,598	7,542	10,434	15,465
4,534	8,695	14,935	21,332	42,700
2,655	5,141	18,996	38,737	59,281
4,152	15,325	27,853	47,514	67,220
2.9	4.8	10.1	16.4	26.4
12	54	183	966	1,980

tion in the international market, the number of corporate R&D laboratories increased from one in 1970 to 2,272 in 1995, reflecting the seriousness with which Korean firms are pursuing high-technology development. Although small and medium-size firms account for more than 50 percent of corporate R&D centers, *chaebols* dominate R&D activities. R&D spending in the manufacturing sector has grown faster than sales. The machinery and electronics industry spent more than 4 percent of sales on R&D activities beginning in the mid-1980s.

Consequently, there has been significant structural change in R&D investment. The government played a major role in R&D activities in early years, when the private sector faltered in R&D investment despite the government's encouragement. More recently, the private sector has assumed an increasingly larger role in the country's R&D efforts in response partly to increasing international competition and partly to a policy environment supportive of private R&D activities. For example, while the private sector accounted for only 2 percent of the nation's total R&D expenditure in 1963, the figure had risen to 84 percent by 1994, which is the highest among both advanced and newly industrialized countries.

TOTAL GLOBALIZATION POLICY

A report by International Management Development (IMD) in Switzerland ranked Korea low in international competitiveness indicators.[69] Its 1994 study shows that of forty-one advanced and newly industrializing countries included in the survey, Korea ranked thirty-ninth in globalization, thirty-ninth in finance, thirty-first in business management, thirtieth in government, twenty-ninth in infrastructure, twentieth in human resources, eighteenth in science and technology, and seventh in domestic competitiveness. Korea ranked near the bottom in many more indicators, including trade policy support for firms' globalization, domestic market liberalization, foreign investment liberalization, openness toward foreign culture, government's price control, balance in fiscal policy, financial support for firms, ease of overseas financing, and autonomy of financial institutions.[70]

Even among eighteen newly industrializing countries Korea slid from the top in 1991 to fifth in 1994 in domestic competitiveness, from fourth to ninth in infrastructure, from fourth to thirteenth in globalization, from third to ninth in business management, from fourth to tenth in government, from top to third in science and technology, and from seventh to tenth in finance during the same period. Korea's incredibly low ranking in the IMD study prompted several local institutes to undertake comparable studies just to find similar results.[71]

Shocked by these reports, the government launched another ambitious scheme, *segyehwa*, "total globalization policy," with a goal to raise various activities in Korea to international standards. The *segyehwa* committee is manned by cabinet members and twenty-three representatives from the private sector and cochaired by the prime minister representing the government and a university president representing the private sector. This committee delineated twelve major tasks including the reform of educational system and foreign language training, human resource development for "future" industries, and the acceleration of information to society. *Segyehwa* manifested Korea's belated determination to make major reforms in human resource development and government bureaucracy. Its efficacy, however, remains to be seen.

SUMMARY

The government played a developmental role in Korea's early industrialization. On the demand side of technological learning, the government created and fostered the growth of large *chaebols* as a vehicle for effective technological learning. The government then sanctioned them to accommodate technologically challenging, government-imposed new industrial projects and overly ambitious export goals and to accomplish them within the planned time frame, inducing a series of challenging crises for the private sector. These crises pushed the private sector into something of a life-or-death struggle and forced them to exert all efforts toward accelerating technological learning. But at the same time, the government provided necessary supports through various incentives to make the crises creative rather than destructive.

On the supply side of technological learning, the government restricted foreign direct investment and foreign licensing, instead promoting technology transfer through such other means as capital-goods imports in the early decades. Such a policy was effective in forcing Korean firms to acquire and assimilate foreign technology primarily through imitative reverse engineering of imported foreign goods in the early decades, when learning by doing was relatively easy. Consequently, none of the policy instruments to stimulate the country's own

58 EVOLUTION OF PUBLIC POLICY

R&D were effective. But anticipating increasing demands for S&T, the government established S&T infrastructure and GRIs when the private sector faltered in R&D investment.

Significant changes in Korea's economic environment in recent decades have, however, forced the Korean government to make a major policy shift from protection of the local market, regulation of foreign investment, and direct support of exports and R&D to liberalization of trade, foreign investment and financial market, antitrust legislation to enhance competition, and indirect support for R&D activities. This policy shift was designed to introduce market mechanisms and to undertake a structural change toward relatively more technology-based industries. Despite efforts in the 1980s, several indicators show that Korea's international competitiveness has dwindled mainly as a result of inertia in bureaucracy.

One encouraging sign is rapid growth in indigenous industrial R&D activities, an important indicator of learning in industry. The private sector has assumed a major role in Korea's R&D efforts in response partly to increasing international competition and partly to a policy environment supportive of private R&D activities. The private sector accounted for more than 80 percent of the nation's total R&D expenditures in the 1990s. Korea is, however, far behind advanced countries in R&D activities.

The policy environment described in this chapter, together with education and sociocultural environment, discussed in the following chapter, shaped the way firms have developed technological capability.

CHAPTER 2

1. "Developmental state" is the term Chalmers Johnson coined in his analysis of Japan's economic transformation to describe the orchestrating role of the state in Japanese industrialization. See Chalmers Johnson, *MITI and the Japanese Miracle: The Growth of Industrial Policy, 1925–1975*, (Stanford: Stanford University Press, 1982).

2. See, for example, World Bank, *The East Asian Miracle: Economic Growth and*

Public Policy (New York: Oxford University Press, 1993); Kiwhan Kim and Danny Leipziger, "Korea: A Case of Government-led Development: Lessons from East Asia, a Country Studies Approach," (Washington, D.C.: World Bank, 1993); and Robert Hassink, "South Korea: Economic Miracle by Policy Miracle?" a Maastricht Economic Research Institute on Innovation and Technology mimeograph, 1994.

3. Among monographs, the most comprehensive may be Lee-Jay Cho and Yoon-Hyung Kim, eds., *Economic Development in the Republic of Korea: A Policy Perspective* (Honolulu: East-West Center, University of Hawaii Press, 1992). Others include Alice H. Amsden, *Asia's Next Giant: South Korea and Late Industrialization* (New York: Oxford University Press, 1989); Dilip K. Das, *Korean Economic Dynamism* (London: Macmillan, 1992); World Bank, *The East Asian Miracle: Economic Growth and Public Policy* (New York: Oxford University Press, 1993); A. Chowdhury and I. Islam, *The Newly Industrializing Economies of East Asia* (London: Routledge, 1993). Informative articles include Robert Wade, "Industrial Policy in East Asia: Does It Lead or Follow the Market?" in Gary Gereffi and Donald L. Wyman, eds., *Manufacturing Miracles: Paths of Industrialization in Latin America and East Asia* (Princeton: Princeton University Press, 1990), 231–266; Manuel Castells, "Four Asian Tigers with a Dragon Head: A Comparative Analysis of the State, Economy, and Society in the Asian Pacific Rim," in Richard Applebaum and Jeffrey Henderson, eds., *States and Development in the Asian Pacific Region* (Newbury Park, Calif.: Sage Publications, 1992), 33–70.

4. The discussions in this and subsequent paragraphs draw heavily on Linsu Kim and Carl J. Dahlman, "Technology Policy and Industrialization: An Integrative Framework and Korea's Experience," *Research Policy* 21 (1992): 437–452.

5. On the other hand, he created and used the Korean CIA to oppress his dissidents.

6. Low wages in civil service and strong power given to bureaucrats in allocating business licenses and financial resources led to serious corruption.

7. Ezra F. Vogel, *The Four Little Dragons: The Spread of Industrialization in East Asia* (Cambridge, Mass.: Harvard University Press, 1991), 93.

8. Ibid., 49.

9. A study undertaken in 1993 by the International Exchange Foundation of Japan revealed that Korea had the largest number (820,000) studying Japanese, followed by China (250,000), Australia (170,000), Indonesia (73,000), and the United States (50,000). "Segye ileo hakseopja jeolbani hankookin." (Koreans comprise half the students of Japanese), *Kookmin Ilbo*, (Korea daily, Seoul), February 21, 1995, 5.

10. Alice H. Amsden, "The Specter of Anglo-Saxonization Is Haunting South Korea," in Lee-Jay Cho and Yoon Hyung Kim, eds., *Korea's Political Economy: An Institutional Perspective* (Boulder, Colo.: Westview Press, 1994), 87–126.

11. Vogel, *The Four Little Dragons*, 54. He, however, rightly criticizes Koreans' copying the Japanese institutions they learned during the Japanese occupation in the 1930s and 1940s rather than more recent variants.

12. Trade policy is also included here.

13. Richard M. Steers, Yoo Keun Shin, and Gerardo R. Ungson, *The Chaebols: Korea's New Industrial Might* (New York: Harper & Row, 1989), 34.

14. For excellent discussions of how the government promoted the growth of chaebols, see Seok-Ki Kim, *Business Concentration and Government Policy*, D.B.A. diss., Harvard Business School, 1987.

15. The data here are based on "The World's Largest Industrial Corporations," *Fortune*, July 26, 1993, 188–234.

16. The 1994 global 100 included only Daewoo among Korean *chaebols*. Unlike the 1992 list, the 1994 global 100 included not only manufacturing but also service firms. Consequently, Ssangyong and Sunkyung were pushed out, and Samsung, like Hyundai and LG, did not reveal its group revenue.

17. Amsden, *Asia's Next Giant*.

18. Chung-Yum Kim, *Hankuk Kyungje Jungchek 30 Nyunsa* (Korea's thirty-year economic policy history), Seoul: Chung-Ang Ilbo Press, 1990.

19. Linsu Kim, "Toward Reinventing Korea's National Management System in the Changing Global Environment," Institute report, East Asian Institute, Columbia University, October 1993.

20. For example, Samsung began as a small trader, Hyundai as one of 3,000 small construction subcontractors, LG as a primitive face cream producer, and Daewoo was a small spin-off from a trading company.

21. H. Chenery, S. Robinson, and M. Syrquin, *Industrialization and Growth: A Comparative Study* (New York: Oxford University Press, 1986), as quoted in Amsden, *Asia's Next Giant*.

22. The import-substitution policy refers to a mechanism that provides high protection to local markets in attempts to substitute foreign imports.

23. See Chapters 5, 6, and 8 for discussions of these industries.

24. Linsu Kim, "Korea," in Surendra Patel, ed., *Technological Transformation in the Third World, Volume 1: Asia* (Aldershot, England: Avebury Publishers, 1993).

25. Kwang-Suk Kim, "The 1964–1965 Exchange Rate Reform, Export-Promotion Measures, and Import-Liberalization Program," in Cho and Kim, *Economic Development in the Republic of Korea*.

26. Mason et al., *Economic and Social Modernization*, 265.

27. Linsu Kim, "National System of Industrial Innovation: Dynamics of Capability Building in Korea," in Richard Nelson, ed., *National Innovation Systems: A Comparative Analysis* (New York: Oxford University Press, 1993), 357–383.

28. For a more detailed discussion of export incentives see Kwang-Suk Kim, "Dynamics of Industrial Policy: Export-oriented Industrialization," paper presented at Korea's State-Guided Modernization Conference at East West Center, Honolulu, August 9–12, 1994.

29. World Bank, *World Bank Atlas*, various years.

30. For a detailed discussion of HCIs, see Suk-Chae Lee, "The Heavy and Chemical Industries Promotion Plan (1973–1979)," in Cho and Kim, *Economic Development in the Republic of Korea*, 431–472. From Lee's Table 17.11 (p. 452), total

HCI investment of W 6,166 billion is divided by the exchange rate of W 484 per dollar.

31. T. Watanabe, "Economic Development in Korea: Lessons and Challenges," in Toshio Shishido and Ryuzo Sato, eds., *Economic Policy and Development: New Perspectives* (Dover, Del.: Auburn House, 1985), quoted from Robert Wade, "Industrial Policy in East Asia: Does It Lead or Follow the Market?" in Gary Gereffi and Donald L. Wyman, eds., *Manufacturing Miracles: Paths of Industrialization in Latin America and East Asia* (Princeton: Princeton University Press, 1990), 231–266.

32. Walden Bello and Stephanie Rosenfeld, *Dragons in Distress: Asia's Miracle Economies in Crisis* (San Francisco: Institute for Food and Development Policy, 1992), 58.

33. Paul Samuelson, "Truths, Hard Truths, for Korea," *Dateline*, March 1990: 4–7.

34. For excellent discussions of labor subordination in Korea and other East Asian countries, see Frederic C. Deyo, ed., *Beneath the Miracle: Labor Subordination in the New Asian Industrialism* (Berkeley: University of California Press, 1989). For Korea, see Jang-Jip Choi, *Labor and Authoritarian State: Labor Unions in South Korean Manufacturing Industries, 1961–1980* (Seoul: Korea University Press, 1989).

35. Bello and Rosenfeld, *Dragons in Distress*.

36. Robert P. Kearney, *The Warrior Worker: The Challenge of the Korean Way of Working* (New York: Henry Holt, 1991), 25.

37. Byung-Nak Song, *The Rise of the Korean Economy* (Hong Kong: Oxford University Press, 1990).

38. There are two types of affiliates: *jahoisa* (child company) and *gyeyulsa* (affiliate companies). See "Largest Business Groups Continue Affiliate Expansion," *Korea Economic Weekly*, September 5, 1994, 26.

39. *Chaebols* divided some of their affiliates to give them to other family members.

40. A 1994 survey conducted by the Korea Economic Research Institute shows that of the thirty largest *chaebols*, six are owned and managed predominantly by the founders and their family groups and nine are managed by the mother firm, also managed by the founders and their family members. In other words, half the thirty largest *chaebols* are still run traditionally, but they are relatively smaller ones. The larger firms have significantly dispersed their ownership and modernized management style. See "KERI Report Reveals *Chaebol's* Ownership, Management Structure," *Korea Economic Weekly*, August 15, 1994, 18.

41. Net export subsidies represent the sum of direct cash subsidies, export dollar premium, direct tax reductions for exporters, and interest preference for exporters. See Kwang Suk Kim, "Industrial Policy and Trade Regimes," in Cho and Kim, *Korea's Political Economy*, 531–555.

42. The Korean government protects the local market from such Japanese imports as electronic goods and automobiles in an attempt to control trade imbalance with Japan.

43. Denise Chai, "Skeletons in the Closet," *Asia Money* 4, no. 7 (September 1993): 67–69.

44. Korea submitted its formal membership application to OECD in March 1995. However, it takes at least a year for a final decision to be made.
45. "Learning the Soft Way," *Far Eastern Economic Review*, December 3, 1992, 54–56.
46. "Korea Draws Legal Lines to Protect Property Rights," *Korea Business World*, September 1987, 84–87.
47. "Jijaekwon bumjae 5nyunse 5bae" (The number of violations of intellectual property rights quintupled in five years), *Chosun Ilbo* (Seoul daily), April 10, 1995, 39.
48. In a private conversation, Alice Amsden claimed that the Korean state, compared with that of other countries, is still relatively powerful in the marketplace.
49. For brevity of presentation, linking mechanisms are also included in this section.
50. My earlier examination of foreign license contract agreements through the end of the 1960s shows that all licensers that demanded payment above the 3 percent royalty ceiling later agreed to that figure.
51. Korea Exchange Bank, "Direct Foreign Investment in Korea," *Monthly Review*, October 1987, 18–19.
52. Dong-Sae Cha, *Weja Doipeo Hyogwa Boonsuk* (The effects of direct foreign investment) (Seoul: Korean Institute of Economics and Trade Press, 1983).
53. Linsu Kim and Youngbae Kim, "Innovation in a Newly Industrializing Country: A Multiple Discriminant Analysis," *Management Science* 31, no. 3 (1985): 312–322.
54. Larry E. Westphal, Linsu Kim, and Carl J. Dahlman "Reflections on the Republic of Korea's Acquisition of Technological Capability," in Nathan Rosenberg and C. Frischtak, eds., *International Technology Transfer: Concepts, Measures, and Comparisons* (New York: Praeger, 1985), 167–221.
55. The automatic approval system expedites foreign investors' applications by okaying them unless an applicant is otherwise notified within fifteen days in principle and within forty-five days if the application requires the evaluation of environmental effects and diversification of farmland.
56. "Foreign Investment Soars 43% in First Seven Months," *Korea Economic Weekly*, September 12, 1994, 6.
57. The current system stipulates that reporting to the appropriate ministry is necessary for the licensing of foreign technology with a fixed royalty of more than $300,000 or a running royalty of more than 3 percent of sales and a down payment of $50,000.
58. Even in the reporting system, the government often exercised its veto power by refusing to accept a report. For instance, until 1995 it refused to accept the reporting of Samsung's technology licensing agreement with Nissan as a way to block Samsung's entry into the automobile industry.
59. "Firms Receive 23 Percent More Foreign Technology," *Korea Economic Weekly*, September 11–18, 1995, 8.
60. Linsu Kim and Jeffrey B. Nugent, "Korean SMEs and Their Support Mecha-

252 NOTES

nisms: An Empirical Analysis of the Role of Government and Other Nonprofit Organizations," paper presented at the World Bank Conference "Can Intervention Work? The Role of Government in SME Success," Washington, D.C., February 9, 1994.

61. This institution was renamed the Korea Advanced Institute of Science and Technology in 1980.

62. Ministry of Science and Technology, Korea, *1994 Report on the Survey of Research and Development in Science and Technology* (Seoul: MOST, December 1994).

63. The only exception may be the Pohang University of Science Technology, founded by the Pohang Iron and Steel Company.

64. The government originally set a goal to reach G-7 status by 2001, but revised the target date to 2020.

65. Ministry of Science and Technology, Korea.

66. National Defense College, "Gukbang yungu gebalkwa mingan yungu gebaleo gwange ganghwa bangane kwanhan yungu" (A proposal to strengthen the link between military and industrial R&D) (Seoul: KIST Center for Science and Technology Policy, 1990).

67. Korea Industrial Technology Association, *Sanup Gisul Baegseo* (Industrial technology white paper), *1994* (Seoul: KITA Press, December 1994), Table 2–39, 109.

68. Korea Trade Promotion Corporation, *World Class Korean Products* (Seoul: KOTRA, no date).

69. IMD generated 381 indicators, some based on objective data and others on the opinions of 2,851 executives in forty-four countries, in eight major categories of international competitiveness. See Samsung Economic Research Institute, *1994 Segye Jooyogukbyul Gyungjaengryuk Bikyo* (International comparison of competitiveness among selected countries) (Seoul: Samsung Economic Research Institute, September 1994).

70. IMD, in cooperation with the World Economic Forum, has undertaken an annual survey of international competitiveness since 1980. In 1994, it studied 16,500 executives in forty-four countries and reported indicators related to various aspects of international competitiveness.

71. These include Korea Economic Research Institute and Korea Institute of Economy and Trade.

D
Corporate Organisation

[17]

THE JOURNAL OF FINANCE • VOL. XLVII, NO. 3 • JULY 1992

The Structure of Corporate Ownership in Japan

STEPHEN D. PROWSE*

ABSTRACT

I examine the structure of corporate ownership in a sample of Japanese firms in the mid 1980s. Ownership is highly concentrated in Japan, with financial institutions by far the most important large shareholders. Ownership concentration in independent Japanese firms is positively related to the returns from exerting greater control over management. This is not the case in firms that are members of corporate groups (keiretsu). Ownership concentration and the accounting profit rate in both independent and keiretsu firms are unrelated. The results are consistent with the notion that there exist two distinct corporate governance systems in Japan —one among independent firms and the other among firms that are members of keiretsu.

WHO ARE THE LARGE shareholders of Japanese firms and how much of the firm do they own? How important are financial institutions, nonfinancial corporations, and individuals as large shareholders? How concentrated is corporate ownership in Japan and how does it compare with corporate ownership in the U.S.? Do large shareholders in Japan respond to incentives for corporate control in the same way that they appear to in U.S. firms? Does the structure of ownership and the behavior of large shareholders differ between firms in keiretsu groups and those that are independent of such groups? Does the ownership structure of a Japanese firm have any bearing on its profitability? This paper attempts to answer these questions by analyzing the ownership structure of a sample of large Japanese firms in the mid 1980s.

Many of these questions were addressed by Demsetz and Lehn (1985) and Morck, Shleifer, and Vishny (1988) for U.S. firms, and this paper borrows from both works in terms of methodology. The interest in addressing these questions for Japan stems from three factors. First, Japan differs from the U.S. because the legal and regulatory environment of Japanese financial institutions permits them to be what Jensen (1989) has termed "active investors" to a much greater extent in corporations. Institutional investors in

---

* Board of Governors of the Federal Reserve System, Washington D.C. I am grateful to seminar participants at the University of Pittsburgh and the Federal Reserve Bank of Chicago Bank Structure Conference, and to Takeo Hoshi, Anil Kashyap, Steven Sharpe, and Paul Clyde for helpful comments. Kelli Mock provided excellent research assistance. The Japanese data used in this study are from the *NEEDS* database obtained from *The Japan Economic Journal* (Nihon Keizai Shimbun, Inc.). The views expressed herein are those of author and not necessarily those of the Federal Reserve System.

Japan are generally given much more latitude to own shares in, and exert control over, firms than they are in the U.S.[1] These differences may be important in determining the firm's ownership structure and the importance of financial institutions as large shareholders.

Second, within Japan there exist differences between firms that are affiliated with keiretsu groups and unaffiliated, independent firms concerning institutional arrangements with suppliers, customers, and financiers. Japanese industrial organization is characterized by groups of enterprises (keiretsu) composed of firms based in different industries, but bound by ties of fractional ownership, and reliant on a large commercial bank as the major lender. The large shareholders of keiretsu firms often are also large creditors of the firm as well as important long-term commercial business partners. Keiretsu firms differ from independent firms that have more arms-length type relationships with other firms and financiers. These differences in institutional arrangements may influence the firm's ownership structure and the behavior of shareholders as monitors.[2]

Finally, the role played by shareholders in Japan is subject to some controversy. The belief that shareholders have little power to exercise control over management is widespread.[3] Recent work, however, has suggested that the large shareholders of keiretsu firms do monitor and influence management, albeit in different ways than in the U.S. Kester (1990) characterizes the corporate governance of a keiretsu firm as relying on a complex interaction between the shareholding, credit holding, and long-term business relationships that exist between the firm and its stakeholders. Prowse (1990) suggests that because large shareholders are also large debtholders in the same keiretsu firms, they may preclude policies that attempt to transfer wealth from debtholders to shareholders.

Existing research on the structure of corporate ownership in Japan does not extend much beyond the citation of the aggregate statistics on the shareownership of listed companies published by the Tokyo Stock Exchange (exceptions are Flath (1990), Prowse (1990) and Hoshi and Ito (1991)). This study uses data on shareownership for a sample of 734 companies to discern the relative importance of different types of shareholders (financial institutions, nonfinancial companies, and individuals) and to see how the structure and concentration of shareownership varies with the affiliation of the firm and other firm characteristics.

The rest of the paper is divided into five sections. In the first, I set out some of the basic characteristics of the ownership structures of my sample of

[1] See Jensen (1989), Roe (1990) and Prowse (1990) and (1991).
[2] Recent studies suggest that differences between keiretsu and independent firms are large enough to produce observable differences in behavior. For example, Hoshi et al. (1991) found that keiretsu firms' investment is less liquidity-constrained than is independent firms because of their closer ties to a major creditor and the lower cost of debt financing this implies.
[3] Abegglen and Stalk (1985) suggest that Japanese firms are run for employees and not shareholders. See also "Shareholder Rights Idea Grows in Japan," *Wall Street Journal*, August 28, 1989 and "Stakes, shares and digestible poison pills," *The Economist*, February 2, 1991.

Japanese companies. Comparisons are made with existing data for U.S. firms. The second section discusses the Demsetz and Lehn (1985) framework of the determinants of corporate ownership concentration and attempts to apply it to the different institutional and regulatory environment of the Japanese firm. The third section contains empirical work on the determinants of ownership concentration in Japan in keiretsu and independent firms. The fourth analyzes whether ownership structure influences the profitability of keiretsu or independent firms. The final section concludes.

I. The Structure of Corporate Ownership in Japan

Table I shows how the ownership of all listed Japanese corporations in the aggregate breaks down between financial institutions, nonfinancial corporations, and individuals, with data for the U.S. provided as a standard of comparison. One major difference between the two countries is the far heavier weight of financial institutions (particularly banks) in the ownership of common stock in Japan. In 1984, commercial banks in Japan owned more than 20% of the outstanding stock of all firms. In the U.S., commercial banks

Table I

Percentage of Outstanding Corporate Equity Held by Various Sectors in the U.S. and Japan in 1984

	Japan	U.S.
All corporations	67.3	37.7
Financial institutions	43.3	26.6
Commercial banks	20.5	0.2
Insurance companies	17.7	4.6
Other financial	5.1	21.8
Nonfinancial corporations	24.0	11.1
Households	26.7	58.1
Foreign	5.0	4.2
Other	1.0	0.0

Sources: Federal Reserve Board, Flow of Funds Accounts, Financial Assets and Liabilities 1966–1989 (September 1990) and Japanese Securities Research Institute (1988). Commercial Banks for Japan refers to city banks, long-term credit banks and regional banks; for U.S., refers to commercial and mutual savings banks, and bank holding companies. Other financial includes pension funds, mutual funds, and securities companies. For both countries, trust holdings are counted among household holdings. For the U.S., nonfinancial corporations holdings are netted out of the Flow of Funds estimates. I follow French and Poterba (1991) in using IRS data on the ratio of dividends paid by U.S. corporations to domestic dividends received by U.S. corporations to estimate nonfinancial holdings.

have been prevented by law from holding any corporate stock on their own account. (Bank holding companies in the U.S. are allowed to hold up to 5% of the voting stock of any nonbank. However, the figures in Table I suggest that their holdings are minuscule). Insurance companies in Japan (life and non-life) held more than 17% of the outstanding shares of firms, more than three times the amount held by their U.S. counterparts. Holdings by nonfinancial corporations in Japan are more than twice what they are in the United States. Overall, corporate shareholdings in Japan are close to twice what they are in the U.S., where individual shareownership predominates.[4]

Aggregate ownership figures such as those in Table I do not reveal anything about the *concentration* of ownership, nor about who the largest shareholders are in a typical firm. Table II gives some information on the concentration of ownership in a sample of Japanese firms. Data on the five largest owners of 734 Japanese firms in 1984 were obtained from two

Table II

Panel A: Summary statistics of ownership concentration (S5) and market value of equity (MVE) for 734 Japanese nonfinancial corporations in 1984 and 457 U.S. nonfinancial corporations in 1980.[a]

	Mean	Median	Standard Deviation	Minimum	Maximum
Japanese sample					
S5	33.1	29.7	13.8	10.9	85.0
MVE ($millions)	990	327	1883	22.2	27182.1
U.S. sample					
S5	25.4	20.9	16.0	1.3	87.1
MVE ($millions)	1287.2	425	2833.4	22.3	40587.2

Panel B: Summary statistics of ownership concentration (S5) and its composition among financial institutions (F5), nonfinancial corporations (NF5), individuals (I5) and other agents (O5) in 734 Japanese firms in 1984.[b]

	S5	F5	NF5	I5	O5
Mean	33.1	25.0	4.9	3.0	0.2
Median	29.7	24.2	0.0	0.0	0.0
Standard deviation	13.8	8.3	8.3	6.6	1.0
Minimum	10.9	0.0	0.0	0.0	0.0
Maximum	85.0	48.8	42.1	35.2	8.9

[a] Data for the sample of U.S. firms is taken from Corporate Data Exchange directories. Market value of equity for Japanese firms is converted to dollars at an exchange rate of 225 yen = $1.
[b] F5 measures the percentage of outstanding shares held by financial institutions that are among the top five shareholders of the firm. NF5, I5, and O5 are the measures for nonfinancial corporations, individuals and other agents, respectively.

[4] Both the Japanese and U.S. financial systems changed somewhat in the 1980s, and in many ways have recently become more alike (see Jensen (1989) and Hoshi et al. (1990)). For example, the U.S. system has seen a significant increase in the shareholdings of corporations (financial and nonfinancial) at the expense of household holdings.

publications: *The Japan Company Handbook* (1985) and *Industrial Groupings in Japan* (1985). The sample consists of all nonfinancial firms listed on the Tokyo Stock Exchange for which shareholding data was available and whose market value of equity was greater than 5 billion Yen at year-end 1984 (roughly $22 million at the prevailing exchange rate in 1984). All major nonfinancial sectors (manufacturing, transportation, wholesale and retail, and services) are represented in the sample. As a measure of ownership concentration I use the percentage of outstanding shares held by the top five shareholders of the company (S5). The choice of the top five shareholders was dictated by the fact that data for larger numbers of shareholders were unavailable for many firms.

For these firms, Figure I and Table II gives the frequency distribution and other summary statistics of ownership concentration. Panel A of Table II also provides summary statistics for the same measure of ownership concentration for a sample of 457 U.S. nonfinancial corporations (collected from the Corporate Data Exchange directories) as a standard of comparison. Ownership concentration appears to vary quite widely in Japan; the percentage of outstanding shares held by the top five shareholders ranges from a minimum of 10.9% to a maximum of 85%, with a mean of 33.1%. Ownership concentration in Japanese firms is significantly higher than in U.S. firms; the mean concentration ratio in Japan is over 30% higher than in the U.S., a difference that is significant at the 1% level, while the median concentration ratio is over 40% higher in Japan.[5]

Frequency

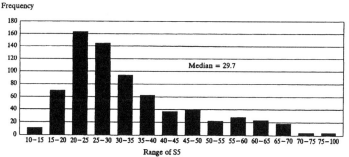

Figure 1. Frequency distribution of ownership concentration for 734 Japanese nonfinancial corporations in 1984. The measure of ownership concentration, S5, is the percentage of outstanding shares held by the top five shareholders of the firm.

[5] These differences appear too large to be explained by the $300 million greater market value of equity (MVE) exhibited by the sample of U.S. firms. Assuming the exchange rate used to convert the Japanese MVE to dollars is the correct one for these purposes, the regression results presented later indicate that a $300 million increase in the mean MVE for the Japanese sample would lower the mean concentration ratio by only about 1 percentage point to 32.1%.

Panel B of Table II provides information on the identity of the large shareholders. Each of the largest five shareholders in each firm was classified as either a financial institution, nonfinancial corporation, individual, or "other" agent.[6] Then the percentage of outstanding shares held by each shareholder class was calculated. For example, F5 measures the percentage of outstanding shares held by those financial institutions that rank among the top five shareholders. NF5, I5, and O5 measure the same thing for nonfinancial corporations, individuals and other agents, respectively. Panel B provides summary statistics for these measures. Financial institutions clearly predominate in importance as large shareholders. On average financial institutions ranking among the top five shareholders hold 25% of the firm's shares. This contrasts with the much smaller holdings of financial institutions in the U.S., and probably reflects the tighter U.S. restrictions on financial institutions' equity holdings and how they can use the shares they do own for governance purposes.[7]

Because I have recorded only the largest five shareholders of the firm, my data are not conducive to measuring the size of management's shareholdings. However, some tentative comparisons with U.S. data can be made. Two studies document significant management shareholding in U.S. firms. Demsetz and Lehn (1985) report that the largest five family and individual investors in their sample of U.S. firms owned a combined 9.1% of the firm's outstanding equity. Morck, Shleifer, and Vishny (1988) found that in a sample of Fortune 500 companies, the mean combined stake of all board members was 10.6%. While I have no figures directly comparable with those cited in these two reports,[8] the figures presented in Panel B for individual shareholdings suggest that management shareholding in Japanese companies may be rather less important. Individuals ranking among the top five shareholders of the firm hold on average 3% of the firm's outstanding shares. Even if we assume these individuals are all managers, this still appears low compared to the Demsetz and Lehn (1985) and Morck et al. (1988) numbers, notwithstanding the differences in definitions. This impression is bolstered by data recently reported by Kaplan (1992) that in a sample of large Japanese and U.S. firms, only 12.2% of Japanese presidents held more than 0.5% of their company's stock in 1981, compared to 22.6% of U.S. chief executive officers.[9]

[6] The "other" category consists primarily of holdings by employee stock ownership plans and foreigners.

[7] In the Demsetz and Lehn (1985) sample of 511 nonfinancial firms, the mean holdings of the *largest five* financial institution shareholders were 18.4%. I count the holdings of only those financial institutions *among the largest five* shareholders, so it is clear that equity holdings of financial institutions are much larger in Japan than in the United States.

[8] Morck et al. (1988) measure shareholdings by all board members holding a greater than 0.2% stake, and Demsetz and Lehn (1985) measure shares held by the largest five individuals, whereas I measure only those individual shareholding that *rank among the five largest*.

[9] There is also anecdotal evidence to suggest that management shareholding is less important in Japan. Kester (1986) notes that management shareholding is not widespread in Japan and that there are laws prohibiting officers of the firm from owning stock options.

In sum, Japanese firms exhibit much higher degrees of ownership concentration than do U.S. firms. Financial institutions predominate among the top five shareholders, and take significantly larger equity positions in firms than they do in the U.S. Management ownership appears to be rather less important in Japan.

These differences appear at least consistent with the notion that firms in Japan rely on different methods to discipline managers than do U.S. firms. For example, the market for corporate control in Japan appears much less active (at least among large firms) than in the United States.[10] In addition, if management shareholding in Japanese firms is indeed rather less important than it is in the U.S., then the structure of management compensation in Japanese firms by itself might plausibly give managers less incentive than their U.S. counterparts to follow value-maximizing policies.[11] Overall, there seems to be less scope in Japan for the promotion of managerial discipline through the market for corporate control or the structure of management compensation.[12] Kester (1990) and Prowse (1991) suggest that this may mean greater reliance in Japan on direct shareholder monitoring, which may be reflected in the higher levels of ownership concentration observed in Japan in Panel B.

There also seems to be a significant amount of variation in ownership concentration among firms in Japan. The next section attempts to explain some of this variation.

II. The Determinants of Ownership Structure in Japan

Demsetz and Lehn (1985) propose a number of potential determinants of ownership concentration in U.S. firms. This study uses their framework with some refinements where differences in the Japanese institutional or regulatory environment make it appropriate.

One determinant of ownership concentration is the value-maximizing size of the firm. The larger the firm, the greater is the cost of obtaining a given fraction of ownership. In addition, risk aversion implies that large shareholders will increase their ownership of the firm only at lower, risk-compensating prices. This increased cost of capital will discourage owners of large firms from attaining as highly concentrated ownership as owners of smaller firms. In order to control for the effects of leverage, firm size is measured by the market value of equity (MVE). I expect MVE to have a negative effect on ownership concentration in Japan, as Demsetz and Lehn (1985) found for U.S. firms.

---

[10] Kaplan (1992) reports that only 2.5% of his sample of Japanese firms was taken over or merged between 1980 and 1989, in contrast to 22.6% of his sample of U.S. firms over the same period.

[11] Kester (1986) notes that explicit profit sharing contracts with management are rare among Japanese firms.

[12] On the other hand, higher management shareholdings in the U.S. could conceivably give managers more scope to become entrenched.

A second factor influencing ownership concentration is what Demsetz and Lehn (1985) term the control potential of the firm—the profit potential from exercising more effective monitoring of managerial performance by the firm's owners. They postulate that a firm's control potential is likely correlated with the instability of the firm's environment, and proxy this by the variation of the firm's profit rate (measured by both stock and accounting returns). A firm with a more volatile profit rate is more likely to be operating in a less predictable environment, where managerial behavior is both more difficult to monitor and also is likely to be more crucial in affecting profitability. The less stable is the firm's environment therefore, the larger is the potential benefit to shareholders from maintaining tighter control over managerial behavior via more concentrated ownership structures.

I expect the influence of control potential to differ between keiretsu and independent firms. Within a keiretsu, large shareholders typically have a variety of relationships with the firm, including credit and trading contracts. For example, a large shareholder of a keiretsu firm is also typically a large creditor of that firm. In my sample of 85 keiretsu firms (described in Section III), the largest shareholder is also the largest creditor (in terms of the share of outstanding bank and bond debt held) in 55 cases. The largest creditor, which is almost always either the main bank or an insurance company in the same keiretsu, holds on average 21.9% of the firm's outstanding debt and 6% of its outstanding equity. The firm's largest five creditors (that are members of the same keiretsu) hold 49.8% of its debt and 18% of its equity. Moreover, the simultaneous holding of a keiretsu firm's debt and equity is not restricted to the financial institutions within the group. Many nonfinancial firms within the keiretsu extend large amounts of trade credit to those firms in which they have equity interests.

Large shareholders of keiretsu firms also typically have strong commercial and trading relationships with them. Trading ties between keiretsu firms are strong. Most keiretsu firms do much of their buying and selling within their own group through implicit reciprocal trade agreements. Kester (1990) cites some examples of the shareholding and commercial relationships between firms in the Mitsubishi keiretsu. Mitsubishi Heavy Industries is the largest shareholder in Mitsubishi Steel (with a 7% interest in the firm) and also is a large purchaser of its output and important supplier of its equipment and construction services. Similarly, Mitsubishi Bank holds 3.7% of Mitsubishi Electric's shares, more than 15% of its debt and in addition is a major purchaser of its computer equipment.

In contrast to these tight financial and commercial relationships between customers, suppliers, and financiers, independent firms are much more similar to U.S. firms in their arms-length relationships with financiers and trading partners. These differences between keiretsu and independent firms in their relationships with stakeholders suggest differences in the way in which their corporate governance systems work. For example, the tight, long-term commercial and financial relationships that exist between keiretsu members mean that there may exist a number of methods of monitoring and influencing a firm's management aside from simply exerting influence as a large shareholder. A main bank or major corporation may be able to obtain information about a firm's prospects and policies and influence management just as easily through its role as a large lender or long-term commercial partner of the firm as it can in its role as a large shareholder.[13] In contrast, the weaker ties that exist between independent firms and their stakeholders suggest that methods of monitoring and influencing management may rely more directly on the size of the shareholder's equity holdings, as is the case in the U.S.

Ownership concentration by itself may thus not be a good proxy for the control shareholders have over management in the keiretsu firm because they are also typically creditors and long-term business partners of the firm and may be able to monitor and influence management through these alternative channels. Ownership concentration may be a much better proxy for the control shareholders have over management in the independent firm. This issue is addressed in the empirical section, where the sensitivity of ownership concentration to control potential is examined in keiretsu and independent firms separately.

Regulation is another factor that may influence the concentration of a firm's ownership. Demsetz and Lehn (1985) propose that in the U.S. regulation restricts the options available to owners, thus reducing the profit potential from exercising more effective control. It may in addition provide some subsidized monitoring of management by regulators, thereby reducing the need for shareholders themselves to engage in monitoring. Demsetz and Lehn account for this factor by using dummies that identify regulated industries such as utilities and financial companies in their regressions for ownership concentration. They find that regulated industries in the U.S. exhibit significantly less ownership concentration than unregulated firms.

I do not include a proxy for regulation in my regressions for two reasons. First, some regulation in Japan takes the form of informal "administrative guidance" by the Ministry of Trade and Industry (MITI).[14] Consequently, it is difficult to identify the degree to which particular industries are subject to such informal regulation and monitoring. Second, while it is possible that some forms of more explicit regulation in Japan may lessen the need for high levels of ownership concentration in firms, it is plausible that firms subject to informal guidance by MITI may depend crucially for their success on how the managers of the firm respond to such guidance. High ownership concentration might help owners monitor and influence the way in which the managers

---

[13] This is not to say that shareholders are not the legal owners of the firm in Japan with ultimate power over who runs it, merely that there are more avenues for monitoring and influencing the firm open to the typical shareholder in Japan who is also a creditor and long-term business partner than there are in the United States. Note, however, that there is no doctrine of equitable subordination in Japanese corporate law, which effectively means that creditors are much less reluctant to exert influence over the firm's management when they feel the need to do so (see Kester (1990) and Prowse (1990)).

[14] See, for example, Wheeler et al. (1982).

of the firm negotiate with MITI bureaucrats in order to maximize share-holder wealth.[15]

Demsetz and Lehn (1985) also refer to the amenity potential of the firm's output as a potential determinant of the degree to which ownership is concentrated in an individual's or family's hands. They define amenity potential as the ability to influence the type of goods produced by the firm, and identify two industries that are likely to generate concentrated ownership so that the owners can indulge their personal preferences: professional sports clubs and mass media firms. The sample of 143 firms on which I perform regression analysis (described in Section III) are in the manufacturing and mining sectors of the economy and do not include firms that I could clearly identify as having high degrees of amenity potential. Consequently, I do not attempt to measure this variable. However, since the firm's amenity potential is likely to be strongly governed by personal tastes, it is likely that it is a less important factor in determining ownership concentration in Japan, where individual shareholders are rarely of importance among the top five shareholders.

III. Data and Measurements

From the original sample of 734 firms, a smaller sample was constructed consisting of all firms for which I was able to obtain consolidated accounting data (from the NEEDS tapes), stock price data (from the NEEDS monthly stock price tapes for firms listed on the Tokyo Stock Exchange), and which Nakatani (1984) classifies as either a keiretsu member or an independent firm.[16] This smaller sample consists of 143 firms from the mining and manufacturing sector of the economy: 85 keiretsu and 58 independent firms.

In the following regressions I apply a *log* transformation to the percentage of outstanding shares held by the top five shareholders, using the formula.

$$LS5 = \log \frac{S5}{100 - S5}$$

The transformation follows Demsetz and Lehn's methodology and is used to convert an otherwise bounded dependent variable into an unbounded one.

---

[15] Wheeler et al. (1982) identify three industries: shipbuilding, aluminum refining, and petroleum refining, that are subject to regulation by explicit bills passed in the Diet. Unfortunately, my sample contains only one or two firms in each of these industries. When dummy variables for these industries are included in the regressions, the coefficient on each dummy is negative, but insignificant. I leave a fuller examination of the effects of regulation on Japanese ownership concentration for a later time.

[16] Membership of a keiretsu is not clearly definable. There are no dues or other formalities that classify a firm as a group member. Several publications attempt to make this classification. I use Nakatani's (1984) refinement of the *Keiretsu no Kenkyu* classification, which has previously been used by Hoshi et al. (1991) to compare differences between keiretsu and independent firms.

The measure of firm size (MVE) is the market value of the firm's common equity at the end of 1984 measured in millions of dollars.[17] The instability of the firm's environment is proxied by three measures of the instability of the firm's profit rate. Two of these measures, (SE and STDS, see Table III) are based on stock market rates of return as determined by 72 monthly stock

Table III
Description of Variables

S5	Percentage of outstanding common shares owned by the top five shareholders in 1984.[a,b]
F5, NF5, I5, O5	Percentage of outstanding shares held by those financial institutions (F5), nonfinancial corporations (NF5), individuals (I5), and other agents (O5) ranking among the top five shareholders in 1984.[a,b]
MVE	Market value of common equity in millions of dollars at year-end 1984.[c,d]
SE	Standard error of estimate from market model in which firm's monthly returns for 1979–1984 are regressed on the monthly returns of the market portfolio for the same period.[d]
STDS	Standard deviation of monthly stock market rates of return, 1979–1984.[d]
RETURNA	Accounting rate of return (annual average of net income to book value of shareholders' equity 1979–1984).[d]
STDA	Standard deviation of annual accounting rates of return, 1979–1984.[d]
CAP	Ratio of capital expenditures to total sales (annual average 1979–1984).[d]
ADV	Ratio of advertising expenditures to total sales (annual average 1979–1984).[d]
RD	Ratio of research and development expenditures to total sales (annual average 1979–1984).[d]
ASSET	Value of total assets in millions of dollars (annual average 1979–1984).[c,d]
D5	Percentage of outstanding bank and bond debt held by the top five debtholders of the firm who are members of the same keiretsu in 1984.[b]

[a] Source: *Japan Company Handbook* (1985).
[b] Source: *Industrial Groupings in Japan* (1985).
[c] Yen values are converted to dollar values at the approximate exchange rate existing in 1984 of 225 Yen = $1.
[d] Source: *NEEDS* consolidated accounts tape and monthly stock price stape.

[17] All yen values in this study are converted to dollars at the approximate exchange rate existing in 1984 of 225 Yen = $1.

1132   *The Journal of Finance*

market returns during the 6-year period 1979–1984. SE is calculated as the standard error of the regression of each firm's monthly returns on the returns to the market portfolio. STDS is the standard deviation of the firm's monthly stock market rates of return. The third measure of profit instability is the standard deviation of accounting profit rates of the firm (STDA) and is based on six annual profit rates over the period 1979–1984.

Table III provides definitions of all variables in the study and Table IV provides their summary statistics for 85 keiretsu and 58 independent firms. Table IV suggests little difference in levels of ownership concentration between keiretsu and independent firms. Financial institutions appear more

Table IV

Means and Standard Deviations of Variables for 143 Japanese Firms[a]

Variable	For 85 Keiretsu Firms	For 58 Independent Firms
S5	33.2	32.8
	(8.8)	(8.0)
F5	26.1	22.9
	(7.0)	(6.2)
NF5	5.1	5.3
	(6.5)	(4.4)
I5	1.9	4.4
	(4.4)	(5.1)
O5	0.1	0.2
	(0.7)	(0.1)
MVE ($millions)	1019	624.2
	(1964)	(1689)
SE	0.086	0.088
	(0.036)	(0.031)
STDS	0.091	0.094
	(0.036)	(0.031)
STDA	0.015	0.021
	(0.017)	(0.018)
RETURNA	0.032	0.042
	(0.037)	(0.089)
CAP	0.026	0.027
	(0.027)	(0.039)
ADV	0.144	0.184
	(0.065)	(0.095)
RD	0.026	0.023
	(0.022)	(0.019)
ASSET ($millions)	2239	1505.0
	(3725)	(3848)
D5	49.8	NA
	(17.0)	NA

NA = not applicable.
[a] For descriptions of variables see Table III. Standard deviations are in parentheses.

important as large shareholders in keiretsu firms, reflecting the closer financial ties between them, whereas individuals appear more important in independent firms. Table IV also indicates that keiretsu firms are on average larger and less profitable than independent firms. They also show less volatility in their profit rates. However, none of the differences in the means are statistically significant and so caution should be used in drawing conclusions from them.[18]

Table V provides OLS regression estimates of LS5 on the three alternative measures of profit instability and the market value of equity for keiretsu and independent firms separately.[19] The two samples exhibit markedly different behavior. For independent firms, all three measures of profit instability are positively and significantly related to ownership concentration. Firm size (MVE) enters with the expected sign (negative) and is significant in all three specifications of the model. In contrast, for keiretsu firms none of the measures of profit instability are significant and one coefficient (on STDA) is negative. Firm size enters with the expected sign (negative), but is not significant in any specification of the model. Overall, the variation in LS5

Table V
Regression Results for the Log of Ownership Concentration (LS5) for 85 Keiretsu Firms and 58 Independent Firms on Measures of Profit Instability (SE, STDS, STDA) and the Market Value of Equity of the Firm (MVE).

Absolute values of t-statistics are in parentheses.

Independent Variables[a]	Keiretsu Firms			Independent Firms		
Intercept	−1.2	−1.2	−1.1	−1.3	−1.3	−1.0
	(8.8)	(8.4)	(19.7)	(10.2)	(9.7)	(13.4)
MVE[b]	−2.8	−2.8	−3.1	−17.3	−17.3	−19.4
	(1.6)	(1.6)	(1.8)	(3.3)	(3.3)	(3.9)
SE	0.7	—	—	4.3	—	—
	(0.7)			(3.2)		
STDS	—	0.4	—	—	3.6	—
		(0.8)			(3.0)	
STDA	—	—	−0.1	—	—	1.7
			(0.05)			(2.2)
N	85	85	85	58	58	58
Adjusted R^2	0.02	0.02	0.02	0.24	0.24	0.26
F-statistic	1.7	1.7	1.6	9.8	9.4	9.7

[a] See Table III for descriptions of variables.
[b] All coefficient estimates on MVE should be multiplied by 10^{-5}.

[18] Nonetheless, the differences are in accord with Nakatani (1984), who found that keiretsu firms exhibited less volatile, though lower, profitability over time than did independent firms.
[19] Demsetz and Lehn include in some of their regressions the squared value of the measure of profit instability. This variable proved insignificant for my samples of Japanese firms. I also included two-digit industry dummies in my regressions. These proved insignificant and did not affect the results presented here.

explained by these equations is markedly higher for independent firms than for keiretsu firms.

The estimated coefficients of all three profit instability variables are much larger for independent firms than for keiretsu firms, more than six times as large in the SE and STDS regressions, and also much larger in the STDA regression (where the coefficient enters with a negative sign for keiretsu firms). The differences in the SE and STDS coefficients between samples are statistically significant at the 10% confidence level.[20] Note also that the absolute size of the MVE coefficient is much larger for independent firms than for keiretsu firms, roughly six times as large. The differences in these coefficients are also statistically significant at the 1% confidence level.[21] Thus I can reject the null hypothesis of equality of the profit instability coefficients in two out of three cases, and also of the firm size coefficients between independent and keiretsu firms.

These results suggest that the shareholders of independent and keiretsu firms behave differently in two respects. First, large shareholders in keiretsu firms show no sign of a wealth constraint, whereas they do in independent firms. This may be due to the greater importance of individuals as large shareholders of independent firms, who face a tighter wealth constraint than corporate investors. Second, in independent firms, the top shareholders take larger positions in firms where there appear to be greater returns from exerting control over management. In keiretsu firms, the top shareholders do not seem to take larger positions in those firms where greater control over management might imply improved firm performance.

Table VI attempts to identify the type of shareholder that is producing the behavior observed in the independent firms. It provides OLS estimates of a regression on measures of the importance of financial institutions (F5), nonfinancial corporations (NF5), and individuals (I5) among the top five shareholders of the firm on a measure of profit instability (SE) and firm size (MVE).[22] The results indicate that financial institutions are largely responsible for the positive relationship between ownership concentration and profit instability in independent Japanese firms. The coefficient on SE is positive and significant in the F5 regression, positive and marginally significant in the NF5 regression, and negative and insignificant in the I5 regression.[23] These results suggest that financial institutions' equity investments in independent firms are particularly sensitive to the benefits that exist from exerting control over firms with unstable environments. Nonfinancial firms' equity investments in independent firms show less sensitivity to these benefits, and individual equity investments show none at all.

---

[20] The *t*-statistic of the difference in the coefficients is 2.1 for SE and 2.0 for STDS.

[21] The *t*-statistic of the difference in the MVE coefficients ranges from 2.6 to 3.0 in the three specifications.

[22] Since F5, NF5, and I5 occasionally take on values of zero, for which the log transformation used in the Table V regressions is undefined, these variables are not logistically transformed.

[23] Similar results (not reported here) were obtained in regressions using the other two measures of profit instability (STDS and STDA).

Table VI

**Regression Results for the Percentage of
Outstanding Shares Held by Financial
Institutions (F5), Nonfinancial Corporations
(NF5) and Individuals (I5) that Rank Among
the Top Five Shareholders of the Firm,
for 58 Independent Japanese Firms.**

Absolute values of t-statistics are in parentheses.

Independent Variables[a]	Dependent Variables		
	F5	NF5	I5
Intercept	13.2	3.4	4.2
	(4.5)	(1.1)	(1.9)
MVE[b]	−1.0	−1.0	−5.0
	(0.7)	(0.8)	(3.0)
SE	66.8	12.7	−11.7
	(3.2)	(1.5)	(0.5)
N	58	58	58
Adjusted R^2	0.10	0.04	0.04
F-statistic	3.2	1.5	1.5

[a] See Table III for descriptions of variables.
[b] All coefficients on MVE should be multiplied by 10^{-3}.

Note also the coefficient on MVE. For financial and nonfinancial corporations it is insignificant, suggesting that they are large enough so as not to have the size of their investment in a given firm be constrained by their wealth. As one might expect, individuals' equity investments in firms do show evidence of a wealth constraint.

The hypothesis outlined in the previous section suggests that the results in Table V for keiretsu firms do not necessarily imply irrational behavior on the part of their shareholders, since they may have means other than increased shareholding through which to assert influence over the firm, such as through a creditor or trading partner relationship. Unfortunately, these means are not as easily observable or measurable as a simple shareholding relationship.

One aspect of the relationship among keiretsu firms that is potentially measurable is the creditor relationship. For example, the more concentrated the outstanding loans of a keiretsu firm are in the hands of other group members, then the more influence these group members can plausibly have over the firm. My measure of the concentration of debt ownership is the percentage of outstanding bank and bond debt held by the five largest debtholders of the firm who are members of the same keiretsu (D5). I rerun the Table V regressions for keiretsu firms, using as the dependent variable the interaction variable S5∗D5.[24] This variable attempts to capture *two*

---

[24] Since I am now considering share and debt ownership together, I use the total assets of the firm as the measure of firm size rather than the market value of equity.

margins along which stakeholders of the keiretsu firm may move in order to exert more or less control over the firm. It essentially assumes that share and debt ownership are substitute methods of exerting control over the firm.[25]

Table VII provides some limited support for the notion that large stakeholders in the keiretsu firm react to the control potential of the firm by adjusting share *and* debt ownership together. Compare the three regression results reported in Table V for keiretsu firms and those reported in Table VII. In the two regressions using SE and STDS, the level of statistical significance of their coefficients is markedly larger in Table VII (the t-statistics double). In the regression using STDA the sign changes from negative in Table V to positive in Table VII. It is still the case, however, that in the Table VII regressions the levels of statistical significance on the profit instability variables are somewhat above the 10% level. This is not surprising since many aspects of the firm's relationship with its stakeholders are still being left out in the dependent variable. Overall, I take these results as being suggestive (although certainly not conclusive) of the notion that stakeholders

Table VII

Regression Results for the Product of Ownership Concentration (S5) and Outstanding Debt Concentration (D5) for 85 Keiretsu Firms on Measures of Profit Instability (SE, STDS, STDA) and the Total Assets of the Firm (ASSET).

Absolute values of t-statistics are in parentheses.

Independent Variables[a]			
Intercept	636.3	666.2	535.1
	(5.0)	(14.9)	(11.4)
ASSET[b]	−2.9	−2.9	−2.9
	(3.3)	(3.4)	(3.5)
SE	853.9	—	—
	(1.5)		
STDS	—	1156.3	—
		(1.6)	
STDA	—	—	2110.3
			(1.5)
N	85	85	85
Adjusted R^2	0.20	0.25	0.24
F-statistic	7.5	7.6	7.2

[a] See Table III for descriptions of variables.
[b] All coefficients on ASSET should be multiplied by 10^{-2}.

[25] Of course, there are many other margins along which stakeholders of keiretsu firms may operate which are not captured by my measure. For example, my measure ignores the degree to which a keiretsu firm has long-term reciprocal trading contracts with other group firms which could plausibly yield access to information about the firm's prospects and some ability to influence firm policy.

of the keiretsu firm do act to increase their control over those firms within their group where there appear to be greater benefits from exerting control over management.

In addition, indirect evidence as to whether keiretsu shareholders are behaving irrationally may be found by examining the ownership concentration-profitability relationship among keiretsu firms. If keiretsu shareholders are behaving irrationally, then keiretsu firms with higher ownership concentration should perform better than keiretsu firms with lower levels of ownership concentration. This is examined in the following section.

IV. Ownership Concentration and Profitability

Table VIII provides OLS estimates of a regression of the accounting profit rate of the firm on the measure of ownership concentration (LS5) and other variables for the samples of keiretsu and independent firms. The dependent variable (RETURNA) is the mean value of annual net profit as a percentage of the book value of equity for the 6-year period 1979–1984.[26] Following

Table VIII
Regression Results for the Mean Accounting Profit Rate for 85 Keiretsu and 58 Independent Firms

Absolute values of t-statistics are in parentheses.

Independent Variables[a]	Keiretsu Firms	Independent Firms
Intercept	−0.007	0.2
	(0.2)	(1.7)
CAP	0.46	0.95
	(1.6)	(2.3)
ADV	0.18	0.07
	(2.5)	(0.5)
RD	−0.1	0.2
	(0.5)	(0.3)
ASSET[b]	−0.73	−12.0
	(0.4)	(0.4)
SE	−0.21	−0.70
	(1.0)	(1.5)
LS5	0.01	0.11
	(0.6)	(0.6)
N	85	58
Adjusted R^2	0.16	0.24
F-statistic	2.5	2.2

[a] See Table III for descriptions of variables.
[b] Coefficients on ASSET should be multiplied by 10^{-6}.

[26] Stock market rates of return presumably adjust for any divergences between the interests of management and shareholders, so I rely on accounting rates of return to reveal such differences.

Demsetz and Lehn (1985) and Morck, Shleifer, and Vishny (1988), I include several other independent variables in the regression: capital, research and development, and advertising expenditures (all as a percentage of sales) and firm size measured by the book value of assets in millions of dollars. The instability of the firm's profit rate (SE) is also included in the regressions. Tables III and IV provide full descriptions and summary statistics for these variables.

Table VIII shows no significant relationship between ownership concentration and accounting profit rate for either sample, where in both cases the coefficient on ownership concentration is positive, but insignificant (and, for keiretsu firms, particularly small). In sum, there is little evidence of any relationship between ownership concentration and profitability for keiretsu or independent firms.[27]

Morck, Shleifer, and Vishny (1988) suggest that the failure of Demsetz and Lehn (1985) to find a relationship between ownership concentration and profitability among U.S. firms may be due to their use of a linear specification that does not capture an important nonmonotonicity. In their analysis of the relationship between management ownership and the market valuation of a sample of U.S. firms, Morck et al. find evidence of just such a nonmonotonic relationship. The results in Table VIII are potentially subject to a similar criticism. However, following the Morck et al. methodology and using various differently specified piecewise linear regressions, I find no evidence of any nonmonotonic relationship between ownership concentration and profitability in either sample of Japanese firms. This may not be surprising given the previous observation that management ownership is probably rather less important in Japan than in the U.S.

I conclude that, given there is no significant relationship between profitability and ownership concentration in keiretsu firms, then the behavior of their large shareholders observed in Table V cannot be explained by claiming they are not maximizing the returns from their equity investments. This provides some indirect evidence that large shareholders of keiretsu firms may have means to monitor and control management other than through their role as a shareholder.

V. Conclusion

The empirical work suggests the following:

1. Ownership concentration in Japanese firms is higher than in U.S. firms. Financial institutions are the most important large shareholders of the firm,

---

[27] An alternative hypothesis for the behavior of keiretsu shareholders shown in Table V is that keiretsu provide their members with an insurance mechanism that stabilizes their performance (see Nakatani (1984)). If high ownership concentration proxies for the strength of attachment to a keiretsu, then such a mechanism would produce a negative relation between ownership concentration and profit volatility, which may offset the shareholder monitoring effect that we would otherwise observe. However, Table VIII shows no evidence of an insurance premium paid by keiretsu members, since ownership concentration appears unrelated to profitability.

and hold larger equity positions in firms than do U.S. financial institutions. Management ownership appears rather less important in Japan than in the United States.

2. Ownership concentration does not differ significantly between keiretsu and independent firms. In independent firms, ownership concentration is sensitive to the returns from exerting greater control over management. This appears to be largely driven by the behavior of financial institutions. In keiretsu firms, ownership concentration appears unrelated to the returns from exerting greater control over management.

3. Keiretsu firms do exhibit a somewhat stronger (although only marginally significant) relationship between the returns from exercising greater control over management and a measure of the degree of concentration of *both* share and loan ownership.

4. Ownership concentration and profitability in both keiretsu and independent firms are unrelated. In particular, higher ownership concentration is not related to higher profitability.

These results are consistent with two notions. First, the corporate governance mechanism in Japanese firms (both keiretsu and independent) appears to rely more on direct monitoring of managers by shareholders achieved through concentrated ownership structures than in the U.S. This reliance appears to reflect a number of factors, including the greater latitude given Japanese financial institutions to be active investors in firms and the less active market for corporate control in Japan.

Second, within Japan there exist two distinct corporate governance systems. Among independent firms, which have more arms-length relationships with their suppliers, customers, and financiers, management appears to be disciplined in part by large shareholders taking larger equity positions in those firms where increased control brings the largest benefits.

Among keiretsu firms, a different governance system appears to operate, where management is disciplined through a complex interaction of monitoring and control conducted by suppliers, customers, and financiers who typically have long-term commercial relationships with the firm in addition to being major creditors and shareholders. In this system, there are other avenues through which shareholders can more intensively monitor and influence management than simply by increasing their shareholdings of the firm.

That these two systems appear to have existed side by side with each other in the postwar period suggests that neither system has had an overwhelming advantage over the other, although the fact that keiretsu firms have generally been much larger than independent firms suggests that the keiretsu system may have had a significant comparative advantage. However, as Kester (1990) points out, the dramatic changes in the Japanese corporate sector in the last decade, including improved access to global capital markets and the deregulation of domestic capital markets, the slowing of growth opportunities for Japanese firms in their traditional lines of business and the huge build-up of cash on Japanese firms' balance sheets, may have weakened the governance mechanism in the keiretsu groups. For example, there is evidence that many keiretsu firms are becoming increasingly independent of their main banks as sources of capital.[28] This suggests that, if these trends continue, the corporate governance mechanism in keiretsu firms may in the future evolve into something more resembling the mechanism that appears to operate in independent firms.

[28] See Hoshi, Kashyap, and Scharfstein (1990).

REFERENCES

Abegglen, James and George Stalk, 1985, *Kaisha: The Japanese Corporation* (Basic Books, New York).

Demsetz, Harold and Kenneth Lehn, 1985, The structure of corporate ownership: Causes and consequences, *Journal of Political Economy* 93, 1155–1177.

Dodwell Marketing Consultants, 1985, *Industrial Groupings in Japan* (Dodwell Marketing Consultants, Tokyo).

Flath, David, 1990, Shareholding interlocks in the keiretsu, Japan's financial groups, Unpublished manuscript, North Carolina State University, Raleigh, NC.

French, Ken and James Poterba, 1991, Were Japanese stock prices too high? *Journal of Financial Economics* 29, 337–363.

Hoshi, Takeo, and Takatoshi Ito, 1991, Measuring coherence of Japanese enterprise groups, Unpublished manuscript, University of California, La Jolla, CA.

Hoshi, Takeo, Anil Kashyap, and David Scharfstein, 1990, Bank monitoring and investment: Evidence from the changing structure of Japanese corporate banking relationships, in R. Glenn Hubbard, ed.: *Information, Investment and Capital Markets* (University of Chicago Press, Chicago, IL).

————, 1991, Corporate structure, liquidity and investment: Evidence from Japanese panel data, *Quarterly Journal of Economics* 106, 33–60.

————and Takatoshi Ito, 1991, Measuring coherence of Japanese enterprise groups, Unpublished manuscript, University of California, La Jolla, CA.

Japan Company Handbook, 1985, (Oriental Economist, Tokyo)

Japanese Securities Research Institute, 1988, *Securities Markets in Japan* (Japanese Securities Research Institute, Tokyo)

Jensen, Michael C., 1989, Eclipse of the public corporation, *Harvard Business Review* 5, 61–75.

Kaplan, Steven, 1992, Internal corporate governance in Japan and the U.S.: Differences in activity and horizons, Unpublished manuscript, University of Chicago, Chicago, IL.

Kester, W. Carl, 1986, Capital and ownership structure: A comparison of United States and Japanese manufacturing corporations, *Financial Management*, Spring, 5–16.

————, 1990, *Japanese Takeovers: The Global Contest for Corporate Control* (Harvard Business School Press, Cambridge, MA).

Morck, R., Andrei Shleifer, and Robert Vishny, 1988, Management ownership and market valuation: An empirical analysis, *Journal of Financial Economics* 20, 293–316.

Nakatani, I., 1984, The economic role of corporate financial grouping, in M. Aoki, ed.: *Economic Analysis of the Japanese Firm* (Elsevier, New York).

Prowse, Stephen D., 1990, Institutional investment patterns and corporate financial behavior in the U.S. and Japan, *Journal of Financial Economics* 27, 43–66.

————, 1991. The changing role of institutional investors in the financial and governance markets, in A. Sametz, ed.: *Institutional Investing: The Challenges and Responsibilities of the Twenty-first Century* (Business One Irwin, Homewood, IL).

Roe, Mark J., 1990, Political and legal restraints on ownership control of public companies, *Journal of Financial Economics* 27, 7–42.

Wheeler, Jimmy, Merit Janow, and Thomas Pepper, 1982, *Japanese Industrial Development Policies in the 1980s* (Hudson Institute, New York).

[18]

PAUL SHEARD

The Economics of Japanese Corporate Organization and the "Structural Impediments" Debate: A Critical Review

Introduction

In recent years Japanese corporate organization and business and management practices have attracted widespread attention, although the focus of that attention has been shifting over time. After the high growth of the 1960s and the favorable structural adjustment to the "oil shocks" of the 1970s, Japan has continued to exhibit strong economic performance, to the point where per capita gross national product (GNP) now exceeds that in the United States. Much attention has been directed to understanding the organization and behavior of the firms whose operations have contributed to this economic performance. The perception that Japanese firm organization, both internal (the employment system) and external (capital structure and interfirm relations), differs in important ways from firm organization elsewhere, particularly in the other dominant economy, the United States, has intensified this interest, and has helped to stimulate a large body of literature on Japanese corporate organization and behavior in such disciplinary areas as economics, management science,

---

The author is a member of the department of economics, Faculty of Economics and Commerce, Australian National University, and visiting in the department of economics, Stanford University

and sociology, and in more popular and journalistic writings.[1]

A particular focus of interest, and some controversy, in recent years concerns the international context and implications of Japanese corporate organization. It is argued widely that various aspects of Japanese corporate organization have played important roles in, or are important elements in piecing together an understanding of, Japan's economic performance and behavior in the international economy involving such aspects as its economic growth, its propensity for macro- and micro-level structural adjustment, and its trade structure and trade flows. Corporate organization here is meant to refer to how production and exchange activities are organized within and between firms and in the Japanese context refers to such things as the organization and operation of internal labor markets and employment systems, bank-firm financial and capital relations, interfirm supply networks, subcontracting hierarchies and distribution systems, and innovative activities.

While many observers would agree that the issue of corporate organization and Japanese economic performance are related, opinions differ as to what the nature of that link is and what its implications are. One school of thought emphasizes the contribution of Japanese corporate organization to the achievement of favorable economic outcomes by facilitating longer-term structural adjustment (reallocation of capital and labor resources between declining and growing sectors) and higher levels of economic growth and innovative activity. Writers in this strand of literature tend to positively evaluate Japanese corporate organization, at least as the system works in Japan, and to focus on the motivational, incentive-aligning, risk-sharing, and informational-processing properties arising from the organization of firms around such institutional mechanisms as the "lifetime" employment system and enterprise unionism, close bank-firm ties, quasi-integrated subcontracting networks, and long-term interfirm trading arrangements (see, for example, Aoki, 1988, 1989; Dore, 1986).

Quite a different interpretation is given by another set of observers who view, basically the same aspects of, Japanese corporate organization as leading to a high degree of effective closure of the Japanese market, to a distorted trade structure, and to a tendency for Japan to accumulate excessive trade surpluses with major trading partners such as the United States and Western European countries (see, for example, Christelow, 1985–86; Gerlach, 1989; Johnson, 1990a; Lincoln, 1990a; Rapp, 1986; Yamamura, 1990). For instance, Lawrence (1987, pp. 517, 551) cites, and indicates agreement with, the view that "Japanese imports are also discouraged by unofficial practices, such as the strong relationships ('invisible handshakes') between local suppliers and buyers, 'just-in-time' inventory practices that give nearby suppliers an edge, and an unusually complex distribution system that creates substantial entry barriers for newcomers, whether Japanese or foreign."

Much of the discussion of this issue has taken place in the context of Japan-U.S. trade friction and trade negotiations. In particular, U.S. businessmen, policy makers and academics have argued that close interfirm ties in Japan in financial markets, intermediate product markets, and in parts supply systems represent "structural impediments" to penetration by foreign firms into the Japanese import market. According to the Office of the United States Trade Representative (1989, p. 112), "Japan's *keiretsu* system involves close intercompany linkages which impede the importation of many U.S. products into the Japanese market." It is fair to say that the *keiretsu* or corporate grouping form of corporate organization has become one of the most contentious issues in the analysis of Japan's international economic relations, as reflected in the issue becoming a major item on the agenda for discussion and policy action in the Structural Impediments Initiative talks between the United States and Japanese governments that commenced in 1989.[2] Johnson (1990b, p. 17) has gone so far as to characterize keiretsu as "the rigging of a market system in order to cause it to achieve political goals."

The purpose of this paper is to critically examine the structural impediments view of Japanese corporate organization and to sug-

The Economic Development of Northeast Asia IV

gest an alternative framework for approaching the issue. A word or two about the motivation for the paper is in order. As noted above, much of the popular and policy discussion of this issue has taken place in, or has been motivated by, the macroeconomic context of Japanese international economic relations and trade structure. Corporate organization has been perceived as contributing to the "problem" of excessive accumulation of current account surpluses via the mechanism of distorting the trade structure. In this paper we take a more microeconomic perspective that draws on the literature on Japanese corporate organization and on recent developments in the economics of organization. In a certain sense, we are positioned between the major protagonists in the debate: we disagree with the extreme view that says that corporate organization is irrelevant as an influence on, or component of, international trade, structural adjustment, and macroeconomic performance; we also feel that the arguments of many observers lack a convincing basis in microeconomic analysis.

The evidence that has been put forward to suggest that corporate organization is a structural impediment to imports has been of two different kinds. On the one hand, analyses of Japanese trade structure that purport to show that Japan's import and export patterns are not consistent with traditional theories have been used as indirect evidence of a distorting effect of corporate organization (and of other factors such as governmental nontariff barriers, industrial policy, and peculiar consumer preferences) (Lincoln, 1990a). On the other hand, there are numerous "stories" and anecdotes emanating from the first-hand experience of businessmen, officials and others dealing with Japan (but told n-th hand) testifying to the difficulty or impossibility of penetrating the Japanese market (e.g., Saxonhouse, 1988, pp. 233–34). Rather than go through the debates over whether or not Japanese trade structure is an outlier, and if it is why it is,[3] or try to "second guess" what was happening in the situations referred to in the numerous anecdotes, we concentrate in this paper on making some general points that relate directly to the interpretation of corporate organization and that may serve as a framework or benchmark for assessing the particular arguments that are encountered in the literature and in popular discussion.

Some conceptual issues

We begin by attempting to clarify what it means in economic terms to say that corporate organization might constitute a "structural impediment" to international trade. There are, at least, three ways to approach the issue. One is to interpret the notion of a structural impediment from the viewpoint of international trade as a nontariff barrier to trade, as many participants in the structural impediments debate do. While it is generally accepted that Japan now has a comparatively low level of tariff and other direct trade barriers, critics of Japan have argued that there are many nontariff barriers to trade, including various aspects of corporate organization. It is argued that just as tariffs raise the costs of exporting goods to a given country so does a complicated distribution system or the existence of close interfirm relations or "the need" to channel transactions through trading companies.

While superficially there appears to be an analogy between tariffs and corporate organization, it is not really a valid one, and analyzing corporate organization in terms of nontariff barriers is not very fruitful. The appropriate way to view the distinction between tariff and nontariff barriers is not in terms of the identity of the agent responsible for creating the barriers (e.g., government versus private sector) but in terms of the instrument employed by the government (in particular, its degree of "directness"). A distinction needs to be made between barriers to trade that result, directly or indirectly, from government policies and intervention—and which in principle the government could remove by undoing the actions—and "institutional" or "systemic" barriers, which may just reflect the real costs of operating the economic system, or at least whose "removal" is not a feasible policy option. To take an extreme example, the Japanese language is a barrier to new firms wishing to get their products into the Japanese market, and so to the firm concerned might appear to be just like the additional costs created by a tariff. In economic and policy terms, the two kinds of barriers are quite distinct.

A second approach is to appeal to the notion of "barriers to entry" that is used more widely in industrial economics than just the specific case of international trade (Gilbert, 1989). The interpretation from the viewpoint of the claim that corporate organization is a structural impediment would be that Japanese firms, acting individually or in cartels, are able to erect barriers to the entry of foreign producers into their markets. There are a number of problems with this interpretation of the structural impediments hypothesis. The notion of barriers to entry in industrial economics has been quite controversial, and economists use the term in a much more restricted sense than is the case in popular discussion. Indeed, according to one school of thought, barriers to entry could seldom, if ever, exist in the absence of some form of direct or indirect governmental activity or sanctioning. Second, it does not appear that barriers to entry, using the term in the looser sense, are particularly high in Japanese markets as compared to other industrialized countries. Third, to the extent that barriers do exist, there is no particular reason to expect that these would apply differentially to domestic as opposed to foreign entrants. Fourth, the concept of barriers to entry is a "market-oriented" concept in the tradition of the "market structure-conduct-performance" paradigm of industrial organization: there is a market in existence and some aspect of the structure of the market or conduct of the firms operating in it leads to there being a barrier to new entry. Most of the writers who adhere to the structural impediments view of Japanese corporate organization appear to have something else in mind, namely that firm organization itself influences the nature of the market to be entered.

These observations lead to consideration of a third, and more fruitful, approach, which is to locate the discussion of structural impediments in the context of the theory of economic organization (or theory of the firm). The essence of the structural impediments arguments appears to be that the very way in which the activities of firms are organized constitutes a systemic barrier to entry, particularly by foreign firms. This suggests that the notion of barriers to entry itself may need to be modified to take account of the possibility that the way firms are organized influences the nature and extent of the market in which these firms operate. It also suggests that the thesis that corporate organization affects market entry is one that applies in principle to any economy, not just Japan.

The relevance of the recent literature on the theory of economic organization is that it views "firms" and "markets" as alternative modes for organizing economic activity. It is not just the case that firms are economic agents that act in markets; as recognized by Coase (1937) and taken up in a serious way by Williamson (1975) firms can also be seen as supplanting, or being supplanted by, markets. To cite some specific examples, an automobile assembly firm can arrange for the production of parts to be done in-house or it may choose to purchase them from independent parts suppliers through a market transaction; the firm may raise finance from an external capital market through share or bond issues or, if it is one division in a larger business organization, it may receive its funding from a head office; the firm's employees may be permanent employees supplying labor inputs under long-term contractual arrangements or the firm may hire its workers on a short-term basis from the external labor market. The modern theory of economic organization is concerned largely with understanding what governs these kinds of choices and what their economic implications are. Some questions are: What is the difference between markets and hierarchy (internal organization of firms)? What determines whether economic activity takes place within firms or between firms in markets? And what are the comparative advantages and attributes of firms and markets? Interest in these questions dates back at least to Coase (1937) but received renewed interest with the work of Williamson (1975, 1985) and with developments in the economics of information in the past fifteen or so years (Kreps, 1990).[4]

The literature also recognizes that organization design is not a matter of a series of binary choices—internalization or spot-market procurement—as the above examples might suggest but rather usually there exists a large range of possible organizational forms, or degrees of firm-like and market-like aspects for any given transaction.

Treating firms and markets as alternative transaction governance structures, raises the question of what the essential difference between these is. This issue continues to be debated in the literature. One predominant view associates with firm-like activity such attributes as centralized decision making, administration by fiat, and adjustment of key variables in terms of quantities rather than prices; market-like activity, on the other hand, is characterized by decentralized decision making and coordination of decisions through the price mechanism. In a firm, resources move to alternative uses because they are directed to by a higher "authority" (a manager, boss, or entrepreneur) and often those resources (equipment, skills, materials, and parts) are to some extent specialized, they are not fungible perfectly between internal uses and redeployment to the market (other firms), and the identity of the agents supplying them is a relevant variable. In a pure market transaction, information and decision-making authority is dispersed, resources move in response to price signals, which convey to agents in an economical form information about the opportunities and constraints that they face, and transactions are anonymous in the sense that the identity of the agents involved is not important.

While these distinctions provide important insights, an alternative approach has been to play down somewhat the distinction between firms and markets by arguing that the firm is best viewed as a "nexus of contractual relationships" among various factors of production and consumers of output (Alchian and Demsetz, 1972; Jensen and Meckling, 1976; Fama, 1980; Cheung, 1983). This represents a subtle but powerful shift in viewing the firm from the traditional way. One implication is that we should not take too seriously the notion that there exists a well-defined boundary to the firm. In the pure theory of markets, the firm has a boundary in the sense that it is a well-defined economic agent endowed with a technology (production function) and a consistent decision-making capacity (objective function). The firm operates in markets and is treated analogously to the consumer or household in consumer theory. The Coase-Williamson line of literature argues that the line between firms and markets is not given but itself should be the subject of economic analysis, but implicitly views the line itself as being well defined.

The nexus-of-contracts view suggests that, while the firm may exist as a legal entity that can enter into enforceable contracts, we should not worry too much about whether the parties that are being contracted with are "inside" the firm or "outside" of it (Tirole, 1988a, p. 16). What is of interest not so much where the contracting agent is notionally located in relation to the boundary of the firm as the nature of the transactional relationship. For instance, it is normal to think of an employee as being located inside the firm but an input supplier or customer as being outside the firm (transacting with the firm "across" a market). But it may be the case that from an economic viewpoint the customer is more a part of the firm than the employee is. As an example, the customer may have undertaken shared investments and be transacting with the firm on a continual basis (what Itoh and Matsui [1987] term "organizational transactions") whereas the employee might be supplying labor services of a nonspecific kind on a short-term basis from the labor market.

Another implication is that the notion of ownership of the firm needs to be qualified, if not dispensed with entirely. As Fama (1980, p. 290) puts it, "ownership of capital should not be confused with ownership of the firm. Each factor in a firm is owned by somebody. The firm is just the set of contracts covering the way inputs are joined to create outputs and the way receipts from outputs are shared among inputs." Shareholders are normally thought as being the owners of the firm. The point being made here is that shareholders do not "own the firm," they own shares in the firm, which define a bundle of rights. Conceptually shareholders are like other suppliers of factors to the firm such as bondholders or lending banks which supply the same factor but under different contractual arrangements, or employees who supply a different factor, but may do so under contractual arrangements resembling those commonly associated with that of a shareholder (a long-term arrangement and such that they have "a say" in the running of the firm). One view of ownership, put forward by Grossman and Hart (1986), is that it defines the party with residual decision rights, that is, the rights to specify what actions to take in situations not explicitly contracted for.

These theoretical developments are helpful for providing insights into some controversies concerning the Japanese firm. For instance, a common argument has been that shareholders in a Japanese firm are not really the owners of the firm and that the employees, because of their "lifetime" employment status, are the "real" owners of the firm (Abegglen and Stalk, 1984; Nishiyama, 1980). On this basis, it is sometimes argued that the Japanese firm is fundamentally different from firms elsewhere and not amenable to economic analysis. But the above discussion suggests the basis for this assertion may not be sound. The institutional form of the firm reflects the underlying contractual arrangements entered into by suppliers of inputs and consumers of output. A more accurate observation may be that the Japanese firm takes on a particular contractual form, not that it is fundamentally different from firms elsewhere. The central task becomes to understand why the contracts, which are generally implicit in nature and incompletely specified, take on the particular form that they do, and what this means for economic performance.

Viewed from the economics of organization perspective, arguments about Japanese corporate organization as structural impediments to trade become arguments about how and why firms and markets are organized in Japan. This shift in analytical focus has important implications for policy assessment. In the traditional industrial organization literature, barriers to entry if they exist are usually associated with attempts to exercise, maintain or obtain monopoly power and are thought to be undesirable from a welfare viewpoint. In the Coase-Williamson framework, economic organization evolves in such a way as to reduce transaction costs, which in some circumstances means that transactions will be organized within firms rather than in markets, or between firms but in ways that differ from the benchmark of competitive armslength market transactions (Williamson, 1989). It would be erroneous from a public policy viewpoint to regard aspects of corporate organization as constituting "barriers to entry" to markets; in the Williamson world, corporate organization is a *solution* to a problem not a source of one.

Long-term contracts and Japanese corporate organization

A common claim in the literature and policy discussion is that the prevalence of long-term contractual arrangements in Japanese business makes penetration of the Japanese market inherently difficult and gives Japanese industry a form of "natural immunity" against import competition (Dore, 1986, p. 248). Tyson and Zysman (1989a, p. xix) argue that "even when the government reduces policy barriers to market access in Japan, foreign firms continue to confront barriers that stem from the long-term contractual relationships among Japanese firms" and that "long-term business relationships ... serve to slow or impede shifts provoked by price changes in the market," meaning that business practices "seal off" the market "at very low levels of import penetration" (1989b, p. 126). Dore (1986, p. 248) makes the point this way: "Imports penetrate into markets, and where there *are* no markets, only a network of established 'customer relationships,' it is hard for them to make headway" (emphasis in original).

A number of aspects of long-term interfirm ties have been cited in this context, including long-term supply/purchasing relations in parts supply systems, in vertical distribution systems, and between firms in "horizontal" corporate groups, often involving mediation by general trading companies (*sogo shosha*), intercorporate shareholding relations based on "stable shareholding arrangements," and close bank-firm ties, centering on the main bank system.[5] These phenomena are quite extensively observed in the large corporate sector but find particular manifestation in the context of the large firms associated with the six bank-centered corporate groupings (*kigyo shudan*).

A number of facets of distribution systems in Japan have been cited as factors contributing to the alleged closedness of the Japanese market to foreign imports, particularly of manufactured goods. Some of these relate to regulatory issues such as the infamous large-scale retail stores law (*Daikibo kouri tenpo ho*), but a recurring theme has been the nature of corporate organization in the multilayered distribution system. For example, Chalmers Johnson (1990a, p. 16) has recently argued that "so-called distribution *keiretsu* are actually cartels to gouge domestic consumers and keep out foreign competitors," and elsewhere (1990b, p. 122) that, although the distribution system inflates the markup in price on imported goods, "price is actually irrelevant because foreign goods are normally not allowed in the distribution system." Lincoln (1990a, p. 124) argues that "the inefficiency or convoluted nature of the system is not the problem . . . the real difficulty lies in the tight relationships between distributors and manufacturers." Similar observations have been made with regard to parts supply procurement systems in Japan, such as those of the automobile manufacturers.

A feature of Japanese corporate capital structure is the prevalence of corporate cross-shareholding, centering on identifiable financial corporate groupings. A notable aspect is that these shareholdings appear to be based on implicit self-enforcing agreements among firms to hold the shares as "friendly insiders" and not, for instance, to tender them to outside third parties such as might occur in the case of a hostile takeover. Japanese businessmen refer to these arrangements as "stable shareholding arrangements" (*antei kabunushi kosaku*) and the practice is thought to be one important factor behind the absence, for all intents and purposes, of an active external takeover market in Japan. While some writers evaluate positively this aspect of Japanese financial corporate organization, in the sense of allowing management to adopt a longer-run decision-making horizon and avoiding some of the pitfalls of a U.S.-style system,[6] it has also been cited as a further aspect of the closed nature of Japanese corporate organization and markets: in this case the market for the control of corporate assets. For instance, Johnson (1990a, pp. 119–20) argues that "Japan's structure also blocks foreign acquisitions of Japanese firms as a way of entering the Japanese market. . . . Japan's blocking of acquisitions is not only an anticompetitive practice but also a nontariff barrier to trade" and elsewhere identifies cross-shareholding as one of "the instruments that are currently being employed in the administration of Japan's long-standing mercantilist industrial policy" (1990a, p. 17).[7] The recent attempt by the United States "corporate raider" T. Boone Pickens to gain control, or at least a say in the running, of Toyota affiliate (19 percent owned) and headlamp supplier, Koito Manufacturing Company, focused sharp attention in international policy circles on this institutional phenomenon of corporate ownership and control in Japan. Pickens became the largest shareholder in Koito with 26 percent of its stock but was unsuccessful in his attempt to exert control over the firm, and recently announced that he was withdrawing from the company.

Importance of the comparative benchmark

An important issue in an assessment of the above kinds of claims concerns the comparative benchmark that is used to assess the degree of interpenetration of market and hierarchy, or the pervasiveness of long-term contractual arrangements in Japan (Imai and Itami, 1984). For simplicity, call the degree to which market has been supplanted by hierarchy the degree of "market-orientedness" in an economy. Most writers cite the pervasiveness of long-term contracts as evidence of the lack of market-orientedness and, by extension, of the closedness of the Japanese economy.

The Economic Development of Northeast Asia IV

Without specifying a comparative benchmark, however, it is not clear conceptually or empirically whether the Japanese economy is less or more infused with market elements than any other economy, such as that of the United States with which it is commonly compared.

At one extreme, one could envision a completely internalized economy in which there was one giant firm and in which all economy activity was decided upon according to information collected by the central planning authority (the head office or central government) and executed according to plans and directions laid down by the central authority. At the other extreme, one could posit the existence of a completely "externalized" or market economy in which all firms were atomistic price-taking agents and all activity took place through competitive markets. The earlier discussion suggests however that there are two dimensions along which the degree of "market-orientedness" should be measured. One is the degree of concentration of activity within the boundaries of firms; the other is the degree to which relations between firms in the economy conform to market transactions as opposed to resembling intrafirm transactions. The first point refers to where the boundary of the firm is drawn (how extensive or integrated the firm is); the second to what is going on at, and lies beyond, the boundary of the firm.

The importance of this distinction can be appreciated by considering two prototypical economies. In one, firms are extensive—there is a high degree of integration within firms—but interactions between firms are governed by the market. In another, firms are nonextensive—there is little integration—but interfirm ties are strong. It is not clear a priori which of these two economies should be said to be more market oriented. At the risk of oversimplification, the Japanese mode seems to be that of the type-one economy, and the Western mode, particularly the Anglo-American economies, seems to correspond to that of the type-two economy.

Two generalizations or "stylized facts" can be gleaned form the literature on Japanese corporate organization that support the above characterization.[8] The first is the prevalence of long-term contractual relationships in Japanese business which has been analyzed variously in such terms as the prevalence of "visible handshakes" (Aoki, 1984b), "relational contracting" (Dore, 1986), "business alliances" (Gerlach, 1987), and "organizational transactions" (Itoh and Matsui, 1987). Examples include the long-term employment contracts embodied in the "lifetime" employment system, the close relationship between the firm and its main bank, stable intercorporate shareholdings, close association with and intermediation of interfirm transactions by general trading companies, and long-term supply relationships with parts suppliers and subcontractors. In all of these cases, the firm's links with labor, financial, product and services markets depart markedly from the theoretical benchmark of competitive, arms-length market transactions.

The second stylized fact is the tendency for Japanese business units to be relatively 'dis-integrated' (Aoki, 1984b, 1984d; Clark, 1979, chap. 3). By this is meant that the core activities and contracts of a Japanese business units are probably less extensive and more narrowly circumscribed than those of a typical Western firm. Several aspects of this generalization can be cited, relating to employment, in-house production, organizational structure and diversification.

At the level of the business unit, in a legal, accounting and corporate identity sense, the typical large firm in Japan is relatively specialized, nonintegrated, and centralized organizationally. Horizontally, Japanese firms tend to be quite specialized in terms of the range of industries in which they operate (typically it is one) (Goto, 1981). Vertically, the Japanese firm tends to be relatively dis-integrated in terms of the operations and production activities actually located "in-house" (Aoki, 1984b, 1984d). Operations such as maintenance, parts supply, and sales and distribution are often carried out by affiliated firms or subcontractors, whereas the parent firm concentrates on the core production activities such as technology-intensive processing and assembly operations.

This is true of the employment system also. Only core managerial and skilled blue-collar workers are covered by the lifetime employment system and many other labor inputs are provided by workers who are not formally integrated into the employment structure of the firm such as "outside workers" (*shagaiko*), temporary workers (*rinjiko*), and part-time workers (usually female employees). In terms of organizational structure, the typical Japanese firm is closer to the unitary, functional structure (Williamson's [1975] U-form) than the decentralized, divisionalized structure (M-form). This is partly because firms are less diversified horizontally and partly because parts-supplying subsidiaries and affiliates are one step removed from the core firm and handled through a "Related Firms' Office" (*kanren jigyobu*) rather than being incorporated into divisions of the firm.

Putting the two aspects together, and positing a typical Western firm as a comparative yardstick, it is possible to make the following generalization: if we draw a boundary around what would normally be considered the firm we find that there typically is less activity inside the boundary of the Japanese firm, but that the contracts or interactions that the firm has with other economic agents "outside the firm" are less market oriented and have more of the transactional features normally associated with intrafirm activity. To give a frequently cited example, a Japanese auto maker such as Toyota has a relatively low level of in-house production but maintains close "firm-like" ties with it suppliers, whereas a U.S. auto maker like General Motors has (or at least traditionally had) a relatively high level of in-house production but more market-based ties with outside suppliers. A priori it is an open question which of these two production systems is more "closed" to new suppliers.

The issue of long-term contracts and the closeness of interfirm ties is, to a certain extent, an empirical matter, in the sense that in principle it should be possible to measure or quantify the extent of these in the economy. Survey evidence does indicate that large firms in Japan make extensive use of long-term trading arrangements. One recent survey of large nonfinancial firms showed that

61 percent of firms considered that "almost all" of their transactions involving production materials were continuous ones and 37 percent considered that a "considerable proportion" were (Nihon keizai chosa kyogikai, 1989, p. 2). Restricting attention to the top thirty suppliers, the survey found that 63 percent of these had had dealings with the firm for ten or more years (p. 10). On the other hand, it would appear that observers often impute too much cohesion to the horizontal groupings of firms (*kigyo shudan*), that are usually defined with respect to the membership of a presidents' committee (*shachokai*). The "members" of these groups have varying degrees of overlapping financial and transactional ties but each firm is an independent corporate entity. For instance, in the 1987 FY the group financial institutions provided an average of 17 percent of the borrowings of member firms, 23 percent of issued shares were held within the group, and in 1981 FY 12 percent of material inputs were purchased from and 11 percent of sales made to other group members (Ryutsu torihiki kanko nado to kyoso seisaku ni kansuru kento iinkai, 1990, pp. 55–58). These figures can be viewed as being "high" or "low" depending on one's perspective. It is quite misleading, however, to treat the group as a whole as a single more-or-less cohesive business entity, as is suggested by the common practice of quoting figures such as that the big six groups account for 15 percent of sales turnover in the economy.

Effects of long-term ties

Another set of issues concerns the implications and effects of long-term contracts. To understand the economic logic behind long-term contracts it is necessary to work within a framework where decision making in at least two periods is considered. From the vantage point of period 1, a long-term contract among economic agents would be one that specified certain actions (or placed constraints on the choice sets) of the agents in period 2, whereas a short-term contract would specify actions only in period 1, and leave it until period 2 had arrived to determine period

2 actions, including such issues as who to trade with and on what terms. A number of points can be made within this general framework.

The first point, harking back to the earlier comments, is that, viewed from the perspective of the economic organization literature, associating various aspects of how firms and interfirm relationships are organized with the notion of "market closure" may be misguided.[9] Assume, as in most of economic theory, that "firms" exist in order to produce goods that will be consumed by individual "consumers." Suppose that entry into the final goods markets is free (there are no differential barriers to entry across potential competitors in the market); then the final consumer markets are not "closed." To produce the goods that consumers demand, a firm typically will require numerous inputs (even for simple consumer items such as pencils or tissue paper, not to mention complex articles such as automobiles or computers). How the firm chooses to organize itself—that is, the supply of those inputs—for example, by purchasing various components from spot markets or through in-house production or through complicated long-term relationships with subcontractors and suppliers, is normally thought of as an aspect of the firm's competitive, market strategy. One firm may choose to organize itself in one way, and another firm in quite a different way, but we would not normally say that one firm's choice had "closed the market" to the other firm, unless we meant it in the sense that the firm made a better choice which made it more competitive in the final market place.[10] But that is like saying that one firm "closed the market" to another because it developed a better product or provided better service to consumers.

This point can be pushed a bit further by reference to the following illustrative example. Consider an industry that has two distinct production stages, "upstream operations," such as manufacture of basic parts, and "downstream operations," such as the assembly of those parts into the final consumer product. Consider two countries, A and B, so that the respective upstream industries can be labeled A_U and B_U, and similarly for the downstream industries. A number of points can be made with reference to this basic framework.

The first is to notice that, in principle, various forms of industrial organization are possible. The two stages of production could be vertically integrated, there could be long-term trading relations, or firms could interact across arms-length markets. Suppose that industrial organization in the two countries is such that in country A firms tend to have a high proportion of long-term contractual arrangements whereas in B there is more reliance on short-term transacting. For expository purposes, take the extreme case where in a certain period input-output transactions in country A are totally governed by complete long-term contracts and in country B there are no contractual constraints, only short-term contracting. Then it might appear that there is a "market closure" problem for firms in industry B_U (the upstream industry in country B) with respect to A_D in that those firms cannot export to industry A_D: the A_D market appears to be closed to them in the period under consideration. The point that was made above is that this market closure pertains to an input market in country A, not the final consumer market, which is the one that matters: for instance, the market in country A is not really closed to firms in B_U because as long as firms in B_D can sell their output to final consumers in country A, firms in B_U are selling their output there indirectly (not through firms in A_U but this is irrelevant). From a policy perspective, there is no need for concern about the "closure" of the input market to A_D as long as the final market remains open, and, as long as firms in A_D do not control an essential input to firms in B_D, their strategy with respect to the organization of their inputs cannot have an effect on the capacity of firms in country B to compete in the D market (in either country). A further point to note is that it is always open to firms in B to organize themselves in the same way as firms in A.

A second set of points relates to viewing the effects of long-term contracts in their entirety both in a temporal sense and in terms of their associated costs and benefits. To continue with the above example, observing that in a given period B_U firms were not able to supply A_D firms because A_D firms were being supplied by A_U firms under long-term contracts could reflect two very different things: one, that B_U firms had the opportunity to compete with A_U firms for the right to supply A_D firms at the time A_D firms were entering into long-term contracts, but they chose not to; and two, B_U firms were excluded from the opportunity to enter into long-term contracts with A_D firms in the earlier period. That is, the period over which the arrangement is said to be exclusionary is quite critical. An arrangement can be exclusionary in the short run—by virtue of there being prior commitments associated with long-term contracts—or exclusionary in the long run.

This distinction is a critical one in the context of assessing the many claims of exclusionary behavior and practices by so-called keiretsu firms. It is one thing to say that a foreign firm cannot supply to a Japanese firm because it is unwilling to supply under a long-term contractual basis and quite another to say that it is excluded from ever being able to supply under a long-term contractual arrangement. The latter case is what presents a real policy problem.

Long-term contracts involve both costs and benefits for the various parties involved, and much of the popular discussion implicitly focuses selectively on just the costs or the benefits. In terms of the case under consideration, an A_U firm benefits from its long-term contract with the A_D industry in that it has secured its future demand. But there is a corresponding opportunity cost of doing this; to the extent that the contract is binding, it cannot switch the output dedicated under the long-term contract to other sources of demand even should external market conditions make this more beneficial. Long-term contracts make the future less uncertain, but correspondingly limit the flexibility to take advantage of the profitable opportunities that come having a wider choice set.

From the viewpoint of the B_U firms also there is a tendency to focus only on the costs to them and overlook the possible benefits they may enjoy as result of A_U firms—their direct competitors—having entered into long-term contracts. The popular discussion tends to focus on the fact that B_U firms are disadvantaged by A_U contracts with A_D but overlooks the fact that B_U firms may benefit from this. One way they may benefit is in not facing as much competition from A_U firms in their dealings with B_D. To bring this point out starkly, assume that there is just one firm in each industry in each country and that, a la Bertrand price competition, two firms would be sufficient to induce competitive outcomes. Suppose that the A_U firm is able to dedicate its total output to the A_D firm under a long-term supply contract; then this shuts firm B_U out of any dealings with A_D which appears to hurt B_U. But now B_U does not face any competition from A_U in its dealings with B_D and so is effectively transformed into a monopolist with respect to its position in the B market. What appears to disadvantage B_U, A_U's ability to tie up the A_D input market, actually works to B_U's advantage. To make the point graphically, firm A_U's shutting of B_U out of its market also implies shutting its own self out of B_U's output market. This example, of course, is somewhat contrived, and it is unlikely to be an equilibrium course of action for A_D to enter into the contract in the first place. The example serves to sharply point out, however, that long-term contracts entail costs and benefits to the firms concerned, and focusing on only one side of the equation is likely to be misleading.

Economic rationale for long-term ties

So far we have focused on examining the possible effects of long-term contracts; we need to look also at the reasons for employing long-term contracts. It should be noted that the literature in economics literature on the reasons for and effects of long-term contracting is still developing.[11] One quite general insight, however, is that there may be "good" efficiency reasons for economic agents utilizing long-term contracts in their dealings with one another. Among the reasons that have been identified are to facilitate risk-sharing, to economize on transactions costs, and to facilitate transactions that involve one or more agent making specific investments or revealing private information.

Consider a simple two-period model where agents take actions in both periods and the payoffs to the agents, which are functions potentially of first-period actions, are subject to uncertainty in the second period (payoffs are state-dependent). Then a basic insight of contract theory is that the agent may take different actions in period 1, and arrive in period 2 with different attributes, depending on what payoff is specified in the contract for the agent in period 2. For instance, if exposed to spot-market conditions in period 2, an employee with an opportunity to make a risky but potentially valuable specific investment in period 1 may refrain from doing so, but be induced to make the investment if offered a long-term contract that specifies in advance what he/she will receive in the second period.

How do these general observations apply to the Japanese firm? One insight is that long-term contractual arrangements, of the kind that tend to characterize Japanese business, may perform such economic functions as facilitating risk sharing, providing incentives to make specific investments, and limiting the scope for opportunistic behavior. For instance, workers in a Japanese firm who develop firm-specific skills in the context of the lifetime employment system may be putting themselves at considerable risk of having the value of their human capital reduced by financial failure of the firm or takeover by an agent who reneges on the implicit agreements. The financial contracts of the firm, such as those with the main bank and stable shareholders, may be crucial in providing employees with incentives to enter into the kinds of employment contracts with the firm that they do, and neither the financial contracts nor the employment contracts would make complete sense viewed in isolation from one another or without reference to the intertemporal nature of the firm's investments and activities.

The argument outlined earlier that it is only competition in the final consumer market that matters would be challenged by those who argue, as in the earlier quotations, that the Japanese distribution itself is a major barrier to the entry of foreign firms and products. Again, the issues are more complex and subtle than the popular discussion might convey. Several points can be made. First, distribution can be viewed as another input that the firm contracts for, although temporally it enters differently from other material inputs. The earlier logic carries over: how firms choose to organize the supply of this input is an aspect of their corporate organizational strategy, and does not necessarily imply (and in general will not) that a firm that integrates forward into distribution is able to exercise any market power in so doing.[12] Second, although it is generally recognized that distribution in the Japanese market is difficult and costly, these costs must be borne by all firms in the market. Firms that have already sunk considerable costs in setting up distribution channels may have an absolute cost advantage over new entrants (but as with any asset there is an opportunity cost that needs to be taken into account), but foreign firms that are not committed to existing distribution networks may have an advantage in certain circumstances in being less constrained in their choices.

Itoh (forthcoming 1992) carries these arguments further in an analysis of the Japanese distribution system from the viewpoint of recent developments in economic theory.[13] Itoh challenges the view that Japanese distribution systems are inefficient and argues instead that they reflect the importance of what he terms "organizational transactions" in the Japanese business sphere. Itoh's point is that quite complicated transactional arrangements such as are found in Japanese distribution systems reflect the outcome of attempts by transaction partners to organize their transactions in long-term efficient ways in the presence of problems of contractual incompleteness, uncertainty, possible opportunistic behavior and highly nonstandardized products. While not denying that such distribution systems may represent, at least a short-term, barrier to entry to foreign firms, Itoh's analysis provides a timely caution against taking this fact too much at face value rather than probing more deeply into the complex of economic and other factors that lie behind it.

Sheard's (1989a) analysis of the role of general trading companies in interfirm transactions makes a similar point. Even though there exists a voluminous literature on the general trading companies,[14] there has been surprisingly little detailed examination of the nature of, and reasons for, the trading companies' role in interfirm transactions from an analytical as opposed to descriptive perspective. As with other aspects of Japanese corporate organization, such an analysis is crucial if any informed judgment is to be made about the many claims that have made regarding the GTCs.

Sheard argues that one of the important economic functions that large trading companies perform is that of a risk-absorbing agent in interfirm transactions involving large exposure by suppliers to trade credit default risk by purchasers. One point that Sheard makes is that a seemingly curious aspect of distribution system complexity—the entering of a trading company into a transaction between two firms—can be given a natural economic interpretation if approached from the viewpoint of the more recent perspective of the theory of economic organization. Thus the analysis complements the more general approach of Itoh.

A series of papers by Asanuma (1985a, 1985b, 1989) has helped to clarify the economic mechanisms at work in parts supply networks in Japan, particularly in the automobile industry. Asanuma points out that U.S. firms typically have more suppliers of parts than their Japanese counterparts but that the trading relationship is of longer duration in Japan. As noted above, the tendency of Japanese firms to enter into long-term trading relationships is frequently cited as a source of "market closure" in Japan.[15] Asanuma makes a key contribution to aiding our understanding of this issue. He shows that a key feature of the Japanese system is that suppliers are involved earlier and to a greater degree in the design and development stages of parts production; on the other hand, suppliers do not escape competitive pressures and are expected, and given incentives, to engage in cost-reducing technical innovations, are subject to long-run evaluation via ratings and "promotion" or "demotion" in the subcontracting hierarchy, and are expected to be able to supply customized parts and respond flexibly to variations in the short-run requirements of their parent firms. Asanuma (forthcoming 1992) also discusses recent international adjustments in both the U.S. and Japan. He argues that since the early 1980s there has been some convergence of the U.S. system toward that of Japan.

Transmission of shocks and structural adjustment

The structural impediments view of Japanese corporate organization tends to conjure up an image of Japanese firms protected from external competition by a network of "cozy" interfirm relations with banks, trading companies, suppliers and purchasers, and even competitors. This image is quite at odds with another set of perceptions and literature about Japanese corporate organization suggesting that the organization of Japanese industry has been an important factor underpinning the resilience of the economy in the face of external shocks to competitiveness and its propensity to carry out longer term structural adjustments in response to such shifts in competitiveness. A common theme in this strand of literature is that Japanese corporate organizational forms, while incorporating extensively long-term contractual elements, possess quite flexible institutional mechanisms for adapting to changes in competitive conditions, as suggested by Dore's (1986) phrase "flexible rigidities."

How an economy reacts to exogenous shocks and disturbances such as short-term price shocks or longer term structural changes in competitiveness, is often viewed as a macroeconomic question and analyzed with the help of macroeconomic models and tools. There is also an important question, however, as to whether and in what ways the organization of economic activity at the micro level can affect the economy's response to shocks and the process of structural adjustment. As noted earlier, this issue has attracted attention in the Japanese context.

At a theoretical level, there is some justification for being interested in the link between corporate organization and structural adjustment. One general proposition, drawing on the above discussion, would be that how factors of production are affected by and respond to exogenous shocks will depend in part on how those factors of production are organized within and between such institutions as "firms" and "markets." Putting the point in a somewhat neoclassical way, factors of production are supplied to firms according to particular contractual arrangements and how factors are remunerated and "behave" in various states of nature will reflect the nature of those contractual arrangements.

A direct link between corporate organization and structural adjustment concerns the risk-shifting properties of economic organization. Implicit in the economic organization of firms are arrangements for shifting risks between various participants in the firm. For instance, in the neoclassical firm, the shareholders are the residual risk bearers, and shareholders and bondholders, although supplying the same factor, differ in the risk that they have contracted to accept (and in their control rights over the firm). These risk-shifting arrangements have implications for structural adjustment because they influence who bears the costs of structural adjustment, these costs being the ex post manifestations of what, ex ante, represent risks to the agents concerned. If a complete set of risk-insurance markets existed, structural adjustment would be a trivial process as all the costs would be fully accounted for and internalized ex ante. In the real world, however, this is manifestly not the case, and sorting out and devising solutions to the problem of how the costs of adjustment are distributed is usually a critical issue in the public policy process surrounding structural adjustment.

The literature has focused on a number of dimensions of corporate organization in considering implications for transmission of shocks and structural adjustment in Japan.[16] It is possible to distinguish two related aspects. One is how corporate organization affects the way in which shocks to demand or costs impinge on the firm. A second is how corporate organization affects the way that the firm responds to these shocks. The distinction is between how adjustment pressures are manifest and how these are played out, or between short-term impacts and long-run responses.

A general observation is that contractual arrangements in various markets incorporate implicit risk-sharing devices that serve to cushion the impact of external shocks on the firm. These risk-sharing mechanisms include flexibility in employment contracts, the main bank system, intercorporate shareholdings, long-term contracts governing the supply of inputs and sale of outputs, and the intermediation of general trading companies in interfirm transactions. The effect of these mechanisms is that Japanese firms are not as vulnerable in the short-run to shocks to their competitiveness as might be suggested by the fact of their typically relatively narrow product specialization, highly-levered financial structure and lifetime employment-related obligations.

Much attention in this context has focused on labor market adjustment and the implications of the lifetime employment system (Komiya and Yasui, 1984; Dore, 1986, chap. 4; Freeman and Weitzman, 1987; Koike, 1983, 1988). A number of points about the lifetime employment system are now clear. The first is that only a certain fraction of the total effective work force of a large Japanese firm is covered by permanent employment contracts. To adopt the terminology introduced earlier, the permanent employment contract is a rather special contract within the set of contracts called the firm in Japan. In the context of labor adjustment, because there are different categories of employees, that differ in the level of contractual obligation (including the firm's risk sharing vis-à-vis the employee), the Japanese firm has several margins of adjustment even in the relatively short run when the number of core permanent employees is fixed.

A second point that is frequently made with regard to adjustment flexibility is that, because of such features of the lifetime employment system as on-the-job training, job rotation with the firm, and the system of enterprise unionism, reallocation of labor within the firm in response to changing competitive conditions is facilitated, compared with the typical situation in a Western-type firm.

Other observers make a somewhat different but related point, namely that the lifetime employment system encourages structural adjustment at the firm level because of incentive effects. The argument is that firms have an incentive to innovate and diversify into new product lines in order to redeploy the labor force to which they have extended guarantees of lifetime employment (these guarantees are not absolute but the costs of reneging in an opportunistic way may be so high as to give these incentives to the firm); workers have corresponding incentives to cooperate in the process of internal adjustment given the alignment of their interests with those of the firm. While these incentive and motivational effects are no doubt significant, these are frequently overstated in the literature.

The empirical evidence suggests that there is more flexibility in the intrafirm labor markets, both in terms of labor inputs in the short run and the number of employees in the medium to long run, than is suggested by the lifetime employment stereotype.[17] In cases where there is a structural decline in demand, firms implement the necessary reductions in the size of their work forces, including the redeployment and retrenchment of regular or lifetime employees (Rohlen, 1979). The feature of this process in Japan appears to be the careful way in which firms go about implementing these voluntary retirement and redeployment schemes. There is a good deal of evidence to suggest that large Japanese firms cushion the impact of exogenous shocks on their work forces, suggesting that lifetime employment contracts incorporate a significant risk-insurance element, but the extent of this is easily overstated (the capacity of the firm to honor the risk insurance component of its employment contracts is limited, and most severely so in bad states of nature when it is most demanded by employees).

Another focus of interest has been the link between the capital market aspects of firm organization and firm behavior and industrial adjustment (Nakatani, 1984; Sheard, 1985, 1986a, 1986b). One prevalent notion has been that various institutional features of the capital market organization of firms—the main-bank financing system and prevalence of intercorporate shareholdings—incorporate implicit risk-sharing mechanisms and may have important implications for the way in which competitive shocks impinge upon firms and the way in which firms respond to these shocks. Many observers have argued that these capital market links facilitate the adoption of a longer-term decision making horizon by management, with implications for firm investment and adjustment (disinvestment) decisions. A recent example of an argument along these lines with implications for aggregate performance concerns the performance of the Tokyo stock market at the time of the October 1987 stock market "crash." It has been suggested that the capital market organization of firms, in the form of extensive and closely knit intercorporate shareholdings, was a factor contributing to the relatively "favorable" performance of the Tokyo market.[18]

A feature of corporate organization in Japan is the prevalence of intercorporate shareholdings and close bank-firm ties (main bank system) associated with the existence of identifiable financial corporate groupings (Nakatani, 1984). Nakatani has suggested an interesting link between this form of corporate organization and how the economy responds to shocks and undergoes adjustment, which is further explored in a series of papers by Sheard (1985, 1986a, 1986b, 1987) on the role of the main bank system, intercorporate shareholdings and general trading companies.

Nakatani's claim, which is backed up by an extensive statistical analysis of the performance and attributes of group-aligned and more independent firms, is that the grouping arrangements serve as a form of implicit mutual insurance scheme which enables firms to absorb shocks to competitiveness by sharing the costs of adjustment within the group (1984, p. 244). An interesting link can be made to the labor market side of the firm's organization by noting that such arrangements may be conducive to sustaining the viability of the internal employment system. The key insight is that lifetime employment guarantees are only meaningful if two conditions are satisfied: the firm continues as a

viable financial entity and the firm can commit itself not to re-
nege on its employment contracts in the future. The first condition would be violated if the firm were to fail financially or go
bankrupt and the second might fail if a competing management
or ownership team were able to take control of the firm and
renegotiate existing contracts.[19]

This capital market organization has important implications
for the way in which competitive shocks impinge upon firms and
corporate assets are redeployed. In a market economy, the takeover and bankruptcy mechanisms together with active secondary
asset and factor markets are viewed as playing a key role in
structural adjustment by facilitating the reallocation of capital,
managerial, entrepreneurial and other resources. While these
market-mediated mechanisms do operate in Japan to a certain
extent, more so in the small and medium-sized firm sector, a
further set of mechanisms has operated in the large firm sector,
centering on the implicit financial contracts underpinning the
main bank system. One interpretation of the phenomenon of financial corporate grouping is that it is an institutional mechanism
that enables firms to secure a measure of insurance against corporate failure and external takeover. The main bank system provides a critical role in providing a form of corporate monitoring
and takeover role in the capital market that is intermediate between the internalized control structure of a multidivisional business organization and the external control structure of a
competitive capital market.

An implication for how structural adjustment takes place is as
follows. When a shock hits a group-affiliated firm, it is unlikely
to go bankrupt or become a target of takeover because of its
implicit financial contracts with its main bank and other stable
corporate shareholders. Rather the main bank of the firm will
provide financial assistance to the firm such as emergency finance or interest payment deferrals and exemptions. The main
bank provides this assistance in the context of close monitoring
of and to various degrees direct intervention in the management
of the firm. This intervention typically involves requiring the

firm to devise and implement a restructuring plan centering on asset sales, organizational changes, and labor force rationalization, and often involves sending in bank officers to assist with, or in extreme cases virtually take control of, the management of the firm.

Attention has also been focused on the attributes of subcontracting systems and supply networks in Japanese industry. There are conflicting views on the role of subcontracting and its implications for structural adjustment. An old idea in the literature, still held by many writers, is that extensive reliance on subcontractors provides core assembly firms in Japan with a shock absorber mechanism.[20] More recent literature has focused on the incentive and informational aspects of hierarchical subcontracting relations and has argued that rather than parent firms "exploiting" subcontractors by shifting risks onto them, quite the opposite might be the case, with parent firms absorbing some (but for incentive reasons not all) of the risks faced by parts suppliers.[21]

The focus on risk-sharing mechanisms can give a rather one-sided picture of the firm's capacity to withstand shocks. It should be noted that these devices provide a short run buffer but do not dull the longer run incentives to take necessary adjustments. A key point here is that, to the extent that the firm has opportunities to shift some of the costs of shocks to risk-sharing business partners, these firms have corresponding incentives to ensure that the costs that they bear are minimized subject to their fulfilling their part of the implicit contractual arrangement. Thus a purchaser of an ailing firm's output may continue to purchase the output of the firm in quantities (or at a price) that would not occur if the transaction were a pure spot-market one but its own desire to remain competitive will limit the amount of insurance it can provide and give it an interest in ensuring that the firm quickly take whatever actions are required to regain a competitive position. A similar and perhaps stronger point can be made with respect to the main bank's insuring role: it provides financial support but also requires that the firm undertake certain actions, partly because the main bank's own incentives, as the principal "residual risk bearer," dictate that the firm be restored to financial health (Sheard, 1989b). These observations seem to reflect a more general point, that any insuring agent has incentives to take actions to mitigate moral hazard on the part of the insured agent.

Corporate organization and international trade

The argument that corporate organization makes the Japanese market closed to foreign firms can be looked at from quite a different viewpoint, namely that of the theory of economic organization as applied to international exchange. Viewed from this perspective, the question is not "is corporate organization a structural impediment?" but rather what explains the choice of contractual or organizational form, or in Williamson's (1989) terminology "transaction governance structure," that is adopted?

In traditional theories of international trade and structural adjustment, the firm or corporate organization played little substantive role. In international trade theory, resource endowments and assumptions about factor mobility and the operation of competitive markets play critical roles but the firm as such does not.[22] In much of the literature on structural adjustment, the firm is treated as a very simple mechanism that responds in a predictable and mechanical way to shifts in relative prices and so it can be ignored as a contributor to performance.

This kind of simplifying approach to the firm, adopted in much economic analysis, is extremely powerful and useful for answering certain kinds of questions. As noted earlier, however, there is also a need to introduce the firm into such models as more than a mechanical "black box" and much progress has been made in the economics of organization literature in this direction in recent years. One of the aims of this literature is to understand why exchange between economic agents takes on the particular institutional and contractual forms that it does. The literature observes that, depending on such attributes of the transaction as the degree of asset specificity, frequency, and extent of uncertainty and distribution of information, different organizational modes may be chosen to execute the transaction, ranging from organization of the transaction within the firm (in-house production or vertical integration), through some form of long-term contract or quasi-integration, to reliance on the spot market.

The same question arises in the case of international transactions involving trade in goods and services and/or cross-border investments. The question then becomes: given that there is scope for a transaction to take place across national borders—there are potential gains from trade involving goods, services or perhaps know-how—what determines the choice of contractual or business arrangement for organizing the transaction, as between, for instance, in the case of exports, export of the good into "world markets" determined by world prices, entering into various forms of long-term supply contracts, vertical integration through direct foreign investment and host country production, or licensing of production know-how to overseas producers. Similarly for imports such options exist as importing at world prices from world spot markets (assuming this is possible), utilizing long-term import contracts, entering into international joint ventures, and engaging in direct foreign investment in off-shore production capacity and importing the output through transfer within a vertically integrated corporate structure. To these choices could be added delegating or sharing responsibility for import or export with a general trading company. A second question, which bears on the earlier discussion, is: can the contractual mode chosen influence the distribution of rents or gains from trade between the respective parties to the trade? Whereas international trade theory will have something to say about the activities in which a country is likely to have some comparative advantage, insights from the economics of organization may prove helpful in explaining and predicting the actual form that any particular transaction will take on and the distribution of benefits that obtains.

The positive question of what contractual arrangement *is* chosen assumes a normative aspect when viewed from the perspective of the corporate strategist. A variation of the "market closure" theme is the argument that aspects of Japanese corporate strategy and organization (and more broadly industrial policy) enable Japanese firms to capture a disproportionately large share of the gains from international trade. This "expropriation" hypothesis, like the "market closure" hypothesis, comes in many forms. It has been frequently suggested, for example, that Japanese importers of raw materials have been able to extract rents from foreign suppliers through the strategic choice of imports arrangements such as by forming buyer-cartels, by using long-term contracts rather than committing themselves to direct foreign investment, and by diversifying their sources of inputs (Anderson, 1987). The expropriation hypothesis is also manifest in much of the discussion relating to Japanese direct foreign investment. There appears to be an implicit concern on the part of policy makers and others that when Japanese firms invest directly in overseas production and service facilities they do so in such a way as to skew the benefits toward themselves through such means as preferential purchasing strategies and the monopolization of domestic and foreign distribution channels.

The foreign firm that wishes to trade with Japan or do business with Japanese firms overseas can be thought of as facing a menu of choices of contract, including such options as arms-length export or import of goods, some form of long-term contract or joint venture, and direct foreign investment. The question then becomes what form of contract *should* the firm choose in order to maximize its strategic objectives? Viewed in this way, the market access issue and the expropriations of rents issue are really ones of choice of organization form for doing international business, taking account of the various constraints faced including the nature of the economic organization in the target market.

One feature of international transactions is that what we normally think of as a single transaction, such as the export of a good, can often be broken up into a number of parts or separate transactions. Formally, this is to recognize Williamson's (1981, p. 1544) point that a transaction occurs when a good or service is transferred across a "technologically separable interface," and that there are typically many such interfaces between the producer of a good in an exporting country and the consumer of the good in the importing country. In principle, there is scope for separate ownership or competitive trading of the product at every stage in its production, transportation and distribution of the product; on the other hand, complete vertical integration may obtain and the product is transferred along a logistics chain that is owned and controlled by a single firm. The insight from the literature is that the choice is determined largely by "transaction cost" or economics of organization considerations, as opposed to international trade theoretic considerations since this theory offers no guidance on the question.

Another slightly different way to look at this issue is to note that for many international transactions it is the case that what is being traded is a bundle of goods and services and various options exist for packaging this bundle together. Tourism is a case where a package of goods and services is provided and consumers (importers) may purchase various elements of the package separately and do the packaging themselves or purchase them as a bundle. The nature of the distribution system will constrain the choices of the consumer—it may not be possible to purchase items separately or unbundle a given package—but, to the extent that competitive pressures exist, the distribution system can be expected to respond to consumer preferences, that is, to minimize various forms of transactions costs on behalf of the consumer.

Changing nature of Japanese corporate organization

The international profile and orientation of Japanese firms has increased quite dramatically in the past few years particularly since the mid-1980s when the yen began to appreciate sharply, and corporate organization within Japan has been subject to various pressures for change. In 1980, 66 of the 500 largest manufacturing companies in the world (by sales) were Japanese but by 1987 this number had risen to 97 (Tsusho sangyosho, 1988, p. 177). The number of cases of new overseas direct foreign invest-

ment each year was in the region of two and a half thousand per
year from the late 1970s to mid-1980s but rose from 2,613 in
1985 to 6,076 by 1988, and in value terms from U.S. $12.2
billion to $47.0 billion (on a reported basis) (Tsusho sangyosho
sangyo seisakukyoku kokusai kigyoka, 1990, pp. 227–28). One
major facet of this internationalization process has been the shifting offshore of manufacturing activity. According to a survey by
the Ministry of International Trade and Industry, the ratio of
overseas to domestic manufacturing output by Japanese firms
increased from 1.6 percent in 1979 to 4.9 percent in 1988 and an
estimate of 5.8 percent in 1989 (Tsusho sangyosho sangyo
seisakukyoku kokusai kigyoka, 1990, pp. 14–15). The industries
exhibiting the highest ratios of overseas production are the as-
sembly-type industries, notably precision equipment (13.9 percent in 1988), electrical equipment (10.6 percent) and transport
equipment (including motor vehicles) (9.4 percent). An issue of
interest in this context is whether and in what ways traditional
forms of corporate organization and ways of conducting business
in Japan may change as a result of structural changes in the
domestic and international environment and the process of internationalization of Japanese business.

One source of impetus for such changes would be from what
could be termed feedback and spillover effects of internationalization. Feedback effects refer to domestic changes that occur as
a result of Japanese business becoming more international or
having a higher profile internationally. One source of feedback
effects could be learning effects that gradually permeate back
through the home organization. As Japanese firms gain greater
experience of ways of operating in different market environments, they may import some of these practices and attitudes
back into Japan.

Another source of feedback effects could be induced or secondary effects that occur as third parties (such as foreign governments or firms) take actions or alter their behavior in such as way
as to have an effect on the domestic operating environment of
Japanese firms. It could be argued that this has already occurred

to a considerable extent but the trend may continue and accelerate. For example, as Japanese firms become more active in foreign markets, pressures are generated for various forms of reciprocity to be granted to foreign firms in Japanese markets or for Japanese firms to conform in their behavior or structure to international standards of business. This phenomenon has been evident in the context of Japan-U.S. bilateral trade negotiations and the structural impediments initiative talks in particular; another example is the requirement that Japanese banks take steps to raise their net capital ratios to meet Bank of International Settlements standards.

An example can be given to lend some content to these general remarks. Consider the takeover market or market for corporate control in Japan. It is often said that there is no takeover market to speak of in Japan and hostile takeovers rarely occur. This fact is directly related to the forms of corporate organization that have evolved to handle corporate control and managerial incentive problems in Japan, and the regulation or administrative guidance that has facilitated these business ways.

As explained earlier in the paper and in more detail in Sheard (1985, 1986a), the takeover market in Japan has taken on a rather specific "quasi-internalized" form in Japan: roughly speaking, firms have employed a system of multilateral intercorporate shareholding arrangements to provide mutual insulation against the possibility of hostile takeover through the share market and the major city banks, in their capacity as main banks, have provided a mechanism for capital market monitoring and intervention in failing or poorly managed firms that has substituted for, and paralleled the effects of, a more market-mediated set of monitoring and takeover mechanisms. A question of considerable interest is whether this system will persist in the future, or whether it could be supplanted by a more Anglo-American kind of takeover system.

While it is too early to predict with any certainty whether the Japanese system will persist in its current form in the future, one possible scenario is that a more open market for corporate control may develop, along the lines of the situation in the United States or Australia where hostile takeover bids by "corporate raiders" are everyday events.

One way that this might occur is if Japanese firms and banks changed their attitude toward launching and acceding to take-overs (as shareholders or financiers) after accumulating experience with takeover strategies overseas. It is pertinent to note that Japanese firms, including banks, increasingly are expanding their overseas operations through merger and acquisition strategies that include hostile takeovers as one element.[23] Not only are Japanese banks actively expanding their merger and acquisition departments in order to facilitate their Japanese clients' overseas expansion strategies, they are buying up American banks themselves and have started to finance hostile takeover bids by firms in the United States.[24]

As well as feedback effects of this kind, there may be spillover effects. Spill-over effects refer to the changes that may occur in one arena of business or aspect of corporate organization as a result of changes in another area or market. The previous analysis has shown that the capital market, managerial labor market and product market aspects of Japanese corporate organization are closely related through risk-sharing and other long-term contractual arrangements. This very interconnectedness suggests that such spill-over effects may be potentially important.

A likely area for spillover effects is between the capital market and the labor market, particularly the managerial labor market. There is also a possibility of corporate organization changing as a result of spillover effects between product markets and the capital market. For instance, McKenzie (forthcoming 1992) examines the corporate shareholding motivations of life insurance companies, which occupy a pivotal position in stable shareholding arrangements, and suggests that deregulation of the insurance product market, were it to occur, could trigger, or accelerate a shift in behavior of insurance companies away from acting as stable shareholders to firms. This could have far-reaching effects on the operation of the market for corporate control in Japan. A

similar implication can be drawn from Sheard's (1989a) analysis
of the general trading company's role in interfirm transactions:
changes in the capital market may have spillover effects in intermediate product markets by weakening the traditionally dominant role of trading companies as conduits for the channeling of
funds from the banking to the small and medium-sized firm sector.

Conclusion

It is perhaps not surprising, given the Japanese economic success,
that Japanese corporate organization has become a hotly debated
and controversial topic. Some observers argue that the organization of firms is a central aspect of Japanese-style capitalism;
others that it is institutional detail of little import in interpreting
the central aspects of the Japanese economy. Some view Japanese corporate organization as innovative and as contributing new
organizational technologies and prototypes to the industrial
world; others view it, in terms bordering on the conspiratorial, as
insular and as distorting Japanese economic interaction with the
world. It is hoped that this paper, by drawing on the modern
theory of economic organization, will go some way to clarifying
these puzzles and controversies, or at least provide a more solid
foundation on which to further that task.

Notes

This paper draws heavily on material from a joint paper with Christopher
Findlay to be published in a forthcoming book edited by the author entitled
International Adjustment and the Japanese Firm. The paper was prepared
while the author was visiting the department of economics, Stanford Univer-
sity, and enjoying the hospitality of the Northeast Asia-United States Forum on
International Policy, Stanford University. At various stages, helpful comments
have been provided by Kevin Davis, Robert Dekle, Peter Drysdale, Mark
Fruin, Michael Gerlach, Bob Gregory, Leonard Lynn, Iwao Nakatani, Greg
Noble, and Tom Roehl, none whom of bears any responsibility for the final
product.
    1. Some of the more important or notable works include Aoki (1984a,

1988, 1990), Abegglen and Stalk (1985), Clark (1979), Imai and Itami (1984), Koike (1988), Kono (1984), Ouchi (1981), Pascale and Athos (1981), Sato and Hoshino (1984), Shirai (1983), and Thurow (1985). The literarure in Japanese is voluminous: among academic works by economists and management scientists, Imai and Komiya (1989), Imai and Kaneko (1988), and Kagono et al. (1983) warrant citation.

2. For recent discussion of the relationship between *keiretsu* business organization and the market access issue, see Gerlach (1989), Haley (1990), Imai (1990), Johnson (1990a, 1990b), Lawrence (1991a), Lincoln (1990a, chap. 3; 1990b), Okimoto (1987), Wassmann and Yamamura (1989), and Yamamura (1990). For critical counter views, see Komiya and Irie (1990), Yoshitomi (1990) and Bergsten and Cline (1985, pp. 65–68).

3. See Lincoln (1990a) and Saxonhouse (1988) for a comprehensive discussion of this issue. Recent further contributions are Fung (forthcoming 1992) and Lawrence (1991b).

4. For recent surveys of the theory of the firm and economic organization, see Holmstrom and Tirole (1989), Milgrom and Roberts (1988), Putterman (1986), Tirole (1988a; 1988b), Williamson (1989), and the book by Milgrom and Roberts (forthcoming 1992).

5. See, for instance, Gerlach (1989), Lincoln (1990a, pp. 89–90), Yamamura (1990).

6. See, for example, Nakatani (1984), Aoki (1988, chap. 4), Dore (1986, chap. 3), Abegglen and Stalk (1985, chap. 7). Recent papers by Dewatripont and Maskin (1990) and von Thadden (1990) attempt to formalize these kinds of arguments.

7. Further discussion of this issue can be found in Gerlach (1989, pp. 156–62, 167–69), Imai (1990), and Lincoln (1990b, p. 3).

8. On the Japanese firm, see Aoki (1984a, 1987, 1988, 1990), Abegglen and Stark (1985), Dore (1986), Clark (1979), Imai and Itami (1984), Komiya (1987), and Kono (1984).

9. This is not to say that firms can never act strategically or with the aid of government intervention to place competitors at a disadvantage in the markets in which they operate. The issue then, however, is the strategic behavior or government intervention rather than the nature of corporate organization which is what we wish to focus on here.

10. Again, at the risk of being repetitive, one can easily conceive of cases where one firm's (or set of firms') strategy in terms of organizational design has an element of strategic behavior aimed at limiting other firms' access to the final market, but such cases are hardly likely to be pervasive. For some analysis in this direction, see the discussion in Tirole (1988a, chap. 4).

11. An important recent contribution is the paper by Fudenberg, Holmstrom, and Milgrom (1990), which establishes conditions under which long-term contracting provides no additional benefits over a series of short-term contracts. See also the earlier survey by Hart and Holmstrom (1987).

12. Like barriers to entry, the issue of the competitive effects of vertical contracts (also called vertical restraints) has been a hotly debated one in the

industrial organization literature. An emerging view is that vertical contracts
have more to do with attempts to ameliorate various forms of vertical and
horizontal externalities than with any exercise of market power. See Tirole
(1988a, chap. 4) for an introduction to the debate.

13. For a similar perspective, see also Itoh (1991) and Ito and Maruyama
(1991).

14. See, for instance, Young (1979), Yoshino and Lifson (1986), Tsurumi
(1984). For an insightful analysis using a transactions cost approach, see Roehl
(1983), and for a useful historical perspective, see Yamamura (1976).

15. See, for instance, Gerlach (1989), Lincoln (1990a, pp. 89–90),
Yamamura (1990).

16. Government policy has also been an important aspect of the structural
adjustment of declining industries in Japan, but we do not address that issue
here, although Sheard's (1991) study of aluminium industry adjustment sheds
light on the role of government policy and assistance vis-à-vis that of the
private sector. For a fuller account of Japanese adjustment policies, see the
excellent review by Peck, Levine, and Goto (1987).

17. Koshiro (1986, p. 56) concludes an extensive survey of the Japanese
empirical literature by stating that "Japan's labor markets as a whole [are]
unexpectedly flexible to economic changes in spite of the very existence of the
lifetime employment system in the core sector of the economy." See Shimada
(1977) for evidence and discussion of the range of measures that firms use for
reducing their labor costs and size of labor force in recession or structural
depression. Shimada (1977, p. 60) quotes the results of a study by Shinozuka
and Ishiwara showing that Japanese firms took more than three times as long
to adjust numbers employed as American firms (as did British firms) but that
they were just as fast in adjusting labor input.

18. For example, Shibata (1988, p.56) quotes the view of the president of
Daiwa International Capital Management on this point. The (then) chief economist of the Bank of Japan, Yoshio Suzuki, expressed a similar view at a
conference at the Australian National University in November 1987.

19. The latter kind of possibility has recently been raised by Shleifer and
Summers (1988) as an important issue in interpreting takeover experience in
the United States.

20. Johnson (1990b, p.16) has recently argued that "The subcontractors of
Japan's big assemblers, such as Toyota and Nissan, are the shock absorbers of
the Japanese business cycle." This issue is also discussed in Okimoto (1987).

21. See the important contributions by Asanuma (1985a, 1985b, 1989),
Asanuma and Tatsuta (1990), Aoki (1984b, 1984c, 1988, chap. 6; 1990, pp.
24–26), and Kawasaki and McMillan (1987), and the surveys by McMillan
(1990), Roehl (1989), and Minato (1989).

22. For some recent attempts to integrate the firm, particularly the multinational enterprise, into international trade theory, see Casson (1987), Caves
(1982), Ethier (1986), Horstmann and Markusen (1987), and Markusen (1984).

23. The *Japan Economic Journal*, January 30, 1988, p. 23, reported that in
1987 Japanese companies spent a record U.S. $5.9 billion buying eighty-one

businesses in the United States. The Japanese ink-maker Dainippon Ink &
Chemicals has succeeded in two hostile takeover bids in the United States,
taking over one of the divisions of Sun Chemical Company for $550 million in
1986 and Reichold Chemicals for $535 million in 1987 (*Japan Economic
Journal*, December 19, 1987, p. 3).

24. See *Japan Economic Journal*, December 19, 1987, pp. 1–4. Among
the major Japanese banks, Sanwa Bank purchased Lloyds Bank California for
U.S. $263 milion in 1986; Sumitomo Bank moved to buy a more than 50
percent stake in the American investment bank Goldman, Sachs for $500
million in 1986 (although severe conditions were later placed on the deal by
the U.S. Federal Reserve) (*Japan Economic Journal*, August 16, 1986, p. 1;
November 29, 1986, p. 3); and Bank of Tokyo announced a $750 million
proposal to acquire the California-based Union Bank (*Japan Economic Journal*, March 5, 1988, p. 2). The *Japan Economic Journal*, March 19, 1988, p.
12, also reported that in February 1988 seven Japanese banks including the
Industrial Bank of Japan, Fuji Bank, and Sumitomo Bank loaned $1,475 mil-
lion to Eastman Kodak for its bid for Sterling Drug and that Sumitomo Bank
was to make a loan of $500 million to Campeau Corporation of Canada for its
takeover of a leading American Department store chain.

References

Abegglen, James C., and George Stalk, Jr. 1985. *Kaisha, the Japanese Corpo-
ration*. New York: Basic Books.
Alchian, Armen A., and Harold Demsetz. 1972. "Production, Information
Costs, and Economic Organization," *American Economic Review* 62, 5:
777–95.
Anderson, David L. 1987. *An Analysis of Japanese Coking Coal Procurement
Policies: The Canadian and Australian Experience*. Centre for Resource
Studies, Queens University, Ontario.
Aoki, Masahiko, ed. 1984a. *The Economic Analysis of the Japanese Firm*.
Amsterdam: North-Holland.
————. 1984b. "Aspects of the Japanese Firm," in Masahiko Aoki, ed., *The
Economic Analysis of the Japanese Firm*. Amsterdam: North-Holland, pp.
3–43.
————. 1984c. "Risk-sharing in the Corporate Group," in Masahiko Aoki, ed.,
The Economic Analysis of the Japanese Firm, pp. 259–64.
————. 1984d. "Innovative Adaptation through the Quasi-tree Structure: An
Emerging Aspect of Japanese Entrepreneurship," *Zeitschrift fur
Nationalokonomie* 4: 177–98.
————. 1987. "The Japanese Firm in Transition," in Kozo Yamamura and
Yasukichi Yasuba, eds., *The Political Economy of Japan*, vol. 1, *The Domestic Transformation*. Stanford: Stanford University Press, pp. 262–88.
————. 1988. *Information, Incentives and Bargaining in the Japanese Economy*. Cambridge: Cambridge University Press.

————. 1989. "The Nature of the Japanese Firm as a Nexus of Employment and Financial Contracts: An Overview," *Journal of the Japanese and International Economies* 3: 345–66.

————. 1990. "Towards an Economic Model of the Japanese Firm," *Journal of Economic Literature* 28: 1–27.

Asanuma, Banri. 1985a. "The Organization of Parts Purchases in the Japanese Automotive Industry," *Japanese Economic Studies* 13, 4: 32–53.

————. 1985b. "The Contractual Framework for Parts Supply in the Japanese Automotive Industry," *Japanese Economic Studies* 13, 4: 54–78.

————. 1989. "Manufacturer-Supplier Relationships in Japan and the Concept of Relation-specific Skill," *Journal of the Japanese and International Economies* 3: 1–30.

————. Forthcoming 1992. "Japanese Manufacturer-Supplier Relationships in International Perspective: The Automobile Case," in Paul Sheard, ed., *International Adjustment and the Japanese Firm.* Sydney: Allen and Unwin.

———— and Kikutani, Tatsuya. 1990. "Risk Absorption in Japanese Subcontracting: A Microeconometric Study on the Automobile Industry," Centre for Economic Policy Research Technical Paper no. 218, Stanford University, Stanford.

Bergsten, C. Fred, and William R. Cline. 1985. *The United States-Japan Economic Problem,* Policy Analyses in International Economics 13. Washington, DC: Institute for International Economics.

Casson, Mark. 1987. *The Firm and the Market: Studies on Multinational Enterprise and the Scope of the Firm.* Cambridge: MIT Press.

Caves, R. E. 1982. *Multinational Enterprise and Economic Analysis.* Cambridge: Cambridge University Press.

Clark, Rodney. 1979. *The Japanese Company.* New Haven: Yale University Press.

Cheung, Stephen N. S. 1983. "The Contractual Nature of the Firm," *Journal of Law and Economics* 26: 1–21.

Christelow, Dorothy. 1985–86. "Japan's Intangible Barriers to Trade in Manufactures," *Federal Reserve Bank of New York Quarterly Review* 10: 11–18.

Coase, Ronald H. 1937. "The Nature of the Firm," *Economica* 4: 386–405.

Dewatripont, M., and E. Maskin. 1990. "Credit and Efficiency in Centralized and Decentralized Economies," Discussion Paper no. 1512, Harvard Institute of Economic Research.

Dore, Ronald. 1986. *Flexible Rigidities: Industrial Policy and Structural Adjustment in the Japanese Economy 1979–80.* Stanford: Stanford University Press.

Ethier, Wilfred J. 1986. "The Multinational Firm," *Quarterly Journal of Economics* 86: 805–33.

Fama, Eugene F. 1980. "Agency Problems and the Theory of the Firm," *Journal of Political Economy* 88, 2: 288–307.

Freeman, Richard B., and Martin L. Weitzman. 1987. "Bonuses and Employment in Japan," *Journal of the Japanese and International Economies* 1: 168–94.

Fudenberg, D., B. Holmstrom, and P. Milgrom. 1990. "Short-term Contracts and Long-term Agency Relationships," *Journal of Economic Theory* 51: 1–31.

Fung, K. C. Forthcoming 1992. "Characteristics of Japanese Industrial Groups and Their Potential Impact on U.S.-Japan Trade," in Robert Baldwin, ed., *Empirical Studies of Commercial Policy*. Chicago: Chicago University Press.

Gerlach, Michael. 1987. "Business Alliances and the Strategy of the Japanese Firm," *California Management Review,* Fall, pp. 126–42.

Gerlach, Michael. 1989. *"Keiretsu* Organization in the Japanese Economy: Analysis and Trade Implications," in Chalmers Johnson, Laura D'Andrea Tyson, and John Zysman, eds., *Politics and Productivity: The Real Story of Why Japan Works.* Ballinger Publishing Company, pp. 141–74.

Gilbert, Richard J. 1989. "Mobility Barriers and the Value of Incumbency," in Richard Schmalensee and Robert D. Willig, eds., *Handbook of Industrial Organization,* vol. 1. Amsterdam: North-Holland, pp. 475–535.

Goto, Akira. 1981. "Statistical Evidence on the Diversification of Japanese Large Firms," *Journal of Industrial Economics* 29, 3: 271–78.

Grossman, Sanford, and Oliver Hart. 1986. "The Costs and Benefits of Ownership: A Theory of Vertical and Lateral Integration," *Journal of Political Economy* 94: 691–19.

Haley, John O. 1990. "Weak Law, Strong Competition, and Trade Barriers: Competitiveness as a Disincentive to Foreign Entry into Japanese Markets," in Kozo Yamamura, ed., *Japan's Economic Structure: Should It Change?* Seattle: Society for Japanese Studies, pp. 203–35.

Hart, Oliver, and Bengt Holmstrom. 1987. "The Theory of Contacts," in Truman F. Bewley, ed., *Advances in Economic Theory: Fifth World Congress.* Cambridge: Cambridge University Press, pp. 71–155.

Holmstrom, Bengt, and Jean Tirole. 1989. "The Theory of the Firm," in Richard Schmalensee and Robert D. Willig, eds., *Handbook of Industrial Organization,* vol. 1. Amsterdam: North-Holland, pp. 61–133.

Horstmann, Ignatius, and James R. Markusen. 1987. "Licensing versus Direct Investment: A Model of Internationalization by the Multinational Enterprise," *Canadian Journal of Economics* 20, 3: 464–81.

Imai, Ken-ichi. 1990. "Japanese Business Groups and the Structural Impediments Initiative," in Kozo Yamamura, ed., *Japan's Economic Structure: Should It Change?* Seattle: Society for Japanese Studies, pp. 167–202.

Imai, Ken-ichi, and Hiroyuki Itami. 1984. "Interpenetration of Organization and Market: Japan's Firm and Market in Comparison with the U.S.," *International Journal of Industrial Organization* 2: 285–310.

Imai, Ken-ichi, and Ikuyo Kaneko. 1988. *Nettowaku soshikiron* (Theory of network organization). Tokyo: Iwanami shoten.

Imai, Ken-ichi, and Ryutaro Komiya, eds. 1989. *Nihon no kigyo* (The Japanese firm). Tokyo: University of Tokyo Press.

Ito, Takatoshi, and Masayoshi Maruyama. 1991. "Is the Japanese Distribution System Really Inefficient?" in Paul Krugman, ed., *Trade with Japan: Has*

74   PAUL SHEARD

the Door Opened? Chicago: Chicago University Press, pp. 151–75.

Itoh, Motoshige. 1991. "The Japanese Distribution System and Access to the Japanese Market," in Paul Krugman, ed., *Trade with Japan: Has the Door Opened?*, pp. 177–89.

————. Forthcoming 1992. "Organisational Transactions and Access to the Japanese Import Market," in Paul Sheard, ed., *International Adjustment and the Japanese Firm*. Sydney: Allen and Unwin.

———— and Akihiko Matsui. 1987. "Organizational Transactions: One Aspect of Japanese-style Business Relations," mimeo, University of Tokyo.

Jensen, Michael C., and William H. Meckling. 1976. "Theory of the Firm: Managerial Behavior, Agency Costs and Ownership Structure," *Journal of Financial Economics* 3, 4: 305–60.

Johnson, Chalmers. 1990a. "Trade, Revisionism, and the Future of Japanese-American Relations," in Kozo Yamamura, ed., *Japan's Economic Structure: Should It Change?* Seattle: Society for Japanese Studies, pp. 105–36.

————. 1990b. "*Keiretsu*: An Outsider's View," *International Economic Insights* 1, 2: 15–17.

Kagono, Tadao, et al. 1983. *Nichibei kigyo no keiei hikaku: senryakuteki kankyo tekio no riron* (A comparison of the management of Japanese and U.S. firms: A theory of strategic adaptation to the environment). Tokyo: Nihon keizai shimbunsha (published in English in 1985 as *Strategic vs. Evolutionary Management: A U.S.-Japan Comparison of Strategy and Organization*. Amsterdam: North-Holland).

Kawasaki, Seiichi, and John McMillan. 1987. "The Design of Contracts: Evidence from Japanese Subcontracting," *Journal of the Japanese and International Economies* 1: 327–49.

Koike, Kazuo. 1983. "Internal Labor Markets: Workers in Large Firms," in Taishiro Shirai, ed., *Contemporary Industrial Relations in Japan*. Madison: University of Wisconsin Press, pp. 29–61.

————. 1988. *Industrial Relations in Japan*. London: Macmillan.

Komiya, Ryutaro. 1987. "Japanese Firms, Chinese Firms: Problems for Economic Reform in China, part I," *Journal of the Japanese and International Economies* 1: 31–61.

Komiya, Ryutaro, and Kazutomo Irie. 1990. "The U.S.-Japan Trade Problem: An Economic Analysis from a Japanese Viewpoint," in Kozo Yamamura, ed., *Japan's Economic Structure: Should It Change?* Seattle: Society for Japanese Studies, pp. 65–104.

Komiya, Ryutaro, and Kazuo Yasui. 1984. "Japan's Macroeconomic Performance since the First Oil Crisis: Review and Appraisal," *Carnegie-Rochester Conference Series on Public Policy* 20: 69–114.

Kono, Toyohiro. 1984. *Strategy and Structure of Japanese Enterprises*. Armonk, NY: M. E. Sharpe.

Koshiro, Kazutoshi. 1986. "Job Security: Redundancy Arrangements and Practices in Japan," *Ekonomia* 89: 32–58.

Kreps, David M. 1990. *A Course in Microeconomic Theory*. Princeton:, Princeton University Press.

Lawrence, Robert Z. 1987. "Imports in Japan: Closed Markets or Minds?" *Brookings Papers on Economic Activity* 2: 517–52.

———. 1991a. "How Open is Japan?" in Paul Krugman, ed., *Trade with Japan: Has the Door Opened Wider?* Chicago: Chicago University Press, pp. 9–40.

———. 1991b. "Efficient or Exclusionist? The Import Behavior of Japanese Corporate Groups," *Brookings Papers on Economic Activity* 1: 311–30.

Lincoln, Edward J. 1990a. *Japan's Unequal Trade*. Washington, DC: The Brookings Institution.

———. 1990b. "U.S.-Japan Trade Talks: Hope for Progress," *The Heritage Lectures* 234. Washington, DC: The Heritage Foundation.

McKenzie, Colin. Forthcoming 1992. "Stable Shareholdings and the Role of Japanese Life Insurance Companies," in Paul Sheard, ed., *International Adjustment and the Japanese Firm*. Sydney: Allen and Unwin.

McMillan, John. 1990. "Managing Suppliers: Incentive Systems in Japan and the U.S.," *California Management Review* 32, 4: 38–55.

Markusen, James R. 1984. "Multinationals, Multi-plant Economies and the Gains from Trade," *Journal of International Economics* 16: 205–26.

Milgrom, Paul, and John Roberts. 1988. "Economic Theories of the Firm: Past, Present, and Future," *Canadian Journal of Economics* 21, 3: 444–58.

———. Forthcoming 1992. *Economics, Organization and Management*. Prentice-Hall.

Minato, Tetsuo. 1989. "A Comparison of Japanese and American Interfirm Production Systems," in Kichiro Hayashi, ed., *The U.S.-Japanese Economic Relationship: Can It Be Improved?* New York, New York University, pp. 87–122.

Nagasaka, Toshihisa. 1988. "Globalisation of Japanese Corporations and the Changing Role in Asia-Pacific Development," paper presented to a Symposium on the Changing Role of Transnational Corporations in Asia-Pacific Development. Sydney: Sydney University, July 14–15.

Nakatani, Iwao. 1984. "The Economic Role of Financial Corporate Grouping," in Masahiko Aoki, ed., *The Economic Analysis of the Japanese Firm*. Amsterdam: North-Holland, pp. 227–58.

Nihon keizai chosa kyogikai. 1989. *Wagakuni kigyo no keizokuteki torihiki no jittai ni tsuite* (On the actual state of continuous transactions among Japanese firms). Tokyo: Nihon keizai chosa kyogikai.

Nishiyama, Tadanori. 1980. *Shihai kozoron: Nihon shihon shugi no hokai* (On control structure: The collapse of Japanese capitalism). Tokyo: Bunchindo.

Office of the United States Trade Representative. 1989. *1989 National Trade Estimate Report on Foreign Trade Barriers*. Washington, DC: Government Printing Office.

Okimoto, Daniel I. 1987. "Outsider Trading: Coping with Japanese Industrial Organization," in Kenneth B. Pyle, ed., *The Trade Crisis: How Will Japan Respond?* Seattle: Society for Japanese Studies, pp. 85–116.

Ouchi, William G. 1981. *Theory Z: How American Business Can Meet the Japanese Challenge*. Reading, MA: Addison-Wesley.

Pascale, Richard T., and Anthony G. Athos. 1981. *The Art of Japanese Management: Applications for American Executives.* New York: Simon and Schuster.

Peck, M. J., R. C. Levine, and A. Goto. 1987. "Picking Losers: Public Policy towards Declining Industries in Japan," *Journal of Japanese Studies* 13, 1: 79–123.

Putterman, Louis. 1986. "The Economic Nature of the Firm: Overview," in Louis Putterman, ed., *The Economic Nature of the Firm: A Reader.* Cambridge: Cambridge University Press, pp. 1–29.

Rapp, William V. 1986. "Japan's Invisible Barriers to Trade," in Thomas A. Pugel and Robert G. Hawkins, eds., *Fragile Interdependence: Economic Issues in U.S.-Japanese Trade and Investment.* Lexington, MA: Lexington Books, pp. 21–45.

Roehl, Thomas. 1983. "A Transactions Cost Approach to International Trading Structures: The Case of Japanese General Trading Companies," *Hitotsubashi Journal of Economics* 24: 19–35.

————. 1989. "A Comparison of U.S.-Japanese Firms' Parts-Supply Systems: What Besides Nationality Matters?" in Kichiro Hayashi, ed., *The U.S.-Japanese Economic Relationship: Can It Be Improved?* New York: New York University Press, pp. 127–54.

Rohlen, Thomas P. 1979. " 'Permanent Employment' Faces Recession, Slow Growth and an Aging Work Force," *Journal of Japanese Studies* 5, 2: 235–72.

Ryutsu torihiki kanko nado to kyoso seisaku ni kansuru kento iinkai. 1990. *Ryutsu torihiki kanko to kore kara no kyoso seisaku fuzoku shiryohen* (Distribution and transactional practices and competition policy from now on: Attached data edition), booklet.

Sato, Kazuo, and Yasuo Hoshino, eds. 1984. *The Anatomy of Japanese Business.* Armonk, NY: M. E. Sharpe.

Saxonhouse, Gary R. 1988. "Comparative Advantage, Structural Adaptation, and Japanese Performance," in Takashi Inoguchi and Daniel I. Okimoto, eds., *The Political Economy of Japan,* vol. 2, *The Changing International Context.* Stanford: Stanford University Press, pp. 225–48.

Sheard, Paul. 1985. "Main Banks and Structural Adjustment in Japan," *Pacific Economic Papers* no. 129, Australia-Japan Research Centre, Australian National University, Canberra.

————. 1986a. "Intercorporate Shareholdings and Structural Adjustment in Japan," *Pacific Economic Papers* no.140, Australia-Japan Research Centre, Australian National University, Canberra.

————. 1986b. "General Trading Companies and Structural Adjustment in Japan," *Pacific Economic Papers* no. 132, Australia-Japan Research Centre, Australian National University, Canberra.

————. 1987. "How Japanese Firms Manage Industrial Adjustment: The Case of Aluminium," *Pacific Economic Papers* no. 151, Australia-Japan Research Centre, Australian National University, Canberra.

————. 1989a. "The Japanese General Trading Company as an Aspect of

Interfirm Risk-sharing," *Journal of the Japanese and International Economies* 3, 3: 308–22.

———. 1989b. "The Main Bank System and Corporate Monitoring and Control in Japan," *Journal of Economic Behavior and Organization* 11: 399–422.

———. 1991. "The Role of Firm Organization in the Adjustment of a Declining Industry in Japan: The Case of Aluminum," *Journal of the Japanese and International Economies* 5, 1: 19–40.

Shibata, Yoko. 1988. "Japan Begins to Rethink Cross-ownership," *Global Finance*, January, pp. 54–57.

Shimada, Haruo. 1977. "The Japanese Labor Market after the Oil Crisis: A Factual Report (I), (II)," *Keio Economic Studies* 14, 1: 49–65; 14, 2: 37–59.

Shirai, Taishiro, ed. 1983. *Contemporary Industrial Relations in Japan.* Madison: University of Wisconsin Press.

Shleifer, Andrei, and Lawrence H. Summers. 1988. "Breach of Trust in Hostile Takeovers," in Alan J. Auerbach, ed., *Corporate Takeovers: Causes and Consequences.* Chicago: University of Chicago Press, pp. 33–67.

Thurow, Lester C., ed. 1985. *The Management Challenge: Japanese Views.* Cambridge: MIT Press.

Tirole, Jean. 1988a. *The Theory of Industrial Organization.* Cambridge: MIT Press.

———. 1988b. "The Multicontract Organization," *Canadian Journal of Economics* 21, 3: 459–66.

Tsurumi, Yoshi. 1984. *Sogoshosha: Engines of Export-Based Growth.* Montreal: Institute for Research on Public Policy.

Tsusho sangyosho. 1988. *Tsusho hakusho heisei gannenban* (International trade white paper: 1988 edition). Tokyo: Okurasho insatsukyoku.

Tsusho sangyosho sangyo seisakukyoku kokusai kigyoka. 1990. *Wagakuni kigyo no kaigai jigyo katsudo (dai 18 19kai)* (Overseas business activities of Japanese firms (18th/19th time). Tokyo: Okurasho insatsukyoku.

Tyson, Laura D'Andrea, and John Zysman. 1989a. "Preface: The Argument Outlined," in Chalmers Johnson, Laura D'Andrea Tyson, and John Zysman, eds., *Politics and Productivity: The Real Story of Why Japan Works.* Ballinger Publishing Company, pp. xiii-xxi.

———. 1989b. "Developmental Strategy and Production Innovation in Japan," in Johnson, Tyson, and Zysman, eds., *Politics and Productivity*, pp. 59–140.

von Thadden, E-L. 1990. "Bank Finance and Long Term Investment," *WWZ Discussion Paper* 9010, University of Basel.

Wassmann, Ulrike, and Kozo Yamamura. 1989. "Do Japanese Firms Behave Differently? The Effects of *Keiretsu* in the United States," in Kozo Yamamura, ed., *Japanese Investment in the United States: Should We Be Concerned?* Seattle: Society for Japanese Studies, pp. 119–49.

Williamson, Oliver E. 1975. *Markets and Hierarchies.* New York: The Free Press.

———. 1981. "The Modern Corporation: Origins, Evolution, Attributes," *Journal of Economic Literature* 19, 4: 1537–68.

78   PAUL SHEARD

————. 1985. *The Economic Institutions of Capitalism.* New York: The Free Press.

————. 1989. "Transaction Cost Economics," in Richard Schmalensee and Robert D. Willig, eds., *Handbook of Industrial Organization*, vol. 1. Amsterdam: North-Holland, pp. 135–82.

Yamamura, Kozo. 1976. "General Trading Companies in Japan: Their Origins and Growth," in Hugh Patrick, ed., *Japanese Industrialization and Its Social Consequences.* Berkeley: University of California Press, pp. 161–99.

————. 1990. "Will Japan's Economic Structure Change? Confessions of a Former Optimist," in Kozo Yamamura, ed., *Japan's Economic Structure: Should It Change?* Seattle: Society for Japanese Studies, pp. 13–64.

Yoshino, M. Y., and T. B. Lifson. 1986. *The Invisible Link: Japan's Sogo Shosha and the Organization of Trade.* Cambridge: MIT Press.

Yoshitomi, Masaru. 1990. *"Keiretsu*: An Insider's Guide to Japan's Conglomerates," *International Economic Insights* 1, 2: 10–14.

Young, A. K. 1979. *The Sogo Shosha: Japan's Multinational Trading Companies.* Boulder: Westview Press.

[19]

The Developing Economies, XXXV-4 (December 1997): 382–400

A DISTRIBUTIVE COMPARISON OF ENTERPRISE SIZE IN KOREA AND TAIWAN

Makoto ABE
Momoko KAWAKAMI

INTRODUCTION

WITHIN the existing research dealing with the economic development of the Republic of Korea (hereafter Korea) and Taiwan there is a broad consensus that the backbone of industrialization in Korea has been the *chaebol*s (conglomerate business groups) rather than small and medium-size enterprises (SMEs) (Kuramochi 1992, p. 380), while in Taiwan's economic development, SMEs have been the driving force for growth (Yu 1993, p. 338). In this special issue as well, the article by Hattori (1997) analyzing Korea's economic development likewise focuses on the *chaebol*s as central in carrying out the economy's development since the 1960s, while Numazaki's article (1997) analyzing Taiwan depicts SMEs supported by horizontal networks of *laoban* (owner-managers) as playing the major role in that island's economic development. In sum, the general consensus in the research to date that has focused on the main players of industrialization in the two economies is that "Korea is a big business economy while Taiwan is an SME economy." The purpose of this study is to verify by means of statistical data the appropriateness of this general perception which sharply contrasts the sizes of the enterprises that have been central to economic development in the two economies.

In Section I we will utilize census data for the Korean and Taiwanese manufacturing sectors, the most comprehensive source for evaluating the actual conditions of enterprises in both economies, in order to examine whether or not the above general perception reflects reality. This examination will entail comparing the changes in the distribution pattern of the sizes of production units in both Korea and Taiwan during a time series and at given points of time. This examination will show that both economies have been moving away from large-scale businesses, but it will also show a noticeable dichotomy in the distribution of the sizes of enterprises in the two economies. In Section II we will compare the position of large-scale business groups in both economies, as we consider that the contrasting perception of a *chaebol*-centered Korean economy and an SME-oriented Taiwanese economy derives in part from the much greater economic presence of large-scale business groups (the *chaebols*) in Korea when compared with such groups in Taiwan.[1] In Section III we will compare the share of exports that SMEs account for in both economies, and will compare the relationship between enterprise size and the ratio of export sales. Exports have played an extremely large part in the economic development of Korea and Taiwan; and the perceived dichotomy of the two economies is very likely to be derived partly from the difference in the size of the enterprises that have been the important exporters in both economies: big businesses in Korea and SMEs in Taiwan. The last section presents our conclusions.

I. ANALYZING THE CENSUS DATA

Before taking up the intended examination of this study, we first need to check the nature and compatibility of the census data for the manufacturing sectors in Korea and Taiwan and point out the limitations of such data for comparing the size distribution of production units (establishments[2]/enterprises) in both economies. After clarifying these limitations, we will utilize this data to compare the changes that took place in this distribution over time in each economy and the distribution pattern of the sizes of production units at given points in time, in order to examine the appropriateness of the general perception that contrasts the size of the enterprises that were the main engines of growth in the two economies.[3]

A. The Nature of the Data

In Korea a total of ten censuses were conducted between 1958 and 1993.[4] These were taken at irregular intervals until 1968, then in 1969 it was decided to conduct them every five years. To be compatible with the pertinent census data for Taiwan,

---

[1] Taniura (1988, p. 5) points out that (1) Taiwanese large business groups are smaller in number than their Korean counterparts, and their position in the economy is less important than in Korea, and (2) Taiwan has no general trading companies, which increases the role of SMEs in foreign trade.

[2] An "establishment" means "a physical unit engaging in industrial activities such as a factory, workshop, office, or mine." (ROK, NSO, *Report on Industrial Census*, 1993).

[3] Enterprise size can be determined by indices other than the number of employees; capitalization, sales volume, or the value of assets can also be used. At present in Taiwan capitalization is used; an SME in the manufacturing sector is defined as a firm with capital of N.T.$40 million or less. In Korea, firms in the manufacturing sector with 20 employees or less are defined as small enterprises while those with between 21 and 300 employees are defined as medium-size enterprises. In this study we have used the number of employees for defining an SME.

[4] Census titles have differed over the years. Between 1963 and 1978 they were published as *Report on Mining and Manufacturing Census* (ROK, EPB, various years), while in 1983 and 1988 they were published as *Report on Industrial Census* (ROK, NSO, 1983, 1988). Censuses are conducted every five years, and in years when no census is taken, surveys are carried out (see ROK, NSO, *Report on the Mining and Manufacturing Census*, various years). However in the surveys no data appears on "small establishments" with less than five employees.

we used the six Korean censuses taken since 1968. However the 1968 census did not contain statistics for small establishments with four workers or less which caused problems for a strict comparison with Taiwan at given points of time. For this reason, we used data since 1968 when looking only at the time-series changes for Korea, and when making comparisons with Taiwan at given points of time, we used only the data available since 1973.

The first census in Taiwan was carried out in 1954, then from the second one in 1961, they were conducted every five years, the eighth census taking place in 1991 (ROC, DGBAS, various years). We obtained the results of the last seven censuses. However there is a discontinuity in the data between the 1961 census and the later ones. For this reason we used the data from the censuses since 1966 for our analysis. We carried out our analysis of Korea using the data up to 1988, and that of Taiwan using the data up to 1986. Changes which have taken place during the 1990s will be discussed in the Conclusion.

The categories of the census data, such as classifications for number of workers and industries, for the two economies differs from year to year which put limitations on the framing of the time-series data so that it would meet the purposes of our analysis. The most severe limitation was the difference in the basic production unit used in the statistics. The Korean statistical data takes the individual establish-ment as the basic unit for which the most detailed information is available, while the data for Taiwan takes the whole enterprise as the basic unit. There were other less severe differences in the data for which we also had to make adjustments, but we consider that our overall statistical results remain valid.

The ideal situation for comparing the pattern of distribution of the enterprises in the two economies would be to have data that is as identical as possible. However we found that if we attempted to analyze the distribution of the size of enterprises in the two economies either based on "establishments" or "enterprises," there was only one similar point in time prior to the 1990s where we could compare the two in the area of output; this was Taiwan-1981/Korea-1983. We carried out a comparative analysis for this point in time, and for the other points in time we decided to use the data on establishments for Korea and that on enterprises for Taiwan. We will discuss below the possible problems for our analysis arising from this difference in the nature of the data.

Fortunately from the Taiwanese census data we were able to work out the size distribution for the total number of enterprises, the number of employees, and the expenses of labor compensation both on establishments and on enterprises (see Table I-B). Through a comparison of these, we were able to make some inferences about the differences between the results obtained from enterprise-based data and from establishment-based data regarding the pattern of size distribution for Taiwan.

We concluded that in the case of Taiwan, utilizing the enterprise-based data gave

DISTRIBUTIVE COMPARISON   385

TABLE I

ENTERPRISE AND ESTABLISHMENT SIZE DISTRIBUTION IN KOREA AND TAIWAN

A.   Korean Manufacturing Sector, 1973–93

(%)

		Establishment-Base Data			
	No.	No. of Employees	Employee Remuneration[a]	Production Output	Value Added
1973					
1–9	87.0	17.6	6.9	4.7	5.8
10–49	9.3	12.3	10.3	7.3	7.2
50–99	1.6	7.4	7.6	6.5	6.5
100–499	1.7	24.2	26.5	28.6	27.8
500–	0.5	38.5	48.2	52.8	52.7
1978					
1–9	82.9	11.4	4.6	3.6	4.6
10–49	11.3	12.2	10.6	7.4	7.9
50–99	2.5	8.6	8.2	6.7	6.9
100–499	2.8	27.6	28.1	26.9	26.6
500–	0.6	40.2	48.4	55.4	54.0
1983					
1–9	81.6	12.6	5.2	3.2	4.3
10–49	13.0	16.5	14.1	8.1	9.2
50–99	2.6	10.6	10.2	7.3	7.5
100–499	2.3	26.3	27.9	26.0	26.3
500–	0.4	33.9	42.8	55.4	52.7
1988					
1–9	77.0	11.6	5.3	3.5	4.8
10–49	17.3	20.8	16.5	11.3	13.2
50–99	3.0	11.5	10.5	8.7	9.0
100–499	2.3	24.1	25.2	25.8	25.0
500–	0.4	32.1	42.5	50.6	48.0
1993					
1–9	79.7	19.0	5.9	3.7	4.5
10–49	16.7	27.3	24.5	17.1	18.3
50–99	2.1	11.4	11.8	9.9	10.1
100–499	1.3	19.7	23.7	24.0	24.5
500–	0.2	22.5	34.1	45.3	42.6

Source: ROK, NSO, *Report on Industrial Census* (various years).
[a] Includes salaries, wages, bonuses, and fringe benefits.

Continued overleaf

large-scale production units a greater weight in the economy than when using the establishment-based data. This becomes apparent on examining Taiwan's statistics for enterprises and establishments for 1981 and 1991, the only two years which provide statistics for both categories (see Table I-B). Furthermore, it is possible to estimate the distribution of the size of production based on the distribution of the

TABLE I (Continued)

B. Taiwan Manufacturing Sector, 1966–91

(%)

		Enterprise-Base Data					Establishment-Base Data			
	No.	No. of Em-ployees	Expenses of Labor Compens-ation[a]	Produc-tion Output	Value Added	No.	No. of Em-ployees	Expenses of Labor Compens-ation[a]	Produc-tion Output
1966										
1–9	72.1	12.8	9.4	14.2	n.a.	71.6	13.4	10.0	n.a.
10–49	22.4	21.2	15.9	13.9	n.a.	22.7	22.5	18.0	n.a.
50–99	2.7	8.7	7.7	6.4	n.a.	2.7	9.2	8.8	n.a.
100–499	2.3	22.5	20.2	19.9	n.a.	2.5	26.9	26.9	n.a.
500–	0.5	34.8	46.9	45.6	n.a.	0.5	28.0	36.2	n.a.
1971										
1–9	68.7	9.4	7.3	7.9	6.0	n.a.	n.a.	n.a.	n.a.
10 49	23.0	17.0	13.7	11.9	9.9	n.a.	n.a.	n.a.	n.a.
50–99	3.8	9.2	8.0	6.9	5.7	n.a.	n.a.	n.a.	n.a.
100–499	3.8	28.2	26.7	26.0	20.5	n.a.	n.a.	n.a.	n.a.
500–	0.8	36.1	44.3	47.3	57.9	n.a.	n.a.	n.a.	n.a.
1976										
1–9	68.1	10.2	7.9	6.6	5.8	n.a.	n.a.	n.a.	n.a.
10–49	22.8	17.7	14.4	11.9	10.3	n.a.	n.a.	n.a.	n.a.
50–99	4.3	11.1	9.9	8.8	6.8	n.a.	n.a.	n.a.	n.a.
100–499	4.1	30.4	28.9	29.1	24.8	n.a.	n.a.	n.a.	n.a.
500–	0.6	30.6	38.9	43.6	52.3	n.a.	n.a.	n.a.	n.a.
1981[b]										
1–29	87.1	22.3	17.9	12.0	13.0	86.8	23.5	19.5	12.4
30–299	11.8	39.7	36.9	32.9	28.3	12.1	42.6	41.2	37.0
300–499	0.5	8.4	8.5	8.2	8.1	0.6	9.9	10.5	10.9
500–	0.5	29.5	36.7	47.0	50.6	0.5	24.1	28.8	39.7
1986										
1–9	63.6	10.4	7.6	5.6	6.4	63.2	10.9	8.7	n.a.
10–49	27.7	24.0	19.2	16.7	15.1	28.1	25.6	22.1	n.a.
50–99	4.7	13.5	12.3	11.6	9.4	4.7	14.2	13.8	n.a.
100–499	3.5	28.1	29.2	29.0	25.1	3.6	30.8	33.3	n.a.
500–	0.4	24.1	31.7	37.2	44.0	0.4	18.4	22.1	n.a.
1991										
1–9	66.1	14.1	10.5	7.3	8.5	65.7	14.8	11.4	8.1
10–49	28.0	29.6	23.5	19.5	18.1	28.1	31.5	26.1	22.6
50–99	3.6	12.8	11.5	10.9	9.0	3.7	13.9	13.1	12.9
100–499	2.1	21.3	22.6	23.8	20.0	2.3	24.3	27.7	29.5
500–	0.3	22.2	31.9	38.5	44.4	0.3	15.6	21.8	26.8

Source: ROC, DGBAS (various years).
[a] Includes salaries, wages, bonuses, and fringe benefits.
[b] Size classification by number of employees for 1981 is broader than for other years.

expenses of labor compensation at establishments.[5] Through this procedure we found that the distribution of small-scale production units becomes greater when relying on the establishment-based rather than enterprise-based statistics.

Thus in Section B when comparing the Taiwanese data based on enterprises with the Korean data based on individual establishments, it is very possible that the importance of large-scale production units in the Taiwanese economy will be over-emphasized than if we were able to analyze both economies using data for individual establishments.

B.   *Evolution in the Size-Distribution Pattern*

Table I presents the size-distribution pattern in the Korean and Taiwanese manufacturing sector for the number of establishments/enterprises, the number of employees, employee remuneration/expenses of labor compensation, production output, and value added.[6] The table indicates, though not sharply, that big business tends to predominate in the Korean economy while in Taiwan SMEs tend to be more important players in the economy.

In the discussion below we will focus mainly on establishments/enterprises with 500 employees or more, and on those with less than 10 employees, to give a general picture of the evolution in the pattern of size distribution for these particular production units in the two economies.

1.   *Establishments/enterprises with 500 employees or more*

(1)   Trends

We will begin by comparing time-series changes in the position within both economies of establishments/enterprises with more than 500 employees. In both Korea and Taiwan the percentage of such large-scale establishments/enterprises in the total number of businesses is small and has decreased over time. In terms of output, the decreasing trend has been even more pronounced. In Korea from 1973 to 1983, the share of output accounted for by large-scale establishments first rose somewhat then leveled off, then dropped by about 5 points between 1983 and 1988. In Taiwan the share of output by such large-scale enterprises remained stable in the 40 per cent range between 1966 and 1981, then declined by 10 points between

---

[5] For the enterprise-based statistical data, the adjusted coefficient of determination between the distribution of the expenses of labor compensation and that of production is as high as 0.944. Assuming that a similarly high correspondence would be found for the establishment-based figures, we can assume the distribution of production among establishments of different size. Table I-B shows that the establishment-based data produces a larger distribution of expenses of labor compensation among smaller businesses compared to the enterprise-based statistics, and it is presumable that the same relationship holds for the distribution of production.

[6] The Korean censuses do not provide output figures for establishments with less than five employees. Therefore for these small establishments we used "value of shipments" instead.

1981 and 1986. Thus in both economies since the 1980s, the share of total production accounted for by establishments/enterprises with 500 or more employees has decreased somewhat.

Looking at this trend away from large-scale businesses in more detail and analyzing the factors that brought it about, Table II shows the percentages of change that took place in the number of establishments/enterprises and the output of these production units, and attributes these changes to two factors: (1) changes in industrial structure and (2) changes in the size distribution of establishments/enterprises within (each) specific industry. Table II presents the calculations for the two economies for the two periods that are closest to each other in point of time for (1) Ko-

TABLE II

FACTORS FOR CHANGE IN ENTERPRISE AND ESTABLISHMENT SIZE DISTRIBUTION:
MANUFACTURING SECTOR IN KOREA AND TAIWAN

A. Korea

		(Percentage points)	
	Change in Ratio to Total Manufacturing Sector (a) + (b)	Change Attributed to Factor 1 (a)	Change Attributed to Factor 2 (b)
1968–78			
Establishments with over 500 employees:			
No. of establishments	1.4	0.3	1.1
Production output	10.0	−0.7	10.6
Establishments with 5–9 employees:			
No. of establishments	−16.7	−6.0	−10.7
Production output	−3.6	−0.1	−3.5
1978–88			
Establishments with over 500 employees:			
No. of establishments	−0.9	0.3	−1.3
Production output	−4.9	0.1	−5.0
Establishments with 5–9 employees:			
No. of establishments	−6.7	−3.7	−3.0
Production output	0.0	−0.2	0.2

Source: ROK, NSO, *Report on Industrial Census* (various years).
Note: Change attributed to Factor 1 = change attributable to changes in industrial structure; Change attributed to Factor 2 = change attributable to changes in establishment size in specific industries.

For example, the change in the ratio between period $t-1$ and t for establishments with over 500 employees was as follows.

$$\left(\frac{Y_i}{Y}\right)_t - \left(\frac{Y_i}{Y}\right)_{t-1} = \sum_i l_i^t \Gamma_i^t - \sum_i l_i^{t-1} \Gamma_i^{t-1} = \sum_i \Gamma_i^t (l_i^t - l_i^{t-1}) + \sum_i l_i^{t-1} (\Gamma_i^t - \Gamma_i^{t-1}),$$

where Y = total manufacturing sector output, Y_i = production output of enterprises with over 500 employees, i = the ith industry, t = the tth period, l_i = share of enterprises with over 500 employees in the ith industry, and Γ_i = ith industry's share of total manufacturing sector production.

DISTRIBUTIVE COMPARISON 389

TABLE II (Continued)

B. Taiwan

(Percentage points)

	Change in Ratio to Total Manufacturing Sector (a) + (b)	Change Attributed to Factor 1 (a)	Change Attributed to Factor 2 (b)
1966–76			
Enterprises with over 500 employees:			
No. of enterprises	0.2	0.2	0.0
Production output	−2.2	−0.1	−2.0
Enterprises with 1–9 employees:			
No. of enterprises	−3.8	−9.6	5.7
Production output	−7.5	−4.9	−2.6
1976–86			
Enterprises with over 500 employees:			
No. of enterprises	−0.2	0.1	−0.3
Production output	−6.5	−1.0	−5.6
Enterprises with 1–9 employees:			
No. of enterprises	−4.4	−2.0	−2.3
Production output	−1.0	−0.2	−0.8

Source: ROC, DGBAS (various years).
Note: Change attributed to Factor 1 = change attributable to changes in industrial structure: Change attributed to Factor 2 = change attributable to changes in enterprise size in specific industries.

rean establishments and Taiwanese enterprises with more than 500 employees and (2) Korean establishments with 5–9 employees and Taiwanese enterprises with less than 10 employees.[7] The Korean side of the table shows that during the decade of 1968–78, establishments employing 500 or more workers increased their share of production by 10 points due to the increase in output by establishments in this specific size category in each specific industry. This indicated an overall trend toward large-scale production units during the ten years. However during the decade of 1978–88, the change in the size-distribution pattern in each industry, which had trended toward large-scale businesses during the previous decade turned negative resulting in a drop of 4.9 points in total output.

In Taiwan the share of total output for enterprises with 500 workers or more declined slightly during the decade of 1966–76, then dropped by a significant 6.5 points during the ten years of 1976–86. This trend away from large-scale enterprises in Taiwan could also be attributed mainly to the second factor; change in the size distribution of enterprises within each specific industry. In sum, Korea experienced a move toward large-scale establishments during the late 1960s and early 1970s followed by a move away from such large businesses in the 1980s, while in

[7] Since the Korean 1968 census data does not contain data on establishments with 4 workers or less, we had to use data for those with 5–9 workers for Korea in Table II.

Taiwan there was a gradually accelerating trend away from large-scale enterprises during the same decades.

(2)   Size distribution at given points of time

In this sub-section we will look at the pattern of size distribution at similar given points of time in the Korean and Taiwanese economies and compare the share of total manufacturing output accounted for by establishments/enterprises with 500 employees or more. First we will compare the data for Korea-1983 and Taiwan-1981, the only two points for which data on establishments is available for both economies. The share of total output accounted for by establishments with 500 employees or more was 55.4 per cent in Korea in 1983 compared with only 39.7 per cent in Taiwan in 1981. Furthermore, when comparing the size distribution of output for the two economies at the same points in time, we can see that for Taiwan-1981 small-scale establishments with 49 employees or less has a larger distribution than in Korea. In this particular instance the data clearly shows the dichotomy between Korea's big-business-centered economy and Taiwan's SME-oriented economy.

In order to compare the distribution of large-scale production units in the two economies at more points in time, we will now utilize data for establishments in Korea and for enterprises in Taiwan. As shown in Table I, the share of production for Korean establishments with over 500 employees continuously surpassed that of Taiwanese enterprises of the same size category, and the gap widened markedly especially in the late 1980s; in Korea the share was 50.6 per cent in 1988 while in Taiwan it was only 37.2 per cent in 1986. Thus the data attests to the much greater importance of big business in Korea. Moreover, the enterprise-based data for Taiwan tends to overstate the presence of large businesses in the economy than does the establishment-based data, as noted earlier. Thus the actual difference between the two economies in the share of output produced by large-scale establishments/enterprises is likely to be greater than what the above figures indicate.

2.   *Establishments/enterprises with less than ten employees*

(1)   Trends

As shown in Table I, up to the end of the 1980s the position in both economies of establishments/enterprises employing less than ten workers followed a long-term decline. In Korea the position in the economy of establishments employing between five and nine workers continued to decline during both the 1968–78 and 1978-86 periods. As seen from Table II-A, this decline was most apparent in the number of establishments. The causes for this decline were the changes taking place in the industrial structure of the economy and changes in the distribution of the size of establishments within each industrial sector as well.[8]

---

[8] The decline in the number of establishments with between five and nine employees was especially

In Taiwan the position in the economy of enterprises employing between one and nine workers also continued to decline during both the 1966–76 and 1976–86 periods. During the 1966–76 period in particular, the share of output of these small-scale enterprises fell by 7.5 points due mainly to the overall change in the industrial structure (Table II-B). The decline in the position of the food processing industry, in particular, where small-scale manufacturers played a large role, contributed significantly to the steep drop in the share of output by small enterprises.

(2)   Size distribution at given points of time

When comparing at given points of time the position in both economies of establishments/enterprises with less than ten employees, Table I shows that although the percentage of the number of small-scale establishments in Korea exceeded that of enterprises of the same size in Taiwan by almost 10 points, the share of output accounted for by these small enterprises in Taiwan was higher than Korea employing less than ten people. Thus the scale of production for Korean establishments employing between one and nine workers was comparatively smaller than that of similar-sized enterprises in Taiwan.

C.   *Summation*

As shown in the patterns of size distribution of establishments/enterprises in Korea and Taiwan, there has been a clear trend away from both large- and small-scale businesses. Since the 1980s this trend has been particularly marked in the share of output accounted for by large-scale businesses in both economies. Looking at the factors behind this phenomenon, during the 1970s just before the move away from large-scale businesses began in both economies, Korea and Taiwan both passed through a transition point marking a change from a surplus of labor to a scarcity of labor in their economies. Previous studies show that this transition took place around 1970 in Taiwan and around 1975 in Korea.[9] Following this transition large-scale businesses were confronted with a scarcity of labor and concomitant rising wages. In response they began to subcontract production to SMEs, while at the same time automating their production processes and shifting to non-labor-intensive industries. Several studies have reported the rise of subcontracting during the 1980s,[10] and the results of our research showing a decline in the output of large businesses concur with these findings. The rise in subcontracting along with grow-

---

marked in the food processing and machinery manufacturing industries during 1968–78 and in the apparel industry during 1978–88.

[9] For example, Kuo et al. (1981) and Sumiya and Liu (1992) date the transition in Taiwan in 1968, and Bai (1982) dates the transition in Korea around 1975.

[10] For Taiwan, Ka (1993) and Wei (1993) found that subcontracting started to increase from the 1980s in response to growing labor scarcity. According to Levy (1991), in Korea the footwear industry showed a steady shift from internal production to subcontracting to SMEs during the 1980s.

392   THE DEVELOPING ECONOMIES

ing scarcity of labor and rising wages in both economies since the 1980s seems to be one of the important factors that has brought on the trend away from large-scale businesses.

The present section has relied on census data to examine the appropriateness of the widely held perception that the main drivers of the Korean economy have been large-scale businesses while in Taiwan they have been the SMEs. However, as mentioned earlier, a comparative analysis of the two economies based on this data has definite limitations, the most critical being the absence of establishment-based statistics for both economies prior to the 1990s with the sole exception being two comparable dates in the early 1980s. Therefore we relied on data on establishments in Korea and on enterprises in Taiwan.[11] Thus the results presented in this section have been affected to some degree by the incompatibility of the categories found in the data.

In the following section we will examine the generally perceived dichotomy between the two economies by comparing and contrasting, first, the size of business groups and their position in their respective economies, and second, the size of the major exporters in both economies. As was mentioned earlier, the research to date on the Korean economy has directed most of its attention at the *chaebol* groups while that on Taiwan has focused on SMEs. We consider that such differing points of focus is due to the contrast in the positions that large-scale business groups have in their respective economies and the contrast in the size of the major exporters.

II. A COMPARISON OF THE SIZE OF BUSINESS GROUPS

A. *The Data*

A *chaebol*, or Korean conglomerate, is defined in the Monopoly Regulation and Fair Trade Act and its Rules for Implementation as a "large-scale business group."[12] Certified *chaebol*s must report to the Fair Trade Commission about their

---

[11] Also we had to use a rather loose classification for size categories for establishments/enterprises in order to standardize categories for comparing the number of employees. For example, if the category of establishments/establishments with 100–499 employees could be broken down into smaller segments, we could probably see the contrast between the two economies more clearly. Also, in pre-1973 Korea, establishments employing five workers or less were excluded from the census making it impossible to do an adequate comparison for the 1960s, a decade when both economies experienced accelerated economic growth.

[12] Article 2, Section 2 of the Act defines a "business group" as a collection of companies whose business affairs are under the control of a single individual. A detailed definition is also given for the meaning of "control over business affairs." A large-scale business group is defined in Article 3 of the Rules for Implementation as a business group with total assets ranking within the top thirty groups, and the government imposes various restrictions on the groups certified as being large-scale. Those large-scale business groups with a dispersed shareholding structure are excluded from the definition, as the Korean government offers incentives to promote the dispersion of shareholding in large-scale business groups.

financial situation and who their present stockholders are, and the following analysis is based on a portion of this reported information which is published in "The Financial Analysis of the Korean Thirty Largest *Chaebols*, 1996" (NIMA 1995; hereafter referred to as "Korean *Chaebols*"). Regarding business groups in Taiwan, we relied on surveys which the China Credit Information Service has conducted continuously since 1974 and published as "Research on Business Groups in the Taiwan-Fukien Area" (CCIS, various years; hereafter referred to as "Taiwan Research").

The criteria used in "Taiwan Research" for including business groups in its survey have been revised over the years. In the 1996/97 issue, the criterion for inclusion is to have either (1) total assets and total sales of over N.T.$400 million,[13] or (2) a sum of assets and sales exceeding N.T.$1 billion. For determining the physical size of a group, "Taiwan Research" uses "objective" criteria such as capital investment and managerial relationships among the individual member companies, and "subjective" criteria such as the existence of a mutual identity among the businesses that they belong to the same group.[14]

B. *Comparison of the Top Groups*

Using the information in Tables III and IV, we will first look at the change that has taken place in the position of large-scale business groups in the economies of Korea and Taiwan. Table III presents the shares for the top 5, 10, and 20 Korean business groups in the nominal GDP; and in Table IV we calculated total sales for the approximately 100 groups surveyed in "Taiwan Research" as a percentage of nominal GDP. Here it should be mentioned that in Table IV these absolute values have no special economic meaning themselves. First, total sales does not theoretically correspond to nominal GDP, the total amount of value added, and second, since a business group's total sales include the value of transactions among its member companies, the ratio of these total sales to GDP has little significance itself. However we have no alternative, and since our aim is to see how the position of large business groups in Taiwanese economy has changed, this indicator is sufficiently useful for the purpose.

---

[13] During 1995, N.T.$26.49 averaged U.S.$1.

[14] "Taiwan Research" lists five "objective" criteria: (1) the parent company owns at least 50 per cent of its subsidiaries' stock, or member companies of the group mutually own at least 25 per cent or a fair percentage of each other's stock; (2) the same individual invests over half of the capital in the parent and subsidiary companies; (3) the majority of director (*dongshi*), general manager (*zongjingli*), and auditor (*jiancharen*) positions in the parent and subsidiary companies are assumed by the same individuals or immediate family members, i.e., spouses and relatives within the third degree of kinship; and (4) the group is directed and supervised under the same managerial organ. The "subject" criterion means the commonly shared identity among the affiliated companies. If a collection of companies fulfills one of the "objective" criteria and meets the "subjective" condition, it is classified as a "business group" in "Taiwan Research."

TABLE III

KOREAN *CHAEBOL* VALUE ADDED AS A PERCENTAGE OF GDP, 1973–94

					(%)
	1973	1978	1983	1989	1994
Top 5 groups	3.5	8.1	10.0	8.4	8.4
Top 10 groups	5.1	10.9	13.0	10.4	11.2
Top 20 groups	7.1	14.0	16.0	13.5	13.5

Sources: For 1973–89, Hattori (1994); for 1994, NIMA (1996).

TABLE IV

ECONOMIC POSITION OF TAIWANESE BUSINESS GROUPS: TOTAL SALES OF BUSINESS
GROUPS AS A PERCENTAGE OF GDP, 1970–94

	Total Group Sales (N.T.$ Billion) (a)	Nominal GDP (N.T.$ Billion) (b)	No. of Groups[a]	(a)/(b) (%)
1970	54.7	226.8	100	24.1
1975	165.5	589.7	106	28.1
1980	456.9	1,491.1	100	30.6
1985	735.4	2,473.8	97	29.7
1990	1,688.6	4,222.0	101	40.0
1994	2,700.7	6,376.5	115	42.5

Source: CCIS (various years).
[a] The number of groups surveyed by the table's source. Criteria for their inclusion in the survey are detailed in footnote 14.

Table III shows that the position of the top *chaebol*s within the Korean economy grew in importance throughout the 1970s; however, in the mid-1980s this importance reached its peak and started to decline. Table IV indicates that in Taiwan the position of large business groups within the economy has been rising continuously since the 1970s.

We will now compare the position of business groups in the two economies during the past few years. Table V shows the ratio of total sales for the top thirty business groups to the nominal GDP in both economies. The figures for the latest available year, 1994—73.7 per cent in Korea and 31.3 per cent in Taiwan—are strikingly different, and an even larger difference can be seen in the calculations for the five top groups—49.0 per cent in Korea and 12.3 per cent in Taiwan. Clearly the importance of the *chaebol*s is far greater in the Korean economy than is that of large business groups in the Taiwanese economy.

The remarkably larger presence of Korean *chaebol*s in the economy shown in Table V is mainly due to the very large scale of the top *chaebol*s. For example, the total sales and assets expressed in U.S. dollars of the Cathay Group, Taiwan's largest business group in 1994, would rank only ninth in sales and fifth in assets for that

TABLE V

TOTAL SALES OF TOP BUSINESS GROUPS AS A PERCENTAGE OF
GDP: KOREA AND TAIWAN, 1994

		(%)
	Korea	Taiwan
Top 5 groups	49.0	12.3
Top 10 groups	60.4	19.7
Top 30 groups	73.7	31.3

Sources: For Korea, NIMA (1995). For Taiwan,
CCIS (1996/97).

year among Korea's business groups. Furthermore, the number of corporations comprising Korean *chaebol*s is considerably greater than the number of member companies making up Taiwanese business groups. In 1994 twelve groups in Korea had more than twenty companies while in Taiwan there were only three such groups. Research to date has often referred to *chaebol*s as "world-class big businesses" (Watanabe 1986, p. 116) while Taiwanese business groups are described as "small-scale conglomerates mainly under the control of family management" (Liu 1992, p. 137). One can see that there is indeed a marked contrast in the size of business groups in the two economies.

In this section we have seen the substantially clear contrast between the position of the *chaebol*s in the Korean economy and that of large business groups in the Taiwanese economy. It is very likely that this dichotomy has been an important factor behind the general perception that big business has had a far more important position in Korea's economy than in Taiwan's.

III. EXPORTERS AND BUSINESS SIZE

A. *The Data*

Table VI-A provides the export sales ratios (export sales / total sales) for Korean SME manufacturers by size, and Table VI-B shows export sales ratios for SME and non-SME manufacturers in Taiwan. Table VII shows the share of exports shipped by SMEs to total exports.[15]

The definition of "SME" in Taiwanese statistics is based on capitalization while for Korea it is defined by the number of employees. To determine whether the Korean data was sufficiently comparable to the Taiwanese data, we calculated the

---

[15] Table VII includes not only SME manufacturers but also SME trading companies. Therefore goods exported by SME trading companies, whether produced by large-scale enterprises or not, are included as SME exports, while goods manufactured by SMEs and exported by large trading companies may be included in SME exports.

TABLE VI

ENTERPRISE SIZE AND EXPORT SALES RATIO

A.   Export Sales Ratio of Korean SMEs

(%)

	Enterprise Size (No. of Employees)						
	5–9	10–19	20–49	50–99	100–199	200–299	Total
1977	6.0	19.1	10.4	12.8	28.0	42.9	21.8
1979	0.4	12.4	9.5	17.2	22.9	30.3	19.1
1981	2.7	16.3	19.3	29.9	29.3	31.4	25.5
1983	3.7	6.5	22.4	31.6	32.6	33.4	26.6
1989	7.6	11.7	16.0	21.7	26.6	33.0	21.3
1993	13.6	19.0	20.9	25.0	30.2	28.5	23.7

Source: ROK, KFSB (various years).
Notes: 1. Export sales ratio = export sales / total sales.
        2. Export sales include indirect export sales.

B.   Taiwan

	SMEs		Non-SMEs		Average SME Size (No. of Employees)	Average Non-SME Size (No. of Employees)
	Domestic Sales (%)	Export Sales (%)	Domestic Sales (%)	Export Sales (%)		
1973	41.8	58.2	53.6	47.5	n.a.	n.a.
1974	58.1	41.9	59.6	40.4	n.a.	n.a.
1975	45.1	54.9	62.7	37.3	n.a.	n.a.
1976	42.4	57.6	60.4	39.6	n.a.	n.a.
1977	47.5	52.5	62.7	37.3	n.a.	n.a.
1978	43.6	56.4	63.6	36.4	n.a.	n.a.
1979	42.8	57.2	59.8	40.2	117.5	611.5
1980	40.6	59.4	60.9	39.1	104.2	579.6
1981	26.4	73.6	57.9	42.1	122.5	523.2
1982	24.1	75.9	60.8	39.2	151.4	628.3
1983	28.4	71.6	65.4	34.6	n.a.	n.a.
1984	28.1	71.9	64.3	35.7	127.4	610.8
1985	28.9	71.1	64.5	35.5	105.6	534.1
1986	33.4	66.6	67.5	32.5	99.7	546.8
1987	34.8	65.2	67.9	32.1	86.8	534.4
1988	59.5	37.4	68.8	30.3	n.a.	n.a.
1989	63.3	32.7	69.7	26.9	63.8	468.1
1990	58.8	40.8	68.6	30.6	52.9	417.0
1991	61.9	37.7	68.8	30.0	46.7	354.9
1992	64.0	35.0	71.8	27.0	45.0	423.3

Source: Bank of Taiwan (various years).
Note: The definition of SMEs in the manufacturing sector has varied in the following ways:
    1973–76: Enterprises capitalized at N.T.$10 million or less.
    1977–81: Enterprises capitalized at N.T.$20 million or less.
    1982–92: Enterprises capitalized at N.T.$40 million or less.

DISTRIBUTIVE COMPARISON 397

TABLE VII

Total Exports for SMEs: Korea and Taiwan, 1981–94

(U.S.$ million)

	Korea			Taiwan		
	Total Exports	SME Exports	SME Share (%)	Total Exports	SME Exports	SME Share (%)
1981	n.a	n.a.	n.a.	22,600	15,390	68.1
1982	21,850	4,820	22.1	22,200	15,470	69.7
1983	24,450	4,890	20.0	25,120	15,930	63.4
1984	29,240	7,440	25.4	30,460	18,050	59.2
1985	30,280	8,410	27.3	30,720	18,800	61.2
1986	34,710	12,230	35.2	39,790	26,410	66.4
1987	47,280	17,810	37.7	53,540	35,900	67.1
1988	60,700	23,000	37.9	60,590	36,350	60.0
1989	62,380	26,050	41.8	66,200	40,770	61.6
1990	65,020	27,380	42.1	67,210	38,520	57.3
1991	71,870	28,700	39.3	76,180	43,330	56.9
1992	76,630	30,680	40.0	81,470	45,560	55.9
1993	82,240	35,170	42.8	84,920	46,510	54.8
1994	96,010	40,700	42.4	93,050	48,910	52.6

Sources: For Korea, SMIPC (various years); for Taiwan, ROC, MSBA (1995).
Note: SMEs include nonmanufacturing enterprises.

percentage of Taiwanese enterprises with less than 300 employees (the Korean definition of an SME) among the enterprises with N.T.$40 million or less capital worth (the Taiwanese definition of an SME) and found that as of 1990, 99.9 per cent of Taiwan's "SMEs" employed less than 300 workers. Hence, the enterprises defined statistically by the two economies as "SMEs" were largely the same size in terms of the number of employees. This indicates that the data in Table VI is sufficiently comparable.[16]

B. *Comparison*

From Table VI we can see that there is a contrast between the two economies in the relationship between enterprise size and the ratio of export sales. For Korea we were able to obtain data on the export sales ratios for SMEs (enterprises with less

[16] However there are definite problems in the quality of the data for the statistics on Taiwan contained in Table VI-B. First, the average number of employees of the enterprises surveyed shows a very discontinuous change over time: 151.4 in 1982 and 45.0 in 1992. Second, there is also a strange discontinuity in the movement of export ratios. For example, from 1987 to 1988 the share of exports shipped by SMEs dropped by 28 points. During these two years accelerated evaluation of the Taiwan dollar caused SME exports to stagnate, and it is quite possible that SMEs turned their marketing strategies away from exports and toward domestic demand. However, such a steep drop of 28 points indicates the possibility that some bias may have occurred in the survey methodology during the period covered by the survey.

than 300 employees) by size and found that there is a positive relationship between the size and the export sales ratios for SMEs (Table VI-A). In contrast, the share of exports to total sales for SMEs in Taiwan has consistently far exceeded that of non-SME exporters, and a comparison at given points of time also shows that the share of exports for SMEs in Taiwan was always higher than that for their counterparts in Korea.

We will now compare the share of SME exports as a portion of total exports in each economy. Table VII indicates that the share of SME exports is much higher in Taiwan than it is in Korea, especially up to the late 1980s. Comparing the time-series changes, we see that in Korea since 1982, the SME export ratio has steadily increased, while in Taiwan the share of SME exports to total exports remained at a comparably stable 60 per cent until the 1990s. Since then their share has decreased slightly, and the contrast between the two economies is becoming less sharp.

Despite definite data quality problems, the analysis in this section indicates that the Taiwanese SMEs have played a far more important role in the export sector than have their counterparts in Korea.[17] Both economies represent successful cases of export-oriented industrialization, but the export drive in Korea has been borne mainly by non-SMEs while in Taiwan it has been carried on by SMEs.

CONCLUSION

In the present study we examined the appropriateness of the generally held perception within research literature that contrasts the *chaebol*-led Korean economy and the SME-oriented Taiwanese economy.

In Section I we confirmed via census data a contrasting pattern of distribution in the size of establishments / enterprises in the two economies, although there were various limitations with the data due to the differing ways of categorizing the statistics. In Sections II and III we compared the position of large business groups in both economies and the position of SMEs in the export sector. Despite limitation with the data, we showed in Section II that the position of the *chaebol*s in the Korean economy is more important than is the position of large business groups in the Taiwanese economy. In Section III we showed the contrasting position of SMEs in the export sector of the two economies. In conclusion we can say that the statistical data to the end of the 1980s confirms the generally held perception contrasting enterprise size in the two economies has had its basis in those differences in the two economies that have been pointed out in this study.

---

[17] One more limitation is that the intermediate input-output relationship is not analyzed in this study. The export products of SMEs often contain intermediate goods supplied by large-scale enterprises and vice versa. The input-output relationship among manufacturing sectors should be taken into consideration in more detail when analyzing the relative roles played by big business and SMEs in the exporting sector.

In future follow-up research there are two points which will need to be examined further. First, starting from the eighth census conducted in 1991, Taiwan began publishing statistics at the level of the establishment providing data on the output and value added by industry and establishment size. Therefore, more adequate comparison between the two economies will be possible for the 1990s and beyond. Second, looking at the trend during the 1990s, we can see from Table I that in Korea the number of establishments employing 500 or more workers and their production as a ratio declined between 1988 and 1993, with the ratio for production dropping by 5.3 points. On the other hand, between 1986 and 1991 the position of enterprises employing more than 500 workers in the Taiwanese economy increased in importance, if only slightly. In other words, the dichotomy in the position of big business in the two economies seems to have lessened since the mid-1980s. Whether this trend will continue is a subject deserving further observation and future study.

REFERENCES

Bai, Moo-Ki. 1982. "The Turning Point in the Korean Economy." *Developing Economies* 20, no. 2: 117–40.

Bank of Taiwan. Various years. *Zhonghua minguo Taiwan diqu gongye caiwu zhuangkuang diaocha baogao* [Report on survey of financial statements of manufacturing industry in Taiwan Area, the Republic of China]. Taipei: Bank of Taiwan.

China, Republic of (ROC), Executive Yuan, Directorate-General of Budget, Accounting and Statistics (DGBAS). Various years. *Zhonghua minguo taiwan diqu gongshangye pucha baogao* [The report on industrial and commercial census, Taiwan-Fukien Area, the Republic of China]. Taipei.

China, Republic of (ROC), Executive Yuan, Ministry of Economic Affairs, Medium and Small Business Administration (MSBA). 1995. *Zhongxiao qiye baipishu, 1995* [White paper on small and medium business, 1995]. Taipei.

China Credit Information Service [Zhonghua Zhengxinsuo] (CCIS). Various years. *Taiwan diqu jituan qiye yanjiu* [Research on business groups in the Taiwan-Fukien Area]. Taipei: China Credit Information Service.

Hattori, Tamio. 1994. "Keizai seichō to 'zaibatsu' no keisei" [Economic growth and the formation of Korean zaibatsu]. In *Kōza gendai Ajia* [Contemporary Asia]. Vol. 2, *Kindai-ka to kōzō hendō* [Modernization and structural transformation], ed. Katsuji Nakagane. Tokyo: University of Tokyo Press.

———. 1997. "*Chaebol*-Style Enterprise Development in Korea." *Developing Economies* 35, no. 4: 458–77.

Ka, Chihming. 1993. *Taiwan dushi xiaoxing zhizaoye de chuangye jingying yu shengchan zuzhi: Yi Wufenpu chengyi zhizaoye wei anli de fenxi* [Market, social networks, and the production organization of small-scale industry in Taiwan: The garment industries in Wufenpu]. Taipei: Institute of Ethnology, Academia Sinica.

Korea, Republic of (ROK), Economic Planning Board (EPB). Various years. *Report on Mining and Manufacturing Census*. Seoul.

Korea, Republic of (ROK), Ministry of Trade, Industry and Energy, Korea Federation of

Small Business (KFSB). Various years. *Report on Actual State of Small and Medium Enterprises.* Seoul.

Korea, Republic of (ROK), National Statistical Office (NSO). Various years. *Report on Industrial Census.* Seoul.

———. Various years. *Report on Mining and Manufacturing Survey.* Seoul.

Kuo, Shirley W. Y.; Gustav Ranis; and John C. H. Fei. 1981. *The Taiwan Success Story: Rapid Growth with Improved Distribution in the Reublic of China, 1952–1979.* Boulder, Colo.: Westview Press.

Kuramochi, Kazuo. 1992. "Kankoku no tassei" [The achievement of Korea]. In *Gendai Nihon shakai* [Contemporary Japanese society], ed. University of Tokyo, Institute of Social Science. Vol. 3, *Kokusai hikaku* [International comparison]. No. 2. Tokyo: University of Tokyo, Institute of Social Science.

Levy, Brian. 1991. "Transaction Costs, the Size of Firms and Industrial Policy: Lessons from a Comparative Case Study of the Footwear Industry in Korea and Taiwan." *Journal of Development Economics* 34, nos. 1/2: 151–78.

Liu, Jin Qing. 1992. "Sangyō: Kanmin kyōsei no kōzu" [Industry: Coexistence between the public and private sectors]. In *Taiwan no keizai: Tenkei NIES no hikari to kage* [Taiwan's economy: The bright and dark sides of a typical NIE], by Mikio Sumiya, Liu Jin Qing, and Two Jaw-yaan. Tokyo: University of Tokyo Press.

New Industry Management Academy [Sin Sanob Gyongyongwon] (NIMA), ed. 1995. *Hanguk 30 dae chaebol jaemu bunsok, 1996* [The financial analysis of the Korean thirty largest *chaebol*s, 1996]. Seoul: New Industry Management Academy.

Numazaki, Ichiro. 1997. "The *Laoban*-Led Development of Business Enterprises in Taiwan: An Analysis of the Chinese Entrepreneurship." *Developing Economies* 35, no. 4: 440–57.

Small and Medium Industry Promotion Corporation (SMIPC). Various years. *Major Statistics of Small and Medium Industries.* Seoul: Small and Medium Industry Promotion Corporation.

Sumiya, Mikio; Liu Jin Qing; and Two Jaw-yaan. 1992. *Taiwan no keizai: Tenkei NIES no hikari to kage* [Taiwan's economy: The bright and dark sides of a typical NIE]. Tokyo: University of Tokyo Press.

Taniura, Takao. 1988. "Taiwan kōgyōkaron josetsu" [Introduction to the study of industrialization in Taiwan]. In *Taiwan no kōgyōka: Kokusai kakō kichi no keisei* [Industrialization in Taiwan: The formation of an international export manufacturing base], ed. Takao Taniura. Tokyo: Institute of Developing Economies.

Watanabe, Toshio. 1986. *Kankoku: Benchā kyapitarizumu* [Korea: Venture capitalism]. Tokyo: Kōdansha.

Wei, Yinping. 1993. "Chanye waiyi zhong shengchan zuzhi zhuanbian de jizhi: Yi Taiwan zhixieye wei li" [Mechanism of production organization change in the course of industry's relocation: A case of Taiwan's footwear industry]. Master's thesis, National Tsing Hua University.

Yu, Zong-xian. 1993. "Zhongxiao qiye" [Small and medium-size industries]. In *Taiwan jingyan sishi nian* [The Taiwan experience: 1949–89], ed. Kao Hsichun and Li Cheng. Taipei: Commonwealth Publishing Co.

[20]

EVOLUTION OF INDUSTRIAL ORGANIZATION AND POLICY RESPONSE IN KOREA: 1945-1995

Seong Min Yoo
Korea Development Institute

Sung Soon Lee
Sung Kyun Kwan University

Introduction

In quantitative terms, the Korean economy recorded a remarkable growth for the past half century. This growth record, however, may not constitute what we call "development," if we define development as a continuous upward movement of the overall socio-economic system. Economic development is meant to incorporate not only the expansion of physical production inputs like labor and capital, or the enhancement of production technology and entrepreneurial talents, but also the improvement of surrounding institutions and people's minds. Economic development under capitalism is the process of building up socio-economic orders based on autonomous and independent decisions of individual economic agents, and thus, is the process of nurturing a society's own market economy.

In this respect, economic development in Korea for the past 50 years can be explained in terms of how certain important characteristics of the market economy have evolved in Korea. At first glance, one can easily agree that even today's Korean economy cannot be identified as a typical market economy, given the role of the state in the economy. In the past the Korean economy was even further from being a market economy: after the devastating war, there were neither consumers, producers, nor any markets. It was an unaffordable luxury to pursue a market economy in the early days of development in Korea. Rather, the ability to manage the economy and to run the industries and business firms was badly needed for a long period, and the government was considered the most appropriate means for meeting these demands. As the economy grew more complicated, however, the once significant role of the Korean government began to decline and a market mechanism began to replace the state. This gradual process of the market substituting for the state has taken place in accordance with the evolution of Korea's industrial organization, which is the subject of this paper.

In this chapter, the objective is to trace back the development history of the industrial organization in Korea for the past 50 years. In doing so, we will focus on how the Korean version of a capitalist market economy has evolved, how the role of the government vis-a-vis the private sector has changed over time, and what were the policy issues in question, including industrial policy, competition policy, deregulation and privatization policy, corporate policy, and so forth. Section II will summarize the birth of a market economy system and the appearance of entrepreneurs and firms in Korea after its liberation in 1945. Section III illustrates the evolution of industrial organization during the 1960s and 1970s, when much of the process of concentration was taking place under the government-led management of the economy. Section IV deals with the period after 1980, when the market had more distinctly substituted for the state and the confrontation between various pro-competitive and anti-competitive forces began to determine the Korean version of a market economy. In Section V, we choose a special topic in Korea's industrial organization, that is, the concentration of economic power, also known as the chaebol issue. Section VI will conclude this chapter and suggest important tasks ahead in the area of industrial organization.

The Beginning of a Market Economy in Korea: 1945-1960

Emergence of Market Mechanism and Entrepreneurs

Although the basic direction toward a free market economy was assumed under the U.S. military administration in 1945, the institutions to support the economy were founded after the establishment of the Korean government and its Constitution in 1948. Since then, numerous laws were enacted and the disposal of vested properties once owned by the Japanese began to be implemented.

Institutional Arrangements for a Market Mechanism

Soon after Korea's liberation, there were debates, especially among the intellectuals, concerning the adoption of a free market economy or a planned economy, the implementation of land reform, striking balance between state-owned enterprises and private enterprises, etc. The establishment of the Korean government and its Constitution in 1948 drew an end to this debate.

The Constitution of 1948 had certain implications regarding the new republic's economic system: first, it is fundamentally to be a free and democratic system (Article 5); second, social welfare should be maximized and the state can intervene, if necessary (Article 84); third, agricultural land should in principle be owned by farmers and the agricultural land reform is called for (Article 86); fourth, state ownership or public management of enterprises is to be expanded (Article 87); fifth, labor rights are to be protected and workers should be allowed their share of profits (Article 18). In addition to these constitutional principles, many laws were enacted to lay down the institutional groundwork of a market economy; they included laws to establish the central bank and state-run enterprises, tax laws, capital market laws, etc. In December 1948, the U.S. and Korea entered into an agreement for economic aid. The eight principles included in the agreement to stabilize and strengthen the Korean economy, were the backbone of economic policy of the ruling Liberal Party. The basic policy stance was to minimize the intervention of the government and pursue a laissez-faire type of free market economy.

Vested Properties and the Evolution of Firms

Disposal or sale of the properties reverted from Japanese ownership was an important and sensitive issue after the liberation, since it involved conflict of interest among different groups of people. The Rhee Syngman administration, the National Assembly and the U.S. military administration had different views on "to whom the properties should be sold" and "which institution should administer this process of disposal." The Rhee administration clashed with the National Assembly in setting the priority, since the former placed top priority upon those with managerial capability while the latter preferred the landlord class which collapsed due to the land reform. In 1949, the Vested Properties Disposal Law was enacted to support the government's idea, and those given top priority in the distribution of vested properties included former employees of the company, businessmen, skilled workers in the same line of business, and technocrats. We note that these people were believed to be the most experienced in commerce and industry, and the government policy was realistically aiming for fast economic growth.

Actual sales of the vested properties were made under highly preferential conditions. The sale prices of properties were set a great deal below the real values of the properties. Moreover, the installment repayment plan spanned 15 years, making the properties almost free. Thus, the disposal of vested properties combined with land reform resulted in the collapse of the landlord class and the emergence of new commercial or industrial capital. It also resulted in a change in the production share of large firms. As 36 out of 89 vested companies (over 300 employees) were either sold or transformed into state-run enterprises, these large firms began to actively manufacture goods, and the market structure previously dominated by small- and medium-sized firms began to change.

An Appraisal of the Role of Government

The disposal of the vested properties and the subsequent privatization of state-owned enterprises exemplifies the nature of government intervention in those years. Again, the administration and the National Assembly differed in their view of ownership of vested properties. While most of the politicians supported the idea of state ownership of vested properties, the government, as well as the businessmen (the Chosun Chamber of Commerce, in particular), supported private ownership or at least contracting out those properties for private use. The principle of property ownership by private individuals was established amidst this debate, and in 1951 state-owned enterprises (then 54 in total) began to be privatized. Most of these state-owned enterprises were privatized by the year 1954, and the commercial banks which were reverted from Japanese ownership were also privatized.

It appears that the Rhee Syngman administration tried to provide an institutional setting necessary for a new market economy. While the administration tried to foster the development of business firms through the disposal and privatization of vested properties, efforts were rather indirect and government intervention in the economy was kept at a minimum level. Although the strategy was not successful in terms of the growth record, it served a critical role in the initial stages of the capitalist economy in Korea, and it constitutes a sharp contrast with the economic policies of the Park Chung Hee administration in the 1960s and 1970s.

Growth of Firms and Industrial Policies in the 1950s

Expansion of Big Business after the Korean War

Although the disposal and privatization of vested properties provided physical capital to entrepreneurs, the Korean War destroyed most of it, and there was a severe shortage of capital goods after the war. Foreign aid in the form of capital or raw material contributed significantly to solving this problem, which was another important moment in the growth history of firms in Korea. Aided raw materials and production facilities were distributed directly to the producers at prices much lower than the market level. Since the acquisition of foreign aid meant in itself huge profits, it was critical to maintain access to this aid. Firms began to organize cartels to monopolize the procurement of raw materials, and trade associations appeared in such industries as textile and flour milling in order to monopolize the procurement of raw materials and distribute them among its member companies. These trade associations engaged in such cartel-like practices as price fixing, deterrence of new entry, etc. Although the government discouraged imports to protect the domestic market, it was insensitive to the monopolistic conduct of trade associations.

The profits accumulated in the industries based on foreign aid, however, were not invested towards the production sector, but rather used for speculative purposes or went to curb market, since a mature capital market did not exist. In the so-called "three white" industries (cement, sugar, and wheat flour), investments in plants and other production facilities were made only to meet the requirements to obtain the aid raw materials, and thus, were not productive investments. As we look back on the emergence of business firms and the process of capital accumulation after the Korean War, it was inevitable that manufacturing industries lacked capital investments due to many limitations in the commodity market, capital market, and business mind of entrepreneurs, while most of the capital accumulations were made in the commercial or speculative sectors. It was still difficult to encounter genuine entrepreneurship due to a lack of creativity in product development and a reluctance to make risky ventures into new markets.

A sharp decline in foreign aid after 1958, coupled with a recession in 1956 and 1957, led to the bankruptcy of many firms followed by a wave of mergers and acquisitions. This M&A wave resulted in a change in distribution of sellers, widening the size gap between large and small firms, facilitating diversification of many firms, and the restructuring of consumer goods industries. Although rapid growth of the so-called *chaebols* was a phenomenon of the 1960s and 1970s, their core or founding companies existed from the 1950s and were quite successful in their businesses. Out of today's 10 largest *chaebols*, nine (except the Daewoo group) had already established their core companies in the 1950s. These firms grew in subsequent decades and are now the leading conglomerates of Korea, through rapid expansion of their traditional businesses, as well as diversifications into new businesses. Thus, the 1950s can be defined as an embryonic period for most of the *"chaebols"* in Korea.

Underdevelopment of Small and Medium Industries

Large firms were able to accumulate their capital through import substitution, profits in consumer goods industries, and also via the disposal of vested properties and access to foreign aid. However, small- and medium-sized businesses were isolated from these opportunities, lacked modern managerial know-how and production technology, and suffered from a sub-optimal scale of production. They had to rely upon raw materials and intermediate goods either supplied by domestic big business or imported by speculative commercial capital, which were available at high prices. They could not obtain capital from the banking sector and were exposed to the uncertainties and instabilities of the commodity markets where they ran their business. The bad harvest in the late 1950s caused a decline in the demand for products of small- and medium-sized businesses in rural areas and many as a result went bankrupt.

There existed a significant market failure in the sense that no form of cooperation or division of labor emerged spontaneously in the market. The large firms differed significantly in many respects from small and medium firms. They differed in their method of investment financing, line of business, production technology, etc. A dichotomy between the big business sector and the small and medium industries emerged, and a long period of time passed before any changes in this dual structure could be observed.

An Appraisal of Industrial Policy in the 1950s

Industrial policies of the 1950s, if there were any, were to promote the development of import substituting industries in order to satisfy the urgent needs of the people in consuming daily necessities. Under the assumption that foreign aid was a major source of capital supply, a decline in aid in the late 1950s called for a fundamental shift of policies, which did not take place under the Rhee Syngman administration. Although there were government plans to promote such industries as textile, milling, sugar, paper, leather, and rubber, the plans failed to have well-designed financing programs. Under these circumstances, it was inconceivable to derive an industrial policy that would prepare for the future restructuring of industries.

An Age of Concentration: 1960-1980

A Shift in Development Strategy and Government-Business Relationship

The military coup in 1960 created an authoritarian government which differed substantially from the previous administration in terms of economic policies. In order to induce the support of the general public, the military government placed top priority on enhancing the living standard of people and maximizing economic growth. At first, though, the military government under the control of Park Chung Hee promised to develop agriculture and small and medium industries and penalize some of the businessmen for conducting unethical and illegal business practices. This line of policy, though dubious in its real effects on economic growth, highlighted the reform plaform of the new power group and helped gain political support from Korean people. Through these measures, the new power elites were also successful in turning the political support into a consensus of people's commitment to economic growth.

It is interesting to note how the policies against shady business deals transformed over the years, since punishment would directly affect many of the big businesses at that time. Recognizing that outright punishment of businessmen would seriously undermine growth potential, at least in the short-run, the Park administration soon switched its position by allowing some businessmen to participate in important development projects targeted by the government. In this process, the big businesses of the 1950s were divided into two groups of contrasting destiny. Although a clear-cut selection criteria did not exist, it is interesting to observe that those businessmen who made a fortune in speculative or commercial activities in the 1950s collapsed, while those running large scale manufacturing plants survived the political turmoil in the early 1960s. The authoritarian nature of the military administration over private businessmen in the early 1960s signalled the beginning of a "government-the leader, business-the follower" relationship in Korea, which later developed into a government-led growth model.

There also came other important policy shifts, most of which consolidated the dominant position of the government in managing the economy. Nationalization of several key industries was one of the major steps toward government initiative. Nationalization of the once privatized commercial banks was particularly significant, because it enabled the government to fully control the creation and supply of credit thereafter. For decades, the government's control over banks was an essential element in the government-led economic growth, and much of the investment financing was subject to government approval. As long as access to credit was the key to business success, the private sector was willing to be subordinate to the directives of the government. In this way, the so-called "policy loan" became a symbol of government intervention. Five-year plans which started in 1962 were another aspect of the government's dominance over the market.

Export Drive, HCI Drive and the Expansion of Big Business

The 1960s

Various incentives to promote the growth of exports were introduced in the early 1960s and were maintained until the mid-1980s with minor modifications. Export-oriented industrialization strategy inevitably increased Korea's dependence on foreign raw material and capital goods. Export opportunities, however, helped domestic producers overcome the diseconomy arising from the sub-optimal scale of the domestic market. More importantly, the competition in the world market put competitive pressure on Korean exporters who had no other choice but to make every effort to strengthen their competitiveness. Thus, an export-oriented growth strategy was important not only from a macroeconomic perspective, but also from an industrial organizational perspective, since it introduced a new source of competition to Korean firms.

The rapid growth of exports and the development of such new industries as fertilizer, oil refinery, petrochemicals, textile, and cement, diversified the expansion path of big businesses in the 1960s. The industrial policies to promote cement, chemical, and steel industries facilitated the growth of large firms in these industries. Bankruptcy of some of the foreign-loan-financed companies led to another wave of M&As under the supervision of the government, and those acquiring these failing firms at preferential terms expanded very rapidly (Daewoo, Hyundai, Hanjin, Dong-Ah, Hyosung, etc.). Various laws enacted to promote the development of target industries accelerated the growth of big business in such industries as shipbuilding, electronics, steel, petrochemical, etc. Thanks to the land development boom, cement and construction businesses grew rapidly (Hyundai, Dong-Ah, Ssangyong, etc.). The Vietnam War brought about a sharp increase of demand for certain products and services (Daewoo, Hanjin, Kukje, etc.). Among the large firms of the 1960s, there were state-owned enterprises, as well. Pohang Iron and Steel Company (POSCO) established in 1968 was a representative case.

The export drive was carried out under a tight control of investment resources by the government. Since foreign loans guaranteed by the government were an important source of capital in the 1960s, the government was never free from the bad performance of individual firms, and in many cases had to rescue them by providing even more credit. As the government found it necessary to maintain profitable investments, it aimed to protect the market position of those foreign-debt-invested firms, and introduced a strong license and permit system. This government-made barrier to entry consolidated the monopoly position of the incumbent firms and resulted in a highly concentrated market structure. The incumbent firms on their part formed cartel-like trade associations and engaged in many anti-competitive activities. Although there were many criticisms of the ill effects of protecting monopolies and oligopolies, the prevailing view at the time was that economic growth should be maximized at the expense of anything, including competition. We note that during 1964-1972 there were four attempts to enact a competition law, all of which were in vain.

The 1970s

Although the 1960s witnessed the rise of a few heavy industries, it was not until 1973 that Korea embarked upon a drive to develop heavy and chemical industries (HCIs hereafter). The "HCI Declaration" announced in January 1973 by President Park Chung Hee included an ambitious plan to increase the share of HCI products in total exports to above 50% by the year 1980. Although details of the HCI drive were modified according to changing economic conditions, the basic policy stance did not change until 1979.

The HCI drive in the 1970s was by far the most important industrial policy in the history of Korea's industrialization, and its effects on the industrial structure as well as industrial organization have been profound. If there had not been a policy to concentrate available investment resources into HCIs, Korea would not have today's advanced industrial structure. However, there were at the same time distortions caused by the concentration of investments in HCIs: the neglect of light industries sacrificed their growth potential; some of the government-led investments in HCIs turned out to be inefficient, leading to the subsequent realignment of investments and rationalization measures in the 1980s; the industrial organization dominated by the *chaebol* was also consolidated due to the HCI drive.

The HCI drive made big business grow dramatically in the 1970s. First of all, the HCI drive created an environment in which active participation in the HCIs targeted by the government was a must for any firm who wished to grow. In view of the scale economies inherent in many HCIs, it was believed that the size of production should exceed minimum efficient scale in order to be competitive. In many cases, this led the government to protect the monopolistic positions of many firms who already enjoyed various kinds of support from the government.

The *chaebols'* growth in the 1970s was quite explosive in terms of the number of subsidiaries as well as their size. The number of subsidiaries of the 30 largest *chaebols* increased from 126 in 1970 to 429 in 1979, and many of the new subsidiaries were *de novo* entry into new businesses while the rest became *chaebol* subsidiaries through M&A. For *chaebols* participating in the HCI drive, the rapid industrial restructuring meant quick expansion through diversification into new industries, which was mostly financed by policy loans from the state-controlled banks and equity investments from other subsidiaries within the same group. The Middle East construction boom, the development of non-bank financial institutions and general trading companies were all behind the rapid diversification of *chaebols*. In particular, the establishment of general trading companies by the largest *chaebols* was important for their diversification. For *chaebols* licensed to operate a general trading company, it was easier to obtain greater access to preferential policy loans, employ higher quality manpower, and flexibly switch any managerial know-how to new business opportunities. Thus, the general trading companies served as the headquarters for conglomerate diversification.

Throughout the 1970s, big business in Korea was able to develop into conglomerate business groups which had diverse businesses under a single control, covering most of the important manufacturing industries, distribution, construction, finance, etc. By the end of the 1970s, these conglomerates came to have the characteristics of today's *chaebols*: family ownership, control, and management; numerous subsidiaries under a single control and seemingly excessive diversification; cross shareholding among the subsidiaries within a group through equity investment and mutual loan guarantee by subsidiaries, etc.

Legacies of the 1960s and 1970s: Concentrated Industrial Organization

To understand the evolution of industrial organization in Korea, the term "concentration" should be given a broader and deeper meaning than what the traditional textbook of industrial organization defines it to be. Concentration in Korea was not only the result of what we observed in the structure of markets and industries, but also an essential element of the development strategy that had been maintained at least throughout the 1960s and 1970s. It is widely accepted that several structural features of Korea's industrial organization — such as the predominance of the state over the market, the strong favoritism of producers at the expense of consumers, the dominant position of *chaebols* in the economy, the monopoly or oligopoly status of many markets — are all the result of the development strategy of the 1960s and 1970s. However, a closer look at the phenomenon would verify that it constitutes the very ingredients of that development strategy. Leadership of the government, protection and support of producers, concentration of investment resources into large firms, and entry regulations for industrial policy objectives, were a means of concentrating any available resources in to the economy along with the efforts of the people.

The economic development in the 1960s and 1970s was accompanied by a greater concentration of industrial organization, which became a tradition that could not easily change. Since the legacies of the 1960s and 1970s are still important in understanding today's industrial organization in Korea, there is a need to explore what the legacies are.

Predominance of the State over the Market

The relationship between the state and the market saw a new swing in the 1960s. As liberalism and inactivity of the government in the 1950s proved to be ineffective, the new administration first tried to establish the leading role of the government in the economy. The authoritarian political power's strong commitment to economic development, nationalization of many industries, control of the financial and fiscal policy tools, and short and long-term plans all helped the government override the market mechanism. As the situation persisted for two decades, the dominant position of the government as the problem-solver became even stronger, and there seemed to be a belief among the political elites as well as technocrats that the government was omnipotent in achieving economic growth in Korea.

The idea that the government can successfully replace the market mechanism was at a peak during the HCI drive of the 1970s, and it then began to weaken as the HCI drive entailed serious problems. Once established, however, the predominance of the state over the market developed its own inertia and it did not easily change. In what follows, we look into certain features of this phenomenon.

Discretion Rather Than the Rule: The Government-Business Relationship   The state's dominance over the market resulted in a situation in which discretionary judgment was important in most of the government decisions. Even though rules such as constitutional principles or legal provisions existed, economic policies based upon discretion sometimes violated the rules. To the eyes of policymakers, resort to discretion rather than the rules was justified on the grounds of flexibility and efficiency. Under these circumstances, businessmen tended to appeal to the discretionary decision of the government instead of abiding by the rules. In many markets, it was not competitive process but a discretionary ·choice by the government in giving out licenses and permits or the allocation of preferential loans that decided the winners. The situation created many businessmen who were highly dependent upon the government. Even today, private sector firms to some extent expects the government to do something for them, although they pretend to support an unfettered market mechanism. On the part of the government, it was even more difficult to move away from the past inertia of discretion, though the government was professing the need for liberalization and a freer market economy in the 1980s.

The Cobweb of Government Regulations   In an economy where discretion overrides any rules, government regulations in actual practice are much more expansive than those stipulated in laws and legal regulations. The idea of an omnipotent government during the 1960s and 1970s was specified in many interventionist measures in the name of industrial policy. The nature of industrial policy was either industrial support through various measures or regulatory interventions in the market. The HCI drive of the 1970s, in particular, produced innumerable interventionist regulations, many of which were hard to remove even at a time when they were no longer desirable. The rapid increase of government regulations was paralleled by the expansion of the government body, which in turn made it more difficult to reform the regulations.

Government regulations in the name of industrial policy included both economic regulations such as entry regulations, price regulations, investment regulations, and administrative or procedural regulations that were designed to implement economic regulations. As these regulations persisted over a long period, they became a hotbed of corruption. With regards to the private sector, the cost of abiding by or detouring regulations increased, while regulations were suspected of yielding the original effects. In addition, the regulatory industrial policy affected Korea's industrial organization in a significant manner. Entry regulations explain why many of the important markets in Korea have been maintained as monopolies or oligopolies. The heated debate in recent years over the entry regulations in such industries as petrochemicals, aircraft manufacturing, passenger cars, steel, telecommunications, illustrates how difficult it is to remove a single regulation. Price regulations were even more pervasive in Korea and had a nullifying effect on the most important weapon of competition among firms. Reform of price regulations was difficult partly because it was easy to blame price deregulation as being the source of inflation.

Although the government apparently shifted to liberalization and to pro-competition policies in the 1980s, the strong tradition of regulatory industrial policy still exists even today. The overall trend has been a gradual shift to a freer market mechanism, but interventionist industrial policy was revived in the years of economic recession.

The Proliferation of Public Enterprises   State-owned and managed enterprises are an extreme form of government regulation. The rapid expansion of public enterprises in Korea in the 1960s and 1970s could be understood in the context of a prevailing belief in an omnipotent government in those years. In addition to the textbook explanation of the raison *d'etre* for public enterprises, such as natural monopoly and externality, public enterprises in developing countries can be justified when the input markets suffer from serious imperfections. Korea in the 1960s and 1970s was no exception in this regard, and the markets for capital, labor, and entrepreneurship, were all suffering from market failures. The government believed that it could promote the development of key industries by establishing public enterprises. Nationalization of banks was carried out for a different reason, to control the supply of credit, since it was essential to the government-led management of the economy. Once many industries were nationalized, they contributed to consolidating the economic power of the government through the direct ownership and control of the industries. In addition to the banking sector, such social infrastructure as electricity, telecommunication, roads, railways, port facilities and such key industries as fertilizers, oil refineries, and steel were all owned and controlled by the government, which consolidated the economic power of the government vis-a-vis the private sector in the 1960s and 1970s.

As far as the public enterprises were concerned, the legacy of the 1960s and 1970s was the difficulty of privatization. Not only did the prevalence of government regulations combined with the expansion of government body make it difficult to shift to a freer market economy in the 1980s, the public enterprises, once established and maintained for many years, had built up their own inertia. In many cases, the government officials who controlled the public enterprises and the managers and employees of the enterprises seemed to enjoy vested interests, which made it more difficult to implement reforms.

Expansion of the Industrial Base and the Emerging Forces of Market Mechanism

It cannot be denied that the strong and consistent interventionist drive of the Park Chung Hee administration significantly affected industrial growth, industrial restructuring and the evolution of industrial organization in Korea. It is also true, however, that government policies and actions were not the only factors which determined the evolution of industrial organization in the 1960s and 1970s. Thus, legacies of the past should include changes in market structural factors, which are basically the result of diverse causes that appear along the growth path, and which do not necessarily and exactly correspond to policy changes. The simple truth — that rapid economic growth was accompanied by significant broadening of the industrial base as well as the emergence of many new industries along the spectrum of industrial restructuring from simple light industries to sophisticated and large-scale heavy industries — had great implications for development of market mechanism and industrial organization in Korea.

Macroeconomic growth and the growth of firms and industries represent two sides of a coin. The rapid growth of firms and industries both in number and size was what broadened the industrial base. Between 1960 and 1980, the economy grew at 8.1% per annum, which was driven by the 16.6% annual average growth of the manufacturing sector. The manufacturing sector during the period of 1970-80 recorded an increase in shipments by 6 times, value added by 21.6 times, employment by 2.3 times, the average size of establishment by 3.2 times (in terms of shipments), and the net addition to the number of establishments in the manufacturing sector was 6,700 during the same period. While broadening their base, industries in Korea experienced a rapid restructuring: The share of heavy industries in the manufacturing sector rose from 46.1% in 1970 to 58.8% in 1980 in terms of value added (Lee and Yoo, 1994). The industrial base expansion and the rapid industrial restructuring were accompanied by the following structural changes in the market, which can also be regarded as legacies of the 1960s and 1970s.

Emerging Markets and Greater Pressures of Competition   In the 1960s and 1970s, there emerged new markets not only in the manufacturing sector but also in the non-manufacturing sector, including electricity, telecommunication, gas, construction, transportation, real estate development, finance, etc. Emerging markets provided valuable opportunities to businessmen and created a new demand for credit. While some of the traditional markets continued to be the source of profits, the emerging markets sometimes offered huge windfall profits and rents, when the market demand grew rapidly and the government protected first-comers with entry regulations.

Acknowleging the potential profits of emerging markets, the private sector naturally made vigorous efforts to diversify into these new business opportunities. Even though there existed entry regulations or investment coordination measures of the government designed to block entry, firms made every concerted effort to avoid such regulations, which sometimes was realized due to the discretionary changes of the government's position. Entrepreneurship in those years was meant to include the ability to gain access to preferential loans and permit to new businesses. Obviously, there existed a great dispersion among firms in this ability, which contributed to a dispersion in their growth rates.

The fact that firms grew in number and size meant changes in the size distribution of sellers and the increase of competitive pressures in the markets concerned. On average, each market became populated with a greater number of competitors, leading to a more competitive market structure and to an increased amount of actual or potential competition.

Competition in Export Markets and its Efficiency Results   The export drive in the 1960s and 1970s created an environment in which the exporting firms continued to face competitive threats in the export markets and had to improve their efficiency in order to survive. Although many domestic markets were protected from foreign competition as well as domestic competition, the export drive alone must have contributed to augmenting efficiency and to the rapid growth of the manufacturing sector. In microeconomic terms, the export drive meant that the individual industries and firms tried to overcome the limitations of a small domestic market by creating demand abroad and thus achieving economies of scale in their production.

The fact that the industrial development in the 1960s and 1970s witnessed the growth of firms and industries, the emergence of many new markets, the expansion of entrepreneurship and increasing pressures of competition both domestically and abroad, implies that certain fundamental driving forces of the market mechanism began to be fostered in the Korean economy. Although the economy was still under strong government control, these forces began forming a main trend in substituting for the role of the government.

Monopolistic Markets and *Chaebols*

If the industrial development in the 1960s and 1970s began to form a trend toward a market economy, is the general perception true that the government-led growth strategy consolidated the monopolistic market structure and the concentration of economic power by the *chaebols*?

Changes in Market Structure   Due to a lack of hard evidence, partial evidence will be presented on the changes in market structure of the 1960s and 1970s. Table 10-1 compares the three-firm concentration ratios (CR3) of five-digit manufacturing industries in 1966 and 1974. In Table 10-1, the CR3 estimates measured in shipments and those measured in employment exhibit slightly different results: the former indicates that manufacturing industries became more concentrated in 1974 relative to 1966, while the opposite is true with the latter indicator. At any rate, both results show weak support for any significant changes in the concentration ratios of manufacturing industries in Korea during the eight year period. It is fair to conclude from Table 10-1 that the monopolistic market structure of the 1960s did not change much in the 1970s. This observation can be supplemented by the estimates given in Table 10-2, which compares CR3 of manufacturing industries for the years 1970, 1977 and 1981.

In Table 10-2, we can see that the industrial concentration peaked around 1977, and then the share of monopoly or duopoly declined while that of oligopoly rose sharply. From these estimates, we can at least infer that there were important changes in the seller distribution of many industries in the late 1970s, which is consistent with the aforementioned argument that the industrial development of the

Table 10-1. Changes in Market Structure: 1966 and 1974

CR3(%)	Shipments				Employment			
	Number of industries		Share(%)		Number of industries		Share(%)	
	1966	1974	1966	1974	1966	1974	1966	1974
80-100	50	50	22.0	26.9	38	36	6.7	4.9
60-80	50	51	20.2	17.9	34	29	12.3	8.8
40-60	49	61	27.3	27.3	51	67	24.1	30.4
20-40	41	35	15.3	21.9	62	51	31.2	31.2
0-20	15	8	15.2	6.0	20	22	25.7	24.7
Total	205	205	100.0	100.0	205	205	100.0	100.0

Note: CR3 is the share accounted for by the largest three firms in each market (in terms of shipments or other indices).

Source: Kyu Uck Lee, *Market Structure and Monopoly Regulation,* Korea Development Institute, 1977. (in Korean)

444 *Seong Min Yoo & Sung Soon Lee*

Table 10-2. Market Structure in the 1970s

(Unit: %)

	Shipment			Number of commodities		
	1970	1977	1981	1970	1977	1981
Monopoly	8.7	16.3	11.0	29.6	31.6	23.5
Duopoly	16.3	11.0	4.7	18.7	20.1	9.6
Oligopoly	35.1	33.9	50.9	33.2	32.0	49.0
Competitive	39.9	38.8	33.4	18.5	16.3	17.9

Notes: Monopoly: CR1≥80%, S1/S2≥10,
Duopoly: CR2≥80%, S1/S2<5, S3<5.0%
Oligopoly: CR3≥60%, (monopoly and duopoly are excluded)
Competitive: CR3<60%
(CRi indicates i-firm concentration ratio and Si is market share of the largest ith firm)
Source: Kyu Uck Lee, Jae-Hyung Lee, and Joo-Hoon Kim, *Market and Market Structure*, Korea Development Institute, 1984. (in Korean)

1960s and 1970s began to generate a structural trend toward a more competitive market economy.

Changes in *Chaebol* Structure   While market structure refers to the seller distribution of individual industries, the concept of the concentration of economic power by the *chaebols* critically hinges upon how we define the 'boundary' of *chaebols*. The growth of the chaebol would depend upon the growth in size of individual subsidiaries and the growth in the number of the subsidiaries under the same corporate control. Thus, the concept of a single corporate control is the key to understanding the process of economic power concentration. Unlike a single firm, a chaebol or a business group can grow simply by increasing the number of subsidiaries as long as it adds to the size of the entire business group. During the 1960s and 1970s, the Korean *chaebols* increased the number of their subsidiaries in many ways: they either acquired failing firms, state-owned enterprises that were privatized, small- and medium-sized firms, or established new firms to diversify into new businesses.

There exists evidence that the concentration of economic power by the *chaebols* intensified during the 1960s and 1970s. The economic growth in the 1970s consolidated the economic power into a small number of *chaebols*, and since the late 1970s most of them continued to be the largest business conglomerates even today. Table 10-3 shows how the concentration of economic power changed over time during the period 1973-1981. The share of the 46 largest *chaebols* in GDP increased from 9.8% in 1973 to 24.0% in 1981. The concentration by *chaebols* was especially noticeable in the manufacturing sector, as shown in Table 10-3 for the years 1973, 1975 and 1978. Table 10-4, on the other hand, reports the aggregate concentration ratio which differs from *chaebol* concentration ratio.

For our purposes, it seems clear that the concentration of economic power by the *chaebols* was one of the legacies of the industrial development in the 1960s and 1970s. However, the causes of this concentration process cannot be reduced into one or two factors. Although the big business-oriented growth strategy and the HCI drive of the 1960s and 1970s must have fueled this process of concentration, there existed other factors as well, including the monopolization process that can be found in other capitalist market economies. The HCI drive of the 1970s has been especially criticized by many people for creating inefficiencies in the allocation of investment resources and increasing the concentration of economic power. The HCI drive,

Table 10-3. *Chaebol* Concentration Ratios : 1973-1981

(Unit: %)

	GDP									Manufacturing		
	1973	1974	1975	1976	1977	1978	1979	1980	1981	1973	1975	1978
Top 5	3.5	3.8	4.7	5.1	8.2	8.1	–	–	–	8.8	12.6	18.4
Top 10	5.1	5.6	7.1	7.2	10.6	10.9	–	–	–	13.9	18.9	23.4
Top 20	7.1	7.8	9.8	9.4	13.3	14.0	–	–	–	21.8	28.9	33.2
Top 46	9.8	10.3	12.3	12.3	16.3	17.1	16.6	19.5	24.0	31.8	36.5	43.0

Source: Il SaKong, *Korea in the World Economy*, 1993.

Table 10-4. Aggregate Concentration Ratio: 1970-1981

(Unit: %)

	Percentage share of shipments						Percentage share of employment					
	1970	1977	1978	1979	1980	1981	1970	1977	1978	1979	1980	1981
Top 50	17.8	34.7	34.1	33.7	36.4	36.6	15.4	14.1	14.9	14.6	13.6	12.4
Top 100	28.7	45.0	43.6	43.1	46.3	46.2	22.8	20.8	20.8	20.6	19.4	19.1

Source: National Statistical Office; Fair Trade Commission.

however, should be given a more balanced evaluation, since today's industrial structure could not have been established if there had not been such a drive in the 1970s.

Interaction of Market and State: 1980s and 1990s

The economic policies of the early 1980s under the Chun Doo Whan administration emphasized economic stabilization and tried to cure the imbalances caused by the HCI drive of the 1970s. In view of the development of a market mechanism, however, there were not many changes in the early 1980s, since the predominance of the state over the market was maintained throughout Chun's administration. Strong leadership by the government and ensuing government regulations were deemed necessary to carry out such policies as price stabilization, investment realignment in heavy industries, anti-speculation measures, etc. As the government resorted to price regulations, entry regulations and exit orders to rationalize some of the heavy industries, there was insufficient room for a market mechanism to function properly. Although the agenda of industrial policy changed relative to the Park administration, the anti-competitive nature of government regulations did not easily change under Chun's administration.

Even under these circumstances, the prevailing opinion supported market principles as an effective tool for solving the problems the Korean economy faced in the 1980s. In fact, the 1980s witnessed a series of new policies to strengthen the functions of the market mechanism and to cure the imperfections found in the government's management of the economy. These included trade liberalization, competition law and policy, deregulation and privatization of public enterprises, most of which are still on-going policy issues in Korea. For the past 15 years or so, these policies have had significant implications for the development of a free market economy system in Korea, although the overall progress has been slow.

Thus, it is fair to say that the 1980s and 1990s have been a period during which the traditional predominance of the state over the market, represented by regulations, protection and support, was actively interacting with new forces of the market, represented by trade liberalization, competition, deregulation and privatization. These two forces have been contradicting each other, and the conflict and confusion still exist today.

Changes in the Market Structure

As the industrial development of the 1960s and 1970s sowed the seeds of competition, economic growth in the 1980s was also accompanied by important changes in Korea's industrial organization. First, there was an unprecedented growth in the size and number of firms which far surpassed the industrial growth in the 1960s and 1970s. In the manufacturing sector alone, the number of establishments increased from 30,823 in 1980 to 74,679 in 1992, and the total number of shipments increased fourfold during the same period (46 trillion won in 1980 and 179 trillion won in 1992, all in 1985 prices). The industrial development in the 1980s was similar to that of the earlier decades in broadening the industrial base and restructuring the industries. Table 10-5 extends Table 10-2 into the 1980s, and clearly illustrates that the share of competitive industries (CR3<50%) increased steadily throughout the 1980s.

Although Table 10-5 reveals the changes to a more competitive market structure, it simultaneously shows that the absolute level of the share of monopolistic industries (CR3>50%) was still high, recording 63.7% of the total shipments of manufacturing industries in 1990. The high concentration ratios of many industries in Korea reflect that they existed for a long time as monopolies, duopolies or oligopolies. One of the plausible explanations of how these industries could maintain their monopolistic status is the implicit or explicit government regulations of entry and the investment and ownership of these industries. Table 10-6 presents the number of market dominating firms and commodity markets defined under the Monopoly Regulation and Fair Trade Act. The government regulations were protecting the long time monopoly status of many of the market dominating firms in Table 10-6.

It should also be noted that the estimates in Tables 10-2 and 10-5 do not take into account the effects of imports and exports. Since the shipments data obtained from the manufacturing census do not include imports but exports, the estimates do not correctly reflect the

448

Table 10-5. Changes in Market Structure in the 1980s

(Unit : %)

		1981	1982	1983	1984	1985	1986	1987	1988	1989	1990
Monopoly/ Oligopoly (CR3≥50)	Number of commodities	87.8	88.0	86.3	86.9	85.1	83.9	83.5	82.5	80.6	80.9
	Value of shipment	73.9	74.8	74.8	73.9	69.9	68.1	64.8	65.1	62.7	63.7
Competitive (CR3<50)	Number of commodities	12.2	12.0	13.7	13.1	14.9	16.1	16.5	17.5	19.4	19.1
	Value of shipment	26.1	25.2	25.2	26.1	30.1	31.9	35.2	34.9	37.3	36.3

Source : Fair Trade Commission.

Table 10-6. Market Dominating Firms and Commodities.

(in numbers)

	1976	1977	1978	1979	1981	1982	1983	1984	1985	1986	1987	1988	1989	1990	1991	1992	1993	1994	1995
Number of commodities	148	157	148	155	42	48	58	71	85	100	106	122	131	135	136	144	140	140	138
Number of Firms	247	272	257	63	102	115	148	179	216	266	240	286	307	314	320	352	335	332	316

Notes : Until 1979 designation of market dominating firms and commodities was subject to the Price Stabilization and Fair Trade Act and included basic necessities and public utilities as well. Since 1981 they were designated by the Monopoly Regulation and Fair Trade Act under the criteria that CR1>50% or CR3>75% in markets exceeding 30 billion won (50 billion won after 1993) of domestic shipments.

Source : Fair Trade Commission.

seller distribution of the domestic market. Such a bias will be greater in markets for producer goods where imports were an important source of supply.

Open Door Policy and Competition from Abroad

The trade liberalization in the 1960s and 1970s can be described as a "producer-oriented, protectionist and selective open door policy." Around 1980, criticisms called for modifications of the producer-oriented trade liberalization policy. In fact, the government's strong commitment to a more liberal policy in those years was apparent, such as the import liberalization measures in May 1978, the liberalization of technology imports in April 1979, the measures to promote foreign direct investment in September 1980, and the Fifth Five-Year Social and Economic Development Plan which emphasized liberalization, and so on. Again in 1984, tariff reduction and the revision of the foreign investment regulations expanded the scope of liberalization policy.

It is true that the open door policy of the early 1980s lowered the tariff barriers to imports and increased the number of industries open to foreign investment. However, the speed of liberalization was quite slow and the scope was limited mainly to some of the manufacturing industries. The slow progress in the liberalization policy was not surprising in view of the strong tradition of industrial policy that placed top priority on promoting the development of domestic industries. The vested interests of domestic firms and the protectionist characteristic of technocrats also formed a strong thrust against liberalization. Since the mid-1980s, however, liberalization was on the agenda in trade talks with Korea's major trade partners, especially the U.S. Demands of trade partners for further liberalization of imports and investment began to shape Korea's trade and investment policies and accelerated market opening.

The official statistics show that the import liberalization ratio has how approached a level close to that of advanced economies. However, Majority of imports were non-consumer goods, and thus, the imports did not produce the effects of competitive liberalization of many consumer goods markets. There were other reasons why the import liberalization had limitations in increasing competitive pressures in the domestic markets. These include the import diversification policy which was aimed at prohibiting imports of certain products from Japan, monopolization of domestic distribution of imports either through trade association of domestic producers or by a single domestic supplier of a competing product, and other non-tariff barriers to imports based upon special laws and regulations. The limited liberalization of foreign direct investment also did not have the effects of increasing competitive pressures, which can be explained by the traditional dominance of debt-financing over equity-financing and the limited and selective liberalization of foreign investment.

The fact that the liberalization policy of the 1980s was slow in introducing foreign competition into the domestic market, implies the dominance of the protectionist argument which favored the producers at the expense of the consumers. As long as the surplus of these "captured consumers" continues to be sacrificed, trade and investment liberalization will remain an important policy issue in Korea.

Evolution of Competition Law and Policy

The enactment of the Monopoly Regulation and Fair Trade Act (MRFTA hereafter) in 1980 was an important turning point in the history of interaction between the market and state in Korea. As Korea's competition law, the MRFTA tried to establish a market economy by setting the rules of the game, and thus, claimed to be the economic constitution which would precede other economic laws and regulations. It is interesting to see that Korea adopted a competition law as early as 1980, when most of the other developing countries and even some of the advanced economies did not have one. This reflects the urgent need for a competition law at a time when the economic growth in the 1960s and 1970s resulted in a concentrated industrial organization. It also implies that the newly enacted MRFTA had serious limitations under a regime characterized by the dominance of the state over the market tangled in a cobweb of government regulations.

When the MRFTA was enacted in 1980, the main provisions of the Act included sections dealing with abuse of market dominant position, anti-competitive business integration, undue collaborative activities, unfair trade practices, restraints of competition by trade associations, resale price maintenance, anti-competitive international contracts, etc. The contents of the Act were known to have incorporated various contents of the competition laws of Japan and Germany. Since then, the MRFTA has been amended five times in 1986, 1990, 1992, 1994 and 1996. The amendments were made to add new substantive provisions to the Act or strengthen the enforcement of the Act. In particular, new provisions against the concentration of economic power of *chaebols* were introduced in the amendments, such as regulations of cross shareholdings in 1986, and regulations of mutual loan guarantees. By incorporating many provisions against the economic power concentration of *chaebols*, the MRFTA has been regarded as one of the central instruments of chaebol policy. The chaebol regulations have resulted in the MRFTA reaching beyond the traditional scope of competition law. The incorporation of chaebol regulations in the MRFTA has been criticized by the legal profession.

Along with the enactment of the MRFTA, the Fair Trade Commission was established in 1981 as the competition policy authority in Korea, and the four amendments of MRFTA strengthened the power and independent status of the Commission. Although the MRFTA is the basic concern of the Fair Trade Commission, it is also responsible for the implementation of the Law on Fair Subcontracting Trade enacted in 1984, the Law on Regulating Business Stipulations enacted in 1986. The Consumer Protection Law enacted in 1986 is also closely associated with the MRFTA and the policy concerning the Fair Trade Commission, though there exists the Consumer Protection Board which enforces the law.

Table 10-7 summarizes the enforcement record of the MRFTA during 1981-1994, measured in the number of corrective measures taken by the Fair Trade Commission. The statistics in Table 10-7 clearly indicate that most of the law enforcement activities were related to unfair trade practices, undue international contracts, and unfair subcontracting trade, while corrective measures against abusive practices of market dominating firms, anti-competitive business integration, collusive activities and violations of chaebol regulations were much smaller in number. This does not necessarily indicate the existence of any bias in implementing the MRFTA. It is still questionable, however, whether the violations of the important provisions in the MRFTA have been challenged and given appropriate punitive decisions. One might suspect that cartel practices and restraints of competition have been widespread in the Korean business community, but the statistics in Table 10-7 show a weak law enforcement record against cartels and trade associations, implying a possible bias in law enforcement in the past. Another important characteristic of the MRFTA is that it is basically a conduct regulation which challenges the misconduct of business concerns and the ill-effects arising from market power. Thus, Korea's competition law differs from those of the U.S. or Japan in that it does not stipulate any provisions to dismantle a monopoly.

As we review the evolution of competition law and policy in Korea, we may agree that the MRFTA symbolized a discontinuity from previous decades and contributed to the establishment of a freer market economy in Korea by promoting free and fair competition and also mitigating the concentration of economic power, as spelled out in Article 1 of the Act. We also note that there exists numerous explanations why competition law and policy had to face serious limitations in Korea during the 1980s and even in the 1990s. First, the strong tradition of the state dominance over the market led many to question whether free and fair competition in the market would help promote industrial development. Although everyone seemed to agree that competition was good for captured consumers, the question was: "Does competition enhance the competitiveness of domestic industries and firms?" It can be said that even the government officials at the Fair Trade Commission were not confident enough to say yes to this question often posed by protectionists and interventionists. On the other hand, the old government interventions based upon industrial policy considerations were maintained, not leaving much room for competition law and policy. Government regulations of entry, price and investment as well as the government ownership and control of public enterprises, for example, created many industries and firms which were exempt, either explicitly or implicitly, from competition law. The more exemptions from a law, the weaker the law, which was the case with the Korean competition law in the past.

Table 10-7. Enforcement of the MRFTA : 1981-1994

(in number of corrective measures)

	1981-84	1985	1986	1987	1988	1989	1990	1991	1992	1993	1994	Total
Abuse of market-dominating position	3	1	1	4	–	–	2	–	6	2	1	20
Combination of enterprises[a]	140	27	22	35	37	32	12	22	19	24	13	383
Violation of economic power concentration	–	–	–	1	27	11	21	3	37	5	12	117
Undue collaborative activities	7	10	4	6	15	11	12	20	9	16	20	130
Restricting competition of trade association	30	8	37	16	41	24	23	31	45	50	52	357
Unfair trade practices	269	138	264	240	275	320	177	336	292	397	430	3,138
– Large enterprise group	–	–	–	–	–	–	–	–	–	(26)	(50)	(76)
– Concerned market–dominating business	(61)	(32)	(31)	(29)	(8)	(55)	(23)	(19)	(46)	(38)	(18)	(360)
Unfair stipulation[b]	–	–	–	2	8	7	10	8	8	34	83	160
Unfair subcontract	89	141	153	141	144	144	97	199	149	223	220	1,700
Unreasonable international agreement[c]	703	234	273	242	70	39	288	235	57	65	55	2,261
Total	1,241	559	754	687	617	588	642	854	622	816	886	8,266

Notes: a. Most of the corrective measures were taken for violations of reporting requirements.

b. The numbers include minor revisions of international contracts.

c. The numbers include the activities of the Coordinating Committee on Subcontract Dispute.

Source : Fair Trade Commission.

Deregulation and Privatization: Urgent Policy Issues in Industrial Organization

In view of the past government-led industrial development, deregulation and privatization have been considered two of the most important policy issues which bear great significance to industrial organization. In this accord, there have been a few rounds of deregulation and privatization efforts in the 1980s and 1990s. Both policies, however, involved abrupt readjustments of interests of different groups of people including owners, managers, workers, consumers and even the government officials themselves. Thus, deregulation and privatization have never been easy in the history of any economy. In Korea, the difficulty is even greater in view of its history of heavy regulatory interventions and state control of both private and public enterprises.

The first round of deregulation was attempted in 1988 under the Roh Tae Woo administration. The industries in which anti-competitive government regulations were deemed to impede their development were first selected by the government and an economic analysis was conducted to investigate the rationale and problems of existing regulations and to seek an optimal solution of deregulation. Since then, deregulation became a vogue in Korea, and the Roh Tae Woo administration put a lot of effort into deregulating many industries.

However, the deregulation policy soon deteriorated and the policy objective was often confused. As the economic downturn began in 1989, deregulation of industries was treated as a policy tool to overcome economic difficulties in the short-run. Although this perception itself was not seriously mistaken, it led to the naive misconception that deregulation was a policy that would "help the producers strengthen their competitiveness." Although in actually economic deregulation just promotes competition and may or may not enhance the competitiveness of domestic industries and firms, this misconception resulted in a distorted deregulation policy in Korea. We note that the original deregulation policy in 1988 started as an effort to reform the anti-competitive regulations stemming from the industrial policy of the past. At that time, deregulation of entry, price and investment was called for in order to promote competition and expand the functioning of a market principle in the economy. As later efforts of deregulation focused more on relieving the difficulties of domestic industries, the subsequent deregulation programs concentrated on removing or simplifying the administrative and procedural regulations instead of addressing more important economic regulations.

Since the inauguration of the Kim, Young Sam administration in 1993, deregulation was selected as one of the most important economic reforms, and most of the economic ministries have been seemingly willing to undertake the deregulation policy. However, the misconception and confusion around the policy objective of deregulation have not changed at all. It is interesting to observe that businessmen strongly support deregulation policies in Korea, since they are, as incumbents who wish to protect their vested interests, expected to oppose deregulation which would imply more competition. The deregulation policy businessmen supported was defined in their own terms; that is, the businessmen wanted to see those cumbersome government interventions of the past removed. It cannot be denied that numerous regulations have increased the cost of doing business in Korea, and deregulation of this type should be pursued to improve the business environment and stop corruption. However, this should not be the focus of deregulation policy, as long as such key economic variables as entry, pricing, investment, and ownership, are heavily regulated as a means of achieving industrial policy objectives.

Privatization of public enterprises has a longer history in Korea relative to deregulation policy. Except for the divestiture of the vested properties in the 1950s, the first round of privatization came as early as 1968, when the government privatized the airline, trucking, and a few of the mining and heavy manufacturing industries. In 1980, the second round of privatization was carried out in the banking and oil refinery industries. In 1987, an ambitious privatization program was drafted by the government, which included the largest public enterprises in Korea such as Korea Telecom, Korea Electric Power Corp., POSCO, but the plan was only partially implemented for many reasons including the downturn of the stock market.

It is interesting to see that the two rounds of privatization programs in the 1980s were not exactly acts of privatization, since the government sold out part or all of its ownership shares but did not give away corporate control over the enterprises. Thus, privatization of ownership, with the exception of control and management, did not free the enterprises from the control of the state. The commercial banks privatized in the early 1980s were a typical example. Recognizing the limitations of the past privatization policies in augmenting the efficiency of the privatized firms, the Kim Young Sam administration announced a new privatization program in 1993, which was the most ambitious in the history of privatization in Korea. The program included the privatization of 58 state-owned enterprises and the restructuring of 10 more public enterprises out of the total of 133 state-owned enterprises. This time, the government announced that it would sell out the entire government shares and leave the management in the hands of the private sector, in order for privatization to produce the desired effects of efficiency gain. As privatization under Kim's administration is still in effect, it is too early to evaluate any results. However, the policy is unlikely to be implemented as originally planned if we consider strong opposition from vested interest groups including managers and workers of the public enterprises, government officials and politicians and the concerns about the effects of privatization on the concentration of economic power, stock market, etc.

Though not yet widely acknowledged, clear lessons have emerged from the experiences of the deregulation and privatization policies of the 1980s and 1990s. Korean experience shows that it takes a strong political commitment as well as the right vision and philosophy to implement deregulation and privatization policies successfully. Without the right vision and philosophy, the policy objectives are easily forgotten and distorted. A strong commitment by the political leader is also crucial, since without it opposition from vested interest groups including technocrats, present businesses and workers cannot be overcome. Compared to the strong commitment for economic growth and industrialization made by President Park Chung Hee, the political commitment necessary for deregulation and privatization has to be even stronger simply because they face stronger opposition. It is yet uncertain if today's political leaders are committed at all.

Understanding the *Chaebol* Issue

Evolution of Chaebol Policy

Concentration of economic power has long been identified with the so-called *"chaebol* issue," although the latter is not necessarily confined to the former. Depending on how we define it, the *chaebol* issue may include or at least relate to such wide-ranging issues as government-business relationships, income and wealth distribution, industrial relations, small and medium industries, land, financial development, etc. Given the complex nature of the *chaebol* issue, it has been particularly difficult to verify what the real problems of *chaebols* are, and the list of problems associated with *chaebols* have varied depending on the subjective views of individuals and groups of people.

Although there did not exist any consensus on the real problems of *chaebols*, the so-called *"chaebol* policy" or the policies against the concentration of economic power have an established tradition in Korea. The policies to repress or mitigate the concentration of economic power have in certain instances been justified on the grounds of equity and fairness, and in other instances by efficiency and growth. The overall direction of *chaebol* policy has changed due to the business cycle and socio-political considerations influenced by *"anti-chaebol"* attitudes deemed to exist among the general public. Thus, Korea's *chaebol* policy during the last decade tended to strengthen regulations, but these were eased or became less effective during periods of economic recession. Socio-political considerations include the anti-*chaebol* slogans of most candidates in the presidential elections of 1987 and 1992.

The first policy attempt to regulate big businesses appeared in 1974, when the concentration of credit supply and corporate ownership and the unhealthy financial status of *chaebols* were recognized as serious problems. The credit control system was newly introduced and public listing in the stock market was encouraged to promote the deconcentration of corporate ownership. These policies, however, were not actively enforced and were neglected during the rest of the 1970s. There were no more *chaebol* policies during the 1970s, and amidst the HCI drive, the concentration of economic power was not checked at all. In 1980, another set of regulations was introduced to discourage *chaebols'* real estate holdings, induce the restructuring of *chaebols'* subsidiaries, strengthen the credit control system, etc. These regulations, however, essentially aimed at improving the financial status of *chaebols*, and did not continue after one year of implementation.

The year 1987 earmarked an important turning point in the history of *chaebol* policy in Korea. The cross shareholding regulation was newly introduced and the so-called basket control of credit was strengthened in the amended MRFTA and the credit control system, respectively. Since then, these regulations have constituted two of the most important *chaebol* regulations in Korea. Additional diverse *chaebol* regulations have appeared in the late 1980s and early 1990s. The MRFTA has added a new provision in 1992 to regulate mutual loan guarantees of *chaebols'* subsidiaries, and a guideline was announced to regulate the anti-competitive behavior of *chaebols* based upon in-group transactions. The so-called specialization policy announced in 1991 was reinforced in 1993 to induce *chaebols* from refraining from excessive diversification and focus their investment resources into their core businesses in order to strengthen their competitiveness. Deconcentration of corporate ownership appeared as a new *chaebol* policy issue in 1992 when the 7th Five-Year Plan was announced, and various measures have been introduced since then to encourage the ownership deconcentration process. In addition to these policy instruments, privatization of public enterprises, inducement of private investments in social infrastructure construction, deregulation of entry, investment, and ownership in many industries, are all closely related to the growth of the *chaebol* sector in Korea, and thus, cannot be discussed independently of the *chaebol* policy.

With these policy developments, the decade since the mid-1980s was an era of *chaebol* regulations. It is not a clear issue, however, if the *chaebol* regulations have had the desired effects. There was the possibility that the diverse *chaebol* regulations might have been the wrong prescriptions based upon the wrong diagnoses of the real problems associated with *chaebols*. It is true that many of the *chaebol* regulations were only symptomatic treatments that could not cure the fundamental problems of *chaebols*, if there were any; and in many cases, it was not clear at all what the regulations were ultimately

Table 10-8. *Chaebol* Concentration Ratio: 30 Largest *Chaebols*, Mining
and Manufacturing

(Unit: %)

	1977	1978	1979	1980	1981	1982	1983	1984	1985	1986	1987	1988	1989	1990
Shipments	32.0	34.1	35.2	36.0	39.7	40.7	39.9	40.3	40.2	37.7	36.8	35.7	35.2	35.0
Value Added	29.1	–	–	–	30.8	33.2	31.6	33.5	33.1	32.4	31.9	30.4	29.6	30.0
Fixed Assets	–	–	–	–	36.7	37.2	37.1	40.3	39.6	39.1	37.9	37.3	35.3	32.2
Employment	20.5	–	–	–	19.8	18.6	17.9	18.1	17.6	17.2	17.6	16.9	16.6	16.0

Source : Fair Trade Commission.

pursuing. This is why we need a new understanding of the *chaebol*
issue in Korea. A new framework for decomposing the concentration
of economic power into three concrete aspects has been suggested
for understanding and analysis. These aspects are: a) the size and relative economic share of the *chaebols*; b) *chaebol* diversification; and c)
the corporate ownership, control, governance and management structure of *chaebols*.

Understanding the Facts and Causes

Changes in the *Chaebol* Concentration Ratios

The share of *chaebols* in the national economy increased sharply
in the 1970s and early 1980s. In 1989, the share of the five largest
chaebols in GNP was 9.2%, while that of the 30 largest *chaebols* was
16.3% (Chung and Yang, 1992). In mining and manufacturing industries, the share of the 30 largest *chaebols* increased steadily until the
mid-1980s, and then declined, as shown in Table 10-8. As discussed
earlier, changes in the *chaebol* concentration ratio are determined by
the growth of individual subsidiaries both in number and size. Thus,
changes in corporate control through business integrations may significantly affect the *chaebol* concentration ratio. M&As involving large
corporations or privatization of large public enterprises may result
in a discontinuous increase of the *chaebols'* share in the economy.

Any attempts to evaluate the absolute level of *chaebol* concentration have raised questions. Are the shares in Table 10-8 too high, or
are they "tolerable"? Although there is no definite answer, Table 10-9
gives an indirect reference by comparing aggregate concentration ratios found in several market economies. The partial evidence given
in Table 10-9 indicates that the aggregate concentration ratio, which

460   Seong Min Yoo & Sung Soon Lee

Table 10-9. Aggregate Concentration Ratios: 100 Largest Firms

	Korea (1990)	Japan (1984)	U.S.A. (1985)	W. Germany (1984)	Canada (1983)
Shipments	37.7	27.3[a]	–	39.5	–
Value Added	35.1	–	33.0[b]	24.8	47.1
Fixed Assets	40.8	33.0	49.1	–	52.2

Notes: a. 1980; b. 1982.
Sources: Fair Trade Commission; Marfels (1988).

differs considerably across countries, is not abnormally high in Korea. A more direct comparison can be made between Japanese business groups and Korean *chaebols*; in 1987, six business groups accounted for 25.2% of the total sales of non-financial corporations in Japan, while the five largest *chaebols* accounted for 21.3% of the total value of shipments of the manufacturing sector in Korea (Yoo, 1992).

Diversification of *Chaebols*: The Puzzle

No one can deny that *chaebols* in Korea have highly diversified business portfolios. As shown in Table 10-10, the five largest *chaebols* have, on average, 42 subsidiaries and run businesses in more than 30 KSIC 3-digit industries. This evidence is enough to confirm that the extent of Korean *chaebols'* diversification has been rather extraordinary.

This dimension of the *chaebol* issue is puzzling because the traditional association of diversification and inefficiency or weak com-

Table 10-10. Number of *Chaebol*'s Subsidiaries and Industries

	Subsidiaries[a]	Financial Companies[b]	Industries Covered[c]
Top 5	210	20	30.4
Hyundai	49	5	36
Samsung	50	5	34
Daewoo	25	2	27
LG	53	6	32
Sunkyong	33	2	23
Top 30	626	64	19.1

Notes: a. June 1994.
   b. April 1993, the numbers include only non-bank financial institutions.
   c. 1993, the numbers are counted for 2-digit KSIC industries.
Source: Fair Trade Commission.

petitiveness is now being seriously questioned. In the past, many believed that excessive diversification by *chaebols* seriously undermined their competitiveness. The five-year-long economic recession in 1989-1993 led many people to believe that the "competitiveness crisis" was the result of excessive *chaebol* diversification. Although there has been little effort to prove the validity of this belief, the argument has prevailed and has contributed to the introduction of direct and indirect regulations of *chaebols'* diversification. However, one observes that today's most successful *chaebols* are highly diversified, while many of the specialized *chaebols* of the 1960s and 1970s went out of business.

The big-business-oriented, growth-first strategy was implemented for decades via a discriminatory industrial policy by which the government selected target industries to promote and firms to act as principal agents. There is no doubt that the government's industrial policy was crucial in determining today's business structure. However, there were other fundamental factors as well, most of which were elementary economics of cost minimization and profit maximization as shown below.

In a rapidly growing economy, many new markets continued to emerge which guaranteed high rates of return on investments, especially when the markets were protected from foreign as well as domestic competition. Thus, the capital accumulated in the early phase of success, combined with a preferential supply of loans from the government-controlled credit market, could easily be channelled into a new activity. In this process, managerial know-how and technological capabilities grew and often produced synergistic effects. Thus, *chaebol* diversification simply reflects the process of rapid industrial restructuring in Korea. Even when participating in a new market did not prove profitable, there still existed other important incentives to diversify: operating a financial company significantly reduced the risk of business when the financial sector suffered from market imperfections; owning a newspaper or broadcasting company were in some cases a key element of business success; the capital gains from holding the real estate of a new subsidiary by far exceeded any losses from business when real estate prices soared. These factors served as a profitability incentive to diversify. There existed other non-economic explanations as well, of which an important one was the psychological traits of many owner-managers of Korean *chaebols*. For example, they never wanted to close one of their businesses since they regarded such behavior as a failure of management.

In sum, we argue that diversification of *chaebols* was the logical response to changing market fundamentals and the government-business relationship. Some studies have produced partial evidence on the efficiency-neutrality of *chaebols'* diversification; that is, there is neither a strong case for the traditional link between diversification and inefficiency, nor one for the opposite correlation. Nevertheless, regulations to curb the "octopus-like" diversification of *chaebols* have constituted the core of *chaebol* policy in Korea. For example, entry regulations that existed or still exist in such industries as automobiles, steel, telecommunications, and the financial sector are often justified by their effect on discouraging *chaebol* diversification. The regulations on *chaebol* investment decisions based upon the credit control system were classic examples of diversification regulations. The specialization policy of 1991 was yet another example.

With all these efforts of control, why has the extent of *chaebol* diversification continued to intensify over the last decade? One obvious problem with the regulations was that they restrained competition and the functioning of the market mechanism, intensified the close intertwining of politics and business, and severely restricted creativity in the private sector. Investment regulations based upon the credit control system have turned the banks into regulators of industrial firms, resulting in a distorted relationship between banks and their customers. The randomness of these regulations in selecting the winners and losers has also been criticized.

In light of the regulations' insufficient deterrence effects and serious negative effects, the regulations concerning *chaebol* diversification have recently come under harsh criticism. New studies, however, identified the market fundamentals and other factors explaining *chaebol* diversification. The important policy implication is that appropriate cures must not entail symptomatic treatments, but must directly address these fundamentals. Appropriate cures include introducing effective and workable competition, removing market imperfections in input markets such as the financial sector and real estate, developing a well-functioning market for corporate control so that exit decisions can be appropriately timed, and finally, a negative list of a few direct regulations which are deemed necessary even after these efforts.

A special topic of concern is industrial *chaebols'* diversification into the banking sector. For any country, the relationship between big business and banks in terms of mutual ownership and control has been a key factor in determining its model of capitalism. Different models reflect differences in the history of capitalism in different places, and an *a priori* ideal model for Korea to follow does not seem to exist. It is unclear whether the defense against *chaebol* control of banks will remain valid after the liberalization of the banking industry. Another question arises from the weakening distinction between banks and non-bank financial institutions when most of the latter are owned and controlled by *chaebols* in Korea.

Ownership, Control and Management

The New Agenda: As with a high degree of diversification, the concentration of corporate ownership of *chaebols* is also extraordinary. The "in-group shareholding ratio," a measure of *chaebol* ownership concentration, was on average as high as 43.3% for the 30 largest *chaebols* in 1995, although the ratio has been falling gradually from 57% over the last decade, as can be seen in Table 10-11. The essential feature of 43.3% of ownership is that a family-owned share of almost 10.5% combined with 32.8% of ownership by the subsidiaries is high enough to consolidate firm control over the subsidiaries in the hands

Table 10-11. In-Group Ownership Concentration

(Unit: %)

	1983.9	1987.4	1989.4	1990.4	1991.4	1992.4	1993.4	1994.4	1995.4
Top 30	57.2	56.2	46.2	45.4	46.9	46.1	43.4	42.7	43.3
family	(17.2)	(15.8)	(14.7)	(13.7)	(13.9)	(12.6)	(10.3)	(9.7)	(10.5)
subsidiaries	(40.0)	(40.4)	(32.5)	(31.7)	(33.0)	(33.5)	(33.1)	(33.0)	(32.8)
Top 5	–	60.3	49.4	49.6	51.6	51.9	49.0	47.5	–
family	–	15.6	13.7	13.3	13.2	13.3	11.8	12.5	–
subsidiaries	–	44.7	35.7	36.3	38.4	38.6	37.2	35.0	–
Hyundai	81.4	79.9	–	60.2	67.8	65.7	57.8	61.3	60.4
Samsung	59.5	56.5	–	51.4	53.2	58.3	52.9	48.9	49.3
Daewoo	70.6	56.2	–	49.1	50.4	48.8	46.9	42.4	41.4
L G	30.2	41.5	–	35.2	38.3	39.7	38.8	37.7	39.7

Notes: The so-called 'in-group ownership' means the ownership shares held by chairman (*chongsu*) and his/her family members plus those held by other subsidiaries.
Source: Fair Trade Commission.

of the owner-managers and their family members. Thus, the owner-ship structure is the root of the concentration of corporate control and management in Korea.

In some recent studies, the concentration of ownership and control is recognized as the central feature of the concentration of economic power, since many of the *chaebol* organizational characteristics basically come from the ownership and control structure. However, highly concentrated corporate ownership and control is not simply a *chaebol*-specific characteristic, but it is also found in non-*chaebol* companies in Korea. The natural question is: how can they maintain concentrated ownership in the course of rapid growth? The answer lies in the method of financing. Korean firms have grown via debt financing rather than equity financing. The desire of owner-managers to maintain a high level of ownership share coupled with debt financing has resulted in ownership concentration.

Although ownership deconcentration may be desirable for such goals as achieving more equitable distribution of income and wealth, which is often dubious in itself, ownership deconcentration occurs over a long period of time and requires the development of a mature stock market. Since ownership deconcentration is a long-term vision, the policies and laws to expedite the process are important but have limitations.

This ownership structure of *chaebols* has resulted in a simple corporate control and management structure. For most *chaebols*, there is an owner-manager who exercises full control over all subsidiaries. In this centralized structure of grouped control and management, the role of professional managers is limited. As ownership deconcentration is regarded as a long-term goal, criticism of corporate control and management by the owner-managers has also surfaced, leading to discussions for establishing professional management in Korea. There are now many who support the earliest possible separation of ownership and management.

Although the present form of corporate control and management of *chaebol* companies obviously suffers from certain problems, a basic question is whether we can choose a priori between owner-management and professional management based upon an efficiency criteria. The answer must be negative, because for both types of management structures, pros and cons exist. Introducing professional management requires ownership deconcentration, the existence of a market for managers, and the development of a corporate control and governance mechanism which can replace the present one based upon concentrated ownership. These requirements will not be easy to achieve in a short period of time. Japanese corporate capitalism, American managerial capitalism, and German financial capitalism were all established over long periods of time, and each model exhibits its own mechanism of corporate control and management with its own merits and demerits. The separation of ownership and control is neither desirable for efficiency reasons nor supported by practical requirements, and it is better to leave this issue to the private sector. Strengthening competition in output markets will produce better results, since the owner-managers facing severe competition will have a strong incentive to optimize the corporate control and management mechanism. The role of the government is to develop the institution of the joint stock company so that corporate control and management can be made more transparent.

Summary and Conclusions

The legacies of economic growth during 1945-1995 are clear concerning the industrial organization in Korea. The protection and regulation of industries were the rule, severely restricting competition. On the other hand, the export drive worked as a stimulus to promote efforts to reach the efficiency frontier in the world market, and contributed to enhancing the competitiveness and rapid restructuring of Korean industries. The big-business-oriented growth strategy resulted in the appearance of world-class companies, but at the same time, brought about the underdevelopment of small and medium industries and the concentration of economic power. The largest firms representing Korean industries are still family-owned and managed. Repression of the financial sector under government-led growth undermined its own competitiveness, and distorted the relationship between banks and firms. The overall government-business relationship is still not free from the patriarchal authoritarianism, which hinders the establishment of a free market economy in Korea.

Among the legacies of past economic growth, there are both assets and liabilities. Toward the 21st century, the two important challenges in industrial organization are: first, enhancing industrial efficiency and competitiveness, and second, developing a Korean model of a capitalist market economy that can secure a healthy economic system and support the Korean people. As abrupt and discontinuous changes in the history of economic growth are neither feasible nor desirable, the appropriate way to approach these challenges is to develop assets and reduce liabilities.

For efficiency and competitiveness, it will be important to reform government regulations and the public sector, and to establish the rules of competition. The government-business relationship will have to develop into one based upon rules instead of discretion. The relationship between large and small firms should be more complementary, while the role of the government must be limited to correcting any market failures in small and medium industries.

To establish a Korean model of a market economy is a long-term issue that requires gradual improvement and continuous awakening in the short- and medium-term. *Chaebols* should be as free as possible in pursuing profits and growth. The society's intellectual energy should concentrate on exploring what will be the tomorrow's model of today's family capitalism in Korea. The different models of corporate ownership, control, management and governance structure prevailing in advanced economies will provide important lessons, but none of these can be simply imitated. The relationship between industrial *chaebols* and the financial sector is another issue of concern, but again, the models of other economies cannot be simulated. Privatization of large public enterprises will be another important experiment in seeking a new corporate control and governance mechanism of big business in Korea.

References

Chung, Byung Hyu and Young Sik Yang, *An Economic Analysis of Chaebol in Korea*, Seoul: Korea Development Institute, 1992. 8. (in Korean)

Economi Planning Board, *The White Paper of Fair Trade in Korea: Toward a New Economic Orders*, June 1984. (in Korean)

Fair Trade Commission, *The Fair Trade Statistics in Korea*, Seoul, 1995. (in Korean)

Fair Trade Commission and Korea Development Institute, *10 Years of Fair Trade*, Seoul, 1991. (in Korean)

Koo, Bon Ho and Kyu Uck Lee (eds.), *A Retrospect of the History of Korean Economy*, Korea Development Institute, Seoul, June 1991. (in Korean)

Korea Economic Research Institute, *Big Business Groups in Korea*, Seoul, July 1995.

Lee, Jae Hyung and Seong Min Yoo, "Growth and Productivity of Large Establishments and *Chaebol*'s Establishments," *Korea Development Review*, Vol. 16, No. 3, Seoul: Korea Development Institute, November 1994. (in Korean)

Lee, Kyu Uck, Jae Hyung Lee, and Joo Hoon Kim, *Markets and Market Structure in Korea*, Seoul: Korea Development Institute, 1984. (in Korean)

Lee, Kyu Uck and Jae Hyung Lee, *Business Groups and the Concentration of Economic Power*, Seoul: Korea Development Institute, 1990. (in Korean)

Lee, Kyu Uck and Sung Soon Lee, *Business Integration and the Concentration of Economic Power*, Seoul: Korea Development Institute, 1985. (in Korean)

Lee, Sung Soon, "Liberalization and a New Direction of Industrial Organization Policy in Korea," *The Korea Economic Research*, Vol. 2, No. 1, 1988, pp.75-95. (in Korean)

Marfels, Christian, "Aggregate Concentration in International Perspective," Chapter 3 in Khemani et al. (ed.), *Mergers, Corporate Concentration and Power in Canada*, The Institute for Research on Public Policy, 1988.

SaKong, Il, "Economic Growth and Concentration of Economic Power," *Korea Development Review*, Vol. 2, No. 1, Seoul: Korea Development Institute, March 1980. (in Korean)

_____, *Korea in the World Economy*, Washington, D.C.: Institute for International Economics, 1993.

Yoo, Seong Min, "The Ownership Structure of Korea's Big Business Conglomerates and Its Policy Implications," *Korea Development Review*, Vol. 14, No. 1, Seoul: Korea Development Institute, April 1992. (in Korean)

Name Index